W9-BUL-896

APPLYING CULTURAL ANTHROPOLOGY

APPLYING CULTURAL ANTHROPOLOGY
An Introductory Reader

SIXTH EDITION

Aaron Podolefsky
University of Northern Iowa

Peter J. Brown
Emory University

Boston   Burr Ridge, IL   Dubuque, IA   Madison, WI   New York   San Francisco   St. Louis
Bangkok   Bogotá   Caracas   Kuala Lumpur   Lisbon   London   Madrid   Mexico City
Milan   Montreal   New Delhi   Santiago   Seoul   Singapore   Sydney   Taipei   Toronto

McGraw-Hill Higher Education

A Division of The **McGraw-Hill** Companies

1 2 3 4 5 6 7 8 9 0 PBT/PBT 0 9 8 7 6 5 4 3 2

Library of Congress Cataloging-in-Publication Data

Applying cultural anthropology : an introductory reader / [edited by] Aaron Podolefsky, Peter J. Brown.—6th ed.
     p. cm.
   Includes bibliographical references and index.
   ISBN 0-07-256425-3
   1. Applied anthropology.   2. Ethnology.   I. Podolefsky, Aaron.   II. Brown, Peter J.

GN397.5. A68 2002
306—dc21

                                                                            2002075350

Publisher, Phillip A. Butcher; sponsoring editor, Kevin M. Witt; production editors, Vicki Moran and Jen Mills; manuscript editor, Jennifer Gordon; art director, Jeanne Schreiber; art manager, Robin Mouat; cover designer, Cassandra Chu; illustrators, Lotus Art, Joan Carol, and Robin Mouat; production supervisor, Rich DeVitto. The text was set in 10/12 Palatino by TBH Typecast, Inc. and printed on acid-free 45# New Era Matte by Phoenix Color Corp. Book Technology Park.

Cover: A chief in Cameroon places a red feather in the cap of a tribesman. Symbols—such as a red feather—are used in cultures to evoke meaning on a thing or event. © Adam Koons/Anthro-Photo

www.mhhe.com

We dedicate this book to our families
in appreciation for their love, support,
and encouragement. From Aaron to Ronnie,
Noah, Isaac, and Abby. From Peter to Betsy,
Nico, Patrick, Thomas, and Georgia.

To the Student

An introductory course in any discipline is full of new terminology, concepts, and facts. Sometimes students forget that these new ideas and vocabulary are actually intellectual tools that can be put to work for analyzing and solving problems. In preparing this book, we have selected readings that will show you how anthropological concepts, discoveries, and methods can be applied in today's world.

The study of anthropology can help you view the world in a completely different way than you ever have before. You can come to appreciate the great diversity of human cultures and the interrelatedness of economic, sociopolitical, and religious systems. Anthropology can give you a broad perspective on humanity and help you understand other people's beliefs and customs. In doing so, it can help you become a better citizen in an increasingly global society. But your motivation need not be completely altruistic—there are many examples in this book of how cross-cultural awareness can improve performances in business, negotiations, and clinical medicine.

The fascinating side of anthropology seems obvious to most educated people, but there is also a lesser-known practical side of the discipline. The readings we have selected demonstrate that practical, applied side. Many of the articles depict anthropological ideas and research methods in action—as they are used to understand and solve practical problems. We have included career profiles of anthropologists working outside the academic setting to show how they are applying anthropology. We believe that the fundamental lessons of anthropology can be applied to many careers and all areas of human endeavor.

To benefit from the study of anthropology, you need to study effectively. Over the years, we have found that students often read assignments without planning, and this actually makes studying less efficient. Before you read a selection, spend a few moments skimming it to get an idea of what it is about, where it is going, and what you should look for. This kind of preliminary reading is a poor idea for mystery novels but is essential for academic assignments. Without this preparation, the article may become a hodgepodge of facts and figures; details may be meaningless because you have missed the big picture. By planning your reading, you can see how the details are relevant to the central themes of an article.

To help you plan your reading, at the beginning of each article we have included questions and a list of glossary terms. Looking at these questions in advance, you may gain an idea of what is to come and why the article is important. This will help make the time you spend reading more fruitful. Most of the questions highlight the central themes of the selection or draw your attention to interesting details. Some of the questions, however, do not have straightforward answers—they are food for thought and topics for discussion. Some of the selections refer directly to current debates on topics like welfare reform, education reform, bilingualism, environmentalism, and affirmative action. Our idea is to challenge you to think about how anthropology can be applied to your own life and education.

These articles have been selected with you, the student, in mind. We hope they convey our excitement about the anthropological adventure, and we trust that you will find them both enjoyable and thought-provoking.

If you are interested in reading more about applied anthropology, there are several excellent books available, such as *Applied Anthropology: A Practical Guide*, by Erve Chambers; *Applied Anthropology: An Introduction*, by John van Willigen; *Anthropological Praxis: Translating Knowledge into Action*, by Robert M. Wulff and Shirley J. Fiske; *Applied Anthropology in America*, by Elizabeth M. Eddy and William L. Partridge; and *Making Our Research Useful*, by John van Willigen, Barbara Rylko-Bauer, and Anne McElroy. If you are interested in medical matters, you may want to consult *Understanding and Applying Medical Anthropology*, by Peter J. Brown or *Anthropology and Public Health*, by Robert Hahn. You may also want to look at the journals *Human Organization* and *Practicing Anthropology*, both of which are published by the Society for Applied Anthropology. The National Association of Practicing Anthropologists (NAPA) also publishes interesting works on specific fields such as medical anthropology.

To the Instructor

Introductory anthropology has become an established part of the college curriculum, and through this course our profession communicates with a large and diverse undergraduate audience. Members of that audience differ in experience, academic concentration, and career aspirations. For those students considering anthropology as a major, we need to provide (among other things) a vision of the future, a view of anthropological work to be done in the public domain as well as within academia. For them, we need to provide some answers to the question, What can I do with a degree in anthropology? For students majoring in other areas, such as business, engineering, or psychology, we need to address the question, How can anthropological insights or research methods help me understand and solve human problems? If we can provide such a service, we increase the likelihood that students will find creative solutions to the professional problems that await them, and we brighten the future for our anthropology majors by underscoring the usefulness of an anthropological perspective in attempts to solve the practical problems of today's world.

Over the years we have found that many introductory texts do little more than include a chapter on applied anthropology at the end of the book. This suggests, at least to students, that most of anthropology has no relevance to their lives. Such treatment also implies that the application of anthropological knowledge is a tangent or afterthought—at best an additional subject area, such as kinship or politics.

We disagree. We believe that the applications of anthropology cut across and infuse all the discipline's subfields. This book is a collection of articles that provide examples of both basic and applied research in cultural anthropology and linguistic anthropology.

One of our primary goals is to demonstrate some of the ways our discipline is used outside the academic arena. We want anthropology to be seen as a field that is interesting as well as relevant to the real world. Like the public at large, students seem well aware that the subject matter of anthropology is fascinating, but they seem unaware of both the fundamental questions of humanity addressed by anthropologists and the practical applications of the field. Increased public awareness of the practical contributions of anthropology is a goal that we share with many in the profession. In fact,

this is a major long-term goal of the American Anthropological Association.

Although people distinguish between basic and applied research, much of anthropology falls into a gray area, having elements of both. Many selections in this book fall into that gray zone—they are brief ethnographic accounts that contain important implications for understanding and resolving problems. We could have included a large number of articles exemplifying strictly applied research—an evaluation report of agency performance, for example. Although this sort of research is fascinating and challenging to do, it is usually not exciting for students to read. We have selected articles that we believe are fascinating for students and convey the dual nature (basic/applied) of social science research. We think that it is not the scholarly writing style that is most important, but rather the content of the research as a way to get students to think, and to challenge their own assumptions about the world.

Any student who completes an introductory course in anthropology should learn that anthropological work, in its broadest sense, may include (or at least contribute to) international business, epidemiology, program evaluation, social impact studies, conflict resolution, organizational analysis, market research, and nutrition research, even though their introductory anthropology texts make no mention of those fields. The selections in this book should help students understand why anthropology is important in today's world and also make the course more memorable and meaningful.

FEATURES OF THIS EDITION

- To spark student discussion and thinking about public policy issues, we have included selections dealing with contemporary issues like environmentalism, affirmative action, education reform, multicultural and bilingual education, refugees, and AIDS. All of these selections are clearly anthropological in their approach.
- We chose the readings in this book to complement the typical course in introductory cultural anthropology. The sequence of articles follows the

organization of standard anthropology textbooks, grouped under traditional headings such as kinship and marriage, rather than headings based on the applied areas such as medical anthropology or the anthropology of development. As in most contemporary textbooks, linguistic anthropology is included under culture and communication. Had we meant this book to be a reader on applied anthropology, our organization would have been different. Although this book could be used by students in courses on applied anthropology (earlier editions have been), they are not our intended audience. And for this reason, we have not provided extensive discussion of the history or definition of applied anthropology. For students interested in this, there are a number of fine books on the subject. These include *Applied Anthropology: A Practical Guide,* by Erve Chambers; *Applied Anthropology: An Introduction,* by John van Willigen; *Anthropological Praxis: Translating Knowledge into Action,* by Robert M. Wulff and Shirley J. Fiske; *Applied Anthropology in America,* by Elizabeth M. Eddy and William L. Partridge; and *Making Our Research Useful,* by John van Willigen, Barbara Rylko-Bauer, and Anne McElroy. Students interested in medical matters may want to consult *Understanding and Applying Medical Anthropology,* by Peter J. Brown, or *Anthropology and Public Health,* by Robert Hahn.

- To emphasize how anthropology can be put to work in different settings, we have included a number of profiles of anthropologists whose careers involve applying anthropology outside the university setting.
- To help students better understand the subject matter, we have included a number of pedagogical aids: introductions, a list of glossary terms, and guiding questions for each article; a world map that pinpoints the locations of places and peoples discussed in the articles; and, for easy reference, an extensive glossary and index.
- To help busy instructors, we have provided an instructor's manual that includes a brief summary, glossary terms, and test questions for each article.

NEW TO THIS EDITION

In this edition we have continued our previous commitment to the introduction of race as a salient topic for introductory cultural anthropology. Race and ethnicity are important topics both for our discipline and for society at large. Race is a cultural construction, not a biological fact. In this regard, students need to understand that "whiteness" is a cultural construction also. Racism is a continuing reality in our society, and it deserves to be confronted directly.

We have also added some new readings directly related to current public policy debates. These additions fit the long-term goal of the American Anthropological Association to increase the voice of anthropology in public discourse about important social issues. In addition to the issue of race, and clearly related to it, are topics like bilingual education and Ebonics, education reform, multiculturalism, and refugees. These are cogent issues in North America, and we have integrated these additions throughout the book.

A new section addresses anthropology and education. We felt that this topic deserved some direct attention, not only because it appears to be a flash point in our society but also because both students and professors are engaged in the education process and it is useful to be reflexive about what we are doing.

Additionally, we have changed readings in other areas, such as economics and economic development. In all cases, the changes were made to offer better examples of the relevance of anthropology to solving practical problems in today's world.

ACKNOWLEDGMENTS

We wish to thank the staff at McGraw-Hill, especially Kevin Witt, Vicki Moran, and Jen Mills. Also, we would like to express our appreciation to Stacy Bowers, Jaime Tokheim, and Pat Woelber for their efforts in compiling *Applying Anthropology* and *Applying Cultural Anthropology.*

We are grateful to the many instructors who returned questionnaires evaluating the selections: C. Adams, Indiana University; S. Adrian, University of Arizona; N. Allison, Toccoa Falls College; L. Ammons, Assumption College; P. Barlett, Emory University; K. Barlow, University of Minnesota; E. Bigler, Rhode Island College; B. Bigony, University of Wisconsin at Menomonie; G. Bogdan, Orange Coast College; A. Bolyanatz, Wheaton College; C. Bretell, Southern Methodist University; J. Brown, Oakland University; D. Bruner, University of North Carolina at Greensboro; J. Cahoon, College of St. Scholastica; D. Chasin, Newport Beach, CA; J. Coggeshall, Clemson University; K. Costa, Fall River, MA; J. Culbert, San Diego State University; D. Darlington, Western Wyoming Community College; S. Dauria, Bloomsburg University; J. Dempsey, Phoenix, AZ; D. Duchon, Georgia State University; M. Findlay, California State University at Chico; T. Fitzgerald, University of North Carolina at Greensboro; M. Fong, Chaffey College;

P. Fontane, St. Louis College of Pharmacy; F. Freedman, Syracuse University; D. Gamble, Southwest Baptist University; D. Gibson, El Camino College; D. Gordon, Fort Lewis College; T. Greaves, Bucknell University; C. Hartse, Olympic College; T. Headland, Summer Institute of Linguistics; E. Hegeman, John Jay College, City University of New York; M. Helms, University of North Carolina at Greensboro; J. Herron, Ottawa, KS; B. Howell, University of Tennessee at Knoxville; C. Hull, Grand Valley State University; S. Jen, California State University at Fresno; B. Joans, Merritt College; C. Johnson, Indiana University Northwest; C. Kahrs, Saddleback Community College; P. Kilbride, Bryn Mawr College; S. Kus, Rhodes College; S. Lamb, Brandeis University; G. Landsman, State University of New York at Albany; J. Levi, Carleton College; P. Little, University of Kentucky; W. Lohrer, California State University at Chico; K. Lorenz, Shippensburg University; K. Maines, Pennsylvania State University; B. Mathieu, West Los Angeles College; M. Mazzarelli, Massachusetts Bay Community College; C. McCall, Hiwassee College; J. McCall, Southern Illinois University at Carbondale; C. Moyers, Cabrillo College; B. Nelson, University of Utah; C. Nowak, Chicago, IL; B. Pate, University of Tennessee; K. Piatt, Babson College; K. Porter, Rochester, NY; M. Pulford, University of Wisconsin at Superior; S. Rachelle, Mt. San Jacinto College; R. Rajner, University of Toledo; S. Rasmussen, University of Houston; S. Rorbakken, University of Iowa; J. Ryan, Texas Christian University; B. Schmitz, Orange Coast College; D. Seelow, State University of New York at Old Westbury; D. Shepherd, Rubbindale, MN; V. Smith, California State University at Chico; J. Stimpfl, University of Nebraska at Lincoln; H. Swanson, Mohave Community College; M. Taylor, University of Memphis; T. M. Taylor, University of South Colorado; J. Thompson, Tennessee Wesleyan College; J. Tizon, University of Southern Maine; K. Wilcoxson, University of Sioux Falls; P. Wohlt, Ball State University; Z. Zelazo, Montclair State University.

Contents

Culture and Communication

Culture and Food

Culture and Agriculture

Culture and Race

Economy and Business

Gender and Socialization

Religion, Ritual, and Curing

Cultural Change and Globalization

Introduction

Understanding Humans and Human Problems

To the uninitiated, the term *anthropology* conjures up images of mummies' tombs, Indiana Jones, and treks through steaming jungles or over high alpine peaks. Anthropologists agree that their chosen field is exciting, that they have been places and seen things that few experience firsthand, and that they have been deeply and emotionally involved in understanding the human condition. At the same time, however, the vision of anthropology presented by Hollywood has probably done more to obscure the true nature of the profession than it has to enlighten the public about what we really do.

Providing an accurate image of anthropology and anthropological work is both simple and complex. Essentially, anthropology is the study of people, or more properly, of humankind. But, you may say, many disciplines study people: psychology, sociology, history, biology, medicine, and so on. True, but anthropology is different in that it seeks to integrate these separate and perhaps narrower views of humanity. To understand ourselves, we need to join these disparate views into a single framework, a process that begins with our biological and evolutionary roots, explores the development of culture through the prehistoric and historical periods, probes the uniquely human ability to develop culture through communication, and examines the diversity of recent and present-day cultures that inhabit the globe.

From this conception of the *holistic* and *comparative* study of humankind emerge what are termed the four fields of anthropology: biological (or physical) anthropology, archaeology, anthropological linguistics, and cultural anthropology. Some universities offer an introductory course that covers all four subfields. Other schools cover the subfields in two or three separate introductory courses. Each approach has its advantage. The former may more fully integrate the biocultural and historical dimensions of humanity; the latter allows students to explore each subfield in greater depth. This book introduces you to the four fields of anthropology and how they are used in today's world.

Another way to divide the discipline—in fact almost any discipline—is into *basic* and *applied* research. These categories are important in this reader because we would like students to appreciate both the basic and the applied sides of anthropology. A survey of natural and social scientists and engineers conducted by the U.S. Census Bureau for the National Science Foundation used the following definitions of these fundamental concepts: *Basic research* is study directed toward gaining scientific knowledge primarily for its own sake. *Applied research* is study directed toward gaining scientific knowledge in an effort to meet a recognized need.

Anthropology is a discipline concerned primarily with basic research. It asks "big" questions concerning the origins of humankind, the roots of human nature, the development of civilization, and the functions of our major social institutions (such as marriage and religion). Nevertheless, anthropologists have put the methods and skills developed in basic research to use in solving human problems and fulfilling the needs of society. Anthropologists have, for example, worked with medical examiners in the identification of skeletal remains. They have also helped communities preserve their cultural heritage and businesses and government agencies understand the social impact of programs or development projects.

Although the application of anthropology has a long history, it has until recent years remained in the shadows of pure or basic research. The last twenty-five years have seen a change. Anthropologists have moved beyond their traditional roles in universities and museums and now work in a broad range of settings. They are employed in many government agencies, in the private sector, and in a variety of nonresearch capacities (such as administrator, evaluator, or policy analyst).

In response to the growing opportunities for anthropologists outside academia and to the demands of students, an increasing number of master's degree and doctoral programs provide training specifically in the applications of anthropology. This is not to say that the classified ads list jobs titled "anthropologist." Rather, for those interested in anthropology, there are increasing opportunities to find careers that draw on anthropological training and skills. Profiles of people in nonacademic careers (consumer marketing, high-tech industry, and refugee policy) can be found in this reader. At the same time, studies have shown that there will be increasing job opportunities for anthropologists in universities and colleges during the next decade and beyond.

These new opportunities are particularly evident in this era of multiculturalism and in the increasing public recognition that our society must be a culturally diverse social mosaic. Exploration of this reality has always been the domain of cultural anthropology; a usual pedagogical goal of teachers of cultural anthropology is to increase a student's appreciation and tolerance of cultural differences. Living in a multicultural society presents real challenges of social tensions caused by chronic persistent ethnocentrism and racism. But living in a multicultural society also brings a cultural richness, a luxuriant wealth, to our lives.

School administrators, engineers, doctors, business leaders, lawyers, medical researchers, and government officials have become aware that the substantive knowledge, the unique perspective, and the research skills of anthropologists are applicable to practical problems—in the United States as well as other countries.

As we explore anthropology, keep in mind the interplay between and interdependence of basic cultural research and the applications of anthropological knowledge and research methods to the solution of human problems.

CULTURAL ANTHROPOLOGY

Cultural anthropology is concerned with the description and analysis of people's lives and traditions. In the past, cultural anthropologists almost always did research in far-off "exotic" societies, but today we have expanded our research interests to include our own society. Cultural anthropology can add much to both the basic and the applied scientific understanding of human behaviors and beliefs. The study and interpretation of other societies—of their traditions, history, and view of the world—is inherently interesting and important because it documents the diversity of human lifestyles. The anthropological approach to understanding other societies also has practical value for addressing contemporary human problems and needs.

The concept of *culture* is central to anthropology. It refers to the patterns of economy, social organization, and belief that are learned and shared by members of a social group. Culture is traditional knowledge that is passed down from one generation to the next. Although generally stable over time, culture is flexible and fluid, changing through borrowing or invention. The influential American anthropologist Franz Boas championed the concept of culture for understanding human diversity; culture, Boas argued, is distinct from biological "race" or language. Anthropologists believe that all cultural lifestyles have intrinsic value and

validity. Other societies deserve to be studied and understood without being prejudged using our own narrow (and sometimes intolerant) beliefs and values; this universal tendency to prejudge based on the supposed superiority of one's own group, called *ethnocentrism*, is something everyone should avoid.

Culture is the crowning achievement of human evolution. To understand ourselves is to appreciate cultural diversity. Dependence on culture as our primary mechanism of survival sets humans apart from other members of the animal kingdom. This dependence is responsible for the tremendous evolutionary success of our species, which has grown in population (sometimes to the point of overpopulation) and can inhabit nearly every niche on the planet.

The paradox of culture is that, as we humans learn to accept our own cultural beliefs and values, we unconsciously learn to reject those of other peoples. At birth, we are capable of absorbing any culture and language. We are predisposed to cultural learning, but we are not programmed to adopt a particular culture. As we grow, our parents, our schools, and our society teach us what is right and wrong, good and evil, acceptable and unacceptable. At the subconscious level, we learn the symbolic meanings of behavior and through them interpret the meanings of actions. Beliefs, values, and symbols must be understood within the context of a particular culture. This is the principle of *cultural relativity*. At the same time, culture supplies us with the cognitive models—software programs, if you will—that allow us to perceive or "construct" a particular version of reality. Culture permeates our thinking and our expectations; this is the principle of *culture construction*.

In addition to the concept of culture, the anthropological approach to the study of human behavior and belief has two essential characteristics: a holistic approach and a comparative framework. The *holistic approach* means that anthropologists see a particular part of culture—for example, politics, economy, or religion—in relation to the larger social system. Individuals are viewed, not in isolation, but as part of an intricate web of social relationships. Although an anthropological study may have a particular focus, the holistic approach means that the broader cultural context is always considered important because the different parts of a cultural system are interrelated. When, for example, the economy or the technology changes, other aspects of the culture will change as well.

The *comparative framework* means that explanations or generalizations are achieved through cross-cultural research. Questions about humanity cannot be based on information from a single society or a single type of society such as the industrial societies of the United States and Europe. Such a limited framework is simply to narrow for understanding the big picture that basic anthropological research seeks. By studying others within a comparative framework, we can better understand ourselves. If other cultures are a mirror in which we see ourselves, then anthropology is a mirror for humankind.

The broad generalizations about culture and society that we have been talking about are based on detailed knowledge of the world's cultures. To gain this knowledge, anthropologists go to the people. Often accompanied by spouses and children, we pack our bags and travel to far-off lands—to the highlands of New Guinea, the frozen Arctic, the savannas of Africa, or the jungles of South America. Increasingly, anthropologist are bringing their research methods and comparative, holistic perspective into the cities and suburbs of America, the American schoolroom, and the corporate jungle. This "research adventure" has become the hallmark of cultural anthropology.

The research methods used by the cultural anthropologist are distinctive because they depend to a large extend on the firsthand experiences and interpretations of the field researcher. Cultural anthropologists conduct research in natural settings rather than in laboratories or over the telephone. This method for studying another society is often called *participant observation, ethnography,* or *qualitative methods.* The goal of describing, understanding, and explaining another culture is a large task. It is most often accomplished by living in the society for an extended period, by talking with people, and, as much as possible, by experiencing their lives.

One important tool that cultural anthropologists depend on in field research is *language.* They need to learn the local language not only for their own survival in the field but, more important, because language is a key to understanding someone else's culture. Many anthropologists study descriptive linguistics to make it easier for them to learn an unwritten language in the field. By looking at speech and language in Apache culture (Selection 7) or the complex problems of male-female miscommunication (Selection 8), anthropologists can learn a great deal about the culture they are studying.

The fieldwork experience usually involves a kind of culture shock in which the researcher questions his or her own assumptions about the world. In this way, fieldwork is often a rewarding period of personal growth. In their work, anthropologists expect to find that other people's behavior, even when it seems bizarre when seen from the outside, makes sense when viewed from the people's own point of view. This is why anthropological research often means letting people speak for themselves. While doing research, the anthropologist often thinks of herself or himself as a child—as being ignorant or uninformed and needing to be taught by the people being studied. This approach often involves in-depth interviewing with a few key informants and then interpreting (and writing about) that other culture for the researcher's own society. The ethnographic method, pioneered and developed in anthropology, is now being used in a range of applied areas, including marketing, management research, and school evaluation. Although ethnography is an important research style, the selection in this book demonstrate that many different methods are used in anthropology today.

The applications of cultural anthropology are diverse. Internationally, anthropologists are involved in programs of technical assistance and economic aid to Third World nations. Theses programs address needs in such areas as agriculture and rural development; health, nutrition, and family planning; education; housing and community organizing; transportation and communication; and energy. Anthropologists do many of the same things domestically as well. They evaluate public education, study agricultural extension programs, administer projects, analyze policy (such as U.S. refugee resettlement programs), and research crime and crime prevention, for example.

In the private sector, cultural anthropologists can add a fresh perspective to market research. They analyze office and industrial organization and culture. They create language and cultural training workshops for businesspeople and others who are going overseas. These workshops reduce the likelihood of crosscultural misunderstanding and the problems of culture shock for the employee and, often more important, for his or her family. A good example is the work of Richard Reeves-Ellington (Selection 22), who has demonstrated how the training of corporate managers in Japanese culture significantly improves their business productivity.

Applied anthropological work can be divided into four categories. In the first group, applied research and basic research look very much alike, except that the goal of applied research is more directly linked to a particular problem or need. For example, in Selection 34, Aaron Podolefsky studies the causes of the re-emmergence of tribal warfare in New Guinea. Such studies provide planners and policymakers with important insights for understanding the problem. This knowledge can help in the design and implementation of programs that help bring an end to warfare in the region. Similarly, Philippe Bourgois' sensitive ethnography of the culture of crack users may help in the implementation of drug treatment programs (Selection 4).

In the second category, anthropologists may work as researchers for a government agency, corporation, or interest group on a specific task defined by the client.

In the third category, anthropologists work as consultants to business and industry or to government agencies that need in-depth cultural knowledge to solve or prevent a problem. Anthropologists often act as cultural brokers, mediating and translating between groups who are miscommunicating not because of their words but because of cultural meanings.

Finally, a few anthropologists have developed and administered programs. Gerald F. Murray's work in reforestation in Haiti (Selection 14) exemplifies the development and actual administration of a project in which cultural understanding is a fundamental component. The overwhelming success of this agroforestry project attests to the practical value of cultural understanding for solving human problems.

A great deal of anthropological work remains to be done, although this seems to be a well-kept secret. People have a far easier time focusing on the individual as the level of analysis. When divorce, drug abuse, or suicide affects small numbers of people, we may look to the individual and to psychology for answers. When divorce rates climb to 50 percent of all marriages and the suicide rate increases tenfold, however, we must look beyond the individual to forces that affect society at large. Because we are so immersed in our own culture, we have difficulty seeing it as a powerful force that guides—even controls—our behavior. We begin these readings, therefore, with several selections that convey the hidden, but powerful, nature of culture.

The readings in this book are subdivided into traditional anthropological categories, such as economy, gender, social organization, politics, and religion. In each category you will find reading selections that demonstrate not only the relevance of anthropology theory and methods in the understanding of human problems but also the application of anthropology to specific problems or issues.

1

Body Ritual Among the Nacirema

Horace Miner

Generations of anthropologists have traveled the globe, reaching to the far corners of the five continents to discover and describe the many ways of humankind. Anthropologists have gathered a diverse collection of exotic customs, from the mundane to the bizarre. Understanding and appreciating other societies requires us to be culturally relative. But people tend to judge others by their own cultural values in a way that is *ethnocentric*. This is because people take their cultural beliefs and behaviors for granted; they seem so natural that they are seldom questioned. Among the most interesting social customs on record are the rituals of the Nacirema. By viewing Nacirema behaviors as *rituals*, we gain insight into their culture and into the meaning of the concept of *culture*. We also gain insight into the problem of ethnocentrism.

Ritual is a cultural phenomenon. Ritual can be found in all societies. It can be defined as a set of acts that follow a sequence established by tradition.

Throughout the world, ritual reflects the fundamental cultural beliefs and values of a society by giving order to important activities and particular life crises like death and birth. Every day, however, mundane rituals are performed unconsciously. In fact, most Nacirema people do these things without being aware of their underlying symbolic meanings. Pay particular attention to the quotation at the end of the selection.

As you read this selection, ask yourself the following questions:

- How do the Nacirema feel about the human body?
- Do you think that the charms and magical potions used by the Nacirema really work?
- Can you list those aspects of social life in which magic plays an important role?
- What is your opinion of the importance of body ritual, and if you went to live among the Nacirema, would you tell them of your opinion?
- Living among the Nacirema, you might find that their behaviors sometimes appear bizarre. Do you think the Nacirema themselves feel this way?

The following terms discussed in this selection are included in the Glossary at the back of the book:

clan	*ethnocentrism*
culture	*ritual*

The anthropologist has become so familiar with the diversity of ways in which different peoples behave in similar situations that he is not apt to be surprised by even the most exotic customs. In fact, if all of the logically possible combinations of behavior have not been found somewhere in the world, he is apt to suspect that they must be present in some yet undescribed tribe. This point has, in fact, been expressed with respect to clan organization by Murdock (1949:71). In this light, the magical beliefs and practices of the Nacirema present such unusual aspects that it seems desirable to describe them as an example of the extremes to which human behavior can go.

Professor Linton first brought the ritual of the Nacirema to the attention of anthropologists twenty years ago (1936:326), but the culture of this people is still very poorly understood. They are a North American group living in the territory between the Canadian Cree, the Yaqui and Tarahumare of Mexico, and the Carib and Arawak of the Antilles. Little is known of their origin, although tradition states that they came from the east. According to Nacirema mythology, their nation was originated by a culture hero, Notgnihsaw, who is otherwise known for two great feats of strength —the throwing of a piece of wampum across the river

Reproduced by permission of the American Anthropological Association from *American Anthropologist* 58:3, 1956. Not for further reproduction.

Pa-To-Mac and the chopping down of a cherry tree in which the Spirit of Truth resided.

Nacirema culture is characterized by a highly developed market economy which has evolved in a rich natural habitat. While much of the people's time is devoted to economic pursuits, a large part of the fruits of these labors and a considerable portion of the day are spent in ritual activity. The focus of this activity is the human body, the appearance and health of which loom as a dominant concern in the ethos of the people. While such a concern is certainly not unusual, its ceremonial aspects and associated philosophy are unique.

The fundamental belief underlying the whole system appears to be that the human body is ugly and that its natural tendency is to debility and disease. Incarcerated in such a body, man's only hope is to avert these characteristics through the use of the powerful influences of ritual and ceremony. Every household has one or more shrines devoted to this purpose. The more powerful individuals in the society have several shrines in their houses and, in fact, the opulence of a house is often referred to in terms of the number of such ritual centers it possesses. Most houses are of wattle and daub construction, but the shrine rooms of the more wealthy are walled with stone. Poorer families imitate the rich by applying pottery plaques to their shrine walls.

While each family has at least one such shrine, the rituals associated with it are not family ceremonies but are private and secret. The rites are normally only discussed with children, and then only during the period when they are being initiated into these mysteries. I was able, however, to establish sufficient rapport with the natives to examine these shrines and to have the rituals described to me.

The focal point of the shrine is a box or chest which is built into the wall. In this chest are kept the many charms and magical potions without which no native believes he could live. These preparations are secured from a variety of specialized practitioners. The most powerful of these are the medicine men, whose assistance must be rewarded with substantial gifts. However, the medicine men do not provide the curative potions for their clients, but decide what the ingredients should be and then write them down in an ancient and secret language. This writing is understood only by the medicine men and by the herbalists who, for another gift, provide the required charm.

The charm is not disposed of after it has served its purpose, but is placed in the charm-box of the household shrine. As these magical materials are specific for certain ills, and the real or imagined maladies of the people are many, the charm-box is usually full to overflowing. The magical packets are so numerous that people forget what their purposes were and fear to use them again. While the natives are very vague on this point, we can only assume that the idea in retaining all the old magical materials is that their presence in the charm-box, before which the body rituals are conducted, will in some way protect the worshipper.

Beneath the charm-box is a small font. Each day every member of the family, in succession, enters the shrine room, bows his head before the charm-box, mingles different sorts of holy water in the font, and proceeds with a brief rite of ablution. The holy waters are secured from the Water Temple of the community, where the priests conduct elaborate ceremonies to make the liquid ritually pure.

In the hierarchy of magical practitioners, and below the medicine men in prestige, are specialists whose designation is best translated "holy-mouth-men." The Nacirema have an almost pathological horror of and fascination with the mouth, the condition of which is believed to have a supernatural influence on all social relationships. Were it not for the rituals of the mouth, they believe that their teeth would fall out, their gums bleed, their jaws shrink, their friends desert them, and their lovers reject them. They also believe that a strong relationship exists between oral and moral characteristics. For example, there is a ritual ablution of the mouth for children which is supposed to improve their moral fiber.

The daily body ritual performed by everyone includes a mouth-rite. Despite the fact that these people are so punctilious about care of the mouth, this rite involves a practice which strikes the uninitiated stranger as revolting. It was reported to me that the ritual consists of inserting a small bundle of hog hairs into the mouth, along with certain magical powders, and then moving the bundle in a highly formalized series of gestures.

In addition to the private mouth-rite, the people seek out a holy-mouth-man once or twice a year. These practitioners have an impressive set of paraphernalia, consisting of a variety of augers, awls, probes, and prods. The use of these objects in the exorcism of the evils of the mouth involves almost unbelievable ritual torture of the client. The holy-mouth-man opens the client's mouth, and using the above mentioned tools,

The author of this article used the term *man* to refer to humanity in general. This term is not used by modern anthropologists because, to many people, it reflects an unconscious sexist bias in language and rhetoric. At the time that this article was written, however, the generalized *man* was a common convention in writing. In the interest of historical accuracy we have not changed the wording in this article, but students should be aware that nonsexist terms (*humans, people, Homo sapiens,* and so on) are preferred.—The Editors.

enlarges any holes which decay may have created in the teeth. Magical materials are put into these holes. If there are no naturally occurring holes in the teeth, large sections of one or more teeth are gouged out so that the supernatural substance can be applied. In the client's view, the purpose of these ministrations is to arrest decay and to draw friends. The extremely sacred and traditional character of the rite is evident in the fact that the natives return to the holy-mouth-men year after year, despite the fact that their teeth continue to decay.

It is to be hoped that, when a thorough study of the Nacirema is made, there will be careful inquiry into the personality structure of these people. One has to but watch the gleam in the eye of a holy-mouth-man as he jabs an awl into an exposed nerve, to suspect that a certain amount of sadism is involved. If this can be established, a very interesting pattern emerges, for most of the population shows definite masochistic tendencies. It was to these that Professor Linton referred in discussing a distinctive part of the daily body ritual which is performed only by men. This part of the rite involves scraping and lacerating the surface of the face with a sharp instrument. Special women's rites are performed only four times during each lunar month, but what they lack in frequency is made up in barbarity. As part of this ceremony, women bake their heads in small ovens for about an hour. The theoretically interesting point is that what seems to be a preponderantly masochistic people have developed sadistic specialists.

The medicine men have an imposing temple, or *latipso*, in every community of any size. The more elaborate ceremonies required to treat very sick patients can only be performed at this temple. These ceremonies involve not only the thaumaturge but a permanent group of vestal maidens who move sedately about the temple chambers in distinctive costume and headdress.

The *latipso* ceremonies are so harsh that it is phenomenal that a fair proportion of the really sick natives who enter the temple ever recover. Small children whose indoctrination is still incomplete have been known to resist attempts to take them to the temple because "that is where you go to die." Despite this fact, sick adults are not only willing but eager to undergo the protracted ritual purification, if they can afford to do so. No matter how ill the supplicant or how grave the emergency, the guardians of many temples will not admit a client if he cannot give a rich gift to the custodian. Even after one has gained admission and survived the ceremonies, the guardians will not permit the neophyte to leave until he makes still another gift.

The supplicant entering the temple is first stripped of all his or her clothes. In everyday life the Nacirema avoids exposure of his body and its natural functions. Bathing and excretory acts are performed only in the secrecy of the household shrine, where they are ritualized as part of the body-rites. Psychological shock results from the fact that body secrecy is suddenly lost upon entry into the *latipso*. A man, whose own wife has never seen him in an excretory act, suddenly finds himself naked and assisted by a vestal maiden while he performs his natural functions into a sacred vessel. This sort of ceremonial treatment is necessitated by the fact that the excreta are used by a diviner to ascertain the course and nature of the client's sickness. Female clients, on the other hand, find their naked bodies are subjected to the scrutiny, manipulation and prodding of the medicine men.

Few supplicants in the temple are well enough to do anything but lie on their hard beds. The daily ceremonies, like the rites of the holy-mouth-men, involve discomfort and torture. With ritual precision, the vestals awaken their miserable charges each dawn and roll them about on their beds of pain while performing ablutions, in the formal movements of which the maidens are highly trained. At other times they insert magic wands in the supplicant's mouth or force him to eat substances which are supposed to be healing. From time to time the medicine men come to their clients and jab magically treated needles into their flesh. The fact that these temple ceremonies may not cure, and may even kill the neophyte, in no way decreases the people's faith in the medicine men.

There remains one other kind of practitioner, known as a "listener." This witch-doctor has the power to exorcise the devils that lodge in the heads of people who have been bewitched. The Nacirema believe that parents bewitch their own children. Mothers are particularly suspected of putting a curse on children while teaching them the secret body rituals. The counter-magic of the witch-doctor is unusual in its lack of ritual. The patient simply tells the "listener" all his troubles and fears, beginning with the earliest difficulties he can remember. The memory displayed by the Nacirema in these exorcism sessions is truly remarkable. It is not uncommon for the patient to bemoan the rejection he felt upon being weaned as a babe, and a few individuals even see their troubles going back to the traumatic effects of their own birth.

In conclusion, mention must be made of certain practices which have their base in native esthetics but which depend upon the pervasive aversion to the natural body and its functions. There are ritual fasts to make fat people thin and ceremonial feasts to make thin people fat. Still other rites are used to make women's breasts larger if they are small, and smaller if they are large. General dissatisfaction with breast shape is symbolized in the fact that the ideal form is virtually outside the range of human variation. A few women afflicted with almost inhuman hypermammary development are so idolized that they make a handsome living by simply going from village to village and permitting the natives to stare at them for a fee.

Reference has already been made to the fact that excretory functions are ritualized, routinized, and relegated to secrecy. Natural reproductive functions are similarly distorted. Intercourse is taboo as a topic and scheduled as an act. Efforts are made to avoid pregnancy by the use of magical materials or by limiting intercourse to certain phases of the moon. Conception is actually very infrequent. When pregnant, women dress so as to hide their condition. Parturition takes place in secret, without friends or relatives to assist, and the majority of women do not nurse their infants.

Our review of the ritual life of the Nacirema has certainly shown them to be a magic-ridden people. It is hard to understand how they have managed to exist so long under the burdens which they have imposed upon themselves. But even such exotic customs as these take on real meaning when they are viewed with the insight provided by Malinowski when he wrote (1948:70):

> Looking from far and above, from our high places of safety in the developed civilization, it is easy to see all the crudity and irrelevance of magic. But without its power and guidance early man could not have mastered his practical difficulties as he has done, nor could man have advanced to the higher stages of civilization.

REFERENCES

Linton, Ralph, 1936, *The Study of Man*. New York, D. Appleton-Century Co.

Malinowski, Bronislaw, 1948, *Magic, Science, and Religion*. Glencoe, The Free Press.

Murdock, George P., 1949, *Social Structure*. New York, The Macmillan Co.

2

Slumber's Unexplored Landscape

Bruce Bower

Why might our sleep be shaped by culture? All people need to sleep, but our expectations of what is normal sleep and how we go about arranging sleep are dictated by our cultural background. Therefore, our need for sleep may be a biological universal, but there are significant variations in the way that our need for sleep is satisfied. Similarly, culture shapes the way that our need for food is satisfied—what and when we eat and which foods we most enjoy. Of course, we can learn to enjoy and desire new foods. In fact, expanding our palates through cultural learning can be a delicious experience. From another perspective, we might consider pain as a way that culture shapes biology. All people experience pain, but there are cultural rules about the way in which we communicate our discomfort. For example, some societies may have gender-specific rules about the expression of pain ("boys don't cry") that become internalized so that adult men seek health care less frequently than women and children and consequently die at earlier ages.

Human biologists do not completely understand what the neurophysiological and psychological functions of dreams might be. In this selection, we see that nearly all scientific sleep research is conducted in artificial laboratory settings and based on the particular patterns of sleep found in Western culture. In this way, medical definitions of insomnia are based upon cultural assumptions of what "normal" sleep patterns are. In traditional societies, sleep is often communal and in contexts that are noisy. People in these societies see the North American pattern of putting babies in their own cribs in their own rooms as strange and barbaric. Cross-cultural comparison based on direct observations of people in the field is the hallmark of research in cultural anthropology. In this selection we find that people in traditional societies sleep in eye-opening ways.

As you read this selection, ask yourself the following questions:

- Many students find that their sleeping patterns change when they go to college. What are the ways that your social and cultural contexts determine your sleep?
- Does the two-phase sleep pattern described at the end of this selection make sense to you?
- When we sleep, we dream. Does culture affect the content of our dreams? Why are dreams more discussed in some other societies?
- What is the value of cross-cultural anthropological research in sleep research?

The following terms discussed in this selection are included in the Glossary at the back of the book:

communal	*rapid eye movement (REM)*
cross-cultural	*séance*

Ah, the sweet simplicity of sleep. You tramp into your bedroom with sagging eyelids and stifle a yawn. After disrobing, you douse the lights and climb into bed. Maybe a little reading or television massages the nerves, loosening them up for slumber's velvet fingers. In a while, you nod off. Suddenly, an alarm clock's shrill blast breaks up the dozefest as the sun pokes over the horizon. You feel a bit drowsy but shake it off and face the new day. Images of a dream dissolve like sugar in the morning's first cup of coffee.

There's a surprising twist, however, at the heart of this familiar ritual. It simply doesn't apply to people currently living outside of the modern Western world —or even to inhabitants of Western Europe as recently as 200 years ago.

In such contexts, and probably throughout human evolution, solitary shut-eye organized around a regular bedtime and a single bout of sleep proves about as

Reprinted with permission from *Science News* 1999, vol. 156:205–207.

common as stock car racing or teleconferencing. Surprisingly, anthropologists have rarely scrutinized the sleep patterns and practices of different cultures, much less those of different classes and ethnic groups in the United States.

An initial attempt to draw back the veils of sleep in hunter-gatherer groups and other traditional societies has uncovered a wide variety of sleep customs, reports anthropologist Carol M. Worthman of Emory University in Atlanta. None of these snooze styles, however, looks anything like what modern Western folk take for granted.

This finding raises profound questions for the burgeoning discipline of sleep research, Worthman says. Over the past 50 years, scientists have avidly delved into slumber's biology. Early research identified periods of rapid-eye-movement (REM) sleep, during which intense dreams often occur. Current efforts pursue genes involved in wakefulness and sleeping (SN: 8/14/99, p. 100). Researchers have also taken strides toward treating insomnia and other sleep disturbances.

While investigators readily concede that they don't yet know why people sleep and dream, they assume that they at least know how people should sleep: alone or with a partner for a solid chunk of the night. Sleep studies therefore take place in laboratories where individuals catch winks while hooked up to a bevy of brain and body monitors.

However, the distinctive sleep styles of non-Western groups may mold sleep's biology in ways undreamed of in sleep labs, Worthman suggests. They may influence factors ranging from sleep-related genes to the brain's electrical output during various sleep phases.

"It's time for scientists to get out into natural sleep environments," Worthman remarks. "It's embarrassing that anthropologists haven't done this, and the lack of such work is impeding sleep research."

A seemingly innocent question awakened Worthman to her discipline's ignorance of how people sleep. In 1994, she had a conversation with pediatrician Ronald E. Dahl of the University of Pittsburgh School of Medicine, who studies the effects of mood disorders on sleep. He asked the Emory scientist to tell him what anthropologists know about the history and prehistory of sleep. "[My] bald, if somewhat overstated, answer was 'zero,'" she says.

Sleep scarcely figures in the literature on either cross-cultural differences or human evolution, Worthman realized. Investigators generally relegate slumber to the sidelines, treating it as a biological given with little potential for variation from one place to another, she holds.

A few researchers have bucked this trend. For instance, anthropologist James J. McKenna of the University of Notre Dame in Indiana has reported that babies in many countries outside the United States sleep next to or in the same room as their parents. Contact with a parent's body helps regulate an infant's breathing and other physiological functions, he asserts, perhaps lowering the risk for sudden infant death syndrome (SN:12/4/93, p. 380).

McKenna's work should have roused investigators of traditional societies out of their sleep-related torpor, Worthman says. Yet, even seasoned fieldworkers have tended to ignore sleep—at least in their published works—while describing food production, sexual practices, and other facets of daily life.

So, Worthman contacted seven researchers who she knew had intimate knowledge of one or more traditional societies, including nomadic foragers, herders, and village-based farmers. Among these far-flung populations, none of the investigators, by their own admission, had systematically studied how people sleep. After plumbing what the researchers had absorbed about nighttime activities, Worthman has assembled a preliminary picture of sleep practices in 10 non-Western populations.

Worthman's findings rip the covers off any lingering suspicions that people everywhere sleep pretty much alike. Far from the wallpapered confines of middle-class bedrooms, sleep typically unfolds in shared spaces that feature constant background noise emanating from other sleepers, various domestic animals, fires maintained for warmth and protection from predators, and other people's nearby night-time activities.

Groups in Worthman's analysis include Ache foragers in Paraguay, !Kung hunter-gatherers in Africa, Swat Pathan herders in Pakistan, and Balinese farmers in Indonesia. For all these groups and six others, communal sleep equals safe sleep, because sleepers can count on there being someone else up or easily awakened at all hours of the night to warn others of a threat or emergency.

Adult sleepers in traditional societies recline on skins, mats, wooden platforms, the ground, or just about anything except a thick, springy mattress. Pillows or head supports are rare, and people doze in whatever they happen to be wearing. Virtually no one, including children, keeps a regular bedtime. Individuals tend to slip in and out of slumber several times during the night. In these unplugged worlds, darkness greatly limits activity and determines the time allotted to sleep. Folks there frequently complain of getting too much sleep, not too little.

Many rituals occur at night and exploit the need to sleep. For instance, initiation rites often force participants to cope with sleep deprivation. In other ceremonies, individuals enter somnolent, or near-sleep, states in order to magnify an occasion's psychological impact and to induce spiritual visions.

Consider the communal sleep of the Gebusi, New Guinea, rainforest dwellers, who grow fruit in small gardens and occasionally hunt wild pigs. Women, girls, and babies crowd into a narrow section of a community longhouse to sleep on mats. Men and boys retreat to an adjacent, more spacious longhouse area, where they sleep on wooden platforms.

Gebusi females retire at dark for about 10 hours of rest and sleep. In contrast, the men stay up later and frequently conduct rituals. About once a month, everyone attends an all-night dance and feast, catching up on sleep the next day.

Each week or two, Gebusi men go to séances led by a "spirit medium," at which they try to keep spirits awake throughout the night. Participants attempt to slip in and out of a near-sleep state as the medium, who's usually adept at operating in this half-conscious condition, sings about the spirit world and other matters.

As in most of the other studied societies, the Gebusi express concerns about exposure to ghosts, evil spirits, and witchcraft during sleep. They consider deep sleep risky, since a sleeper's spirit may wander off too far and fail to return. The Gebusi view group slumber as a way to lessen the danger of spirit loss, which they view as especially likely while a person dreams.

Whether or not one believes that sleeping puts a person's spirit at risk, slumber appears to have crucial effects on body and mind. A culture's sleeping style serves as a growing child's training ground for managing biologically based systems of attention and alertness, Worthman contends. Balinese farmers provide a striking example of this sleep-related tutoring.

Balinese infants are carried and held continuously by caregivers so that they learn to fall asleep even in hectic and noisy situations. This grooms them to exhibit what the Balinese call "fear sleep" later in life, Worthman says. Children and adults enter fear sleep by suddenly slumping over in a deep slumber when they or family members confront intense anxiety or an unexpected fright. They are literally scared into sleep.

Infants in middle-class American homes, who usually sleep alone, may not learn to ground their sleeping and waking cycles in a flow of sensations that include bodily contact, smells, and background noises, Worthman proposes. In fact, babies forced to bounce back and forth between the sensory overload of the waking world and the sensory barrenness of dark, quiet bedrooms may often find it difficult to relax, fall asleep, wake up, or concentrate, she theorizes.

Only cross-cultural studies of children's sleep and behavior can clarify such issues, Worthman says.

She described her findings and their implications in June at the annual meeting of the Associated Professional Sleep Societies in Orlando, Fla.

Sleep researchers at the meeting expressed considerable excitement about the potential for cross-cultural studies. "Worthman is doing innovative and important work," comments neuroscientist Robert A. Stickgold of the Massachusetts Mental Health Center in Boston. "It's awakening us to the many different ways in which people organize sleep."

Stickgold has developed snug-fitting, electrode-studded caps that people can wear in their own beds to measure brain activity linked to REM and other sleep stages. Worthman plans to take these "nightcaps," which hook up to mobile recorders, into the field to study sleep biology in traditional societies.

"I've been hoping anthropologists would examine sleep cross-culturally for the past 20 years," remarks psychologist Mary A. Carskadon of the Brown University School of Medicine in Providence, R.I.

Carskadon has directed studies that indicate that the body's so-called biological clock gets pushed back during adolescence. Teenagers may require more sleep than adults and may have a natural tendency to go to sleep later and wake up later than at other ages, she says.

A related study, directed by neuroscientist Louis J. Ptáček of the University of Utah in Salt Lake City, finds that a specific gene yanks the biological clock forward in some adults. People who have this gene tend to fall asleep by 8:30 P.M. and to awaken before 5:30 A.M., the researchers report in the September *Nature Medicine*.

In modern Western cultures, teens' backward shift in sleep timing is considered a nuisance or a sign of rebellion, while extreme early birds get diagnosed as sleep disordered. In traditional settings, however, highly variable sleep schedules among individuals and age groups prove invaluable, since they allow for someone to be awake or easily roused at all times should danger arise, Worthman holds.

If sleeping patterns in traditional societies remain little known, those of prehistoric humans are a total mystery. Still, in settings that roughly mimic ancient night-time conditions, sleep undergoes an intriguing shift, says psychiatrist Thomas A. Wehr of the National Institute of Mental Health (NIMH) in Bethesda, Md.

When prohibited from using artificial light from dusk until dawn, people who formerly slumbered in solid blocks of time begin to sleep in two periods separated by an hour or two of quiet rest and reflection.

Wehr and his coworkers asked 15 healthy adults to rest and sleep in darkness for 14 hours (6 P.M. to 8 A.M.) each night for several weeks. Volunteers slept for 11 hours each of the first few nights, apparently to catch up on their sleep. They then settled into a pattern of lying awake for a couple of hours before falling asleep for 3 to 5 hours in the evening. An hour or so of quiet wakefulness ensued, followed by about 4 more hours of sleep in the early morning.

Many mammals sleep in two major bouts during the night or day, Wehr says. Animals from rodents to giraffes and the experimental human sleepers secrete elevated amounts of the hormone prolactin when they rest quietly, even if they are not asleep. Prolactin may promote a state of calmness that accompanies sleep, the NIMH scientist suggests.

Participants in Wehr's study usually awoke out of REM sleep to end their first slumber session. During REM sleep, the brain becomes about as active as it is when wide awake. One function of this sleep phase may be to set the stage for waking up, Wehr holds.

If prehistoric people slept in two nightly periods, then regularly awakening out of REM sleep may have allowed them to reflect on and remember their dreams in a semiconscious state that's generally unavailable to modern sleepers. Sleep compressed into a single stint may thus encourage modern humans to lose touch with dreams, myths, and fantasies, Wehr argues.

These results, first reported in 1993, also raise the possibility that people who wake up once or twice each night don't necessarily suffer from insomnia. "A natural human sleep pattern may reassert itself in an unwelcome world and get labeled as a disorder," Wehr says.

The two-phase sleep pattern observed by Wehr corresponds remarkably closely to the way in which most Western Europeans slept between 500 to 200 years ago, according to historian A. Roger Ekirch of Virginia Polytechnic Institute and State University in Blacksburg. While doing research for a book on nighttime behaviors during that era, Ekirch came across several hundred references to what he identifies as "segmented sleep."

From country farms and villages to city apartments, early modern Europeans usually sank each evening into what they called a "first sleep," which lasted for several hours. Shortly after midnight, they awoke and spent 1 or 2 hours in a "watching period." A "second," or "morning," sleep followed.

The watching period presented many opportunities, Ekirch notes. People coming out of their first sleep often stayed in bed to pray, converse with a bedfellow, contemplate the day's events or the meaning of a dream, or simply let their minds wander in a semiconscious state of contentment that was prized at the time.

A 16th-century physician wrote that many laborers dozed off exhausted at the start of each night. Sexual intercourse with their wives typically occurred in the watching period, after a recuperative first sleep.

These days, Western societies treat sleep more as an unavoidable stretch of downtime than as a prelude to sex or a time for inner reflection. Only intensive investigations across cultures and classes will illuminate the lushness of sleep's landscape, Worthman predicts.

Adds Wehr, "We're going to have to reconceptualize what it means to sleep normally."

3

Tricking and Tripping: Fieldwork on Prostitution in the Era of AIDS

Claire E. Sterk

Students often think of anthropological fieldwork as requiring travel to exotic tropical locations, but that is not necessarily the case. This reading is based on fieldwork in the United States—on the streets in New York City as well as Atlanta. Claire Sterk is an anthropologist who works in a school of public health and is primarily interested in issues of women's health, particularly as it relates to sexual behavior. In this selection, an introduction to a book by the same title, she describes the basic fieldwork methods she used to study these women and their communities. Like most cultural anthropologists, Sterk's primary goal was to describe "the life" of prostitution from the women's own point of view. To do this, she had to be patient, brave, sympathetic, trustworthy, curious, and nonjudgmental. You will notice these characteristics in this selection; for example, Sterk begins her book with a poem written by one of her informants. Fieldwork is a slow process, because it takes time to win people's confidence and to learn their language and way of seeing the world. In this regard, there are probably few differences between the work of a qualitative sociologist and that of a cultural anthropologist (although anthropologists would not use the term "deviant" to describe another society or a segment of their own society).

Throughout the world, HIV/AIDS is fast becoming a disease found particularly in poor women. Sex workers or prostitutes have often been blamed for AIDS, and they have been further stigmatized because of their profession. In reality, however, entry into prostitution is not a career choice; rather, these women and girls are themselves most often victims of circumstances such as violence and poverty. Public health officials want to know why sex workers do not always protect their health by making men wear condoms. To answer such questions, we must know more about the daily life of these women. The way to do that, the cultural anthropologist would say, is to ask and to listen.

As you read this selection, ask yourself the following questions:

- What happens when Sterk says, "I'm sorry for you" to one of her informants? Why?
- Why do you think fieldwork might be a difficult job?
- Do you think that the fact that Sterk grew up in Amsterdam, where prostitution is legal, affected her research?
- Which of the six themes of this work, described at the end of the article, do you think is most important?

The following terms discussed in this selection are included in the Glossary at the back of the book:

demography	*sample*
fieldwork	*stroll*
key respondent	

Prostitution is a way of life. IT IS THE LIFE.
We make money for pimps who promise us
    love and more,
but if we don't produce, they shove us out the door.

We turn tricks who have sex-for-pay.
They don't care how many times we serve every day.

The Life is rough. The Life is tough.
We are put down, beaten up, and left for dead.
It hurts body and soul and messes with
    a person's head.
Many of us get high. Don't you understand it is
    a way of getting by?

Reprinted with permission of the author and publisher from *Tricking and Tripping: Prostitution in the Era of AIDS*. Putnam Valley, NY: Social Change Press, 2000.

The Life is rough. The Life is tough.
We are easy to blame because we are lame.

—Piper, 1987[1]

One night in March of 1987 business was slow. I was hanging out on a stroll with a group of street prostitutes. After a few hours in a nearby diner/coffee shop, we were kicked out. The waitress felt bad, but she needed our table for some new customers. Four of us decided to sit in my car until the rain stopped. While three of us chatted about life, Piper wrote this poem. As soon as she read it to us, the conversation shifted to more serious topics—pimps, customers, cops, the many hassles of being a prostitute, to name a few. We decided that if I ever finished a book about prostitution, the book would start with her poem.

This book is about the women who work in the lower echelons of the prostitution world. They worked in the streets and other public settings as well as crack houses. Some of these women viewed themselves primarily as prostitutes, and a number of them used drugs to cope with the pressures of the life. Others identified themselves more as drug users, and their main reason for having sex for money or other goods was to support their own drug use and often the habit of their male partner. A small group of women interviewed for this book had left prostitution, and most of them were still struggling to integrate their past experiences as prostitutes in their current lives.

The stories told by the women who participated in this project revealed how pimps, customers, and others such as police officers and social and health service providers treated them as "fallen" women. However, their accounts also showed their strengths and the many strategies they developed to challenge these others. Circumstances, including their drug use, often forced them to sell sex, but they all resisted the notion that they might be selling themselves. Because they engaged in an illegal profession, these women had little status: their working conditions were poor, and their work was physically and mentally exhausting. Nevertheless, many women described the ways in which they gained a sense of control over their lives. For instance, they learned how to manipulate pimps, how to control the types of services and length of time bought by their customers, and how to select customers. While none of these schemes explicitly enhanced their working conditions, they did make the women feel stronger and better about themselves.

In this book, I present prostitution from the point of view of the women themselves. To understand their current lives, it was necessary to learn how they got started in the life, the various processes involved in their continued prostitution careers, the link between prostitution and drug use, the women's interactions with their pimps and customers, and the impact of the AIDS epidemic and increasing violence on their experiences. I also examined the implications for women. Although my goal was to present the women's thoughts, feelings, and actions in their own words, the final text is a sociological monograph compiled by me as the researcher. Some women are quoted more than others because I developed a closer relationship with them, because they were more able to verbalize and capture their circumstances, or simply because they were more outspoken.

THE SAMPLE

The data for this book are qualitative. The research was conducted during the last ten years in the New York City and Atlanta metropolitan areas. One main data source was participant observation on streets, in hotels and other settings known for prostitution activity, and in drug-use settings, especially those that allowed sex-for-drug exchanges. Another data source was in-depth, life-history interviews with 180 women ranging in age from 18 to 59 years, with an average age of 34. One in two women was African-American and one in three white; the remaining women were Latina. Three in four had completed high school, and among them almost two-thirds had one or more years of additional educational training. Thirty women had graduated from college.

Forty women worked as street prostitutes and did not use drugs. On average, they had been prostitutes for 11 years. Forty women began using drugs an average of three years after they began working as prostitutes, and the average time they had worked as prostitutes was nine years. Forty women used drugs an average of five years before they became prostitutes, and on the average they had worked as prostitutes for eight years. Another forty women began smoking crack and exchanging sex for crack almost simultaneously, with an average of four years in the life. Twenty women who were interviewed were ex-prostitutes.

COMMENTS ON METHODOLOGY

When I tell people about my research, the most frequent question I am asked is how I gained access to the women rather than what I learned from the research. For many, prostitution is an unusual topic of conversation, and many people have expressed surprise that I, as a woman, conducted the research. During my research some customers indeed thought I was a working woman, a fact that almost always amuses those who hear about my work. However, few people want to hear stories about the women's struggles and sadness. Sometimes they ask questions about the reasons why women become prostitutes. Most of the time, they are surprised when I tell them that the prostitutes as well as their customers represent all layers of society. Before presenting the findings, it seems important to discuss the research process, including gaining access to the women, developing relationships, interviewing, and then leaving the field.[2]

LOCATING PROSTITUTES AND GAINING ENTREE

One of the first challenges I faced was to identify locations where street prostitution took place. Many of these women worked on strolls, streets where prostitution activity is concentrated, or in hotels known for prostitution activity. Others, such as the crack prostitutes, worked in less public settings such as a crack house that might be someone's apartment.

I often learned of well-known public places from professional experts, such as law enforcement officials and health care providers at emergency rooms and sexually transmitted disease clinics. I gained other insights from lay experts, including taxi drivers, bartenders, and community representatives such as members of neighborhood associations. The contacts universally mentioned some strolls as the places where many women worked, where the local police focused attention, or where residents had organized protests against prostitution in their neighborhoods.

As I began visiting various locales, I continued to learn about new settings. In one sense, I was developing ethnographic maps of street prostitution. After several visits to a specific area, I also was able to expand these maps by adding information about the general atmosphere on the stroll, general characteristics of the various people present, the ways in which the women and customers connected, and the overall flow of action. In addition, my visits allowed the regular actors to notice me.

I soon learned that being an unknown woman in an area known for prostitution may cause many people to notice you, even stare at you, but it fails to yield many verbal interactions. Most of the time when I tried to make eye contact with one of the women, she quickly averted her eyes. Pimps, on the other hand, would stare at me straight on and I ended up being the one to look away. Customers would stop, blow their horn, or wave me over, frequently yelling obscenities when I ignored them. I realized that gaining entree into the prostitution world was not going to be as easy as I imagined it. Although I lacked such training in any of my qualitative methods classes, I decided to

move slowly and not force any interaction. The most I said during the initial weeks in a new area was limited to "how are you" or "hi." This strategy paid off during my first visits to one of the strolls in Brooklyn, New York. After several appearances, one of the women walked up to me and sarcastically asked if I was looking for something. She caught me off guard, and all the answers I had practiced did not seem to make sense. I mumbled something about just wanting to walk around. She did not like my answer, but she did like my accent. We ended up talking about the latter and she was especially excited when I told her I came from Amsterdam. One of her friends had gone to Europe with her boyfriend, who was in the military. She understood from her that prostitution and drugs were legal in the Netherlands. While explaining to her that some of her friend's impressions were incorrect, I was able to show off some of my knowledge about prostitution. I mentioned that I was interested in prostitution and wanted to write a book about it.

Despite the fascination with my background and intentions, the prostitute immediately put me through a Streetwalker 101 test, and apparently I passed. She told me to make sure to come back. By the time I left, I not only had my first conversation but also my first connection to the scene. Variations of this entry process occurred on the other strolls. The main lesson I learned in these early efforts was the importance of having some knowledge of the lives of the people I wanted to study, while at the same time refraining from presenting myself as an expert.

Qualitative researchers often refer to their initial connections as gatekeepers and key respondents. Throughout my fieldwork I learned that some key respondents are important in providing initial access, but they become less central as the research evolves. For example, one of the women who introduced me to her lover, who was also her pimp, was arrested and disappeared for months. Another entered drug treatment soon after she facilitated my access. Other key respondents provided access to only a segment of the players on a scene. For example, if a woman worked for a pimp, [she] was unlikely . . . to introduce me to women working for another pimp. On one stroll my initial contact was with a pimp whom nobody liked. By associating with him, I almost lost the opportunity to meet other pimps. Some key respondents were less connected than promised—for example, some of the women who worked the street to support their drug habit. Often their connections were more frequently with drug users and less so with prostitutes.

Key respondents tend to be individuals central to the local scene, such as, in this case, pimps and the more senior prostitutes. Their function as gatekeepers often is to protect the scene and to screen outsiders.

Many times I had to prove that I was not an undercover police officer or a woman with ambitions to become a streetwalker. While I thought I had gained entree, I quickly learned that many insiders subsequently wondered about my motives and approached me with suspicion and distrust.

Another lesson involved the need to proceed cautiously with self-nominated key respondents. For example, one of the women presented herself as knowing everyone on the stroll. While she did know everyone, she was not a central figure. On the contrary, the other prostitutes viewed her as a failed streetwalker whose drug use caused her to act unprofessionally. By associating with me, she hoped to regain some of her status. For me, however, it meant limited access to the other women because I affiliated myself with a woman who was marginal to the scene. On another occasion, my main key respondent was a man who claimed to own three crack houses in the neighborhood. However, he had a negative reputation, and people accused him of cheating on others. My initial alliance with him delayed, and almost blocked, my access to others in the neighborhood. He intentionally tried to keep me from others on the scene, not because he would gain something from that transaction but because it made him feel powerful. When I told him I was going to hang out with some of the other people, he threatened me until one of the other dealers stepped in and told him to stay away. The two of them argued back and forth, and finally I was free to go. Fortunately, the dealer who had spoken up for me was much more central and positively associated with the local scene. Finally, I am unsure if I would have had success in gaining entrance to the scene had I not been a woman.

DEVELOPING RELATIONSHIPS AND TRUST

The processes involved in developing relationships in research situations amplify those involved in developing relationships in general. Both parties need to get to know each other, become aware and accepting of each other's roles, and engage in a reciprocal relationship. Being supportive and providing practical assistance were the most visible and direct ways for me as the researcher to develop a relationship. Throughout the years, I have given countless rides, provided child care on numerous occasions, bought groceries, and listened for hours to stories that were unrelated to my initial research questions. Gradually, my role allowed me to become part of these women's lives and to build rapport with many of them.

Over time, many women also realized that I was uninterested in being a prostitute and that I genuinely was interested in learning as much as possible about their lives. Many felt flattered that someone wanted to learn from them and that they had knowledge to offer. Allowing women to tell their stories and engaging in a dialogue with them probably were the single most important techniques that allowed me to develop relationships with them. Had I only wanted to focus on the questions I had in mind, developing such relationships might have been more difficult.

At times, I was able to get to know a woman only after her pimp endorsed our contact. One of my scariest experiences occurred before I knew to work through the pimps, and one such man had some of his friends follow me on my way home one night. I will never know what plans they had in mind for me because I fortunately was able to escape with only a few bruises. Over a year later, the woman acknowledged that her pimp had gotten upset and told her he was going to teach me a lesson.

On other occasions, I first needed to be screened by owners and managers of crack houses before the research could continue. Interestingly, screenings always were done by a man even if the person who vouched for me was a man himself. While the women also were cautious, the ways in which they checked me out tended to be much more subtle. For example, one of them would tell me a story, indicating that it was a secret about another person on the stroll. Although I failed to realize this at the time, my field notes revealed that frequently after such a conversation, others would ask me questions about related topics. One woman later acknowledged that putting out such stories was a test to see if I would keep information confidential.

Learning more about the women and gaining a better understanding of their lives also raised many ethical questions. No textbook told me how to handle situations in which a pimp abused a woman, a customer forced a woman to engage in unwanted sex acts, a customer requested unprotected sex from a woman who knew she was HIV infected, or a boyfriend had unrealistic expectations regarding a woman's earnings to support his drug habit. I failed to know the proper response when asked to engage in illegal activities such as holding drugs or money a woman had stolen from a customer. In general, my response was to explain that I was there as a researcher. During those occasions when pressures became too severe, I decided to leave a scene. For example, I never returned to certain crack houses because pimps there continued to ask me to consider working for them.

Over time, I was fortunate to develop relationships with people who "watched my back." One pimp in particular intervened if he perceived other pimps, customers, or passersby harassing me. He also was the one who gave me my street name: Whitie (indicating my racial background) or Ms. Whitie for those who disrespected me. While this was my first street name, I subsequently had others. Being given a street name was a symbolic gesture of acceptance. Gradually, I developed an identity that allowed me to be both an insider and an outsider. While hanging out on the strolls and other gathering places, including crack houses, I had to deal with some of the same uncomfortable conditions as the prostitutes, such as cold or warm weather, lack of access to a rest room, refusals from owners for me to patronize a restaurant, and of course, harassment by customers and the police.

I participated in many informal conversations. Unless pushed to do so, I seldom divulged my opinions. I was more open with my feelings about situations and showed empathy. I learned quickly that providing an opinion can backfire. I agreed that one of the women was struggling a lot and stated that I felt sorry for her. While I meant to indicate my genuine concern for her, she heard that I felt sorry for her because she was a failure. When she finally, after several weeks, talked with me again, I was able to explain to her that I was not judging her, but rather felt concerned for her. She remained cynical and many times asked me for favors to make up for my mistake. It took me months before I felt comfortable telling her that I felt I had done enough and that it was time to let go. However, if she was not ready, she needed to know that I would no longer go along. This was one of many occasions when I learned that although I wanted to facilitate my work as a researcher, that I wanted people to like and trust me, I also needed to set boundaries.

Rainy and slow nights often provided good opportunities for me to participate in conversations with groups of women. Popular topics included how to work safely, what to do about condom use, how to make more money. I often served as a health educator and a supplier of condoms, gels, vaginal douches, and other feminine products. Many women were very worried about the AIDS epidemic. However, they also were worried about how to use a condom when a customer refused to do so. They worried particularly about condom use when they needed money badly and, consequently, did not want to propose that the customer use one for fear of rejection. While some women became experts at "making" their customers use a condom—for example, by hiding it in their mouth prior to beginning oral sex—others would carry condoms to please me but never pull one out. If a woman was HIV positive and I knew she failed to use

a condom, I faced the ethical dilemma of challenging her or staying out of it.

Developing trusting relationships with crack prostitutes was more difficult. Crack houses were not the right environment for informal conversations. Typically, the atmosphere was tense and everyone was suspicious of each other. The best times to talk with these women were when we bought groceries together, when I helped them clean their homes, or when we shared a meal. Often the women were very different when they were not high than they were when they were high or craving crack. In my conversations with them, I learned that while I might have observed their actions the night before, they themselves might not remember them. Once I realized this, I would be very careful to omit any detail unless I knew that the woman herself did remember the event.

IN-DEPTH INTERVIEWS

All interviews were conducted in a private setting, including women's residences, my car or my office, a restaurant of the women's choice, or any other setting the women selected. I did not begin conducting official interviews until I developed relationships with the women. Acquiring written informed consent prior to the interview was problematic. It made me feel awkward. Here I was asking the women to sign a form after they had begun to trust me. However, often I felt more upset about this technicality than the women themselves. As soon as they realized that the form was something the university required, they seemed to understand. Often they laughed about the official statements, and some asked if I was sure the form was to protect them and not the school.[3] None of the women refused to sign the consent form, although some refused to sign it right away and asked to be interviewed later.

In some instances the consent procedures caused the women to expect a formal interview. Some of them were disappointed when they saw I only had a few structured questions about demographic characteristics, followed by a long list of open-ended questions. When this disappointment occurred, I reminded the women that I wanted to learn from them and that the best way to do so was by engaging in a dialogue rather than interrogating them. Only by letting the women identify their salient issues and the topics they wanted to address was I able to gain an insider's perspective. By being a careful listener and probing for additional information and explanation, I as the interviewer, together with the women, was able to uncover the complexities of their lives. In addition, the nature of the interview allowed me to ask questions about contradictions in a woman's story. For example, sometimes a woman would say that she always used a condom. However, later on in the conversation she would indicate that if she needed drugs she would never use one. By asking her to elaborate on this, I was able to begin developing insights into condom use by type of partner, type of sex acts, and social context.

The interviewer becomes much more a part of the interview when the conversations are in-depth than when a structured questionnaire is used. Because I was so integral to the process, the way the women viewed me may have biased their answers. On the one hand, this bias might be reduced because of the extent to which both parties already knew each other; on the other, a woman might fail to give her true opinion and reveal her actions if she knew that these went against the interviewer's opinion. I suspected that some women played down the ways in which their pimps manipulated them once they knew that I was not too fond of these men. However, some might have taken more time to explain the relationship with their pimp in order to "correct" my image.

My background, so different from that of these women, most likely affected the nature of the interviews. I occupied a higher socioeconomic status. I had a place to live and a job. In contrast to the nonwhite women, I came from a different racial background. While I don't know to what extent these differences played a role, I acknowledge that they must have had some effect on this research.

LEAVING THE FIELD

Leaving the field was not something that occurred after completion of the fieldwork, but an event that took place daily. Although I sometimes stayed on the strolls all night or hung out for several days, I always had a home to return to. I had a house with electricity, a warm shower, a comfortable bed, and a kitchen. My house sat on a street where I had no fear of being shot on my way there and where I did not find condoms or syringes on my doorstep.

During several stages of the study, I had access to a car, which I used to give the women rides or to run errands together. However, I will never forget the cold night when everyone on the street was freezing, and I left to go home. I turned up the heat in my car, and tears streamed down my cheeks. I appreciated the heat, but I felt more guilty about that luxury than ever

before. I truly felt like an outsider, or maybe even more appropriate, a betrayer.

Throughout the years of fieldwork, there were a number of times when I left the scene temporarily. For example, when so many people were dying from AIDS, I was unable to ignore the devastating impact of this disease. I needed an emotional break.

Physically removing myself from the scene was common when I experienced difficulty remaining objective. Once I became too involved in a woman's life and almost adopted her and her family. Another time I felt a true hatred for a crack house owner and was unable to adhere to the rules of courteous interactions. Still another time, I got angry with a woman whose steady partner was HIV positive when she failed to ask him to use a condom when they had sex.

I also took temporary breaks from a particular scene by shifting settings and neighborhoods. For example, I would invest most of my time in women from a particular crack house for several weeks. Then I would shift to spending more time on one of the strolls, while making shorter and less frequent visits to the crack house. By shifting scenes, I was able to tell people why I was leaving and to remind all of us of my researcher role.

While I focused on leaving the field, I became interested in women who had left the life. It seemed important to have an understanding of their past and current circumstances. I knew some of them from the days when they were working, but identifying others was a challenge. There was no gathering place for ex-prostitutes. Informal networking, advertisements in local newspapers, and local clinics and community settings allowed me to reach twenty of these women. Conducting interviews with them later in the data collection process prepared me to ask specific questions. I realized that I had learned enough about the life to know what to ask. Interviewing ex-prostitutes also prepared me for moving from the fieldwork to writing.

It is hard to determine exactly when I left the field. It seems like a process that never ends. Although I was more physically removed from the scene, I continued to be involved while analyzing the data and writing this book. I also created opportunities to go back, for example, by asking women to give me feedback on parts of the manuscript or at times when I experienced writer's block and my car seemed to automatically steer itself to one of the strolls. I also have developed other research projects in some of the same communities. For example, both a project on intergenerational drug use and a gender-specific intervention project to help women remain HIV negative have brought me back to the same population. Some of the women have become key respondents in these new projects, while others now are members of a research team. For example, Beth, one of the women who has left prostitution, works as an outreach worker on another project.

SIX THEMES IN THE ETHNOGRAPHY OF PROSTITUTION

The main intention of my work is to provide the reader with a perspective on street prostitution from the point of view of the women themselves. There are six fundamental aspects of the women's lives as prostitutes that must be considered. The first concerns the women's own explanations for their involvement in prostitution and their descriptions of the various circumstances that led them to become prostitutes. Their stories include justifications such as traumatic past experiences, especially sexual abuse, the lack of love they experienced as children, pressures by friends and pimps, the need for drugs, and most prominently, the economic forces that pushed them into the life. A number of women describe these justifications as excuses, as reflective explanations they have developed after becoming a prostitute.

The women describe the nature of their initial experiences, which often involved alienation from those outside the life. They also show the differences in the processes between women who work as prostitutes and use drugs and women who do not use drugs.

Although all these women work either on the street or in drug-use settings, their lives do differ. My second theme is a typology that captures these differences, looking at the women's prostitution versus drug-use identities. The typology distinguishes among (a) streetwalkers, women who work strolls and who do not use drugs; (b) hooked prostitutes, women who identify themselves mainly as prostitutes but who upon their entrance into the life also began using drugs; (c) prostituting addicts, women who view themselves mainly as drug users and who became prostitutes to support their drug habit; and (d) crack prostitutes, women who trade sex for crack.

This typology explains the differences in the women's strategies for soliciting customers, their screening of customers, pricing of sex acts, and bargaining for services. For example, the streetwalkers have the most bargaining power, while such power appears to be lacking among the crack prostitutes.

Few prostitutes work in a vacuum. The third theme is the role of pimps, a label that most women dislike and for which they prefer to substitute "old man" or "boyfriend." Among the pimps, one finds entrepreneur lovers, men who mainly employ streetwalkers and hooked prostitutes and sometimes prostituting addicts. Entrepreneur lovers engage in the life for business reasons. They treat the women as their employees or their property and view them primarily as an economic commodity. The more successful a woman is in earning them money, the more difficult it is for that woman to leave her entrepreneur pimp.

Most prostituting addicts and some hooked prostitutes work for a lover pimp, a man who is their steady partner but who also lives off their earnings. Typically, such pimps employ only one woman. The dynamics in the relationship between a prostitute and her lover pimp become more complex when both partners use drugs. Drugs often become the glue of the relationship.

For many crack prostitutes, their crack addiction serves as a pimp. Few plan to exchange sex for crack when they first begin using; often several weeks or months pass before a woman who barters sex for crack realizes that she is a prostitute.

Historically, society has blamed prostitutes for introducing sexually transmitted diseases into the general population. Similarly, it makes them scapegoats for the spread of HIV/AIDS. Yet their pimps and customers are not held accountable. The fourth theme in the anthropological study of prostitution is the impact of the AIDS epidemic on the women's lives. Although most are knowledgeable about HIV risk behaviors and the ways to reduce their risk, many misconceptions exist. The women describe the complexities of condom use, especially with steady partners but also with paying customers. Many women have mixed feelings about HIV testing, wondering how to cope with a positive test result while no cure is available. A few of the women already knew their HIV-infected status, and the discussion touches on their dilemmas as well.

The fifth theme is the violence and abuse that make common appearances in the women's lives. An ethnography of prostitution must allow the women to describe violence in their neighborhoods as well as violence in prostitution and drug-use settings. The most common violence they encounter is from customers. These men often assume that because they pay for sex they buy a woman. Apparently, casual customers pose more of a danger than those who are regulars. The types of abuse the women encounter are emotional, physical, and sexual. In addition to customers, pimps and boyfriends abuse the women. Finally, the women discuss harassment by law enforcement officers.

When I talked with the women, it often seemed that there were no opportunities to escape from the life. Yet the sixth and final theme must be the escape from prostitution. Women who have left prostitution can describe the process of their exit from prostitution. As ex-prostitutes they struggle with the stigma of their past, the challenges of developing a new identity, and the impact of their past on current intimate relationships. Those who were also drug users often view themselves as ex-prostitutes and recovering addicts, a perspective that seems to create a role conflict. Overall, most ex-prostitutes find that their past follows them like a bad hangover.

NOTES

1. The names of the women who were interviewed for this study, as well as those of their pimps and customers, have been replaced by pseudonyms to protect their privacy. The use of pseudonyms is suggested by guidelines to protect the privacy of study participants (American Anthropological Association; American Sociological Association).

2. For more information about qualitative research methods, see, for example, Patricia Adler and Peter Adler, *Membership Roles in Field Research* (Newbury Park: Sage, 1987); Michael Agar, *The Professional Stranger* (New York: Academic Press, 1980) and *Speaking of Ethnography* (Beverly Hills: Sage, 1986); Howard Becker and Blanche Geer, "Participant Observation and Interviewing: A Comparison," *Human Organization* 16 (1957): 28–32; Norman Denzin, *Sociological Methods: A Sourcebook* (Chicago: Aldine, 1970); Barney Glaser and Anselm Strauss, *The Discovery of Grounded Theory: Strategies for Qualitative Research* (Chicago: Aldine, 1967); Y. Lincoln and E. Guba, *Naturalistic Inquiry* (Beverly Hills: Sage, 1985); John Lofland, "Analytic Ethnography: Features, Failings, and Futures," *Journal of Contemporary Ethnography* 24 (1996): 30–67; and James Spradley, *The Ethnographic Interview* (New York: Holt, Rinehart and Winston, 1979) and *Participant Observation* (New York: Holt, Rinehart and Winston, 1980).

3. For a more extensive discussion of informed consent procedures and related ethical issues, see Bruce L. Berg, *Qualitative Research Methods for the Social Sciences*, 3rd edition, Chapter 3: "Ethical Issues" (Boston: Allyn and Bacon, 1998).

4

Crack in Spanish Harlem

Philippe Bourgois

Urban America vibrates with the intensity of a taut drum. The cadence of street life is a constant reminder that things are different here. Suburban folks who meander into some of these inner-city neighborhoods immediately notice the contrasts between these streets and their hometowns. Beset by what have been called the "signs of incivility," outsiders are uneasy and often afraid. Outsiders seldom understand the subculture of the inner city, and most don't want to.

Yet it is in the inner city that many of our most serious social problems are found, including unemployment, homelessness, broken families, poor medical care, and crime. Survival in this milieu, particularly in the drug scene, requires a deep understanding of the subculture. In the same way, effective public policy is more likely to result if policymakers understand the cultural meaning of people's behavior. But how can they achieve such an understanding?

This riveting account reveals how anthropological work can lend an important dimension to our comprehension of a way of life almost as foreign to most of us as is the life of an Amazon warrior, a !Kung bushman, or a rain forest pygmy.

As you read this selection, ask yourself the following questions:

- What is meant by the culture of resistance, and what effects does this culture have on a community and society?
- In what ways is the underground economy like a business?
- How is a job in the underground economy different from a legal job in terms of respect and an individual's feeling of self-worth?
- What is meant by the culture of terror, and what is the role of violence in maintaining social status?
- What can be learned through ethnographic fieldwork as opposed to questionnaires and surveys?

The following terms discussed in this selection are included in the Glossary at the back of the book:

cultural reproduction

ethnography

ghetto

A MUGGING IN SPANISH HARLEM

The heavy-set, white undercover policeman pushed me across the ice-cream counter, spreading my legs and poking me around the groin. As he came dangerously close to the bulge in my right pocket I hissed in his ear "It's a tape recorder." He snapped backwards, releasing his left hand's grip on my neck and whispering a barely audible "Sorry." Apparently, he thought he had clumsily intercepted an undercover from another department because before I could get a close

"Crack in Spanish Harlem: Culture and Economy in the Inner City" by Philippe Bourgois, from *Anthropology Today,* vol. 5, no. 4, 1989. Royal Anthropological Institute of Great Britain and Ireland. Reprinted with permission.

look at his face he had left the *bodega* grocery-store cum numbers-joint. Meanwhile, the marijuana sellers stationed in front of the *bodega* that Gato and I had just entered to buy 16-ounce cans of Private Stock (beer), observing that the undercover had been rough with me when he searched through my pants, suddenly felt safe and relieved—finally confident that I was a white drug addict rather than an undercover.

As we hurried to leave this embarrassing scene we were blocked by Bennie, an emaciated teenager high on angel dust who was barging through the door along with two friends to mug us. I ran to the back of the *bodega* but Gato had to stand firmly because this was the corner he worked, and those were his former partners. They dragged him onto the sidewalk surrounding him on all sides, shouting about the money he still owed, and began kicking and hitting him with a baseball bat. I found out later that Gato owed them for his share of the supply of marijuana confiscated in a drug bust last week. . . . After we finished telling the story at the crack/*botanica*[1] house where I had been spending most of my evening hours this summer, Chino, who was on duty selling that night with Julio (pronounced Jew-Lee-oh), jumped up excitedly calling out "what street was that on? Come on, let's go, we can still catch them—How many were they?" I quickly stopped this mobilization for a revenge posse, explaining that it was not worth my time, and that we should just forget about it. Chino looked at me disgustedly sitting back down on the milk crate in front of the *botanica*'s door and turned his face away from me, shrugging his shoulders. Julio, whom I knew better and had become quite close to for a number of weeks last year, jumped up in front of me raising his voice to berate me for being "pussy." He also sat back down shortly afterwards feigning exasperated incredulity with the comment "Man you still think like a *blanquito*." A half dozen spectators—some of them empty-pocketed ("thirsty!") crack addicts, but most of them sharply dressed teenage drug-free girls competing for Chino's and Julio's attentions—giggled and snickered at me.

CULTURE AND MATERIAL REALITY

The above extract from sanitized fieldwork notes is merely a personalized glimpse of the day-to-day struggle for survival *and for meaning* by the people who stand behind the extraordinary statistics on inner city violent crime in the United States.[2] These are the same Puerto Rican residents of Spanish Harlem, New York City, that Oscar Lewis in *La Vida* declared to be victims of a "culture of poverty" enmired in a "self-perpetuating cycle of poverty" (Lewis 1966:5). The culture of poverty concept has been severely criticized for its internal inconsistencies, its inadequate understanding of "culture" and ethnicity, its ethnocentric/middle class bias, its blindness to structural forces, and its blame-the-victim implications (cf. Leacock ed. 1971, Valentine 1968, Waxman 1977, Stack 1974). Despite the negative scholarly consensus on Lewis's theory, the alternative discussions either tend towards economic reductionism (Ryan 1971, Steinberg 1981, Wilson 1978) or else ultimately minimize the reality of profound marginalization and destruction—some of it internalized—that envelop a disproportionate share of the inner city poor (cf. Stack 1974, Valentine 1978; see critiques by Maxwell 1988, Wilson 1987). More importantly, the media, public policy-makers and a large proportion of inner city residents themselves continue to subscribe to a popularized blame-the-victim/culture of poverty concept that has not been adequately rebutted by scholars.

The inner city residents described in the ethnographic vignette above are the pariahs of urban industrial US society. They seek their income and subsequently their identity and the meaning in their life through what they perceive to be high-powered careers "on the street." They partake of ideologies and values and share symbols which form the basis of an "inner city street culture" completely excluded from the mainstream economy and society but ultimately derived from it. Most of them have a few direct contacts with non–inner city residents, and when they do it is usually with people who are in a position of domination: teachers in school, bosses, police officers, and later parole or probation officers.

How can one understand the complicated ideological dynamic accompanying inner city poverty without falling into a hopelessly idealistic culture of poverty and blame-the-victim interpretation? Structural, political economy reinterpretations of the inner city dynamic emphasize historical processes of labour migration in the context of institutionalized ethnic discrimination. They dissect the structural transformations in the international economy which are destroying the manufacturing sector in the United States and are swelling the low wage, low prestige service sector (cf. Davis 1987; Sassen-Koob 1986; Steinberg 1981; Tabb and Sawers, eds., 1984; Wilson 1978, 1987). These analyses address the structural confines of the inner city dynamic but fall prey to a passive interpretation of human action and subscribe to a weakly dialectic interpretation of the relationship between ideological processes and material reality, or between culture and class.

Although ultimately traceable directly to being products of international labour migrations in a transnational world economy, street-level inner city residents are more than merely passive victims of historical economic transformations or of the institutionalized discrimination of a perverse political and economic system. They do not passively accept their fourth-class citizen fate. They are struggling determinedly—just as ruthlessly as the railroad and oil robber-barons of the previous century and the investment-banker "yuppies" of today—to earn money, demand dignity and lead meaningful lives. Tragically, it is that very process of struggle against—yet within —the system which exacerbates the trauma of their community and which destroys hundreds of thousands of lives on the individual level.

In the day-to-day experience of the street-bound inner city resident, unemployment and personal anxiety over the inability to provide one's family with a minimal standard of living translates itself into intra-community crime, intra-community drug abuse, intra-community violence. The objective, structural desperation of a population without a viable economy, and facing systematic barriers of ethnic discrimination and ideological marginalization, becomes charged at the community level into self-destructive channels.

Most importantly, the "personal failure" of those who survive on the street is articulated in the idiom of race. The racism imposed by the larger society becomes internalized on a personal level. Once again, although the individuals in the ethnographic fragment at the beginning of this paper are the victims of long-term historical and structural transformations, they do not analyse their difficult situation from a political economy perspective. In their struggle to survive and even to be successful, they enforce on a day-to-day level the details of the trauma and cruelty of their lives on the excluded margins of US urban society.

CULTURAL REPRODUCTION THEORY

Theorists of education have developed a literature on processes of social and cultural reproduction which focus on the ideological domination of the poor and the working class in the school setting (cf. Giroux 1983). Although some of the social reproduction approaches tend towards an economic reductionism or a simple, mechanical functionalism (cf. Bowles and Gintis 1977), the more recent variants emphasize the complexity and contradictory nature of the dynamic of ideological domination (Willis 1983). There are several ethnographies which document how the very process whereby students resist school channels them into marginal roles in the economy for the rest of their lives (cf. Willis 1977; Macleod 1987). Other ethnographically-based interpretations emphasize how success for inner city African-American students requires a rejection of their ethnic identity and cultural dignity (Fordham 1988).

There is no reason why these theories of cultural resistance and ideological domination have to be limited to the institutional school setting. Cultural reproduction theory has great potential for shedding light on the interaction between structurally induced cultural resistance and self-reinforced marginalization at the street level in the inner city experience. The violence, crime and substance abuse plaguing the inner city can be understood as the manifestations of a "culture of resistance" to mainstream, white racist, and economically exclusive society. This "culture of resistance," however, results in greater oppression and self-destruction. More concretely, refusing to accept the outside society's racist role playing and refusing to accept low wage, entry-level jobs, translates into high

crime rates, high addiction rates and high intra-community violence.

Most of the individuals in the above ethnographic description are proud that they are not being exploited by "the White Man," but they feel "like fucking assholes" for being poor. All of them have previously held numerous jobs in the legal economy in their lives. Most of them hit the street in their early teens working odd jobs as delivery boys and baggers in supermarkets and *bodegas*. Most of them have held the jobs that are recognized as among the least desirable in US society. Virtually all of these street participants have had deeply negative personal experiences in the minimum-wage labour market, owing to abusive, exploitative and often racist bosses or supervisors. They see the illegal, underground economy as not only offering superior wages, but also a more dignified workplace. For example, Gato had formerly worked for the ASPCA, cleaning out the gas chambers where stray dogs and cats are killed. Bennie had been fired six months earlier from a night shift job as security guard on the violent ward for the criminally insane on Wards Island; Chino had been fired a year ago from a job installing high altitude storm windows on skyscrapers following an accident which temporarily blinded him in the right eye. Upon being disabled he discovered that his contractor had hired him illegally through an arrangement with a corrupt union official who had paid him half the union wage, pocketing the rest, and who had not taken health insurance for him. Chino also claimed that his foreman from Pennsylvania was a "Ku Klux Klanner" and had been especially abusive to him as he was a black Puerto Rican. In the process of recovering from the accident, Chino had become addicted to crack and ended up in the hospital as a gunshot victim before landing a job at Papito's crack house. Julio's last legal job before selling crack was as an off-the-books messenger for a magazine catering to New York yuppies. He had become addicted to crack, began selling possessions from out of his home and finally was thrown out by his wife who had just given birth to his son, who carried his name as Julio the IIIrd, on public assistance. Julio had quit his messenger job in favour of stealing car radios for a couple of hours at night in the very same neighbourhood where he had been delivering messages for ten hour days at just above minimum wage. Nevertheless, after a close encounter with the police, Julio begged his cousin for a job selling in his crack house. Significantly, the sense of responsibility, success and prestige that selling crack gave him enabled him to kick his crack habit and replace it by a less expensive and destructive powder cocaine and alcohol habit.

The underground economy, consequently, is the ultimate "equal opportunity employer" for inner city youth (cf. Kornblum and Williams 1985). As Davis (1987:75) has noted for Los Angeles, the structural economic incentive to participate in the drug economy is overwhelming:

> With 78,000 unemployed youth in the Watts-Willowbrook area, it is not surprising that there are now 145 branches of the rival Crips and Bloods gangs in South L.A., or that the jobless resort to the opportunities of the burgeoning "Crack" economy.

The individuals "successfully" pursuing careers in the "crack economy" or any other facet of the underground economy are no longer "exploitable" by legal society. They speak with anger at their former low wages and bad treatment. They make fun of friends and acquaintances—many of whom come to buy drugs from them—who are still employed in factories, in service jobs, or in what they (and most other people) would call "shitwork." Of course, many others are less self-conscious about the reasons for their rejection of entry-level, mainstream employment. Instead, they think of themselves as lazy and irresponsible. They claim they quit their jobs in order to have a good time on the street. Many still pay lip service to the value of a steady, legal job. Still others cycle in and out of legal employment supplementing their bouts at entry-level jobs through part-time crack sales in an almost perverse parody of the economic subsidy of the wage labour sector by semi-subsistence peasants who cyclically engage in migratory wage labour in third world economies (cf. Meillassoux 1981; Wallerstein 1977).

THE CULTURE OF TERROR IN THE UNDERGROUND ECONOMY

The culture of resistance that has emerged in the underground street-level economy in opposition to demeaning, underpaid employment in the mainstream economy engenders violence. In the South American context of extreme political repression and racism against Amerindians and Jews, anthropologist Michael Taussig has argued that "cultures of terror" emerge to become ". . . a high-powered tool for domination and a principal medium for political practice" (1984:492). Unlike Taussig's examples of the 1910s Putumayo massacres and the 1970s Argentine torture chambers, domination in the case of the inner city's culture of terror is self-administered even if the root cause is generated or even imposed externally. With the exception of occasional brutality by policemen or the bureaucratized repression of the social welfare and

criminal justice institutions (cf. Davis 1988), the physical violence and terror of the inner city are largely carried out by inner city residents themselves.

Regular displays of violence are necessary for success in the underground economy—especially at the street-level drug dealing world. Violence is essential for maintaining credibility and for preventing rip-off by colleagues, customers and hold-up artists. Indeed, upward mobility in the underground economy requires a systematic and effective use of violence against one's colleagues, one's neighbours and, to a certain extent, against oneself. Behaviour that appears irrationally violent and self-destructive to the middle class (or the working class) outside observer, can be reinterpreted according to the logic of the underground economy, as a judicious case of public relations, advertising, rapport building and long-term investment in one's "human capital development."

The importance of one's reputation is well illustrated in the fieldwork fragment at the beginning of this paper. Gato and I were mugged because Gato had a reputation for being "soft" or "pussy" and because I was publicly unmasked as *not being* an undercover cop: hence safe to attack. Gato tried to minimize the damage to his future ability to sell on that corner by not turning and running. He had pranced sideways down the street, though being beaten with a baseball bat and kicked to the ground twice. Significantly, I found out later that it was the second time this had happened to Gato this year. Gato was not going to be upwardly mobile in the underground economy because of his "pussy" reputation and he was further cementing his fate with an increasingly out-of-control addiction to crack.

Employers or new entrepreneurs in the underground economy are looking for people who can demonstrate their capacity for effective violence and terror. For example, in the eyes of Papito, the owner of the string of crack franchises I am currently researching, the ability of his employees to hold up under gunpoint is crucial as stick-ups of dealing dens are not infrequent. In fact, since my fieldwork began in 1986, the *botanica* has been held up twice. Julio happened to be on duty both times. He admitted to me that he had been very nervous when they held the gun to his temple and had asked for money and crack. Nevertheless, not only did he withhold some of the money and crack that was hidden behind the bogus *botanica* merchandise, but he also later exaggerated to Papito the amount that had been stolen in order to pocket the difference.

On several occasions in the midst of long conversations with active criminals (i.e., once with a dealing-den stick-up artist, several times with crack dealers, and once with a former bank robber) I asked them to explain how they were able to trust their partners in crime sufficiently to ensure the longevity and effectiveness of their enterprise. To my surprise I was not given any righteous diatribes about blood-brotherhood trustworthiness or any adulations of boyhood loyalty. Instead, in each case, in slightly different language I was told somewhat aggressively: "What do you mean how do I trust him? You should ask 'How does he trust me?'" Their ruthlessness is their security: "My support network is me, myself and I." They made these assertions with such vehemence as to appear threatened by the concept that their security and success might depend upon the trustworthiness of their partner or their employer. They were claiming—in one case angrily—that they were not dependent upon trust: because they were tough enough to command respect and enforce all contracts they entered into. The "How can they trust me?" was said with smug pride, perhaps not unlike the way a stockbroker might brag about his access to inside information on an upcoming hostile takeover deal.

At the end of the summer Chino demonstrated clearly the how-can-I-be-trusted dynamic. His cocaine snorting habit had been degenerating into a crack addiction by the end of the summer, and finally one night he was forced to flee out of state to a cousin's when he was unable to turn in the night's receipts to his boss Papito following a binge. Chino also owed Papito close to a thousand dollars for bail that Papito had posted when he was arrested for selling crack at the *botanica* a few months ago. Almost a year later when Papito heard that Chino had been arrested for jumping bail he arranged through another associate incarcerated in the same prison (Rikers Island) to have Chino beaten up before his trial date.

My failure to display a propensity for violence in several instances cost me the respect of the members of the crack scene that I frequented. This was very evident when I turned down Julio and Chino's offer to search for Bennie after he mugged Gato and me. Julio had despairingly exclaimed that I "still [thought] like a *blanquito*," genuinely disappointed that I was not someone with common sense and self-respect.

These concrete examples of the cultivation of violent public behaviour are the extreme cases of individuals relying on the underground economy for their income and dependent upon cultivating terror in order to survive. Individuals involved in street activity cultivate the culture of terror in order to intimidate competitors, maintain credibility, develop new contacts, cement partnerships, and ultimately to have a good time. For the most part they are not conscious of this process. The culture of terror becomes a myth and a role model with rules and satisfactions all its own which ultimately has a traumatic impact on the majority of Spanish Harlem residents—who are drug free and who work honestly at poorly remunerated legal jobs, 9 to 5 plus overtime.

PURSUING THE AMERICAN DREAM

It is important to understand that the underground economy and the violence emerging out of it are not propelled by an irrational cultural logic distinct from that of mainstream USA. On the contrary, street participants are frantically pursuing the "American dream." The assertions of the culture of poverty theorists that the poor have been badly socialized and do not share mainstream values is wrong. On the contrary, ambitious, energetic, inner city youths are attracted into the underground economy in order to try frantically to get their piece of the pie as fast as possible. They often even follow the traditional US model for upward mobility to the letter by becoming aggressive private entrepreneurs. They are the ultimate rugged individualists braving an unpredictable frontier where fortune, fame and destruction are all just around the corner. Hence Indio, a particularly enterprising and ambitious young crack dealer who was aggressively carving out a new sales point, shot his brother in the spine and paralysed him for life while he was high on angel dust in a battle over sales rights. His brother now works for him selling on crutches. Meanwhile, the shooting has cemented Indio's reputation and his workers are awesomely disciplined: "If he shot his brother he'll shoot anyone." Indio reaffirms this symbolically by periodically walking his turf with an oversized gold chain and name plate worth several thousand dollars hanging around his neck.

The underground economy and the culture of terror are experienced as the most realistic routes to upward mobility. Entry-level jobs are not seen as viable channels to upward mobility by high school dropouts. Drug selling or other illegal activity appear as the most effective and realistic options for getting rich within one's lifetime. Many of the street dealers claim to be strictly utilitarian in their involvement with crack and they snub their clients despite the fact that they usually have considerable alcohol and powder cocaine habits themselves. Chino used to chant at his regular customers "Come on, keep on killing yourself; bring me that money; smoke yourself to death; make me rich."

Even though street sellers are employed by the owner of a sales point for whom they have to maintain regular hours, meet sales quotas and be subject to being fired, they have a great deal of autonomy and power in their daily (or nightly) routine. The boss only comes once or twice a shift to drop off drugs and pick up money. Frequently, it is a young messenger who is sent instead. Sellers are often surrounded by a bevy of "thirsty" friends and hanger-oners—frequently young teenage women in the case of male sellers—willing to run errands, pay attention to conversations, lend support in arguments and fights and provide sexual favours for them on demand because of the relatively large amounts of money and drugs passing through their hands. In fact, even youths who do not use drugs will hang out and attempt to befriend respectfully the dealer just to be privy to the excitement of people coming and going, copping and hanging; money flowing, arguments, detectives, and stick-up artists—all around danger and excitement. Other nonusers will hang out to be treated to an occasional round of beer, Bacardi or, on an off night, Thunderbird.

The channel into the underground economy is by no means strictly economic. Besides wanting to earn "crazy money," people choose "hoodlum" status in order to assert their dignity at refusing to "sling a mop for the white man" (cf. Anderson 1976:68). Employment or better yet self-employment—in the underground economy—accords a sense of autonomy, self-dignity and an opportunity for extraordinary rapid short-term upward mobility that is only too obviously unavailable in entry-level jobs. Opulent survival without a "visible means of support" is the ultimate expression of success and it is a viable option. There is plenty of visible proof of this to everyone on the street as they watch teenage crack dealers drive by in convertible Suzuki Samurai jeeps with the stereo blaring, "beem" by in impeccable BMWs, or—in the case of the middle-aged dealers—speed around in well waxed Lincoln Continentals. Anyone can aspire to be promoted to the level of a seller perched on a 20-speed mountain bike with a beeper by their side. In fact, many youths not particularly active in the drug trade run around with beepers on their belts just pretending to be big-time. The impact of the sense of dignity and worth that can accompany selling crack is illustrated by Julio's ability to overcome his destructive addiction to crack only after getting a job selling it: "I couldn't be messin' up the money. I couldn't be fucking up no more! Besides, I had to get respect."

In New York City the insult of working for entry-level wages amidst extraordinary opulence is especially painfully perceived by Spanish Harlem youths who have grown up in abject poverty only a few blocks from all-white neighbourhoods commanding some of the highest real estate values in the world. As messengers, security guards or Xerox machine operators in the corporate headquarters of the *Fortune* 500

companies, they are brusquely ordered about by young white executives who sometimes make monthly salaries superior to their yearly wages and who do not even have the time to notice that they are being rude.

It could be argued that Manhattan sports a *de facto* apartheid labour hierarchy whereby differences in job category and prestige correlate with ethnicity and are often justified—consciously or unconsciously—through a racist logic. This humiliating confrontation with New York's ethnic/occupational hierarchy drives the street-bound cohort of inner city youths deeper into the confines of their segregated neighbourhood and the underground economy. They prefer to seek out meaning and upward mobility in a context that does not constantly oblige them to come into contact with people of a different, hostile ethnicity wielding arbitrary power over them. In the underground economy, especially in the world of substance abuse, they never have to experience the silent subtle humiliations that the entry-level labour market—or even merely a daily subway ride downtown—invariably subjects them to.

In this context the crack high and the rituals and struggles around purchasing and using the drug are comparable to the millenarian religions that sweep colonized peoples attempting to resist oppression in the context of accelerated social trauma—whether it be the Ghost dance of the Great Plains Amerindians, the "cargo cults" of Melanesia, the Mamachi movement of the Guaymi Amerindians in Panama, or even religions such as Farrakhan's Nation of Islam and the Jehovah's Witnesses in the heart of the inner city (cf. Bourgois 1986, 1989). Substance abuse in general, and crack in particular, offer the equivalent of a millenarian metamorphosis. Instantaneously users are transformed from being unemployed, depressed high school dropouts, despised by the world—and secretly convinced that their failure is due to their own inherent stupidity, "racial laziness" and disorganization—into being a mass of heart-palpitating pleasure, followed only minutes later by a jaw-gnashing crash and wideawake alertness that provides their life with concrete purpose: get more crack—fast!

One of the most dramatic illustrations within the dynamic of the crack economy of how a cultural dynamic of resistance to exploitation can lead contradictorily to greater oppression and ideological domination is the conspicuous presence of women in the growing cohort of crack addicts. In a series of ten random surveys undertaken at Papito's crack franchises, women and girls represented just under 50% of the customers. This contrasts dramatically to the estimates of female participation in heroin addiction in the late 1970s.

The painful spectacle of young, emaciated women milling in agitated angst around crack copping corners and selling their bodies for five dollars, or even merely for a puff on a crack stem, reflects the growing emancipation of women in all aspects of inner city life, culture and economy. Women—especially the emerging generation which is most at risk for crack addiction—are no longer as obliged to stay at home and maintain the family. They no longer so readily sacrifice public life or forgo independent opportunities to generate personally disposable income. This is documented by the frequent visits to the crack houses by pregnant women and by mothers accompanied by toddlers.

A more neutral illustration of the changed position of women in street culture outside the arena of substance abuse is the growing presence of young women on inner city basketball courts. Similarly, on the national level, there are conclusive statistics documenting increased female participation in the legal labour market—especially in the working class Puerto Rican community. By the same token, more women are also resisting exploitation in the entry-level job market and are pursuing careers in the underground economy and seeking self-definition and meaning through intensive participation in street culture.

Although women are using the drug and participating intensively in street culture, traditional gender relations still largely govern income-generating strategies in the underground economy. Most notably, women are forced disproportionately to rely on prostitution to finance their habits. The relegation of women to the traditional street role of prostitution has led to a flooding of the market for sex, leading to a drop in the price of women's bodies and to an epidemic rise in venereal disease among women and newborn babies.

Contradictorily, therefore, the underlying process of emancipation which has enabled women to demand equal participation in street culture and to carve out an expanded niche for themselves in the underground economy has led to a greater depreciation of women as ridiculed sex objects. Addicted women will tolerate a tremendous amount of verbal and physical abuse in their pursuit of a vial of crack, allowing lecherous men to humiliate and ridicule them in public. Chino, who is married and is the father of nine children, refers to the women who regularly service him with oral sex as "my moufs" [mouths]. He enjoys calling out to these addicted women from across the street, "Yo, there goes my mouf! Come on over here." Such a public degradation of a cohort of women who are conspicuously present on the street cannot be neutral. It ultimately reinforces the ideological domination of women in general.

DE-LEGITIMIZING DOMINATION

How can one discuss and analyse the phenomenon of street-level inner city culture and violence without reproducing and confirming the very ideological relationships that are its basis? In his discussion of the culture of terror, Taussig notes that it is precisely the narratives about the torture and violence of the repressive societies which ". . . are in themselves evidence of the process whereby a culture of terror was created and sustained" (1984:279). The superhuman power that the media has accorded to crack serves a similar mythical function. The *New York Times* has run articles and interviews with scientists that portray crack as if it were a miraculous substance beyond the power of human beings to control (cf. 25 June, 1988: 1). They "prove" this by documenting how quickly rats will ecstatically kill themselves when provided with cocaine upon demand. Catheterized rats push the cocaine lever to the exclusion of the nutrient lever until they collapse exhausted to die of thirst.

The alleged omnipotence of crack coupled with even the driest recounting of the overpowering statistics on violence ultimately allows US society to absolve itself of any real responsibility for the inner city phenomena. The mythical dimensions of the culture of terror push economics and politics out of the picture and enable the US to maintain in some of its larger cities a level of ethnic segregation and economic marginalization that are unacceptable to any of the other wealthy, industrialized nations of the world, with the obvious exception of South Africa. Worse yet, on the level of theory, because of the continued domination—even in their negation—of the North America-centred culture of poverty theories, this discussion of the ideological implications of the underground economy may take readers full circle back to a blame-the-victim interpretation of inner city oppression.

NOTES

1. A *botanica* is a herbal pharmacy and *santeria* utility store.
2. This research was funded by the United States Bureau of the Census, the Wenner-Gren Foundation for Anthropological Research, two Washington University Junior Faculty Summer Research grants, and Lottery Funds and an Affirmative Action Grant from San Francisco State University. An expanded version of this article will be appearing in a special issue of *Contemporary Drug Problems* devoted to crack in the United States.

   Pseudonyms have been used in order to disguise identities of persons referred to.

REFERENCES

Anderson, Elijah. 1976. *A Place on the Corner*. Chicago: U. of Chicago.

Bourgois, Philippe. 1986. The Miskitu of Nicaragua: Politicized Ethnicity. *A.T.* 2(2): 4–9.

———. 1989. *Ethnicity at Work: Divided Labour on a Central American Banana Plantation*. Baltimore: Johns Hopkins U.P.

Bowles, Samuel, and Herbert Gintis. 1977. *Schooling in Capitalist America*. New York: Basic Books.

Davis, Mike. 1987. *Chinatown*, Part Two? The "Internationalization" of Downtown Los Angeles. *New Left Review* 164: 65–86.

Davis, Mike, with Sue Ruddick. 1988. Los Angeles: Civil Liberties Between the Hammer and the Rock. *New Left Review* 1970: 37–60.

Fordham, Signithia. 1988. Racelessness as a Factor in Black Students' School Success: Pragmatic Strategy or Pyrrhic Victory? *Harvard Educational Review* 58(1): 54–84.

Giroux, Henry. 1983. Theories of Reproduction and Resistance in the New Sociology of Education: A Critical Analysis. *Harvard Educational Review* 53(3): 257–293.

Kornblum, William, and Terry Williams. 1985. *Growing Up Poor*. Lexington, MA: Lexington Books.

Leacock, Eleanor Burke, ed. 1971. *The Culture of Poverty: A Critique*. New York: Simon and Schuster.

Lewis, Oscar. 1966. The Culture of Poverty. In *Anthropological Essays*, pp. 67–80. New York: Random House.

Macleod, Jay. 1987. *Ain't No Makin' It*. Boulder, Colorado: Westview P.

Maxwell, Andrew. 1988. The Anthropology of Poverty in Black Communities: A Critique and Systems Alternative. *Urban Anthropology* 17(2&3): 171–191.

Meillassoux, Claude. 1981. *Maidens, Meal and Money*. Cambridge: Cambridge U.P.

Ryan, William. 1986[1971]. Blaming the Victim. In *Taking Sides: Clashing Views on Controversial Social Issues*, pp.

45–52, ed. Kurt Finsterbusch and George McKenna. Guilford, CT: Dushkin Publishing Group.

Sassen-Koob, Saskia. 1986. New York City: Economic Restructuring and Immigration. *Development and Change* 17(1): 87–119.

Stack, Carol. 1974. *All Our Kin: Strategies for Survival in a Black Community*. New York: Harper & Row.

Steinberg, Stephen. 1981. *The Ethnic Myth: Race, Ethnicity and Class in America*. New York: Atheneum.

Tabb, William, and Larry Sawers, eds. 1984. *Marxism and the Metropolis: New Perspectives in Urban Political Economy*. New York: Oxford U.P.

Taussig, Michael. 1984. Culture of Terror—Space of Death, Roger Casement's Putumayo Report and the Explanation of Torture. *Comparative Studies in Society and History* 26(3): 467–497.

Valentine, Charles. 1968. *Culture and Poverty*. Chicago: U. of Chicago P.

Valentine, Bettylou. 1978. *Hustling and Other Hard Work*. NY: Free Press.

Wallerstein, Emanuel. 1977. Rural Economy in Modern World Society. *Studies in Comparative International Development* 12(1): 29–40.

Waxman, Chaim. 1977. *The Stigma of Poverty: A Critique of Poverty Theories and Policies*. NY: Pergamon.

Willis, Paul. 1983. Cultural Production and Theories of Reproduction. In *Race, Class and Education*, pp. 107–138, ed. Len Barton and Stephen Walker. London: Croom-Helm.

———. 1977. *Learning to Labor: How Working Class Kids Get Working Class Jobs*. Aldershot, England: Gower.

Wilson, William Julius. 1978. *The Declining Significance of Race: Blacks and Changing American Institutions*. Chicago: U. of Chicago P.

———. 1987. *The Truly Disadvantaged: The Inner City, the Underclass and Public Policy*. Chicago: U. of Chicago Press.

5

PROFILE OF AN ANTHROPOLOGIST

Corporate Anthropologists

Jennifer J. Laabs

Most anthropological work is still done in other cultures. Today, however, an increasing number of anthropologists are bringing their expertise to the corporate world. The concept of culture and the ethnographic methods of anthropology that originally developed on the African savannas, the Australian outback, the Arctic tundra, and the bush country of the New Guinea highlands are now being applied to understand and advance corporate cultures as well as to enhance the social organization of shops and offices. From Xerox to General Motors to Nissan, corporate executives find that anthropologists can help them to see through different eyes.

Recent business anthropology aims to improve working conditions within offices, develop an understanding of the importance of corporate culture, provide market research insights through participant observation rather than survey research, develop products through observation of people in natural settings, and provide insights into other cultures to facilitate a corporation's expansion into the global economy.

Although anthropologists have been working with businesses since the 1930s, the 1980s witnessed exceptional growth in this field because of the globalization of business activity and the increased awareness of the importance of culture for business.

As you read this selection, ask yourself the following questions:

- What are the four fields of anthropology, and what are some of the areas of applied anthropological work?
- What are the similarities and differences between business anthropology and other forms of cultural anthropology?
- What is meant by the culture of a business?
- How can anthropologists help corporations perform better in a global environment?
- How can a corporate origin myth stimulate creative thinking?

The following terms discussed in this selection are included in the Glossary at the back of the book:

archaeology

biological anthropology

corporate culture

cultural anthropology

linguistic anthropology

origin myth

Chances are, an anthropologist wouldn't be the first business expert you'd call if you wanted to build a better mousetrap—or a better HR program. Anthropologists aren't exactly listed as consultants in the phone book between *accountant* and *attorney*. But maybe they should be.

Although calling an anthropologist might seem like an unusual answer to a business dilemma, many companies have found that anthropologists' expertise as cultural scientists is quite useful in gaining insight about human behavior within their corporate digs.

Anthropology, by definition, is "the science of human beings," and studies people in relation to their "distribution, origin, classification, relationship of races, physical character, environmental and social relations and culture" (according to *Webster's Ninth New Collegiate Dictionary*).

Although there are many types of anthropologists (see "They Dig up Rocks, Don't They?"), most people

THEY DIG UP ROCKS, DON'T THEY?

When most people think of anthropologists, they think of the most popular kind—those who dig up ancient artifacts and try to make sense of past life forms and cultures. These "stones and bones" scientists are only a fraction of the forms that anthropology takes: *Academic anthropology* dates back to the late 19th century. It was formalized by the establishment of the American Anthropological Association (AAA) in 1902, which currently has 11,000 members. In contrast with anthropology in Europe and Latin America, American academic anthropology is distinguished by its "four-field approach" including:

- Cultural anthropology
- Archaeology
- Biological anthropology
- Linguistic anthropology.

There are many other subgroups within these four areas.

Applied anthropology dates back to World War II when anthropologists worked for the federal government

The Society for Applied Anthropology (SFAA), founded in 1941, has 3,000 members. The National Association for the Practice of Anthropology (NAPA) was formed in 1983 and overlaps membership of the SFAA. Many of these *applied* and *practicing* anthropologists work for government agencies and non-profit groups. Their work includes:

- Agricultural development
- Education
- Family planning
- Legal system development
- Natural resources management
- Public health and nutrition
- Social impact assessment.

Business anthropology traces its origins to the 1930s, but only since the early 1980s have anthropologists been working for such major corporations as General Motors, Xerox, Nissan and McDonnell Douglas.   —J.L.

have only heard of the archaeology (stones and bones) variety. But there's much more to them than that.

Anthropologists study many different areas of business, but essentially they're all people-watchers of one sort or another. Business anthropologists have been studying the corporate world for years (since the early 1900s), on such varied topics as how to encourage more creativity or how best to integrate multicultural learning techniques into an organization's training program.

There are only a dozen business anthropologists who actually use the title of *anthropologist,* but there are about 200 currently working in and for corporate America.

Lorna M. McDougall, a staff anthropologist at Arthur Andersen's Center for Professional Education in St. Charles, Illinois, for example, currently is studying why people from some cultures learn best from lectures, although others learn best through interactive learning.

Her background includes linguistics study at Trinity College in Dublin, Ireland, and social anthropological study at Oxford. She also has a specialty in medical anthropology, and has worked in a variety of organizations and universities.

McDougall has been a key player in shaping the firm's Business English Language Immersion Training

(ELIT) program, directed by the company's management development group, to which McDougall reports.

The ELIT program builds both a common language skill for communication between people who speak English as a second language (there are approximately 800 million in the world), and an awareness of each culture's unique approach to business encounters. The results of her work have helped instructors, who train Andersen consultants working in 66 countries, be better teachers. They've also helped students become better learners.

The center is almost a mini-United Nations, and has many of the same kinds of intercultural opportunities and challenges, but also is a melting pot of sorts in which she studies many types of cultural issues. "We're in a unique position to be able to use people's information and exchange it," says McDougall.

Arthur Andersen's product essentially is its people, and keeping them trained and in top shape to consult alongside other Andersen employees in many different countries is a cultural and business challenge that many global firms are facing these days. Although the company has been global for many years, delivering clear, effective training for consultants continues to be an issue.

AN ANTHROPOLOGIST'S TOOL KIT
By Lorna M. McDougall

Anthropologists rely on a large historical and current geographical data bank for new ideas and new applications of old ideas. For example, when we look at the history of work, we can trace it from the survival activities common to higher primates—getting food and shelter—through the stages of human evolution and history.

What we see is that, as work becomes further removed from the direct provision of needs, the issue of motivation arises. We know that many of the great states: Greek, Roman, Mayan, Egyptian, African, Indian, Chinese, to mention only a few, approached work and productivity using a variety of rewards, incentives and disciplinary measures. They also had to deal with what we would recognize as business issues: strategic planning, accounting, finance and inventory management.

A wide-ranging cultural approach shows us that the issues any society faces today aren't necessarily new—nor are the issues new for management. On the contrary, approaching things from a comparative perspective, we can see that in our time we have made progress in finding creative alternatives for productivity in the context of today's values and culturally diverse work force.

The value of this knowledge is that it can readily stimulate creative thinking. It helps us to realize that nothing is written in stone, and that we are dealing with situations that always have been challenging. We aren't deficient just because these situations continue.

On the contrary, we need to realize that our current proactive approach to such situations, which involves actually studying how to improve them, rather than just wrestling with them, is a significant advancement. Management problems have been around a long time, but management development is our creative response to dealing with them.

McDougall is part of Andersen's corporate strategy, says Pete Pesce, managing director for Arthur Andersen's human resources worldwide. "An anthropologist brings a lot of value to an organization," says Pesce. Although McDougall is the company's first on-site anthropologist and has been with Arthur Andersen only one year, she's going to be even more valuable in the future because of the increasing worldwide scope of the company's operations, says Pesce.

Because the organization has more than 56,000 employees and has spent, for example, 7.4% of its annual revenue in 1990 ($309 million) on training and education, the company is committed to enhancing its education programs using expertise that such disciplines as anthropology can offer.

What is that expertise? "Business anthropology, like all anthropology, is based on observing and analyzing group values and behavior in a cultural context. We focus on *what* people in a cultural group do, *how many* of them do it and *how what they do* affects the individuals in the group," she says.

"Business anthropologists seek to identify the connections between national culture and organizational culture," explains McDougall. Just as other cultural scientists, she helps identify some of the major cultural variables within and between organizations and the various ways that these differences impact:

- Structure
- Strategy
- Operations
- Communications
- Behavior

From a cross-cultural standpoint, McDougall's job was to analyze what Arthur Andersen instructors (usually partners) and students do in the classroom and how they interpret those events.

"When I came in to study this program, I used an anthropological methodology to take a look at what was happening," she says. She listened in on classroom sessions and conducted many face-to-face interviews. "I then analyzed that data from an anthropological perspective," says McDougall. She noticed, for example, that people from certain cultures are used to two-way communication in the classroom, although others just sit quietly while the "professor lectures." To do otherwise, in their minds, would be disrespectful.

"It isn't necessarily an inherent feature of the human mind that people learn in one way or another," says McDougall. It's more a question of how people have *learned to learn,* and how the company's training can incorporate all types of learning styles for the best possible retention of the material by everyone. "What we're really doing is facilitating," she says.

Changes were made in the objectives of the training program. For example, another component was added—a cultural orientation module, which helps the company's staff and managers become more aware of multicultural diversity issues and how those behaviors are affecting their business interactions.

As a result of the changes, the "students" have been more cooperative and better learners inside the classroom, explains McDougall. Noticeably more intercultural socializing has taken place outside the classroom as well—something management hadn't anticipated. "It's important to realize that when you're looking at the effectiveness of cross-cultural training, you want to look at the outcome in improved relations between the people involved," she explains.

Pesce, from a human resources perspective, has found that the organizational values are the same throughout the firm's many offices globally because of the company's emphasis on homogeneous training and orientation. "I've travelled around the world and talked to employees," he says. "What I see clearly is that the values of the firm are very, very consistent. When our people talk about our organization, they talk about it in the same light in terms of quality, values, delivering client service and developing our people."

McDougall also teaches some of the management development classes, and is involved in the company's "train the trainers" program. In addition, she presents special classes to the company's human resources managers on cultural sensitivity issues.

"Recently, I was in London meeting with our directors of human resources for our Europe, the Middle East, India and Africa divisions," says Pesce. "Their interest in dealing with working standards is very keen. The challenge is to understand the differences in cultures, and in work and family values—the differences between Spain and Germany, for example. Lorna will be very helpful to us in that whole process."

Other areas she is studying involve such topics as:

- Leadership
- Creativity
- Productivity
- Delegation

Areas for McDougall's anthropological study have been identified in a variety of ways. Sometimes members of the management development team propose ideas; other times, McDougall identifies them. Some recent topics have included teaching associates the cultural meaning of gestures and selecting colors for computer screens used in training.

"Colors have symbolic connections that are culture-specific," explains McDougall. "For example, in some cultures, white is associated with marriage, but in others it's associated with death. Others associate blue with death. In some cultures pink is considered feminine and in others yellow is."

Another project that McDougall is helping develop is an Experienced Hire Orientation program to help new hires assimilate more rapidly into the company's corporate culture. "We would apply what anthropologists call *oral transmission* of beliefs, practices and values by having established personnel pass on the firm's history and traditions by word of mouth, rather than in writing," explains McDougall.

For now, her work has been centered at the St. Charles facility, but in the future she might travel to the company's other worldwide locations for other research projects.

ANTHROPOLOGY BOOSTS CREATIVITY

"What good are zero defects, if you aren't even making the right product?" asks Roger P. McConochie, a St. Charles, Illinois-based anthropologist who consults with businesses on a variety of topics.

McConochie asks a thought-provoking question. Some companies are looking to people like him to help answer it, because it opens up the corporate agenda to the bigger picture: What really is a company's business all about?

One business person, who has benefited from the anthropological approach, came to this conclusion: "What is our product? It isn't hardware, and it isn't even customer satisfaction, excellence, quality, TQM, or those other buzzwords from the '80s," says Mark T. Grace, operations development manager for Houston-based Generon Systems (a division of Dow Chemical and British Oxygen Corp.). Although the company manufactures nitrogen-separation equipment, Grace says: "We have only one product: innovation."

"Today we're the best in the world at what we do," says Grace, "but if we keep doing things the same way for another two or three years, we'll be out of business. That's how quickly this industry is changing and that's how tough our competition is. Our challenge on a daily basis is to redesign our equipment so that it's more efficient: space-efficient, weight-efficient, cost-efficient."

In his business, creativity is everything, he continues. "The problem is putting people into a group and having them freely share their ideas. Each person wants individual credit for his or her ideas, yet the best ideas emerge from interaction." Although the company even has "idea rooms" in which people can draw their ideas and put them up on the wall, Grace explains, "We were stuck. So at one meeting, I said, 'We've tried everything else, why not bring in an anthropologist?'"

He called McConochie, president of Corporate Research International, for suggestions on how to incorporate culturally correct ways of getting staff to contribute. Since then, McConochie, and his associate, Harvard-educated Anthony Giannini, president of

TEN DIMENSIONS OF CORPORATE BEAUTY

1. Purpose. Is there a clear and unifying purpose to the product or service you're auditing?

2. Integrity. Does the product or service do what it was originally designed to do?

3. Simplicity. Is the product or service as simple as possible in structure, content, operation, and so on? Do corporate standards exist for simplicity in design?

4. Symmetry/Asymmetry. Is it physically symmetrical? Pleasing to the eye? Is it logically symmetrical? Pleasing to the mind? Is there operational harmony between the various parts? Pleasing to the ear? Does it feel symmetrical? Pleasing to the touch? Smell? Taste? Is it pleasing to your sense of proportional order in all respects? Pleasing to the emotions?

5. Balance. Does the product or service justify its existence? Are its gains worth its costs? Does it fit in with the rest of your product or service family?

6. Brilliancy. Compared to other competitive products and services, does this product or service sparkle on its own? Where does it lack sparkle?

7. Suggestiveness. Does the use of this product or service strongly evoke images of client or customer success in multiple domains, such as how designer clothes may suggest a boost in social status?

8. Clarity. Is the product or service easily understood? Is it easily used?

9. Adaptability. How adaptable to sudden change in the marketplace is the product or service? Are there any breakthroughs looming on the technology horizon that will change the picture?

10. Perenniality. Is the product or service an annual or perennial entity? Will it last at least two years? More than 5, 10 or 15 years?

The Corporate DaVinci, Ltd., have been an anthropological sounding board for Grace.

Generon's problem is fairly typical in business. But it isn't the company's fault, say these anthropologists, because today's business people are products of the competitive jungle in which they live and work. Although competition may be good among rivals, it often doesn't work within a single organizational culture, as evidenced by the fact that creativity gets stifled. People have a hard time leaving their cultural imprints at the front door.

To understand present society, anthropologists look to the past. From their perspective, McConochie and Giannini liken successful business strategy to the Renaissance period in Europe (between the 14th and 16th centuries), when such individuals as Leonardo da Vinci were guided by many values, including the aesthetics of beauty and the spiritual and emotional sides of humanity.

"During the Renaissance, new institutions were being formed and reformed and the individual was rediscovered," says Giannini. Da Vinci's *The Last Supper,* for example, was the first painting that got away from depicting human figures in a flat and monochromatic way. "You had, for the very first time, real people," he notes.

At that time, there was a blending of many human interests and cultures into almost every facet of life, including work. But that approach, for the most part, was abandoned somewhere along the way.

What was lost? "A concern with the human side of things, a concern with the non-quantifiable," says McConochie. He and Giannini say they think business would benefit from getting back to that holistic approach to thinking. "We believe in numbers; and we believe in measurements, but we also believe that there are elements to life and elements to corporate practice that can't be put into numbers."

Today, compartmentalization of human thinking is rampant, but the challenge of globalization requires businesses to rethink that strategy. Such techniques as "bridging" or "scaffolding" allow workers to use the many facets of their collective conscious to come up with solutions to current problems. It also can help them better understand colleagues from other cultures. Anything less, they say, falls short.

Giannini and McConochie created *The Corporate DaVinci*—a program for corporate Renaissance, in which they help organizations rethink their corporate history and recreate their corporate myths. "In anthropological terms, we would call it an *origin myth.* Every tribe in the jungle has a story of how it came to be," says McConochie. And so do companies. They don't usually think about it, but it often helps people remember how they came to be, and how they fit into history.

For example, when Giannini took the program to Ford Motor Co., he began the first session with a brief history of the wheel: From its invention to modern-day transportation. "In just 15 minutes, they had a fresh way of looking at the work they were doing day by day," says McConochie. "It was no longer just going out and pushing cars off the assembly line and selling them to get their sales figures up for the year. They were participating in the human drama."

Why is this so important? Because companies need a clear "ego sense": a continual sense of organizational self over time, says McConochie. Most anthropologists talk in terms of thousands, or even millions, of years. People begin to see that their lives, in the grander scheme of things, last only an instant. They also see, however, that what they do has an impact on the historical continuum and gives workers a feeling of oneness.

"What defines us as human beings is that, despite the differences across cultures, we're all trying to create meaning in our lives," says McConochie. "From my experience in corporations, the people on the shop floor have as much need for meaning in their lives as the people in the boardroom," he explains. "Everybody wants fewer defects at a lower cost. That's fine," says McConochie. "I'm not sure that's enough."

Corporations have been trapped by the concept that all that people on the shop floor need is to sleep, eat and get paid at the end of the week—and if you give them those basics, it's enough to motivate them. This isn't so, explains McConochie, who has consulted with many types of businesses, including aviation companies. Even chief executive officers won't work any harder if you double their salaries. "What you need to do is give them an opportunity to be creative, and an opportunity for challenge and growth," he explains. Creativity also must be supported in corporate culture—in word and deed.

"Right at the top of their corporate mission statement, organizations ought to have a special credo that reads 'Beauty in our products and services, and in the creative means of their production, is a corporate goal of the highest order,'" says Giannini.

Everyone can be creative—they just need some tools to help broaden their thinking. Giannini and McConochie's *Corporate DaVinci* program includes a segment called *The Aesthetic Audit* (see "Ten Dimensions of Corporate Beauty"), which gives people a guide to use as a springboard into the creative process.

For example, if you went to the hardware store, and picked up a simple screw or nut, you could examine it and ask, "Does it suit its purpose?" Then you'd move on to the other points. Does it demonstrate integrity? If it's corroded, has sharp edges that might cut the person using it, or lacks brilliancy and symmetry, for example, you might round the edges and paint it.

"Typically, I find that executives give low ratings to 60 to 70% of their products and services in at least half of these dimensions," says Giannini. Looking at their own products with *focused eyes*, companies then go on to make better products, and also create new ones. It gives colleagues a set of questions from which to start, so they can work together creatively.

Employees also can benefit from cognitive and cultural training, so they understand where ideas come from and how those ideas vary across societal boundaries. For example, these anthropologists include such topics in their program as:

- Organization of Thought Across Cultures
- The Multicultural Technician
- Cognitive Emotions Across Cultures
- Multicultural Business Thinking in Action

Can corporations actually blend science with poetry? Production with art? Business with aesthetics? Anthropologists who reach from one culture to another —bringing the best cognitive and cultural artifacts from the past into the present—say it *is* possible, and may be just the bridge that sparks innovation of the future.

6

Shakespeare in the Bush

Laura Bohannan

Communication is an essential characteristic of human social life. Through language we socialize our children and pass down cultural values from generation to generation. Communication forms and defines relations among individuals as well as among groups. Because communication is so natural, we seldom ask a critical question: When we speak, does the listener understand?

At a minimum, communication involves a sender, a receiver, and a shared code for exchanging information. When an individual or a group sends a message, the sender anticipates that those who receive the message will interpret and understand the message in the way the sender intended. Miscommunication is, of course, an unfortunately common phenomenon that can lead to fistfights, divorces, and wars.

What most of us do not appreciate is the degree to which culture affects our interpretation of messages. As Laura Bohannan tells the tale of *Hamlet*, we gradually discover how particular behaviors or events can have very different meanings in different places. What is interesting is that the miscommunication of interpretational differences is not a result of poor language or translation abilities. Miscommunication is not a result of speaking too quickly or not loudly enough. It reflects cultural differences.

As you read this selection, ask yourself the following questions:

- What were the author's original beliefs about the universality of the classics—such as *Hamlet?*
- How did the Tiv elders react to the marriage of Hamlet's mother to his uncle? How was this different from Hamlet's own emotional reaction?
- Why do the Tiv believe that a chief should have more than one wife?
- As the author tells the story, consider how the elders interpret various actions to fit Tiv culture and in so doing redefine the central meaning of the play.

The following terms discussed in this selection are included in the Glossary at the back of the book:

age grade	levirate
agnatic	polygyny
chiefdom	socialization
cultural relativism	

Just before I left Oxford for the Tiv in West Africa, conversation turned to the season at Stratford. "You Americans," said a friend, "often have difficulty with Shakespeare. He was, after all, a very English poet, and one can easily misinterpret the universal by misunderstanding the particular."

I protested that human nature is pretty much the same the whole world over; at least the general plot and motivation of the greater tragedies would always be clear—everywhere—although some details of custom might have to be explained and difficulties of translation might produce other slight changes. To end an argument we could not conclude, my friend gave me a copy of *Hamlet* to study in the African bush: it would, he hoped, lift my mind above its primitive surroundings, and possibly I might, by prolonged meditation, achieve the grace of correct interpretation.

It was my second field trip to that African tribe, and I thought myself ready to live in one of its remote sections—an area difficult to cross even on foot. I eventually settled on the hillock of a very knowledgeable old man, the head of a homestead of some hundred and forty people, all of whom were either his close relatives or their wives and children. Like the other elders of the vicinity, the old man spent most of

From *Natural History*, 1966. Reprinted by permission of the author.

his time performing ceremonies seldom seen these days in the more accessible parts of the tribe. I was delighted. Soon there would be three months of enforced isolation and leisure, between the harvest that takes place just before the rising of the swamps and the clearing of new farms when the water goes down. Then, I thought, they would have even more time to perform ceremonies and explain them to me.

I was quite mistaken. Most of the ceremonies demanded the presence of elders from several homesteads. As the swamps rose, the old men found it too difficult to walk from one homestead to the next, and the ceremonies gradually ceased. As the swamps rose even higher, all activities but one came to an end. The women brewed beer from maize and millet. Men, women, and children sat on their hillocks and drank it.

People began to drink at dawn. By midmorning the whole homestead was singing, dancing, and drumming. When it rained, people had to sit inside their huts: there they drank and sang or they drank and told stories. In any case, by noon or before, I either had to join the party or retire to my own hut and my books. "One does not discuss serious matters when there is beer. Come, drink with us." Since I lacked their capacity for the thick native beer, I spent more and more time with *Hamlet*. Before the end of the second month, grace descended on me. I was quite sure that *Hamlet* had only one possible interpretation, and that one universally obvious.

Early every morning in the hope of having some serious talk before the beer party, I used to call on the old man at his reception hut—a circle of posts supporting a thatched roof above a low mud wall to keep out wind and rain. One day I crawled through the low doorway and found most of the men of the homestead sitting huddled in their ragged clothes on stools, low plank beds, and reclining chairs, warming themselves against the chill of the rain around a smoky fire. In the center were three pots of beer. The party had started.

The old man greeted me cordially. "Sit down and drink." I accepted a large calabash full of beer, poured some into a small drinking gourd, and tossed it down. Then I poured some more into the same gourd for the man second in seniority to my host before I handed my calabash over to a young man for further distribution. Important people shouldn't ladle beer themselves.

"It is better like this," the old man said, looking at me approvingly and plucking at the thatch that had caught in my hair. "You should sit and drink with us more often. Your servants tell me that when you are not with us, you sit inside your hut looking at a paper."

The old man was acquainted with four kinds of "papers": tax receipts, bride price receipts, court fee receipts, and letters. The messenger who brought him letters from the chief used them mainly as a badge of office, for he always knew what was in them and told the old man. Personal letters for the few who had relatives in the government or mission stations were kept until someone went to a large market where there was a letter writer and reader. Since my arrival, letters were brought to me to be read. A few men also brought me bride price receipts, privately, with requests to change the figures to a higher sum. I found moral arguments were of no avail, since in-laws are fair game, and the technical hazards of forgery difficult to explain to an illiterate people. I did not wish them to think me silly enough to look at any such papers for days on end, and I hastily explained that my "paper" was one of the "things of long ago" of my country.

"Ah," said the old man. "Tell us."

I protested that I was not a storyteller. Storytelling is a skilled art among them; their standards are high and the audiences critical—and vocal in their criticism. I protested in vain. This morning they wanted to hear a story while they drank. They threatened to tell me no more stories until I told them one of mine. Finally, the old man promised that no one would criticize my style "for we know you are struggling with our language." "But," put in one of the elders, "you must explain what we do not understand, as we do when we tell you our stories." Realizing that here was my chance to prove Hamlet universally intelligible, I agreed.

The old man handed me some more beer to help me on with my storytelling. Men filled their long wooden pipes and knocked coals from the fire to place in the pipe bowls; then, puffing contentedly, they sat back to listen. I began in the proper style, "Not yesterday, not yesterday, but long ago, a thing occurred. One night three men were keeping watch outside the homestead of the great chief, when suddenly they saw the former chief approach them."

"Why was he no longer their chief?"

"He was dead," I explained. "That is why they were troubled and afraid when they saw him."

"Impossible," began one of the elders, handing his pipe on to his neighbor, who interrupted, "Of course it wasn't the dead chief. It was an omen sent by a witch. Go on."

Slightly shaken, I continued. "One of these three was a man who knew things"—the closest translation for scholar, but unfortunately it also meant witch. The second elder looked triumphantly at the first. "So he spoke to the dead chief saying, 'Tell us what we must do so you may rest in your grave,' but the dead chief did not answer. He vanished, and they could see him no more. Then the man who knew things—his name was Horatio—said this event was the affair of the dead chief's son, Hamlet."

There was a general shaking of heads round the circle. "Had the dead chief no living brothers? Or was this son the chief?"

"No," I replied. "That is, he had one living brother who became the chief when the elder brother died."

The old men muttered: such omens were matters for chiefs and elders, not for youngsters; no good could come of going behind a chief's back; clearly Horatio was not a man who knew things.

"Yes, he was," I insisted, shooing a chicken away from my beer. "In our country the son is next to the father. The dead chief's younger brother had become the great chief. He had also married his elder brother's widow only about a month after the funeral."

"He did well," the old man beamed and announced to the others, "I told you that if we knew more about Europeans, we would find they really were very like us. In our country also," he added to me, "the younger brother marries the elder brother's widow and becomes the father of his children. Now, if your uncle, who married your widowed mother, is your father's full brother, then he will be a real father to you. Did Hamlet's father and uncle have one mother?"

His question barely penetrated my mind; I was too upset and thrown off balance by having one of the most important elements of *Hamlet* knocked straight out of the picture. Rather uncertainly I said that I thought they had the same mother, but I wasn't sure—the story didn't say. The old man told me severely that these genealogical details made all the difference and that when I got home I must ask the elders about it. He shouted out the door to one of his younger wives to bring his goatskin bag.

Determined to save what I could of the mother motif, I took a deep breath and began again. "The son Hamlet was very sad because his mother had married again so quickly. There was no need for her to do so, and it is our custom for a widow not to go to her next husband until she has mourned for two years."

"Two years is too long," objected the wife, who had appeared with the old man's battered goatskin bag. "Who will hoe your farms for you while you have no husband?"

"Hamlet," I retorted without thinking, "was old enough to hoe his mother's farms himself. There was no need for her to remarry." No one looked convinced. I gave up. "His mother and the great chief told Hamlet not to be sad, for the great chief himself would be a father to Hamlet. Furthermore, Hamlet would be the next chief: therefore he must stay to learn the things of a chief. Hamlet agreed to remain, and all the rest went off to drink beer."

While I paused, perplexed at how to render Hamlet's disgusted soliloquy to an audience con-vinced that Claudius and Gertrude had behaved in the best possible manner, one of the younger men asked me who had married the other wives of the dead chief.

"He had no other wives," I told him.

"But a chief must have many wives! How else can he brew beer and prepare food for all his guests?"

I said firmly that in our country even chiefs had only one wife, that they had servants to do their work, and that they paid them from tax money.

It was better, they returned, for a chief to have many wives and sons who would help him hoe his farms and feed his people; then everyone loved the chief who gave much and took nothing—taxes were a bad thing.

I agreed with the last comment, but for the rest fell back on their favorite way of fobbing off my questions: "That is the way it is done, so that is how we do it."

I decided to skip the soliloquy. Even if Claudius was here thought quite right to marry his brother's widow, there remained the poison motif, and I knew they would disapprove of fratricide. More hopefully I resumed, "That night Hamlet kept watch with the three who had seen his dead father. The dead chief again appeared, and although the others were afraid, Hamlet followed his dead father off to one side. When they were alone, Hamlet's dead father spoke."

"Omens can't talk!" The old man was emphatic.

"Hamlet's dead father wasn't an omen. Seeing him might have been an omen, but he was not." My audience looked as confused as I sounded. "It was Hamlet's dead father. It was a thing we call a 'ghost.'" I had to use the English word, for unlike many of the neighboring tribes, these people didn't believe in the survival after death of any individuating part of the personality.

"What is a 'ghost'? An omen?"

"No, a 'ghost' is someone who is dead but who walks around and can talk, and people can hear him and see him but not touch him."

They objected. "One can touch zombis."

"No, no! It was not a dead body the witches had animated to sacrifice and eat. No one else made Hamlet's dead father walk. He did it himself."

"Dead men can't walk," protested my audience as one man.

I was quite willing to compromise. "A 'ghost' is the dead man's shadow."

But again they objected. "Dead men cast no shadows."

"They do in my country," I snapped.

The old man quelled the babble of disbelief that arose immediately and told me with that insincere, but courteous, agreement one extends to the fancies of the young, ignorant, and superstitious, "No doubt in your country the dead can also walk without being zombis." From the depths of his bag he produced a withered fragment of kola nut, bit off one end to show it wasn't poisoned, and handed me the rest as a peace offering.

"Anyhow," I resumed, "Hamlet's dead father said that his own brother, the one who became chief, had poisoned him. He wanted Hamlet to avenge him. Hamlet believed this in his heart, for he did not like his father's brother." I took another swallow of beer. "In the country of the great chief, living in the same homestead, for it was a very large one, was an important elder who was often with the chief to advise and help him. His name was Polonius. Hamlet was courting his daughter, but her father and her brother . . . (I cast hastily about for some tribal analogy) warned her not to let Hamlet visit her when she was alone on her farm, for he would be a great chief and so could not marry her."

"Why not?" asked the wife, who had settled down on the edge of the old man's chair. He frowned at her for asking stupid questions and growled, "They lived in the same homestead."

"That was not the reason," I informed them. "Polonius was a stranger who lived in the homestead because he helped the chief, not because he was a relative."

"Then why couldn't Hamlet marry her?"

"He could have," I explained, "but Polonius didn't think he would. After all, Hamlet was a man of great importance who ought to marry a chief's daughter, for in his country a man could have only one wife. Polonius was afraid that if Hamlet made love to his daughter, then no one else would give a high price for her."

"That might be true," remarked one of the shrewder elders, "but a chief's son would give his mistress's father enough presents and patronage to more than make up the difference. Polonius sounds like a fool to me."

"Many people think he was," I agreed. "Meanwhile Polonius sent his son Laertes off to Paris to learn the things of that country, for it was the homestead of a very great chief indeed. Because he was afraid that Laertes might waste a lot of money on beer and women and gambling, or get into trouble by fighting, he sent one of his servants to Paris secretly, to spy out what Laertes was doing. One day Hamlet came upon Polonius's daughter Ophelia. He behaved so oddly he frightened her. Indeed"—I was fumbling for words to express the dubious quality of Hamlet's madness—"the chief and many others had also noticed that when Hamlet talked one could understand the words but not what they meant. Many people thought that he had become mad." My audience suddenly became more attentive. "The great chief wanted to know what

was wrong with Hamlet, so he sent for two of Hamlet's age mates (school friends would have taken long explanation) to talk to Hamlet and find out what troubled his heart. Hamlet, seeing that they had been bribed by the chief to betray him, told them nothing. Polonius, however, insisted that Hamlet was mad because he had been forbidden to see Ophelia, whom he loved."

"Why," inquired a bewildered voice, "should anyone bewitch Hamlet on that account?"

"Bewitch him?"

"Yes, only witchcraft can make anyone mad, unless, of course, one sees the beings that lurk in the forest."

I stopped being a storyteller, took out my notebook and demanded to be told more about these two causes of madness. Even while they spoke and I jotted notes, I tried to calculate the effect of this new factor on the plot. Hamlet had not been exposed to the beings that lurk in the forest. Only his relatives in the male line could bewitch him. Barring relatives not mentioned by Shakespeare, it had to be Claudius who was attempting to harm him. And, of course, it was.

For the moment I staved off questions by saying that the great chief also refused to believe that Hamlet was mad for the love of Ophelia and nothing else. "He was sure that something much more important was troubling Hamlet's heart."

"Now Hamlet's age mates," I continued, "had brought with them a famous storyteller. Hamlet decided to have this man tell the chief and all his homestead a story about a man who had poisoned his brother because he desired his brother's wife and wished to be chief himself. Hamlet was sure the great chief could not hear the story without making a sign if he was indeed guilty, and then he would discover whether his dead father had told him the truth."

The old man interrupted, with deep cunning, "Why should a father lie to his son?" he asked.

I hedged: "Hamlet wasn't sure that it really was his dead father." It was impossible to say anything, in that language, about devil-inspired visions.

"You mean," he said, "it actually was an omen, and he knew witches sometimes send false ones. Hamlet was a fool not to go to one skilled in reading omens and divining the truth in the first place. A man-who-sees-the-truth could have told him how his father died, if he really had been poisoned, and if there was witchcraft in it; then Hamlet could have called the elders to settle the matter."

The shrewd elder ventured to disagree. "Because his father's brother was a great chief, one-who-sees-the-truth might therefore have been afraid to tell it. I think it was for that reason that a friend of Hamlet's father—a witch and an elder—sent an omen so his friend's son would know. Was the omen true?"

"Yes," I said, abandoning ghosts and the devil; a witch-sent omen it would have to be. "It was true, for when the storyteller was telling his tale before all the homestead, the great chief rose in fear. Afraid that Hamlet knew his secret, he planned to have him killed."

The stage set of the next bit presented some difficulties of translation. I began cautiously. "The great chief told Hamlet's mother to find out from her son what he knew. But because a woman's children are always first in her heart, he had the important elder Polonius hide behind a cloth that hung against the wall of Hamlet's mother's sleeping hut. Hamlet started to scold his mother for what she had done."

There was a shocked murmur from everyone. A man should never scold his mother.

"She called out in fear, and Polonius moved behind the cloth. Shouting, 'A rat!' Hamlet took his machete and slashed through the cloth." I paused for dramatic effect. "He had killed Polonius!"

The old men looked at each other in supreme disgust. "That Polonius truly was a fool and a man who knew nothing! What child would not know enough to shout, 'It's me!'" With a pang, I remembered that these people are ardent hunters, always armed with bow, arrow, and machete; at the first rustle in the grass an arrow is aimed and ready, and the hunter shouts "Game!" If no human voice answers immediately, the arrow speeds on its way. Like a good hunter Hamlet had shouted, "A rat!"

I rushed in to save Polonius's reputation. "Polonius did speak. Hamlet heard him. But he thought it was the chief and wished to kill him to avenge his father. He had meant to kill him earlier that evening . . ." I broke down, unable to describe to these pagans, who had no belief in individual afterlife, the difference between dying at one's prayers and dying "unhousell'd, disappointed, unaneled."

This time I had shocked my audience seriously. "For a man to raise his hand against his father's brother and the one who has become his father—that is a terrible thing. The elders ought to let such a man be bewitched."

I nibbled at my kola nut in some perplexity, then pointed out that after all the man had killed Hamlet's father.

"No," pronounced the old man, speaking less to me than to the young men sitting behind the elders. "If your father's brother has killed your father, you must appeal to your father's age mates; they may avenge him. No man may use violence against his senior relatives." Another thought struck him. "But if his father's brother had indeed been wicked enough to bewitch Hamlet and make him mad that would be a good story indeed, for it would be his fault that Hamlet, being mad, no longer had any sense and thus was ready to kill his father's brother."

There was a murmur of applause. *Hamlet* was again a good story to them, but it no longer seemed quite the same story to me. As I thought over the coming complications of plot and motive, I lost courage and decided to skim over dangerous ground quickly.

"The great chief," I went on, "was not sorry that Hamlet had killed Polonius. It gave him a reason to send Hamlet away, with his two treacherous age mates, with letters to a chief of a far country, saying that Hamlet should be killed. But Hamlet changed the writing on their papers, so that the chief killed his age mates instead." I encountered a reproachful glare from one of the men whom I had told undetectable forgery was not merely immoral but beyond human skill. I looked the other way.

"Before Hamlet could return, Laertes came back for his father's funeral. The great chief told him Hamlet had killed Polonius. Laertes swore to kill Hamlet because of this, and because his sister Ophelia, hearing her father had been killed by the man she loved, went mad and drowned in the river."

"Have you already forgotten what we told you?" The old man was reproachful. "One cannot take vengeance on a madman; Hamlet killed Polonius in his madness. As for the girl, she not only went mad, she was drowned. Only witches can make people drown. Water itself can't hurt anything. It is merely something one drinks and bathes in."

I began to get cross. "If you don't like the story, I'll stop."

The old man made soothing noises and himself poured me some more beer. "You tell the story well, and we are listening. But it is clear the elders of your country have never told you what the story really means. No, don't interrupt! We believe you when you say your marriage customs are different, or your clothes and weapons. But people are the same everywhere; therefore, there are always witches and it is we, the elders, who know how witches work. We told you it was the great chief who wished to kill Hamlet, and now your own words have proved us right. Who were Ophelia's male relatives?"

"There were only her father and her brother." Hamlet was clearly out of my hands.

"There must have been many more; this also you must ask of your elders when you get back to your country. From what you tell us, since Polonius was dead, it must have been Laertes who killed Ophelia, although I do not see the reason for it."

We had emptied one pot of beer, and the old men argued the point with slightly tipsy interest. Finally one of them demanded of me, "What did the servant of Polonius say on his return?"

With difficulty I recollected Reynaldo and his mission. "I don't think he did return before Polonius was killed."

"Listen," said the elder, "and I will tell you how it was and how your story will go, then you may tell me if I am right. Polonius knew his son would get into trouble, and so he did. He had many fines to pay for fighting, and debts from gambling. But he had only two ways of getting money quickly. One was to marry off his sister at once, but it is difficult to find a man who will marry a woman desired by the son of a chief. For if the chief's heir commits adultery with your wife, what can you do? Only a fool calls a case against a man who will someday be his judge. Therefore Laertes had to take the second way: he killed his sister by witchcraft, drowning her so he could secretly sell her body to the witches."

I raised an objection. "They found her body and buried it. Indeed Laertes jumped into the grave to see his sister once more—so, you see, the body was truly there. Hamlet, who had just come back, jumped in after him."

"What did I tell you?" The elder appealed to the others. "Laertes was up to no good with his sister's body. Hamlet prevented him, because the chief's heir, like a chief, does not wish any other man to grow rich and powerful. Laertes would be angry, because he would have killed his sister without benefit to himself.

In our country he would try to kill Hamlet for that reason. Is this not what happened?"

"More or less," I admitted. "When the great chief found Hamlet was still alive, he encouraged Laertes to try to kill Hamlet and arranged a fight with machetes between them. In the fight both the young men were wounded to death. Hamlet's mother drank the poisoned beer that the chief meant for Hamlet in case he won the fight. When he saw his mother die of poison, Hamlet, dying, managed to kill his father's brother with his machete."

"You see, I was right!" exclaimed the elder.

"That was a very good story," added the old man, "and you told it with very few mistakes. There was just one more error, at the very end. The poison Hamlet's mother drank was obviously meant for the survivor of the fight, whichever it was. If Laertes had won, the great chief would have poisoned him, for no one would know that he arranged Hamlet's death. Then, too, he need not fear Laertes' witchcraft; it takes a strong heart to kill one's only sister by witchcraft.

"Sometime," concluded the old man, gathering his ragged toga about him, "you must tell us some more stories of your country. We, who are elders, will instruct you in their true meaning, so that when you return to your own land your elders will see that you have not been sitting in the bush, but among those who know things and who have taught you wisdom."

7

"To Give up on Words"

Silence in Western Apache Culture

Keith H. Basso

Can you imagine working on a four-person cattle crew for several days without being introduced to or speaking with one of the other members, whom you did not know? For the Apache, this is a normal occurrence; they do not feel obligated to introduce strangers to one another. Instead, the Apache believe that when the time is right, the strangers will begin speaking to one another.

Would you find it uncomfortable to go on a date and sit in silence for an hour because you had only recently met your companion? What would you think if after returning home from several months' absence your parents and relatives didn't speak to you for several days? Although these situations seem unusual to us, they are considered appropriate among the Apache. Although it seems natural to us that when people first meet introductions are in order and that when friends and relatives reunite greetings and catching up will immediately follow, this is not the case for all cultures.

Those familiar with the television show "Northern Exposure" may consider how the reticence of Native American character Marilyn Whirlwind contrasts with the behavior of the other characters. This example demonstrates how communicating across cultural boundaries can be fraught with uncertainty and misunderstanding. In this selection Keith Basso shows how, among the Apache, certain situations call for silence rather than communication and how silence makes sense within its cultural context.

As you read this selection, ask yourself the following questions:

- What are some of the ways silence is used in European American communication, and how are they different from those in Apache culture?
- How are the meaning and function of silence affected by the social and cultural context?
- What is the critical factor in an Apache's decision to speak or keep silent?
- How do Apaches interact upon meeting a stranger, courting, welcoming children home, "getting cussed out," and being with people who are sad?
- Despite the variety of situations in which Apaches are silent, what is the underlying determinant?

The following terms discussed in this selection are included in the Glossary at the back of the book:

hypothesis	socialization
informant	sociolinguistics
kinship	status

It is not the case that a man who is silent says nothing.

—Anonymous

I[1]

Anyone who has read about American Indians has probably encountered statements which impute to

From *Southwestern Journal of Anthropology,* vol. 26, no. 3, Autumn 1970, pp. 213–230. Reprinted with permission.

them a strong predilection for keeping silent or, as one writer has put it, "a fierce reluctance to speak except when absolutely necessary." In the popular literature, where this characterization is particularly widespread, it is commonly portrayed as the outgrowth of such dubious causes as "instinctive dignity," "an impoverished language," or, perhaps worst of all, the Indians' "lack of personal warmth." Although statements of this sort are plainly erroneous and dangerously misleading, it is noteworthy that professional anthropologists have made few attempts to correct them. Traditionally, ethnographers and linguists have paid little attention to cultural interpretations given to silence or, equally important, to the types of social contexts in which it regularly occurs.

This study investigates certain aspects of silence in the culture of the Western Apache of east-central Arizona. After considering some of the theoretical issues involved, I will briefly describe a number of situations —recurrent in Western Apache society—in which one or more of the participants typically refrain from speech for lengthy periods of time.[2] This is accompanied by a discussion of how such acts of silence are interpreted and why they are encouraged and deemed appropriate. I conclude by advancing an hypothesis that accounts for the reasons that the Western Apache refrain from speaking when they do, and I suggest that, with proper testing, this hypothesis may be shown to have relevance to silence behavior in other cultures.

II

A basic finding of sociolinguistics is that, although both language and language usage are structured, it is the latter which responds most sensitively to extra-linguistic influences (Hymes 1962, 1964; Ervin-Tripp 1964, 1967; Gumperz 1964; Slobin 1967). Accordingly, a number of recent studies have addressed themselves to the problem of how factors in the social environment of speech events delimit the range and condition the selection of message forms (cf. Brown and Gilman 1960; Conklin 1959; Ervin-Tripp 1964, 1967; Frake 1964; Friedrich 1966; Gumperz 1961, 1964; Martin 1964). These studies may be viewed as taking the now familiar position that verbal communication is fundamentally a decision-making process in which, initially, a speaker, having elected to speak, selects from among a repertoire of available codes that which is most appropriately suited to the situation at hand. Once a code has been selected, the speaker picks a suitable channel of transmission and then, finally, makes a choice from a set of referentially equivalent expressions within the code. The intelligibility of the expression he chooses will, of course, be subject to grammatical constraints. But its acceptability will not. Rules for the selection of linguistic alternates operate on features of the social environment and are commensurate with rules governing the conduct of face-to-face interaction. As such, they are properly conceptualized as lying outside the structure of language itself.

It follows from this that for a stranger to communicate appropriately with the members of an unfamiliar society it is not enough that he learn to formulate messages intelligibly. Something else is needed: a knowledge of what kinds of codes, channels, and expressions to use in what kinds of situations and to what kinds of people—as Hymes (1964) has termed it, an "ethnography of communication."

There is considerable evidence to suggest that extra-linguistic factors influence not only the use of speech but its actual occurrence as well. In our own culture, for example, remarks such as "Don't you know when to keep quiet?" "Don't talk until you're introduced," and "Remember now, no talking in church" all point to the fact that an individual's decision to speak may be directly contingent upon the character of his surroundings. Few of us would maintain that "silence is golden" for all people at all times. But we feel that silence is a virtue for some people some of the time, and we encourage children on the road to cultural competence to act accordingly.

Although the form of silence is always the same, the function of a specific act of silence—that is, its interpretation by and effect upon other people—will vary according to the social context in which it occurs. For example, if I choose to keep silent in the chambers of a Justice of the Supreme Court, my action is likely to be interpreted as a sign of politeness or respect. On the other hand, if I refrain from speaking to an established friend or colleague, I am apt to be accused of rudeness or harboring a grudge. In one instance, my behavior is judged by others to be "correct" or "fitting"; in the other, it is criticized as being "out of line."

The point, I think, is fairly obvious. For a stranger entering an alien society, a knowledge of when *not* to speak may be as basic to the production of culturally acceptable behavior as a knowledge of what to say. It stands to reason, then, that an adequate ethnography of communication should not confine itself exclusively to the analysis of choice within verbal repertoires. It should also, as Hymes (1962, 1964) has suggested, specify those conditions under which the members of the society regularly decide to refrain from verbal behavior altogether.

III

The research on which this paper is based was conducted over a period of sixteen months (1964–1969) in the Western Apache settlement of Cibecue, which is located near the center of the Fort Apache Indian Reservation in east-central Arizona. Cibecue's 800 residents participate in an unstable economy that combines subsistence agriculture, cattle-raising, sporadic wage-earning, and Government subsidies in the form of welfare checks and social security benefits. Unemployment is a serious problem, and substandard living conditions are widespread.

Although Reservation life has precipitated far-reaching changes in the composition and geographical distribution of Western Apache social groups, consanguineal kinship—real and imputed—remains the single most powerful force in the establishment and regulation of interpersonal relationships (Kaut 1957; Basso 1970). The focus of domestic activity is the individual "camp," or *gowąą́*. This term labels both the occupants and the location of a single dwelling or, as is more apt to be the case, several dwellings built within a few feet of each other. The majority of *gową́ą́* in Cibecue are occupied by nuclear families. The next largest residential unit is the *gotáá* (camp cluster), which is a group of spatially localized *gową́ą́*, each having at least one adult member who is related by ties of matrilineal kinship to persons living in all the others. An intricate system of exogamous clans serves to extend kinship relationships beyond the *gową́ą́* and *gottáá* and facilitates concerted action in projects, most notably the presentation of ceremonials, requiring large amounts of manpower. Despite the presence in Cibecue of a variety of Anglo missionaries and a dwindling number of medicine men, diagnostic and curing rituals, as well as the girls' puberty ceremonial, continue to be performed with regularity (Basso 1966, 1970). Witchcraft persists in undiluted form (Basso 1969).

IV

Of the many broad categories of events, or scenes, that comprise the daily round of Western Apache life, I shall deal here only with those that are coterminous with what Goffman (1961, 1964) has termed "focused gatherings" or "encounters." The concept *situation*, in keeping with established usage, will refer inclusively to the location of such a gathering, its physical setting, its point in time, the standing behavior patterns that accompany it, and the social attributes of the persons involved (Hymes 1962, 1964; Ervin-Tripp 1964, 1967).

In what follows, however, I will be mainly concerned with the roles and statuses of participants. The reason for this is that the critical factor in the Apache's decision to speak or keep silent seems always to be the nature of his relationships to other people. To be sure, other features of the situation are significant, but apparently only to the extent that they influence the perception of status and role.[3] What this implies, of course, is that roles and statuses are not fixed attributes. Although they may be depicted as such in a static model (and often with good reason), they are appraised and acted upon in particular social contexts and, as a result, subject to redefinition and variation.[4] With this in mind, let us now turn our attention to the Western Apache and the types of situations in which, as one of my informants put it, "it is right to give up on words."

V

1. "Meeting strangers" *(nda dòhwáá iłtsééda)*. The term, *nda*, labels categories at two levels of contrast. At the most general level, it designates any person—Apache or non-Apache—who, prior to an initial meeting, has never been seen and therefore cannot be identified. In addition, the term is used to refer to Apaches who, though previously seen and known by some external criteria such as clan affiliation or personal name, have never been engaged in face-to-face interaction. The latter category, which is more restricted than the first, typically includes individuals who live on the adjacent San Carlos Reservation, in Fort Apache settlements geographically removed from Cibecue, and those who fall into the category *kii dòhandáágo* (non-kinsmen). In all cases, "strangers" are separated by social distance. And in all cases it is considered appropriate, when encountering them for the first time, to refrain from speaking.

The type of situation described as "meeting strangers" *(nda dòhwáá iłtsééda)* can take place in any number of different physical settings. However, it occurs most frequently in the context of events such as fairs and rodeos, which, owing to the large number of people in attendance, offer unusual opportunities for chance encounters. In large gatherings, the lack of verbal communication between strangers is apt to go unnoticed, but in smaller groups it becomes quite conspicuous. The following incident, involving two strangers who found themselves part of a four-man round-up crew, serves as a good example. My informant, who was also a member of the crew, recalled the following episode:

> One time, I was with A, B, and X down at Gleason Flat, working cattle. That man, X, was from East Fork [a community nearly 40 miles from Cibecue] where B's wife was from. But he didn't know A, never knew him before, I guess. First day, I worked with X. At night, when we camped, we talked with B, but X and A didn't say anything to each other. Same way, second day. Same way, third. Then, at night on fourth day, we were sitting by the fire. Still, X and A didn't talk. Then A said, "Well, I know there is a stranger to me here, but I've been watching him and I know he is all right." After that, X and A talked a lot. . . . Those two men didn't know each other, so they took it easy at first.

As this incident suggests, the Western Apache do not feel compelled to "introduce" persons who are unknown to each other. Eventually, it is assumed, strangers will begin to speak. However, this is a decision that is properly left to the individuals involved, and no attempt is made to hasten it. Outside help in the form of introductions or other verbal routines is viewed as presumptuous and unnecessary.

Strangers who are quick to launch into conversation are frequently eyed with undisguised suspicion. A typical reaction to such individuals is that they "want something," that is, their willingness to violate convention is attributed to some urgent need which is likely to result in requests for money, labor, or transportation. Another common reaction to talkative strangers is that they are drunk.

If the stranger is an Anglo, it is usually assumed that he "wants to teach us something" (i.e., give orders or instructions) or that he "wants to make friends in a hurry." The latter response is especially revealing, since Western Apaches are extremely reluctant to be hurried into friendships—with Anglos or each other. Their verbal reticence with strangers is directly related to the conviction that the establishment of social relationships is a serious matter that calls for caution, careful judgment, and plenty of time.

2. "Courting" (*líígoláá*). During the initial stages of courtship, young men and women go without speaking for conspicuous lengths of time. Courting may occur in a wide variety of settings—practically anywhere, in fact—and at virtually any time of the day or night, but it is most readily observable at large public gatherings such as ceremonials, wakes, and rodeos. At these events, "sweethearts" (*zééde*) may stand or sit (sometimes holding hands) for as long as an hour without exchanging a word. I am told by adult informants that the young people's reluctance to speak may become even more pronounced in situations where they find themselves alone.

Apaches who have just begun to court attribute their silence to "intense shyness" ('*isté*) and a feeling of acute "self-consciousness" (*dàyéézí*) which, they claim, stems from their lack of familiarity with one another. More specifically, they complain of "not knowing what to do" in each other's presence and of the fear that whatever they say, no matter how well thought out in advance, will sound "dumb" or "stupid."[5]

One informant, a youth 17 years old, commented as follows:

> It's hard to talk with your sweetheart at first. She doesn't know you and won't know what to say. It's the same way towards her. You don't know how to talk yet . . . so you get very bashful. That makes it sometimes so you don't say anything. So you just go around together and don't talk. At first, it's better that way. Then, after a while, when you know each other, you aren't shy anymore and can talk good.

The Western Apache draw an equation between the ease and frequency with which a young couple talks and how well they know each other. Thus, it is expected that after several months of steady companionship sweethearts will start to have lengthy conversations. Earlier in their relationship, however, protracted discussions may be openly discouraged. This is especially true for girls, who are informed by their mothers and older sisters that silence in courtship is a sign of modesty and that an eagerness to speak betrays previous experience with men. In extreme cases, they add, it may be interpreted as a willingness to engage in sexual relations. Said one woman, aged 32:

> This way I have talked to my daughter. "Take it easy when boys come around this camp and want you to go somewhere with them. When they talk to you, just listen at first. Maybe you won't know what to say. So don't talk about just anything. If you talk with those boys right away, then they will know you know all about them. They will think you've been with many boys before, and they will start talking about that."

3. "Children, coming home" (*čogoše nakáii*). The Western Apache lexeme *iltá inatsáá* (reunion) is used to describe encounters between an individual who has returned home after a long absence and his relatives and friends. The most common type of reunion, *čogoše nakáii* (children, coming home), involves boarding school students and their parents. It occurs in late May or early in June, and its setting is usually a trading post or school, where parents congregate to await the arrival of buses bringing the children home. As the latter disembark and locate their parents in the crowd, one anticipates a flurry of verbal greetings. Typically, however, there are few or none at all. Indeed, it is not unusual for parents and child to go without speaking for as long as 15 minutes.

When the silence is broken, it is almost always the child who breaks it. His parents listen attentively to everything he says but speak hardly at all themselves. This pattern persists even after the family has reached the privacy of its camp, and two or three days may pass before the child's parents seek to engage him in sustained conversation.

According to my informants, the silence of Western Apache parents at (and after) reunions with their children is ultimately predicated on the possibility that the latter have been adversely affected by their experiences away from home. Uppermost is the fear that, as a result of protracted exposure to Anglo attitudes and values, the children have come to view their parents as ignorant, old-fashioned, and no longer deserving of respect. One of my most thoughtful and articulate informants commented on the problem as follows:

> You just can't tell about those children after they've been with White men for a long time. They get their minds turned around sometimes . . . they forget where

they come from and get ashamed when they come home because their parents and relatives are poor. They forget how to act with these Apaches and get mad easy. They walk around all night and get into fights. They don't stay at home.

At school, some of them learn to want to be White men, so they come back and try to act that way. But we are still Apaches! So we don't know them anymore, and it is like we never knew them. It is hard to talk to them when they are like that.

Apache parents openly admit that, initially, children who have been away to school seem distant and unfamiliar. They have grown older, of course, and their physical appearance may have changed. But more fundamental is the concern that they have acquired new ideas and expectations which will alter their behavior in unpredictable ways. No matter how pressing this concern may be, however, it is considered inappropriate to directly interrogate a child after his arrival home. Instead, parents anticipate that within a short time he will begin to divulge information about himself that will enable them to determine in what ways, if any, his views and attitudes have changed. This, the Apache say, is why children do practically all the talking in the hours following a reunion, and their parents remain unusually silent.

Said one man, the father of two children who had recently returned from boarding school in Utah:

Yes, it's right that we didn't talk much to them when they came back, my wife and me. They were away for a long time, and we didn't know how they would like it, being home. So we waited. Right away, they started to tell stories about what they did. Pretty soon we could tell they liked it, being back. That made us feel good. So it was easy to talk to them again. It was like they were before they went away.

4. "Getting cussed out" (*sìɫditéé*). This lexeme is used to describe any situation in which one individual, angered and enraged, shouts insults and criticism at another. Although the object of such invective is in most cases the person or persons who provoked it, this is not always the case, because an Apache who is truly beside himself with rage is likely to vent his feelings on anyone whom he sees or who happens to be within range of his voice. Consequently, "getting cussed out" may involve large numbers of people who are totally innocent of the charges being hurled against them. But whether they are innocent or not, their response to the situation is the same. They refrain from speech.

Like the types of situations we have discussed thus far, "getting cussed out" can occur in a wide variety of physical settings: at ceremonial dancegrounds and trading posts, inside and outside wickiups and houses, on food-gathering expeditions and shopping trips—in short, wherever and whenever individuals lose control of their tempers and lash out verbally at persons nearby.

Although "getting cussed out" is basically free of setting self-imposed restrictions, the Western Apache fear it most at gatherings where alcohol is being consumed. My informants observed that especially at "drinking parties" (*dá'idlą́ą́*), where there is much rough joking and ostensibly mock criticism, it is easy for well-intentioned remarks to be misconstrued as insults. Provoked in this way, persons who are intoxicated may become hostile and launch into explosive tirades, often with no warning at all.

The silence of Apaches who are "getting cussed out" is consistently explained in reference to the belief that individuals who are "enraged" (*haškéé*) are also irrational or "crazy" (*bìné'idíí*). In this condition, it is said, they "forget who they are" and become oblivious to what they say or do. Concomitantly, they lose all concern for the consequences of their actions on other people. In a word, they are dangerous. Said one informant:

When people get mad they get crazy. Then they start yelling and saying bad things. Some say they are going to kill somebody for what he has done. Some keep it up that way for a long time, maybe walk from camp to camp, real angry, yelling, crazy like that. They keep it up for a long time, some do.

People like that don't know what they are saying, so you can't tell about them. When you see someone like that, just walk away. If he yells at you, let him say whatever he wants to. Let him say anything. Maybe he doesn't mean it. But he doesn't know that. He will be crazy, and he could try to kill you.

Another Apache said:

When someone gets mad at you and starts yelling, then just don't do anything to make him get worse. Don't try to quiet him down because he won't know why you're doing it. If you try to do that, he may just get worse and try to hurt you.

As the last of these statements implies, the Western Apache operate on the assumption that enraged persons—because they are temporarily "crazy"—are difficult to reason with. Indeed, there is a widely held belief that attempts at mollification will serve to intensify anger, thus increasing the chances of physical violence. The appropriate strategy when "getting cussed out" is to do nothing, to avoid any action that will attract attention to oneself. Since speaking accomplishes just the opposite, the use of silence is strongly advised.

5. "Being with people who are sad" (*nde dòbiɫgòzóóda bigáá*). Although the Western Apache phrase that labels this situation has no precise equivalent in English, it refers quite specifically to gatherings in which an individual finds himself in the company of

someone whose spouse or kinsman has recently died. Distinct from wakes and burials, which follow immediately after a death, "being with people who are sad" is most likely to occur several weeks later. At this time, close relatives of the deceased emerge from a period of intense mourning (during which they rarely venture beyond the limits of their camps) and start to resume their normal activities within the community. To persons anxious to convey their sympathies, this is interpreted as a sign that visitors will be welcomed and, if possible, provided with food and drink. To those less solicitous, it means that unplanned encounters with the bereaved must be anticipated and prepared for.

"Being with people who are sad" can occur on a foot-path, in a camp, at church, or in a trading post; but whatever the setting—and regardless of whether it is the result of a planned visit or an accidental meeting—the situation is marked by a minimum of speech. Queried about this, my informants volunteered three types of explanations. The first is that persons "who are sad" are so burdened with "intense grief" (dóɬgozóóda) that speaking requires of them an unusual amount of physical effort. It is courteous and considerate, therefore, not to attempt to engage them in conversation.

A second native explanation is that in situations of this sort verbal communication is basically unnecessary. Everyone is familiar with what has happened, and talking about it, even for the purpose of conveying solace and sympathy, would only reinforce and augment the sadness felt by those who were close to the deceased. Again, for reasons of courtesy, this is something to be avoided.

The third explanation is rooted in the belief that "intense grief," like intense rage, produces changes in the personality of the individual who experiences it. As evidence for this, the Western Apache cite numerous instances in which the emotional strain of dealing with death, coupled with an overwhelming sense of irrevocable personal loss, has caused persons who were formerly mild and even-tempered to become abusive, hostile, and physically violent.

> That old woman, X, who lives across Cibecue Creek, one time her first husband died. After that she cried all the time, for a long time. Then, I guess she got mean because everyone said she drank a lot and got into fights. Even with her close relatives, she did like that for a long time. She was too sad for her husband. That's what made her like that; it made her lose her mind.

> My father was like that when his wife died. He just stayed home all the time and wouldn't go anywhere. He didn't talk to any of his relatives or children. He just said, "I'm hungry. Cook for me." That's all. He stayed that way for a long time. His mind was not with us. He was still with his wife.

> My uncle died in 1911. His wife sure went crazy right after that. Two days after they buried the body, we went over there and stayed with those people who had been left alone. My aunt got mad at us. She said, "Why do you come back over here? You can't bring my husband back. I can take care of myself and those others in my camp, so why don't you go home." She sure was mad that time, too sad for someone who died. She didn't know what she way saying because in about one week she came to our camp and said, "My relatives, I'm all right now. When you came to help me, I had too much sadness and my mind was no good. I said bad words to you. But now I am all right and I know what I am doing."

As these statements indicate, the Western Apache assume that a person suffering from "intense grief" is likely to be disturbed and unstable. Even though he may appear outwardly composed, they say, there is always the possibility that he is emotionally upset and therefore unusually prone to volatile outbursts. Apaches acknowledge that such an individual might welcome conversation in the context of "being with people who are sad," but, on the other hand, they fear it might prove incendiary. Under these conditions, which resemble those in Situation No. 4, it is considered both expedient and appropriate to keep silent.

6. "Being with someone for whom they sing" (ndebìdádìstááha bigáá). The last type of situation to be described is restricted to a small number of physical locations and is more directly influenced by temporal factors than any of the situations we have discussed so far. "Being with someone for whom they sing" takes place only in the context of "curing ceremonials" (gòjitáɬ). These events begin early at night and come to a close shortly before dawn the following day. In the late fall and throughout the winter, curing ceremonials are held inside the patient's wickiup or house. In the spring and summer, they are located outside, at some open place near the patient's camp or at specially designated dance grounds where group rituals of all kinds are regularly performed.

Prior to the start of a curing ceremonial, all persons in attendance may feel free to talk with the patient; indeed, because he is so much a focus of concern, it is expected that friends and relatives will seek him out to offer encouragement and support. Conversation breaks off, however, when the patient is informed that the ceremonial is about to begin, and it ceases entirely when the presiding medicine man commences to chant. From this point on, until the completion of the final chant next morning, it is inappropriate for anyone except the medicine man (and, if he has them, his aides) to speak to the patient.[6]

In order to appreciate the explanation Apaches give for this prescription, we must briefly discuss the concept of "supernatural power" (diyí) and describe some of the effects it is believed to have on persons at whom it is directed. Elsewhere (Basso 1969:30) I have defined "power" as follows:

> The term *diyí* refers to one or all of a set of abstract and invisible forces which are said to derive from certain classes of animals, plants, minerals, meteorological phenomena, and mythological figures within the Western Apache universe. Any of the various powers may be acquired by man and, if properly handled, used for a variety of purposes.

A power that has been antagonized by disrespectful behavior towards its source may retaliate by causing the offender to become sick. "Power-caused illnesses" (*kásití̜ kiyí bił*) are properly treated with curing ceremonials in which one or more medicine men, using chants and various items of ritual paraphernalia, attempt to neutralize the sickness-causing power with powers of their own.

Roughly two-thirds of my informants assert that a medicine man's power actually enters the body of the patient; others maintain that it simply closes in and envelops him. In any case, all agree that the patient is brought into intimate contact with a potent supernatural force which elevates him to a condition labeled *gòdiyò'* (sacred, holy).

The term *gòdiyò'* may also be translated as "potentially harmful" and, in this sense, is regularly used to describe classes of objects (including all sources of power) that are associated with taboos. In keeping with the semantics of *gòdiyò'*, the Western Apache explain that, besides making patients holy, power makes them potentially harmful. And it is this transformation, they explain, that is basically responsible for the cessation of verbal communication during curing ceremonials. Said one informant:

> When they start singing for someone like that, he sort of goes away with what the medicine man is working with (i.e., power). Sometimes people they sing for don't know you, even after it (the curing ceremonial) is over. They get holy, and you shouldn't try to talk to them when they are like that . . . it's best to leave them alone.

Another informant made similar comments:

> When they sing for someone, what happens is like this: that man they sing for doesn't know why he is sick or which way to go. So the medicine man has to show him and work on him. That is when he gets holy, and that makes him go off somewhere in his mind, so you should stay away from him.

Because Apaches undergoing ceremonial treatment are perceived as having been changed by power into something different from their normal selves, they are regarded with caution and apprehension. Their newly acquired status places them in close proximity to the supernatural and, as such, carries with it a very real element of danger and uncertainty. These conditions combine to make "being with someone for whom they sing" a situation in which speech is considered disrespectful and, if not exactly harmful, at least potentially hazardous.

VI

Although the types of situations described above differ from one another in obvious ways, I will argue in what follows that the underlying determinants of silence are in each case basically the same. Specifically, I will attempt to defend the hypothesis that keeping silent in Western Apache culture is associated with social situations in which participants perceive their relationships *vis-à-vis* one another to be ambiguous and/or unpredictable.

Let us begin with the observation that, in all the situations we have described, *silence is defined as appropriate with respect to a specific individual or individuals.* In other words, the use of speech is not directly curtailed by the setting of a situation nor by the physical activities that accompany it but, rather, by the perceived social and psychological attributes of at least one focal participant.

It may also be observed that, in each type of situation, *the status of the focal participant is marked by ambiguity*—either because he is unfamiliar to other participants in the situation or because, owing to some recent event, a status he formerly held has been changed or is in a process of transition.

Thus, in Situation No. 1, persons who earlier considered themselves "strangers" move towards some other relationship, perhaps "friend" (*šìdikéé*), perhaps "enemy" (*šìkédndíí*). In Situation No. 2, young people who have relatively limited exposure to one another attempt to adjust to the new and intimate status of "sweetheart." These two situations are similar in that the focal participants have little or no prior knowledge of each other. Their social identities are not as yet clearly defined, and their expectations, lacking the foundation of previous experience, are poorly developed.

Situation No. 3 is somewhat different. Although the participants—parents and their children—are well known to each other, their relationship has been seriously interrupted by the latter's prolonged absence from home. This, combined with the possibility that recent experiences at school have altered the children's attitudes, introduces a definite element of unfamiliarity and doubt. Situation No. 3 is not characterized by the absence of role expectations but by the participants' perception that those already in existence may be outmoded and in need of revision.

Status ambiguity is present in Situation No. 4 because a focal participant is enraged and, as a result, considered "crazy." Until he returns to a more rational condition, others in the situation have no way of predicting how he will behave. Situation No. 5 is similar in that the personality of a focal participant is seen to have undergone a marked shift which makes his actions more difficult to anticipate. In both situations, the status of focal participants is uncertain because of real or imagined changes in their psychological makeup.

In situation No. 6, a focal participant is ritually transformed from an essentially neutral state to one which is contextually defined as "potentially harmful." Ambiguity and apprehension accompany this transition, and, as in Situations No. 4 and 5, established patterns of interaction must be waived until the focal participant reverts to a less threatening condition.

This discussion points up a third feature characteristic of all situations: *the ambiguous status of focal participants is accompanied either by the absence or suspension of established role expectations.* In every instance, nonfocal participants (i.e., those who refrain from speech) are either uncertain of how the focal participant will behave towards them or, conversely, how they should behave towards him. Stated in the simplest way possible, their roles become blurred with the result that established expectations—if they exist—lose their relevance as guidelines for social action and must be temporarily discarded or abruptly modified.

We are now in a position to expand upon our initial hypothesis and make it more explicit.

1. In Western Apache culture, the absence of verbal communication is associated with social situations in which the status of local participants is ambiguous.

2. Under these conditions, fixed role expectations lose their applicability and the illusion of predictability in social interaction is lost.

3. To sum up and reiterate: keeping silent among the Western Apache is a response to uncertainty and unpredictability in social relations.

VII

The question remains to what extent the foregoing hypothesis helps to account for silence behavior in other cultures. Unfortunately, it is impossible at the present time to provide anything approaching a conclusive answer. Standard ethnographies contain very little information about the circumstances under which verbal communication is discouraged, and it is only within the past few years that problems of this

sort have engaged the attention of sociolinguists. The result is that adequate cross-cultural data are almost completely lacking.

As a first step towards the elimination of this deficiency, an attempt is now being made to investigate the occurrence and interpretation of silence in other Indian societies of the American Southwest. Our findings at this early stage, though neither fully representative nor sufficiently comprehensive, are extremely suggestive. By way of illustration, I quote below from portions of a preliminary report prepared by Priscilla Mowrer (1970), herself a Navajo, who inquired into the situational features of Navajo silence behavior in the vicinity of Tuba City on the Navajo Reservation in east-central Arizona.

> I. *Silence and Courting:* Navajo youngsters of opposite sexes just getting to know one another say nothing, except to sit close together and maybe hold hands. . . . In public, they may try not to let on that they are interested in each other, but in private it is another matter. If the girl is at a gathering where the boy is also present, she may go off by herself. Falling in step, the boy will generally follow. They may just walk around or find some place to sit down. But, at first, they will not say anything to each other.
>
> II. *Silence and Long Absent Relatives:* When a male or female relative returns home after being gone for six months or more, he (or she) is first greeted with a handshake. If the returnee is male, the female greeter may embrace him and cry—the male, meanwhile, will remain dry-eyed and silent.
>
> III. *Silence and Anger:* The Navajo tend to remain silent when being shouted at by a drunk or angered individual because that particular individual is considered temporarily insane. To speak to such an individual, the Navajo believe, just tends to make the situation worse. . . . People remain silent because they believe that the individual is not himself, that he may have been witched, and is not responsible for the change in his behavior.
>
> IV. *Silent Mourning:* Navajos speak very little when mourning the death of a relative. . . . The Navajo mourn and cry together in pairs. Men will embrace one another and cry together. Women, however, will hold one another's hands and cry together.
>
> V. *Silence and the Ceremonial Patient:* The Navajo consider it wrong to talk to a person being sung over. The only people who talk to the patient are the medicine man and a female relative (or male relative if the patient is male) who is in charge of food preparation. The only time the patient speaks openly is when the medicine man asks her (or him) to pray along with him.

These observations suggest that striking similarities may exist between the types of social contexts in which Navajos and Western Apaches refrain from speech. If this impression is confirmed by further research, it will lend obvious cross-cultural support to the hypothesis advanced above. But regardless of the final outcome, the situational determinants of silence seem eminently deserving of further study. For as we become better informed about the types of contextual variables that mitigate against the use of verbal codes, we should also learn more about those variables that encourage and promote them.

NOTES

1. At different times during the period extending from 1964–1969 the research on which this paper is based was supported by U. S. P. H. S. Grant MH-12691-01, a grant from the American Philosophical Society, and funds from the Doris Duke Oral History Project at the Arizona State Museum. I am pleased to acknowledge this support. I would also like to express my gratitude to the following scholars for commenting upon an earlier draft: Y. R. Chao, Harold C. Conklin, Roy G. D'Andrade, Charles O. Frake, Paul Friedrich, John Gumperz, Kenneth Hale, Harry Hoijer, Dell Hymes, Stanley Newman, David M. Schneider, Joel Sherzer, and Paul Turner. Although the final version gained much from their criticisms and suggestions, responsibility for its present form and content rests solely with the author. A preliminary version of this paper was presented to the Annual Meeting of the American Anthropological Association in New Orleans, Louisiana, November 1969. A modified version of this paper is scheduled to appear in *Studies in Apachean Culture and Ethnology* (ed. by Keith H. Basso and Morris Opler), Tucson: University of Arizona Press, 1970.

2. The situations described in this paper are not the only ones in which the Western Apache refrain from speech. There is a second set—not considered here because my data are incomplete—in which silence appears to occur as a gesture of respect, usually to persons in positions of authority. A third set, very poorly understood, involves ritual specialists who claim they must keep silent at certain points during the preparation of ceremonial paraphernalia.

3. Recent work in the sociology of interaction, most notably by Goffman (1963) and Garfinkel (1967), has led to the suggestion that social relationships are everywhere the major determinants of verbal behavior. In this case, as Gumperz (1967) makes clear, it becomes methodologically unsound to treat the various components of communicative events as independent variables. Gumperz (1967) has presented a hierarchical model, sensitive to dependency, in which components are seen as stages in the communication process. Each stage serves as the input for the next. The basic stage, i.e., the initial input, is "social identities or statuses." For further details see Slobin 1967:131–134.

4. I would like to stress that the emphasis placed on social relations is fully in keeping with the Western Apache interpretation of their own behavior. When my informants were asked to explain why they or someone else was silent on a particular occasion, they invariably did so in terms of *who* was present at the time.

5. Among the Western Apache, rules of exogamy discourage courtships between members of the same clan (*kii àɬhánigo*) and so-called "related" clans (*kii*), with the result that sweethearts are almost always "non-matrilineal kinsmen" (*dòhwàkìida*). Compared to "matrilineal kinsmen" (*kii*), such individuals have fewer opportunities during childhood to establish close personal relationships and thus, when courtship begins, have relatively little knowledge of each other. It is not surprising, therefore, that their behavior is similar to that accorded strangers.

6. I have witnessed over 75 curing ceremonials since 1961 and have seen this rule violated only 6 times. On 4 occasions, drunks were at fault. In the other 2 cases, the patient fell asleep and had to be awakened.

REFERENCES

Basso, Keith H. 1966. *The Gift of Changing Woman.* Bureau of American Ethnology, bulletin 196.

——. 1969. *Western Apache Witchcraft.* Anthropological Papers of the University of Arizona, no. 15.

——. 1970. *The Cibecue Apache.* New York: Holt, Rinehart and Winston, Inc.

Brown, R. W., and Albert Gilman. 1960. "The Pronouns of Power and Solidarity," in *Style and Language* (ed. by T. Sebeok), pp. 253–276. Cambridge: The Technology Press of Massachusetts Institute of Technology.

Conklin, Harold C. 1959. Linguistic Play in Its Cultural Context. *Language* 35:631–636.

Ervin-Tripp, Susan. 1964. "An Analysis of the Interaction of Language, Topic and Listener," in *The Ethnography of Communication* (ed. by J. J. Gumperz and D. Hymes), pp. 86–102. *American Anthropologist,* Special Publication, vol. 66, no. 6, part 2.

——. 1967. *Sociolinguistics.* Language-Behavior Research Laboratory, Working Paper no. 3. Berkeley: University of California.

Frake, Charles O. 1964. "How to Ask for a Drink in Subanun," in *The Ethnography of Communication* (ed. by J. J. Gumperz and D. Hymes), pp. 127–132. *American Anthropologist,* Special Publication, vol. 66, no. 6, part 2.

Friedrich, P. 1966. "Structural Implications of Russian Pronominal Usage," in *Sociolinguistics* (ed. by W. Bright), pp. 214–253. The Hague: Mouton.

Garfinkel, H. 1967. *Studies in Ethnomethodology.* Englewood Cliffs, N.J.: Prentice-Hall, Inc.

Goffman, E. 1961. *Encounters: Two Studies in the Sociology of Interaction.* Indianapolis: The Bobbs-Merrill Co., Inc.

——. 1963. *Behavior in Public Places.* Glencoe, Ill.: Free Press.

——. 1964. "The Neglected Situation," in *The Ethnography of Communication* (ed. by J. J. Gumperz and D. Hymes), pp.

133–136. *American Anthropologist*, Special Publication, vol. 66, no. 6, part 2.

Gumperz, John J. 1961. Speech Variation and the Study of Indian Civilization. *American Anthropologist* 63: 976–988.

——. 1964. "Linguistic and Social Interaction in Two Communities," in *The Ethnography of Communication* (ed. by J. J. Gumperz and D. Hymes), pp. 137–153. *American Anthropologist*, Special Publication, vol. 66, no. 6, part 2.

——. 1967. "The Social Setting of Linguistic Behavior," in *A Field Manual for Cross-Cultural Study of the Acquisition of Communicative Competence (Second Draft)* (ed. by D. I. Slobin), pp. 129–134. Berkeley: University of California.

Hymes, Dell. 1962. "The Ethnography of Speaking," in *Anthropology and Human Behavior* (ed. by T. Gladwin and W. C. Sturtevant), pp. 13–53. Washington, D. C.: The Anthropological Society of Washington.

——. 1964. "Introduction: Toward Ethnographies of Communication" in *The Ethnography of Communication* (ed. by J. J. Gumperz and D. Hymes), pp. 1–34. *American Anthropologist*, Special Publication, vol. 66, no. 6, part 2.

Kaut, Charles R. 1957. *The Western Apache Clan System: Its Origins and Development.* University of New Mexico Publications in Anthropology, no. 9.

Martin, Samuel. 1964. "Speech Levels in Japan and Korea," in *Language in Culture and Society* (ed. by D. Hymes), pp. 407–415. New York: Harper & Row.

Mowrer, Priscilla. 1970. Notes on Navajo Silence Behavior. MS, University of Arizona.

Slobin, Dan I. (ed.). 1967. *A Field Manual for Cross-Cultural Study of the Acquisition of Communicative Competence (Second Draft).* Berkeley: University of California.

8

A Cultural Approach
to Male-Female Miscommunication

Daniel N. Maltz and Ruth A. Borker

Of the 60,000 or so words in the English language, the typical educated adult uses about 2,000. Five hundred of these words alone can convey over 14,000 meanings. But even with all these alternatives, this is not the central problem of miscommunication in North America. Rather, interethnic and cross-sex conversations are the central problem, because the participants possess different subcultural rules for speaking.

Conversation is a negotiated activity. Within a given culture, conversations rely on unspoken understandings about tone of voice, visual cues, silence, minimal responses (such as "mm hmm"), and a variety of other subtle conventions. A cultural approach to male-female conversation highlights unconscious meanings that can lead members of one group to misinterpret the intent of others. Evidence suggests, for example, that women use the response "mm hmm" to indicate they are listening, whereas men use the same response to indicate they are agreeing. Thus, a man who does not provide such cues may indicate to a female conversation partner that he is not listening, whereas a woman may appear to keep changing her mind when giving the same cue. This and similar insights are found throughout this selection and indicate the need for paying attention to communication across cultural and subcultural boundaries.

As you read this selection, ask yourself the following questions:

- What are some of the differences in the ways men and women talk to each other that have been noted in earlier research?

- How do differences between men and women in conversational style reflect differences in power in the larger society?

- If men and women exist in different linguistic subcultures, how and when were these subcultures learned? How does the world of girls differ from the world of boys?

- What kinds of miscommunications occur in cross-sex conversation?

- Can you think of situations that have occurred in your own life that can be better understood after reading this cultural analysis of cross-sex conversation?

The following terms discussed in this selection are included in the Glossary at the back of the book:

gender	*social networks*
metalinguistics	*sociolinguistics*
sex roles	*subculture*

INTRODUCTION

This chapter presents what we believe to be a useful new framework for examining differences in the speaking patterns of American men and women. It is based not on new data, but on a reexamination of a wide variety of material already available in the scholarly literature. Our starting problem is the nature of the different

roles of male and female speakers in informal cross-sex conversations in American English. Our attempts to think about this problem have taken us to preliminary examination of a wide variety of fields often on or beyond the margins of our present competencies: children's speech, children's play, styles and patterns of friendship, conversational turn-taking, discourse analysis, and interethnic communication. The research which most influenced the development of our present model includes John Gumperz's work on problems in interethnic communication (1982) and Marjorie Goodwin's study of the linguistic aspects of play among black children in Philadelphia (1978, 1980a, 1980b).

From *Language and Social Identity*, John L. Gumperz, ed., 1982. Reprinted with the permission of Cambridge University Press.

Our major argument is that the general approach recently developed for the study of difficulties in cross-ethnic communication can be applied to cross-sex communication as well. We prefer to think of the difficulties in both cross-sex and cross-ethnic communication as two examples of the same larger phenomenon: cultural difference and miscommunication.

THE PROBLEM OF CROSS-SEX CONVERSATION

Study after study has shown that when men and women attempt to interact as equals in friendly cross-sex conversations they do not play the same role in interaction, even when there is no apparent element of flirting. We hope to explore some of these differences, examine the explanations that have been offered, and provide an alternative explanation for them.

The primary data on cross-sex conversations come from two general sources: social psychology studies from the 1950s such as Soskin and John's (1963) research on two young married couples and Strodbeck and Mann's (1956) research on jury deliberations, and more recent sociolinguistic studies from the University of California at Santa Barbara and the University of Pennsylvania by Candace West (Zimmerman and West 1975; West and Zimmerman 1977; West 1979), Pamela Fishman (1978), and Lynette Hirschman (1973).

WOMEN'S FEATURES

Several striking differences in male and female contributions to cross-sex conversation have been noticed in these studies.

First, women display a greater tendency to ask questions. Fishman (1978:400) comments that "at times I felt that all women did was ask questions," and Hirschman (1973:10) notes that "several of the female-male conversations fell into a question-answer pattern with the females asking the males questions."

Fishman (1978:408) sees this question-asking tendency as an example of a second, more general characteristic of women's speech, doing more of the routine "shitwork" involved in maintaining routine social interaction, doing more to facilitate the flow of conversation (Hirschman 1973:3). Women are more likely than men to make utterances that demand or encourage responses from their fellow speakers and are therefore, in Fishman's words, "more actively engaged in insuring interaction than the men" (1978:404). In the earlier social psychology studies, these features have been coded under the general category of "positive reactions" including solidarity, tension release, and agreeing (Strodbeck and Mann 1956).

Third, women show a greater tendency to make use of positive minimal responses, especially "mm hmm" (Hirschman 1973:8), and are more likely to insert "such comments throughout streams of talk rather than [simply] at the end" (Fishman 1978:402).

Fourth, women are more likely to adopt a strategy of "silent protest" after they have been interrupted or have received a delayed minimal response (Zimmerman and West 1975; West and Zimmerman 1977:524).

Fifth, women show a greater tendency to use the pronouns "you" and "we," which explicitly acknowledge the existence of the other speaker (Hirschman 1973:6).

MEN'S FEATURES

Contrasting contributions to cross-sex conversations have been observed and described for men.

First, men are more likely to interrupt the speech of their conversational partners, that is, to interrupt the speech of women (Zimmerman and West 1975; West and Zimmerman 1977; West 1979).

Second, they are more likely to challenge or dispute their partners' utterances (Hirschman 1973:11).

Third, they are more likely to ignore the comments of the other speaker, that is, to offer no response or acknowledgment at all (Hirschman 1973:11), to respond slowly in what has been described as a "delayed minimal response" (Zimmerman and West 1975:118), or to respond unenthusiastically (Fishman 1978).

Fourth, men use more mechanisms for controlling the topic of conversation, including both topic development and the introduction of new topics, than do women (Zimmerman and West 1975).

Finally, men make more direct declarations of fact or opinion than do women (Fishman 1978:402), including suggestions, opinions, and "statements of orientation" as Strodbeck and Mann (1956) describe them, or "statements of focus and directives" as they are described by Soskin and John (1963).

EXPLANATIONS OFFERED

Most explanations for these features have focused on differences in the social power or in the personalities of men and women. One variant of the social power argument, presented by West (Zimmerman and West 1975; West and Zimmerman 1977), is that men's dominance in conversation parallels their dominance in society. Men enjoy power in society and also in conversation. The two levels are seen as part of a single social-political system. West sees interruptions and topic control as male displays of power—a power based in the larger social order but reinforced and expressed in face-to-face interaction with women. A second variant of this argument, stated by Fishman (1978), is that while the differential power of men and women is crucial, the specific mechanism through which it enters conversation is sex-role definition. Sex roles serve to obscure the issue of power for participants, but the fact is, Fishman argues, that norms of appropriate behavior for women and men serve to give power and interactional control to men while keeping it from women. To be socially acceptable as women, women cannot exert control and must actually support men in their control. In this casting of the social power argument, men are not necessarily seen to be consciously flaunting power, but simply reaping the rewards given them by the social system. In both variants, the link between macro and micro levels of social life is seen as direct and unproblematic, and the focus of explanation is the general social order.

Sex roles have also been central in psychological explanations. The primary advocate of the psychological position has been Robin Lakoff (1975). Basically, Lakoff asserts that, having been taught to speak and act like "ladies," women become as unassertive and insecure as they have been made to sound. The impossible task of trying to be both women and adults, which Lakoff sees as culturally incompatible, saps women of confidence and strength. As a result, they come to produce the speech they do, not just because it is how women are supposed to speak, but because it fits with the personalities they develop as a consequence of sex-role requirements.

The problem with these explanations is that they do not provide a means of explaining why these specific features appear as opposed to any number of others, nor do they allow us to differentiate between various types of male-female interaction. They do not really tell us why and how these specific interactional phenomena are linked to the general fact that men dominate within our social system.

AN ALTERNATIVE EXPLANATION: SOCIOLINGUISTIC SUBCULTURES

Our approach to cross-sex communication patterns is somewhat different from those that have been previously proposed. We place the stress not on psychological differences or power differentials, although these may make some contribution, but rather on a notion of cultural differences between men and women in their conceptions of friendly conversation, their rules for engaging in it, and, probably most important, their rules for interpreting it. We argue that American men and women come from different sociolinguistic sub-

cultures, having learned to do different things with words in a conversation, so that when they attempt to carry on conversations with one another, even if both parties are attempting to treat one another as equals, cultural miscommunication results.

The idea of distinct male and female subcultures is not a new one for anthropology. It has been persuasively argued again and again for those parts of the world such as the Middle East and southern Europe in which men and women spend most of their lives spatially and interactionally segregated. The strongest case for sociolinguistic subcultures has been made by Susan Harding from her research in rural Spain (1975).

The major premise on which Harding builds her argument is that speech is a means for dealing with social and psychological situations. When men and women have different experiences and operate in different social contexts, they tend to develop different genres of speech and different skills for doing things with words. In the Spanish village in which she worked, the sexual division of labor was strong, with men involved in agricultural tasks and public politics while women were involved in a series of networks of personal relations with their children, their husbands, and their female neighbors. While men developed their verbal skills in economic negotiations and public political argument, women became more verbally adept at a quite different mode of interactional manipulation with words: gossip, social analysis, subtle information gathering through a carefully developed technique of verbal prying, and a kind of second-guessing the thoughts of others (commonly known as "women's intuition") through a skillful monitoring of the speech of others. The different social needs of men and women, she argues, have led them to sexually differentiated communicative cultures, with each sex learning a different set of skills for manipulating words effectively.

The question that Harding does not ask, however, is, if men and women possess different subcultural rules for speaking, what happens if and when they try to interact with each other? It is here that we turn to the research on interethnic miscommunication.

INTERETHNIC COMMUNICATION

Recent research (Gumperz 1977, 1978a, 1978b, 1979; Gumperz and Tannen 1978) has shown that systematic problems develop in communication when speakers of different speech cultures interact and that these problems are the result of differences in systems of conversational inference and the cues for signalling speech acts and speaker's intent. Conversation is a negotiated activity. It progresses in large part because of shared assumptions about what is going on.

Examining interactions between English-English and Indian-English speakers in Britain (Gumperz 1977, 1978a, 1979; Gumperz et al. 1977), Gumperz found that differences in cues resulted in systematic miscommunication over whether a question was being asked, whether an argument was being made, whether a person was being rude or polite, whether a speaker was relinquishing the floor or interrupting, whether and what a speaker was emphasizing, whether interactants were angry, concerned, or indifferent. Rather than being seen as problems in communication, the frustrating encounters that resulted were usually chalked up as personality clashes or interpreted in the light of racial stereotypes which tended to exacerbate already bad relations.

To take a simple case, Gumperz (1977) reports that Indian women working at a cafeteria, when offering food, used a falling intonation, e.g., "grạvy," which to them indicated a question, something like "do you want gravy?" Both Indian and English workers saw a question as an appropriate polite form, but to English-English speakers a falling intonation signalled not a question, which for them is signalled by a rising intonation such as "grạvy," but a declarative statement, which was both inappropriate and extremely rude.

A major advantage of Gumperz's framework is that it does not assume that problems are the result of bad faith, but rather sees them as the result of individuals wrongly interpreting cues according to their own rules.

THE INTERPRETATION OF MINIMAL RESPONSES

How might Gumperz's approach to the study of conflicting rules for interpreting conversation be applied to the communication between men and women? A simple example will illustrate our basic approach: the case of positive minimal responses. Minimal responses such as nods and comments like "yes" and "mm hmm" are common features of conversational interaction. Our claim, based on our attempts to understand personal experience, is that these minimal responses have significantly different meanings for men and women, leading to occasionally serious miscommunication.

We hypothesize that for women a minimal response of this type means simply something like "I'm listening to you; please continue," and that for men it has a somewhat stronger meaning such as "I agree with you" or at least "I follow your argument so far." The fact that women use these responses more often than men is in part simply that women are listening more often than men are agreeing.

But our hypothesis explains more than simple differential frequency of usage. Different rules can lead to repeated misunderstandings. Imagine a male speaker who is receiving repeated nods or "mm hmm"s from the woman he is speaking to. She is merely indicating that she is listening, but he thinks she is agreeing with everything he says. Now imagine a female speaker who is receiving only occasional nods and "mm hmm"s from the man she is speaking to. He is indicating that he doesn't always agree; she thinks he isn't always listening.

What is appealing about this short example is that it seems to explain two of the most common complaints in male-female interaction: (1) men who think that women are always agreeing with them and then conclude that it's impossible to tell what a woman really thinks, and (2) women who get upset with men who never seem to be listening. What we think we have here are two separate rules for conversational maintenance which come into conflict and cause massive miscommunication.

SOURCES OF DIFFERENT CULTURES

A probable objection that many people will have to our discussion so far is that American men and women interact with one another far too often to possess different subcultures. What we need to explain is how it is that men and women can come to possess different cultural assumptions about friendly conversation.

Our explanation is really quite simple. It is based on the idea that by the time we have become adults we possess a wide variety of rules for interacting in different situations. Different sets of these rules were learned at different times and in different contexts. We have rules for dealing with people in dominant or subordinate social positions, rules which we first learned as young children interacting with our parents and teachers. We have rules for flirting and other sexual encounters which we probably started learning at or near adolescence. We have rules for dealing with service personnel and bureaucrats, rules we began learning when we first ventured into the public domain. Finally, we have rules for friendly interaction, for carrying on friendly conversation. What is striking about these last rules is that they were learned not from adults but from peers, and that they were learned during precisely that time period, approximately age 5 to 15, when boys and girls interact socially primarily with members of their own sex.

The idea that girls and boys in contemporary America learn different ways of speaking by the age of five or earlier has been postulated by Robin Lakoff (1975), demonstrated by Andrea Meditch (1975), and more fully explored by Adelaide Haas (1979). Haas's research on school-age children shows the early appearance of important male-female differences in patterns of language use, including a male tendency toward direct requests and information giving and a female tendency toward compliance (1979:107).

But the process of acquiring gender-specific speech and behavior patterns by school-age children is more complex than the simple copying of adult "genderlects" by preschoolers. Psychologists Brooks-Gunn and Matthews (1979) have labelled this process the "consolidation of sex roles"; we call it learning of gender-specific "cultures."

Among school-age children, patterns of friendly social interaction are learned not so much from adults as from members of one's peer group, and a major feature of most middle-childhood peer groups is homogeneity; "they are either all-boy or all-girl" (Brooks-Gunn and Matthews 1979). Members of each sex are learning self-consciously to differentiate their behavior from that of the other sex and to exaggerate these differences. The process can be profitably compared to accent divergence in which members of two groups that wish to become clearly distinguished from one another socially acquire increasingly divergent ways of speaking.[1]

Because they learn these gender-specific cultures from their age-mates, children tend to develop stereotypes and extreme versions of adult behavior patterns. For a boy learning to behave in a masculine way, for example, Ruth Hartley (1959, quoted in Brooks-Gunn and Matthews 1979:203) argues that:

> both the information and the practice he gets are distorted. Since his peers have no better sources of information than he has, all they can do is pool the impressions and anxieties they derived from their early training. Thus, the picture they draw is oversimplified and overemphasized. It is a picture drawn in black and white, with little or no modulation and it is incomplete, including a few of the many elements that go to make up the role of the mature male.

What we hope to argue is that boys and girls learn to use language in different ways because of the very different social contexts in which they learn how to carry on friendly conversation. Almost anyone who remembers being a child, has worked with school-age children, or has had an opportunity to observe school-age children can vouch for the fact that groups of girls and groups of boys interact and play in different ways. Systematic observations of children's play have tended to confirm these well-known differences in the ways girls and boys learn to interact with their friends.

In a major study of sex differences in the play of school-age children, for example, sociologist Janet Lever (1976) observed the following six differences between the play of boys and that of girls: (1) girls more often play indoors; (2) boys tend to play in larger groups; (3) boys' play groups tend to include a wider age range of participants; (4) girls play in predomi-nantly male games more often than vice versa; (5) boys more often play competitive games, and (6) girls' games tend to last a shorter period of time than boys' games.

It is by examining these differences in the social organization of play and the accompanying differences in the patterns of social interaction they entail, we argue, that we can learn about the sources of male-female differences in patterns of language use. And it is these same patterns, learned in childhood and carried over into adulthood as the bases for patterns of single-sex friendship relations, we contend, that are potential sources of miscommunication in cross-sex interaction.

THE WORLD OF GIRLS

Our own experience and studies such as Goodwin's (1980b) of black children and Lever's (1976, 1978) of white children suggest a complex of features of girls' play and the speech within it. Girls play in small groups, most often in pairs (Lever 1976; Eder and Hallinan 1978; Brooks-Gunn and Matthews 1979), and their play groups tend to be remarkably homogeneous in terms of age. Their play is often in private or semi-private settings that require participants be invited in. Play is cooperative and activities are usually organized in noncompetitive ways (Lever 1976; Goodwin 1980b). Differentiation between girls is not made in terms of power, but relative closeness. Friendship is seen by girls as involving intimacy, equality, mutual commitment, and loyalty. The idea of "best friend" is central for girls. Relationships between girls are to some extent in opposition to one another, and new relationships are often formed at the expense of old ones. As Brooks-Gunn and Matthews (1979:280) observe, "friendships tend to be exclusive, with a few girls being exceptionally close to one another. Because of this breakups tend to be highly emotional," and Goodwin (1980a:172) notes that "the non-hierarchical framework of the girls provides a fertile ground for rather intricate processes of alliance formation between equals against some other party."

There is a basic contradiction in the structure of girls' social relationships. Friends are supposed to be equal and everyone is supposed to get along, but in fact they don't always. Conflict must be resolved, but a girl cannot assert social power or superiority as an individual to resolve it. Lever (1976), studying fifth-graders, found that girls simply could not deal with quarrels and that when conflict arose they made no attempt to settle it; the group just broke up. What girls learn to do with speech is cope with the contradiction created by an ideology of equality and cooperation and a social reality that includes differences and conflict. As they grow up they learn increasingly subtle ways of balancing the conflicting pressures created by a female social world and a female friendship ideology.

Basically girls learn to do three things with words: (1) to create and maintain relationships of closeness and equality, (2) to criticize others in acceptable ways, and (3) to interpret accurately the speech of other girls.

To a large extent friendships among girls are formed through talk. Girls need to learn to give support, to recognize the speech rights of others, to let others speak, and to acknowledge what they say in order to establish and maintain relationships of equality and closeness. In activities they need to learn to create cooperation through speech. Goodwin (1980a) found that inclusive forms such as "let's," "we gonna," "we could," and "we gotta" predominated in task-oriented activities. Furthermore, she found that most girls in the group she studied made suggestions and that the other girls usually agreed to them. But girls also learn to exchange information and confidences to create and maintain relationships of closeness. The exchange of personal thoughts not only expresses closeness but mutual commitment as well. Brooks-Gunn and Matthews (1979:280) note of adolescent girls:

> much time is spent talking, reflecting, and sharing intimate thought. Loyalty is of central concern to the 12- to 14-year-old girl, presumably because, if innermost secrets are shared, the friend may have "dangerous knowledge" at her disposal.

Friendships are not only formed through particular types of talk, but are ended through talk as well. As Lever (1976:4) says of "best friends," "sharing secrets binds the union together, and 'telling' the secrets to outsiders is symbolic of the 'break-up.'"

Secondly, girls learn to criticize and argue with other girls without seeming overly aggressive, without being perceived as either "bossy" or "mean," terms girls use to evaluate one another's speech and actions. Bossiness, ordering others around, is not legitimate because it denies equality. Goodwin (1980a) points out that girls talked very negatively about the use of commands to equals, seeing it as appropriate only in role play or in unequal relationships such as those with younger siblings. Girls learn to direct things without seeming bossy, or they learn not to direct. While disputes are common, girls learn to phrase their arguments in terms of group needs and situational requirements rather than personal power or desire (Goodwin 1980a). Meanness is used by girls to describe nonlegitimate acts of exclusion, turning on someone, or withholding friendship. Excluding is a frequent occurrence (Eder and Hallinan 1978), but girls learn over time to discourage or even drive away other girls in ways that don't seem to be just personal whim. Cutting someone is justified in terms of the target's failure to meet group norms and a girl often

rejects another using speech that is seemingly supportive on the surface. Conflict and criticism are risky in the world of girls because they can both rebound against the critic and can threaten social relationships. Girls learn to hide the source of criticism; they present it as coming from someone else or make it indirectly through a third party (Goodwin 1980a, 1980b).

Finally, girls must learn to decipher the degree of closeness being offered by other girls, to recognize what is being withheld, and to recognize criticism. Girls who don't actually read these cues run the risk of public censure or ridicule (Goodwin 1980a). Since the currency of closeness is the exchange of secrets which can be used against a girl, she must learn to read the intent and loyalty of others and to do so continuously, given the system of shifting alliances and indirect expressions of conflict. Girls must become increasingly sophisticated in reading the motives of others, in determining when closeness is real, when conventional, and when false, and to respond appropriately. They must learn who to confide in, what to confide, and who not to approach. Given the indirect expression of conflict, girls must learn to read relationships and situations sensitively. Learning to get things right is a fundamental skill for social success, if not just social survival.

THE WORLD OF BOYS

Boys play in larger, more hierarchically organized groups than do girls. Relative status in this ever-fluctuating hierarchy is the main thing that boys learn to manipulate in their interactions with their peers. Nondominant boys are rarely excluded from play but are made to feel the inferiority of their status positions in no uncertain terms. And since hierarchies fluctuate over time and over situation, every boy gets his chance to be victimized and must learn to take it. The social world of boys is one of posturing and counterposturing. In this world, speech is used in three major ways: (1) to assert one's position of dominance, (2) to attract and maintain an audience, and (3) to assert oneself when other speakers have the floor.

The use of speech for the expression of dominance is the most straightforward and probably the best-documented sociolinguistic pattern in boys' peer groups. Even ethological studies of human dominance patterns have made extensive use of various speech behaviors as indices of dominance. Richard Savin-Williams (1976), for example, in his study of dominance patterns among boys in a summer camp uses the following speech interactions as measures of dominance: (1) giving of verbal commands or orders, such as "Get up," "Give it to me," or "You go over there"; (2) name calling and other forms of verbal ridicule, such as "You're a dolt"; (3) verbal threats or boasts of authority, such as "If you don't shut up, I'm gonna come over and bust your teeth in"; (4) refusals to obey orders; and (5) winning a verbal argument as in the sequence: "I was here first"/"Tough," or in more elaborate forms of verbal duelling such as the "dozens."[2]

The same patterns of verbally asserting one's dominance and challenging the dominance claims of others form the central element in Goodwin's (1980a) observations of boys' play in Philadelphia. What is easy to forget in thinking about this use of words as weapons, however, is that the most successful boy in such interaction is not the one who is most aggressive and uses the most power-wielding forms of speech, but the boy who uses these forms most successfully. The simple use of assertiveness and aggression in boys' play is the sign not of a leader but of a bully. The skillful speaker in a boys' group is considerably more likeable and better liked by his peers than is a simple bully. Social success among boys is based on knowing both how and when to use words to express power as well as knowing when not to use them. A successful leader will use speech to put challengers in their place and to remind followers periodically of their nondominant position, but will not browbeat unnecessarily and will therefore gain the respect rather than the fear of less dominant boys.

A second sociolinguistic aspect of friendly interaction between boys is using words to gain and maintain an audience. Storytelling, joke telling, and other narrative performance events are common features of the social interaction of boys. But actual transcripts of such storytelling events collected by Harvey Sacks (Sacks 1974; Jefferson 1978) and Goodwin (1980a), as opposed to stories told directly to interviewers, reveal a suggestive feature of storytelling activities among boys: audience behavior is not overtly supportive. The storyteller is frequently faced with mockery, challenges and side comments on his story. A major sociolinguistic skill which a boy must apparently learn in interacting with his peers is to ride out this series of challenges, maintain his audience, and successfully get to the end of his story. In Sacks's account (1974) of some teenage boys involved in the telling of a dirty joke, for example, the narrator is challenged for his taste in jokes (an implication that he doesn't know a dirty joke from a non-dirty one) and for the potential ambiguity of his opening line "Three brothers married three sisters," not, as Sacks seems to imply, because audience members are really confused, but just to hassle the speaker. Through catches,[3] put-downs, the building of suspense, or other interest-grabbing devices, the speaker learns to control his audience. He also learns to continue when he gets no encouragement whatever, pausing slightly at various points for possible audience response but going on if there is nothing but silence.

A final sociolinguistic skill which boys must learn from interacting with other boys is how to act as audience members in the types of storytelling situations just discussed. As audience member as well as storyteller, a boy must learn to assert himself and his opinions. Boys seem to respond to the storytelling of other boys not so much with questions on deeper implications or with minimal-response encouragement as with side comments and challenges. These are not meant primarily to interrupt, to change topic, or to change the direction of the narrative itself, but to assert the identity of the individual audience member.

WOMEN'S SPEECH

The structures and strategies in women's conversation show a marked continuity with the talk of girls. The key logic suggested by Kalčik's (1975) study of women's rap groups, Hirschman's (1973) study of students and Abrahams's (1975) work on black women is that women's conversation is interactional. In friendly talk, women are negotiating and expressing a relationship, one that should be in the form of support and closeness, but which may also involve criticism and distance. Women orient themselves to the person they are talking to and expect such orientation in return. As interaction, conversation requires participation from those involved and back-and-forth movement between participants. Getting the floor is not seen as particularly problematic; that should come about automatically. What is problematic is getting people engaged and keeping them engaged—maintaining the conversation and the interaction.

This conception of conversation leads to a number of characteristic speech strategies and gives a particular dynamic to women's talk. First, women tend to use personal and inclusive pronouns, such as "you" and "we" (Hirschman 1973). Second, women give off and look for signs of engagement such as nods and minimal response (Kalčik 1975; Hirschman 1973). Third, women give more extended signs of interest and attention, such as interjecting comments or questions during a speaker's discourse. These sometimes take the form of interruptions. In fact, both Hirschman (1973) and Kalčik (1975) found that interruptions were extremely common, despite women's concern with politeness and decorum (Kalčik 1975). Kalčik (1975) comments that women often asked permission to speak but were concerned that each speaker be allowed to finish and that all present got a chance to speak. These interruptions were clearly not seen as attempts to grab the floor but as calls for elaboration and development, and were taken as signs of support and interest. Fourth, women at the beginning of their utterances explicitly acknowledge and respond to what has been said by others. Fifth, women attempt to link their utterance to the one preceding it by building on the previous utterance or talking about something parallel or related to it. Kalčik (1975) talks about strategies of tying together, filling in, and serializing as signs of women's desire to create continuity in conversation, and Hirschman (1973) describes elaboration as a key dynamic of women's talk.

While the idiom of much of women's friendly talk is that of support, the elements of criticism, competition, and conflict do occur in it. But as with girls, these tend to take forms that fit the friendship idiom. Abrahams (1975) points out that while "talking smart" is clearly one way women talk to women as well as to men, between women it tends to take a more playful form, to be more indirect and metaphoric in its phrasing and less prolonged than similar talk between men. Smartness, as he points out, puts distance in a relationship (Abrahams 1975). The target of criticism, whether present or not, is made out to be the one violating group norms and values (Abrahams 1975). Overt competitiveness is also disguised. As Kalčik (1975) points out, some stories that build on preceding ones are attempts to cap the original speaker, but they tend to have a form similar to supportive ones. It is the intent more than the form that differs. Intent is a central element in the concept of "bitchiness," one of women's terms for evaluating their talk, and it relates to this contradiction between form and intent, whether putting negative messages in overtly positive forms or acting supportive face to face while not being so elsewhere.

These strategies and the interactional orientation of women's talk give their conversation a particular dynamic. While there is often an unfinished quality to particular utterances (Kalčik 1975), there is a progressive development to the overall conversation. The conversation grows out of the interaction of its participants, rather than being directed by a single individual or series of individuals. In her very stimulating discussion, Kalčik (1975) argues that this is true as well for many of the narratives women tell in conversation. She shows how narrative "kernels" serve as conversational resources for individual women and the group as a whole. How and if a "kernel story" is developed by the narrator and/or audience on a particular occasion is a function of the conversational context from which it emerges (Kalčik 1975:8), and it takes very different forms at different tellings. Not only is the dynamic of women's conversation one of elaboration and continuity, but the idiom of support can give it a distinctive tone as well. Hannerz (1969:96), for example, contrasts the "tone of relaxed sweetness, sometimes bordering on the saccharine," that characterizes

approving talk between women, to the heated argument found among men. Kalčik (1975:6) even goes so far as to suggest that there is an "underlying esthetic or organizing principle" of "harmony" being expressed in women's friendly talk.

MEN'S SPEECH

The speaking patterns of men, and of women for that matter, vary greatly from one North American subculture to another. As Gerry Philipsen (1975:13) summarizes it, "talk is not everywhere valued equally; nor is it anywhere valued equally in all social contexts." There are striking cultural variations between subcultures in whether men consider certain modes of speech appropriate for dealing with women, children, authority figures, or strangers; there are differences in performance rules for storytelling and joke telling; there are differences in the context of men's speech; and there are differences in the rules for distinguishing aggressive joking from true aggression.

But more surprising than these differences are the apparent similarities across subcultures in the patterns of friendly interaction between men and the resemblances between these patterns and those observed for boys. Research reports on the speaking patterns of men among urban blacks (Abrahams 1976; Hannerz 1969), rural Newfoundlanders (Faris 1966; Bauman 1972), and urban blue-collar whites (Philipsen 1975; LeMasters 1975) point again and again to the same three features: storytelling, arguing and verbal posturing.

Narratives such as jokes and stories are highly valued, especially when they are well performed for an audience. In Newfoundland, for example, Faris (1966: 242) comments that "the reason 'news' is rarely passed between two men meeting in the road—it is simply not to one's advantage to relay information to such a small audience." Loud and aggressive argument is a second common feature of male-male speech. Such arguments, which may include shouting, wagering, name-calling, and verbal threats (Faris 1966:245), are often, as Hannerz (1969:86) describes them, "debates over minor questions of little direct import to anyone," enjoyed for their own sake and not taken as signs of real conflict. Practical jokes, challenges, put-downs, insults, and other forms of verbal aggression are a third feature of men's speech, accepted as normal among friends. LeMasters (1975:140), for example, describes life in a working-class tavern in the Midwest as follows:

> It seems clear that status at the Oasis is related to the ability to "dish it out" in the rapid-fire exchange called "joshing": you have to have a quick retort, and prefer-

ably one that puts you "one up" on your opponent. People who can't compete in the game lose status.

Thus challenges rather than statements of support are a typical way for men to respond to the speech of other men.

WHAT IS HAPPENING IN CROSS-SEX CONVERSATION

What we are suggesting is that women and men have different cultural rules for friendly conversation and that these rules come into conflict when women and men attempt to talk to each other as friends and equals in casual conversation. We can think of at least five areas, in addition to that of minimal responses already discussed, in which men and women probably possess different conversational rules, so that miscommunication is likely to occur in cross-sex interaction.

1. There are two interpretations of the meaning of questions. Women seem to see questions as a part of conversational maintenance, while men seem to view them primarily as requests for information.

2. There are two conventions for beginning an utterance and linking it to the preceding utterance. Women's rules seem to call for an explicit acknowledgment of what has been said and making a connection to it. Men seem to have no such rule and in fact some male strategies call for ignoring the preceding comments.

3. There are different interpretations of displays of verbal aggressiveness. Women seem to interpret overt aggressiveness as personally directed, negative, and disruptive. Men seem to view it as one conventional organizing structure for conversational flow.

4. There are two understandings of topic flow and topic shift. The literature on storytelling in particular seems to indicate that men operate with a system in which topic is fairly narrowly defined and adhered to until finished and in which shifts between topics are abrupt, while women have a system in which topic is developed progressively and shifts gradually. These two systems imply very different rules for and interpretations of side comments, with major potential for miscommunication.

5. There appear to be two different attitudes towards problem sharing and advice giving. Women tend to discuss problems with one another, sharing experiences and offering reassurances. Men, in contrast, tend to hear women, and other men, who present them with problems as

making explicit requests for solutions. They respond by giving advice, by acting as experts, lecturing to their audiences.[4]

CONCLUSIONS

Our purpose in this paper has been to present a framework for thinking about and tying together a number of strands in the analysis of differences between male and female conversational styles. We hope to prove the intellectual value of this framework by demonstrating its ability to do two things: to serve as a model both of and for sociolinguistic research.

As a model *of* past research findings, the power of our approach lies in its ability to suggest new explanations of previous findings on cross-sex communication while linking these findings to a wide range of other fields, including the study of language acquisition, of play, of friendship, of storytelling, of cross-cultural miscommunication, and of discourse analysis. Differences in the social interaction patterns of boys and girls appear to be widely known but rarely utilized in examinations of sociolinguistic acquisition or in explanations of observed gender differences in patterns of adult speech. Our proposed framework should serve to link together these and other known facts in new ways.

As a model *for* future research, we hope our framework will be even more promising. It suggests to us a number of potential research problems which remain to be investigated. Sociolinguistic studies of school-age children, especially studies of the use of speech in informal peer interaction, appear to be much rarer than studies of young children, although such studies may be of greater relevance for the understanding of adult patterns, particularly those related to gender. Our framework also suggests the need for many more studies of single-sex conversations among adults, trying to make more explicit some of the differences in conversational rules suggested by present research. Finally, the argument we have been making suggests a number of specific problems that appear to be highly promising lines for future research:

1. A study of the sociolinguistic socialization of "tomboys" to see how they combine male and female patterns of speech and interaction;

2. An examination of the conversational patterns of lesbians and gay men to see how these relate to the sex-related patterns of the dominant culture;

3. An examination of the conversational patterns of the elderly to see to what extent speech differences persist after power differences have become insignificant;

4. A study of children's cultural concepts for talking about speech and the ways these shape the acquisition of speech styles (for example, how does the concept of "bossiness" define a form of behavior which little girls must learn to recognize, then censure, and finally avoid?);

5. An examination of "assertiveness training" programs for women to see whether they are really teaching women the speaking skills that politically skillful men learn in boyhood or are merely teaching women how to act like bossy little girls or bullying little boys and not feel guilty about it.

We conclude this paper by reemphasizing three of the major ways in which we feel that an anthropological perspective on culture and social organization can prove useful for further research on differences between men's and women's speech.

First, an anthropological approach to culture and cultural rules forces us to reexamine the way we interpret what is going on in conversations. The rules for interpreting conversations are, after all, culturally determined. There may be more than one way of understanding what is happening in a particular conversation and we must be careful about the rules we use for interpreting cross-sex conversations, in which the two participants may not fully share their rules of conversational inference.

Second, a concern with the relation between cultural rules and their social contexts leads us to think seriously about differences in different kinds of talk, ways of categorizing interactional situations, and ways in which conversational patterns may function as strategies for dealing with specific aspects of one's social world. Different types of interaction lead to different ways of speaking. The rules for friendly conversation between equals are different from those for service encounters, for flirting, for teaching, or for polite formal interaction. And even within the apparently uniform domain of friendly interaction, we argue that there are systematic differences between men and women in the way friendship is defined and thus in the conversational strategies that result.

Third and finally, our analysis suggests a different way of thinking about the connection between the gender-related behavior of children and that of adults. Most discussions of sex-role socialization have been based on the premise that gender differences are greatest for adults and that these adult differences are learned gradually throughout childhood. Our analysis, on the other hand, would suggest that at least some aspects of behavior are most strongly gender-differentiated during childhood and that adult patterns of friendly interaction, for example, involve learning to overcome at least partially some of the gender-specific cultural patterns typical of childhood.

NOTES

1. The analogy between the sociolinguistic processes of dialect divergence and genderlect divergence was pointed out to us by Ron Macaulay.

2. In the strict sense of the term, "dozens" refers to a culturally specific form of stylized argument through the exchange of insults that has been extensively documented by a variety of students of American black culture and is most frequently practiced by boys in their teens and pre-teens. Recently folklorist Simon Bronner (1978) has made a convincing case for the existence of a highly similar but independently derived form of insult exchange known as "ranking," "mocks," or "cutting" among white American adolescents. What we find striking and worthy of note is the tendency for both black and white versions of the dozens to be practiced primarily by boys.

3. "Catches" are a form of verbal play in which the main speaker ends up tricking a member of his or her audience into a vulnerable or ridiculous position. In an article on the folklore of black children in South Philadelphia, Roger Abrahams (1963) distinguishes between catches which are purely verbal and tricks in which the second player is forced into a position of being not only verbally but also physically abused, as in the following example of a catch which is also a trick:

    A. Adam and Eve and Pinch-Me-Tight
    Went up the hill to spend the night.
    Adam and Eve came down the hill.
    Who was left?

    B: Pinch-Me-Tight

    [A pinches B]

    What is significant about both catches and tricks is that they allow for the expression of playful aggression and that they produce a temporary hierarchical relation between a winner and loser, but invite the loser to attempt to get revenge by responding with a counter-trick.

4. We thank Kitty Julien for first pointing out to us the tendency of male friends to give advice to women who are not necessarily seeking it and Niyi Akinnaso for pointing out that the sex difference among Yoruba speakers in Nigeria in the way people respond verbally to the problems of others is similar to that among English speakers in the U.S.

REFERENCES

Abrahams, R. D. 1963. The "Catch" in negro Philadelphia. Keystone Folklore Quarterly 8(3):107–116.

Abrahams, R. D. 1975. Negotiating respect: patterns of presentation among black women. In *Women in Folklore*. C. R. Farrat, ed. Austin: University of Texas Press.

Abrahams, R. D. 1976. *Talking Black*. Rowley, Mass.: Newbury House.

Bauman, R. 1972. The La Have Island General Store: Sociability and verbal art in a Nova Scotia community. *Journal of American Folklore* 85:330–43.

Bronner, S. J. 1978. A Re-examining of white dozens. *Western Folklore* 37(2):118–28.

Brooks-Gunn, J. and Matthews, W. S. 1979. *He and She: How Children Develop Their Sex-Role Identity*. Englewood Cliffs, NJ: Prentice Hall.

Eder, D. and Hallinan, M. T. 1978. Sex differences in children's friendships. *American Sociological Review* 43: 237–50.

Faris, J. C. 1966. The dynamics of verbal exchange: A Newfoundland example. *Anthropologica* (Ottawa) 8(2): 235–48.

Fishman, P. M. 1978. Interaction: The work women do. *Social Problems* 25(4):397–406.

Goodwin, M. 1978. Conversational practices in a peer group of urban black children. Doctoral dissertation. University of Pennsylvania, Philadelphia.

Goodwin, M. 1980a. Directive-response speech sequences in girls' and boys' task activities. In *Women and Language in Literature and Society*. S. McConnell-Ginet, R. Borker, and N. Furman, eds. New York: Praeger.

Goodwin, M. 1980b. He-said-she-said: Formal cultural procedures for the construction of a gossip dispute activity. *American Ethnologist* 7(4):674–95.

Gumperz, J. J. 1977. Sociocultural knowledge in conversational inference. In *Linguistics and Anthropology*. M. Saville-Troike, ed. Washington DC: Georgetown University Press (Georgetown University Round Table on Languages and Linguistics), 1977.

Gumperz, J. J. 1978a. The conversational analysis of interethnic communication. In *Interethnic Communication*. E. Lamar Ross, ed. Athens, Ga.: University of Georgia Press.

Gumperz, J. J. 1978b. Dialect and conversational inference in urban communication. *Language in Society* 7(3):393–409.

Gumperz, J. J. 1979. The sociolinguistic basis of speech act theory. In *Speech Act Ten Years After*. J. Boyd and S. Fertara, eds. Milan: Versus.

Gumperz, J. J. 1982. *Discourse Strategies*. Cambridge: Cambridge University Press.

Gumperz, J. J., Agrawal, A., and Aulakh, G. 1977. Prosody, paralinguistics and contextualization in Indian English. Language Behavior Research Laboratory, typescript. University of California, Berkeley.

Gumperz, J. J. and Tannen, D. 1978. Individual and social differences in language use. In *Individual Differences in Language Ability and Language Behavior*. W. Wang and C. Fillmore, eds. New York: Academic Press.

Haas, A. 1979. The acquisition of genederlect. In Language, Sex and Gender: Does La Différence Make a Difference? J. Orasnu, M. Slater, and L. Adler, eds. *Annals of the New York Academy of Sciences* 327:101–13.

Hannerz, U. 1969. *Soulside*. New York: Columbia University Press.

Harding, S. 1975. Women and words in a Spanish village. In *Towards an Anthropology of Women*. R. Reiter, ed. New York: Monthly Review Press.

Hirschman, L. 1973. Female–male differences in conversational interaction. Paper presented at Linguistic Society of America, San Diego.

Jefferson, G. 1978. Sequential aspects of storytelling in conversation. In *Studies in the Organization of Conversation Interaction*. J. Schenker, ed. New York: Academic Press.

Kalčik, S. 1975. ". . . Like Anne's gynecologist or the time I was almost raped": Personal narratives in women's rap groups. In *Women and Folklore*. C. R. Farrar, ed. Austin: University of Texas Press.

Lakoff, R. 1975. *Language and Women's Place*. New York: Harper and Row.

LeMasters, E. E. 1975. *Blue Collar Aristocrats: Life-Styles at a Working-Class Tavern*. Madison: University of Wisconsin Press.

Lever, J. 1976. Sex differences in the games children play. *Social Problems* 23:478–83.

Lever, J. 1978. Sex differences in the complexity of children's play and games. *American Sociological Review* 43:471–83.

Meditch, A. 1975. The development of sex-specific speech patterns in young children. *Anthropological Linguistics* 17:421–33.

Philipsen, G. 1975. Speaking "like a man" in Teamsterville: Cultural patterns of role enactment in an urban neighborhood. *Quarterly Journal of Speech* 61:13–22.

Sacks, H. 1974. An analysis of the course of a joke's telling in conversation. In *Explorations in the Ethnography of Speaking*. R. Bauman and J. Scherzer, eds. Cambridge: Cambridge University Press.

Savin-Williams, R. C. 1976. The ethological study of dominance formation and maintenance in a group of human adolescents. *Child Development* 47:972–79.

Soskin, W. F. and John, V. P. 1963. The study of spontaneous talk. In *The Stream of Behavior*. R. G. Barker, ed. New York: Appleton-Century-Croft.

Strodbeck, F. L. and Mann, R. D. 1956. Sex role differentiation in jury deliberations. *Sociometry* 19:3–11.

West, C. 1979. Against our will: Male interruptions of females in cross-sex conversation. In Language, Sex and Gender: Does La Différence Make a Difference? J. Oranzanu, M. Slater and L. Adler, eds. *Annals of the New York Academy of Sciences* 327:81–100.

West, C. and Zimmerman, D. H. 1977. Women's place in everyday talk: Reflections on parent–child interaction. *Social Problems* 24(5):521–9.

Zimmerman, D. H. and West, C. 1975. Sex roles, interruptions, and silences in conversation. In *Language and Sex: Differences and Dominance*. B. Thorne and N. Henley, eds. Rowley, Mass.: Newbury House.

9

Suite for Ebony and Phonics

John R. Rickford

The musical *My Fair Lady* is the story of a lower-class flower girl, Eliza Doolittle, who is transformed by a linguistics professor, Henry Higgins. The transformation is based on teaching Eliza "proper" patterns of speech, grammar, and presentation of self. Motivated by a simple wager, this human experiment in social and linguistic transformation is a success, at least in the sense that Eliza is able to pass as a lady at a society ball. The experiment also exposes the professor's class-based arrogance and dehumanized attitudes about the poor. The relationship between speech patterns and social class is real and observable, but what is the significance of that connection?

Linguistic anthropologists often make a distinction between language and speech. Language is a rule-based and patterned system; speech refers to the actual performance—how people talk. The study of sociolinguistics focuses on how speech patterns reflect social realities like social class. Sociolinguists document regional differences in dialects, specialized vocabularies of particular groups, and "code switching" to exclude or include people in a conversation.

This selection concerns linguistic relativity in a multicultural society. In 1996 the Oakland City School District passed a resolution recognizing Ebonics, or black English vernacular (BEV), as the primary language of African American students in this poor urban area. As such, school officials reasoned, the differences between Standard English and Ebonics needed to be explicitly recognized in the classroom. As you will see in this selection, there was a national uproar in the media against this idea. Ebonics was ridiculed, in part because nonstandard dialects of English are stigmatized in our society. This selection argues that the debate over Ebonics missed the point, which was, just as in *My Fair Lady*, the significance of the social con-

struction of class differences and the politics of economic opportunity. The connection between this argument and the idea of the social construction of race (Selections 16, 17, and 18) in U.S. society should be clear.

As you read this selection, ask yourself the following questions:

- What are the five present tenses of black English vernacular?
- How are differences between Ebonics and Standard English both phonological and grammatical?
- Do you think it would be easier for children who regularly speak a dialect at home to learn Standard English if the differences between Standard English and the vernacular were made explicit?
- Who speaks Ebonics? What role might speech play in marking and maintaining ethnic identity or social class?
- Why did the Oakland schools' decision about Ebonics prompt such a negative public outcry?
- In a multicultural and multiethnic society, what are the goals of bilingual education programs? What are the best ways to provide educational opportunities to all?

The following terms discussed in this selection are included in the Glossary at the back of the book:

Afrocentric	*language*
Creole	*linguistic relativity*
dialect	*slang*
Ebonics	

To James Baldwin, writing in 1979, it was "this passion, this skill . . . this incredible music." Toni Morrison, two years later, was impressed by its "five present tenses" and felt that "the worst of all possible things that could happen would be to lose that language." What these novelists were talking about was Ebonics, the informal speech of many African Americans, which rocketed to public attention a year ago this

John R. Rickford/© 1997 *Discover* magazine.

month [1996] after the Oakland School Board approved a resolution recognizing it as the primary language of African American students.

The reaction of most people across the country—in the media, at holiday gatherings, and on electronic bulletin boards—was overwhelmingly negative. In the flash flood of e-mail on America Online, Ebonics was described as "lazy English," "bastardized English," "poor grammar," and "fractured slang." Oakland's decision to recognize Ebonics and use it to facilitate mastery of Standard English also elicited superlatives of negativity: "ridiculous, ludicrous," "VERY, VERY STUPID," "a terrible mistake."

However, linguists—who study the sounds, words, and grammars of languages and dialects—though less rhapsodic about Ebonics than the novelists, were much more positive than the general public. Last January, at the annual meeting of the Linguistic Society of America, my colleagues and I unanimously approved a resolution describing Ebonics as "systematic and rule-governed like all natural speech varieties." Moreover, we agreed that the Oakland resolution was "linguistically and pedagogically sound."

Why do we linguists see the issue so differently from most other people? A founding principle of our science is that we describe *how* people talk; we don't judge how language should or should not be used. A second principle is that all languages, if they have enough speakers, have dialects—regional or social varieties that develop when people are separated by geographic or social barriers. And a third principle, vital for understanding linguists' reactions to the Ebonics controversy, is that all languages and dialects are systematic and rule-governed. Every human language and dialect that we have studied to date—and we have studied thousands—obeys distinct rules of grammar and pronunciation.

What this means, first of all, is that Ebonics is not slang. Slang refers just to a small set of new and usually short-lived words in the vocabulary of a dialect or language. Although Ebonics certainly has slang words —such as *chillin* ("relaxing") or *homey* ("close friend"), to pick two that have found wide dissemination by the media—its linguistic identity is described by distinctive patterns of pronunciation and grammar.

But is Ebonics a different language from English or a different dialect of English? Linguists tend to sidestep such questions, noting that the answers can depend on historical and political considerations. For instance, spoken Cantonese and Mandarin are mutually unintelligible, but they are usually regarded as "dialects" of Chinese because their speakers use the same writing system and see themselves as part of a common Chinese tradition. By contrast, although Norwegian and Swedish are so similar that their speakers can generally understand each other, they are usually regarded as different languages because their speakers are citizens of different countries. As for Ebonics, most linguists agree that Ebonics is more of a dialect of English than a separate language, because it shares many words and other features with other informal varieties of American English. And its speakers can easily communicate with speakers of other American English dialects.

Yet Ebonics is one of the most distinctive varieties of American English, differing from Standard English —the educated standard—in several ways. Consider, for instance, its verb tenses and aspects. ("Tense" refers to *when* an event occurs, "aspect" to *how* it occurs, whether habitual or ongoing.) When Toni Morrison referred to the "five present tenses" of Ebonics, she probably had usages like these—each one different from Standard English—in mind:

1. He runnin. ("He is running.")
2. He be runnin. ("He is usually running.")
3. He be steady runnin. ("He is usually running in an intensive, sustained manner.")
4. He bin runnin. ("He has been running.")
5. He BIN runnin. ("He has been running for a long time and still is.")

In Standard English, the distinction between habitual or nonhabitual events can be expressed only with adverbs like "usually." Of course, there are also simple present tense forms, such as "he runs," for habitual events, but they do not carry the meaning of an ongoing action, because they lack the "-ing" suffix. Note too that "bin" in example 4 is unstressed while "BIN" in example 5 is stressed. The former can usually be understood by non-Ebonics speakers as equivalent to "has been" with the "has" deleted, but the stressed BIN form can be badly misunderstood. Years ago, I presented the Ebonics sentence "She BIN married" to 25 whites and 25 African Americans from various parts of the United States and asked them if they understood the speaker to be still married or not. While 23 of the African Americans said yes, only 8 of the whites gave the correct answer. (In real life a misunderstanding like this could be disastrous!)

Word pronunciation is another distinctive aspect of dialects, and the regularity of these differences can be very subtle. Most of the "rules" we follow when speaking Standard English are obeyed unconsciously. Take for instance English plurals. Although grammar books tell us that we add "s" to a word to form a regular English plural, as in "cats" and "dogs," that's true only for writing. In speech, what we actually add in the case of "cat" is an s sound; in the case of "dog" we add z. The difference is that s is voiceless, with the vocal cords spread apart, while *z* is voiced, with the vocal cords held closely together and noisily vibrating.

Now, how do you know whether to add *s* or *z* to form a plural when you're speaking? Easy. If the word ends in a voiceless consonant, like "*t*," add voiceless *s*. If the word ends in a voiced consonant, like "*g*," add voiced *z*. Since all vowels are voiced, if the word ends in a vowel, like "tree," add *z*. Because we spell both plural endings with "s," we're not aware that English speakers make this systematic difference every day, and I'll bet your English teacher never told you about voiced and voiceless plurals. But you follow the "rules" for using them anyway, and anyone who doesn't—for instance, someone who says "bookz"—strikes an English speaker as sounding funny.

One reason people might regard Ebonics as "lazy English" is its tendency to omit consonants at the ends of words—especially if they come after another consonant, as in "tes(t)" and "han(d)." But if one were just being lazy or cussed or both, why not also leave out the final consonant in a word like "pant"? This is not permitted in Ebonics; the "rules" of the dialect do not allow the deletion of the second consonant at the end of a word unless both consonants are either voiceless as with "st," or voiced, as with "nd." In the case of "pant," the final "t" is voiceless, but the preceding "n" is voiced, so the consonants are both spoken. In short, the manner in which Ebonics differs from Standard English is highly ordered; it is no more lazy English than Italian is lazy Latin. Only by carefully analyzing each dialect can we appreciate the complex rules that native speakers follow effortlessly and unconsciously in their daily lives.

Who speaks Ebonics? If we made a list of all the ways in which the pronunciation and grammar of Ebonics differ from Standard English, we probably couldn't find anyone who always uses all of them. While its features are found most commonly among African Americans (*Ebonics* is itself derived from "ebony" and "phonics," meaning "black sounds"), not all African Americans speak it. The features of Ebonics, especially the distinctive tenses, are more common among working-class than among middle-class speakers, among adolescents than among the middle-aged, and in informal contexts (a conversation on the street) rather than formal ones (a sermon at church) or writing.

The genesis of Ebonics lies in the distinctive cultural background and relative isolation of African Americans, which originated in the slaveholding South. But contemporary social networks, too, influence who uses Ebonics. For example lawyers and doctors and their families are more likely to have more contact with Standard English speakers—in schools, work, and neighborhoods—than do blue-collar workers and the unemployed. Language can also be used to reinforce a sense of community. Working-class speakers, and adolescents in particular often embrace Ebonics features as markers of African American identity, while middle-class speakers (in public at least) tend to eschew them.

Some Ebonics features are shared with other vernacular varieties of English, especially Southern white dialects, many of which have been influenced by the heavy concentration of African Americans in the South. And a lot of African American slang has "crossed over" to white and other ethnic groups. Expressions like "givin five" ("slapping palms in agreement or congratulation") and "Whassup?" are so widespread in American culture that many people don't realize they originated in the African American community. Older, nonslang words have also originated in imported African words. *Tote,* for example, comes from the Kikongo word for "carry," *tota,* and *hip* comes from the Wolof word *hipi,* to "be aware." However, some of the distinctive verb forms in Ebonics—he run, he be runnin, he BIN runnin—are rarer or nonexistent in white vernaculars.

How did Ebonics arise? The Oakland School Board's proposal alluded to the Niger-Congo roots of Ebonics, but the extent of that contribution is not at all clear. What we do know is that the ancestors of most African Americans came to this country as slaves. They first arrived in Jamestown in 1619, and a steady stream continued to arrive until at least 1808, when the slave trade ended, at least officially. Like the forebears of many other Americans, these waves of African "immigrants" spoke languages other than English. Their languages were from the Niger-Congo language family, especially the West Atlantic, Mande, and Kwa subgroups spoken from Senegal and Gambia to the Cameroons, and the Bantu subgroup spoken farther south. Arriving in an American milieu in which English was dominant, the slaves learned English. But how quickly and completely they did so and with how much influence from their African languages are matters of dispute among linguists.

The Afrocentric view is that most of the distinctive features of Ebonics represent imports from Africa. As West African slaves acquired English, they restructured it according to the patterns of Niger-Congo languages. In this view, Ebonics simplifies consonant clusters at the ends of words and doesn't use linking verbs like "is" and "are"—as in, for example, "he happy"—because these features are generally absent from Niger-Congo languages. Verbal forms like habitual "be" and BIN referring to a remote past, it is argued, crop up in Ebonics because these kinds of tenses occur in Niger-Congo languages.

Most Afrocentrists, however, don't cite a particular West African language source. Languages in the Niger-Congo family vary enormously, and some historically significant Niger-Congo languages don't show these forms. For instance, while Yoruba, a major language for many West Africans sold into slavery, does indeed lack a linking verb like "is" for some adjectival constructions, it has another linking verb for other adjectives. And it has *six* other linking verbs for nonadjectival constructions, where English would use "is" or "are." Moreover, features like dropping final consonants can be found in some vernaculars in England that had little or no West African influence. Although many linguists acknowledge continuing African influences in some Ebonics and American English words, they want more proof of its influence on Ebonics pronunciation and grammar.

A second view, the Eurocentric—or dialectologist—view, is that African slaves learned English from white settlers, and that they did so relatively quickly and successfully, retaining little trace of their African linguistic heritage. Vernacular, or non-Standard features of Ebonics, including omitting final consonants and habitual "be," are seen as imports from dialects spoken by colonial English, Irish, or Scotch-Irish settlers, many of whom were indentured servants. Or they may be features that emerged in the twentieth century, after African Americans became more isolated in urban ghettos. (Use of habitual "be," for example, is more common in urban than in rural areas.) However, as with Afrocentric arguments, we still don't have enough historical details to settle the question. Crucial Ebonics features, such as the absence of linking "is," appear to be rare or nonexistent in these early settler dialects, so they're unlikely to have been the source. Furthermore, although the scenario posited by this view is possible, it seems unlikely. Yes, African American slaves and whites sometimes worked alongside each other in households and fields. And yes the number of African slaves was so low, especially in the early colonial period, that distinctive African American dialects may not have formed. But the assumption that slaves rapidly and successfully acquired the dialects of the whites around them requires a rosier view of their relationship than the historical record and contemporary evidence suggest.

A third view, the creolist view, is that many African slaves, in acquiring English, developed a pidgin language—a simplified fusion of English and African languages—from which Ebonics evolved. Native to none of its speakers, a pidgin is a mixed language, incorporating elements of its users' native languages but with less complex grammar and fewer words than either parent language. A pidgin language emerges to facilitate communication between speakers who do not share a language; it becomes a creole language when it takes root and becomes the primary tongue among its users. This often occurs among the children of pidgin speakers—the vocabulary of the language expands, and the simple grammar is fleshed out. But the creole still remains simpler in some aspects than the original languages. Most Creoles, for instance, don't use suffixes to mark tense ("he walk*ed*"), plurals ("boy*s*"), or possession ("John*'s* house").

Creole languages are particularly common on the islands of the Caribbean and the Pacific, where large plantations brought together huge groups of slaves or indentured laborers. The native languages of these workers were radically different from the native tongues of the small groups of European colonizers and settlers, and under such conditions, with minimal access to European speakers, new, restructured varieties like Haitian Creole French and Jamaican Creole English arose. These languages do show African influence, as the Afrocentric theory would predict, but their speakers may have simplified existing patterns in African languages by eliminating more complex alternatives; like the seven linking verbs of Yoruba I mentioned earlier.

Within the United States African Americans speak one well-established English creole, Gullah. It is spoken on the Sea Islands off the coast of South Carolina and Georgia, where African Americans at one time constituted 80 to 90 percent of the local population in places. When I researched one of the South Carolina Sea Islands some years ago, I recorded the following creole sentences. They sound much like Caribbean Creole English today:

1. E. M. run an gone to Suzie house. ("E. M. went running to Suzie's house.")

2. But I does go to see people when they sick. ("But I usually go to see people when they are sick.")

3. De mill bin to Bluffton dem time. ("The mill was in Bluffton in those days.") Note the creole traits: the first sentence lacks the past tense and the possessive form; the second sentence lacks the linking verb "are" and includes the habitual "does"; the last sentence uses unstressed "bin" for past tense and "dem time" to refer to a plural without using an *s*.

What about creole origins for Ebonics? Creole speech might have been introduced to the American colonies through the large numbers of slaves imported from the colonies of Jamaica and Barbados, where Creoles were common. In these regions the percentage of Africans ran from 65 to 90 percent. And some slaves who came directly from Africa may have brought with them pidgins or creoles that developed around West African trading forts. It's also possible that some creole varieties—apart from well-known cases like Gullah—might have developed on American soil.

This would have been less likely in the northern colonies, where blacks were a very small percentage of the population. But blacks were much more concentrated in the South, making up 61 percent of the population in South Carolina and 40 percent overall in the South. Observations by travelers and commentators in the eighteenth and nineteenth centuries record creole-like features in African American speech. Even today, certain features of Ebonics, like the absence of the linking verbs "is" and "are," are widespread in Gullah and Caribbean English creoles but rare or nonexistent in British dialects.

My own view is that the creolist hypothesis incorporates the strengths of the other hypotheses and avoids their weaknesses. But we linguists may never be able to settle that particular issue one way or another. What we can settle on is the unique identity of Ebonics as an English dialect.

So what does all this scholarship have to do with the Oakland School Board's proposal? Some readers might be fuming that it's one thing to identify Ebonics as a dialect and quite another to promote its usage. Don't linguists realize that nonstandard dialects are stigmatized in the larger society, and that Ebonics speakers who cannot shift to Standard English are less likely to do well in school and on the job front? Well, yes. The resolution we put forward last January in fact stated that "there are benefits in acquiring Standard English." But there is experimental evidence both from the United States and Europe that mastering the standard language might be easier if the differences in the student vernacular and Standard English were made explicit rather than entirely ignored.

To give only one example: At Aurora University, outside Chicago, inner-city African American students were taught by an approach that contrasted Standard English and Ebonics features through explicit instruction and drills. After eleven weeks, this group showed a 59 percent reduction in their use of Ebonics features in their Standard English writing. But a control group taught by conventional methods showed an 8.5 percent increase in such features.

This is the technique the Oakland School Board was promoting in its resolution last December. The approach is not new; it is part of the 16-year-old Standard English Proficiency Program, which is being used in some 300 California schools. Since the media uproar over its original proposal, the Oakland School Board has clarified its intent: the point is not to teach Ebonics as a distinct language but to use it as a tool to increase mastery of Standard English among Ebonics speakers. The support of linguists for this approach may strike nonlinguists as unorthodox, but that is where our principles—and the evidence—lead us.

10

Ancient Bodies, Modern Customs, and Our Health

Elizabeth D. Whitaker

Culture determines the way we have children and how we raise children. The American way of childbirth—with the woman in a hospital, lying on her back with her legs up in stirrups, connected to a fetal monitor, and numbed with an epidural anesthetic—is a cultural creation that has developed in recent history. Rarely do we question our cultural traditions, especially when there are experts and expert opinions. People in all cultures take comfort in the fact that they are doing things the "right way," that is, the way things are supposed to be as dictated by tradition. The comfort derived from our traditions is most evident in rituals, like weddings or funerals. But cultural traditions (and dependence on cultural experts) also play a major role in how people go about being parents. In the United States, mothers and fathers try to do the best they can for their children, often unaware how the larger cultural context shapes or limits the possibilities. Children, in turn, get not just their genes but also their ideas, beliefs, and values from their parents, thus perpetuating the culture. But people also have minds of their own, and there are more rational ways to choose one's child-rearing practices than to simply accept the opinions of "experts" and authorities. After all, it is also part of our culture to question authority!

Biological anthropologists believe that evolution has shaped our bodies and therefore strongly influences our health. In this selection, Elizabeth Whitaker reviews evidence from evolutionary medicine about the health implications of infant feeding and sleeping patterns. She demonstrates that American cultural ideas emphasizing the individual have detracted from the fact that mothers and their infants form a biological interacting pair during pregnancy and continuing in infancy. Patterns of breast-feeding in other cultures are undoubtedly linked to health issues such as birth spacing, allergies, and infant diarrhea and dehydration. It is less obvious, however, that the disappearance of evolutionary patterns of breast-feeding is also linked to the increasing incidence of breast cancer in countries like the United States. Finally, there is solid evidence that the cultural pattern of babies sleeping in their own cribs—by themselves, in a separate room, and often placed on their stomachs—is linked to the risk of sudden infant death syndrome.

As you read this selection, ask yourself the following questions:

- What benefits does breast-feeding have for the mother? What benefits does it have for the child?
- Why do people get fevers? Why do people take medicine to stop fevers?
- Does the U.S. socioeconomic system shape our patterns of breast-feeding and weaning?
- Is evolutionary medicine against progress?

The following terms discussed in this selection are included in the Glossary at the back of the book:

diseases of civilization	*ovulation*
evolutionary medicine	*SIDS*
food foragers	

Mothers and infants are physiologically interconnected from conception to the termination of breast-feeding. While this mutual biological relationship is obvious during pregnancy, to many people it is less clear in the period following birth. In Western society, individuals are expected to be autonomous and independent, and this ideal extends to mothers and their babies. Individual autonomy is a core value in our economy, society, and family life: even to our understanding of health and disease. However, it is not a widely shared notion, as more *sociocentric* conceptions of personhood are very common in other cultures and have prevailed in other time periods. Until the Industrial Revolution, Western society also recognized the dependence relationships among individuals and families, and this matched an agrarian social structure involving mutual responsibilities and obligations. Mothers and infants were considered interdependent and there was relatively little cultural intervention in or manipulation of gestation or lactation.

Until a century ago, medical experts followed Aristotle, Hippocrates, and Galen in saying that *not* to breast-feed was to have half a birth, because mother's milk came from the same blood which nourished the fetus. Today, in many cultures around the world, infants are not expected to be independent of their mothers for as long as they breast-feed—that is, for at least the first few years of life. These beliefs reflect an appreciation of the fact that breast-feeding represents a physiological process for both mothers and infants and is more than a simple question of nutrition.

Cultural interventions in the mother–infant relationship are bound to bring significant biological outcomes. Common infant feeding practices in Western societies, such as timed, widely spaced meals, early weaning, pacifier use, and isolated infant sleep with few or no nighttime feedings, are very new and rare in human history, and do not reflect "natural" needs or optimal behaviors, as is commonly presumed. They result in partial or short-term breast-feeding that is very different from the "traditional" or ancient pattern humans have known over evolutionary time. This pattern involves frequent, exclusive, and prolonged breast-feeding, and brings the greatest benefits to mothers and infants. These benefits include reduced risk of breast cancer and the Sudden Infant Death Syndrome (SIDS), diseases which share a common thread in their history: the decline in breast-feeding in the Western industrial societies. By examining them together, we will try to overcome the assumption of individual autonomy, which is so entrenched in Western culture that studies on breast-feeding commonly focus on either the mother or child, but not both.

OLD GENES, NEW LIFESTYLES

Beyond the level of personal experience, breast-feeding concerns both biological processes and cultural interpretation and manipulation. Biocultural anthropology examines such a topic by bringing together cross-cultural comparison and evolutionary considerations. This can mean, for example, comparing human physiology and behavior to those of other primates, such as chimpanzees and gorillas, with whom we share common ancestors and diverge genetically by less than 2%. It also involves looking at differ-

ent strategies for making a living among human populations. In particular, anthropologists are interested in comparing hunter-gatherers, or foragers, to agricultural or industrial societies. We study modern-day foragers such as the !Kung San of Botswana or the Gainj of Papua New Guinea because their diet, exercise, and health patterns roughly represent those of humans for the vast majority of evolutionary history.

With a few exceptions, our genetic endowment has not changed since the first foraging groups began to practice settled agriculture and animal husbandry between 13,000 and 9,000 years ago (the *Neolithic Revolution*). From the start, the lifestyle change produced notable health consequences. Early agriculturists had shorter stature, greater nutritional stress, and higher infant mortality, especially at the age of weaning. Whereas foragers suffered annual seasonal food shortages, these were less severe than the famines that resulted when crops or livestock were lost. Although famines are rare now, especially in the wealthier countries, constant over-nutrition produces new health problems. At the same time, the diet in many impoverished countries remains scanter and less varied than the foraging diet.

In contrast to what we think of as proper nutrition, foragers subsist on a low-calorie diet made up exclusively of wild plant parts (roots, seeds, stalks, leaves, nuts, fruits) and game or fish. There are no dairy products (except mother's milk) or processed grains in their diet. Most of the food comes from plants, while meat is a less reliable but highly valued supply of concentrated protein, fat (though only one-seventh the amount in the meat of domesticated animals), and vitamins and minerals.

Foragers collect these foods over distances of 10 or more kilometers per day, often carried out in a pattern of one or two days of work for six to eight hours and one or two days of other activities. This averages out to more than 6½ kilometers per day. Women routinely carry up to 15 kilograms (almost 35 pounds) of food, a bundle which can reach half their body weight. They also carry children up to three or four years of age, adding up to another 15 kilograms. In addition to this physical activity, foragers move camp several times each year. Because they work outdoors and do not have climate control indoors, they are constantly exposed to the elements.

Unlike people in affluent societies, foragers do not experience any "natural" rise in blood pressure with age. They do not undergo hearing loss or overweight as inevitable consequences of aging, nor does their body mass increase. They are not free of disorders including accidents and injuries, degenerative bone disease, complications of childbirth, and infectious disease, but the major health problems of the Western societies are very rare. These "diseases of civilization" or "chronic diseases" include heart disease, hypertension, strokes, and cancer, as well as emphysema, cirrhosis, diabetes, and obesity and overweight.

While we all share a genetic propensity for the chronic diseases, it is our lifestyle and environment which cause their wide expression today. Our biological characteristics are those of Stone Age humans practicing a hardy foraging lifestyle, making our bodies adept at storing fat against the likelihood of periodic food shortage. This helps to explain why overweight and obesity are so common wherever physical activity and exposure to the elements are minimal while food supplies are plentiful and steady.

Similarly, the perspective of evolutionary medicine helps us to understand cancer as the cost of the beneficial biological adaptation of tissue repair and regeneration through cell division. In all living things, the body's various ways of regulating and suppressing cell division become less effective in older age. However, over the past centuries, cancer rates have risen way beyond those which would result simply from the increase in the proportion of individuals living into old age. Beyond exposure to carcinogenic and viral agents, this can be explained in terms of changes in diet and lifestyle away from the foraging pattern. Our diet is scarce in protective micro-nutrients such as beta-carotene and selenium, but abundant in macro-nutrients such as fat, protein, and calories which, in themselves and in relation to body composition and size, promote cancer.

Compared to the chronic diseases, we have been adapting to infectious organisms for ages, and vice versa. In many cases, fever is an adaptive defense against infection. It raises the body's temperature and speeds up its metabolic processes, helping to eliminate viruses and bacteria. When ectothermic ("cold-blooded") animals are injected with virus, they seek out a hotter place, and are more likely to die from the infection if prevented from doing so. Recent studies have found that people who take antipyretics (drugs such as aspirin or acetaminophen, which suppress fever) are infectious longer and take longer to recover from colds, flu, and chicken pox.

Fever also promotes the sequestration of iron which takes place as a defense against many kinds of infection. The iron is bound more tightly to protein and hidden in the liver, reducing the amount that circulates in the blood. The resulting anemia is typically treated with iron supplements, but iron is a necessary mineral to many bacteria and their need for it is increased by fever. This pair of evolved defensive systems—increased heat and decreased iron—is therefore blocked by human interventions such as iron supplements and antipyretics. On the other hand, some pathogens actually reproduce better or become more toxic in the presence of fever and reduced iron, which would be expected since their rapid reproductive rates and short lives give them an evolutionary advantage. What this suggests is that an evolutionary perspective is needed to better target and treat symptoms appropriately, just as it contributes to our analysis of lactation and the health outcomes of variations in its practice.

MOTHERS AND INFANTS

When breast-feeding patterns are compared across mammals (from *mamma*, Latin for "breast"), non-human primates, and humans, "on-demand" or baby-fed feeding emerges as the evolutionary norm for our species. Many aspects of the ancestral pattern are shared by non-Western societies today and were common in Western populations until a few generations ago. A relationship of interdependence and mutuality is expressed in parent–infant co-sleeping and exclusive, unrestricted breast-feeding well beyond the first year.

The ancestral pattern involves frequent feedings (from several times an hour to once every hour or two) all day and night with no limit on their duration; no supplementary foods before six months and low to moderate use of pre-chewed foods or very ripe fruits thereafter; and complete weaning at 2½ to 4 years, when the child is able to walk long distances on its own. Mother's milk remains the principal food until 15 to 18 months, after which it continues to be a significant source of nutrition. When these conditions prevail, infants are more likely to survive, pregnancy is prevented for 2 to 3 years or more, and births are spaced 3 to 5 years apart. In all but one family of primates, lactation implies *anovulation* (lack of ovulation). In our closest relatives, births are spaced as far as 5 (in chimpanzees) to 8 (in orangutans) years apart.

In foraging societies such as the !Kung, the mother carries her child in a sling against her body, providing constant physical contact and access to the breast. Infants hardly ever cry, and are not expected to cry. Their signs of distress bring an immediate response from their mother or another relative, but never with any kind of pacifier other than the breast. Infants are constantly cuddled and kissed all over the body, including the genitals. Parents are bewildered to hear that Western infants cry and are left alone in a crib, swaddled perhaps, to do so for long periods without being held or allowed to suckle. They do not share the idea that infants and children need to be denied what they want or they will grow up spoiled or dependent. Indeed, the opposition between independence and dependence has relatively little meaning in these societies.

Milk production and release are regulated by pituitary hormones secreted in response to nipple stimulation, the emptying of the breast, and psychological factors. Prolactin is released in response to suckling, stimulating the synthesis of milk in the lacteal cells within a couple of hours. Oxytocin is also released in response to nipple stimulation, and immediately causes the cells around the milk-producing bulbs and ducts to contract and secrete milk. This pathway can be affected by psychological factors in positive and negative ways. A thought, emotion, or sound or sight of an infant can cause the release of oxytocin. Contrariwise, fear and other stressful emotions lead to the secretion of epinephrine, which impedes the circulation of oxytocin to breast tissue by constricting the blood vessels around it.

After the surge following nipple stimulation, prolactin levels drop off quickly, reaching baseline levels within two hours. Consequently, to maintain continuous milk production it is necessary to breast-feed at short intervals and keep prolactin levels high. Especially in the early months, more frequent feedings result in greater milk production. Milk that is not secreted but left in the breast has an independent dampening effect on production through both a substance in the milk and the mechanical pressure it exerts on the surrounding cells. This kind of control over milk production seems to apply in a preponderant way after the first two or three months, against a diminishing but still important background of hormonal regulation. Moreover, more frequent feedings and complete removal of milk lead to higher average fat and calorie content. Infants fed without restrictions are able to vary feed frequencies and the degree of breast-emptying and thereby regulate their nutrition very closely. They tend to be satiated and satisfied after feedings.

High prolactin levels inhibit ovulation, so that infrequent feedings and reduced time at the breast lead to less effective suppression of fertility. In addition, other hormones involved in the menstrual cycle are affected by frequent breast-feeding, interfering with normal follicle growth, ovulation (should an egg mature), development of the endometrium, and implantation of a fertilized ovum. As women space feedings at wider intervals, introduce supplementary foods, and reduce nighttime feeding, the contraceptive effect of breast-feeding weakens and ovulation and menstruation resume.

The composition of human milk also indicates that it is made to be given frequently. Unlike other mammals such as rabbits or tree shrews, who keep their young in nests and leave them all day or even longer, primates carry their babies and thereby provide them with transportation and temperature regulation, for which their milk is less fatty. Primate infants are born less mature and grow more slowly, explaining why protein is relatively scarce in the milk. Continuous breast-feeding and physical contact also protect the infant from predators, as well as illness. Contact with others is reduced, while exposure to the same diseases leads to the production of immunological substances, which are then transmitted in the mother's milk.

In recent years, there has been wide publication of the wonderful properties of breast-milk, from nutritional components to immunological factors, sedative substances to anti-allergenic properties. These benefits make breast-fed infants better able to resist and overcome infections, including those of the gastrointestinal and respiratory tract (which includes the middle ear). Breast-feeding promotes optimal growth and development of the body's systems, such as the cardiovascular, immune, nervous, and gastrointestinal systems. It also protects breast-fed infants from protein malnutrition, even in areas of the world in which it is common. This is because the quality of milk is remarkably constant across mothers, regardless of their diet or nutritional status.

The uniform quality of mother's milk, even in conditions of stress, brings up two points. It implies that we should focus upon infant demand and suckling behavior when there are problems in breast-feeding, but the tendency is instead to search for maternal causes. Secondly, by focusing on the benefits of breast-feeding in terms of the useful properties of the milk, we may fail to acknowledge the impacts of breast-feeding on the mother. Mothers who are overworked and poorly nourished may become depleted, their lives shortened by repeated cycles of gestation and lactation.

On the other hand, assuming good conditions breast-feeding has many positive effects on mothers. It helps the uterus to return to its normal size and shape after childbirth, hastens weight loss and moderates digestion, metabolism, blood circulation, and sensations of well-being. It favors bone consolidation, preventing osteoporosis and hip and other fractures in later life, and reduces the risk of women's reproductive cancers. In order to appreciate these benefits, we must go beyond looking at breast-milk as a mere product manufactured for the advantage of the child.

Whereas in foraging and agricultural societies mothers and their fetuses or infants are considered inseparable, even when physically divided after childbirth, in Western society they are considered independent even during gestation. In evolutionary biology, this is an appropriate concept since the interests of the child and the mother may conflict: for example, the fetus of humans and all placental animals taps into the mother's blood circulation, injecting fetal hormones into it and drawing nutrients from the mother's organs if they are not available through her diet. Yet, the biological concept of individuality simultaneously presumes physiological interdependence. The cultural concept of the autonomous individual denies it. After childbirth, the separation between mother and child is complete, and the physiological interrelationship in breast-feeding is obscured by a focus on the infant's nutritional and psychological independence. This has notable health outcomes for both mothers and infants, some of which we will now examine in light of an evolutionary perspective.

BREAST CANCER

Until the 19th century, European medical philosophers observed that well-off women who lived in cities were much more susceptible to breast cancer than women who lived in the countryside. They attributed this difference to the abandonment of breast-feeding, which, they noted, caused numerous other maladies and grave health effects. Even today, not only is breast cancer more common in affluent societies, but within them it is more frequent among the wealthier classes.

The decline in breast-feeding has been part of a broad change in reproductive and child-rearing patterns since the Industrial Revolution. Urban women were the first to undergo the *secular trend* of earlier maturation and greater achieved stature. They experienced earlier puberty, delayed marriage and first birth, fewer pregnancies, and reduced or forsaken breast-feeding. Over time, these patterns diffused through the entire population.

Many of the things we consider "natural" are therefore more like aberrations or deviations from what evolution has produced. To illustrate, a typical woman of a foraging or pre-industrial society reaches puberty and her first menstrual period (*menarche*) at the age of 16 to 18. She becomes pregnant within three or four years, breast-feeds for three or four years, and has a subsequent child four or five years after the first. This sequence repeats itself between four and six times before she reaches menopause at around the age of 45. As a result, she has about 150 ovulations in her lifetime, taking account of non-ovulatory cycles at the near and far end of her reproductive years. Periodic nutritional and exercise stress reduce the number of ovulations even more. Because only half of her children survive long enough to reproduce, population grows very slowly, as was the case until historical

times. Lactation has represented humankind's main method of birth control for most of our existence.

In contrast, Western women enjoy a stable food supply, including foods concentrated in fat, protein, and calories, and experience very little stress from exercise and exposure. Over the past centuries, this has caused them, and men, to reach higher stature and lower age at puberty. Girls arrive at menarche at the age of 12 or 13, while menopause is delayed to 50 or 55 years. Significantly, the first birth is postponed for 13 or 14 years, to the age of 25 or 26, and the average number of births is reduced to two or three. The average Western woman breast-feeds for a few months, if at all. Because she spaces feedings at long intervals and supplements with other foods, breast-feeding does not inhibit ovulation for long. As a result, population growth was very rapid in Europe for several centuries (and in many developing countries today) not only because mortality rates were falling but also because women did not have a long interval of infertility associated with lactation.

If she does not take oral contraceptives, the average woman will ovulate around 450 times over her lifetime. Ovulation will rarely be suppressed due to physiological constraints associated with nutritional or exercise stress. This amounts to three or four times as many ovulations over the life-span, and some scholars have suggested that the proportion may be as high as nine times.

The differences in reproductive patterns between women in foraging as opposed to affluent societies match some of the currently known risk factors for women's reproductive cancers (breast, endometrium, ovary), including age at menarche and menopause, *parity* (number of births), and breast-feeding. Differences in diet and physical activity, as well as body composition, also agree with identified non-reproductive risk factors such as fat intake and percent body fat. Together with other factors, they give Western women, especially below the age of 60, at least 20 times the risk of reproductive cancer. The risk for breast cancer may be more than 100 times higher. In nonhuman primates, these cancers are extremely rare.

For all three cancers, earlier age at menarche and later age at menopause increase risk, while greater parity reduces risk. Like these factors, breast-feeding is protective against ovarian cancer because it inhibits ovulation. This reduces the monthly mechanical injury to the ovarian epithelium and the release of hormones by the follicle, which are considered the main elements in the etiology of ovarian cancer. For breast cancer, lactation and earlier first birth are also protective factors.

The breast's susceptibility to carcinogenesis is directly related to the rate of epithelial cell proliferation. Consequently, the lengthening of the period between menarche and first birth widens the window of time in which undifferentiated structures destined to become secretory glands are vulnerable to carcinogenic agents and therefore the initiation of tumors. In breast tissue, cell proliferation is promoted by exposure to estrogen, apparently in concert with progesterone, and cell division rates are highest during the first five years after menarche. With pregnancy and lactation, these structures differentiate and develop, devoting themselves less ardently to cell proliferation. Their cell cycle is longer, and they are more resistant to chemical carcinogens. Subsequent pregnancies may also be protective because they increase the proportion of fully differentiated secretory lobules, until in advanced age pregnancy increases risk by favoring the expansion of initiated tumors.

While the age at first pregnancy seems to be of primary importance and may even modulate the protective effect of breast-feeding and later pregnancies, breast-feeding in itself provides protection against breast cancer in step with the number of children breast-fed and the cumulative duration of breast-feeding. The reason some studies have found no effect or a weak one is that they were based upon the experiences of Western women, who do not generally conform to the ancient pattern of breast-feeding at close intervals for at least a year. Short periods of breast-feeding may in fact provide very little protection.

At the level of the breast fluid, there are lower levels of a potential carcinogen, cholesterol-epoxide, as well as cholesterol, in breast-feeding women, a reduction that persists for two years after childbirth or lactation. Estrogen levels are also lower, protecting the breast tissue directly as opposed to systemically through variations in blood estrogen levels. Breast-feeding also affects the turnover rate of substances in the breast fluid, so that prolonged breast-feeding reduces exposure of the breast epithelial tissue to potential exogenous carcinogens.

Exercise, high consumption of dietary fiber, and low fat consumption and percent body fat are all protective against breast and other cancers. High dietary levels of fat and protein (especially from animal sources) and total calories are associated with higher levels of breast cancer across populations and within subpopulations of single countries. Animal studies have shown that dietary protein promotes tumor development while restriction of protein intake inhibits tumor growth. The enzymes in adipose tissue convert precursor adrenal hormones into active estrogens. Dietary fat raises serum estrogen levels and promotes tumor development and may also play a role in originating tumors. In contrast to Western women, women in foraging societies have low serum estrogen levels.

Western women's skinfold thickness (a measure of the proportion of body fat) is almost twice that of pre-agricultural women. Compared to college athletes, women who are not athletic in college (and less active in adolescence and somewhat less active after college) have two to five times the rates of breast, uterine, and ovarian cancer. Women in affluent societies consume 40% or more of their calories in the form of fat, against 20 to 25% among pre-agricultural women, but only 20 as opposed to 100 grams of fiber per day. Dietary fiber is protective because it reduces free estrogen levels in the blood. It helps to prevent bowel dysfunction, which has been associated with breast cancer, and the severe constipation which can lead to the migration of mutagenic substances from the gastrointestinal tract to the breast fluid.

The protective effect of breast-feeding goes beyond the current generation to the next one, for early nutritional influences seem to have an important effect on later susceptibility to cancer. Breast-feeding contributes to the development and regulation of the immune system, which plays a central role in suppressing the initiation and growth of tumors. It prevents over-consumption of fat, protein, and calories. This influences body size and composition, the baseline against which nutrition works throughout life. That is, breast-feeding prevents the accelerated growth of muscles and fat stores associated with breast cancer risk factors: faster growth rates, earlier menarche, and greater achieved stature and size. Women who have been breast-fed themselves are less likely to develop breast cancer.

We have seen that breast-feeding benefits both the mother and child with respect to prevention of breast cancer. In the mother, breast-feeding according to the ancient pattern influences systemic hormone levels and the micro-environment of the breast tissue, reducing exposure to exogenous and endogenous carcinogens. In the child, breast-milk provides an appropriate balance of nutrients that prevents over-nutrition, rapid growth, and early maturation. This circular interaction of factors expresses and can be predicted by the concept of the mother-infant dyad as a biological interacting pair.

SUDDEN INFANT DEATH SYNDROME

From a global perspective, Western society's expectation that infants should sleep alone for long hours away from their parents stands out as anomalous, even if it fits well in its cultural context. One unfortunate consequence is that the diffusion of lone infant sleep over the past several generations may be related to the rise in the frequency of infant death from the Sudden Infant Death Syndrome (SIDS).

The meaning of reproduction and child-rearing changed with the emergence of industrial society and its predominance of small, simple families (couples plus children). In this kind of society, the crib symbolizes the child's place and is usually placed in a separate room. By contrast, in rural pre-industrial Europe and in a survey of over 90 contemporary non-Western societies, infants invariably slept in the same bed or room as their parents. SIDS does not appear to exist in these societies, nor is it found among non-human primates or other mammals. In many Western societies, SIDS is the major cause of infant death, though rates are very low among sub-populations in which there is co-sleeping and nocturnal breast-feeding. Peak mortality is between the ages of two and four months, with 90% of all deaths occurring before the age of six months.

While there seem to be many intrinsic and secondary factors that affect infants in different ways to bring about SIDS events, one common factor is that SIDS usually happens during sleep. While breast-feeding in itself reduces risk, it is the frequent, intensive, prolonged breast-feeding implying mother–infant co-sleeping that may provide the best environment for avoiding the disease.

Co-sleeping infants lie on their backs or sides with their heads turned toward the breast and feed through the night, often without waking their mothers. Even newborns and very young infants are able to attach to the breast on their own, provided it is within reach. In non-industrialized societies, it is rare for infants younger than one year to sleep long hours with only a few arousals or feedings. They do not increase the length of their longest sleep episode within the first few months, nor do they stop feeding at night, as parents in Western societies expect.

These same patterns are observed in sleep laboratories, where mothers report waking up and feeding their child many times fewer than the number recorded on the monitors. They and their infants move through the various stages of sleep in synchrony, shifting between them more frequently and spending less time in the deep sleep which makes arousal more difficult. If in the laboratory the breast-feeding mother spends the night in a separate room from her child, on average she breast-feeds less than half as often. She also tends to put the child on its stomach when leaving it to sleep alone. Notably, breast-feeding mothers who routinely sleep in a separate room from their infants actually sleep for a shorter amount of time during the night, even though they feed their infants less often and for a shorter overall time period than mothers who co-sleep.

One factor common to a majority of cases is that the infant had been placed on its stomach to sleep: the opposite of the position used by infants who sleep with their mothers and breast-feed throughout the night. This may be due to suffocation because the child is unable to move out of pockets of its own carbon dioxide in puffy mattresses or bean bag cushions. It also may be the result of developmental changes related to a shift in the position of the larynx (windpipe) which takes place at four to six months.

At birth, the larynx is in contact with the back of the palate, allowing air inhaled by the nostrils to go by its own route to the lungs. It then begins to descend in the throat to a position below the back of the tongue, so that the two openings leading to the lungs and stomach lie side by side (which is why food sometimes "goes down the wrong tube"). During this shift, problems can occur if breathing through the nose (which infants greatly prefer) is impeded by a cold or other factor. Breathing through the mouth can be blocked by the uvula (the fleshy structure hanging over the back of the tongue) if it enters the descending larynx, especially if the child is lying at the wrong angle. Huge reductions in SIDS rates have taken place over the past decade in many European countries and the United Kingdom since the initiation of campaigns against the face-down position, and the U.S. is also beginning to show rapid improvement in SIDS rates.

There is more to the story than sleep position, which itself inculpates the crib since co-sleeping is associated with the safer position. More directly, the crib implies isolated, prolonged, deep sleep. Like adults, infants are able to fall into deep sleep, but they are less equipped to arouse themselves out of it. All people have temporary lapses in breathing during the night, but their brains generally respond to them appropriately. Infants are different, for they are born at a much earlier stage of neurological development than other primates, even our closest relatives.

During sleep, infants may need frequent arousals to allow them to emerge from episodes of apnea or cardiorespiratory crisis. External stimuli and parental monitoring from co-sleeping and breast-feeding give them practice at doing so, and keep them from spending long periods of time in deep stages of sleep. SIDS deaths peak at the same age at which the amount of deep sleep relative to REM sleep increases dramatically, at two to three months. Moreover, at this time infants begin to exercise more voluntary control of breathing, as parents notice in their more expressive cries. This is a step toward the speech breathing they will use later, but may complicate breathing in the short term.

The rhythm of sound and silence in the mother's breathing gives the infant auditory stimulation, while contact with her body provides tactile stimulation. The carbon dioxide which her breathing releases into the air they share induces the infant to breathe. Frequent waking for breast-feeding is a behavior common to primates and prevents hypoglycemia, which has been implicated in some SIDS deaths. Human milk also provides immunological protection against several infectious organisms (and preparations of them given as immunizations) considered responsible for some deaths. This protection is especially needed after two months, when inherited maternal antibodies become scarce but the infant's own immune system is not yet developed. Breast-feeding and constant physical contact prevent overheating and the exhausting crying spells which seem to be factors in the disease. In addition, the infant is sensitive to other aspects of its microenvironment, including temperature, humidity, and odors.

While many experts and parents advise against or avoid co-sleeping because they fear suffocating the infant, in fact this risk is very low, especially where people sleep on hard bedding or the floor. Modern bedding is dangerous because of the conformation of bed frames and the use of soft mattresses and heavy coverings. Yet, these factors are at least as relevant to cribs as parents' beds. On the other hand, some parents should not sleep with their infants, such as those who go to bed affected by drugs or alcohol. Cigarette smoke in the sleeping room could cancel the benefit of co-sleeping.

While isolated infant sleep may be consistent with parents' desires and the primacy of the conjugal bond and other Western values, it is a new behavioral norm in human history and does not represent a "natural" need. It is neither in the infant's best interest nor in conformity with behavioral patterns and biological conditions established long before our time. By contrast, parent–infant co-sleeping matches evolutionary considerations such as the need for temperature regulation, frequent nutrition, and protection from predators and disease. There may be some wisdom to the popular term, "crib death," or "cot death," for it points to the crib and the Western concept of infant independence as major factors in the disease.

SOCIAL AND CULTURAL INTERVENTION

We have seen that mothers and infants are physiologically bound together from conception to weaning, not just conception to birth. The Western ideal of the autonomous individual, even the neonate, is not shared by other societies today or by those of the past. The biocultural model shows that evolution has favored frequent, exclusive, and prolonged breast-feeding in humans. This entails constant physical contact, parent–infant co-sleeping, and nighttime breast-feeding. It leads to postpartum infertility and protects against SIDS and breast and other reproductive system cancers. Breast-feeding therefore has significant health outcomes, beyond the usual benefits of breast-milk which have been popularized in recent years.

Unfortunately, the health benefits of breast-feeding, especially for mothers, are generally overshadowed by assertions regarding the supposed convenience of bottle feeding and the nutritional adequacy of artificial milk. Even the promotion of breast-feeding on the basis of the milk's value to infants does not always induce women to breast-feed, since there is little if any mention of a benefit to them. To the contrary, there are many disincentives to breast-feeding, such as beliefs that it causes the breasts to sag and makes it difficult to lose weight, or that it makes the husband feel jealous and left out. The lack of familiarity with breast-feeding which has resulted from a couple of generations of preference for the bottle also discourages it. Many people have never seen a woman breast-feed, and would prefer not to.

The degree to which our culture has come to favor intervention in the fundamental relationship between nurslings and mothers is evident in the nearly-universal use of pacifiers. This has been promoted by the notion, sanctioned by professional medicine, that infants need to suckle, and better a scientifically designed object than the thumb or finger (the nipple is not even among the choices). However, in evolutionary perspective, a pacifier is completely unnecessary since infants who are breast-fed according to the ancient pattern are allowed to suckle to their heart's content. Not surprisingly, pacifier use has been found to reduce the duration of breast-feeding.

The birthing process is focused upon the infant, while the mother is considered and often treated as an impediment to the physician's efforts to extract the child. Afterward, the medical care of the two is split between obstetricians and pediatricians, reflecting the conceptual splitting of the mother–infant relationship at birth. There is little or no breast-feeding (in the United States, only one half of all infants begin life feeding at the breast). Weaning takes place within a few months and almost always within the first year, and the mother resumes her menstrual cycle within a few months. Mothers are strongly encouraged to put their children on feeding schedules and eliminate nighttime feeding as quickly as possible, and to teach them to get to sleep and stay asleep on their own, in their own bed and room. Instead of being carried and cuddled throughout the day and night, infants are left in cribs, strollers, and playpens and are touched relatively rarely. They are expected to cry and left to do so, sometimes for hours. Often, the door to their room is closed at nap time and during the night.

On a social-structural level, cultural interference in breast-feeding seems to be more common in societies which are based upon vertical inheritance and the simple family structure, than societies in which families are wide and inheritance is lateral. In the former, the institution of marriage is emphasized over kin relationships. Women's sexual and conjugal duties take precedence over their role as kinswomen and mothers, while children are considered heirs rather than links in a kinship network. These conditions can make breast-feeding seem to interfere with sexuality, and pit the husband against the child in competition over the woman's sexualized breast.

Notably, our culture describes breasts as "secondary *sexual* characteristics," highlighting a tendency to regard them as objects of display rather than functional organs. In medieval to modern Europe, the postpartum taboo against sex during lactation was circumvented among the elite classes by wet-nursing, so that women could be available to their husbands instead of breast-feeding. This was subsequently replaced by formula feeding and practiced by a much wider segment of the population.

The rise of the modern nation-state over the past two centuries meanwhile has brought an expansion of the authority of medical experts. Beginning with early industrialization, the state and its emerging medical system sought to shape public morality and oppose traditional authority by reaching into the private, intimate world of the family. As a result, reproduction and child-rearing became medicalized well before professional medicine had much legitimate knowledge or expertise in these areas. As multiple families broke up due to socioeconomic changes, families became more dependent upon outside experts in areas which had previously been handled by older relatives or other authorities such as midwives and clerics.

By now, it is rare for anyone to question the authority of the medical community in questions such as birth control or infant feeding. This phenomenon has emerged hand-in-hand with the notion of the autonomous individual. By considering fetuses and infants as beings independent of their mothers, Western society has allowed and welcomed experts into the life of the dyad and granted them predominant authority in decisions regarding the care and upbringing of the young. Mothers are not encouraged to think of themselves as competent or knowledgeable enough to breast-feed without expert intervention and surveillance. This is reinforced by the regimen of ever-more numerous obstetric and pediatric examinations before and after childbirth, and the

literature directed at mothers by the medical and pharmaceutical communities.

In contrast to agricultural and foraging societies, in ours breast-feeding does not easily fit into women's work or social lives. Few professions allow women much flexibility in time scheduling, and there is a deep, underlying expectation that the new mother will immediately be independent from her child. Many working women are forced to pump their milk in bathrooms, often in secrecy. Women who do not work outside the home are targeted by formula manufacturers, who capitalize on cultural values such as work and efficiency by suggesting that formula feeding with an increasingly complex array of products demonstrates a woman's capability in scientific mothering.

Firms that sell formula, pacifiers, and other infant care products distribute samples and coupons through hospitals and physicians' offices, lending their products a medical stamp of approval that appeals to many parents. Often, they are able to "hook" babies even before they leave the hospital because the staff supplements the mother's milk with formula or sugar water, and the infant comes to prefer the easier flow of the bottle.

Thus, even when breast-feeding is promoted and women feel committed to it, social and cultural obstacles can make it difficult. A biocultural understanding of breast-feeding as an evolved, two-way process could help to make conditions more favorable. It would highlight the fact that women are normally able to breast-feed without medical approval, surveillance, and intervention and reduce the public's receptiveness to industrially produced formula and baby foods. Most importantly, the biocultural perspective would foster an appreciation of the intricate mechanisms linking mothers and infants together in a dynamic system of nutrition that benefits them both.

SUGGESTED READING

Cohen, Mark Nathan. 1989. *Health and the Rise of Civilization*. New Haven: Yale University Press.

Daly, S. E. J., and P. E. Hartmann. 1995. Infant Demand and Milk Supply. *Journal of Human Lactation* 11(1):21–37.

Dettwyler, Katherine. 1995. A Time to Wean. In Patricia Stuart-Macadam and Katherine Dettwyler (eds.) *Breast-feeding: Biocultural Perspectives*. New York: Aldine de Gruyter.

Eaton, S. Boyd, Melvin Konner, and Marjorie Shostak. 1988. *The Paleolithic Prescription*. New York: Harper and Row.

Eaton, S. Boyd, et al. 1994. Women's Reproductive Cancers in Evolutionary Perspective. *The Quarterly Review of Biology* 69(3):353–367.

Ellison, Peter. 1995. Breast-feeding, Fertility, and Maternal Condition. In Patricia Stuart-Macadam and Katherine

Dettwyler (eds.) *Breast-feeding: Biocultural Perspectives.* New York: Aldine de Gruyter.

Ewald, Paul W. 1994. *Evolution of Infectious Disease.* New York: Oxford University Press.

Konner, Melvin, and Marjorie Shostak. 1987. Timing and Management of Birth among the !Kung. *Cultural Anthropology* 2(1):11–28.

Konner, Melvin, and Carol Worthman. 1980. Nursing Frequency, Gonadal Function, and Birth Spacing among !Kung Hunter-Gatherers. *Science* 207:788–791.

Maher, Vanessa (ed.). 1992. *The Anthropology of Breast-feeding.* Oxford: Berg.

McKenna, James. 1986. An Anthropological Perspective on the Sudden Infant Death Syndrome (SIDS): The Role of Parental Breathing Cues and Speech Breathing Adaptations. *Medical Anthropology* 10(1):9–53.

McKenna, James, and Sarah Mosko. 1990. Evolution and the Sudden Infant Death Syndrome (SIDS). Part 3: Infant Arousal and Parent–Infant Co-Sleeping. *Human Nature* 1(3):291–330.

Micozzi, Marc. 1995. Breast Cancer, Reproductive Biology, and Breast-feeding. In Patricia Stuart-Macadam and Katherine Dettwyler (eds.) *Breast-feeding: Biocultural Perspectives.* New York: Aldine de Gruyter.

Nesse, Randolph M., and George C. Williams. 1994. *Why We Get Sick: The New Science of Darwinian Medicine.* New York: Random House.

Riordan, Jan, and Kathleen Auerbach. 1993. *Breast-feeding and Human Lactation.* Boston: Jones and Bartlett.

Scheper-Hughes, Nancy, and Margaret Lock. 1987. The Mindful Body: A Prolegomenon to Future Work in Medical Anthropology. *Medical Anthropology Quarterly* 1(1):6–41.

Stuart-Macadam, Patricia. 1995. Breast-feeding in Prehistory. In Patricia Stuart-Macadam and Katherine Dettwyler (eds.) *Breast-feeding: Biocultural Perspectives.* New York: Aldine de Gruyter.

Williams, George C., and Randolph M. Nesse. 1991. The Dawn of Darwinian Medicine. *The Quarterly Review of Biology* 66(1):1–22.

Wood, James W. et al. 1985. Lactation and Birth Spacing in Highland New Guinea. *Journal of Biosocial Sciences, Supplement* 9:159–173.

Woolridge, Michael W. 1995. Baby-Controlled Breast-feeding. In Patricia Stuart-Macadam and Katherine Dettwyler (eds.) *Breast-feeding: Biocultural Perspectives.* New York: Aldine de Gruyter.

11

Chinese Table Manners

You Are How *You Eat*

Eugene Cooper

I had been looking forward to this dinner with an important client for over a week. We were going to close the biggest deal of my career. He arrived on time, and I ordered a bit of wine. It was a fancy restaurant and I was trying to behave appropriately; I tucked my napkin neatly on my lap and lifted my wine glass carefully with my little finger extended in the way I had always seen it done. But what began well began to go awry. I looked on in horror as my client ladled a number of different dishes together into a soup bowl, lifted it to his mouth and began to shovel it in. I was so embarrassed by this display of bad manners that I hoped no one I knew would happen by. My face must have betrayed my thoughts, but my client did not let on. He simply asked if I was not enjoying my food because I had left the dishes flat on the table. This took me by surprise, because I realized for the first time that he was looking at me and finding *my* behavior odd. Our smiles became realizations and turned to laughter. Luckily, we had a good sense of humor about our ethnocentrism. Somebody should have warned us; this could have been a real disaster.

Consider yourself warned. Table manners, like a great many everyday events, are heavily laden with cultural meaning. Understanding culturally prescribed behaviors is of practical importance, not merely interesting. More anthropologists need to be involved in cross-cultural training for situations where there is likely to be interaction between people from different cultures or ethnic groups.

As you read this selection, ask yourself the following questions:

- How does one determine which culture's table manners are better? Why do we judge people by their manners?

- What are the important distinctions in Chinese food?

- Which food is the most basic and a necessary part of every Chinese meal? What about your own culture?

- What does it mean in China if you leave your rice bowl on the table while eating from it?

- What is the overriding rule of Chinese table customs?

- How do the Chinese feel about eating alone? Why?

The following terms discussed in this selection are included in the Glossary at the back of the book:

cultural values

ethnology

symbol

"Etiquette of this kind (not putting half eaten meat back in the bowl, [not] wiping one's nose on one's sleeve) is not superficial, a matter for the surface rather than the depths; refined ways of acting are so internalized as to make alternative behavior truly 'disgusting,' 'revolting,' 'nauseous,' turning them into some of the most highly charged and deeply felt of intra-social differences, so that 'rustic' behavior is not merely quaint but barbarous" (Goody 1982:140).

"Probably no common practice is more diversified than the familiar one of eating in company, for what Europeans consider as correct and decent may by other races be looked upon as wrong or indelicate. Similarly, few social observances provide more opportunities for offending the stranger than the etiquette of the table" (Hammerton 1936:23).

Reproduced by permission of Society for Applied Anthropology from *Human Organization* 45(2):179–184, 1986.

Our shrinking world makes encounters with people of other cultures increasingly common in our life experiences. Whether in the conduct of business, in interactions with our "ethnic" neighbors, or as visitors to other countries, we are frequently called on to communicate with others whose assumptions about what constitutes appropriate behavior are widely different from our own.

In such contexts, it is often difficult to know whether habits and customs one takes for granted in one's own home may be creating unfavorable impressions in one's host's home. No less an authority than Confucius, writing more than two thousand years ago, was aware of the potential difficulties involved in intercultural communication, and provided the following advice: "When entering a country inquire of its customs. When crossing a border, inquire of the prohibitions" (Li Chi 1971:17).

Among such customs and prohibitions, those associated with behavior at the table can make an enormous difference in the way one is perceived by a foreign host.

As regards the Chinese in particular, the way one handles oneself at the table gives off signals of the clearest type as to what kind of a person one is, and it is all too easy to offend, as I hope to show. At the same time, however, it is easy enough to equip oneself with a few simple points to bear in mind that will not only pleasantly surprise one's Chinese host, but also convince him or her that one is a sensitive, cultivated, courteous, respectful, and considerate individual.

Surprisingly, for a civilization which has generated so many handbooks of its various cuisines, China has not produced any popular guidebooks for table manners of the Emily Post variety. The field, of course, has for the most part been preempted by the Li Chi—records of etiquette and ceremonial—most of which is said to date from the early Han. Indeed, many of the themes which characterize contemporary Chinese table manners are present in the minute descriptions of behaviors appropriate to people of various stations in all the gradations of Han social structure, such as the prescription to yield or defer. However, one is hard pressed to find a general rough and ready guide to contemporary Chinese table manners of anything more than the most superficial kind, usually present in popular Chinese cookbooks for Western audiences.

The absence of attention to table manners may be the result of the fact that table manners are among those habits most taken for granted—rules no grown-up needs instruction in. A Chinese culinary enthusiast of my acquaintance assures me that table manners are not important in Chinese history, being far outweighed by the scarcity of food generally as the major

issue. Nevertheless, an examination of Chinese table manners provides sufficient contrast with Western table habits in terms of structure and performance, as to make significant features of Chinese etiquette emerge in comparison—features taken for granted by the native.

Those few who have written on the subject (Chang 1977; Hsü and Hsü 1977) generally qualify as bi-cultural individuals with sufficient experience of both Chinese and Western rules to tease out the areas of contrastive significance. My five years of field research (and eating) in Hong Kong, and eight years of marriage to a Chinese woman who taught me Chinese table manners as to a child, also qualify me for the assignment, although my former European colleagues at the University of Hong Kong might question my credentials as an expert on Western etiquette, to be sure.

BASIC STRUCTURES AND PARAPHERNALIA

To begin with, it is useful to consider K. C. Chang's (1977) broad outline of the important distinctions in Chinese food between food (*shih*) and drink (*yin*), and then within the category food, between *fan* (grain/rice) and *ts'ai* (dishes). Chang establishes a hierarchy with grain as the base, vegetables and fruit as next least expendable, and meat as most expendable in the preparation of a meal. Fish would probably fall between vegetables and meat at least as far as contemporary Hong Kong is concerned, particularly if one includes the enormous variety of preserved fish available.

In any event, it is fair to say that a Chinese meal is not a meal without *fan*. The morning food event, at which rice is not normally taken, or if so is taken as gruel, is not thought of as a meal. When Chinese speak of a full day's eating fare, it is two square meals per day rather than three. Thus rice (or grain) defines a meal, and its treatment and consumption are circumscribed in a number of ways.

It will be helpful, however, to lay out the general paraphernalia with which the diner is equipped, and the structure in which it is deployed before returning to the rules governing rice. On this subject, Hsü and Hsü (1977:304) have written:

> The typical Chinese dining table is round or square, the *ts'ai* dishes are laid in the center, and each participant in the meal is equipped with a bowl for *fan*, a pair of chopsticks, a saucer, and a spoon. All at the table take from the *ts'ai* dishes as they proceed with the meal.

The *ts'ai* dishes are typically shared by all, and must be treated much as common property, whereas one's bowl is a private place which comes directly in touch with the mouth. The chopsticks are of both the mouth and the table, and mediate between. They are thin, and when employed appropriately only touch the one piece or small quantity a person touches first. Many Westerners find the habit of sharing from a common plate potentially unhygienic, and one might be tempted to dismiss this as a bit of ethnocentricity. However, the point has recently been made by no less an authority than Communist party secretary Hu Yaobang, who called attention to the unsanitary character of traditional Chinese eating habits and urged change.

One employs the chopsticks to take from the common plate and place food in one's bowl, then one raises the bowl to the mouth and pushes food into the mouth with the chopsticks. Hsü and Hsü state, "The diner who lets his *fan* bowl stay on the table and eats by picking up lumps of *fan* from the bowl is expressing disinterest in or dissatisfaction with the food. If he or she is a guest in someone's house, that is seen as an open insult to the host" (1977:304). Since one's bowl is a private place, "good manners do not preclude resting a piece of meat (or other items) in one's bowl between bites" (1977:304). However, one never puts a partially chewed piece of anything back into one of the common plates (I would not have thought this necessary to mention; however, an otherwise culturally sensitive person I know had the audacity to do so recently so it may bear mentioning.) Also, it is extremely poor manners to suck or bite your chopsticks.

In some cases the bowl may be substituted for by a spoon, as, for example, when one goes out to lunch with one's workmates, and each diner is supplied with a flat plate piled high with rice topped with roast pork, chicken, duck and/or *lap cheong* (Chinese sausage), or with a helping of a single *ts'ai* dish (the latter known as *hui fan*).

Eating rice off a flat plate with chopsticks alone is not an easy task. Westerners exasperated with the use of chopsticks often feel their most intense frustration when trying to accomplish this task, and are often reduced to picking up small bits of rice with the ends of their chopsticks and placing them in the mouth. Seeming to pick at one's food in this way is not good manners and marks one as an incompetent foreign devil, confirming in most Chinese minds all of their previous prejudices about *guailos*.

No self-respecting Chinese would attempt to eat rice directly from a flat plate without first piling the rice onto, or scooping the rice into, a spoon. One eats the *ts'ai* or meat with one's chopsticks, but rice is most often carried to the mouth in a spoon. The spoon stands in for the bowl in the mini-context of an individual serving, and one can also think of the bowl

itself as serving in the capacity of an enlarged spoon in the context of regular dining as well.

Rice is usually doled out from a common pot by the host or hostess. When someone has filled your rice bowl for you, it is accepted with two hands. To accept rice with one hand suggests disinterest, disrespect, and carelessness. One places the full bowl in front of oneself and waits until everyone has been served. It is very impolite to begin eating before everyone at the table has had his bowl filled with rice. When one has finished the rice in one's bowl, one does not continue to eat of the common *ts'ai* dishes. To eat *ts'ai* without rice in one's bowl is to appear a glutton interested only in *ts'ai*, of which one must consume a great deal to get full without rice. Depending on the degree of intimacy of a relationship, one may, when eating at the home of a friend or acquaintance, rise from the table to refill one's bowl with rice from the rice pot in the kitchen. However, at formal occasions one's host will usually be alert enough to notice when one's rice bowl is empty and move to fill it before one might be forced to request more rice. When one rises to get more rice, the host will usually insist on taking one's bowl and filling it. One may decline such assistance if the host is a close friend by simply saying "I'll serve myself."

At banquets one is expected to fill up on *ts'ai*, and consumption of too much rice may be a sign of disrespect to the quality of the *ts'ai* dishes. No rice should ever be left over in one's bowl at the end of the meal.

> As children we were always taught to leave not a single grain of *fan* in our bowl when we finished. Our elders strongly impressed on us that each single grain of rice or corn was obtained through the drops of sweat of the tillers of the soil (Hsü and Hsü 1977:308).

A corollary of this rule is never to take so much rice, or anything else for that matter, in your bowl as to be unable to finish it. It is also extremely disrespectful of the meal and of one's host to leave bits of rice on the table around one's bowl, and Chinese children are often told that each of these grains will materialize as a pockmark on the face of their future spouse.

As regards the *ts'ai*, it is important to note again that it is arrayed for all to share. Generally speaking, especially on formal occasions, one does not serve oneself without first offering to others, at least those seated immediately to either side. This applies also to the taking of tea, and one generally fills a neighbor's cup before taking tea for oneself. When tea is poured for you, it is customary to tap the table with your fingers to convey your thanks.

The overriding rule of Chinese table customs is deference. Defer to others in everything. Be conscious of the need to share what is placed in common. This means don't eat only from those dishes that you like.

One very common point of instruction from parents to children is that the best mannered person does not allow co-diners to be aware of what his or her favorite dishes are by his or her eating pattern (Hsü and Hsü 1977:304).

When taking from the common dishes one should also only take in such proportions that everyone else will be left with a roughly equivalent amount. It is polite to take the remains of a common *ts'ai* dish after a new dish has been brought out. The desirability of the remains is diminished by the introduction of a new dish, and the remains of the old become fair game. However, it is rather poor manners to incline a common plate toward oneself and scrape the remains into one's bowl. This "looking in the mirror" evokes the idea of narcissistic concern with oneself.

In general, young should defer to old in order of eating, and on formal occasions when guests are present children may even be excluded from the dining table until the adults are finished, or seated at a table separate from the adults. In the household of the boss of the factory where I did my fieldwork, apprentices commonly sat with the boss at the family table, but were relegated to the children's table at the New Year's feast.

A host will usually signal that it is appropriate to begin eating, after each person at the table has taken rice, by picking up his chopsticks and saying *"sik fan."* When a guest has eaten his fill, he indicates that he is finished by putting down his chopsticks and encouraging others still eating to take their time. They in turn will inquire if the guest is full, and if he is he should say so. Upon finishing one may either remain at the table or leave. A guest of honor is expected to remain until all are finished.

In addition, one should be careful not to take large mouthfuls, to refrain from making noise while chewing, and to try to maintain the same pace of eating as others at the table. In contrast to Western etiquette in which "toothpicks are never used outside the privacy of one's room" (McLean 1941:63), toothpicks are provided at most Chinese tables and it is not impolite to give one's teeth a thorough picking at the table, provided one covers one's mouth with the opposite hand.

Spitting is not good manners at a Chinese table, although this is a rule often honored more in the breach. Spittoons are often provided in Chinese restaurants, both as a repository for waste water and tea used to sterilize one's utensils, and for expectorations of various sorts. Often the contents of the spittoons threaten to get up and walk away, so vile are the contents. The floor is fair game in many restaurants for just about anything remaining in one's mouth not swallowable, such as small bits of bone or gristle. Hong Kong has improved considerably in this regard in recent years, but in working-class restaurants and *daipaidongs,* spitting is still quite common.

INFLECTIONS OF GENERAL PRINCIPLES

Having laid out these basic ground rules, it remains to explore how these rules are inflected in the various contexts in which food events occur in contemporary Hong Kong. These contexts are many and varied, ranging from informal and intimate occasions when the family is together at home for a meal, to the more formal occasions involving elaborate feasts usually held in restaurants. Somewhat intermediate between these are the meals eaten out, but in somewhat less formal contexts—from breakfast taken at *dim saam* houses, lunches taken at foodstalls with workmates, to evening meals prepared in restaurants for individual diners (*hak fan*), and midnight snacks. Expectations as to appropriate comportment at the table will also vary with region of origin, age, and class position.

For example, for Cantonese a full meal usually includes soup, and many Cantonese feel uncomfortable leaving the table without having partaken of soup. The minimal structure of the Cantonese meal includes not just *fan* (grain) and *ts'ai* (dishes), but also soup. This minimal structure is served up in what is known as *hak fan,* a specialty of some restaurants (usually Shanghainese) in which one may choose from a daily set menu of *hak* dishes, served with an extra large bowl of rice and the soup of the day. *Hak fan* is designed for people who must eat alone for some reason, not considered the most desirable circumstances. Two Chinese who knew each other would not sit down at the same table and order two individual dishes of *hak fan.* They would surely grasp the opportunity of sharing the greater variety available to each through social eating.

Jack Goody has likened eating alone to defecating in public (1982:306) because of the absence of the social in meeting essentially biological needs. *Hak fan* assures that even taken alone, the minimum structural entity of a Cantonese meal is available to be consumed. This basic structure is also revealed in a variety of thermos containers used for carrying lunch to work which are equipped with compartments for rice, *ts'ai* and soup. Since the contexts in which food events occur in Hong Kong are so varied, soup is not always the focus of attention. Proceeding through the ordinary day's food events from morning to evening will give us occasion to note context-linked inflections of our general principles.

As mentioned previously, the morning food event does not pass muster as a meal, largely due to the absence of rice. Still, there are a variety of contexts in which this event may take place. At home, the morning food event usually involves rice from the evening before boiled down to congee with a variety of pickles and condiments tossed in or served on the side. This is usually grabbed quickly in the kitchen on the way out to work, if it is eaten at all, and seldom involves the entire family seated at a single table.

Eaten out, the morning food event may take several forms. Consistent with the quick and superficial character of the event at home is the food event taken at a food stall or *daipaidong,* of which several different types serve suitable breakfast fare—congee (most commonly with preserved egg and pork), *yautiu* (unsweetened fried dough strips), hot *dao-jeung* (soy bean milk), *jucheung fen* (rolled rice noodles), all served with tea, usually in a glass.

Eating at a *daipaidong,* and even in some restaurants, one assumes the probability that the chopsticks, stuffed together in a can and set at the center of the table for individual diners to take, as well as one's cup, bowl, and spoon, will not have been properly washed. A brief ritualized washing usually precedes the meal in which one pours a glass of boiling hot tea into one's glass, stirring the ends of the chopsticks in the water to sterilize them, pouring the still hot water into one's bowl where one's cup and spoon are immersed and sterilized. The wash water is then thrown out, usually on the street in the case of a *daipaidong,* or in a spittoon at a restaurant, and one is prepared to commence eating. Occasionally, one is even provided with a separate bowl for washing one's eating implements, filled by one's waiter with boiling water from a huge kettle.

At a *daipaidong* for breakfast, one usually shares a table with a stranger, or perhaps a neighbor or workmate, depending on whether one eats near home or near work. In any case, one's portion is usually one's own, and the rules of formal dining apply only in the most general terms. Food is usually taken with dispatch, as one is usually rushing to work or to school, and the idea is just to put something in one's stomach to suppress hunger till the first meal of the day—*ng fan* (lunch).

The slightly more formal morning food event is *dim saam,* referred to most often as *yam ch'a* (drink tea). "Drinking tea" again refers to something less than a "meal," although on weekends, taken with one's family at a large table, *dim saam* often involves the consumption of large quantities of buns, dumplings, rice noodles in various shapes, a variety of innards, and the like. One sits down, is approached by one's waiter, or in fancier restaurants by a host or hostess, who will inquire what kind of tea one will be drinking—*sao mei, bo lei, soy sin,* and that old perceived favorite of *guailos* —*heung pien* (jasmine). When the tea arrives the host will fill everyone's cup and the meal may begin.

One acquires food from carts pushed around by young children and/or aged women, and less frequently by older men. One may find oneself sharing a table with strangers, or with regular customers who eat at the same restaurant at the same time every morning. Going to *yam ch'a* on a regular schedule assures one of continuous contact with the usual crowd, and it is common to find oneself seated at the same table with many of the same people each morning. While polite conversation is the general rule, more juicy gossip is not inappropriate as the relationship between morning diners becomes more familiar.

Generally, each diner is aware of what he has consumed, and the position of the plates may be adjusted where they have been ambiguously placed so the waiter can figure the tab. One eats from one's own plates under such circumstances, and pays for one's own plates; however, it is polite to fill the tea cup of one's neighbor from one's own pot if one is acquainted with him or her. There are still some restaurants in Hong Kong which serve tea in a covered bowl, quite literally stuffed with tea, and poured into a cup to be drunk, extremely dark, but the standard tea pot has replaced the bowl as a tea vessel in most restaurants.

A table shared with strangers or neighbors is usually an informal arrangement in which one eats one's own food. However, taking *dim saam* may also be a more formal occasion, especially on weekends, or when one has been *cheng*-ed (asked out). In such circumstances many of the rules of formal dining apply, i.e., the food on the table is common and should only be taken in such proportions that enough is left for others. One may order dishes one likes from the passing wagons, but one should always offer to others before taking from the dish for oneself. The dishes accumulate somewhat at random due to the vagaries of the itinerary of the carts, so there is no formal order to the dishes' arrival, although sweeter dishes are usually taken last.

Dim saam often trails off into lunch on formal or informal occasions, and by noon after the diners have warmed up with a few *dim saam* dishes, it is polite to inquire of one's fellow diners whether a plate of noodles or rice (a real meal) is in order, and if so, to order such dishes from the kitchen from one's waiter. Varieties of *dim saam* are also available from *daipaidong* as well, sometimes served up in individual portions to go.

The midday food event in Hong Kong includes rice or a reasonable substitute (rice noodles, bean noodles, wheat noodles), and is most often taken during a lunch hour break from factory or office labor. A variety of choices confront the Hong Kong worker eating out for lunch. Food stalls serve a variety of dishes, usually in individual portions on flat plates heaped high with rice, and covered with a single *ts'ai* dish. A glass of tea is usually served, and doubles again as a vessel for sterilizing one's chopsticks and spoon. Blue collar workers I knew in Hong Kong would often consume a full-to-the-brim tea tumbler of high octane spirits with such meals, and trundle back to work with the warm glow and slightly glazed look of a two-martini-lunch executive.

A plate of noodles may also be ordered from stalls specializing in such things. These may be served in individual portions, but given the easy divisibility of noodle dishes it is common for workmates to order a variety of noodle dishes and share them in common. A portion is lifted from the plate to one's bowl; with chopsticks initially, when the noodles are easily grasped in quantity; with help from the spoon as the plate gets progressively emptied. The setting of shared common dishes makes the general rules of the table outlined above once again applicable.

Co-workers will often go out to lunch at large *dim saam* restaurants, catch the tail end of the morning *dim saam* and order a variety of more substantial noodle or rice dishes. Where eating has taken place in common, and occasionally even where individual portions have been served, it is unusual for the check to be divided. Someone usually pays the whole tab. Among workmates, or those who often eat together, there is an implicit assumption that in the long run reciprocity will be achieved. It is not impolite among status equals to grab the check and pay for one's fellow diner, but this is not polite if the status difference is too great. Fights over the check occasionally occur in a way which evokes the potlatches of Northwest Coast Indians in which a status hierarchy is confirmed. Paying the check validates one's status superiority over one's fellow diners. Of course, the wider social setting must also be taken into account. One may be desirous of seeking a favor of an important person, in which case paying the check may serve as a mild form of pressure in which the obligation of reciprocity is finessed, enjoining one's fellow diner to comply with one's request. Food events are first and foremost social events.

The evening meal taken at home usually includes some warmed over *ts'ai* from the previous day's meal plus an increment of newly prepared dishes. It is not good manners to ignore the leftovers, despite the fact that they may not be quite as attractive as when served the day before. The general rules of the table apply, although the intimate setting of the family at home makes their application somewhat less formal. Still and all, parents will most commonly instruct children as to the appropriate forms of behavior at the table in this setting, and the children must show that they understand and are learning. In many working-class homes in Hong Kong it is still common for the men to eat first, with the women joining later and/or hovering over the meal without ever formally sitting down.

At more formal dinners or at banquets or feasts associated with weddings, New Year's, funerals or festivals, the primacy of the *fan* and the secondary character of the *ts'ai* dishes is reversed, with attention devoted to the quality of the *ts'ai* dishes (Hsü and Hsü 1977:307), and rice not served till last. Thus at a banquet one may eat *ts'ai* without rice in one's bowl, and one is expected to fill up on *ts'ai* such that when the rice is finally served, one can only take a token portion, which is to say, this has been a real feast.

> During festivals and especially when acting as hosts all Chinese seem to ignore their sense of frugality and indulge in extravagance. *Ts'ai* dishes are served in abundance. The host or hostess will heap the guests' saucers with piece after piece of meat, fish, chicken and so on, in spite of repeated excuses or even protests on the guests' part. When *fan* is finally served, most around the table are full and can at best nibble a few grains (Hsü and Hsü 1977:307).

By the time the rice has been served at a banquet the diner has already had a share of cold appetizer, several stir fry dishes, or whole chickens, ducks, fish, soup, and a sweet/salty dessert. The emphasis on whole items (with head and tail attached) symbolizes completeness and fullness, and evokes these meanings at the table. One tries to serve fish, *yü*, a homophone for surplus, *yü*, to sympathetically bring about that condition in one's guests.

It is not polite to turn over a fish at the table. Rather, when the side facing up has been finished, the skeleton is lifted off to leave the meat underneath exposed. Apparently, turning over the fish is taboo among boat people, since the fish symbolizes the boat which will capsize sympathetically if a fish is turned over. Waiters in Hong Kong are never sure which of their customers are boat folk and might take offense, so they generally refrain from turning over any fish and apparently the practice has now become general.

A variety of prestige foods, such as shark's fin soup and the various eight precious dishes, are served at banquets more for the social recognition they confer than for the pleasure derived from their consumption (see de Garine 1976:150).

Conceptually, whiskey belongs with grain from which it is distilled and may be taken with food as a rice substitute. On formal occasions in Hong Kong scotch or VSOP Cognac is the rule, served straight in water tumblers, and often diluted with Seven-Up.

Another food event of note in Hong Kong is *siu yeh*—loosely translated as snacks. Usually taken late in the evening, they may include anything from congee, noodles and won ton, to roast pork, duck or chicken, to *hung dao sa* (sweet red bean soup—hot or iced) and *daofufa* (sweet bean curd usually flavored with almond). *Siu yeh* is usually served in individual portions. If you go out for won ton mein, everyone gets his own bowl. If you order duck's neck soup with rice, you are served an individual helping of soup, and an individual bowl of rice. Depending on the class of restaurant you take your *siu yeh* in, you may or may not find it advisable to wash your utensils with tea.

Itinerant street vendors with wheeled carts dispense a variety of prepared *siu yeh* in some residential neighborhoods, calling housewives and amahs to the street clutching their large porcelain bowls, or doling out cuttlefish parts to schoolchildren on street corners.

In all these contexts the general pattern that emerges is one that centers on deference, in thinking first of the other, in suppressing one's inclination to satiate oneself before the other has had a chance to begin, in humility. One yields to the other before satisfying one's own urges. At the macro level of China's great tradition, one finds such behavior characteristic of the *chün-tzu*, the individual skilled in the *li* (etiquette, rites, and ceremonies). He is one also skilled in the art of *jang*—of yielding, of accomplishing without activity, of boundless generosity, of cleaving to the *li*. There is even something of a Taoist resonance in all this, getting at things indirectly, without obvious instrumental effort.

Generally, it can be stated that the degree to which a Chinese practices the rules of etiquette marks his class position with respect to his fellow Chinese; although the degree to which the behavior of lower-class people at the table is informed by these rules should not be underestimated. Disregard of the rules on the part of a Chinese is regarded with as much distaste by their fellows as the faux pas normally committed by Westerners, except that the latter can be excused by their hopeless, if expected, ignorance.

It does not take much study for a Westerner to perform well enough at the table to impress most Chinese, since their expectations are exceedingly low. Keeping in mind a few simple things without slavishly parading one's knowledge, one can usually avoid provoking disgust and revulsion, and convince one's fellow diners that one is sensitive to others on their own terms, as well as to the world at large. Among the most basic of cultural patterns, learned early in life, the degree to which one observes these patterns has a lot to do with the way one is perceived as a person in Chinese terms.

Simple knowledge of the structural contexts, behavioral expectations, and symbolic associations of food events can provide access across social boundaries that would otherwise be less easily breached, and make it possible to more easily achieve one's goals. Table manners are part of an inventory of symbolic behaviors that may be manipulated, finessed, and encoded to communicate messages about oneself. For the Chinese, as for almost everyone else, you are *how* you eat.

REFERENCES

Chang, K. C. (ed.), 1977, Introduction. In *Food in Chinese Culture*. New Haven: Yale University Press.

de Garine, I., 1976, Food, Tradition and Prestige. In *Food, Man and Society*. D. Walcher, N. Kretchmer, and H. L. Barnett, eds. New York: Plenum Press.

Goody, J., 1982, *Cooking, Cuisine and Class*. Cambridge: Cambridge University Press.

Hammerton, J. A., 1936, *Manners and Customs of Mankind*, Vol. I. New York: W. M. A. Wise.

Hsü, F. L. K., and V. Y. N. Hsü, 1977, Modern China: North. In *Food in Chinese Culture*. K. C. Chang, ed. New Haven: Yale University Press.

Li Chi, 1971, *Chü Li, Part I*. Taipei: World Publishing.

McLean, N. B., 1941, *The Table Graces: Setting, Service and Manners for the American House without Servants*. Peoria, IL: Manual Arts Press.

12

Culture and the Evolution of Obesity

Peter J. Brown

As a people, Americans rank as one of the fattest societies in history. This epidemiological fact remains despite the tremendous amount of money, effort, and worry that Americans put into diet, exercise, and the quest for the perfect body. For some people, particularly young women, the quest to be thin can become such an obsession that they develop life-threatening eating disorders, like anorexia nervosa. But in other cultures, young women may go to great lengths to try to gain weight to look attractive. There are no universal standards of physical beauty; in fact, there is considerable cross-cultural variation. Culture defines normality.

How do conditions like obesity come to be expressed? Biologists usually say that it is a combination of genes and environment. There is good evidence that genes predispose people toward conditions, but there is seldom evidence that the chain of causation is entirely genetic. A complete explanation must be both biological and cultural. In other words, if a condition like obesity is caused by an interaction of genetic and cultural/behavioral predispositions, then both the genes and culture must be the product of evolutionary processes.

In this selection, Peter Brown provides a cross-cultural and evolutionary analysis of how both biological and cultural factors in obesity evolved. This analysis explains the sociological distribution of obesity today. It also emphasizes that peripheral body fat (characteristic of women) is a small health hazard compared to abdominal fat (characteristic of men).

Dietary patterns are obviously shaped by culture. But human tendencies to value meat, fatty foods, and sweets must be understood in the context of our evolutionary past.

As you read this selection, ask yourself the following questions:

- Have you ever noticed that there are gender differences in the locality of fat storage in the body? Why would this be the case?

- Why are fat people ridiculed and discriminated against in the United States? Are these social reactions worse for men or for women?

- What does the author mean when he says that in a rich society, slenderness can be an individual symbol of conspicuous consumption?

- Given the difference in health risk between peripheral body fat and central body fat, why might weight not be the best way to measure one's risk?

- Why do humans like foods that are "bad" for them?

The following terms discussed in this selection are included in the Glossary at the back of the book:

adipose tissue	gender dimorphism
cultural ideals	ideal body images
culture	obesity
epidemiology	sexual dimorphism
food scarcity	

The etiology or cause of obesity can be understood in the context of human cultural and genetic evolution. The cause of human obesity and overweight involves the interaction of genetic traits with culturally patterned behaviors and beliefs. Both these genes and cul-

ture traits, remarkably common in human societies, are evolutionary products of similar processes of selection related to past food scarcities. This idea is not new: The notion of "thrifty phenotypes rendered detrimental by progress" was introduced more than a quarter-century ago. In recent years, the evidence for the existence of genes that enable individuals to use food energy efficiently and store energy reserves in the form of fat has been increasingly impressive; those

Reproduced by permission of *Human Nature* 2:31–57, 1991.

individuals with "fat phenotypes" are likely to develop adult obesity (Stunkard et al. 1986, 1990).

It is important to recognize that these "thrifty" genes are, at least in the human context, necessary but not sufficient factors in the causation of obesity. In actuality, the new discoveries in the genetics of obesity highlight our ignorance about the role of nongenetic or cultural factors, which are usually subsumed in the term *environment* in the medical literature. The purpose of this paper is to examine why and how cultures have evolved behaviors and beliefs that appear to predispose individuals to develop obesity. I believe that an anthropological model of culture has significant advantages over the commonly used undifferentiated concept of "environment" for generating hypotheses about behavioral causes of obesity. This cultural approach is particularly useful for improving our understanding of the social epidemiological distribution of obesity.

It is valuable to raise an obvious question at the outset: Why do people find it very difficult to reduce their intake of dietary fat and sugar even when the medical benefits of this behavioral change are well known to them? The answer is not obvious, since neither the physiological nor the cultural attraction of these foods is well understood. The proximate mechanisms for this attraction are linked to brain physiology and biochemistry (Wurtman and Wurtman 1987). The ultimate answers are linked to our evolutionary heritage. Human predispositions to obesity are found in both genetic and cultural traits that may have been adaptive in the context of past food scarcities but are maladaptive today in the context of affluence and constant food surpluses.

THE PROBLEMS OF OBESITY AND OVERWEIGHT

Throughout most of human history, obesity was neither a common health problem nor even a realistic possibility for most people. Today, particularly in affluent societies like the United States, obesity is very common, affecting about 12 percent of adult men and women; overweight is even more common, affecting an additional 20 to 50 percent of adult Americans depending on the definitions used (Bray 1987). Not only are overweight and obesity relatively common conditions in our society, they are also extremely complex and intractable. Obesity is a serious public health problem because of its causal connection to major causes of morbidity and mortality from chronic diseases, including cardiovascular disease, type 2 diabetes mellitus (NIDDM), and hypertension. On the individual level, obesity and overweight bring with them an enormous amount of personal psychological pain. The

fact that the obese are subjected to significant social and economic discrimination is well documented.

Fat is extraordinarily difficult to shed because the body guards its fat stores. The evidence concerning the effectiveness over a 5-year period of diet therapies indicates that nearly all of the weight that is lost through diets is eventually regained. The remarkable failure of diet therapies has made some researchers rethink their commonsensical theory of obesity as being caused by overeating; the clinical evidence of the past 40 years simply does not support this simplistic notion.

Even in the absence of scientific data about the effectiveness of diet therapy, the diet and weight-loss industry in the United States is remarkably successful in its ability to capture the hope and money of people who perceive themselves to be overweight. This industry thrives because of a complex of cultural beliefs about the ideal body and sexual attractiveness rather than medical advice and the prevention of chronic diseases per se. The American cultural concern about weight loss and the positive valuation of slenderness for women of the middle and upper classes are difficult to overemphasize. Chernin (1981) has referred to this cultural theme as an "obsession" and the "tyranny of slenderness." In this light, it is impossible to claim that obesity is purely a medical issue.

OBESITY AND HUNGER

It is important to remember that for most citizens of the world today, as it has been in the past, the possibility of obesity is remote whereas the possibility of hunger is close to home. There is a palpable irony in the fact of an epidemic of obesity in a world characterized by hunger. For example, in the United States an estimated 20 million people are hungry because they are on a "serious diet"; generally these people are of the middle and upper classes, and most are women. At the same time in the same rich nation, another estimated 20 million Americans are hungry and poorly nourished largely because they lack sufficient money; generally these people are elderly, homeless, or rural inhabitants. This sad symmetry in the estimates of voluntary and involuntary hunger in the United States is a valuable starting point for a discussion of the etiology of obesity. From an evolutionary standpoint, past food shortages have acted as powerful agents of natural selection, shaping both human genetics and behavior.

A theory of the etiology of obesity must not only account for the influences of genes and learned behaviors but also explain its social distribution. Before the problem of causation is addressed, it is worthwhile to examine the nature of human obesity.

CHANGING DEFINITIONS OF OBESITY

The most basic scientific issues regarding obesity are, in fact, controversial. The definitions of obesity and overweight have been the subject of substantial medical debate, in part because they must be based on inferred definitions of normality or "ideal" body proportions. Although obesity refers to excessive adiposity (fat deposits), the most common measurement is not of fat tissue at all but an indirect inference based on measures of stature and total body weight (Bray 1987).

The social history of height and weight standards in the United States is interesting. Until recently, the task of defining both obesity and ideal weights has been the domain of the life-insurance industry. The most well-known table of desirable weights was developed by the Metropolitan Life Insurance Company using correlation statistics between height/weight and mortality among insurance applicants. Ideal weights were based on data from 25-year-old insurance applicants, despite the nonrepresentative nature of the "sample" pool and the fact that in most human populations, individuals increase in weight until around age 50. Obesity was defined as 120 percent of the Ideal Body Weight (IBW), and overweight was defined as 110 percent IBW. Individual life-insurance applicants outside the recommended weight range were required to pay a surcharge on insurance premiums. In 1959, the concept of "frame size" was introduced, although the resulting categories were never given operational definitions using anthropometric measures.

Definitions of obesity have changed throughout history. From 1943 to 1980, definitions of "ideal weights" for women of a particular height were consistently lowered, while those for men remained approximately the same. In 1983, a major debate on the definition of obesity began when Metropolitan Life revised its tables upward, based on new actuarial studies of mortality. Many organizations and experts in the diet industry, including experts in medical fields, rejected these new standards.

In the current medical literature, weight and height tables have been replaced by the Body Mass Index (BMI), defined as body weight (in kilograms) divided by the square of body height (in meters). BMI (W/H^2) is strongly correlated with total body fat, and a value greater than 30 is generally considered obese. Current recommendations include slight increases in BMI with age (Bray 1987). Nevertheless, there continues to be little agreement on precise definitions of either overweight or obesity.

An important added dimension to the questions of definition of obesity involves the distribution of fat around the body trunk or on the limbs. Central or trunk body fat distribution is closely correlated with serious chronic diseases, such as cardiovascular disease, whereas peripheral body fat in the hips and limbs does not carry similar medical risks. Because of this clinically important distinction, measures of fat distribution like waist to hips ratio (WHR), wherein lower WHR values indicate lower risk of chronic disease consequences, will be a valuable addition to future definitions of obesity.

FOUR FACTS ABOUT THE SOCIAL DISTRIBUTION OF OBESITY

Humans are among the fattest of all mammals, and the primary function of our fat is to serve as an energy reserve. The nonrandom social distribution of adiposity within and between human populations may provide a key to understanding obesity. Four facts about this social distribution are particularly cogent for an evolutionary reconstruction: (1) the gender difference in the total percent and site distribution of body fat, as well as the prevalence of obesity; (2) the concentration of obesity in certain ethnic groups; (3) the increase in obesity associated with economic modernization; and (4) the powerful and complex relationship between social class and obesity. Any useful theory concerning the etiology of obesity must account for these social epidemiological patterns.

Sexual Dimorphism

Humans show only mild sexual dimorphism in variables like stature. Males are only 5 to 9 percent taller than females. The sample of adults from Tecumseh, Michigan, seen in Figure 1 are typical. Men are larger than women in height and total body mass, but women have more subcutaneous fat as measured by skinfold thicknesses in 16 of 17 sites (the exception is the suprailiac region—so-called "love handles"). The greatest degree of sexual dimorphism is found in the site of distribution of fat tissue; women have much more peripheral fat in the legs and hips (Kissebah et al. 1989). This difference is epidemiologically important because the greater proportion of peripheral fat in females may be associated with reduced morbidity compared to males with identical BMI values.

Sex differences are also seen in the prevalence of obesity. Despite methodological differences in the categorization of obesity, data from the 14 population surveys shown in Figure 2 indicate that in all of the studies, females have a higher prevalence of obesity than males. A greater risk of obesity for females appears to be a basic fact of human biology.

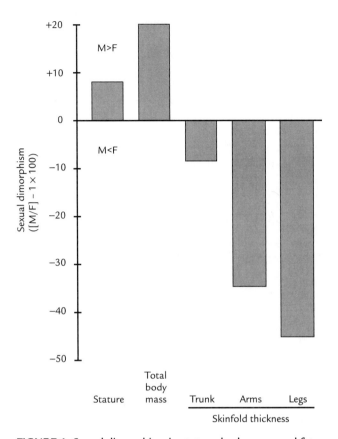

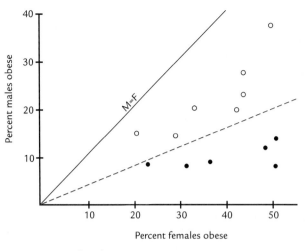

○ Developed

FIGURE 2 Gender differences in prevalences of obesity in 14 populations by general industrial development. Operational definitions of obesity differ between studies. See Brown and Konner (1987) for references. The unbroken line demarcates equal male-female obesity prevalences. The broken line indicates an apparent distinction in gender proportions of obesity in developed and underdeveloped countries. (From Brown, P. J., and M. Konner, An Anthropological Perspective on Obesity. In *Human Obesity*, R. J. Wurtman and J. J. Wurtman, eds. *Annals of New York Academy of Sciences* 499:29–46. Copyright © 1987. Reprinted with permission.)

FIGURE 1 Sexual dimorphism in stature, body mass, and fat measures among white Americans aged 20 to 70 in Techumseh, Michigan. Sexual dimorphism is calculated by comparing male and female means; positive figures refer to greater male measures. Skinfold thicknesses are means of four sites on the trunk or five sites on the arms and legs; the mean dimorphism for all 17 fat measures is –19 percent. (From Brown, P. J., and M. Konner, An Anthropological Perspective on Obesity. In *Human Obesity*, R. J. Wurtman and J. J. Wurtman, eds. *Annals of New York Academy of Sciences* 499:29–46. Copyright © 1987. Reprinted with permission.)

Economic Modernization

The social distribution of obesity varies among societies, depending on their degree of economic modernization. Studies of traditional hunting and gathering populations report *no obesity*. In contrast, numerous studies of traditional societies undergoing the process of economic modernization demonstrate rapid increases in the prevalence of obesity. Trowell and Burkitt's (1981) 15 case studies of epidemiological change in modernizing societies conclude that obesity is the first of the "diseases of civilization" to appear. The rapidity with which obesity becomes a common health problem in the context of modernization underscores the critical role of cultural behaviors in the causation of obesity, since there has been insufficient time for changes in gene frequencies.

Figure 2 also suggests that variations in the male-female ratio of obesity prevalence are related to economic modernization. In less industrially developed societies female obesity is much more common than male obesity, but in more affluent societies the ratio is nearly equivalent. Recent World Health Organization data on global obesity also support this observation (Gurney and Gorstein 1988).

Cultural changes with modernization include the seemingly invariable pattern of diet in industrial countries—decreased fiber intake and increased consumption of fat and sugar. Modernization is also associated with decreased energy expenditures related to work, recreation, or daily activities. From the perspective of the populations undergoing economic modernization, increasing average weight might be seen as a good thing rather than a health problem.

Ethnicity

The idea that particular populations have high rates of a genotype that predisposes individuals to obesity and related diseases is not new but is now supported by a convincing body of adoption and twin data (Stunkard et al. 1986, 1990) and by studies of particular obesity-prone populations like the Pima Indians (Ravussin et al. 1988). In the United States, ethnic groups with elevated rates of obesity include African Americans (particularly in the rural South), Mexican Americans, Puerto Ricans, Gypsies, and Pacific Islanders (Centers for Disease Control 1989).

The fact that certain ethnic groups have high rates of obesity is not easy to interpret because of the entanglement of the effects of genetic heredity, social class, and cultural beliefs. The association of obesity with ethnicity is not evidence for the exclusive role of genetic transmission, since social factors like endogamy (marriage within the group) or group isolation are critical for defining the population structure—that is, the social system through which genes are passed from generation to generation.

Social Class

Social class (socioeconomic status) can be a powerful predictor of the prevalence of obesity in both modernizing and affluent societies, although the direction of the association varies with the type of society. In developing countries, there is a strong and consistent *positive association* between social class and obesity for men, women, and children; correspondingly, there is an inverse correlation between social class and protein-calorie malnutrition. In heterogeneous and affluent societies, like the United States, there is a strong *inverse correlation* of social class and obesity for females. The association between obesity and social class among women in affluent societies is not constant through the life cycle. Economically advantaged girls are initially fatter than their low-income counterparts, but the pattern is reversed beginning at puberty. For females, social class remains the strongest social epidemiological predictor of obesity.

OBESITY AND HUMAN EVOLUTION

Human biology and behavior can be understood in the context of two distinct processes of evolution. Biological evolution involves changes through time in the frequency of particular genes, primarily because of the action of natural selection on individuals. Cultural evolution involves historical changes in the configurations of cultural systems, that is, the learned patterns of behavior and belief characteristics of social groups. Cultural evolution includes the striking and rapid transformation of human lifestyles from small food-foraging societies to large and economically complex states in a span of less than 5,000 years.

The Context of Food Scarcities

Food shortages have been very common in human prehistory and history; in fact, they could be considered a virtually inevitable fact of life for most people. As such, they have been a powerful evolutionary force.

A cross-cultural ethnographic survey of 118 nonindustrial societies (with hunting and gathering, pastoral, horticultural, and agricultural economies) found some form of food shortages for *all* of the societies in the sample (Whiting 1958). Shortages occur annually or even more frequently in roughly half of the societies, and every 2 to 3 years in an additional 24 percent. The shortages are "severe" (i.e., including starvation deaths) in 29 percent of the societies sampled. Seasonal availability of food results in a seasonal cycle of weight loss and weight gain in both hunting and gathering and agricultural societies, although the fluctuation is substantially greater among agriculturalists.

Scarcity and Cultural Evolution

A hunting and gathering economy was characteristic of all human societies for more than 95 percent of our history, yet it is represented by only a handful of societies today. In general, food foragers enjoy high-quality diets, maintain high levels of physical fitness, suffer the risk of periodic food shortages, and are generally healthier than many contemporary populations that rely on agriculture. Without romanticizing these societies, the evidence is persuasive enough to suggest a "paleolithic prescription" of diet and exercise for the prevention of chronic diseases (Eaton et al. 1988). This recommendation refers to the quality of preindustrial diets and not to their dependability or quantity.

Approximately 12,000 years ago, some human groups shifted from a food-foraging economy to one of food production. This economic transformation allowed the evolution of urban civilizations. Many archaeologists believe that people were "forced" to adopt the new agricultural economy because of ecological pressures from population growth and food scarcities or because of military coercion. The archaeological record clearly shows that agriculture was associated with nutritional stress, poor health, and diminished stature (Cohen and Armelagos 1984). The beginning of agriculture is also linked to the emergence of social stratification, a system of inequality that improved the Darwinian fitness of the ruling class relative to that of the lower classes. Social inequality, particularly differential access to strategic resources, plays a critical role in the distribution of obesity in most societies.

Certain ecological zones appear to be prone to severe food shortages. For example, archaeological analysis of tree rings from the southwestern United States shows that the prehistoric past was characterized by frequent and severe droughts. The impressive agricultural societies of the prehistoric Southwest had expanded during an extended period of uncharacteristically good weather and could not be maintained when the lower and more characteristic rainfall patterns resumed. Ecological conditions leading to severe scarcity may have acted as strong forces of selection for "thrifty" genotypes.

Scarcity and Genetic Evolution

Since food shortages were ubiquitous for humans under natural conditions, selection favored individuals who could effectively store calories in times of surplus. For most societies, these fat stores would be called on at least every 2 or 3 years. Malnutrition increases infectious disease mortality, as well as decreasing birth weights and rates of child growth. The evolutionary scenario is this: Females with greater energy reserves in fat would have a selective advantage over their lean counterparts in terms of withstanding the stress of food shortages, not only for themselves but also for their fetuses or nursing children. Humans have evolved the ability to "save up" food energy for inevitable food shortages through the synthesis and storage of fat.

Selection has favored the production of peripheral body fat in females, whose reproductive fitness is influenced by the nutritional demands of pregnancy and lactation. This peripheral fat is usually mobilized after being primed with estrogen during the late stages of pregnancy and during lactation. In addition, a minimal level of fatness increases female reproductive success because of its association with regular cycling and early menarche (Frisch 1987).

In this evolutionary context the usual range of human metabolic variation must have produced many individuals with a predisposition to become obese; yet they would, in all likelihood, never have had the opportunity to do so. Furthermore, in this context there could be little or no natural selection against this tendency. Selection could not provide for the eventuality of continuous surplus simply because it had never existed before.

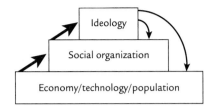

FIGURE 3 A materialist model of culture.

CULTURE AND ADAPTATIONS TO FOOD SCARCITY

Food scarcities have shaped not only our genes but also, and perhaps more important, human cultures. Because the concept of culture is rarely considered in medical research on obesity, and because I am suggesting that this concept has advantages over the more common and undifferentiated term *environment*, it is necessary to review some basic aspects of this anthropological term. *Culture* refers to the learned patterns of behavior and belief characteristic of a social group. As such, culture encompasses *Homo sapiens'* primary mechanism of evolutionary adaptation, which has distinct advantages of greater speed and flexibility than genetic evolution.

Cultural behaviors and beliefs are usually learned in childhood and they are often deeply held and seldom questioned by adults, who pass this "obvious" knowledge and habits to their offspring. In this regard, cultural beliefs and values are largely unconscious factors in the motivation of individual behaviors. Cultural beliefs define "what is normal" and therefore constrain the choices of behaviors available to an individual.

One useful way of thinking about culture in relation to obesity is a cultural materialist model as seen in Figure 3. This model divides culture into three layers. The material foundation of a cultural system is the economic mode of production, which includes the technology and the population size that the productive economy allows and requires. Population size is maintained by the social system, sometimes called the mode of reproduction. Contingent on the first layer is the system of social organization, which includes kinship patterns, marriage and family practices, politics, and status differentiation. Contingent on the social structure is the ideology or belief system, including ideas, beliefs, and values, both secular and sacred. Most anthropologists believe that the ideology is an extremely important part of culture, in part because it rationalizes and reinforces the economy and social structure. Ideology enables people to make sense of their world and to share their common world view through symbols. As such, ideology includes sacred concepts from religion as well as secular concepts (with symbolic components) like health or sexual attractiveness.

A culture is an integrated system: A change in one part causes changes in the other layers. The materialist model indicates that the direction of causal change is from the bottom layer upward (the solid arrows in Figure 3). An economic change, like the invention of agriculture or the Industrial Revolution, has drastic implications for population size, social organization, and associated beliefs. On the other hand, most people within a society tend to explain things from the top down. Of course, people can hold contradictory beliefs and values that are not necessarily linked to their actual behavior.

CULTURAL PREDISPOSITIONS TO OBESITY

Obesity is related to culture in all three levels of the materialist model.

Productive Economy and Food Scarcity

Humans have evolved a wide variety of cultural mechanisms to avoid or minimize the effects of food scarcities. The most important adaptation to scarcity is the evolution of systems of food production and storage. As noted previously, the primary weakness of preindustrial systems of food production is a vulnerability to food shortages. The universality of food shortages discussed above is largely because of the technological limitations in food production and storage.

On the other hand, the energy-intensive (and energy-inefficient) system of agriculture in industrialized societies produces large surpluses of food. These agricultural surpluses are seldom used to eliminate hunger; rather they are used to transform and process foods in particular ways—often to add calories, fat, or salt. For example, we feed "extra" grain to beef cattle to increase the proportion of fat in their meat; consumers say that this overfeeding makes the meat "juicy." Similarly, potatoes are transformed into french fries and potato chips. From a nutritional standpoint the original vegetable is actually reduced to a vehicle for fat and salt. Endemic hunger exists even in the most affluent societies, where it is caused not by poor production but by inequitable distribution.

Technological changes associated with cultural evolution almost exclusively reduce the energy requirements of human labor. In general, cultural evolution has meant the harnessing of greater amounts of energy through technology (one aspect of the mode of production). To prevent obesity, people in developed societies must burn energy through daily workouts rather than daily work.

Reproduction and Energy Expenditure

The concept of the *mode of reproduction* is also related to predispositions to obesity. Pregnancy and lactation represent serious and continuing energy demands on women in societies that have not undergone the demographic transition. Industrial and nonindustrial societies differ in terms of the historical changes from high to low fertility and the reduction of mortality attributable to infectious disease. Higher numbers of pregnancies and longer periods of breast-feeding place high energy demands on women, especially if they cannot supplement their diet during these critical periods. As a result, women suffer greater risk of protein-energy malnutrition. Conversely, with fewer pregnancies and the reduction of breast-feeding, women in industrial societies have less opportunity to mobilize peripheral fat stores and suffer greater risk of obesity. In contemporary societies like the United States, mothers in lower social classes tend to have more children and to feed their infants with bottled formula rather than breast milk. Use of infant formulas allows women to retain their fat stores. These different social patterns in reproduction may play a role in the inverse association of obesity and social class for females.

Social Structure and Obesity

Characteristics of social organization may function as predispositions to obesity. In highly stratified and culturally heterogeneous societies, the distribution of obesity is associated with ethnicity and social class. Marriage patterns typically illustrate ethnic or social class endogamy, that is, marriage within the group. In the United States, members of ethnic minorities choose marriage partners from the same group at extremely high rates. This social practice may concentrate the genetic predispositions to conditions like obesity in particular subpopulations. Similarly, data suggest a pattern of "assortative mating" by social class as well as body type (particularly stature), which may be related to the genetic etiology of obesity. Genetic admixture with Native American groups of the Southwest has been suggested as a cause of elevated rates of type 2 diabetes mellitus and obesity among Mexican Americans (Gardner et al. 1984).

The pervasive and complex relationship between obesity and social class, or socioeconomic status (SES), is important. SES is related to particular behavior patterns that cause obesity. This statement underemphasizes the fact that these learned behaviors are *characteristic* of particular social groups or classes. In other words, the cultural patterns of social class groups are primary, not the individual behaviors themselves.

From a cross-cultural perspective, the general association between obesity and social position is positive: The groups with greater access to economic resources have higher rates of obesity. This pattern is logical and expected because socially dominant groups with better access to strategic resources should have better nutrition, better health, and consequently greater reproductive success.

As discussed earlier, the remarkable and important exception is women in industrial societies, who exhibit a strong *inverse* correlation between obesity and social class. The challenge for researchers is to explain why and how upper-class women in industrial societies remain thin. For many women the ideal of thinness requires considerable effort, restrained eating, and often resources invested in exercise. The social origins of the ideal of thinness in American women are associated with historical changes in women's economic roles, marriage patterns, and family size.

Low-income people in industrial societies might be considered well off by worldwide standards, and this access to resources is reflected in obesity prevalences. Yet in the context of perceived relative deprivation and economic stability, many people in societies like the United States live in stressful conditions—just one paycheck away from hunger. In terms of life priorities, economic security may be a higher and more immediate objective than more elusive goals like an "ideal body" or even long-term health. Amid the daily stresses of poverty, food may be the most common avenue of pleasure and psychological relief. Ethnographic studies of low-income urban black communities in the United States show a social emphasis on food sharing as a tool for marking family ties and demonstrating community cohesiveness.

Cultural Beliefs as Predispositions to Obesity

The third and possibly most important level of the model of culture shown in Figure 3 encompasses cultural symbols, beliefs, and values. Aspects of ideology relevant to the etiology of obesity include the symbolic meaning of fatness, ideal body types, and perceived risks of food shortages.

Fatness is symbolically linked to psychological dimensions, such as self-worth and sexuality, in many societies of the world, but the nature of that symbolic association is not constant. In mainstream U.S. culture,

obesity is socially stigmatized, but for most cultures of the world, fatness is viewed as a welcome sign of health and prosperity. Given the rarity of obesity in preindustrial societies, it is not surprising that they lack ethnomedical terms for obesity. Much more attention is placed on "thinness" as a symptom of starvation, like among the !Kung San (Lee 1979), or in contemporary Africa as a sign of AIDS (sometimes called "the slim disease"). In the context of the AIDS epidemic, plumpness is indeed a marker of health.

Perhaps it is large body size, rather than obesity per se, that is admired as a symbol of health, prestige, prosperity, or maternity in agricultural societies. The Tiv of Nigeria, for example, distinguish between a very positive category, "too big" (kehe), and an unpleasant condition "to grow fat" (ahon) (Bohannan and Bohannan 1969). The first is a compliment because it is a sign of prosperity; the second is a rare and undesirable condition.

For women, fatness may also be a symbol of maternity and nurturance. In traditional societies in which women attain status only through motherhood, this symbolic association increases the cultural acceptability of fatness. A fat woman, symbolically, is well taken care of, and in turn she takes good care of her children. Fellahin Arabs in Egypt describe the proper woman as fat because she has more room to bear the child, lactates abundantly, and gives warmth to her children. The cultural ideal of thinness in industrial societies, in contrast, is found where motherhood is not the sole or even primary means of status attainment for woman. The idea that fat babies and children are healthy children is very widespread. Food can be treated as a symbol of love and nurturance; in some cultures it may be impolite for a guest to refuse food that has been offered, but it is taboo to refuse food from one's mother.

In the industrialized United States, ethnic variation in culturally accepted definitions of obesity is significant. Some Mexican Americans have coined a new term, *gordura mala* (bad fatness), because the original term *gordura* continues to have positive cultural connotations (Ritenbaugh 1982). For this group cultural identity has a stronger and independent effect on risk of obesity than socioeconomic status. An ethnographic study of the cultural meanings of weight in a Puerto Rican community in Philadelphia (Massara 1989) documents the positive associations and lack of social stigma of obesity. Additional quantitative evidence suggests significant differences in ideal body preferences between this ethnic community and mainstream American culture. Positive evaluations of fatness may also occur among lower-class African Americans and Mexican Americans. These ethnic groups are heterogeneous, however, and upwardly mobile ethnics tend to resemble mainstream American culture in their attitudes about obesity and ideal body shape.

In a low-income housing project in Atlanta, Georgia, a sociological interviewer was asked by a group of obese black women, "Don't you know how hard it is to keep this weight *on*?" Their views of the advantages of a large body included being given respect and reduced chances of being bothered by young "toughs" in the neighborhood. For these women, fatness was part of their positive self-identity, and if a friend lost weight she was thought to look sickly. Among lower-income groups, the perceived risk of a food shortage—not for the society as a whole but for the immediate family—may be very important, especially if lack of food was personally experienced in the past. The perception of the risk of future "bad times" and insufficient food is the reality upon which people act.

FATNESS AND CROSS-CULTURAL STANDARDS OF BEAUTY IN WOMEN

Culturally defined standards of beauty vary between societies. In a classic example, Malcom (1925) describes the custom of "fattening huts" for elite Efik pubescent girls in traditional Nigeria. A girl spent up to 2 years in seclusion and at the end of this rite of passage possessed symbols of womanhood and marriageability—a three-tiered hairstyle, clitoridectomy, and fatness. Fatness was a primary criterion of beauty as it was defined by the elites, who alone had the economic resources to participate in this custom. Similarly, fatter brides demand significantly higher bridewealth payments among the Kipsigis of Kenya (Borgerhoff Mulder 1988).

Among the Havasupai of the American Southwest, if a girl is thin at puberty, a fat woman "stands" (places her foot) on the girl's back so she will become attractively plump. In this society, fat legs and, to a lesser extent, arms are considered essential to beauty. The Tarahumara of northern Mexico consider fat legs a fundamental aspect of the ideal feminine body; an attractive woman is called a "beautiful thigh." Among the Amhara of Ethiopia in northern East Africa, thin hips are called "dog hips" in a typical insult (Messing 1957).

It is difficult to know how widespread among the world's cultures is the association of plumpness and beauty. A preliminary indication can be found through a cross-cultural survey based on data from the Human Relations Area Files (a cross-indexed compilation of ethnographic information on more than 300 of the most thoroughly studied societies). The results of this survey are summarized in Table 1. Although conclusions made from these data are weak because of the

TABLE 1 Cross-Cultural Standards of Female Beauty

	Number of societies	Percent of societies
Overall body		
Extreme obesity	0	0
Plump/moderately fat	31	81
Thin/abhorrence of fat	7	19
Breasts		
Large or long	9	50
Small/abhorrence of large	9	50
Hips and Legs		
Large or fat	9	90
Slender	1	10
Stature		
Tall	3	30
Moderate	6	60
Small	1	10

Source: Brown and Konner 1987.

small number and possibly nonrepresentative nature of the cases, as well as the fact that most ethnographies are difficult to code on this variable, some preliminary generalizations are possible. Cultural standards of beauty do not refer to physical extremes. No society on record has an ideal of extreme obesity. On the other hand, the desirability of "plumpness" or being "filled out" is found in 81 percent of the societies for which this variable can be coded. This standard, which probably includes the clinical categories of overweight and mild obesity, apparently refers to the desirability of fat deposits, particularly on the hips and legs.

Although cross-cultural variation is evident in standards of beauty, this variation falls within a certain range. American ideals of thinness occur in a setting in which it is easy to become fat, and preference for plumpness occurs in settings in which it is easy to remain lean. In context, both standards require the investment of individual effort and economic resources; furthermore, each in its context involves a display of wealth. Cultural beliefs about attractive body shape in mainstream American culture place pressure on females to lose weight and are involved in the etiology of anorexia and bulimia.

IDEAL BODY-TYPE, SIZE, AND SYMBOLIC POWER IN MEN

The ethnographic record concerning body preferences for males is extremely weak, yet preliminary research suggests a universal preference for a muscular physique and for tall or moderately tall stature. In general, members of all human societies appear to admire large body size as an attribute of attractiveness in men, because it symbolizes health, economic success, political power, and social status. "Big men," political leaders in tribal New Guinea, are described by their constituents in terms of their size and physical well-being: He is a man "whose skin swells with 'grease' [fat] underneath" (Strahern 1971). The spiritual power (*mana*) and noble breeding of a Polynesian chief is expected to be seen in his large size. In American society vestiges of a similar idea remain; for example, a "fat cat" is a wealthy and powerful man who can "throw his weight around." The political metaphor of weight and power in American society has been explored by social historians. Most male college students in the U.S., in contrast with women, want to gain weight because it is equivalent to gaining muscle mass and physical power in a process called "bulking up."

CONCLUSIONS

Two sets of conclusions can be drawn from this discussion of culture and its relationship to obesity—one practical and one theoretical. First, recognition of cultural variation in beliefs and behaviors related to obesity needs to be incorporated into health programs aimed at reducing the prevalence of obesity. The second conclusion regards the need for more research on the role of culture, as it interacts with genes, on the etiology of obesity.

The Importance of Culture in Health Interventions

Existing cultural beliefs must be taken into account in the design and implementation of health promotion projects. In an obesity prevention campaign in a Zulu community outside of Durban, one health education poster depicted an obese woman and an overloaded truck with a flat tire, with a caption "Both carry too much weight." Another poster showed a slender woman easily sweeping under a table next to an obese woman who was using the table for support; it had the caption "Who do you prefer to look like?" The intended message of these posters was misinterpreted by the community because of a cultural connection between obesity and social status. The woman in the first poster was perceived to be rich and happy, since she was not only fat but had a truck overflowing with her possessions. The second poster was perceived as a scene of an affluent mistress directing her underfed servant.

Health interventions must be culturally acceptable, and we cannot assume that people place the highest priority on their health. The idea of reducing

risk factors for chronic diseases that may develop later may not be an effective strategy for populations who do not feel empowered or who live in a fundamentally risky world.

Implications for the Etiology of Obesity

The frequency of past food shortages, the social distribution of obesity, and the cultural meanings of fatness, when taken together, suggest a biocultural hypothesis of the evolution of obesity. Both genetic and cultural predispositions to obesity may be products of the same evolutionary pressures, involving two related processes: first, genetic traits that cause fatness were selected because they improved chances of survival in the face of food scarcities, particularly for pregnant and nursing women; second, in the context of unequal access to food, fatness may have been socially selected because it is a cultural symbol of social prestige and an index of general health. Under Western conditions of abundance, our biological tendency to regulate body weight at levels above our ideal cannot be easily controlled even with a reversal of the widespread cultural ideal of plumpness.

This evolutionary model is obviously congruent with the current etiological theory about obesity, which combines genetic predispositions with "environmental" causes. Recent research both in epidemiology and human laboratory research demonstrates without a doubt the central role of genetic heredity in the etiology of obesity. Similar genetic evidence exists for variables like the distribution of fat on the body and basal metabolic rates. To an anthropologist, these important studies are welcome and expected.

The recent advances in understanding the genetic bases of obesity remind us, however, of our ignorance about the precise role of the "environment." One problem is that "environment" has been poorly defined and treated as if it were idiosyncratic for every individual or family. Another problem is that "environment" is essentially treated as a residual category—one that cannot be explained by genetic heredity. This paper has attempted to show how the anthropological concept of culture may be useful in conceptualization of the different components of the "environment" and the generation of hypotheses for future research in behavioral medicine.

The most convincing demonstrations of a strong genetic component for obesity have been in populations with relatively high levels of cultural homogeneity. In social contexts like Denmark, Iowa, or among Pima Indians, the influence of culture—including learned behaviors and beliefs—is minimized by the sample selected for study in order to emphasize the importance of genotypical variation. Essentially, cultural variation has been treated as if it were "noise." An essential goal in future research must be the identification of specific cultural factors—whether economic, social, or ideological—that predispose people to obesity.

From the standpoint of the prevention of obesity, it is critical to stress that genetic predisposition is not destiny. Genetic predispositions to obesity have apparently been maintained in populations throughout most of our species' history, yet it has rarely been expressed phenotypically. Culture is adaptive because it can be changed. Habitual patterns of behavior—of an individual or an entire society—can be changed to reduce morbidity and mortality linked to obesity and overweight. These changes must include social and political efforts to reduce the risk of hunger and food scarcity, even in affluent societies.

REFERENCES

Bohannan, P., and L. Bohannan. 1969. *A Source Notebook on Tiv Religion.* New Haven, CT: Human Relations Area Files.

Borgerhoff Mulder, M. 1988. Kipsigis Bridewealth Payments. In *Human Reproductive Behavior,* L. Betzig, M. Borgerhoff Mulder, and P. Turke, eds. Pp. 65–82. Cambridge: Cambridge University Press.

Bray, G. A. 1987. Overweight Is Risking Fate: Definition, Classification, Prevalence and Risks. In *Human Obesity,* R. J. Wurtman and J. J. Wurtman, eds. *Annals of the New York Academy of Sciences* 499:14–28.

Brown, P. J., and M. Konner. 1987. An Anthropological Perspective on Obesity. In *Human Obesity,* R. J. Wurtman and J. J. Wurtman, eds. *Annals of the New York Academy of Sciences* 499:29–46.

Centers for Disease Control. 1989. Prevalence of Overweight —Behavioral Risk Factor Surveillance System, 1987. *Morbidity and Mortality Weekly Report* 38:421–423.

Chernin, K. 1981. *The Obsession: Reflections on the Tyranny of Slenderness.* New York: Harper & Row.

Cohen, M. N., and G. J. Armelagos, eds. 1984. *Paleopathology at the Origins of Agriculture.* New York: Academic Press.

Eaton, S. B., M. Shostak, and M. Konner. 1988. *The Paleolithic Prescription.* New York: Harper & Row.

Frisch, R. E. 1987. Body Fat, Menarche, Fitness and Fertility. *Human Reproduction* 2:521–533.

Gardner, L. I., M. P. Stern, S. M. Haffner, S. P. Gaskill, H. Hazuda, and J. H. Relethford. 1984. Prevalence of Diabetes in Mexican Americans. *Diabetes* 33:86–92.

Gurney, M., and J. Gorstein. 1988. The Global Prevalence of Obesity—An Initial Overview of Available Data. *World Health Statistics Quarterly* 41:251–254.

Kissebah, A. H., D. S. Freedman, and A. N. Peiris. 1989. Health Risks of Obesity. *Medical Clinics of North America* 73:11–138.

Lee, R. B. 1979. *The !Kung Sun: Men, Women, and Work in a Foraging Society.* Cambridge, MA: Harvard University Press.

Malcom, L. W. G. 1925. Note on the Seclusion of Girls Among the Efik at Old Calabar. *Man* 25:113–114.

Massara, E. B. 1989. *Que Gordita! A Study of Weight Among Women in a Puerto Rican Community.* New York: AMS Press.

Messing, S. D. 1957. *The Highland Plateau Amhara of Ethiopia.* Ph.D. dissertation, Department of Anthropology, University of Pennsylvania, Philadelphia.

Ravussin, E., S. Lillioja, and W. C. Knowler, et al. 1988. Reduced Rate of Energy Expenditure as a Risk Factor for Body-Weight Gain. *New England Journal of Medicine* 318:467–472.

Ritenbaugh, C. 1982. Obesity as a Culture-Bound Syndrome. *Culture, Medicine and Psychiatry* 6:347–361.

Strahern, A. 1971. *The Rope of Moka.* New York: Cambridge University Press.

Stunkard, A. J., T. I. A. Sorenson, C. Hanis, T. W. Teasdale, R. Chakaborty, W. J. Schull, and F. Schulsinger. 1986. An Adoption Study of Obesity. *New England Journal of Medicine* 314:193–198.

Stunkard, A. J., J. R. Harris, N. L. Pedersen, and G. McClearn. 1990. The Body-Mass Index of Twins Who Have Been Reared Apart. *New England Journal of Medicine* 322:1483–1487.

Trowell, H. C., and D. P. Burkitt. 1981. *Western Diseases: Their Emergence and Prevention.* Cambridge, MA: Harvard University Press.

Whiting, M. G. 1958. *A Cross-Cultural Nutrition Survey.* Doctoral Dissertation, Harvard School of Public Health, Cambridge.

Wurtman, R. J., and J. J. Wurtman, eds. 1987. *Human Obesity.* Annals of the New York Academy of Sciences 499.

13

The Worst Mistake in the History of the Human Race

Jared Diamond

What we eat and how we eat are important both nutritionally and culturally. This selection suggests that how we get what we eat—through gathering and hunting versus agriculture, for example—has dramatic consequences. This seems pretty obvious. We all imagine what a struggle it must have been before the development of agriculture. We think of our ancestors spending their days searching for roots and berries to eat, or out at the crack of dawn, hunting wild animals. In fact, this was not quite the case. Nevertheless, isn't it really better simply to go to the refrigerator, open the door, and reach for a container of milk to pour into a bowl of flaked grain for your regular morning meal? What could be simpler and more nutritious?

There are many things that we seldom question; the truth seems so evident and the answers obvious. One such sacred cow is the tremendous prosperity brought about by the agricultural revolution. This selection is a thought-provoking introduction to the connection between culture and agriculture. The transition from food foraging to farming (what archaeologists call the Neolithic revolution) may have been the worst mistake in human history or its most important event. You be the judge. But for better or worse, this cultural evolution has occurred, and the world will never be the same again.

As you read this selection, ask yourself the following questions:

- What is the fundamental difference between the progressivist view and the revisionist interpretation?
- How did the development of agriculture affect people's health?
- What three reasons explain the changes brought about by the development of agriculture?
- How did the development of agriculture affect social equality, including gender equality?

The following terms discussed in this selection are included in the Glossary at the back of the book:

agricultural development

civilization

domestication of plants and animals

hunter-gatherers

Neolithic

paleontology

paleopathology

social stratification

To science we owe dramatic changes in our smug self-image. Astronomy taught us that our earth isn't the center of the universe but merely one of billions of heavenly bodies. From biology we learned that we weren't specially created by God but evolved along with millions of other species. Now archaeology is demolishing another sacred belief: that human history over the past million years has been a long tale of progress. In particular, recent discoveries suggest that the adoption of agriculture, supposedly our most decisive step toward a better life, was in many ways a catastrophe from which we have never recovered. With agriculture came the gross social and sexual inequality, the disease and despotism, that curse our existence.

At first, the evidence against this revisionist interpretation will strike twentieth-century Americans as irrefutable. We're better off in almost every respect than the people of the Middle Ages, who in turn had it easier than cavemen, who in turn were better off than apes. Just count our advantages. We enjoy the most

Jared Diamond/© 1987 *Discover* magazine.

abundant and varied foods, the best tools and material goods, some of the longest and healthiest lives, in history. Most of us are safe from starvation and predators. We get our energy from oil and machines, not from our sweat. What neo-Luddite among us would trade his life for that of a medieval peasant, a caveman, or an ape?

For most of our history we supported ourselves by hunting and gathering: we hunted wild animals and foraged for wild plants. It's a life that philosophers have traditionally regarded as nasty, brutish, and short. Since no food is grown and little is stored, there is (in this view) no respite from the struggle that starts anew each day to find wild foods and avoid starving. Our escape from this misery was facilitated only 10,000 years ago, when in different parts of the world people began to domesticate plants and animals. The agricultural revolution gradually spread until today it's nearly universal, and few tribes of hunter-gatherers survive.

From the progressivist perspective on which I was brought up, to ask "Why did almost all our hunter-gatherer ancestors adopt agriculture?" is silly. Of course they adopted it because agriculture is an efficient way to get more food for less work. Planted crops yield far more tons per acre than roots and berries. Just imagine a band of savages, exhausted from searching for nuts or chasing wild animals, suddenly gazing for the first time at a fruit-laden orchard or a pasture full of sheep. How many milliseconds do you think it would take them to appreciate the advantages of agriculture?

The progressivist party line sometimes even goes so far as to credit agriculture with the remarkable flowering of art that has taken place over the past few thousand years. Since crops can be stored, and since it takes less time to pick food from a garden than to find it in the wild, agriculture gave us free time that hunter-gatherers never had. Thus it was agriculture that enabled us to build the Parthenon and compose the B-minor Mass.

While the case for the progressivist view seems overwhelming, it's hard to prove. How do you show that the lives of people 10,000 years ago got better when they abandoned hunting and gathering for farming? Until recently, archaeologists had to resort to indirect tests, whose results (surprisingly) failed to support the progressivist view. Here's one example of an indirect test: Are twentieth-century hunter-gatherers really worse off than farmers? Scattered throughout the world, several dozen groups of so-called primitive people, like the Kalahari Bushmen, continue to support themselves that way. It turns out that these people have plenty of leisure time, sleep a good deal, and work less hard than their farming

neighbors. For instance, the average time devoted each week to obtaining food is only 12 to 19 hours for one group of Bushmen, 14 hours or less for the Hadza nomads of Tanzania. One Bushman, when asked why he hadn't emulated neighboring tribes by adopting agriculture, replied, "Why should we, when there are so many mongongo nuts in the world?"

While farmers concentrate on high-carbohydrate crops like rice and potatoes, the mix of wild plants and animals in the diets of surviving hunter-gatherers provides more protein and a better balance of other nutrients. In one study, the Bushmen's average daily food intake (during a month when food was plentiful) was 2,140 calories and 93 grams of protein, considerably greater than the recommended daily allowance for people of their size. It's almost inconceivable that Bushmen, who eat 75 or so wild plants, could die of starvation the way hundreds of thousands of Irish farmers and their families did during the potato famine of the 1840s.

So the lives of at least the surviving hunter-gatherers aren't nasty and brutish, even though farmers have pushed them into some of the world's worst real estate. But modern hunter-gatherer societies that have rubbed shoulders with farming societies for thousands of years don't tell us about conditions before the agricultural revolution. The progressivist view is really making a claim about the distant past: that the lives of primitive people improved when they switched from gathering to farming. Archaeologists can date that switch by distinguishing remains of wild plants and animals from those of domesticated ones in prehistoric garbage dumps.

How can one deduce the health of the prehistoric garbage makers, and thereby directly test the progressivist view? That question has become answerable only in recent years, in part through the newly emerging techniques of paleopathology, the study of signs of disease in the remains of ancient peoples.

In some lucky situations, the paleopathologist has almost as much material to study as a pathologist today. For example, archaeologists in the Chilean deserts found well preserved mummies whose medical conditions at time of death could be determined by autopsy. And feces of long-dead Indians who lived in dry caves in Nevada remain sufficiently well preserved to be examined for hookworm and other parasites.

Usually the only human remains available for study are skeletons, but they permit a surprising number of deductions. To begin with, a skeleton reveals its owner's sex, weight, and approximate age. In the few cases where there are many skeletons, one can construct mortality tables like the ones life insurance companies use to calculate expected life span and risk of death at any given age. Paleopathologists can also calculate growth rates by measuring bones of people of different ages, examining teeth for enamel defects (signs of childhood malnutrition), and recognizing scars left on bones by anemia, tuberculosis, leprosy, and other diseases.

One straightforward example of what pale-opathologists have learned from skeletons concerns historical changes in height. Skeletons from Greece and Turkey show that the average height of hunter-gatherers toward the end of the ice ages was a gener-ous 5'9" for men, 5'5" for women. With the adoption of agriculture, height crashed, and by 3000 B.C. had reached a low of only 5'3" for men, 5' for women. By classical times heights were very slowly on the rise again, but modern Greeks and Turks have still not regained the average height of their distant ancestors.

Another example of paleopathology at work is the study of Indian skeletons from burial mounds in the Illinois and Ohio river valleys. At Dickson Mounds, located near the confluence of the Spoon and Illinois Rivers, archaeologists have excavated some 800 skele-tons that paint a picture of the health changes that occurred when a hunter-gatherer culture gave way to intensive maize farming around A.D. 1150. Studies by George Armelagos and his colleagues then at the Uni-versity of Massachusetts show these early farmers paid a price for their new-found livelihood. Compared to the hunter-gatherers who preceded them, the farm-ers had a nearly 50 percent increase in enamel defects indicative of malnutrition, a fourfold increase in iron-deficiency anemia (evidenced by a bone condition called porotic hyperostosis), a threefold rise in bone lesions reflecting infectious disease in general, and an increase in degenerative conditions of the spine, prob-ably reflecting a lot of hard physical labor. "Life expectancy at birth in the pre-agricultural community was about twenty-six years," says Armelagos, "but in the post-agricultural community it was nineteen years. So these episodes of nutritional stress and infec-tious disease were seriously affecting their ability to survive."

The evidence suggests that the Indians at Dickson Mounds, like many other primitive peoples, took up farming not by choice but from necessity in order to feed their constantly growing numbers. "I don't think most hunter-gatherers farmed until they had to, and when they switched to farming they traded quality for quantity," says Mark Cohen of the State University of New York at Plattsburgh, co-editor, with Armelagos, of one of the seminal books in the field, *Paleopathology at the Origins of Agriculture*. "When I first started mak-ing that argument ten years ago, not many people agreed with me. Now it's become a respectable, albeit controversial, side of the debate."

There are at least three sets of reasons to explain the findings that agriculture was bad for health. First, hunter-gatherers enjoyed a varied diet, while early farmers obtained most of their food from one or a few starchy crops. The farmers gained cheap calories at the cost of poor nutrition. (Today just three high-carbohydrate plants—wheat, rice, and corn—provide the bulk of the calories consumed by the human species, yet each one is deficient in certain vitamins or amino acids essential to life.) Second, because of dependence on a limited number of crops, farmers ran the risk of starvation if one crop failed. Finally, the mere fact that agriculture encouraged people to clump together in crowded societies, many of which then car-ried on trade with other crowded societies, led to the spread of parasites and infectious disease. (Some archaeologists think it was crowding, rather than agri-culture, that promoted disease, but this is a chicken-and-egg argument, because crowding encourages agriculture and vice versa.) Epidemics couldn't take hold when populations were scattered in small bands that constantly shifted camp. Tuberculosis and diar-rheal disease had to await the rise of farming, measles and bubonic plague the appearance of large cities.

Besides malnutrition, starvation, and epidemic diseases, farming helped bring another curse upon humanity: deep class divisions. Hunter-gatherers have little or no stored food, and no concentrated food sources, like an orchard or a herd of cows: they live off the wild plants and animals they obtain each day. Therefore, there can be no kings, no class of social par-asites who grow fat on food seized from others. Only in farming populations could a healthy, non-producing elite set itself above the disease-ridden masses. Skeletons from Greek tombs at Mycenae *c.* 1500 B.C. suggest that royals enjoyed a better diet than commoners, since the royal skeletons were two or three inches taller and had better teeth (on the average, one instead of six cavities or missing teeth). Among Chilean mummies from *c.* A.D. 1000, the élite were dis-tinguished not only by ornaments and gold hair clips but also by a fourfold lower rate of bone lesions caused by disease.

Similar contrasts in nutrition and health persist on a global scale today. To people in rich countries like the U.S., it sounds ridiculous to extol the virtues of hunt-ing and gathering. But Americans are an élite, depend-ent on oil and minerals that must often be imported from countries with poorer health and nutrition. If one could choose between being a peasant farmer in Ethiopia or a Bushman gatherer in the Kalahari, which do you think would be the better choice?

Farming may have encouraged inequality be-tween the sexes, as well. Freed from the need to trans-port their babies during a nomadic existence, and under pressure to produce more hands to till the fields, farming women tended to have more frequent pregnancies than their hunter-gatherer counterparts— with consequent drains on their health. Among the Chilean mummies, for example, more women than men had bone lesions from infectious disease.

Women in agricultural societies were sometimes made beasts of burden. In New Guinea farming communities today I often see women staggering under loads of vegetables and firewood while the men walk empty-handed. Once while on a field trip there studying birds, I offered to pay some villagers to carry supplies from an airstrip to my mountain camp. The heaviest item was a 110-pound bag of rice, which I lashed to a pole and assigned to a team of four men to shoulder together. When I eventually caught up with the villagers, the men were carrying light loads, while one small woman weighing less than the bag of rice was bent under it, supporting its weight by a cord across her temples.

As for the claim that agriculture encouraged the flowering of art by providing us with leisure time, modern hunter-gatherers have at least as much free time as do farmers. The whole emphasis on leisure time as a critical factor seems to me misguided. Gorillas have had ample free time to build their own Parthenon, had they wanted to. While post-agricultural technological advances did make new art forms possible and preservation of art easier, great paintings and sculptures were already being produced by hunter-gatherers 15,000 years ago, and were still being produced as recently as the last century by such hunter-gatherers as some Eskimos and the Indians of the Pacific Northwest.

Thus with the advent of agriculture an élite became better off, but most people became worse off. Instead of swallowing the progressivist party line that we chose agriculture because it was good for us, we must ask how we got trapped by it despite its pitfalls.

One answer boils down to the adage "Might makes right." Farming could support many more people than hunting, albeit with a poorer quality of life. (Population densities of hunter-gatherers are rarely over one person per ten square miles, while farmers average 100 times that.) Partly, this is because a field planted entirely in edible crops lets one feed far more mouths than a forest with scattered edible plants. Partly, too, it's because nomadic hunter-gatherers have to keep their children spaced at four-year intervals by infanti-

cide and other means, since a mother must carry her toddler until it's old enough to keep up with the adults. Because farm women don't have that burden, they can and often do bear a child every two years.

As population densities of hunter-gatherers slowly rose at the end of the ice ages, bands had to choose between feeding more mouths by taking the first steps toward agriculture, or else finding ways to limit growth. Some bands chose the former solution, unable to anticipate the evils of farming, and seduced by the transient abundance they enjoyed until population growth caught up with increased food production. Such bands outbred and then drove off or killed the bands that chose to remain hunter-gatherers, because a hundred malnourished farmers can still outfight one healthy hunter. It's not that hunter-gatherers abandoned their life style, but that those sensible enough not to abandon it were forced out of all areas except the ones farmers didn't want.

At this point it's instructive to recall the common complaint that archaeology is a luxury, concerned with the remote past, and offering no lessons for the present. Archaeologists studying the rise of farming have reconstructed a crucial stage at which we made the worst mistake in human history. Forced to choose between limiting population or trying to increase food production, we chose the latter and ended up with starvation, warfare, and tyranny.

Hunter-gatherers practiced the most successful and longest-lasting life style in human history. In contrast, we're still struggling with the mess into which agriculture has tumbled us, and it's unclear whether we can solve it. Suppose that an archaeologist who had visited us from outer space were trying to explain human history to his fellow spacelings. He might illustrate the results of his digs by a 24-hour clock on which one hour represents 100,000 years of real past time. If the history of the human race began at midnight, then we would now be almost at the end of our first day. We lived as hunter-gatherers for nearly the whole of that day, from midnight through dawn, noon, and sunset. Finally, at 11:54 p.m., we adopted agriculture. As our second midnight approaches, will the plight of famine-stricken peasants gradually spread to engulf us all? Or will we somehow achieve those seductive blessings that we imagine behind agriculture's glittering façade, and that have so far eluded us?

14

The Domestication of Wood in Haiti

A Case Study in Applied Evolution

Gerald F. Murray

In its annual report on the state of the planet, the Worldwatch Institute describes the growing shortage of wood for fuel and construction throughout the Third World. The problem is most acute in densely populated areas with a long history of agriculture. In these areas, peasant farmers or members of their families can spend several hours each day finding firewood. Because forests take such a long time to grow and such a short time to cut down, reforestation is a worldwide ecological challenge.

As described in this selection, Haiti has a severe deforestation problem that is closely related to wider issues of poverty and overpopulation. In this context, traditional reforestation projects, with ponderous educational components on the value of trees, had failed miserably. Anthropologist Gerald Murray, who had done research on land tenure among rural Haitian peasants, had the rare opportunity to design and implement an alternative project in forestry and agricultural development. His anthropological understanding of the economic system and culture of the Haitian people clearly paid off. The project represents applied cultural anthropology at its best.

As you read this selection, ask yourself the following questions:

- Why does Haiti have a deforestation problem?
- How was Gerald Murray's anthropological alternative project different from traditional reforestation programs?
- Why was using particular kinds of trees important for the project?
- What accounted for the Haitian peasants' enthusiasm for the idea of trees as a cash crop?
- What is meant by the title of this piece?

The following terms discussed in this selection are included in the Glossary at the back of the book:

arable land

cadastral

domestication of plants and animals

horticulture

population pressure

reforestation

swidden cultivation

usufruct rights

PROBLEM AND CLIENT

Expatriate tree lovers, whether tourists or developmental planners, often leave Haiti with an upset stomach. Though during precolonial times the island Arawaks had reached a compromise with the forest, their market-oriented colonial successors saw trees as something to be removed. The Spaniards specialized in exporting wood from the eastern side of the island, whereas the French on the western third found it more profitable to clear the wood and produce sugar cane, coffee, and indigo for European markets. During the nineteenth century, long after Haiti had become an independent republic, foreign lumber companies cut and exported most of the nation's precious hardwoods, leaving little for today's peasants.

The geometric increase in population since colonial times—from an earlier population of fewer than half a million former slaves to a contemporary population of more than six million—and the resulting

From *Anthropological Praxis*, Robert M. Wulff and Shirley J. Fiske, eds., 1987. Copyright © 1987 by Westview Press. Reprinted by permission of Westview Press.

shrinkage of average family holding size have led to the evolution of a land use system devoid of systematic fallow periods. A vicious cycle has set in—one that seems to have targeted the tree for ultimate destruction. Not only has land pressure eliminated a regenerative fallow phase in the local agricultural cycle; in addition the catastrophic declines in per hectare food yields have forced peasants into alternative income-generating strategies. Increasing numbers crowd into the capital city, Port-au-Prince, creating a market for construction wood and charcoal. Poorer sectors of the peasantry in the rural areas respond to this market by racing each other with axes and machetes to cut down the few natural tree stands remaining in remoter regions of the republic. The proverbial snowball in Hades is at less risk than a tree in Haiti.

Unable to halt the flows either of wood into the cities or of soil into the oceans, international development organizations finance studies to measure the volume of these flows (50 million trees cut per year is one of the round figures being bandied about) and to predict when the last tree will be cut from Haiti. Reforestation projects have generally been entrusted by their well-meaning but short-sighted funders to Duvalier's Ministry of Agriculture, a kiss-of-death resource channeling strategy by which the Port-au-Prince jobs created frequently outnumber the seedlings produced. And even the few seedlings produced often died in the nurseries because the peasants were understandably reluctant to cover their scarce holdings with state-owned trees. Project managers had been forced to resort to "food for work" strategies to move seedlings out of nurseries onto hillsides. And peasants have endeavored where possible to plant the trees on somebody else's hillsides and to enlist their livestock as allies in the subsequent removal of this dangerous vegetation.

This generalized hostility to tree projects placed the U.S. Agency for International Development (AID)/Haiti mission in a bind. After several years of absence from Haiti in the wake of expulsion by Francois Duvalier, AID had reestablished its presence under the government of his son Jean Claude. But an ambitious Integrated Agricultural Development Project funded through the Ministry of Agriculture had already given clear signs of being a multimillion-dollar farce. And an influential congressman chairing the U.S. House Ways and Means Committee—consequently exercising strong control over AID funds worldwide—had taken a passionate interest in Haiti. In his worldwide travels this individual had become adept at detecting and exposing developmental charades. And he had been blunt in communicating his conviction that much of what he had seen in

AID/Haiti's program was precisely that. He had been touched by the plight of Haiti and communicated to the highest AID authorities his conviction about the salvific power of contraceptives and trees and his determination to have AID grace Haiti with an abundant flow of both. And he would personally visit Haiti (a convenient plane ride from Washington, D.C.) to inspect for himself, threatening a worldwide funding freeze if no results were forthcoming. A chain reaction of nervous "yes sirs" speedily worked its way down from AID headquarters in Washington to a beleaguered Port-au-Prince mission.

The pills and condoms were less of a problem. Even the most cantankerous congressman was unlikely to insist on observing them in use and would probably settle for household distribution figures. Not so with the trees. He could (and did) pooh-pooh nursery production figures and asked to be taken to see the new AID forests, a most embarrassing request in a country where peasants creatively converted daytime reforestation projects into nocturnal goat forage projects. AID's reaction was twofold—first, to commission an immediate study to explain to the congressman and others why peasants refused to plant trees (for this they called down an AID economist); and second, to devise some program strategy that would achieve the apparently unachievable: to instill in cash-needy, defiant, pleasant charcoalmakers a love, honor, and respect for newly planted trees. For this attitudinal transformation, a task usually entrusted to the local armed forces, AID/Haiti invited an anthropologist to propose an alternative approach.

PROCESS AND PLAYERS

During these dynamics, I completed a doctoral dissertation on the manner in which Haitian peasant land tenure had evolved in response to internal population growth. The AID economist referred to above exhaustively reviewed the available literature, also focusing on the issue of Haitian peasant land tenure, and produced for the mission a well-argued monograph (Zuvekas 1978) documenting a lower rate of landlessness in Haiti than in many other Latin American settings but documenting as well the informal, extralegal character of the relationship between many peasant families and their landholdings. This latter observation was interpreted by some in the mission to mean that the principal determinant of the failure of tree planting projects was the absence among peasants of legally secure deeds over their plots. Peasants could not be expected to invest money on land improvements when at mildest the benefits could accrue to another and at worst the very improvements themselves could lead to expropriation from their land. In short, no massive tree planting could be expected, according to this model, until a nationwide cadastral reform granted plot-by-plot deeds to peasant families.

This hypothesis was reputable but programmatically paralyzing because nobody dreamed that the Duvalier regime was about to undertake a major cadastral reform for the benefit of peasants. Several AID officers in Haiti had read my dissertation on land tenure (Murray 1977), and I received an invitation to advise the mission. Was Haitian peasant land tenure compatible with tree planting? Zuvekas' study had captured the internally complex nature of Haitian peasant land tenure. But the subsequent extrapolations as to paralyzing insecurity simply did not seem to fit with ethnographic evidence. In two reports (Murray 1978a, 1978b) I indicated that peasants in general feel secure about their ownership rights over their land. Failure to secure plot-by-plot surveyed deeds is generally a cost-saving measure. Interclass evictions did occur, but they were statistically rare; instead most land disputes were intrafamilial. A series of extralegal tenure practices had evolved—preinheritance land grants to young adult dependents, informal inheritance subdivisions witnessed by community members, fictitious sales to favored children, complex community-internal share-cropping arrangements. And though these practices produced an internally heterogeneous system with its complexities, there was strong internal order. Any chaos and insecurity tended to be more in the mind of observers external to the system than in the behavior of the peasants themselves. There was a danger that the complexities of Haitian peasant land tenure would generate an unintended smokescreen obscuring the genuine causes of failure in tree planting projects.

What then were these genuine causes? The mission, intent on devising programming strategies in this domain, invited me to explore further, under a contract aimed at identifying the "determinants of success and failure" in reforestation and soil conservation projects. My major conclusion was that the preexisting land tenure, cropping, and livestock systems in peasant Haiti were perfectly adequate for the undertaking of significant tree planting activities. Most projects had failed not because of land tenure or attitudinal barriers among peasants but because of fatal flaws in one or more key project components. Though my contract called principally for analysis of previous or existing projects, I used the recommendation section of the report to speculate on how a Haiti-wise anthropologist would program and manage reforestation activities if he or she had the authority. In verbal debriefings I jokingly challenged certain young program officers in the mission to give me a jeep and carte blanche access to a $50,000 checking account, and I would prove my anthropological assertions about peasant economic behavior and produce more trees in the ground than their current multimillion-dollar Ministry of Agriculture charade. We had a good laugh and shook hands, and I departed confident that the report would be as dutifully perused and as honorably filed and forgotten as similar reports I had done elsewhere.

To my great disbelief, as I was correcting Anthro 101 exams some two years later, one of the program officers still in Haiti called to say that an Agroforestry Outreach Project (AOP) had been approved chapter and verse as I had recommended it; and that if I was interested in placing my life where my mouth had been and would leave the ivory tower to direct the project, my project bank account would have not $50,000, but $4 million. After several weeks of hemming and hawing and vigorous negotiating for leave from my department, I accepted the offer and entered a new (to me) role of project director in a strange upside-down world in which the project anthropologist was not a powerless cranky voice from the bleachers but the chief of party with substantial authority over general project policy and the allocation of project resources. My elation at commanding resources to implement anthropological ideas was dampened by the nervousness of knowing exactly who would be targeted for flak and ridicule if these ideas bombed out, as most tended to do in the Haiti of Duvalier.

The basic structural design of AOP followed a tripartite conceptual framework that I proposed for analyzing projects. Within this framework a project is composed of three essential systemic elements: a technical base, a benefit flow strategy, and an institutional delivery strategy. Planning had to focus equally on all three; I argued that defects in one would sabotage the entire project.

Technical Strategy

The basic technical strategy was to make available to peasants fast-growing wood trees (*Leucaena leucocephala, Cassia siamea, Azadirachta indica, Casuarina equisetifolia, Eucalyptus camaldulensis*) that were not only drought resistant but also rapid growing, producing possible four-year harvest rotations in humid lowland areas (and slower rotations and lower survival rates in arid areas) and that were good for charcoal and basic construction needs. Most of the species mentioned also restore nutrients to the soil, and some of them coppice from a carefully harvested stump, producing several rotations before the need for replanting.

Of equally critical technical importance was the use of a nursery system that produced lightweight microseedlings. A project pickup truck could transport over 15,000 of these microseedlings (as opposed to 250 traditional bag seedlings), and the average peasant could easily carry over 500 transportable seedlings at one time, planting them with a fraction of the ground preparation time and labor required for bulkier bagged seedlings. The anthropological implications of this nursery system were critical. It constituted a technical breakthrough that reduced to a fraction the fossil-fuel and human energy expenditure required to transport and plant trees.

But the technical component of the project incorporated yet another element: the physical juxtaposition of trees and crops. In traditional reforestation models, the trees are planted in large unbroken monocropped stands. Such forests or woodlots presuppose local land tenure and economic arrangements not found in Haiti. For the tree to make its way as a cultivate into the economy of Haitian peasants and most other tropical cultivators, reforestation models would have to be replaced by agroforestry models that entail spatial or temporal juxtaposition of crops and trees. Guided by prior ethnographic knowledge of Haitian cropping patterns, AOP worked out with peasants various border planting and intercropping strategies to make tree planting feasible even for small holding cultivators.

Benefit Flow Strategies

With respect to the second systemic component, the programming of benefit flows to participants, earlier projects had often committed the fatal flaw of defining project trees planted as *pyebwa leta* (the state's trees). Authoritarian assertions by project staff concerning sanctions for cutting newly planted trees created fears among peasants that even trees planted on their own land would be government property. And several peasants were frank in reporting fears that the trees might eventually be used as a pretext by the government or the "Company" (the most common local lexeme used to refer to projects) for eventually expropriating the land on which peasants had planted project trees.

Such ambiguities and fears surrounding benefit flows paralyze even the technically soundest project. A major anthropological feature of AOP was a radical frontal attack on the issue of property and usufruct rights over project trees. Whereas other projects had criticized tree cutting, AOP promulgated the heretical message that trees were meant to be cut, processed, and sold. The only problem with the present system, according to project messages, was that peasants were cutting nature's trees. But once the landowner "mete fos li deyo" (expends his resources) and plants and cares for his or her own wood trees on his or her own

land, the landowner has the same right to harvest and sell wood as corn or beans.

I was inevitably impressed at the impact that this blunt message had when I delivered it to groups of prospective peasant tree planters. Haitian peasants are inveterate and aggressive cash-croppers; many of the crops and livestock that they produce are destined for immediate consignment to local markets. For the first time in their lives, they were hearing a concrete proposal to make the wood tree itself one more marketable crop in their inventory.

But the message would ring true only if three barriers were smashed.

1. The first concerned the feared delay in benefits. Most wood trees with which the peasants were familiar took an impractically long time to mature. There fortunately existed in Haiti four-year-old stands of leucaena, cassia, eucalyptus, and other project trees to which we could take peasant groups to demonstrate the growth speed of these trees.

2. But could they be planted on their scanty holdings without interfering with crops? Border and row planting techniques were demonstrated, as well as intercropping. The average peasant holding was about a hectare and a half. If a cultivator planted a field in the usual crops and then planted 500 seedlings in the same field at 2 meters by 2 meters, the seedlings would occupy only a fifth of a hectare. And they would be far enough apart to permit continued cropping for two or three cycles before shade competition became too fierce. That is, trees would be planted on only a fraction of the peasant's holdings and planted in such a way that they would be compatible with continued food growing even on the plots where they stood. We would then calculate with peasants the potential income to be derived from these 500 trees through sale as charcoal, polewood, or boards. In a best-case scenario, the gross take from the charcoal of these trees (the least lucrative use of the wood) might equal the current annual income of an average rural family. The income potential of these wood trees clearly would far offset any potential loss from decreased food production. Though it had taken AID two years to decide on the project, it took about twenty minutes with any group of skeptical but economically rational peasants to generate a list of enthusiastic potential tree planters.

3. But there was yet a third barrier. All this speculation about income generation presupposed that the peasants themselves, and not the government or the project, would be the sole owners of the

trees and that the peasants would have unlimited rights to the harvest of the wood whenever they wished. To deal with this issue, I presented the matter as an agreement between cultivator and the project: We would furnish the free seedlings and technical assistance; the cultivators would agree to plant 500 of these seedlings on their own land and permit project personnel to carry out periodic survival counts. We would, of course, pay no wages or "Food for Work" for this planting. But we would guarantee to the planters complete and exclusive ownership of the trees. They did not need to ask for permission from the project to harvest the trees whenever their needs might dictate, nor would there be any penalties associated with early cutting or low survival. If peasants changed their minds, they could rip out their seedlings six months after planting. They would never get any more free seedlings from us, but they would not be subject to any penalties. There are preexisting local forestry laws, rarely enforced, concerning permissions and minor taxes for tree cutting. Peasants would have to deal with these as they had skillfully done in the past. But from our project's point of view, we relinquish all tree ownership rights to the peasants who accept and plant the trees on their property.

Cash-flow dialogues and ownership assurances such as these were a far cry from the finger-wagging ecological sermons to which many peasant groups had been subjected on the topic of trees. Our project technicians developed their own messages; but central to all was the principle of peasant ownership and usufruct of AOP trees. The goal was to capitalize on the preexisting fuel and lumber markets, to make the wood tree one more crop in the income-generating repertoire of the Haitian peasant.

Institutional Strategy

The major potential fly in the ointment was the third component, the institutional component. To whom would AID entrust its funds to carry out this project? My own research had indicated clearly that Haitian governmental involvement condemned a project to certain paralysis and possible death, and my report phrased that conclusion as diplomatically as possible. The diplomacy was required to head off possible rage, less from Haitian officials than from certain senior officers in the AID mission who were politically and philosophically wedded to an institution-building strategy. Having equated the term "institution" with "government bureaucracy," and having defined their own career success in terms, not of village-level

resource flows, but of voluminous and timely bureaucracy-to-bureaucracy cash transfers, such officials were in effect marshaling U.S. resources into the service of extractive ministries with unparalleled track records of squandering and/or pilfering expatriate donor funds.

To the regime's paradoxical credit, however, the blatant openness and arrogance of Duvalierist predation had engendered an angry willingness in much of Haiti's development community to explore other resource flow channels. Though the nongovernmental character of the proposal provoked violent reaction, the reactionaries in the Haiti mission were overridden by their superiors in Washington, and a completely nongovernmental implementing mode was adopted for this project.

The system, based on private voluntary organizations (PVOs), worked as follows.

1. AID made a macrogrant to a Washington-based PVO (the Pan American Development Foundation, PADF) to run a tree-planting project based on the principles that had emerged in my research. At the Haiti mission's urging, PADF invited me to be chief of party for the project and located an experienced accountant in Haiti to be financial administrator. PADF in addition recruited three American agroforesters who, in addition to MA-level professional training, had several years of overseas village field experience under their belts. Early in the project they were supplemented by two other expatriates, a Belgian and a French Canadian. We opened a central office in Port-au-Prince and assigned a major region of Haiti to each of the agroforesters, who lived in their field regions.

2. These agroforesters were responsible for contacting the many village-based PVOs working in their regions to explain the project, to emphasize its microeconomic focus and its difference from traditional reforestation models, to discuss the conditions of entry therein, and to make technical suggestions as to the trees that would be appropriate for the region.

3. If the PVO was interested, we drafted an agreement in which our mutual contributions and spheres of responsibility were specified. The agreements were not drafted in French (Haiti's official language) but in Creole, the only language spoken by most peasants.

4. The local PVO selected *animateurs* (village organizers) who themselves were peasants who lived and worked in the village where trees would be planted. After receiving training from us, they contacted their neighbors and kin, generated lists

of peasants interested in planting a specified number of trees, and informed us when the local rains began to fall. At the proper moment we packed the seedlings in boxes customized to the particular region and shipped them on our trucks to the farmers, who would be waiting at specified drop-off points at a specified time. The trees were to be planted within twenty-four hours of delivery.

5. The animateurs were provided with Creole language data forms by which to gather ecological, land use, and land tenure data on each plot where trees would be planted and certain bits of information on each peasant participant. These forms were used to follow up, at periodic intervals, the survival of trees, the incidence of any problems (such as livestock depredation, burning, disease), and—above all—the manner in which the farmer integrated the trees into cropping and livestock patterns, to detect and head off any unintended substitution of food for wood.

RESULTS AND EVALUATION

The project was funded for four years from October 1981 through November 1985. During the writing of the project paper we were asked by an AID economist to estimate how many trees would be planted. Not knowing if the peasants would in fact plant any trees, we nervously proposed to reach two thousand peasant families with a million trees as a project goal. Fiddling with his programmed calculator, the economist informed us that that output would produce a negative internal rate of return. We would need at least two million trees to make the project worth AID's institutional while. We shrugged and told him cavalierly to up the figure and to promise three million trees on the land of six thousand peasants. (At that time I thought someone else would be directing the project.)

Numbers of Trees and Beneficiaries

Though I doubted that we could reach this higher goal, the response of the Haitian peasants to this new approach to tree planting left everyone, including myself, open mouthed. Within the first year of the project, one million trees had been planted by some 2,500 peasant households all over Haiti. My fears of peasant indifference were now transformed into nervousness that we could not supply seedlings fast enough to meet the demand triggered by our wood-as-a-cash-crop strategy. Apologetic village animateurs informed us that some cultivators who had not signed

up on the first lists were actually stealing newly planted seedlings from their neighbors' fields at night. They promised to catch the scoundrels. If they did, I told them, give the scoundrels a hug. Their pilfering was dramatic proof of the bull's-eye nature of the anthropological predictions that underlie the project.

By the end of the second year (when I left the project), we had reached the four-year goal of three million seedlings and the project had geared up and decentralized its nursery capacity to produce several million seedlings per season (each year having two planting seasons). Under the new director, a fellow anthropologist, the geometric increase continued. By the end of the fourth year, the project had planted, not its originally agreed-upon three million trees, but twenty million trees. Stated more accurately, some 75,000 Haitian peasants had enthusiastically planted trees on their own land. In terms of its quantitative outreach, AOP had more than quintupled its original goals.

Wood Harvesting and Wood Banking

By the end of its fourth year the project had already received an unusual amount of professional research attention by anthropologists, economists, and foresters. In addition to AID evaluations, six studies had been released on one or another aspect of the project (Ashley 1986; Balzano 1986; Buffum and King 1985; Conway 1986; Grosenick 1985; McGowan 1986). As predicted, many peasants were harvesting trees by the end of the fourth year. The most lucrative sale of the wood was as polewood in local markets, though much charcoal was also being made from project trees.

Interestingly, however, the harvesting was proceeding much more slowly than I had predicted. Peasants were "clinging" to their trees and not engaging in the clear cutting that I hoped would occur, as a prelude to the emergence of a rotational system in which peasants would alternate crops with tree cover that they themselves had planted. This technique would have been a revival, under a "domesticated" mode, of the ancient swidden sequence that had long since disappeared from Haiti. Though such a revival would have warmed anthropological hearts, the peasants had a different agenda. Though they had long ago removed nature's tree cover, they were extremely cautious about removing the tree cover that they had planted. Their economic logic was unassailable. Crop failure is so frequent throughout most of Haiti, and the market for wood and charcoal so secure, that peasants prefer to leave the tree as a "bank" against future emergencies. This arboreal bank makes particular sense in the context of the recent disappearance from Haiti of the peasant's traditional bank, the pig. A governmentally mandated (and U.S. financed) slaughter of all pigs because of fears of African swine fever created a peasant banking gap that AOP trees have now started to fill.

THE ANTHROPOLOGICAL DIFFERENCE

Anthropological findings, methods, and theories clearly have heavily influenced this project at all stages. We are dealing, not with an ongoing project affected by anthropological input, but with a project whose very existence was rooted in anthropological research and whose very character was determined by ongoing anthropological direction and anthropologically informed managerial prodding.

My own involvement with the project spanned several phases and tasks:

1. Proposal of a theoretical and conceptual base of AOP, and concept of "wood as a cash crop."
2. Preliminary contacting of local PVOs to assess preproject interest.
3. Identification of specific program measures during project design.
4. Preparation of social soundness analysis for the AID project paper.
5. Participation as an outside expert at the AID meetings in Washington at which the fate of the project was decided.
6. Participation in the selection and in-country linguistic and cultural training of the agroforesters who worked for the project.
7. Direction and supervision of field operations.
8. Formative evaluation of preliminary results and the identification of needed midcourse corrections.
9. Generation of several hundred thousand dollars of supplemental funding from Canadian and Swiss sources and internationalization of the project team.
10. Preparation of publications about the project (Murray 1984, 1986).

In addition to my own participation in the AOP, four other anthropologists have been involved in long-term commitments to the project. Fred Conway did a preliminary study of firewood use in Haiti (Conway 1979). He subsequently served for two years as overall project coordinator within AID/Haiti. More recently he has carried out revealing case study research on the harvesting of project trees (Conway 1986). Glenn Smucker likewise did an early feasibility study in the northwest (Smucker 1981) and eventually joined the project as my successor in the directorship. Under his leadership, many of the crucial midcourse corrections were introduced. Ira Lowenthall took over the AID coordination of the project at a critical transitional period and has been instrumental in forging plans for its institutional future. And Anthony Balzano has carried out several years of case study fieldwork on the possible impact of the tree-planting activities on the land tenure in participating villages. All these individuals have PhDs, or are PhD candidates, in anthropology. And another anthropologist in the Haiti mission, John Lewis, succeeded in adapting the privatized umbrella agency outreach model for use in a swine repopulation project. With the possible exception of Vicos, it would be hard to imagine a project that has been as heavily influenced by anthropologists.

But how specifically has anthropology influenced the content of the project? There are at least three major levels at which anthropology has impinged on the content of AOP.

1. *The Application of Substantive Findings.* The very choice of "wood as a marketable crop" as the fundamental theme of the project stemmed from ethnographic knowledge of the cash-oriented foundations of Haitian peasant horticulture and knowledge of current conditions in the internal marketing system. Because of ethnographic knowledge I was able to avoid succumbing to the common-sense inclination to emphasize fruit trees (whose perishability and tendency to glut markets make them commercially vulnerable) and to choose instead a fast-growing wood tree. There is a feverishly escalating market for charcoal and construction wood that cannot be dampened even by the most successful project. And there are no spoilage problems with wood. The peasants can harvest it when they want. Furthermore, ethnographic knowledge of Haitian peasant land tenure—which is highly individualistic—guided me away from the community forest schemes that so many development philosophers seem to delight in but that are completely inappropriate to the social reality of Caribbean peasantries.

2. *Anthropological Methods.* The basic research that led up to the project employed participant observation along with intensive interviewing with small groups of informants to compare current cost/benefit ratios of traditional farming with projected cash yields from plots in which trees are intercropped with food on four-year rotation cycles. A critical part of the project design stage was to establish the likelihood of increased revenues from altered land use behaviors. During project design I also applied ethnographic techniques to the behavior of institutional personnel.

The application of anthropological notetaking on 3-by-5 slips, not only with peasants but also with technicians, managers, and officials, exposed the institutional roots of earlier project failures and stimulated the proposal of alternative institutional routes. Furthermore, ethno-scientific elicitation of folk taxonomies led to the realization that whereas fruit trees are classified as a crop by Haitian peasants, wood trees are not so classified. This discovery exposed the need for the creation of explicit messages saying that wood can be a crop, just as coffee, manioc, and corn can. Finally, prior experience in Creole-language instrument design and computer analysis permitted me to design a baseline data gathering system.

3. *Anthropological Theory.* My own thinking about tree planting was heavily guided by cultural-evolutionary insights into the origins of agriculture. The global tree problem is often erroneously conceptualized in a conservationist or ecological framework. Such a perspective is very short-sighted for anthropologists. We are aware of an ancient food crisis, when humans still hunted and gathered, that was solved, not by the adoption of conservationist practices, but rather by the shift into a domesticated mode of production. From hunting and gathering we turned to cropping and harvesting. I found the analogy with the present tree crisis conceptually overpowering. Trees will reemerge when and only when human beings start planting them aggressively as a harvestable crop, not when human consciousness is raised regarding their ecological importance. This anthropological insight (or bias), nourished by the aggressive creativity of the Haitian peasants among whom I had lived, swayed me toward the adoption of a dynamic "domestication" paradigm in proposing a solution to the tree problem in Haiti. This evolutionary perspective also permitted me to see that the cash-cropping of wood was in reality a small evolutionary step, not a quantum leap. The Haitian peasants already cut and sell natural stands of wood. They already plant and sell traditional food crops. It is but a small evolutionary step to join these two unconnected streams of Haitian peasant behavior, and this linkage is the core purpose of the Agroforestry Outreach Project.

Broader anthropological theory also motivated and justified a nongovernmental implementing mode for AOP. Not only AID but also most international development agencies tend to operate on a service model of the state. This idealized model views the basic character of the state as that of a provider of services to its population. Adherence to this theoretically naive service model has led to the squandering of untold millions of dollars in the support of extractive public bureaucracies. This waste is justified under the rubric of institution building—assisting public entities to provide the services that they are supposed to be providing.

But my anthropological insights into the origins of the state as a mechanism of extraction and control led me to pose the somewhat heretical position that the predatory behavior of Duvalier's regime was in fact not misbehavior. Duvalier was merely doing openly and blatantly what other state leaders camouflage under rhetoric. AID's search of nongovernmental implementing channels for AOP, then, was not seen as a simple emergency measure to be employed under a misbehaving regime but rather as an avenue of activity that might be valid as an option under many or most regimes. There is little justification in either ethnology or anthropological theory for viewing the state as the proper recipient of developmental funds. This theoretical insight permitted us to argue for a radically nongovernmental mode of tree-planting support in AOP. In short, sensitivity to issues in anthropological theory played a profound role in the shaping of the project.

Would AOP have taken the form it did without these varied types of anthropological input? Almost certainly not. Had there been no anthropological input, a radically different scenario would almost certainly have unfolded with the following elements.

1. AID would probably have undertaken a reforestation project—congressional pressure alone would have ensured that. But the project would have been based, not on the theme of "wood as a peasant cash-crop," but on the more traditional approach to trees as a vehicle of soil conservation. Ponderous educational programs would have been launched to teach the peasants about the value of trees. Emphasis would have been placed on educating the ignorant and on trying to induce peasants to plant commercially marginal (and nutritionally tangential) fruit trees instead of cash-generating wood trees.

2. The project would have been managed by technicians. The emphasis would probably have been on carrying out lengthy technical research concerning optimal planting strategies and the combination of trees with optimally effective bench terraces and other soil conservation devices. The outreach problem would have been given second priority. Throughout Haiti hundreds of thousands of dollars have been spent on numerous demonstration projects to create terraced, forested hillsides, but only a handful of cooperative local

peasants have been induced to undertake the same activities on their own land.

3. The project would almost certainly have been run through the Haitian government. When after several hundred thousand dollars of expenditures few trees were visible, frustrated young AID program officers would have gotten finger-wagging lectures about the sovereign right of local officials to use donor money as they see fit. And the few trees planted would have been defined as *pyebwa leta* (the government's trees), and peasants would have been sternly warned against ever cutting these trees, even the ones planted on their own land. And the peasants would soon turn the problem over to their most effective ally in such matters, the free-ranging omnivorous goat, who would soon remove this alien vegetation from the peasants' land.

Because of anthropology, the Agroforestry Outreach Project has unfolded to a different scenario. It was a moving experience for me to return to the village where I had done my original fieldwork (and which I of course tried to involve in the tree-planting activities) to find several houses built using the wood from leucaena trees planted during the project's earliest phases. Poles were beginning to be sold, although the prices had not yet stabilized for these still unknown wood types. Charcoal made from project trees was being sold in local markets. For the first time in the history of this village, people were "growing" part of their house structures and their cooking fuel. I felt as though I were observing (and had been a participant in) a replay of an ancient anthropological drama, the shift from an extractive to a domesticated mode of resource procurement. Though their sources of food energy had been domesticated millennia ago, my former village neighbors had now begun replicating this transition in the domain of wood and wood-based energy. I felt a satisfaction at having chosen a discipline that could give me the privilege of participating, even marginally, in this very ancient cultural-evolutionary transition.

REFERENCES

Ashley, Marshall D. 1986. *A Study of Traditional Agroforestry Systems in Haiti and Implications for the USAID/Haiti Agroforestry Outreach Project.* Port-au-Prince: University of Maine Agroforestry Outreach Research Project.

Balzano, Anthony. 1986. *Socioeconomic Aspects of Agroforestry in Rural Haiti.* Port-au-Prince: University of Maine Agroforestry Outreach Research Project.

Buffum, William, and Wendy King. 1985. *Small Farmer Decision Making and Tree Planting: Agroforestry Extension Recommendations.* Port-au-Prince: Haiti Agroforestry Outreach Project.

Conway, Frederick. 1979. *A Study of the Fuelwood Situation in Haiti.* Port-au-Prince: USAID.

——. 1986. *The Decision Making Framework for Tree Planting Within the Agroforestry Outreach Project.* Port-au-Prince: University of Maine Agroforestry Outreach Research Project.

Grosenick, Gerald. 1985. *Economic Evaluation of the Agroforestry Outreach Project.* Port-au-Prince: University of Maine Agroforestry Outreach Research Project.

McGowan, Lisa A. 1986. *Potential Marketability of Charcoal, Poles, and Planks Produced by Participants in the Agroforestry Outreach Project.* Port-au-Prince: University of Maine Agroforestry Outreach Research Project.

Murray, Gerald F. 1977. *The Evolution of Haitian Peasant Land Tenure: A Case Study in Agrarian Adaptation to Population Growth.* Ph.D. dissertation, Columbia University, New York.

——. 1978a. *Hillside Units, Wage Labor, and Haitian Peasant Land Tenure: A Strategy for the Organization of Erosion Control.* Port-au-Prince: USAID.

——. 1978b. *Informal Subdivisions and Land Insecurity: An Analysis of Haitian Peasant Land Tenure.* Port-au-Prince: USAID.

——. 1979. *Terraces, Trees, and the Haitian Peasant: An Assessment of 25 Years of Erosion Control in Rural Haiti.* Port-au-Prince: USAID.

——. 1984. "The Wood Tree as a Peasant Cash-Crop: An Anthropological Strategy for the Domestication of Energy." In A. Valdman and R. Foster, eds., *Haiti—Today and Tomorrow: An Interdisciplinary Study.* New York: University Press of America.

——. 1986. "Seeing the Forest While Planting the Trees: An Anthropological Approach to Agroforestry in Rural Haiti." In D. W. Brinkerhoff and J. C. Garcia-Zamor, eds., *Politics, Projects, and Peasants: Institutional Development in Haiti.* New York: Praeger, pp. 193–226.

Smucker, Glenn R. 1981. *Trees and Charcoal in Haitian Peasant Economy: A Feasibility Study.* Port-au-Prince: USAID.

Zuvekas, Clarence. 1978. *Agricultural Development in Haiti: An Assessment of Sector Problems, Policies, and Prospects under Conditions of Severe Soil Erosion.* Washington, D.C.: USAID.

15

Two Rights Make a Wrong
Indigenous Peoples Versus Environmental Protection Agencies

Richard Reed

In today's world, environmentalism has become an almost mainstream cultural ideal, as cereal boxes and pop stars beseech us to "save the rainforest." The question of indigenous rights to traditional lands, however, has not received the same degree of popular attention. Indigenous peoples do not have the same political allies as the forests in which they live. In this selection we see that some environmentalists and anthropologists propose combining these two agendas, arguing that the goals of conservation and defending traditional indigenous land use have much in common. For example, both efforts should be aimed at preventing land from being exploited according to models of nonsustainable agrobusiness.

Neither environmental conservation nor indigenous land rights are simple issues, and the alliance between these two sides is far from harmonious. In this selection, anthropologist Richard Reed describes the history of the creation of a national park (or reserve) in Paraguay where, initially, indigenous people were expected both to have access to land for traditional purposes and to be involved in managing and maintaining the park.

Anthropologists began by calling for the creation of the reserve and the inclusion of indigenous people in its management plan. Anthropologists found a powerful ally to make the reserve a reality: The Nature Conservancy, a U.S.-based nonprofit conservation group. Anthropologists were also called on to facilitate communication among indigenous people, biologists, and personnel in a variety of government and non-government organizations. Yet while anthropologists are in a privileged position to understand the viewpoint of these different cultures, they are working in a context of unequal power. By the time the national park was created, only those indigenous people who maintained a traditional economic lifestyle, as defined by The Nature Conservancy, were permitted to have access, while the rest of the "acculturated" indigenous people were excluded.

Indigenous people are not fossils or museum exhibits. They have never been in a "natural" state; they have always had an impact on the local ecology.

Indigenous people themselves should ideally decide how to practice their culture and respond to changing political, economic, and ecological traditions. Because native groups remain as disempowered today as they were five hundred years ago when the first Europeans arrived, they profoundly distrust all who want to come and help them, including well-intentioned anthropologists. As Reed says, to the indigenous people of this region, The Nature Conservancy is just another in a long history of outsider plantation owners (*latifundistas*). Until indigenous peoples can become actors with a voice in the environmental movement, this promising alliance will continue to be problematic.

As you read this selection, ask yourself the following questions:

- What are the different goals that the two sides in this alliance have? Are these goals incompatible?

- How did the fact that there were at least two indigenous groups involved in this case make the situation more complicated?

- How did anthropologists play a role as "culture brokers" in this scenario? Did their efforts fail? Why?

- Why was The Nature Conservancy so interested in Mbaracayu Park, whereas the World Bank was not?

- What cultural ideals of the "native" are involved in this case?

The following terms discussed in this selection are included in the Glossary at the back of the book:

foraging	*peasants*
horticulture	*shifting agriculture*
indigenistas	*swidden cultivation*
indigenous	yerba mate
latifundistas	yerbateros

In lowland Latin America, the struggle to save the forests has forged new alliances between indigenous peoples and environmental foundations. Such alliances link the future of the world's indigenous people with the future of the forests, to the benefit of both. The political and economic capital that environmental agencies bring to the conservation struggle can aid indigenous groups. At the same time, environmental groups gain two things: the indigenous knowledge to understand the complex biological communities in these areas as well as a potent symbol of the importance of the mission (Conklin and Graham 1995).

Problems have begun to surface, however, in the relationship between indigenous peoples and the environmental movement. Agencies find that indigenous populations are often internally divided and that their conflicting demands are difficult to reconcile in the larger fight for environmental protection. Indigenous peoples, in turn, are often dissatisfied with the restrictions imposed by environmental protection organizations.

This article examines a case in which The Nature Conservancy (TNC) and several indigenous groups tried to collaborate in the creation and management of a reserve in northeastern Paraguay. In 1989, TNC purchased 53,000 hectares of the last sustainable stands of subtropical deciduous forest that once covered the Paraguay and Brazil's Paraná Plateau—one of the last open forests for the Aché and the Guaraní peoples. In their fight against colonists and cattle ranchers, the Aché, the Guaraní, and TNC were forced to contend with one another. They also had to contend with misunderstandings based on conceptions of nature and indigenous peoples that emerged as environmentalists and anthropologists negotiated access to and management of the region.

MBARACAYU

Until 1970, far eastern Paraguay was undisturbed by intensive development. The region was protected by plantation owners (*latifundistas*) and multinational corporations that were primarily interested in the limited collection of native *yerba mate* (*Ilex paraguayensis*) and harvesting of hardwood trees. Two indigenous groups occupied the forests, the food-foraging Aché and the horticultural Guaraní. These two groups generally lived in a state of mutual fear and permanent conflict; both have had intermittent contact with *yerba mate* collectors and loggers who penetrated the zone. Throughout history, *latifundistas* restricted colonization of the forest by nonindigenous peoples, but the Guaraní and Aché were tolerated. As a result, the indigenous groups had free access to sufficient resources to control their own lives.

Over the last twenty years, the forests of eastern Paraguay have been expropriated to satisfy land demands by agro-industrialists and the growing peasant population. Between 1963 and 1976, the Paraguay land reform agency (IBR) distributed about four million hectares to 90,000 families. By 1984, 5.1 million hectares, roughly half of the arable land in eastern Paraguay, had been given to peasant colonists (World Bank 1984:11). Foreign investment accompanied colonization. Brazilian, American, and Japanese companies purchased vast areas of forest for clear-cutting and agriculture (Parquet 1985:37). Soybean production and ranching replaced traditional industries in eastern Paraguay. As a result, the forests were reduced by half by 1989, and the rate of continued deforestation in Paraguay was higher than in any other Latin American country (Hanratty and Meditz 1990).

As rural transformation converts Paraguay's subtropical forests into an international breadbasket, the Aché and Guaraní are losing land. As early as the 1970s, voices were raised in defense of Paraguay's indigenous peoples (AIP/Misión 1977). The Aché became an international concern when they were forced to take refuge with missionaries and exploitative patrons (Arens 1976). Anthropologists and *indigenistas* lobbied the national government for land. Although most Aché and Guaraní received guarantees to some land, these *"colonias nacionales"* were insufficient for hunting and shifting agriculture.

In the early 1980s, anthropologists identified a major tract of remaining forested land called "Mbaracayu," which could allow many of the indigenous people to continue traditional hunting and gathering. Since the World Bank then controlled this land (a lumber company had defaulted on a loan), there was hope that this virgin forest could be secured for the indigenous groups.

Traditionally the Guaraní of the region hunted in the forests and collected a variety of goods, including commodities such as *yerba mate* and skins. In 1971, when the land was sold for lumbering, the families living in Mbaracayu were forced from their homes onto adjacent lands. Today, five hundred Guaraní families are located near the land, supplementing their gardens by hunting and gathering on the few large tracts of forest that remain undeveloped.

Mbaracayu also harbored one of the last groups of hunting and gathering Aché. Since being forced out of the forest in 1976, they had been given fields and houses at a religious mission outside the reserve. Nevertheless, the Aché continued their patterns of

TIMELINE OF MBARACAYU RESERVE

- 1531–1960: Indigenous people in Paraguay struggle successfully to maintain traditional lifestyles in the forests of eastern Paraguay.
- 1968: Mbaracayu forest is purchased by timber company.
- 1971: Guaraní communities are forced out of Mbaracayu forest by timber company.
- 1974: Timber company goes bankrupt; World Bank acquires Mbaracayu by default.
- 1976: World Bank and Paraguayan government attempt to force Aché out of Mbaracayu forest.
- 1983: Anthropologists approach World Bank to grant Mbaracayu to indigenous groups.
- 1983: World Bank ignores anthropologists (and their own guidelines on indigenous peoples).
- 1989: TNC purchases 53,000 hectares of the last sustainable stands of subtropical deciduous forest in Paraguay.
- 1989: Anthropologists meet with indigenous groups to discuss the creation of the reserve and its management plan.
- 1989: NGO Fundación Moises Bertoni (FMB) is created to manage the reserve.
- 1991: All Guaraní indigenous people are denied access to the reserve.
- 1991: Aché indigenous people are granted limited access to the reserve, provided they maintain their "traditional," "natural" lifestyles as defined by FMB and TNC.

intermittent nomadic foraging within the dense forests of Mbaracayu.[1]

In 1983, anthropologists approached the World Bank to donate the land for use by Paraguayan indigenous people. When calls to Washington came to naught, the bank was instead asked to provide a small portion of the land to the Aché and Guaraní in compliance with the World Bank's own policy of protecting indigenous peoples in the project areas. Bank personnel ignored the requests, suggesting that the whole idea of indigenous use of the land was preposterous.

Seeking allies, some anthropologists approached TNC. The idea quickly became a plan, was then converted into a project, was embedded in a program, and within days had been granted a budget. There was a reason TNC moved quickly. In the 1980s it was searching for the means to internationalize its work, and Mbaracayu offered a unique opportunity. The region harbored plant and animal life that was disappearing from much of southern Brazil, northern Argentina, and eastern Paraguay. Paraguayan land was cheap and the Paraguayan government was an image-conscious dictatorship. It was a case where a little pull and a little money could accomplish a great deal in a short time.

Whereas anthropologists' inquiries to the World Bank were rebuffed, TNC's interest in acquiring Mbaracayu was warmly received. TNC had important Washington connections, had amassed a considerable war chest for the negotiation of land purchase, and could call on a host of international contacts for such complex transactions as debt-for-nature swaps.

As discussions moved forward quickly, TNC proposed that the land be protected by a joint Paraguayan-international effort. In conformity with World Bank guidelines toward indigenous people, the bank requested that TNC develop a management plan for indigenous peoples' use of the region. To design this component of the management plan, anthropologists (the author included) visited each indigenous community, counted the population, and held a meeting to discuss the plan. In Paraguay, a host country agency called Fundación Moises Bertoni (FMB) was developed to orchestrate the land acquisition and manage the park.

This management plan provided the first arena for the negotiation of the conflicting rights of indigenous people and TNC. The Guaraní and Aché saw the creation of the reserve and TNC's interest in their involvement as a means of acquiring what they considered their primordial right, the forests of Mbaracayu. Although the government's interest in helping indigenous groups was limited, the indigenous groups saw new potential in the international ties and power of TNC. For its part, TNC reinforced the impression that Mbaracayu was a site where indigenous groups could maintain their society and culture. Rhetoric surrounding the project emphasized the agencies' sensitivity to indigenous peoples' needs and rights. Introducing Mbaracayu in its own literature, TNC (1996:17) reported that it purchased the area in 1991 "to help the Aché preserve their traditions and to protect one of the last untouched forest wilderness areas in Paraguay."

In designing the reserve management plan, anthropologists proposed that indigenous people could be important to the future of the region. Guaraní and Aché have the greatest knowledge of the local environment, its resources, and their use. More than a simple biological variable in the forest ecosystem, the plan pointed out that traditional economic activities in the area had directly affected the existing forest. Guaraní and Aché hunting, gathering, fishing, and swidden cultivation had patterned the region's flora and fauna. Anthropologists noted that for five centuries Guaraní had collected *yerba* commercially, while protecting and promoting a series of natural yerba stands (*yerbales*). These activities provided Guaraní with a steady income without destroying the forest. Thus, indigenous commercial extraction had "managed" the so-called "natural" environment (Reed 1997).

Given these models of indigenous resource use, the anthropological team suggested that the indigenous residents be integrated into the maintenance and management of the reserve. Aché would continue to hunt and gather; Guaraní would be allowed to continue traditional, commercial *yerba* gathering. In addition, it was proposed that the Aché be employed as "guarde bosques," manipulating the colonists' fear of "savage Indians" to assure that they remained beyond the park's boundaries. In sum, anthropologists suggested that indigenous groups be given access to the resources that they traditionally used, resources that were vital to their continued social and economic independence (Renshaw and Reed 1989:53).

When the proposed indigenous component of the management plan was presented to the Paraguayan reserve management agency, however, discussions were fraught with conflict and misunderstanding. The team of biologists, TNC, and FMB were skeptical of the plan to give indigenous people rights to use park resources. They were concerned that hunting would undermine endangered animal populations, gardens would damage the forest, and commercial gathering would lead to wholesale destruction of forest resources.

The arguments against the plan rested on two points. First, they suggested that Mbaracayu had been unaffected by past human activity. Second, giving Aché and Guaraní rights to continue hunting, field cutting, or commercial collection would degrade the forest environment.

The management plan that was finally written by the FMB attempted to step gingerly between the conflicting demands. It allowed some Aché limited access to the reserve, provided they had no impact on its floral or faunal populations. The majority of the Aché were to be relocated to land that TNC would purchase elsewhere and title directly to the community. The management plan excluded Guaraní from any access to the land. Instead of being treated as an indigenous people with a right to the reserve, they were integrated into an alternative plan to assist local peasants with agricultural extension work projects.

With the establishment of the reserve, most Aché and Guaraní felt they had lost their primordial right to the forest. They greeted the loss with the same fatalism they had exhibited previously when other large areas were removed from their control. The TNC found that their model was easily imposed on the rural region, creating the reality that fit their ideas. By restricting Guaraní from this last large parcel of forest, they forced them farther into Paraguayan peasant society. Most Aché, in turn, were forced into a plot where a degree of farming was necessary to augment the meager hunting.

DISCUSSION

It would be easy to blame the unhappy result on the parties involved: the environmentalists' insensitivity, the indigenous communities' naivete; the anthropologists' idealism. The reality is more complex. The negotiations surrounding Mbaracayu suffered from a series of erroneous assumptions and conflicting perceptions. Each party created images of the others based on their differing world views. TNC's ideas of forest peoples, the anthropologists' scientific models, and the indigenous groups' attitudes toward the larger power structure all made it impossible for a meaningful dialogue to take place. Consequently, the plan that was implemented reinforced the inequities of power and resources that characterize other relations between small-scale societies and the larger system.

As instructive as it would be to analyze fully all images used in the discussion, the following discussion focuses on the concept of "natural" that dominates much of our thinking about the environment. Despite the word's ubiquity, the concept of nature remains extremely ambiguous. On one hand, it refers to the inherent qualities of things, as in "the nature of." On the other hand, it refers to the original state, as in "the natural world." In the environmental movement, it has taken on both of these meanings. It signifies the world in its original state, following its own (natural) laws and organized according to the (natural) order of things.

In practice, our ideas of nature are most often defined in relation to their opposites; such as grace, in religion; culture, in anthropology; and history, in philosophy. In the environmental debate, our concept of nature is opposed to civilization. In this romantic vision, for which Rousseau can take much of the credit, human civilization destroys the original ideal order of the world. Where French philosophers found the evils of civilization in the growth of the state, today's evil empire is envisioned in the development of expanding technology, markets, and populations. As humans develop the power and need to dominate nature, they destroy its order, its ecological rationality, and its scientific predictability.

Ecologically Noble Savage

The distinction between nature and civilization helps us understand the position of indigenous peoples in the environmental movement. Rousseau suggested that people's natural humanity was destroyed by civilization. As in the seventeenth century, indigenous peoples today are thought to have the capacity to be *either* natural *or* civilized. Presumably, humans in their original state did not destroy nature but lived in conjunction with it—in ideological and biological harmony with the environment in which they lived. Redford (1990) terms this natural conception of humans the "ecologically noble savage."

Anthropologists' own models of indigenous life also promoted the concept of the ecologically noble savage. Since the nineteenth century, anthropologists have portrayed original human societies as in a state of nature. In the ecological anthropology of the 1960s, this perception developed into models of the idealized ecological relationships of indigenous peoples in biotic communities. Indigenous people are presented as elements in stable ecosystems, their adaptive activity perfectly integrated into the larger environment.

As indigenous people enter into agreements with environmental groups in lowland South America, they are preceived within this dichotomy between "natural" and "civilized." In the planning of Mbaracayu, the Aché—who left the mission, shed superfluous clothing, and lived in the forest—were easily defined as forest savages. In the minds of functionaries in Asunción and Washington, they were perceived to be natural elements of the forest ecosystem. Aché culture was described in biological terms in the forest ecosystem. Aché hunters and gatherers were considered as living in harmony with nature, harvesting enough to survive but not seeking to expand or overexploit the flora or fauna.

This conceptualization found expression in the imagery that TNC used in discussing the Aché and advertising their work to the public. Pictures of Aché in TNC articles emphasized the small, light, forest people as a "Stone Age culture." As one publication put it, "For hundreds of years, the Aché roamed over the dense forest in eastern Paraguay, hunting and gathering with no permanent homes and few possessions" (The Nature Conservancy 1996). A writer for *The Nature Conservancy Magazine* almost fully conflates the categories of Aché and animal:

> "Felipe Jakugi scampers 60 feet up a Lapacho tree that sways like a giant waving hand. Jakugi, an Aché Indian, is at home in the treetops of Mbaracayu forest of northeastern Paraguay. For centuries, the Aché have hunted monkeys and escaped enemies in the forest canopy." (Thigpen 1996)

The anthropologists involved with the project (myself included) made full use of the concept of the noble savage. The indigenous component of the management plan depended more on ethnography and theoretical work in tropical ecology (Posey and Baleé 1989, Treachy 1982) than on the ideas and opinions of the local indigenous communities. It stressed the rationality of traditional indigenous use of natural resources. By arguing that these people would continue to treat the forest as a sacred entity, anthropologists forced the diverse hopes, needs, desires, and plans of all the various individuals of several ethnic groups into one neat political package and then tried to sell it to the environmental agencies.

Ecological Half-Breeds

Few, if any, groups in lowland South America conform to the rigid vision of isolated naturalness. As indigenous people become integrated into the environmental movement, the reality of their attitudes and activities often conflicts with the model of forest people as noble. The vast majority of indigenous peoples enter the market economy for cash crops or wage labor; buy clothes and tools from the world markets; and market natural resources. Once sullied by these activities, they are seen to be forever and utterly changed. Once touched by the market, native peoples are thought to lay down the mantle of noble savage and align with the environmentally destructive society.

Indigenous peoples who fail the litmus test of environmental sensitivity are cast as ignoble savages—ecological half-breeds. Indigenous people in contact with the larger society and international economy are assumed to have acquired only the worst of modern society, having adopted the drives and desires of the poor and destitute. Without considering the long-term implications of these ideas, or their coherence in the face of the actual beliefs of indigenous peoples, researchers assume that these peoples lay down indigenous attitudes en masse as if they were broken tools and pick up new ideas as if they were sharper machetes. These new attitudes are considered destructive and unsustainable in the forest, because forest peoples are believed to be especially vulnerable to irrational desires for commodities. Rousseau, like Marx, pointed to private property as the first step toward both civilization and destruction. Today, we harbor the illusion that exposure to commodities seduces forest peoples into making the most unnecessary demands. With the same smug superiority that is used to describe the sale of Manhattan for a few baubles, we expect indigenous peoples to fall into the commodity trap—machetes and running shorts, followed by unquenchable desires for alcohol, tape players, sunglasses, and a host of other luxuries.

In the case of Mbaracayu, native groups that didn't fit the caricature of the noble savage found no place in TNC's forest. Aché who chose to practice a more complex economy, perhaps integrating swidden cultivation or selling labor for wages, were thought to no longer maintain a "traditional" Aché lifestyle (Thigpen 1996). In fact, as Aché expressed growing discordance over the various options presented by TNC, the population became increasingly divided between those Aché whom TNC considered "real" and those whom they considered somehow less authentic. Those who chose to farm or clear forest were restricted from their native forests and offered a parcel in another region. Only those who subscribed to TNC's model of the Aché were permitted to continue to use Mbaracayu.

TNC considered all Guaraní totally degraded by the larger society. The Guaraní are shifting cultivators; as such, they stepped out of a state of nature and became involved in the market economy, practicing a mix of agriculture, wage labor, and petty commodity production. TNC saw such Guaraní activities as a direct threat to the "virgin" forest that supposedly existed. In many ways, the Guaraní were considered peasants—greedy individuals who acted with unenlightened self-interest, predators who would disrupt the equilibrium of nature and destroy the ecosystem.

THE POLITICAL CONTEXT OF THE DEBATE

The environmental dialogue is locked into a simple dichotomy between the natural and the civilized, despite the many recent advances in theory concerning the complexity of human relations with the environment. Biologists and ecologists are aware that the very concept of "virgin" forest as untouched by human hands ignores millennia of human involvement. Indigenous production has not only been sustained in the forest but is an integral factor in maintaining the "natural" biological diversity (Denevan and Padoch 1987, Hecht and Cockburn 1989). In Mbaracayu, gardening, hunting, and even forestry are important influences on the natural forest ecosystem (Baleé 1992:43). Far from destroying nature, humans have created the natural world.

Anthropologists and ecologists appreciate the resilience of the forest and the tenacity of indigenous cultures, but the new understandings are not readily integrated into the discussion of environmental conservation. Why are misperceptions fostered, and why do simple dichotomies still dominate the dialogue about environmental conservation? An awareness of the political context of dialogue makes it clear that misperceptions are created and reinforced in the contemporary conflict over resources.

Graham and Conklin (1995) point out that the dialogue between indigenous peoples and expanding societies takes place in a frontier area. This "middle ground" is not fully controlled by either the small-scale society or the larger system. Since the time of the Jesuits, the Paraguayan government in Asunción has held tenuous control over its rural area. As recently as the 1880s, Paraguay lost over a third of its territory to Brazil. *Latifundios* were organized to take responsibility for protecting Paraguayan sovereignty. Today, the disassembly of these plantations creates a power vacuum. Brazilian ranchers, Japanese lumber firms, and Paraguayan soybean farmers struggle for remnants of control, and no clear state official has the power to enforce the law.

The dialogue between environmental groups and indigenous peoples is a part of this larger conflict over the resources. As environmental groups move to protect the few remaining stands of forests, they find that they are in conflict not only with developers but also with the claims of primordial rights by indigenous residents. Indigenous groups, on the other had, find that a new type of plantation owner (*latifundista*) has arrived on the scene. The need to defend their ancestral land demands that they negotiate with this new "developer"—the environmental protection group.

The terms that are chosen in the dialogue over forest rights fall prey to the power relations of the larger system. Worldwide networks of information, international political connections, and a war chest of capital empower environmental groups in the international scramble for land. TNC, World Wildlife Fund, and the Fund for Animals have the economic and political weapons to confront some of the most powerful corporations and many national governments. They hold a vast amount of institutional power in their relations with indigenous groups—relations that reinforce and are reinforced by the terms of the dialogue. By defining indigenous people with respect to a yardstick of savagery, environmental groups can effectively exclude all those who do not conform to their ideal.

Graham and Conklin also point out that it is politically dangerous for environmental groups to ignore indigenous groups. Indians' presence can develop into a political problem if the conflict over resources moves into the national or international consciousness. Environmental groups are better served by defusing confrontation. On the other hand, the involvement of indigenous peoples, even a contentious and divided group such as the Aché, can be a public relations asset. This was clear in the case of Mbaracayu, where TNC was careful to publicize its defense of the Aché along with its program for protecting the environment (The Nature Conservancy 1996).

Indigenous groups have not had the opportunity to establish their own definitions of themselves or their world in the environmental debate. Despite the attempts of anthropologists and Paraguayans to inform the local residents of TNC and its aims, most indigenous people garnered little understanding of the actors involved or the complex negotiations that were taking place over their land. They had little idea of what to expect, alternating between complete belief that they would get to use the land exclusively and a lack of confidence that anything would happen.

This is not to say they were confused. In the case of Mbaracayu, although indigenous groups had only a hazy idea of TNC, its purpose, or its programs, they had a very clear idea of the structure of power in the struggle for the land of Mbaracayu. Their high hopes and cynicism were born of the long history of relationships with *latifundistas*. From the indigenous standpoint, the environmental agency was virtually indistinguishable from previous ranchers and multinational corporations.

As alliances are formed between indigenous groups and environmental agencies, we are called upon to facilitate the dialogue concerning reserves and indigenous peoples. Anthropologists are brought into the debate because of their distinct knowledge and perspective. They not only offer accurate information about the people and places involved but are also in the privileged position of seeing the conflict from two perspectives. These abilities, however, force anthropologists into the conflicting roles of scientist and political actor. Although knowledge gives anthropologists a responsibility to take action, it offers little power in dictating the terms of the debate or deciding the outcome.

Thus it was TNC, not the Aché, Guaraní, or anthropologists, who defined the terms of the debate over indigenous rights to Mbaracayu in the national and international sphere. By defining some indigenous people as threats to the natural environment, TNC could rally support for the reserve and the relocation of those indigenous residents. Those who chose

to stay needed to abide by the strictures laid down by the agency. On the other had, neither the Aché nor the Guaraní had the opportunity either to portray themselves in all the complexities of their indigenous identity or to declaim TNC as a *latifundista* that was taking indigenous land for its own purposes.

In conclusion, environmental groups are integrating indigenous peoples into the day-to-day management of conservation areas. Despite their common ground, agencies and indigenous groups cannot escape confrontation. Even when their short-term objectives are similar, their respective long-term goals are often very different. Whereas agencies seek to protect the forests in perpetuity and seek indigenous peoples' assistance in the endeavor, indigenous groups are fundamentally concerned with their own survival and see the forests as their primary resource in that struggle. As large areas of the forest are converted to pasture and field, the two groups remain in contention for the remaining undisturbed areas.

NOTE

1. This group has been extensively studied by anthropologists and provided data to further a variety of cultural ecological models (e.g., Hill and Hurtado 1995).

REFERENCES

AIP/Misión (Asociación Indígena del Paraguay y Misión de Amistad). 1977. *Población y tierras indígenas en la región oriental de la República del Paraguay.* Manuscript.

Arens, Richard. 1976. *Genocide in Paraguay.* Philadelphia: Temple University Press.

Baleé, William. 1992. People of the fallow. In *Conservation of Neotropical Forests: Working from Traditional Resource Use,* pp. 35–58, ed. K. Redford and C. Padoch. New York: Columbia.

Clay, Jason. 1988. *Indigenous Peoples and Tropical Forests: Models for Land Use and Management from Latin America.* Cambridge, MA: Cultural Survival.

Denevan, William, and Christine Padoch. 1987. Swidden-fallow agroforestry in the Peruvian Amazon. *Advances in Economic Botany* Number 5. New York: New York Botanical Gardens.

Graham, Laura, and Beth Conklin. 1995. The shifting middle ground: Amazonian Indians and eco-politics. *American Anthropologist* 97(4):695–710.

Hanratty, Dennis, and Sandra Meditz, eds. 1990. *Paraguay: A Country Study.* Washington, DC: U.S. Government Printing Office.

Hecht, Susanna, and Andrew Cockburn. 1989. *The Fate of the Forest.* New York: Verso.

Hill, Kim, and A. Magdalena Hurtado. 1995. *Aché Life History: The Ecology and Demography of a Foraging People.* New York: Aldine de Gruyter.

Laino, Domingo. 1997. *Paraguay: Fronteras y penetracion brasileña.* Asunción: Ediciones Cerro Cora.

The Nature Conservancy. 1996. Profiles: Maracayu. *The Nature Conservancy.* Nov/Dec.

Padoch, Christine et al. 1985. Amazonian agroforestry: A market oriented system in Peru. *Agroforestry Systems* 3(1):47–58.

Parquet, Reinerio. 1985. *Las Empresas Transnacionales en la economia del Paraguay.* Unpublished manuscript prepared for Unidad Conjunta CEPAL/CET: Buenos Aires.

Posey, Darrell, and William Baleé. 1989. Resource management in Amazonia. *Advances in Economic Botany* Number 7. New York: New York Botanical Gardens.

Redford, Kent. 1990. The ecologically noble savage. *Orion Nature Quarterly* 9(3):25–29.

Reed, Richard. 1997. *Forest Dwellers, Forest Protectors: Indigenous Models for International Development.* Boston: Allyn and Bacon.

Renshaw, John, and Richard Reed. 1989. *Analysis socioeconomico y cultural de las poblaciones asentadas en el area de influencia del la reserva Mbaracayu.* Unpublished manuscript prepared for Fundación Moises Bertoni: Asunción.

Thigpen, Jaunita. 1996. Help wanted: Traditional wisdom required. *The Nature Conservancy.* Nov/Dec.

Treachy, Jonathon. 1982. Bora Indian agroforestry: An alternate to deforestation. *Cultural Survival Quarterly* 6(2): 16–17.

16

Race Without Color

Jared Diamond

Looking at the title of this selection, you should ask yourself two questions. First, what is a reading about race doing in a cultural anthropology book? After all, it would seem that race is obviously a biological question. Second, what could the author possibly mean by "race without color"? Doesn't that sound like an oxymoron?

An important aspect of anthropological thinking is examining ideas, beliefs, and values within their own cultural context. Our own cultural ideas and concepts, including scientific ones, are grist for the anthropological mill because they are best understood within a larger cultural framework. Sometimes cultural anthropologists focus on a single cultural concept and take it apart, demonstrating its historical roots and its relation to other social beliefs. In postmodern parlance, this kind of intensive analysis can be called "deconstructing" a concept.

In this selection, a well-known natural scientist "deconstructs" the biological concept of race. Although the term *race* seems to have some use in the description of population variation in birds and in creating a taxonomy, the concept doesn't work very well for understanding human variation. In fact, from a biological standpoint, the concept of race based on skin color is scientifically useless. As the reading demonstrates, there are a lot of different ways to categorize human biological diversity, but these variations are independent from one another so that there is more variation within racial categories than between them. By deconstructing race, we see that it is a cultural category, not a biological one.

On the other hand, race is indeed an important historical and political concept—as a cultural construction that functions as a folk-biological rationalization for enforcing social inequalities. We decided to include this reading within this cultural anthropology book to emphasize the fact that race is a cultural invention. Race is not useful for understanding human biological diversity; it is essentially meaningless, like an oxymoron.

As you read this selection, ask yourself the following questions:

- Why does skin color seem to be such an obvious and commonsensical way to make distinctions among people?
- How might it be acceptable to use the concept of race for talking about birds, but not humans?
- What does it mean that taxonomists are "lumpers" and "splitters"?
- How is our understanding of most biological variations—like resistance to malaria or adults' ability to digest milk—not aided by the concept of race?
- If racial classifications are cultural constructions, what does the author think is the purpose of these arbitrary classifications?

The following terms discussed in this selection are included in the Glossary at the back of the book:

lactose intolerance   sickle-cell anemia
race   species

Basing race on body chemistry makes no more sense than basing race on appearance—but at least you get to move the membership around.

Science often violates simple common sense. Our eyes tell us that the Earth is flat, that the sun revolves around the Earth, and that we humans are not animals. But we now ignore that evidence of our senses. We have learned that our planet is in fact round and revolves around the sun, and that humans are slightly modified chimpanzees. The reality of human races is another commonsense "truth" destined to follow the flat Earth into oblivion. The commonsense view of races goes somewhat as follows. All native Swedes

Jared Diamond/© 1994 *Discover* magazine.

differ from all native Nigerians in appearance: there is no Swede whom you would mistake for a Nigerian, and vice versa. Swedes have lighter skin than Nigerians do. They also generally have blond or light brown hair, while Nigerians have very dark hair. Nigerians usually have more tightly coiled hair than Swedes do, dark eyes as opposed to eyes that are blue or gray, and fuller lips and broader noses.

In addition, other Europeans look much more like Swedes than like Nigerians, while other peoples of sub-Saharan Africa—except perhaps the Khoisan peoples of southern Africa—look much more like Nigerians than like Swedes. Yes, skin color does get darker in Europe toward the Mediterranean, but it is still lighter than the skin of sub-Saharan Africans. In Europe, very dark or curly hair becomes more common outside Scandinavia, but European hair is still not as tightly coiled as in Africa. Since it's easy then to distinguish almost any native European from any native sub-Saharan African, we recognize Europeans and sub-Saharan Africans as distinct races, which we name for their skin colors: whites and blacks, respectively.

What could be more objective?

As it turns out, this seemingly unassailable reasoning is not objective. There are many different, equally valid procedures for defining races, and those different procedures yield very different classifications. One such procedure would group Italians and Greeks with most African blacks. It would classify Xhosas—the South African "black" group to which President Nelson Mandela belongs—with Swedes rather than Nigerians. Another equally valid procedure would place Swedes with Fulani (a Nigerian "black" group) and not with Italians who would again be grouped with most other African blacks. Still another procedure would keep Swedes and Italians separate from all African blacks but would throw the Swedes and Italians into the same race as New Guineans and American Indians. Faced with such differing classifications, many anthropologists today conclude that one cannot recognize any human races at all.

If we were just arguing about races of nonhuman animals, essentially the same uncertainties of classification would arise. But the debates would remain polite and would never attract attention outside the halls of academia. Classification of humans is different "only" in that it shapes our views of other peoples, fosters our subconscious differentiation between "us" and "them," and is invoked to justify political and socioeconomic discrimination. On this basis, many anthropologists therefore argue that even if one *could* classify humans into races, one should not.

To understand how such uncertainties in classification arise let's steer clear of humans for a moment and instead focus on warblers and lions, about which

we can easily remain dispassionate. Biologists begin by classifying living creatures into species. A species is a group of populations whose individual members would, if given the opportunity, interbreed with individuals of other populations of that group. But they would not interbreed with individuals of other species that are similarly defined. Thus all human populations, no matter how different they look belong to the same species because they do interbreed and have interbred whenever they have encountered each other. Gorillas and humans, however, belong to two different species because—to the best of our knowledge—they have never interbred despite their coexisting in close proximity for millions of years.

We know that different populations classified together in the human species are visibly different. The same proves true for most other animal and plant species as well, whenever biologists look carefully. For example, consider one of the most familiar species of bird in North America, the yellow-rumped warbler. Breeding males of eastern and western North America can be distinguished at a glance by their throat color, white in the east, yellow in the west. Hence they are classified into two different races, or subspecies (alternative words with identical meanings), termed the myrtle and Audubon races, respectively. The white-throated eastern birds differ from the yellow-throated western birds in other characteristics as well, such as in voice and habitat preference. But where the two races meet, in western Canada, white-throated birds do indeed interbreed with yellow-throated birds. That's why we consider myrtle warblers and Audubon warblers as races of the same species rather than different species.

Racial classification of these birds is easy. Throat color, voice and habitat preference all vary geographically in yellow-rumped warblers, but the variation of those three traits is "concordant"—that is, voice differences or habitat differences lead to the same racial classification as differences in throat color because the same populations that differ in throat color also differ in voice and habitat.

Racial classification of many other species, though, presents problems of concordance. For instance, a Pacific island bird species called the golden whistler varies from one island to the next. Some populations consist of big birds, some of small birds; some have black-winged males, others green-winged males; some have yellow-breasted females, others gray-breasted females; many other characteristics vary as well. But, unfortunately for humans like me who study these birds, those characteristics don't vary concordantly. Islands with green-winged males can have either yellow-breasted or gray-breasted females, and green-winged males are big on some islands but small on other islands. As a result if you classified golden whistlers into races based on single traits, you would set entirely different classifications depending on which trait you chose.

Classification of these birds also presents problems of "hierarchy." Some of the golden whistler races recognized by ornithologists are wildly different from all the other races, but some are very similar to one another. They can therefore be grouped into a hierarchy of distinctness. You start by establishing the most distinct population as a race separate from all other populations. You then separate the most distinct of the remaining populations. You continue by grouping similar populations, and separating distinct populations or groups of populations as races or groups of races. The problem is that the extent to which you continue the racial classification is arbitrary, and it's a decision about which taxonomists disagree passionately. Some taxonomists, the "splitters," like to recognize many different races, partly for the egotistical motive of getting credit for having named a race. Other taxonomists, the "lumpers," prefer to recognize few races. Which type of taxonomist you are is a matter of personal preference.

How does that variability of traits by which we classify races come about in the first place? Some traits vary because of natural selection: that is, one form of the trait is advantageous for survival in one area, another form in a different area. For example, northern hares and weasels develop white fur in the winter, but southern ones retain brown fur year-round. The white winter fur is selected in the north for camouflage against the snow, while any animal unfortunate enough to turn white in the snowless southern states would stand out from afar against the brown ground and would be picked off by predators.

Other traits vary geographically because of sexual selection, meaning that those traits serve as arbitrary signals by which individuals of one sex attract mates of the opposite sex while intimidating rivals. Adult male lions, for instance, have a mane, but lionesses and young males don't. The adult male's mane signals to lionesses that he is sexually mature, and signals to young male rivals that he is a dangerous and experienced adversary. The length and color of a lion's mane vary among populations, being shorter and blacker in Indian lions than in African lions. Indian lions and lionesses evidently find short black manes sexy or intimidating; African lions don't.

Finally, some geographically variable traits have no known effect on survival and are invisible to rivals and to prospective sex partners. They merely reflect mutations that happened to arise and spread in one area. They could equally well have arisen and spread elsewhere—they just didn't.

RACE BY RESISTANCE

Traditionally we divide ourselves into races by the twin criteria of geographic location and visible physical characteristics. But we could make an equally reasonable and arbitrary division by the presence or absence of a gene, such as the sickle-cell gene, that confers resistance to malaria. By this reckoning, we'd place Yemenites, Greeks, New Guineans, Thai, and Dinkas in one "race," Norwegians and several black African peoples in another.

Nothing that I've said about geographic variation in animals is likely to get me branded a racist. We don't attribute higher IQ or social status to black-winged whistlers than to green-winged whistlers. But now let's consider geographic variation in humans. We'll start with invisible traits, about which it's easy to remain dispassionate.

Many geographically variable human traits evolved by natural selection to adapt humans to particular climates or environments—just as the winter color of a hare or weasel did. Good examples are the mutations that people in tropical parts of the Old World evolved to help them survive malaria, the leading infectious disease of the old-world tropics. One such mutation is the sickle-cell gene, so-called because the red blood cells of people with that mutation tend to assume a sickle shape. People bearing the gene are more resistant to malaria than people without it. Not surprisingly, the gene is absent from northern Europe, where malaria is nonexistent, but it's common in tropical Africa, where malaria is widespread. Up to 40 percent of Africans in such areas carry the sickle-cell gene. It's also common in the malaria-ridden Arabian Peninsula and southern India, and rare or absent in the southernmost parts of South Africa, among the Xhosas who live mostly beyond the tropical geographic range of malaria.

The geographic range of human malaria is much wider than the range of the sickle-cell gene. As it happens, other antimalarial genes take over the protective function of the sickle-cell gene in malarial Southeast Asia and New Guinea and in Italy, Greece, and other warm parts of the Mediterranean basin. Thus human races, if defined by antimalarial genes, would be very different from human races as traditionally defined by traits such as skin color. As classified by antimalarial genes (or their absence), Swedes are grouped with Xhosas but not with Italians or Greeks. Most other peoples usually viewed as African blacks are grouped with Arabia's "whites" and are kept separate from the "black" Xhosas.

RACE BY DIGESTION

We could define a race by any geographically variable trait— for example, the retention in adulthood of the enzyme lactase, which allows us to digest milk. Using this as our divisive criterion, we can place northern and central Europeans with Arabians and such West African peoples as the Fulani; in a "lactase-negative race," we can group most other African blacks with east Asians, American Indians, southern Europeans, and Australian aborigines.

Antimalarial genes exemplify the many features of our body chemistry that vary geographically under the influence of natural selection. Another such feature is the enzyme lactase, which enables us to digest the milk-sugar lactose. Infant humans, like infants of almost all other mammal species, possess lactase and drink milk. Until about 6,000 years ago most humans, like all other mammal species, lost the lactase enzyme on reaching the age of weaning. The obvious reason is that it was unnecessary—no human or other mammal drank milk as an adult. Beginning around 4000 B.C., however, fresh milk obtained from domestic mammals became a major food for adults of a few human populations. Natural selection caused individuals in these populations to retain lactase into adulthood. Among such peoples are northern and central Europeans, Arabians, north Indians, and several milk-drinking black African peoples, such as the Fulani of West Africa. Adult lactase is much less common in southern European populations and in most other African black populations, as well as in all populations of east Asians, aboriginal Australians, and American Indians.

Once again races defined by body chemistry don't match races defined by skin color. Swedes belong with Fulani in the "lactase-positive race," while most African "blacks," Japanese, and American Indians belong in the "lactase-negative race."

Not all the effects of natural selection are as invisible as lactase and sickle cells. Environmental pressures have also produced more noticeable differences among peoples, particularly in body shapes. Among the tallest and most long-limbed peoples in the world are the Nilotic peoples, such as the Dinkas, who live in the hot, dry areas of East Africa. At the opposite extreme in body shape are the Inuit, or Eskimo, who have compact bodies and relatively short arms and legs. The reasons have to do with heat loss. The greater the surface area of a warm body, the more body heat that's lost, since heat loss is directly proportional to

surface area. For people of a given weight, a long-limbed, tall shape maximizes surface area, while a compact, short-limbed shape minimizes it. Dinkas and Inuit have opposite problems of heat balance: the former usually need desperately to get rid of body heat, while the latter need desperately to conserve it. Thus natural selection molded their body shapes oppositely, based on their contrasting climates.

(In modern times, such considerations of body shape have become important to athletic performance as well as to heat loss. Tall basketball players, for example, have an obvious advantage over short ones, and slender, long-limbed tall players have an advantage over stout, short-limbed tall players. In the United States, it's a familiar observation that African Americans are disproportionately represented among professional basketball players. Of course, a contributing reason has to do with their lack of socioeconomic opportunities. But part of the reason probably has to do with the prevalent body shapes of some black African groups as well. However, this example also illustrates the dangers in facile racial stereotyping. One can't make the sweeping generalization that "whites can't jump," or that "blacks' anatomy makes them better basketball players." Only certain African peoples are notably tall and long-limbed; even those exceptional peoples are tall and long-limbed only on the average and vary individually.)

Other visible traits that vary geographically among humans evolved by means of sexual selection. We all know that we find some individuals of the opposite sex more attractive than other individuals. We also know that in sizing up sex appeal, we pay more attention to certain parts of a prospective sex partner's body than to other parts. Men tend to be inordinately interested in women's breasts and much less concerned with women's toenails. Women, in turn, tend to be turned on by the shape of a man's buttocks or the details of a man's beard and body hair, if any, but not by the size of his feet.

But all those determinants of sex appeal vary geographically. Khoisan and Andaman Island women tend to have much larger buttocks than most other women. Nipple color and breast shape and size also vary geographically among women. European men are rather hairy by world standards, while Southeast Asian men tend to have very sparse beards and body hair.

What's the function of these traits that differ so markedly between men and women? They certainly don't aid survival: it's not the case that orange nipples help Khoisan women escape lions, while darker nipples help European women survive cold winters. Instead, these varying traits play a crucial role in sexual selection. Women with very large buttocks are a

Arches   Loops   Whorls

turn-on, or at least acceptable, to Khoisan and Andaman men but look freakish to many men from other parts of the world. Bearded and hairy men readily find mates in Europe but fare worse in Southeast Asia. The geographic variation of these traits, however, is as arbitrary as the geographic variation in the color of a lion's mane.

RACE BY FINGERPRINTS

Probably the most trivial division of humans we could manage would be based on fingerprint patterns. As it turns out, the prevalence of certain basic features varies predictably among peoples: in the "Loops" race we could group together most Europeans, black Africans, and east Asians. Among the "Whorls" we could place Mongolians and Australian aborigines. Finally, in an "Arches" race, we could group Khoisans and some central Europeans.

There is a third possible explanation for the function of geographically variable human traits, besides survival or sexual selection—namely, no function at all. A good example is provided by fingerprints, whose complex pattern of arches, loops, and whorls is determined genetically. Fingerprints also vary geographically: for example, Europeans' fingerprints tend to have many loops, while aboriginal Australians' fingerprints tend to have many whorls.

If we classify human populations by their fingerprints, most Europeans and black Africans would sort out together in one race, Jews and some Indonesians in another, and aboriginal Australians in still another. But those geographic variations in fingerprint patterns possess no known function whatsoever. They play no role in survival: whorls aren't especially suitable for grabbing kangaroos, nor do loops help bar mitzvah candidates hold on to the pointer for the Torah. They also play no role in sexual selection: while you've undoubtedly noticed whether your mate is bearded or has brown nipples, you surely haven't the faintest idea whether his or her fingerprints have more loops than

whorls. Instead it's purely a matter of chance that whorls became common in aboriginal Australians, and loops among Jews. Our rhesus factor blood groups and numerous other human traits fall into the same category of genetic characteristics whose geographic variation serves no function.

RACE BY GENES

One method that seems to offer a way out of arbitrariness is to classify people's degree of genetic distinctness. By this standard the Khoisans of southern Africa would be in a race by themselves. African blacks would form several other distinct races. All the rest of the world's peoples—Norwegians, Navajo, Greeks, Japanese, Australian aborigines, and so on—would, despite their greatly differing external appearance, belong to a single race.

You've probably been wondering when I was going to get back to skin color, eye color, and hair color and form. After all, those are the traits by which all of us members of the lay public, as well as traditional anthropologists, classify races. Does geographic variation in those traits function in survival, in sexual selection, or in nothing?

The usual view is that skin color varies geographically to enhance survival. Supposedly, people in sunny, tropical climates around the world have generally dark skin, which is supposedly analogous to the temporary skin darkening of European whites in the summer. The supposed function of dark skin in sunny climates is for protection against skin cancer. Variations in eye color and hair form and color are also supposed to enhance survival under particular conditions, though no one has ever proposed a plausible hypothesis for how those variations might actually enhance survival.

Alas, the evidence for natural selection of skin color dissolves under scrutiny. Among tropical peoples, anthropologists love to stress the dark skins of African blacks, people of the southern Indian peninsula, and New Guineans and love to forget the pale skins of Amazonian Indians and Southeast Asians living at the same latitudes. To wriggle out of those paradoxes, anthropologists then plead the excuse that Amazonian Indians and Southeast Asians may not have been living in their present locations long enough to evolve dark skins. However, the ancestors of fair-skinned Swedes arrived even more recently in Scandinavia, and aboriginal Tasmanians were black-skinned despite their ancestors' having lived for at least the last 10,000 years at the latitude of Vladivostok.

Besides, when one takes into account cloud cover, peoples of equatorial West Africa and the New Guinea mountains actually receive no more ultraviolet radiation or hours of sunshine each year than do the Swiss. Compared with infectious diseases and other selective agents, skin cancer has been utterly trivial as a cause of death in human history, even for modern white settlers in the tropics. This objection is so obvious to believers in natural selection of skin color that they have proposed at least seven other supposed survival functions of skin color, without reaching agreement. Those other supposed functions include protection against rickets, frostbite, folic acid deficiency, beryllium poisoning, overheating, and overcooling. The diversity of these contradictory theories makes clear how far we are from understanding the survival value (if any) of skin color.

It wouldn't surprise me if dark skins do eventually prove to offer some advantage in tropical climates, but I expect the advantage to turn out to be a slight one that is easily overridden. But there's an overwhelming importance to skin, eye, and hair color that is obvious to all of us—sexual selection. Before we can reach a condition of intimacy permitting us to assess the beauty of a prospective sex partner's hidden physical attractions, we first have to pass muster for skin, eyes, and hair.

We all know how those highly visible "beauty traits" guide our choice of sex partners. Even the briefest personal ad in a newspaper mentions the advertiser's skin color, and the color of skin that he or she seeks in a partner. Skin color, of course, is also of overwhelming importance in our social prejudices. If you're a black African American trying to raise your children in white U.S. society, rickets and overheating are the least of the problems that might be solved by your skin color. Eye color and hair form and color, while not so overwhelmingly important as skin color, also play an obvious role in our sexual and social preferences. Just ask yourself why hair dyes, hair curlers, and hair straighteners enjoy such wide sales. You can bet that it's not to improve our chances of surviving grizzly bear attacks and other risks endemic to the North American continent.

Nearly 125 years ago Charles Darwin himself, the discoverer of natural selection, dismissed its role as an explanation of geographic variation in human beauty traits. Everything that we have learned since then only reinforces Darwin's view.

We can now return to our original questions: Are human racial classifications that are based on different traits concordant with one another? What is the hierarchical relation among recognized races? What is the function of racially variable traits? What, really, are the traditional human races?

Regarding concordance, we *could* have classified races based on any number of geographically variable traits. The resulting classifications would not be at all concordant. Depending on whether we classified ourselves by antimalarial genes, lactase, fingerprints, or skin color, we could place Swedes in the same race as either Xhosas, Fulani, the Ainu of Japan, or Italians.

Regarding hierarchy, traditional classifications that emphasize skin color face unresolvable ambiguities. Anthropology textbooks often recognize five major races: "whites," "African blacks," "Mongoloids," "aboriginal Australians," and "Khoisans," each in turn divided into various numbers of sub-races. But there is no agreement on the number and delineation of the sub-races, or even of the major races. Are all five of the major races equally distinctive? Are Nigerians really less different from Xhosas than aboriginal Australians are from both? Should we recognize 3 or 15 sub-races of Mongoloids? These questions have remained unresolved because skin color and other traditional racial criteria are difficult to formulate mathematically.

A method that could in principle overcome these problems is to base racial classification on a combination of as many geographically variable genes as possible. Within the past decade, some biologists have shown renewed interest in developing a hierarchical classification of human populations—hierarchical not in the sense that it identifies superior and inferior races but in the sense of grouping and separating populations based on mathematical measures of genetic distinctness. While the biologists still haven't reached agreement, some of their studies suggest that human genetic diversity may be greatest in Africa. If so, the primary races of humanity may consist of several African races, plus one race to encompass all peoples of all other continents. Swedes, New Guineans, Japanese, and Navajo would then belong to the same primary race; the Khoisans of southern Africa would constitute another primary race by themselves; and African "blacks" and Pygmies would be divided among several other primary races.

As regards the function of all those traits that are useful for classifying human races, some serve to enhance survival, some to enhance sexual selection, while some serve no function at all. The traits we traditionally use are ones subject to sexual selection, which is not really surprising. These traits are not only visible at a distance but also highly variable; that's why they became the ones used throughout recorded history to make quick judgments about people. Racial classification didn't come from science but from the body's signals for differentiating attractive from unattractive sex partners, and for differentiating friend from foe.

Such snap judgments didn't threaten our existence back when people were armed only with spears and surrounded by others who looked mostly like themselves. In the modern world, though, we are armed with guns and plutonium, and we live our lives surrounded by people who are much more varied in appearance. The last thing we need now is to continue codifying all those different appearances into an arbitrary system of racial classification.

17

Official Statement on "Race"

American Anthropological Association

Race is an incredibly important social and political issue in the United States. News items of national interest—from the Los Angeles riots after the Rodney King verdict to the trial of O. J. Simpson—often center on sensitive cultural issues. Questions about the inclusion of mixed race and ethnicity categories for the U.S. Census for the year 2000 have been hotly debated. The publication of Herrnstein and Murray's *The Bell Curve: Intelligence and Class Structure in American Life* raised a remarkable public debate; despite terrible reviews and scientific criticism, the book sold very well. President Clinton identified the need for a national dialogue about race; such a dialogue may well be an uncomfortable conversation.

As we learned in the last selection, race is an out-of-date and useless concept from the viewpoint of understanding and explaining human biological diversity. Although many biological anthropologists have privately come to this conclusion, the public holds on to the belief that race refers to real biological categories. At the same time, discrimination based on skin color—at times overt and at other times subtle and invidious—continues to exist in the United States.

The American Anthropological Association (AAA) is the oldest and largest professional association for all four fields of anthropology as well as applied anthropology. As a professional association, the AAA has drafted a clear statement about the biology and politics of race. The statement is clear and informational.

As you read this selection, ask yourself the following questions:

- Why would members of a professional academic association think that they need to have an official statement about race?

- Why is the history of a concept like race relevant to understanding its current scientific usefulness?

- What is the relationship between racial categorizations and the distribution of privilege, power, and wealth?

- Why does race distort and prejudge our ideas about human differences and group behavior?

The following terms discussed in this selection are included in the Glossary at the back of the book:

biophysical diversity

culture

race

S ince the mid-20th century there has been a major transformation in thinking about "race" in the academic world, especially in the fields of anthropology and biology. For several hundred years before this time, both scholars and the public had been conditioned to viewing purported "races" as natural, distinct and exclusive divisions among human populations based on visible physical differences. However, with the vast expansion of scientific knowledge in this century, it is clear that human populations are not unambiguous, clearly demarcated, biologically distinct groups. As a result, we conclude that the concept of "race" has no validity as a biological category in the human species. Because it homogenizes widely varying individuals into limited categories, it impedes research and understanding of the true nature of human biological variations.

The following statement summarizes the findings and conclusions of experts on human biophysical variation. For a more full and extensive exploration of this topic, see the statement published by the American Association of Physical Anthropologists in 1996 (AJPA 101:569–570).

The human species is highly diverse, with individuals and populations varying in observable traits such as body size and shape, skin color, hair texture, facial

Reprinted by permission of the American Anthropological Association from *Anthropology Newsletter* 38:6, September 1997.

features and certain characteristics of the skeletal structure. Populations also differ in their percentage frequencies of the blood types (A, B, AB and O) and other known genetic traits. This variation is a product of evolutionary forces operating on human groups as they have adapted to different environments over thousands of years. Some biogenetic variation results from migration and changes within isolated groups. Yet all human groups are capable of interbreeding with others and producing viable and fertile offspring. Throughout history, whenever different groups have come into contact, they have interbred. As a result, all populations share many features with other, neighboring groups.

Variations in any given trait tend to occur gradually rather than abruptly over geographic areas. And because physical traits vary independently of one another, knowing the frequencies of one trait does not predict the presence or frequencies of others. These facts render any attempt to establish lines of division among biological populations both arbitrary and subjective. Genetically there are greater differences among individuals within large geographic populations than the average differences between them. Because of our complex genetic structure, no human groups can be seen as homogeneous or "pure."

Biophysical diversity has no inherent social meaning except what we humans confer upon it. The concept of "race" is in reality a product of that process. "Race" is a set of culturally created attitudes toward, and beliefs about, human differences developed following widespread exploration and colonization by Western European powers since the 16th century. In the North American colonies, European settlers conquered an indigenous population and brought in as slaves alien peoples from Africa. By the end of the 18th century a rising antislavery movement, produced by liberal and humanistic forces mostly in Europe, compelled slave owners to find new defenses for preserving slavery. "Race" was invented as a social mechanism to justify the retention of slavery. "Race" ideology magnified differences among these populations, established a rigid hierarchy of socially exclusive categories, underscored and bolstered unequal rank and status differences and provided the rationalization that such differences were natural or God-given. The different physical traits became markers or symbols of status differences.

As they were constructing this society, white Americans fabricated the cultural/behavioral characteristics associated with each "race," linking superior traits to Europeans and negative and inferior ones to blacks and Indians. Thus arbitrary beliefs about the different peoples were institutionalized and deeply embedded in American thought. Ultimately "race" as an ideology about human differences was reified and

subsequently spread to other areas of the world. It became a mechanism for dividing and ranking people, used by colonial powers everywhere. But it was not limited to the colonial situation; it was employed by Europeans to rank each other and, during World War II, became the motive for the unspeakable brutalities of the Holocaust.

"Race" evolved as a worldview, a body of prejudgments that distorts our ideas about human differences and group behavior. Such beliefs constitute myths about the diversity in the human species and about the abilities and behavior of people homogenized into "racial" categories. The myths fused behavior and physical features together in the public mind, impeding our comprehension of both biology and culture and implying that both are genetically determined. Racial myths bear no relationship to the reality of human capabilities or behavior. Scientists have found that reliance on such folk beliefs about human differences in research has led to countless errors.

At the end of the 20th century, we now understand that human behavior is learned, conditioned into infants beginning at birth and always subject to modification and change. No human is born with built-in culture traits or language. Our temperaments, dispositions and personalities, regardless of genetic propensities, are developed within sets of meanings and values that we call "culture." Studies of infant and early childhood learning and behavior attest to the reality of our cultures in forming who we are.

It is a basic tenet of anthropological knowledge that all normal human beings have the capacity to learn any cultural behavior. In the modern world we humans are constantly experiencing new cultural meanings and are, thus, capable of transforming ourselves. The American experience with immigrants from hundreds of different language and cultural backgrounds who have acquired some variation of American culture traits and behavior is the clearest evidence of this fact. We are all becoming more multicultural as we have access to both material culture and ideas that disseminate around the world.

How people have been accepted and treated within the context of their society and culture has a direct impact on how they perform within that society. The "racial" worldview was invented to assign some groups to perpetual low status while others were permitted access to privilege, power and wealth. The tragedy is that it succeeded all too well in constructing unequal populations. Given what we know about the capacity of normal humans to achieve and function within any culture, we conclude that present-day inequalities between human groups are not consequences of their biological inheritance; rather, these inequalities are products of historical and contemporary social, economic, educational and political circumstances.

18

White Privilege

Unpacking the Invisible Knapsack

Peggy McIntosh

Although many major events of the civil rights movement happened before present-day college students were born, most students have probably seen pictures, films, or videos of police blocking African Americans from entering white schools and signs prohibiting African Americans from sitting at lunch counters or drinking from the same water fountains as whites. Though the signs indicating "for whites only" are fading from the American memory, the legacy of racism certainly remains with us today. In the absence of Cross burnings and other obvious signs of racism, however, there is a tendency for whites to assume that racism is a thing of the past, that inequality no longer plagues our nation.

The frustration in the dialogue about racism in the United States has many of the characteristics of cross-cultural miscommunication. People use the same words but with different meanings. They examine the same social situations and come away with quite different interpretations. The analogy in linguistics is that individuals from one language group may not even hear the phonemes used in a different language. In other words, individuals from one group simply cannot see the world through the eyes of the other. Throughout this book you will be reading about other cultures and trying to understand their lifeways—to see the world as they do. It is often more difficult to set aside our commonsense interpretation of the familiar world that surrounds us each day than to freshly examine a novel situation. We must strive to suspend our judgment and read through this selection with an anthropological imagination.

As you read this selection, ask yourself the following questions:

- What does the author mean by "an invisible package of unearned assets"? How might this relate to the concept of ascribed status?

- Does the author's use of the term *oppressor* imply intentionality, or is this oppression a result of a culture and social organization that is seldom consciously recognized?

- Can you add to the author's list of twenty-six situations that confer privilege?

- Is white privilege a serious threat to equality, or is it merely an inconvenience? What should be done to achieve the U.S. ideal of social equality? Whose responsibility is it to change the culture if it is harmful?

The following terms discussed in this selection are included in the Glossary at the back of the book:

> *hierarchy*
>
> *meritocracy*
>
> *privilege*

Through work to bring materials from Women's Studies into the rest of the curriculum, I have often noticed men's unwillingness to grant that they are overprivileged even though they may grant that women are disadvantaged. They may say they will work to improve women's status, in the society, the university, or the curriculum, but they can't or won't support the idea of lessening men's. Denials which amount to taboos surround the subject of advantages which men gain from women's disadvantages. These denials protect male privilege from being fully acknowledged, lessened or ended.

Thinking through unacknowledged male privilege as a phenomenon, I realized that since hierarchies in our society are interlocking, there was most likely a phenomenon of white privilege which was similarly denied and protected. As a white person, I realized I had been taught about racism as something which puts others at a disadvantage, but had been taught not to see one of its corollary aspects, white privilege, which puts me at an advantage.

I think whites are carefully taught not to recognize white privilege, as males are taught not to recognize male privilege. So I have begun in an untutored way to ask what it is like to have white privilege. I have come to see white privilege as an invisible package of unearned assets which I can count on cashing in each day, but about which I was "meant" to remain oblivious. White privilege is like an invisible weightless knapsack of special provisions, maps, passports, code-books, visas, clothes, tools and blank checks.

Describing white privilege makes one newly accountable. As we in Women's Studies work to reveal male privilege and ask men to give up some of their power, so one who writes about having white privilege must ask, "Having described it, what will I do to lessen or end it?"

After I realized the extent to which men work from a base of unacknowledged privilege, I understood that much of their oppressiveness was unconscious. Then I remembered the frequent charges from women of color that white women whom they encounter are oppressive. I began to understand why we are justly seen as oppressive, even when we don't see ourselves that way. I began to count the ways in which I enjoy unearned skin privilege and have been conditioned into oblivion about its existence.

My schooling gave me no training in seeing myself as an oppressor, as an unfairly advantaged person, or as a participant in a damaged culture. I was taught to see myself as an individual whose moral state depended on her individual moral will. My schooling followed the pattern my colleague Elizabeth Minnich has pointed out: whites are taught to think of their lives as morally neutral, normative, and average, and also ideal, so that when we work to benefit others, this is seen as work which will allow "them" to be more like "us."

I decided to try to work on myself at least by identifying some of the daily effects of white privilege in my life. I have chosen those conditions which I think in my case *attach somewhat more to skin-color privilege* than to class, religion, ethnic status, or geographical location, though of course all these other factors are intricately intertwined. As far as I can see, my African American co-workers, friends and acquaintances with whom I come into daily or frequent contact in this particular time, place, and line of work cannot count on most of these conditions.

1. I can if I wish arrange to be in the company of people of my race most of the time.

2. If I should need to move, I can be pretty sure of renting or purchasing housing in an area which I can afford and in which I would want to live.

3. I can be pretty sure that my neighbors in such a location will be neutral or pleasant to me.

4. I can go shopping alone most of the time, pretty well assured that I will not be followed or harassed.

5. I can turn on the television or open to the front page of the paper and see people of my race widely represented.

6. When I am told about our national heritage or about "civilization," I am shown that people of my color made it what it is.

7. I can be sure that my children will be given curricular materials that testify to the existence of their race.

8. If I want to, I can be pretty sure of finding a publisher for this piece on white privilege.

9. I can go into a music shop and count on finding the music of my race represented, into a supermarket and find the staple foods which fit with my cultural traditions, into a hairdresser's shop and find someone who can cut my hair.

10. Whether I use checks, credit cards, or cash, I can count on my skin color not to work against the appearance of financial reliability.

11. I can arrange to protect my children most of the time from people who might not like them.

12. I can swear, or dress in secondhand clothes. Or not answer letters, without having people attribute these choices to the bad morals, the poverty, or the illiteracy of my race.

13. I can speak in public to a powerful male group without putting my race on trial.

14. I can do well in a challenging situation without being called a credit to my race.

15. I am never asked to speak for all the people of my racial group.

16. I can remain oblivious of the language and customs of persons of color who constitute the world's majority without feeling in my culture any penalty for such oblivion.

17. I can criticize our government and talk about how much I fear its policies and behavior without being seen as a cultural outsider.

18. I can be pretty sure that if I ask to talk to "the person in charge," I will be facing a person of my race.

19. If a traffic cop pulls me over or if the IRS audits my tax return, I can be sure I haven't been singled out because of my race.

20. I can easily buy posters, postcards, picture books, greeting cards, dolls, toys, and children's magazines featuring people of my race.

21. I can go home from most meetings of organizations I belong to feeling somewhat tied in, rather than isolated, out-of-place, outnumbered, unheard, held at a distance, or feared.

22. I can take a job with an affirmative action employer without having co-workers on the job suspect that I got it because of race.

23. I can choose public accommodation without fearing that people of my race cannot get in or will be mistreated in the places I have chosen.

24. I can be sure that if I need legal or medical help, my race will not work against me.

25. If my day, week, or year is going badly, I need not ask of each negative episode or situation whether it has racial overtones.

26. I can choose blemish cover or bandages in "flesh" color and have them more or less match my skin.

I repeatedly forgot each of the realizations on this list until I wrote it down. For me white privilege has turned out to be an elusive and fugitive subject. The pressure to avoid it is great, for in facing it I must give up the myth of meritocracy. If these things are true, this is not such a free country, one's life is not what one makes it; many doors open for certain people through no virtues of their own.

In unpacking this invisible knapsack of white privilege, I have listed conditions of daily experience which I once took for granted. Nor did I think of any of these perquisites as bad for the holder. I now think that we need a more finely differentiated taxonomy of privilege, for some of these varieties are only what one would want for everyone in a just society, and others give license to be ignorant, oblivious, arrogant and destructive.

I see a pattern running through the matrix of white privilege, a pattern of assumptions which were passed on to me as a white person. There was one main piece of cultural turf; it was my own turf, and I was among those who could control the turf. *My skin color was an asset for any move I was educated to want to make.* I could think of myself as belonging in major ways, and of making social systems work for me. I could freely disparage, fear, neglect, or be oblivious to anything outside of the dominant cultural forms. Being of the main culture, I could also criticize it fairly freely.

In proportion as my racial group was being made confident, comfortable, and oblivious, other groups were likely being made inconfident, uncomfortable, and alienated. Whiteness protected me from many kinds of hostility, distress, and violence, which I was being subtly trained to visit in turn upon people of color.

For this reason, the word "privilege" now seems to me misleading. We usually think of privilege as being a favored state, whether earned or conferred by birth or luck. Yet some of the conditions I have described here work to systematically overempower certain groups. Such privilege simply *confers dominance* because of one's race or sex.

I want, then, to distinguish between earned strength and unearned power conferred systematically. Power from unearned privilege can look like strength when it is in fact permission to escape or to dominate. But not all of the privileges on my list are inevitably damaging. Some, like the expectation that neighbors will be decent to you, or that your race will not count against you in court, should be the norm in a just society. Others, like the privilege to ignore less powerful people, distort the humanity of the holders as well as the ignored groups.

We might at least start by distinguishing between positive advantages which we can work to spread, and negative types of advantages which unless rejected will always reinforce our present hierarchies. For example, the feeling that one belongs within the human circle, as Native Americans say, should not be seen as privilege for a few. Ideally it is an *unearned entitlement.* At present, since only a few have it, it is an *unearned advantage* for them. This paper results from a process of coming to see that some of the power which I originally saw as attendant on being a human being in the U.S. consisted [of] *unearned advantage* and *conferred dominance.*

I have met very few men who are truly distressed about systemic, unearned male advantage and conferred dominance. And so one question for me and others like me is whether we will be like them, or whether we will get truly distressed, even outraged, about unearned race advantage and conferred dominance and if so, what we will do to lessen them. In any case, we need to do more work in identifying how they actually affect our daily lives. Many, perhaps most, of our white students in the U.S. think that racism doesn't affect them because they are not people of color; they do not see "whiteness" as a racial identity. In addition, since race and sex are not the only advantaging systems at work, we need similarly to examine the daily experience of having age advantage, or ethnic advantage, or physical ability, or advantage related to nationality, religions or sexual orientation.

Difficulties and dangers surrounding the task of finding parallels are many. Since racism, sexisms and heterosexism are not the same, the advantaging associated with them should not be seen as the same. In addition, it is hard to disentangle aspects of unearned advantage which rest more on social class, economic class, race, religion, sex and ethnic identity than on other factors. Still, all of the oppressions are interlocking, as the Combahee River Collective[1] Statement of 1977 continues to remind us eloquently.

One factor seems clear about all of the interlocking oppressions. They take both active forms which we can see and embedded forms which as a member of the dominant group one is taught not to see. In my class and place, I did not see myself as a racist because I was taught to recognize racism only in individual acts of meanness by members of my group, never in invisible systems conferring unsought racial dominance on my group from birth.

Disapproving of the systems won't be enough to change them. I was taught to think that racism could end if white individuals changed their attitudes. [But] a "white" skin in the United States opens many doors for whites whether or not we approve of the way dominance has been conferred on us. Individual acts can palliate, but cannot end, these problems.

To redesign social systems we need first to acknowledge their colossal unseen dimensions. The silences and denials surrounding privilege are the key political tool here. They keep the thinking about equality or equity incomplete, protecting unearned advantage and conferred dominance by making these taboo subjects. Most talk by whites about equal opportunity seems to me now to be about equal opportunity to try to get into a position of dominance while denying that *systems* of dominance exist.

It seems to me that obliviousness about white advantage like obliviousness about male advantage, is kept strongly inculturated in the United States so as to maintain the myth of meritocracy, the myth that democratic choice is equally available to all. Keeping most people unaware that freedom of confident action is there for just a small number of people props up those in power and serves to keep power in the hands of the same groups that have most of it already.

Though systemic change takes many decades, there are pressing questions for me and I imagine for some others like me if we raise our daily consciousness on the perquisites of being lightskinned. What will we do with such knowledge? As we know from watching men, it is an open question whether we will choose to use unearned advantage to weaken hidden systems of advantage, and whether we will use any of our arbitrarily awarded power to try to reconstruct power systems on a broader base.

NOTE

1. Combahee River Collective: A group of black feminist women in Boston from 1974 to 1980.

19

Of Kwanzaa, Cinco de Mayo, and Whispering

The Need for Intercultural Education

Deborah Freedman Lustig

Living in a multicultural, multiethnic society is a challenge. The U.S. motto *E Pluribus Unum* (out of many, one) implies an ideal of creating national unity while simultaneously respecting cultural diversity. This national challenge is often experienced and played out in our schools, because they are a microcosm of our society. Contemporary political debates often revolve around education policy; from gun control and violence to multiculturalism and bilingualism, the continuing formulation of American society and culture is played out in the social institution of schools.

The expansion of the educational curriculum to be more representative of America's wide ethnic and cultural diversity has been at the center of heated public policy debates. On the one hand, critics of traditional curriculum point out the predominance of the "dead white male" point of view. On the other hand, critics of multicultural programs argue, concern with diversity is "cultural fluff," and the real focus of education reform must be on standards and improving test scores. But students themselves know the reality that our schools are already multicultural societies. In many school districts, students of European ancestry are in the minority, while African American, Latino, and Asian students form youth subcultures that often have strained relations with one another. In response to the overwhelming demands to promote and reflect our rich cultural diversity, many school districts have instituted multicultural programming. In this selection, Deborah Lustig suggests that *superficial* multicultural programs in a high school, largely limited to assemblies and special events, may do more harm than good.

Multicultural programs that are targeted only toward a specific ethnicity create the potential for increased conflict between minority groups. When a Kwanzaa dance performance is organized by a visiting arts teaching team, only African American students feel welcome and empowered to participate. Spanish spoken by Latina women in the classroom is overheard with suspicion by English-speaking students who are certain that "they" must be whispering gossip. By targeting each ethnic group separately with occasional programs, multicultural reforms can exacerbate differences and hostilities because they focus on difference rather than on mutual understanding and trust.

Multicultural reform must start from the ethnographic realities of the school district and classroom. In addition to changing the content of the curriculum to include stories, histories, and arts that better reflect our nation's population, careful attention must be paid to pedagogy and classroom management. No one can learn in a hostile, conflict-ridden environment, and little social change can be expected from a generation educated across ethnic battle lines. In this selection, the anthropologist describes the ethnographic reality of a high school and the way in which opportunities for real *intercultural education* are sometimes missed. Anthropologists sometimes distinguish between cultural ideals, expressed in ambitious statements, and social realities, the observable on-the-ground actions that sometimes reflect conflicting cultural values. This selection demonstrates that there is a significant difference between the ideal and the real.

As you read this selection, ask yourself the following questions:

- How much of your own education reflected your cultural heritage(s), and how much did you learn about the heritages of other cultures?

- How can an analysis and understanding of the social and cultural realities of a school's population be used to avoid misunderstandings and conflict?

Reproduced by permission of the American Anthropological Association from *Anthropology and Education Quarterly* 28(4):574–592, 1997. Not for sale or further reproduction.

- Does focusing educational reform on cultural diversity take away from raising the standards of education?

- How might you as an anthropologist help students, teachers, and administrative staff to understand one another better and promote a supportive, participatory school environment?

- How do the cultural beliefs and values of the teachers themselves contribute to this situation?

The following terms discussed in this selection are included in the Glossary at the back of the book:

Afrocentric

class

ethnic groups

Eurocentric

multiculturalism

pedagogy

race

Throughout much of the world, racial/ethnic tensions and conflicts grow unchecked; schools are a key site for the enactment of these tensions (Macias 1996).[1] Multicultural education attempts to address and alleviate these tensions. The movement toward multicultural education began in the United States after World War II, flourished in the late 1960s, and has continued through the 1990s. Advocates of multicultural education envision a global transformation of the schools. Teacher education texts (Diaz 1992; O'Hair and Odell 1993) call for a true re-visioning of the school, from the curriculum to pedagogy, from extracurricular activities to discipline. A truly multicultural education would teach the histories, literatures, and contemporary experiences of "other Americans" as integral parts of the curriculum. Moreover, because the "hidden" curriculum is just as important as the official curriculum, and the tone and content of interactions are just as important as the demographics of the school (McCarthy 1993; Sleeter and Grant 1988), multicultural education necessitates reforming pedagogy and discipline so that they are culturally sensitive as well.

Proponents of multicultural education affirm that it will improve interethnic relationships (ASCD 1977; Hanna 1994; Sleeter and Grant 1988) as well as educational outcomes for students of color (AACTE 1980; Cummins 1986; Rushton 1981). It is unclear, however, how profound the reforms have to be in order to reap the benefits of multicultural education. In this article, based on ethnographic data from one high school in California, I propose that *superficial* multicultural programs can actually exacerbate interethnic conflict. My evidence suggests that multicultural education must be implemented intensively and systematically, rather than gradually.[2]

I agree with Wallace that we should "view multiculturalism not as an obdurate and unchanging ideological position but as an opportunity for ongoing critical debate" (1993:252). The debate has to include observations and evaluation of (supposedly) multicultural education as it exists in schools today. My critique of multicultural education rests on the contrast between the ideal of multicultural education and the extremely superficial version that I observed.[3]

Token multicultural reforms can intensify ethnic group conflict if they neglect the power relations among the oppressed—between "minority" groups—as well as if they neglect the power relations between the dominant and the oppressed. Discussions of multicultural education usually revolve around the relationship of students of color to European American students, staff, curricula, and pedagogies (McCarthy and Willis 1995). But racial tensions, fears, and hatreds also exist between different "minorities" in many multiethnic schools (Foley 1990, but see Grant and Sleeter 1986 for an exception).[4] In this article I will describe how, at one California high school, interethnic tensions are aggravated by educational reforms that highlight each ethnic group both sequentially and in isolation.

Although at some schools multicultural education *is* implemented intensively, many more schools are quick to claim that they provide multicultural education. "Many well-intentioned but superficial school practices parade as multicultural education, such as food fairs, costume shows, and window-dressing contributions by people of color" (Sleeter 1991:9).

I observed interethnic relations and the attempts at multicultural education at one inner-city high school, King High, in Pineview, California.[5] The Pineview school district and community activists, in their 1990 "Agenda for Positive Change," espouse a thorough multicultural reform.[6]

[Pineview] is a community rich in cultures, ethnicities, and languages. The schools must promote and reflect that richness. This means:

- School personnel are educated about the cultures and histories represented among the children they teach.

- School personnel are as diverse as the student body, providing the sensitivity and language skills to bridge school with home.
- Textbooks are infused with the contributions of all peoples.
- Diverse values and traditions are integrated in every aspect of the educational program.
- Education is no longer presented from an exclusively European-centered point of view.
- Instruction and programs are designed for students to interact harmoniously across racial, ethnic, cultural, and language differences.

Three years after this impressive outline was published, multicultural education at King High was still limited to posters on the wall and special assemblies. Like King High, most schools go no further than a superficial addition of multicultural events and heroes, even though scholars agree that multicultural education should be much more than "add cultures and stir" (Arvizu and Saravia-Shore 1990). At King High, these very superficial attempts at multicultural education actually exacerbated group conflict, but I suggest that a truly multicultural education with a focus on process and boundaries *could* alleviate interethnic tensions.

Twenty years ago, Cortes said that although multicultural education should be more than isolated events and units, their addition was a positive first step.

> The recognition of ethnic groups through school events and the study of single ethnic groups through special units and courses has been a valuable and long overdue addition to our educational process . . . they have intrinsic value and . . . they provide the cutting edge of multicultural educational reform. [Cortes 1977:39]

Most schools have not gone beyond this first step. Moreover, this first step, in isolation, is not only inadequate, but it is actually dangerous. As Hanna warns, "Besides the lack of evidence that multicultural education programs do what they are supposed to do, multicultural programs may have unintended consequences" (1994:72). Token multicultural education can inflame interethnic resentments, surely an unintended consequence. In her case study of the implementation of a multicultural "school within a school," Ulichny found that multiculturalism in practice meant "different foods, festivals, and 'foreign' languages," instead of "an exploration of societal patterns of discrimination and inequality that are based on class, race, and place of origin" (1996:343). The emphasis on cultural heritage worsened interethnic relations because students of some ethnic groups were resentful of those who seemed to have a monopoly on "culture."

I suggest that instead of *starting* from the "special events" approach, we rework the model of multicultural education. Successful multicultural education requires an analysis of the dynamics of student relations across all ethnic groups—"minority" and "majority"—and must begin with the particular culture of each school, as well as encompass broader societal patterns of access to power and privilege. Some scholars have argued for a deepening of multicultural education toward what McCarthy calls "critical multiculturalism, . . . a process that goes beyond 'inclusivity' and emphasizes relationality and multivocality" (1993:290). As I will explain later, I prefer the term *intercultural education* to foreground the relationships between and the diversity within ethnic groups.

ETHNOGRAPHIC SETTING AND RESEARCH METHODS

King High is located in Pineview, a large city in California. Pineview is a poor city, and King High has the highest concentration of low-income students of any Pineview high school.[7] The ethnic makeup of the students is 80 percent African American, 10 percent Latino, and 10 percent other ethnicities. Approximately 1,500 students are enrolled at King High, but on any day only about half of them are present.

My analysis of interethnic relations and the multicultural efforts at King is drawn from a larger ethnographic study of teen mothers and their school experiences (Lustig 1997). King High has a largely self-contained program to enable teen mothers to finish school (the School-Age Parent, or SAP, program). During the year and a half that I spent at the SAP program, about 80 percent of these students were African American, 10 percent were Latina, and 10 percent were Asian American. In the course of the school year over one hundred students enrolled in the SAP program, but only about 25 students attended more or less regularly.[8] I was at the school four full days a week, spending most of my time with the teen mothers in the three classrooms used by the SAP program. Some SAP students were mainstreamed into "regular" (non-SAP) classes, and I occasionally accompanied them there as well. The quotes from students, teachers, and administrators are from my field notes and taped interviews. In the school setting, it often seemed natural to take my field notes during classes and assemblies. During lunch, support group, and other times when it would have been intrusive to take notes, I took notes as soon as possible afterwards, either during the next class period or that afternoon at home.

While my main concern in this article is interethnic relations among students, teachers and administrators could play a vital role in ameliorating those relations. I will address teachers' feelings about interethnic conflict, multicultural education, and their responsibilities as teachers. Although I did not conduct formal interviews with teachers and administrators, I had long conversations with ten teachers (all of the academic and "support services" teachers in the King High SAP program as well as some of the SAP teachers at other Pineview schools) and briefer interactions with several of the administrators. I took notes on these conversations shortly after they took place. I also attended most staff meetings at the King High SAP program and several of the districtwide SAP meetings, including the orientation at the beginning of the year and the midyear retreat, and I took notes during these meetings.

In the SAP program in Pineview and at King High, almost all the administrators are African American. In the SAP program, almost all the academic teachers are European American, while almost all the "support services" teachers, who teach nutrition, parenting, prenatal education, health, and career planning, are African American. This distribution is problematic for four reasons: first, the alignment of European Americans with academic subjects reinforces the association between academic success and "acting white" (Fordham 1988); second, the European American teachers, because of their ethnicity, feel particularly inadequate to deal with the ethnic conflicts that arise; third, the Latinas are left with no Latino adults at school; and fourth, the ethnic makeup of the staff is not seen as problematic by the administrators.

According to one teacher, Ms. Wells, the academic teachers were concerned about the patterning of diversity among the staff and told the administrators that they thought academic teachers of color should be hired. The director downplayed their concerns by referring to the diversity among the staff as a whole and pointed to the undeniable fact of budget cutbacks, which were leading to layoffs, not hiring.

At the SAP staff orientation before the school year began, the director lauded the program for having such an ethnically diverse staff: "Now we can really serve the diverse population of this city and this program." She overlooked the staff distribution and assignments: the few Asian American and Latino staff members were in the district office or the other teen mother programs in the district; the European Americans were all academic teachers; and the African Americans were primarily child care staff, support services teachers, and administrators. Furthermore, her assumption that a diverse staff would automatically make the SAP program culturally sensitive proved to be unfounded.

I conducted taped interviews with 75 teen mothers, of whom half were or had been SAP students at King High. The interviews covered a wide range of subjects, but the questions relevant to this article were,

"What has it been like for you growing up [black/Latina/white/Asian]? Have you ever experienced racism or prejudice against you in school? What do you think about how the different groups get along at school?" I also asked about the ethnic makeup of the schools the informant had attended and asked other questions relevant to each informant's particular situation. For example, if the young woman had a child with a partner of a different ethnic background, I asked about that; if she had been present at one of the problematic events or incidents I had observed, I asked about that.

At best, the relationships between the Latino and African American students at King are characterized by indifference and self-segregation, and at worst, by violence and hostility. In the teen mother program, indifference and self-segregation predominate. I observed that students would not even ask to borrow a pen or a ruler from someone of a different ethnic group. In one instance, a student shared a bag of candy with everyone in the room except the one student of a different ethnic group. When the students group themselves for work or lunch, they almost always self-segregate by ethnicity. In the school at large, there are occasional fights across ethnic lines that sometimes escalate into feuds. At times the principal puts requests in the school bulletin pleading with students of one ethnic group not to respond to an incident in which members of their group have been attacked by another.

The teachers at King High are no less vulnerable to racial tensions than the students. According to one of the SAP teachers, at one volatile faculty meeting teachers openly called each other racists. Moreover, he told me that some King High teachers sit in the staffroom and make racist comments about other teachers and students. (There are 61 teachers at King High; the two full-time and four part-time SAP teachers at King have little to do with the other teachers.) I felt this tension when I introduced myself at a King High faculty meeting. In contrast to my warm reception in the SAP program, other King teachers were quite hostile, not to me personally but to the prospect of another study. One African American teacher exclaimed, "They'll approve rat studies, but they won't approve black studies!" Although the school district has approved "black" studies and offers it as an elective, the teacher's comment indicates that she felt that the "black" studies program was inadequate; she saw a parallel between the dearth of African and African American studies and the potentially colonial implications of a European American researcher at a predominantly African American school. She was metaphorically suggesting a contrast between African American studies, which ideally provides students with a view of African Americans as subjects or agents, and educational research that portrays African Americans as "research subjects" or "rats."

The school situation is a reflection, although not a perfect mirror, of the community, where ethnic conflicts frequently erupt in local politics and on the streets. Ethnic groups battle with each other over shrinking resources: everyone seems to feel that if one group advances, the others lose ground. Conflicts over bilingual education illustrate this general pattern: Latino and Asian American parents struggle to reform inadequate bilingual programs, while African American parents resent the extra funding and attention that their children are not getting. "The battle over whose culture counts, particularly from the perspective of students and the communities they come from, is becoming more *visibly* a battle among so-called minority cultures and only *invisibly* one of white versus other" (Ulichny 1996:334, emphasis in original).

STRENGTH IN NUMBERS

At King, where most of the students and administrators are African American, the African American students appear to be in a position of dominance over the Latino students. This "dominance" is only relative, of course, and does not negate the racism that African American students experience outside school. Moreover, their dominance is not absolute, but rather varies from situation to situation. King High's multicultural efforts overwhelmingly favor African American culture, suggesting that multicultural resources are committed in proportion to the number of students of each group. Kwanzaa and Black History Month are celebrated, African dance is taught, rooms are decorated with posters celebrating Africa and African Americans, and Africa is emphasized in social studies. The school, however, is by no means Afrocentric; rather, it is quite traditional and Eurocentric: the teaching methods are based on individual achievement and competition, and the history books are largely peopled by European and European American men.[9] As one student in U.S. history remarked, "I'm already to page 142, and I haven't read about a single black person." As one teacher remarked, "[Administrators] say we should make the curriculum multicultural, but they never do anything. They never come see what I'm teaching." She was pointing out that there is no follow-through to the rhetoric used by administrators. For example, the SAP mission statement refers to "excellence through diversity," but I saw no concrete manifestations of this philosophy.

In other words, multicultural education at King was a veneer of cultural relevance over a Eurocentric educational system. This veneer was not directly tied to the lives and experiences of the students. For example, most of the African American students did not celebrate Kwanzaa at home, so while they may have enjoyed learning about it, it was not *their* (inner-city African American) culture that they saw reflected as part of the curriculum.[10] Moreover, the African American veneer excluded the Latino, Asian American, and European American students. The Latino and Asian American students did not see their heritage celebrated as the African American and European American students did. The non–African American students were further excluded because it was never clear that the Afrocentric events and materials should be for all the students, although students may have engaged with the activities differently, depending on their own background.

To a large extent—and paradoxically—the exclusion stemmed from the failure of teachers to explicitly acknowledge that they have students of different ethnicities. Race and ethnicity were rarely discussed in classrooms, so during an event like Kwanzaa, there was no discussion of how non–African American students could or should relate to the proceedings. The assumption of exclusivity and the resultant hostility surfaced most clearly during special events that were nominally multicultural but were actually monocultural.

Kwanzaa

To celebrate Kwanzaa, an African theater group came to work with the teen mothers to prepare a performance that included acting, dancing, and a rite of passage for the participants. The production was a major undertaking, involving about two months of preparation. It was a remarkably positive experience for the performers: the directors were skilled at encouraging the students to do their best, and they and the audience were pleased by the results. Rehearsals took place during class time and included frequent references to African women and their strengths and roles. When rehearsals first began, all the students in the SAP program had to go, and everyone participated. Yet as the weeks went by, a few of the African American students and all the non–African American students stopped coming to rehearsals.[11] One of the African American students who stopped participating was pregnant and felt the dancing was too strenuous; perhaps the others were uncomfortable about performing in front of an audience, or did not like the demands placed on them by the directors. The Latinas and Asian Americans stopped because, as one said, "It's all about *African* women—it's not for me." Through this attrition, the nonparticipants missed out on a valuable experience. Since the nonparticipants included some African Americans, the pattern of ethnic separation was less obvious;[12] nevertheless, the process tacitly told everyone involved that African American culture was relevant only to African Americans.

Cinco de Mayo

Up until Cinco de Mayo, no assemblies or special events had celebrated Latino cultures. Just before Cinco de Mayo, the teen mothers went to a conference on African American women. None of the Latinas went. One of them explained, "I'm tired of African American this and African American that. They never have anything for us. I feel left out. Cinco de Mayo is coming and they haven't planned anything." Notice her conviction that an event based on a particular culture is "for" students of that culture.

King High did have a Cinco de Mayo assembly, which included the singing of the Mexican national anthem. Most of the African Americans refused to rise for the singing, although they were repeatedly told to do so. While their reluctance stemmed largely from apathy and a generalized resistance to authority, Latinos interpreted their refusal as hostile and disrespectful. The following year, during the Cinco de Mayo assembly, the Latino students dancing on stage went into the audience and invited other students (mostly African American) to dance with them. They joined in willingly, and the positive and upbeat mood corroborates my intuition that the African American students were unwilling to stand for a national anthem, rather than unwilling to participate in a celebration of Latino cultures.

Cinco de Mayo was the only time I saw an example of truly multicultural education—paradoxically, it took place out of school. The case managers organized a Cinco de Mayo/Mother's Day celebration for teen mothers from the entire county.[13] The event consisted of speeches and performances about Cinco de Mayo and Mexican culture, performances addressed to urban teens in general (skits about violence and safe sex), and performances by African American rappers. In general, the students enjoyed the event, which was more *multi*cultural than others. In particular, one speaker made the only attempt I saw in a year and a half to show how the history or culture of one ethnic group could be relevant to students of other ethnicities. A Latino community leader, talking about Mexican history and Cinco de Mayo, described how the small, under-equipped Mexican army had defeated the seemingly more powerful French army when it invaded Mexico in 1862. He explained, "All of you, whether you're Latina, black, white, Asian, you're fac-

ing a lot. You're trying to bring your kids up right. You're up against drugs, violence, poverty. But you can do it. Just think of the Mexican soldiers—no one thought they could win, but they did, and you can too." The audience responded with cheers and clapping. This speaker was unusual: he acknowledged the presence of different ethnic groups in the room, pointed out to them their common problems, and suggested that they could *all* be inspired by Mexicans of long ago.

The success of the Cinco de Mayo/Mother's Day event provided a model of "something for everyone." Some of the teachers and administrators of the SAP program had been concerned about the relatively heavy emphasis on African American culture throughout the year, discussing at staff meetings their desire to include other cultures. As one administrator said, "We have to do something for the Latina girls." But they did not discuss how the non–African American students could or should relate to African American material, nor did they ever express a concern that the African American students were missing out by not being exposed to Latino cultures. They, like the students, work on the assumption that curricula focusing on one culture are "for" students of that culture.

In an attempt to be more inclusive, the following year's winter holiday event was not only a Kwanzaa celebration. Instead, it was called Winter Holidays Around the World. The event consisted of tabletop displays of different cultures and their holidays and a brief introduction to each one by teachers and community members. The affair was a dismal failure: the students were inattentive and rude during the presentations. The format provided a microcosm of the token multicultural education practiced at King High: the achievements and culture of each group were presented in isolation from other groups, even when they were all included in the same event. In contrast, at the Cinco de Mayo/Mother's Day celebration, connections were forged across ethnic lines.

TEACHERS AND THE "COMFORT ZONE"

I have identified three major weaknesses in the token multicultural education at King High: (1) the allocation of multicultural resources in proportion to the ethnic makeup of the student body; (2) the implication that an event based on one culture is only for members of that ethnic group; and (3) the presentation of different cultures in isolation from each other. These factors combined to drive wedges between the different ethnic groups at the school. True, they did not cause these tensions, but they reflected and reinforced problems that exist in the society at large.

The teachers and the school are culpable, however, for their failure to address ethnic conflict. A problem at King, one that is not addressed by existing multicultural efforts, is that interethnic conflict is quelled as quickly as possible without addressing the underlying tensions that provoke conflict. A classroom incident illustrates how the teachers handle ethnic conflict. The students were all supposedly working on their assignments. The only two Latina students in the room were talking in Spanish and laughing. An African American student, Tasha, asked Lucila, "Do you like talking Spanish more than English?" Lucila replied that she did, and then Tasha said, somewhat aggressively, "Well, I wish you wouldn't. I think it's really rude." The Latinas seemed to want to defuse the situation, perhaps from a fear of conflict. Lucila's response was very conciliatory: "I know what you mean, okay." Her friend Olivia, normally quite outspoken, did not say anything and busied herself with her books. Two other students, both African American, reproached Tasha for her request and defended the rights of Latinos to speak in Spanish. One said, "That's their language. If they didn't speak English, would it be rude for you to speak English [in front of them]?" The other defender took a different tack: "You make them feel bad when you say that. It's disrespecting their language." The interaction among the African Americans almost led to a fight, and the teacher, a European American, responded by taking each of the three African American students outside to talk to them individually. Mr. Gallagher (the teacher) did not talk to the Latina students, nor did he address the class as a whole or open up a class discussion on the subject.

Mr. Gallagher feared that the conflict among the African American students would lead to a fight. The students were not inherently uncontrollable, but there had been several violent fights that year, and a group discussion about ethnicity could have exploded. His primary concern was to maintain order, not to facilitate the students' discussion of ethnicity, language, and exclusion so that it could be conducted in a respectful way. After reading an earlier version of this article, this teacher was upset by my portrayal of him. "I've tried so hard not to be a typical white male, but that's how it makes me seem."[14] I reassured him that I do not think his actions (and inactions) suggest that he is a typical white male, but rather that he, like many teachers, is afraid of conflict in the classroom and reluctant to address ethnic tensions in group discussions. He had no training or preparation in mediating interethnic conflict; an open discussion of Latina/African American relations would have been risky, and he was playing it safe.

In the SAP program, teachers have a heavy administrative and teaching burden. For example, they have to teach different levels of the same subject simultaneously. They may teach remedial math, pre-algebra, and algebra at the same time in the same classroom. They use these constraints to explain and excuse the absence of discussion and innovative teaching in their classrooms. They see discussions of any topic as a luxury that they cannot afford. As one teacher put it, "I want to do well by these girls, but I'm not even able to do the basics [because of the constraints of the program]."[15] Given the challenging nature of their job and the superficial nature of multicultural education as it is implemented at King High, some teachers see multicultural education as a frill, a luxury they cannot afford. When asked whether she was in favor of more multicultural education, one teacher responded, "I don't want to water down the basics."

Even teachers who like to have discussions in their classroom often shy away from openly discussing race and ethnicity with their students (Foley 1990). As bell hooks observes, "The unwillingness to approach teaching from a standpoint that includes awareness of race, sex, and class is often rooted in the fear that classrooms will be uncontrollable, that emotions and passions will not be contained" (1994:39). Teachers' fear of conflict is understandable—I fight to overcome the same fear when I teach, the fear of leaving the "comfort zone," as Jackson and Solis call it.

> Comfort zones are those arenas where multiculturalism has been advocated from . . . essentially additive, procedural, and technical perspectives. The task before us, then, is to force the parameters of those comfort zones outward, pushing for broader and more liberating constructs capable of engendering a pedagogy for transformation in a real and material sense, and not merely a recognition and acknowledgement of difference. [1995:2]

The comfort zone is really not so comfortable when conflict simmers, ignored and unacknowledged.

In fact, confronting and examining conflict can ease tensions, as teachers find when they are willing to address interethnic conflict in their classrooms. Ms. Wells described the atmosphere at another SAP program. She explained that when she was teaching there, students of different ethnicities got along well together. When students made racial slurs, she and the other teacher always discussed those comments in class with all the students, which she saw as important in maintaining the positive atmosphere there. Her experience supports Ulichny's (1996) finding that airing grievances in a respectful way can reduce ethnic tensions. After Ms. Wells and the other teacher left the program, the situation rapidly deteriorated to the point of guarded hostility between the groups, suggesting that their interventions were helpful. As she puts it, "the culture of the program changed."

Ms. Wells and her colleague were unusual in their willingness to discuss interethnic relations with their students as a group. At the King High SAP program, the academic teachers were especially reluctant to intervene in conflicts among students of color because of their "whiteness." As Ms. Wells said, "It's a fear of meddling when you're perceived as an outsider, an oversensitivity [that the students will say], 'Who are you to push us together?'" Most teachers are afraid of conflict and unprepared to mediate interethnic conflict. A teacher described a major interethnic skirmish that had taken place on campus the previous year: "We felt horrible. We wanted to do something, but we didn't know what to do, so we didn't do anything. There was no assembly, no dialogue."

LANGUAGE, VOICE, AND POWER

Earlier, I said that African Americans are in a position of dominance over the Latino students at King High, and I described how Latinas feel left out of "multicultural" activities. African Americans do not always feel dominant. In the incident described above, Tasha was enraged when the Latinas spoke Spanish in front of her. Her anger is symptomatic of the attitude of many, but not all, African Americans toward Latinos. Listen to Tasha: "Where I used to go to school, the Mexican kids would always be talking and laughing, and I never paid any attention. But then a friend of mine who speaks Spanish told me that they were talking about me. They sit up there talking Spanish, and it's just like they're whispering."

The ability to speak Spanish gives the Latinas a dangerous power over the African Americans—"dangerous" because even if they are not talking about their classmates, they can always be suspected of doing so. Indeed, once the African American students learned that I speak Spanish, they frequently asked me what the Latinas were talking about. They did not ask the Latinas, even those who are bilingual. The African Americans assumed that the Latinas would never admit that they were talking about someone in the SAP program. Among high school students, being "talked about" has serious repercussions. A moment of gossip can lead to fighting, death, or being kicked out of school (Lustig 1994). So Tasha's concern should not be dismissed as adolescent vanity. She was expressing a real fear shared by many students in the SAP program and at other schools (Ulichny 1996).

The ability to speak Spanish gives Latino students a distinct advantage, but Latinos also have to be wary of how they conduct their conversations, lest they be misinterpreted.[16] Ulichny (1996) found that multicultural efforts made African American students quite jealous of Latinos (and others) who had their "own" language. A further danger is that by speaking Spanish Latinos are identifying themselves as foreign, non-American, "invaders." As one African American student said of Proposition 187, "Well, I think [the government] should limit the number of people they let in, I mean the [Latino immigrants] are coming in and taking over everything. They have all these businesses we don't have."

COMMON GROUND

The students who defended Olivia and Lucila's right to speak Spanish are not threatened by the speaking of Spanish—a reminder that ethnic groups are far from homogeneous. To avoid stereotyping, any truly multicultural program must attend to the diversity within each ethnic group. The token multicultural efforts at King High define ethnic groups as homogeneous, unchanging, and in opposition to each other. The lived experience of students contradicts this construction of ethnicity, but the school's institutional discourse of ethnicity does not recognize intraethnic differences or interethnic dialogues.

If some students can bridge the gap between ethnic groups, more can as well. For example, a few African American students began asking me to teach them Spanish (no foreign language is offered in the SAP program). Their desire to learn Spanish, as well as the students' defense of Latinas' right to speak Spanish, shows that some students have internalized a respect for cultural difference. Unfortunately, I was only able to teach them a few words, but my microintervention did lead to a moment of rapprochement. Olivia was sitting with me and the African Americans who were "learning" Spanish.[17] Tyisha asked her, "Does your boyfriend speak English?"

OLIVIA: No, but I'm teaching him. I'm trying to anyway. It's hard.

TYISHA: Mhm, I'm teaching my boyfriend English, too.

OLIVIA: Does he speak—

TYISHA: —He speaks that jail English. I want to teach him to talk right.

The connection between Olivia and Tyisha was fleeting, but more and more of such moments would allow the students to know each other as people struggling with (some) similar issues.

I suggest that the best way to improve interethnic relations is to look closely at the few connections that form across ethnic lines and to expand them and develop others in the same vein. It seems clear to me that it is not enough to just put students of different ethnic groups in close proximity. The teen mother program I have been describing is very small—on most days fewer than 20 students spend all day together. Close proximity is simply not enough to break down barriers (Allport 1954). I interviewed most of the students, and they claimed that they got along with people of different ethnicities; many had friends of other ethnicities as children. Yet now in high school, most of them were no longer forming those friendships, nor were they even superficially friendly to students of other ethnicities.

I found an example of a successful interethnic friendship in a small group of Latinas and Asian Americans who attended English as a Second Language classes together two hours a day. Every day, their common experience of not being fluent in English was reinforced when they left the SAP program area and walked to ESL class. However, if common experiences were enough to overcome interethnic tensions, the students in the teen mother program would get along well, since they were all teen mothers. Clearly, this commonality did not, by itself, translate into interethnic friendships.

Nevertheless, when the students occasionally made conversational overtures across ethnic lines, they usually talked about children or pregnancy. If one student was returning from the nursery, she might initiate a conversation by saying, "Your baby is [sleeping/eating/crying]," or she might be asked, "How's my baby?" And then sometimes a more general conversation developed from the initial exchange. Students rarely initiated these conversations without a stimulus such as someone returning from the nursery.

Teachers could build on this potential for communication by encouraging students to explore and discuss their similarities and differences. English and social studies teachers should help students make personal connections to the academic material, even if it does not reflect the experiences of their own ethnic group. This process would deepen students' engagement with the material and help them forge bonds with each other. Sometimes students make these connections on their own: while reading about Native Americans, one African American student exclaimed, "Whites just had to exploit everybody!" Unfortunately, the teacher did not pick up on this remark to start a discussion, and everyone just kept on with their reading. Ulichny (1996) suggests that students of color

can recognize their similar experiences as adolescents and as members of oppressed groups. Clearly, students acknowledge these commonalities at times, but for these glimpses of shared experiences to transcend the divisions between ethnic groups, teachers must actively intervene to facilitate and build on the students' discoveries.

CONCLUSIONS

The hierarchy of power among "minority" groups is not clear. Even when one group apparently dominates another, the hierarchy may be only situational, not absolute. In this article, I have described the complexity of the power relations between African American and Latina teen mothers, a complexity that is not immediately apparent. If multicultural education is to bring students of different ethnicities together, it has to be more sophisticated than the current approach as it is practiced at King High. The "special event approach" can actually worsen existing conflict by encapsulating ethnicities. Instead of relying on posters of notable "other" Americans or textbook "boxes" that present decontextualized incidents and individuals, the curriculum should begin with the experiences of the students and an open examination of ongoing conflict at the school and in the community. Discussing Latino-Anglo relations at a high school in Los Angeles, Patthey-Chavez gives an example of how reluctant school administrators are to listen to students' voices and experiences, "It is much more likely that the district would piece together an in-service about Latino culture, during which a few 'specialists' . . . present their reflections on Latino culture, than it is that the school would ask the students to actually articulate and discuss their needs" (1993:55).

Listening to students' voices and acknowledging their conflicts would form a foundation of understanding on which to build a multicultural education that includes all the cultures of the United States and, even more importantly, includes an analysis of the interrelations among groups and the variations within groups. I suggest we return to the post–World War II term *intercultural education*. In the 1940s, this term was part of an assimilationist rhetoric that reflected an idealistic vision of everyone getting along together (North Central Association of Colleges and Secondary Schools 1946; Warren and Roberts 1945). Enough time has passed for us to reclaim the term (but not the rhetoric or programs) to breathe new life into "multicultural" education. "Inter/between" is preferable to "multi/many" because it calls attention to process and boundaries rather than to a collection of separate cultures. Intercultural education, as I envision it, is a more precise term for the most intensive methods of multi-cultural education (Banks 1996; McCarthy 1993; Sleeter and Grant 1988); yet intercultural education differs slightly from these approaches: it emphasizes the relationships between and within all ethnic groups instead of focusing exclusively on the oppression of minority groups by European Americans. Adopting this term would give some conceptual clarity to a muddied terrain. As it is now, the term *multicultural education* covers too broad a spectrum of programs and approaches. Twenty years ago, Gibson warned that "the vagueness of terms and assumptions [related to multicultural education] appears to be increasing" (1976:1), and her warning still holds true. But adopting the term *intercultural education* is less important than implementing intercultural education, whatever it is called.

The implementation of intercultural education depends on a clear understanding of the specific patterns of interethnic relations at each school and a willingness to investigate those patterns with students from their perspectives. Students, teachers, administrators, and researchers should begin with local ethnography (Carlson 1976; La Belle and Ward 1994) and then look beyond the school to the community and nation to examine inter-"minority" conflict in the context of overarching structures of racism, sexism, and social class. If teachers are to implement an intercultural education, they need training and support to help them acknowledge conflicts and lead students to resolve them. Students deserve more than a smattering of special events. They deserve an education that reflects their histories and experiences and helps them negotiate a society in which traversing cultural borderlands is the norm. "The Borderlands are physically present wherever two or more cultures edge each other, where people of different races occupy the same territory" (Anzaldua 1987). Life in the borderlands can be fraught with tension and fear, for young people and adults, but intercultural education could ease the way.

NOTES

Acknowledgments. An earlier version of this article was presented at the Sacramento Anthropological Society Annual Meetings, March 1994. I would like to thank conference participants, Rose Glickman, Mary Grantham-Campbell, Lawrence Hirschfeld, Deborah Jackson, Kathryn Anderson-Levitt, the AEQ reviewers, and students and teachers at King High for their comments. This article is based on 18 months of fieldwork conducted during 1993–1995. I would like to thank the Spencer Foundation, the Research Institute for the Study of Man, the Abigail Quigley McCarthy Center for Women, the Woodrow Wilson Foundation Women's Studies Program, Rackham College of the University of Michigan, and Sigma Xi for their funding of this research.

1. Throughout this article, I will use *ethnic* as a shorthand for *racial/ethnic*, because it is less clumsy and more "anthropologically correct," although it does not adequately reflect the effects of centuries of assumptions of and about biological races.

2. The second claim of proponents of multicultural education is that it improves educational outcomes for students of color. A discussion of academic achievement is outside the scope of this article, but clearly a *pervasive* multicultural curriculum and pedagogy is more likely to result in greater academic engagement and achievement than a token multiculturalism. Ulichny (1996) found that even a poorly implemented multicultural program had (small) positive effects on students' performance; the program did, however, increase interethnic tension. Moreover, interethnic conflict itself can lead to poor educational outcomes if students become (further) alienated from school. For example, one of my informants dropped out of school because she was getting beaten up by a group of students of a different ethnicity.

3. My critique should not be confused with those who seek to uphold the "canon" of Western civilization (Bloom 1987; Schlesinger 1992); in contrast, I am calling for a more intensive and thorough multiculturalism and a critical look at what passes for multicultural education in (some) schools.

4. The terms *minority* and *majority* are problematic since in many schools and communities, people of color are in the majority and European Americans are in the minority. But I use the terms with their everyday meaning, especially since they reflect power more accurately than they do population.

5. Names of persons, programs, schools, and cities are pseudonyms.

6. This document was prepared by a local nonprofit agency in collaboration with district personnel and community members.

7. Nationwide, 13 percent of the population lives below the poverty line; in Pineview, 20 percent of the population lives below the poverty line.

8. Attendance was poor, but not as bad as these numbers make it seem. The population is very transient: some students enrolled and only came for a short time, others enrolled and later transferred to the comprehensive high school. So there was usually a core group of about 25 out of about 50 who could be expected to show up.

9. As part of my research, I reviewed all the textbooks used in the SAP program.

10. I would like to thank Ms. Wells for drawing my attention to this point.

11. The teachers did urge the students to continue going, but felt they should not force them to participate, given how out of place the students felt.

12. The fact that students do not always split by ethnicity reflects the heterogeneity within each ethnic group, but it also sometimes obscures the divisions that do exist.

13. Case managers are similar to social workers.

14. I gave Mr. Gallagher a more recent copy of this article, and after reading it he e-mailed me that he did "not want to comment further on the incident or topic(s) covered in the paper" and that he did not "have a desire to engage in a continued dialogue related to the paper." I am saddened by his unwillingness to talk with me, but since he *is* unwilling to talk with me about it, I can do no more than record his (implied) objection.

15. This teacher recognizes that she could do better even with the constraints and has requested a mentor teacher, but the program director has not responded to her requests.

16. I never had the opportunity to observe a classroom in which there was more than one student speaking the same Asian language, but presumably a similar situation could arise with Asian American students.

17. I had asked Olivia to help me "teach." I had thought that she could teach them, but then I saw that that would have underscored her greater power as a Spanish speaker.

REFERENCES CITED

Allport, Gordon W. 1954. *The Nature of Prejudice*. Boston: Addison Wesley.

American Association of Colleges for Teacher Education (AACTE), Commission on Multicultural Education, eds. H. P. Baptiste, M. Baptiste, and D. Gollnick. 1980. *Multicultural Teacher Education: Preparing Educators to Provide Educational Equity*. Washington, DC: AACTE.

Anzaldua, Gloria. 1987. *Borderlands/La Frontera: The New Mestiza*. San Francisco: Spinsters/Aunt Lute.

Arvizu, Steven, and Marietta Saravia-Shore. 1990. Cross-cultural literacy: An anthropological approach to dealing with diversity. *Education and Urban Society* 22(4): 364–376.

Association for Supervision and Curriculum Development (ASCD), Multicultural Education Commission. 1977. *Multicultural Education: Commitments, Issues, and Applications*. Washington, DC: ASCD.

Banks, James A. 1996. *Multicultural Education, Transformative Knowledge, and Action*. New York: Teachers College Press.

Bloom, Allan. 1987. *The Closing of the American Mind*. New York: Simon and Schuster.

Carlson, Paul. 1976. Toward a definition of local-level multicultural education. *Anthropology and Education Quarterly* 7:26–30.

Cortes, Carlos E. 1977. Nondecision-making and decision-making in multicultural education. In *Multicultural Education: The Interdisciplinary Approach—A Summary of Conference Proceedings*. Sacramento: Office of Intergroup Relations, California State Department of Education.

Cummins, Jim. 1986. Empowering minority students. *Harvard Educational Review* 56(1):18–36.

Diaz, Carlos, ed. 1992. *Multicultural Education for the 21st Century*. Washington, DC: National Education Association.

Foley, Douglas. 1990. *Learning Capitalist Culture*. Philadelphia: University of Pennsylvania Press.

Fordham, Signithia. 1988. Racelessness as a factor in black students' school success: Pragmatic strategy or pyrrhic victory. *Harvard Educational Review* 58(1):54–84.

Gibson, Margaret A. 1976. Introduction: Anthropological perspectives on multicultural education. *Anthropology and Education Quarterly* 7:1–3.

Grant, Carl A., and Christine E. Sleeter. 1986. *After the School Bell Rings*. London: Falmer.

Hanna, Judith Lynne. 1994. Issues in supporting school diversity: Academics, social relations, and the arts. *Anthropology and Education Quarterly* 25:66–85.

hooks, bell. 1994. *Teaching to Transgress: Education as the Practice of Freedom*. New York: Routledge.

Jackson, Sandra, and Jose Solis. 1995. Introduction: Resisting zones of comfort in multiculturalism. In *Beyond Comfort Zones in Multiculturalism*, pp. 1–14, eds. Sandra Jackson and Jose Solis. Westport, CT: Bergin and Garvey.

La Belle, Thomas, and Christopher Ward. 1994. *Multiculturalism and Education*. Albany: State University of New York Press.

Lustig, Deborah Freedman. 1994. *"Sometimes You Just Have to Fight": Honor, Status, and Violence Among Teen Mothers*. Paper presented at the 93rd Annual Meeting of the American Anthropological Association, Atlanta.

———. 1997. *In and Out of School: How School-Age Mothers Negotiate Gender, Class, and Race/Ethnicity*. Ph.D. dissertation, University of Michigan.

Macias, José, ed. 1996. Racial and ethnic exclusion in education and society. Theme issue. *Anthropology and Education Quarterly* 27(2).

McCarthy, Cameron. 1993. After the canon: Knowledge and ideological representation in the multicultural discourse on curriculum reform. In *Race, Identity, and Representation in Education*, pp. 289–305, eds. Cameron McCarthy and W. Crichlow. New York: Routledge.

McCarthy, Cameron, and Arlette Ingram Willis. 1995. The politics of culture: Multicultural education after the content debate. In *Beyond Comfort Zones in Multiculturalism*, pp. 67–87, eds. Sandra Jackson and Jose Solis. Westport, CT: Bergin and Garvey.

North Central Association of Colleges and Secondary Schools. 1946. *Improving Intergroup Relations in School and Community Life. Committee on In-Service Education of Teachers*. Wichita, KS: North Central Association of Colleges and Secondary Schools.

O'Hair, Mary, and Sandra Odell, eds. 1993. Diversity and Teaching. *Teacher Education Yearbook*, vol. 1. Fort Worth, TX: Harcourt Brace Jovanovich College Publishers.

Patthey-Chavez, G. Genevieve. 1993. High school as an arena for cultural conflict and acculturation for Latino Angelinos. *Anthropology and Education Quarterly* 24: 33–60.

Rushton, James. 1981. Careers and the multicultural curriculum. In *Teaching in the Multicultural School,* pp. 163–170, ed. James Lynch. London: Ward Lock.

Schlesinger, A. M. Jr. 1992. *The Disuniting of America.* New York: Norton.

Sleeter, Christine E. 1991. Introduction: Multicultural education and empowerment. In *Empowerment Through Multicultural Education,* pp. 1–23, ed. Christine E. Sleeter. Albany: State University of New York Press.

Sleeter, Christine E., and Carl A. Grant. 1988. *Making Choices for Multicultural Education.* Upper Saddle River, NJ: Prentice Hall.

Ulichny, Polly. 1996. Cultures in conflict. *Anthropology and Education Quarterly* 27:331–364.

Wallace, Michele. 1993. Multiculturalism and oppositionality. In *Race, Identity, and Representation in Education,* pp. 251–260, eds. Cameron McCarthy and W. Crichlow. New York: Routledge. Originally published in *Afterimage* 19(3):6–9.

Warren, Curtis, and Bertha Roberts. 1945. *Building for World Understanding: To Live in Peace with One Another—San Francisco Elementary Schools' Report on Planned Study in Intercultural Education.* San Francisco: San Francisco Unified School District.

20

Eating Christmas in the Kalahari

Richard Borshay Lee

An economy is a social system for the production, exchange, and consumption of goods and services. Using this definition, anthropologists believe that all human societies have economies and that economic systems can work without money and markets.

People in food-foraging societies, like the !Kung San described in this selection, have received much attention by anthropologists. To a large degree, this is because they represent (at least by analogy) the original lifestyle of our ancestors. A major discovery of research on food foragers is that their life is not "nasty, brutish, and short." In fact, the food forager's diet might be an ideal one for people living in industrialized societies.

In the hunter-gatherer economy, anthropologists have discovered that the exchange of goods is based on rules of gift giving or reciprocity. In this selection, Richard Lee tells of his surprise at the !Kung San's lack of appreciation of a Christmas gift. As we have already seen, a group's customs and rules about appropriate social behavior can reflect important cultural values. When people act in unexpected ways, anthropologists see this as an opportunity to better understand their culture and world view. That is the case in this selection.

All people give gifts to each other, but there are rules and obligations about those gifts. In our own society, there are rules about the polite way to receive a present. We are supposed to act appreciative (even if we hate the gift) because the gift is less important than the social relationship at stake. The !Kung break those rules, but in the process, Richard Lee discovers that there are important cultural messages behind their "impoliteness."

As you read this selection, ask yourself the following questions:

- Why did Richard Lee feel obligated to give a valuable gift to the !Kung at Christmas? Why did they think he was a miser?

- Why did the !Kung people's insults about the impending gift bother the anthropologist so much? Were the people treating him in a special way?

- What does Lee mean by saying, "There are no totally generous acts"? Do you agree?

- What are some cultural rules about gift giving in our own society?

The following terms discussed in this selection are included in the Glossary at the back of the book:

cultural values   hunter-gatherers

economy   reciprocal gift

egalitarian society

The !Kung Bushmen's knowledge of Christmas is thirdhand. The London Missionary Society brought the holiday to the southern Tswana tribes in the early nineteenth century. Later, native catechists spread the idea far and wide among the Bantu-speaking pastoralists, even in the remotest corners of the Kalahari Desert. The Bushmen's idea of the Christmas story, stripped to its essentials, is "praise the birth of white man's god-chief": what keeps their interest in the holiday high is the Tswana-Herero custom of slaughtering an ox for his Bushmen neighbors as an annual goodwill gesture. Since the 1930s, part of the Bushmen's annual round of activities has included a December congregation at the cattle posts for trading, marriage brokering, and several days of trance dance feasting at which the local Tswana headman is host.

As a social anthropologist working with !Kung Bushmen, I found that the Christmas ox custom

With permission from *Natural History,* vol. 78, no. 10. Copyright © 1969 The American Museum of Natural History.

suited my purposes. I had come to the Kalahari to study the hunting and gathering subsistence economy of the !Kung, and to accomplish this it was essential not to provide them with food, share my own food, or interfere in any way with their food-gathering activities. While liberal handouts of tobacco and medical supplies were appreciated, they were scarcely adequate to erase the glaring disparity in wealth between the anthropologist, who maintained a two-month inventory of canned goods, and the Bushmen, who rarely had a day's supply of food on hand. My approach, while paying off in terms of data, left me open to frequent accusations of stinginess and hardheartedness. By their lights, I was a miser.

The Christmas ox was to be my way of saying thank you for the cooperation of the past year; and since it was to be our last Christmas in the field, I determined to slaughter the largest, meatiest ox that money could buy, insuring that the feast and trance dance would be a success.

Through December I kept my eyes open at the wells as the cattle were brought down for watering. Several animals were offered, but none had quite the grossness that I had in mind. Then, ten days before the holiday, a Herero friend led an ox of astonishing size and mass up to our camp. It was solid black, stood five feet high at the shoulder, had a five-foot span of horns, and must have weighed 1,200 pounds on the hoof. Food consumption calculations are my specialty, and I quickly figured that bones and viscera aside, there was enough meat—at least four pounds—for every man, woman, and child of the 150 Bushmen in the vicinity of /ai/ai who were expected at the feast.

Having found the right animal at last, I paid the Herero £20 ($56) and asked him to keep the beast with his herd until Christmas day. The next morning word spread among the people that the big solid black one was the ox chosen by /ontah (my Bushman name; it means, roughly, "whitey") for the Christmas feast. That afternoon I received the first delegation. Ben!a, an outspoken sixty-year-old mother of five, came to the point slowly.

"Where were you planning to eat Christmas?"

"Right here at /ai/ai," I replied.

"Alone or with others?"

"I expect to invite all the people to eat Christmas with me."

"Eat what?"

"I have purchased Yehave's black ox, and I am going to slaughter and cook it."

"That's what we were told at the well but refused to believe it until we heard it from yourself."

"Well, it's the black one," I replied expansively, although wondering what she was driving at.

"Oh, no!" Ben!a groaned, turning to her group. "They were right." Turning back to me she asked, "Do you expect us to eat that bag of bones?"

"Bag of bones! It's the biggest ox at /ai/ai."

"Big, yes, but old. And thin. Everybody knows there's no meat on that old ox. What did you expect to eat off of it, the horns?"

Everybody chuckled at Ben!a's one-liner as they walked away, but all I could manage was a weak grin.

That evening it was the turn of the young men. They came to sit at our evening fire. /gaugo, about my age, spoke to me man-to-man.

"/ontah, you have always been square with us," he lied. "What has happened to change your heart? That sack of guts and bones of Yehave's will hardly feed one camp, let alone all the Bushmen around /ai/ai." And he proceeded to enumerate the seven camps in the /ai/ai vicinity, family by family. "Perhaps you have forgotten that we are not few, but many. Or are you too blind to tell the difference between a proper cow and an old wreck? That ox is thin to the point of death."

"Look, you guys," I retorted, "that is a beautiful animal, and I'm sure you will eat it with pleasure at Christmas."

"Of course we will eat it: it's food. But it won't fill us up to the point where we will have enough strength to dance. We will eat and go home to bed with stomachs rumbling."

That night as we turned in, I asked my wife, Nancy, "What did you think of the black ox?"

"It looked enormous to me. Why?"

"Well, about eight different people have told me I got gypped; that the ox is nothing but bones."

"What's the angle?" Nancy asked. "Did they have a better one to sell?"

"No, they just said that it was going to be a grim Christmas because there won't be enough meat to go around. Maybe I'll get an independent judge to look at the beast in the morning."

Bright and early, Halingisi, a Tswana cattle owner, appeared at our camp. But before I could ask him to give me his opinion on Yehave's black ox, he gave me the eye signal that indicated a confidential chat. We left the camp and sat down.

"/ontah, I'm surprised at you; you've lived here for three years and still haven't learned anything about cattle."

"But what else can a person do but choose the biggest, strongest animal one can find?" I retorted.

"Look, just because an animal is big doesn't mean that it has plenty of meat on it. The black one was a beauty when it was younger, but now it is thin to the point of death."

"Well I've already bought it. What can I do at this stage?"

"Bought it already? I thought you were just considering it. Well, you'll have to kill it and serve it, I suppose. But don't expect much of a dance to follow."

My spirits dropped rapidly. I could believe that Ben!a and /gaugo just might be putting me on about the black ox, but Halingisi seemed to be an impartial critic. I went around that day feeling as though I had bought a lemon of a used car.

In the afternoon it was Tomazo's turn. Tomazo is a fine hunter, a top trance performer . . . and one of my most reliable informants. He approached the subject of the Christmas cow as part of my continuing Bushman education.

"My friend, the way it is with us Bushmen," he began, "is that we love meat. And even more than that, we love fat. When we hunt we always search for the fat ones, the ones dripping with layers of white fat: fat that turns into a clear, thick oil in the cooking pot, fat that slides down your gullet, fills your stomach and gives you a roaring diarrhea," he rhapsodized.

"So, feeling as we do," he continued, "it gives us pain to be served such a scrawny thing as Yehave's black ox. It is big, yes, and no doubt its giant bones are good for soup, but fat is what we really crave and so we will eat Christmas this year with a heavy heart."

The prospect of a gloomy Christmas now had me worried, so I asked Tomazo what I could do about it.

"Look for a fat one, a young one . . . smaller, but fat. Fat enough to make us //gom (evacuate the bowels), then we will be happy."

My suspicions were aroused when Tomazo said that he happened to know a young, fat, barren cow that the owner was willing to part with. Was Tomazo working on commission, I wondered? But I dispelled this unworthy thought when we approached the Herero owner of the cow in question and found that he had decided not to sell.

The scrawny wreck of a Christmas ox now became the talk of the /ai/ai water hole and was the first news told to the outlying groups as they began to come in from the bush for the feast. What finally convinced me that real trouble might be brewing was the visit from u!au, an old conservative with a reputation for fierceness. His nickname meant spear and referred to an incident thirty years ago in which he had speared a man to death. He had an intense manner; fixing me with his eyes, he said in clipped tones:

"I have only just heard about the black ox today, or else I would have come earlier. /ontah, do you honestly think you can serve meat like that to people and avoid a fight?" He paused, letting the implications sink in. "I don't mean fight you, /ontah; you are a white man. I mean a fight between Bushmen. There are many fierce ones here, and with such a small quantity of meat to distribute, how can you give everybody

a fair share? Someone is sure to accuse another of taking too much or hogging all the choice pieces. Then you will see what happens when some go hungry while others eat."

The possibility of at least a serious argument struck me as all too real. I had witnessed the tension that surrounds the distribution of meat from a kudu or gemsbok kill, and had documented many arguments that sprang up from a real or imagined slight in meat distribution. The owners of a kill may spend up to two hours arranging and rearranging the piles of meat under the gaze of a circle of recipients before handing them out. And I knew that the Christmas feast at /ai/ai would be bringing together groups that had feuded in the past.

Convinced now of the gravity of the situation, I went in earnest to search for a second cow; but all my inquiries failed to turn one up.

The Christmas feast was evidently going to be a disaster, and the incessant complaints about the meagerness of the ox had already taken the fun out of it for me. Moreover, I was getting bored with the wisecracks, and after losing my temper a few times, I resolved to serve the beast anyway. If the meat fell short, the hell with it. In the Bushmen idiom, I announced to all who would listen:

"I am a poor man and blind. If I have chosen one that is too old and too thin, we will eat it anyway and see if there is enough meat there to quiet the rumbling of our stomachs."

On hearing this speech, Ben!a offered me a rare word of comfort. "It's thin," she said philosophically, "but the bones will make a good soup."

At dawn Christmas morning, instinct told me to turn over the butchering and cooking to a friend and take off with Nancy to spend Christmas alone in the bush. But curiosity kept me from retreating. I wanted to see what such a scrawny ox looked like on butchering, and if there was going to be a fight, I wanted to catch every word of it. Anthropologists are incurable that way.

The great beast was driven up to our dancing ground, and a shot in the forehead dropped it in its tracks. Then, freshly cut branches were heaped around the fallen carcass to receive the meat. Ten men volunteered to help with the cutting. I asked /gaugo to make the breast bone cut. This cut, which begins the butchering process for most large game, offers easy access for removal of the viscera. But it allows the hunter to spot-check the amount of fat on an animal. A fat game animal carries a white layer up to an inch thick on the chest, while in a thin one, the knife will quickly cut to the bone. All eyes fixed on his hand as /gaugo, dwarfed by the great carcass, knelt to the breast. The first cut opened a pool of solid white in the black skin. The second and third cut widened and deepened the creamy white. Still no bone. It was pure fat; it must have been two inches thick.

"Hey /gau," I burst out, "that ox is loaded with fat. What's this about the ox being too thin to bother eating? Are you out of your mind?"

"Fat?" /gau shot back. "You call that fat? This wreck is thin, sick, dead!" And he broke out laughing. So did everyone else. They rolled on the ground, paralyzed with laughter. Everybody laughed except me; I was thinking.

I ran back to the tent and burst in just as Nancy was getting up. "Hey, the black ox. It's fat as hell! They were kidding about it being too thin to eat. It was a joke or something. A put-on. Everyone is really delighted with it."

"Some joke," my wife replied. "It was so funny that you were ready to pack up and leave /ai/ai."

If it had indeed been a joke, it had been an extraordinarily convincing one, and tinged, I thought, with more than a touch of malice as many jokes are. Nevertheless, that it was a joke lifted my spirits considerably, and I returned to the butchering site where the shape of the ox was rapidly disappearing under the axes and knives of the butchers. The atmosphere had become festive. Grinning broadly, their arms covered with blood well past the elbow, men packed chunks of meat into the big cast-iron cooking pots, fifty pounds to the load, and muttered and chuckled all the while about the thinness and worthlessness of the animal and /ontah's poor judgment.

We danced and ate that ox two days and two nights; we cooked and distributed fourteen potfuls of meat and no one went home hungry and no fights broke out.

But the "joke" stayed in my mind. I had a growing feeling that something important had happened in my relationship with the Bushmen and that the clue lay in the meaning of the joke. Several days later, when most of the people had dispersed back to the bush camps, I raised the question with Hakekgose, a Tswana man who had grown up among the !Kung, married a !Kung girl, and who probably knows the culture better than any other non-Bushman.

"With us whites," I began, "Christmas is supposed to be the day of friendship and brotherly love. What I can't figure out is why the Bushmen went to such lengths to criticize and belittle the ox I had bought for the feast. The animal was perfectly good and their jokes and wisecracks practically ruined the holiday for me."

"So it really did bother you," said Hakekgose. "Well, that's the way they always talk. When I take my rifle and go hunting with them, if I miss, they laugh at me for the rest of the day. But even if I hit and bring one down, it's no better. To them, the kill is always too small or too old or too thin; and as we sit down on the kill site to cook and eat the liver, they keep grumbling, even with their mouths full of meat. They say things like, 'Oh, this is awful! What a worthless animal! Whatever made me think that this Tswana rascal could hunt!'"

"Is this the way outsiders are treated?" I asked.

"No, it is their custom; they talk that way to each other too. Go and ask them."

/gaugo had been one of the most enthusiastic in making me feel bad about the merit of the Christmas ox. I sought him out first.

"Why did you tell me the black ox was worthless, when you could see that it was loaded with fat and meat?"

"It is our way," he said smiling. "We always like to fool people about that. Say there is a Bushman who has been hunting. He must not come home and announce like a braggart, 'I have killed a big one in the bush!' He must first sit down in silence until I or someone else comes up to his fire and asks, 'What did you see today?' He replies quietly, 'Ah, I'm no good for hunting. I saw nothing at all (pause) just a little tiny one.' Then I smile to myself," /gaugo continued, "because I know he has killed something big.

"In the morning we make up a party of four or five people to cut up and carry the meat back to the camp. When we arrive at the kill we examine it and cry out, 'You mean to say you have dragged us all the way out here in order to make us cart home your pile of bones? Oh, if I had known it was this thin I wouldn't have come.' Another one pipes up, 'People, to think I gave up a nice day in the shade for this. At home we may be hungry but at least we have nice cool water to drink.' If the horns are big, someone says, 'Did you think that somehow you were going to boil down the horns for soup?'

"To all this you must respond in kind. 'I agree,' you say, 'this one is not worth the effort; let's just cook the liver for strength and leave the rest for the hyenas. It is not too late to hunt today and even a duiker or steenbok would be better than this mess.'

"Then you set to work nevertheless; butcher the animal, carry the meat back to the camp and everyone eats," /gaugo concluded.

Things were beginning to make sense. Next, I went to Tomazo. He corroborated /gaugo's story of the obligatory insults over a kill and added a few details of his own.

"But," I asked, "why insult a man after he has gone to all that trouble to track and kill an animal and when he is going to share the meat with you so that your children will have something to eat?"

"Arrogance," was his cryptic answer.

"Arrogance?"

"Yes, when a young man kills much meat he comes to think of himself as a chief or a big man, and he thinks of the rest of us as his servants or inferiors. We can't accept this. We refuse one who boasts, for someday his pride will make him kill somebody. So we always speak of his meat as worthless. This way we cool his heart and make him gentle."

"But why didn't you tell me this before?" I asked Tomazo with some heat.

"Because you never asked me," said Tomazo, echoing the refrain that has come to haunt every field ethnographer.

The pieces now fell into place. I had known for a long time that in situations of social conflict with Bushmen I held all the cards. I was the only source of tobacco in a thousand square miles, and I was not incapable of cutting an individual off for noncooperation. Though my boycott never lasted longer than a few days, it was an indication of my strength. People resented my presence at the water hole, yet simultaneously dreaded my leaving. In short I was a perfect target for the charge of arrogance and for the Bushman tactic of enforcing humility.

I had been taught an object lesson by the Bushmen; it had come from an unexpected corner and had hurt me in a vulnerable area. For the big black ox was to be the one totally generous, unstinting act of my year at /ai/ai and I was quite unprepared for the reaction I received.

As I read it, their message was this: There are no totally generous acts. All "acts" have an element of calculation. One black ox slaughtered at Christmas does not wipe out a year of careful manipulation of gifts given to serve your own ends. After all, to kill an animal and share the meat with people is really no more than the Bushmen do for each other every day and with far less fanfare.

In the end, I had to admire how the Bushmen had played out the farce—collectively straight-faced to the end. Curiously, the episode reminded me of the *Good Soldier Schweik* and his marvelous encounters with authority. Like Schweik, the Bushmen had retained a thoroughgoing skepticism of good intentions. Was it this independence of spirit, I wondered, that had kept them culturally viable in the face of generations of contact with more powerful societies, both black and white? The thought that the Bushmen were alive and well in the Kalahari was strangely comforting. Perhaps, armed with that independence and with their superb knowledge of their environment, they might yet survive the future.

21

Strings Attached

Lee Cronk

Anthropologists have traditionally studied how social ties among people are created through a system of kinship and marriage; this is a universal aspect of human social systems. Marriages link families who were previously strangers into kin (affines). Such new social relations are cemented by the exchange of goods—expected gifts—at the time of the marriage; this appears to be a universal aspect of marriage systems.

People give each other gifts all the time, and in all cultures of the world. According to the French anthropologist Marcel Mauss, who first wrote about this phenomenon in 1924, gift giving is a universal way of creating and maintaining social relations among people. This is because gift giving creates social obligations. Gifts "cement" social relationships, and members of a society understand what the implicit rules of gift giving are.

In the beginning of this selection, Lee Cronk discusses possible cultural misunderstandings that were involved in the creation of the unfortunate (and racist) term *Indian giver.* These misunderstandings were offensive to both Native Americans and whites. Europeans thought that gifts should be freely given and that the gift is less valued when there are strings attached. On a worldwide survey of different cultures, however, it is far more common for the strings themselves to be the main consideration of value. Because of this, when anthropologists study economic exchange, they are more interested in the social relationship between the gift giver and the receiver than in the actual gift.

As we saw in the case of Richard Lee and the gift of the Christmas ox among the !Kung San (Selection 20), the cultural rules behind gift giving often involve the principle of reciprocity. There are also cases when gifts can be used to embarrass rivals or to foster feelings of indebtedness. These cases usually involve social groups or nations rather than individuals. It is valuable to reexamine international political relations and economic aid in light of the cross-cultural context of gift giving.

As you read this selection, ask yourself the following questions:

- Is it really true that "there is no such thing as a free gift"?

- How can gift giving be a question of social power and prestige, as in the case of one chief "burying" another with gifts?

- Why was Russian acceptance of humanitarian aid from the United States after the 1988 Armenian earthquake considered to be a breakthrough? How can concessions in arms reduction negotiations be considered as gifts?

- Do Americans devalue a gift that has strings attached? Why?

The following terms discussed in this selection are included in the Glossary at the back of the book:

dependency	*potlatch*
exchange	*reciprocity*
kula	

During a trek through the Rockies in the 1830s, Captain Benjamin Louis E. de Bonneville received a gift of a fine young horse from a Nez Percé chief. According to Washington Irving's account of the incident, the American explorer was aware that "a parting pledge was necessary on his own part, to prove that this friendship was reciprocated." Accordingly, he "placed a handsome rifle in the hands of the venerable chief; whose benevolent heart was evidently touched and gratified by this outward and visible sign of amity."

Even the earliest white settlers in New England understood that presents from natives required reciprocity, and by 1764, "Indian gift" was so common a

Reprinted with permission from *The Sciences* May–June 1989, (3):2–4.

phrase that the Massachusetts colonial historian Thomas Hutchinson identified it as "a proverbial expression, signifying a present for which an equivalent return is expected." Then, over time, the custom's meaning was lost. Indeed, the phrase now is used derisively, to refer to one who demands the return of a gift. How this cross-cultural misunderstanding occurred is unclear, but the poet Lewis Hyde, in his book *The Gift,* has imagined a scenario that probably approaches the truth.

Say that an Englishman newly arrived in America is welcomed to an Indian lodge with the present of a pipe. Thinking the pipe a wonderful artifact, he takes it home and sets it on his mantelpiece. When he later learns that the Indians expect to have the pipe back, as a gesture of goodwill, he is shocked by what he views as their short-lived generosity. The newcomer did not realize that, to the natives, the point of the gift was not to provide an interesting trinket but to inaugurate a friendly relationship that would be maintained through a series of mutual exchanges. Thus, his failure to reciprocate appeared not only rude and thoughtless but downright hostile. "White man keeping" was as offensive to native Americans as "Indian giving" was to settlers.

In fact, the Indians' tradition of gift giving is much more common than our own. Like our European ancestors, we think that presents ought to be offered freely, without strings attached. But through most of the world, the strings themselves are the main consideration. In some societies, gift giving is a tie between friends, a way of maintaining good relationships, whereas in others it has developed into an elaborate, expensive, and antagonistic ritual designed to humiliate rivals by showering them with wealth and obligating them to give more in return.

In truth, the dichotomy between the two traditions of gift giving is less behavioral than rhetorical: our generosity is not as unconditional as we would like to believe. Like European colonists, most modern Westerners are blind to the purpose of reciprocal gift giving, not only in non-Western societies but also, to some extent, in our own. Public declarations to the contrary, we, too, use gifts to nurture long-term relationships of mutual obligation, as well as to embarrass our rivals and to foster feelings of indebtedness. And this ethic touches all aspects of contemporary life, from the behavior of scientists in research networks to superpower diplomacy. Failing to acknowledge this fact, especially as we give money, machines, and technical advice to peoples around the world, we run the risk of being misinterpreted and, worse, of causing harm.

Much of what we know about the ethics of gift giving comes from the attempts of anthropologists to give things to the people they are studying. Richard Lee, of the University of Toronto, learned a difficult lesson from the !Kung hunter-gatherers, of the Kalahari desert, when, as a token of goodwill, he gave them an ox to slaughter at Christmas. Expecting gratitude, he was shocked when the !Kung complained about having to make do with such a scrawny "bag of bones." Only later did Lee learn, with relief, that the !Kung belittle all gifts. In their eyes, no act is completely generous, or free of calculation; ridiculing gifts is their way of diminishing the expected return and of enforcing humility on those who would use gifts to raise their own status within the group.

Rada Dyson-Hudson, of Cornell University, had a similar experience among the Turkana, a pastoral people of northwestern Kenya. To compensate her informants for their help, Dyson-Hudson gave away pots, maize meal, tobacco, and other items. The Turkana reaction was less than heartwarming. A typical response to a gift of a pot, for example, might be, "Where is the maize meal to go in this pot?" or, "Don't you have a bigger one to give me?" To the Turkana, these are legitimate and expected questions.

The Mukogodo, another group of Kenyan natives, responded in a similar way to gifts Beth Leech and I presented to them during our fieldwork in 1986. Clothing was never nice enough, containers never big enough, tobacco and candies never plentiful enough. Every gift horse was examined carefully, in the mouth and elsewhere. Like the !Kung, the Mukogodo believe that all gifts have an element of calculation, and they were right to think that ours were no exception. We needed their help, and their efforts to diminish our expectations and lessen their obligations to repay were as fair as our attempts to get on their good side.

The idea that gifts carry obligations is instilled early in life. When we gave Mukogodo children candies after visiting their villages, their mothers reminded them of the tie: "Remember these white people? They are the ones who gave you candy." They also reinforced the notion that gifts are meant to circulate, by asking their children to part with their precious candies, already in their mouths. Most of the youngsters reluctantly surrendered their sweets, only to have them immediately returned. A mother might take, at most, a symbolic nibble from her child's candy, just to drive home the lesson.

The way food, utensils, and other goods are received in many societies is only the first stage of the behavior surrounding gift giving. Although repayment is expected, it is crucial that it be deferred. To reciprocate at once indicates a desire to end the relationship, to cut the strings; delayed repayment makes the strings longer and stronger. This is especially clear on the Truk Islands, of Micronesia, where a special word—*niffag*—is used to designate objects moving through the island's exchange network. From the Trukese viewpoint, to return niffag on the same day it is received alters its nature from that of a gift to that of a sale, in which all that matters is material gain.

After deciding the proper time for response, a recipient must consider how to make repayment, and that is dictated largely by the motive behind the gift. Some exchange customs are designed solely to preserve a relationship. The !Kung have a system, called *hxaro*, in which little attention is paid to whether the items exchanged are equivalent. Richard Lee's informant !Xoma explained to him that "Hxaro is when I take a thing of value and give it to you. Later, much later, when you find some good thing, you give it back to me. When I find something good I will give it to you, and so we will pass the years together." When Lee tried to determine the exact exchange values of various items (Is a spear worth three strings of beads, two strings, or one?), !Xoma explained that any return would be all right: "You see, we don't trade with things, we trade with people!"

One of the most elaborate systems of reciprocal gift giving, known as *kula*, exists in a ring of islands off New Guinea. Kula gifts are limited largely to shell necklaces, called *soulava*, and armbands, called *mwali*. A necklace given at one time is answered months or years later with an armband, the necklaces usually circulating clockwise, and the armbands counterclockwise, through the archipelago. Kula shells vary in quality and value, and men gain fame and prestige by having their names associated with noteworthy necklaces or armbands. The shells also gain value from their association with famous and successful kula partners.

Although the act of giving gifts seems intrinsically benevolent, a gift's power to embarrass the recipient and to force repayment has, in some societies, made it attractive as a weapon. Such antagonistic generosity reached its most elaborate expression, during the late nineteenth century, among the Kwakiutl, of British Columbia.

The Kwakiutl were acutely conscious of status, and every tribal division, clan, and individual had a specific rank. Disputes about status were resolved by means of enormous ceremonies (which outsiders usually refer to by the Chinook Indian term *potlatch*), at which rivals competed for the honor and prestige of giving away the greatest amount of property. Although nearly everything of value was fair game— blankets, canoes, food, pots, and, until the mid-nineteenth century, even slaves—the most highly prized items were decorated sheets of beaten copper, shaped like shields and etched with designs in the distinctive style of the Northwest Coast Indians.

As with the kula necklaces and armbands, the value of a copper sheet was determined by its history —by where it had been and who had owned it—and a single sheet could be worth thousands of blankets, a fact often reflected in its name. One was called "Drawing All Property from the House," and another, "About Whose Possession All Are Quarreling." After the Kwakiutl began to acquire trade goods from the Hudson's Bay Company's Fort Rupert post, in 1849, the potlatches underwent a period of extreme inflation, and by the 1920s, when items of exchange included sewing machines and pool tables, tens of thousands of Hudson's Bay blankets might be given away during a single ceremony.

In the 1880s, after the Canadian government began to suppress warfare between tribes, potlatching also became a substitute for battle. As a Kwakiutl man once said to the anthropologist Franz Boas, "The time of fighting is past. . . . We do not fight now with weapons: we fight with property." The usual Kwakiutl word for potlatch was *p!Esa*, meaning to flatten (as when one flattens a rival under a pile of blankets), and the prospect of being given a large gift engendered real fear. Still, the Kwakiutl seemed to prefer the new "war of wealth" to the old "war of blood."

Gift giving has served as a substitute for war in other societies, as well. Among the Siuai, of the Solomon Islands, guests at feasts are referred to as attackers, while hosts are defenders, and invitations to feasts are given on short notice in the manner of "surprise attacks." And like the Kwakiutl of British Columbia, the Mount Hagen tribes of New Guinea use a system of gift giving called *moka* as a way of gaining prestige and shaming rivals. The goal is to become a tribal leader, a "big-man." One moka gift in the 1970s consisted of several hundred pigs, thousands of dollars in cash, some cows and wild birds, a truck, and a motorbike. The donor, quite pleased with himself, said to the recipient, "I have won. I have knocked you down by giving so much."

Although we tend not to recognize it as such, the ethic of reciprocal gift giving manifests itself throughout our own society, as well. We, too, often expect something, even if only gratitude and a sense of indebtedness, in exchange for gifts, and we use gifts to establish friendships and to manipulate our positions in society. As in non-Western societies gift giving in America sometimes takes a benevolent and helpful form; at other times, the power of gifts to create obligations is used in a hostile way.

The Duke University anthropologist Carol Stack found a robust tradition of benevolent exchange in an Illinois ghetto known as the Flats, where poor blacks engage in a practice called swapping. Among residents of the Flats, wealth comes in spurts; hard times are frequent and unpredictable. Swapping, of clothes, food, furniture, and the like, is a way of guaranteeing security, of making sure that someone will be there to help out when one is in need and that one will get a share of any windfalls that come along.

Such networks of exchange are not limited to the poor, nor do they always involve objects. Just as the exchange of clothes creates a gift community in the Flats, so the swapping of knowledge may create one among scientists. Warren Hagstrom, a sociologist at the University of Wisconsin, in Madison, has pointed out that papers submitted to scientific journals often are called contributions, and, because no payment is received for them, they truly are gifts. In contrast, articles written for profit—such as this one—often are held in low esteem: scientific status can be achieved only through giving gifts of knowledge.

Recognition also can be traded upon, with scientists building up their gift-giving networks by paying careful attention to citations and acknowledgments. Like participants in kula exchange, they try to associate themselves with renowned and prestigious articles, books, and institutions. A desire for recognition, however, cannot be openly acknowledged as a motivation for research, and it is a rare scientist who is able to discuss such desires candidly. Hagstrom was able to find just one mathematician (whom he described as "something of a social isolate") to confirm that "junior mathematicians want recognition from big shots and, consequently, work in areas prized by them."

Hagstrom also points out that the inability of scientists to acknowledge a desire for recognition does not mean that such recognition is not expected by those who offer gifts of knowledge, any more than a kula trader believes it is all right if his trading partner does not answer his gift of a necklace with an armband. While failure to reciprocate in New Guinean society might once have meant warfare, among scientists it may cause factionalism and the creation of rivalries.

Whether in the Flats of Illinois or in the halls of academia, swapping is, for the most part, benign. But manipulative gift giving exists in modern societies, too —particularly in paternalistic government practices. The technique is to offer a present that cannot be repaid, coupled with a claim of beneficence and omniscience. The Johns Hopkins University anthropologist Grace Goodell documented one example in Iran's Khūzestān Province, which, because it contains most of the country's oil fields and is next door to Iraq, is a strategically sensitive area. Goodall focused on the World Bank–funded Dez irrigation project, a showpiece of the shah's ambitious "white revolution" development plan. The scheme involved the irrigation

of tens of thousands of acres and the forced relocation of people from their villages to new, model towns. According to Goodell, the purpose behind dismantling local institutions was to enhance central government control of the region. Before development, each Khūzestāni village had been a miniature city-state, managing its own internal affairs and determining its own relations with outsiders. In the new settlements, decisions were made by government bureaucrats, not townsmen, whose autonomy was crushed under the weight of a large and strategically placed gift.

On a global scale, both the benevolent and aggressive dimensions of gift giving are at work in superpower diplomacy. Just as the Kwakiutl were left only with blankets with which to fight after warfare was banned, the United States and the Soviet Union now find, with war out of the question, that they are left only with gifts—called concessions—with which to do battle. Offers of military cutbacks are easy ways to score points in the public arena of international opinion and to shame rivals, and failure either to accept such offers or to respond with even more extreme proposals may be seen as cowardice or as bellicosity. Mikhail Gorbachev is a virtuoso, a master potlatcher, in this new kind of competition, and, predictably, Americans often see his offers of disarmament and openness as gifts with long strings attached. One reason U.S. officials were buoyed last December, when, for the first time since the Second World War, the Soviet Union accepted American assistance, in the aftermath of the Armenian earthquake, is that it seemed to signal a wish for reciprocity rather than dominance—an unspoken understanding of the power of gifts to bind people together.

Japan, faced with a similar desire to expand its influence, also has begun to exploit gift giving in its international relations. In 1989, it will spend more than ten billion dollars on foreign aid, putting it ahead of the United States for the second consecutive year as the world's greatest donor nation. Although this move was publicly welcomed in the United States as the sharing of a burden, fears, too, were expressed that the resultant blow to American prestige might cause a further slip in our international status. Third World leaders also have complained that too much Japanese aid is targeted at countries in which Japan has an economic stake and that too much is restricted to the purchase of Japanese goods—that Japan's generosity has less to do with addressing the problems of underdeveloped countries than with exploiting those problems to its own advantage.

The danger in all of this is that wealthy nations may be competing for the prestige that comes from giving gifts at the expense of Third World Nations.

With assistance sometimes being given with more regard to the donors' status than to the recipients' welfare, it is no surprise that, in recent years, development aid often has been more effective in creating relationships of dependency, as in the case of Iran's Khūzestān irrigation scheme, than in producing real development. Nor that, given the fine line between donation and domination, offers of help are sometimes met with resistance, apprehension and, in extreme cases, such as the Iranian revolution, even violence.

The Indians understood a gift's ambivalent power to unify, antagonize, or subjugate. We, too, would do well to remember that a present can be a surprisingly potent thing, as dangerous in the hands of the ignorant as it is useful in the hands of the wise.

22

Using Cultural Skills
for Cooperative Advantage in Japan

Richard H. Reeves-Ellington

Cultural awareness and sensitivity have significant payoffs, helping people avoid major mistakes resulting from cultural ignorance or cultural misunderstanding. In addition, businesspeople who are more culturally aware are also more successful. In this selection, Reeves-Ellington describes a cross-cultural training program that he designed and implemented for an American company doing business in Japan. About fifty employees participated in the on-site cross-cultural training. The long-term results of their training are impressive. Project managers who took the cultural training program were able to cut project completion time nearly in half and increase the financial returns from the projects threefold (see Table 7). After the training program, managers felt much more comfortable and confident about conducting business in Japan on their own.

What might account for this dramatic success? Do the trained managers make no cultural mistakes, and are there no communication misunderstandings? Obviously, some cultural "horror stories" are instructive, like the case of the nervous American who publicly folded and then tore up a Japanese counterpart's business card during a meeting. But there is also evidence that the American efforts to learn Japanese customs and cultural rules of politeness engendered much goodwill and increased trust between employees involved in multinational business cooperation.

Reeves-Ellington teaches businesspeople to use the basic methods developed by cultural anthropologists to describe and analyze cultural settings. In this selection, he describes the cultural values and behavioral rituals implicit in day-to-day business interactions. In many ways, it is more important to recognize the different ways to observe and interpret cultural patterns than to remember the particular details of the cultural rules of business described here. There are practical advantages to being a participant observer rather than a nonobserving participant.

As you read this selection, ask yourself the following questions:

- What Japanese cultural values are illustrated in the stories about business cards and identity?

- Given the cultural expectations for business entertainment described, do you think there may be special challenges facing American women doing business in Japan?

- What are aspects of American culture that Japanese people might find particularly perplexing?

- In what ways do the rules of a business meeting seem to be ritualized?

- How would you convince an American company of the value of intercultural training?

The following terms discussed in this selection are included in the Glossary at the back of the book:

artifact	ritual
intercultural communication	values
participant observation	

Through trial and error, American managers who do business in Japan have learned to gain insight into the Japanese culture. Nonetheless, most American man-agers remain uneasy dealing with their Japanese counterparts, and "home office" continues to be suspicious of Japanese business practices. This situation produces ineffective business relationships and poor business results. The paradigm of discomfort and suspicion must be replaced by one of confidence and trust if American business is to succeed in Japan.

Reproduced by permission of Society for Applied Anthropology from *Human Organization* 52(2), 1993.

Pharmco, a pharmaceutical subsidiary of a major United States multinational, was saddled with this "home office" attitude of suspicion. Having done business in Japan for more than 20 years, it was dissatisfied with the relationships and financial arrangements with its Japanese licensees. The advent of innovative pharmaceutical technologies provided an opportunity to develop a new strategic alliance with a major Japanese company, Diversity KK. Pharmco anticipated that the alliance would facilitate rapid introduction of its technology in Japan, yield tenfold greater financial returns, and furnish the framework for learning to operate more successfully in Japan. Senior managers in the company understood that they and their staff needed to work effectively at many levels with Japanese managers and scientists in both the Japanese and American cultural environments. They had, however, no plan for learning about Japanese culture; the initial meetings between employees of the two companies resulted in more "damage control" than was desirable. The Pharmco senior manager responsible for Japanese operations, a trained anthropologist, proposed a program offering United States-based managers and scientists assistance in learning about Japanese culture. As a result of the program, American-Japanese relations at Pharmco improved considerably and business operations are running smoothly.

This paper . . . demonstrates how individuals used a cultural understanding process, ethnographic data, and participant observation (PO) to get through a business day in Japan, build their own database, and eventually, predict Japanese social behavior in different settings. Empirical evidence is provided to demonstrate the value the program had for one company.

UNDERPINNINGS OF THE PROGRAM

Employee Needs

The purpose of education in the business setting is to resolve problems. . . . Within the Pharmco context, the people who needed cultural information were based in the United States, worked in a variety of functions, and had to operate in several different cultures, not only Japan. Two common learning methods were thereby excluded, i.e., general reading and the use of culture-specific training courses. The manager-anthropologist had to devise another method.

To determine the educational needs, he set up small-group and one-on-one meetings with managers and scientists who would be required to work on the Japanese strategic alliance. He discovered that two questions deterred employees from wanting to work with Japanese in particular and all non-Americans in

general: "What do I do during a business day?" and "How can I learn to respond to the various situations I might find myself in while travelling in foreign cultures?" The initial training objective, therefore, was to offer assistance in getting through a Japanese business day while at the same time providing the tools and processes to enable employees to gain cultural understanding and apply their learning to other cultural contexts.

Involvement of an Insider Anthropologist

The manager-anthropologist responsible for Japan operations provided all training that took place over a five-year period and involved ten sets of employees. Training content included "horror" stories of what goes wrong in U.S.-Japanese relationships, examples of successful activities and processes for increasing the chances of success, and practice in using all the material discussed and presented. Material selection depended on the previous experience of members of the group in multicultural settings. Initial sessions were timed approximately two weeks before contacts with Japanese counterparts. This timing coincided with the peak interest employees had in learning the information. All training was done at the employees' work site, allowing them a greater comfort level. The manager-anthropologist was present at all initial meetings between U.S. employees and their Japanese contacts, and he continued to be present until the Americans expressed confidence that he was not needed at future meetings. . . .

The goal of training was that, through better understanding of Japan, employees would change their normal behavior patterns when working with Japanese counterparts. All improved their ability to work cross-culturally, but not all applied the material learned equally. Managers, in particular, had less patience to learn "how to do things," but rather just wanted to know "what to do." Scientists, on the other hand, tended to apply the models and processes in a much more diligent manner. . . .

Application of the "Understanding and Predicting Culture Process" in Japan

Pharmco employees started gaining understanding of Japanese culture by gathering and understanding cultural generalities. . . . Employees became more involved in the learning process by working on the tools to be used as well as applying them in a Japanese context.

Employees gathered information through visits, while in Japan, to museums, theaters, shrines, baseball games, and business meetings. . . . The initial work session was led by the manager-anthropologist but the trainees at the session participated in data entry. . . . After the introduction of the model, the anthropologist made no effort to suggest data classification according to anthropological criteria. Rather, Pharmco employees using the model defined classifications acceptable to and understood by them. For example, in the case of "insider-outsider," discussed under "artifacts" below, the visual artifact was the way people sat at business and dinner tables, with the concept rightly belonging in the cultural logic. Employees, however, skipped the visual and placed the cultural logic in the artifacts section. The point is that they understood what they meant.

The following analysis of Japanese culture used by Pharmco as baseline data is:

Artifacts. How are things classified or what are the artifacts of an agreed classification system? In Japan there are two basic classification systems commonly used: (1) insider-outsider and (2) front-rear. The insider is determined in the first instance by what Nakane (1970) refers to as a "frame." By frame, she means criteria that classify and identify individuals as part of a group. In business, the most obvious is the identification by company. When introducing oneself, one says, for example, "I am Pharmco's Reeves-Ellington." Japanese frames can also be determined by locality, such as the city in which one is born or family or household affiliations. In all cases frame indicates a criterion that sets a boundary and gives a common basis to a group of individuals who are located or involved in it. Outsiders are all those who are excluded from the frame. Hence, the use of the word "foreigner" (*gaijin*) is frequent in Japan. If one is not part of the frame, i.e., Japanese (insider), then one is a foreigner (outsider) (Nakane 1970).

Front and rear in the Japanese concept are not linear, as in the western world, but circular. The front, which embodies the concept of *tatamae*, is what is seen or what is commonly known, or frontstage, whereas the rear is what is hidden or backstage. This rear embodies the concept of *honne*, commonly referred to as what is "true." In the western world, these two concepts are the flip sides of a coin existing in a dichotomous relationship, but in Japan, the two concepts are a circular continuum. One folds into the next as do the rooms of a house as one walks through it. Outsiders are always kept to the front, whereas insiders are introduced to the rear (Matsumoto 1988).

The artifacts of the classifications are always determined by the situation in which people come together (Hall and Hall 1987). For example, in the inside-outside relationship, obvious manifestations are the family, localities, schools, companies, and associations. Tour groups are formed to make a group of people insiders. Outsiders are those not in a particular group, e.g., family members are outsiders to the company inside group. On the other hand, fellow employees are typically outsiders to a colleague's family group. In another context, such as going on a trip together, the family and business colleagues could both be insiders, as members of the XYZ tour group. The artifacts of the front and rear classifications can be exemplified by business meetings. Humans typically belong to a complex of groups that can be concentrically layered and are variably mutually inclusive and exclusive. The front artifacts are expressed in how people are arranged at a table and the courtesy that is extended to guests. The rear artifacts are expressed in terms of who is attending and the body language that occurs.

Social knowledge (values). What are proper principles for behavior? What are the values that drive the categories and artifacts described above? In Japan, adoption of the classification systems discussed above keeps as many people on the outside as possible. One keeps one's social obligations to a level that encourages self gain but eliminates all that offer less gain than one is required to give. One sees this principle in action in the Tokyo subway system. The proverbial Japanese politeness is totally absent, replaced with a "survival of the fittest" behavior pattern, which is accomplished, in part, by avoiding eye contact, thereby assuring that everyone around stays on the outside.

Keeping people on the outside embodies another principle: Minimize obligations to others. The personal value that drives this principle is the desire and need for personal relationships of a meaningful nature. If too many people are insiders, personal relationships would be weakened and a fundamental value diluted.

There is a third human principle at work: Everyone needs to be an insider somewhere. All Japanese are striving to be an insider in situations that will provide personal gain. In companies, they have a strong sense of being inside: On tour groups, they all do things together as insiders in a travel experience. The driving value that leads Japanese to strive for insider status is the value of acknowledging and accepting mutual interdependencies with others (*amae*) (Doi 1990).

Cultural logic. Social knowledge or values are based on underlying cultural logic around relationships to the environment, the nature of reality, truth, human nature, human activities, human relationships, and use of time. Within a culture, these are all taken for granted, rarely understood, and almost never expressible by those living in the culture, but they are

TABLE 1 Cultural Logic

Environmental relationships

Japanese, as well as other Asians, view the physical environment and human environment as intertwined and not in opposition as do most Christians (Campbell 1960, 1989; Pelzel 1974). As exemplified in Japanese gardens, humans control and shape the environment in ways that suit the artistic feeling of people. The garden denotes the desire for environmental harmony and orderliness.

Nature of truth and reality

Truth and reality are determined by situations and social contexts in which people find themselves (Hall and Hall 1987; Lebra 1976). In a social group, only the insiders determine what is true and real. The accuracy of this determination is based on the degree of harmony and orderliness obtained within the insider group.

Nature of human nature

Humans are driven by emotion and not by logic (Doi 1990b). Mutuality of love and obligation (within the context of the concept of obligation) ties closely with that of hate (Ishida 1974). This mutuality in human relations forces the concept of consensus into human society organization. Since human nature is not believed to be inherently "bad," it is assumed this behavior is caused by ignorance and not evil intent.

Nature of human relationships

Using the concept of relational value orientation (Kluckhohn and Strodbeck 1961), collaterality in human relationships is highly valued. Within this concept is the perception that uncertainty is to be avoided and much effort is put into avoiding it. Within the basic collateral value, there exists a strong power distance within organizations and generational structures (Hofstede 1980).

Nature of human activities

Activity is focused on working toward ideals of harmonious relationships and involves an orientation toward human interdependency (Doi 1990; Lebra 1976; Hayashi 1988). Activity is necessarily done in groups and by groups.

Use of time

Time is polychronic (Hall and Hall 1987). The time system is characterized by the simultaneous occurrence of many things and by a deep involvement with people. There is more emphasis on completing transactions than holding to a schedule. A person confronted with too many subjects to be covered in too short a time chooses to expand the time available to complete the tasks rather than reduce the number of tasks.

---

of utmost importance to foreigners wishing to live and work in that culture. An explanation of Japanese cultural logic is contained in Table 1. . . .

THEORY INTO PRACTICE

To get theory into practice, Pharmco decided to learn how to do introductions, meetings, leavings, dinner, and drinking in Japan.

This analysis brings to life Pharmco's learning by relating incidents about just how badly things can go wrong when there is no basis for successful behaviors leading to appropriate judgements in the course of cross-cultural activities. In spite of the mistakes made, Diversity employees were gracious and appreciative of the efforts made to behave properly. They understand that Pharmco, being foreign, will never get it exactly right in Japan—just as the Japanese will never get it exactly right in the United States. Pharmco

employees constantly remind themselves that they are involved in a continuous process they may never get entirely "right." There are always new and more subtle nuances to learn.

The Business Card (*meishi*)

During the initial meeting with the Japanese, the first item of business is introductions. (See Table 2.) Proper introductions require proper business cards (*meishi*). The word *meishi* is used by all people in Japan, including foreigners because the two words, business card and *meishi*, refer to the same card but the meaning behind the card is substantially different. For this reason, *meishi* should be prepared in Japan and be ready upon arrival to do business. At the time of presenting the *meishi*, the Japanese expect the viewer of the *meishi* to examine it carefully and to remember both name and title.

TABLE 2 Introductions at Business Meetings

Artifacts	Social knowledge	Cultural logic
Technology • Business cards • *Meishi* Visual behavior • Presentation of *meishi* by presenting card, facing recipient. • Senior people present *meishi* first. • Guest presents first, giving name, company affiliation and bowing. • Host presents *meishi* in same sequence. • Upon sitting at conference table, all *meishi* are placed in front of recipient to assure name use.	• Once given a card is kept—not discarded. • *Meishi* are not exchanged a second time unless there is a position change. • Before the next meeting between parties, the *meishi* are reviewed for familiarization with the people attending the meeting. • The *meishi* provides status for the owner.	Human relations • *Meishi* provide understanding of appropriate relations between parties. • *Meishi* take uncertainty out of relationships. Environment • *Meishi* establish insider/outsider environment. • *Meishi* help establish possible obligations to environment. Human activity • *Meishi* help to establish human activities.

Mistreatment of a Japanese businessman's *meishi* will ruin a relationship, whether new or established. Since the *meishi* is an extension of self, damage to the card is damage to the individual. Explaining this to Pharmco staff was not sufficient. They did not understand the implications of the *meishi* until two stories were told to help their understanding.

The importance of this point is demonstrated in the following story. A major U.S. company was having problems with one of its distributors, and the parties seemed unable to resolve their differences. The president of the U.S. company decided to visit Japan, meet with his counterpart in the wholesaler organization, and attempt to resolve their differences. The two had not met previously and, upon meeting, each followed proper *meishi* ritual. The American, however, did not put the Japanese counterpart's *meishi* on the table; instead he held on to it. As the conversation became heated, the American rolled up the *meishi* in his hand. Horror was recorded on the face of the Japanese businessman. The American then tore the *meishi* into bits. This was more than the Japanese could stand; he excused himself from the meeting. Shortly afterward the two companies stopped doing business with each other.

How Japanese use the *meishi* also helped Pharmco staff understand its importance. Japanese companies value a high degree of consistency in those with whom they work and in the handling of personnel within a company. Failure to demonstrate consistency toward internal employees indicates a probable inconsistency in relationships outside the company. The *meishi* can provide the Japanese executive with some indication of a company's attitude toward its employees. The Pharmco employees learned this lesson with a particu-

larly painful outcome at a meeting with a senior Japanese executive. After the Pharmco team explained the purpose of the visit, this executive took a number of *meishi* from his desk. As he turned each of them up, he asked, "I see that I met with Mr. Hansen of your company ten years ago. Where is he now?" Then came the next card. "I see I met with Mr. Harman of your company eight years ago. Where is he now?" The questioning went through eight separate *meishi*. The Pharmco team leader responded each time that the particular person was no longer with the company. At the end, the Japanese executive said, "People are not treated well in your company. In our company, people do not leave until retirement." The meeting was not successful.

With this background, Pharmco staff visiting Japan have a good understanding of the *meishi* and treat it and its presentation with the respect Japanese expect.

The Conference Table

As soon as introductions are complete both sides take a seat at the conference table. In Japan, there are no round tables at business meetings. The expression "head of the table" is meaningless in a Japanese context. Understanding conference table arrangements (Table 3) leads to a successful meeting.

Seating is highly ritualistic and stylized. The power position is flanked by advisors; next come suppliers of data and information, should they be requested; and finally interested parties are seated at the extremities of the conference table (Figure 1). The person in the power seat performs all ritualistic duties

TABLE 3 Conference Seating Arrangements

Artifacts	Social knowledge	Cultural logic
Technology • Rectangular table Visual behavior • Hosts on one side of the table and guests on the other. • Guests are framed by most attractive background. • The power seat is in the middle of the table. • Junior people are closest to the door.	• Set seating allows all parties social/business understanding. • Person responsible for success has the authority. • Guests are treated as customers.	Human relations • Seating arrangements allow established order to be known, allowing a proper order and power structure to function between people. Reality and truth • Responsibility and authority are combined for success. • The inside and outside are maintained at the conference table. Environment • Used to honor customers and guests. • Used to maintain inside-outside definitions.

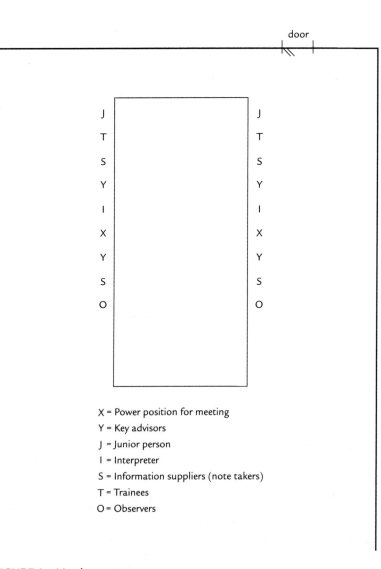

X = Power position for meeting

Y = Key advisors

J = Junior person

I = Interpreter

S = Information suppliers (note takers)

T = Trainees

O = Observers

FIGURE 1   Meeting room

TABLE 4 Leaving the Conference

Artifacts	Social knowledge	Cultural logic
Visual behavior • Ritualistic thank yous end the meeting while all are seated. • Conclusion of exchange means guests initiate standing. All arise. • Power person stays with guests until they are off company premises. • Bows start upon arising and continue each time one of either side leaves.	• Politeness demands guests be treated as though they were visiting the Japanese at home.	Environment • Guests are under control while in the insider environment. They are left only when they achieve the outside environment. Truth and reality • All exchanges assure a smooth transition from one status to another. Human relations • All structured interactions require a host and a guest role.

for the side represented. That person directs all comments or questions to particular members of his team who are best qualified to answer them and also functions as the go-between for his team and the other side.

Contrary to usual western practice, the person in the power seat is not necessarily the most senior person present. Rather, the person designated as the official contact for his company or the person most knowledgeable about the subject matter to be discussed takes the seat. The Japanese want the powerful person to be the one who can accomplish the business at hand.

Not understanding this point led to Pharmco embarrassment. Pharmco managers believed at first that the senior person present always occupied the power seat. This assumption was based on meetings between senior managers of the companies who were addressing subject matter only they could decide. When Pharmco's R&D senior manager led Pharmco's initial discussions with Diversity regarding research philosophy and programs, he correctly took the power seat. At a subsequent meeting, called to address program execution, the senior R&D manager again took the power seat. The Japanese body language indicated he should not be there. A new lesson was learned that day: expertise and subject matter, not status, determine the occupant of the power seat. In the case of program execution, the Pharmco power seat occupant should have been the senior scientist for toxicology, not the head of R&D. By taking the power seat, the R&D manager offended the Japanese scientist because he had less status and therefore felt ineffectual. The meeting was inconclusive.

Knowing who is in the power seat offers insights to the other side's agenda. At a negotiating meeting between Diversity KK and Pharmco, the Pharmco team expected the meeting to be a confirmation of

work done. When the meeting started, however, the Diversity power seat was occupied by an attorney, not the familiar businessman known by Pharmco. Pharmco immediately excused themselves for a few minutes. In private caucus, the team discussed the change of people and decided that major changes in the contract under negotiation were about to be introduced. This proved to be a correct interpretation. Even this short notice helped the Pharmco team stay in control of unfolding events. At the conclusion of the meeting, leaving is as ritualistic as arriving. Table 4 provides a grasp of the ritual.

At the conclusion of a business meeting, both sides stand up to leave; the host leads the guests out of the conference room; the host's team escorts the guests to the elevator; the entire team, excluding the host, leaves the guests as the elevator doors close, both sides bowing profusely; the host joins his guests in the elevator. The remaining host and his guests then go to the front door of the office, where, if a car has been arranged, the host will get into the car if there is room and accompany his guests back to their hotel. If no car is arranged, the host will stay with the guests until a taxi is found and the guests are safely in it and driving off. The host will remain at the curb, bowing, until the taxi is well into the traffic. The guests keep eye contact, heads nodding and arms waving until the car leaves the curb.

The respect ritualistically shown is based on the status of the individual's company, not on that of the individual. By showing this level of courtesy, the hosts expect the guests to recognize that they have an obligation to reciprocate in the future, when he is on their turf.

Once Pharmco staff understood the social importance of what the Japanese were doing in seeing them off, they immediately instituted the same policy of courtesy for the Japanese when they visited the Pharmco facilities.

Going out to Dinner

When foreigners are invited to dinner, they must be prepared to express a preference for the nationality of food to be eaten; in Japan, a preference for Japanese is obligatory because it demonstrates a willingness to engage in things "Japanese." The Japanese restaurant is likely to be more comfortable and offer more privacy than others, thus creating a better relationship. A Japanese menu includes raw fish. The Japanese host will inevitably ask "Do you like raw fish?" The answer is "yes." Accepting what is offered is a necessity for relationship building in Japan, but it does not include the necessity of eating everything. Being a guest is a simple task as all that is necessary is responding to what the Japanese host suggests or discusses. The intricacies of the organization are the responsibility of the hosts.

Hosting a dinner is much more difficult than being a guest. The host is responsible for assuring a successful relationship-building event. Hosting requires an understanding of Japanese social knowledge if the event is to be successful. Three principles of social knowledge are at work in dinner meetings: (1) have an environment that permits individual members of the companies to start to become acquainted and either start building a relationship or support and maintain one; (2) provide a setting and a meal befitting the guests' social position and thereby show that the host respects this position; and (3) send indirect signals of the status of the relationship in terms of the locale and quality of food. The meal can offer a form of celebration, a basis of apology[1] or just a feeling of comfort. The atmosphere created at dinner should be relaxed and enjoyable. The host is responsible for the comfort of the guests and, should that comfort be threatened for any reason, the host must make certain that conviviality is restored.

Execution of these social values requires one to know when to host, how to select the right guests, how to select a proper restaurant, how to assure that the meal is a proper one, how to keep the conversation in an acceptable mood and assure that the event starts and ends within a culturally acceptable time frame.

Determination of who hosts must be settled well in advance of the date of the dinner. The decision should not be left open until the close of a formal business meeting. If one side has an apology to make or if they have a difficult request, then they should certainly offer to host. For dinners following routine meetings, Pharmco works on the basis that if the meet-

ings are in Japan, then the Japanese host, and if they are in the United States, Pharmco hosts. This works well. If, however, the Japanese are insistent upon acting as host, it is best to follow their lead.

The attendees of any particular dinner must correlate to reciprocal status of individuals from both companies. Therefore the attendees must be agreed upon well in advance of the dinner. Any changes of attendee by one side must be announced well in advance of the dinner. For one side to change the status level of attendance at the last minute causes problems for the other. If the side making changes lowers the level of attendance, the other side has two problems to sort out. First, is a *honne* message being sent and why? For example, Japanese companies have been known to use this type of last-minute change as a way to tell the other company that they want to downgrade the existing relationship between the two companies. Second, how can a Japanese manager explain such changes to his superior? If, on the other hand, the level of attendance is increased at the last minute, the other might not be able to reciprocate, leading to embarrassment and a weakening of friendly relations. Attendance, once set, should not change.

The class of the restaurant must be in keeping with the status of the senior member of the party being invited, for Japanese executives have a clear understanding of where their status allows them to dine. Selection of a restaurant considered below a Japanese guest's status results in the guest losing face with his colleagues. Anticipation of this problem makes the Japanese uncomfortable during the meal, precluding the building of good social relationships. An example demonstrates the point.

Pharmco headquarters decided that the cost of entertaining in Tokyo was too high and dictated that cheaper places be found. The dictum was followed and, on the occasion of the next business meeting with a middle manager of Diversity, disaster resulted. When the guest arrived, his first comment was that one of his subordinates often brought suppliers to the restaurant. Pharmco had clearly insulted him in the choice of eating establishment, causing Pharmco managers to spend the rest of the night apologizing. Trying to rectify the situation, the next time they hosted the manager, Pharmco managers went to a very exclusive place. The first comment received was, "the president of our company likes this restaurant but I have never been here." This time, Pharmco embarrassed the Diversity manager by taking him to a location beyond his status, causing him to explain to his colleagues the next day why he was there.

Avoiding these problems requires only that foreigners ask a Japanese for a restaurant preference. The answer will be "no," followed by a comment indicat-

TABLE 5 Going to Dinner

Artifacts	Social knowledge	Cultural logic
Physical • Guests • Restaurant • Meals • Transportation Visual behavior • Hosting • Guesting • Timing to eat	• Relationship building is purpose of eating. • Status is honored by correct dinners. • Dinner group has some "insider" attributes.	Use of time • Time at dinners is effective use of time for relations. Relationships • Identifies how two companies view people's position in hierarchy. • Confirms status matching through acceptance or nonacceptance of invitations.

ing a restaurant in which he has never eaten but would like to do so. If this approach fails, a visit to the social director of the hotel in which the foreigner is staying will yield dividends. By showing the director the card of the individual to be entertained, she will make appropriate selections, based on the *meishi* information of the name of the company and the title of the person. She never errs in judgement.

Selection of the restaurant leads to the selection of a suitable menu, which is done by the host in advance and must reflect the status of the guests and the nature of the occasion. For example, if it is a dinner just to end the day, a simple meal is in order. If the relationship is particularly strong, a stop in a noodle shop can be totally appropriate. If the dinner is one of celebration or a form of apology, however, a more elaborate meal is required. As with the choice of a restaurant, use Japanese expertise. A visit to the restaurant with the guest's business card and a discussion of the room and the meal with the majordomo of the restaurant (a discussion that should also cover who will attend and the purpose of the meal) assures a proper menu and setting.

When Pharmco management decided to enter a strategic alliance with Diversity KK, they had to inform Nippon Pharmaceutical, a potential partner, that they had decided not to work with them. The business aspects of the decision were discussed with Nippon Pharma at their offices, but then at dinner the relationship aspects of the decision were covered. The choice of location and meal was more elaborate than would normally be the case, given the state of the relationship. At the end of the meal, the Nippon Pharma representatives complimented Pharmco on their ability to be a good Japanese host.

Conversation at dinners does not include heavy business negotiations under any but the most unusual circumstances. Talk focuses on recreational activities, current politics, travel, or other "cocktail party" chat.

The point of conversation, as well as of the food, is to put everyone at ease. Failure to follow this principle can cause discomfort.

At a dinner hosted by Diversity management, a Pharmco manager discussed matters relating to fundamental changes in the Japanese health care system. He did not notice that the Japanese were becoming upset until one of them exploded that "these matters were not the business of foreigners and they should not express opinions. Rather they should wait to be taught the right way to do business by the Japanese." While the foreigner thought himself at fault by not avoiding the delicate subject matter, he received an extensive apology by a colleague of the Japanese who expressed such a forceful opinion. He said "As host, I should not permit such things to happen!"

In Japan, dinners are arranged for the end of the business day, which is around 6:30 p.m. The foreign host should plan to invite his guests for a 7 p.m. dinner, as doing so will give them a half an hour to get to the restaurant. Always offer an exact time. The American habit of "let's make it around 6:30 to 7" is not acceptable. The host always should arrive a few minutes early and be there to greet his guests. At the close of the meal, the host walks the guest to the front of the restaurant, where he has had the restaurant arrange transportation. The host stands at the curb and stays there, preferably bowing or waving, until the guests have been driven off. Table 5 summarizes the critical cultural factors concerning dinner engagements.

Drinking in Bars

Going out to drink after dinner is the first opportunity for colleagues of different companies to have the chance to behave as a set of "insiders." It also provides a setting in which anyone of the group can express a *honne* sentiment. Drinking provides the foreigner a

TABLE 6 Going Out Drinking

Artifacts	Social knowledge	Cultural logic
Physical • Karaoke bars • Tabs • Female social managers Visual behavior • Singing • Joking • Honest opinion	• Freedom of speech acceptable. • Drunken behavior acceptable. • Place to get things "off the chest." • Everyone can be an "insider."	Human relations • Provides a time for *honne* talk. • Fills the need for business associates to be a set of "insiders." Environment • Setting is outside a traditional "insider" setting, allowing a new set of "insiders" to be formed on "neutral" ground. Reality and truth • Feelings (reality) must be expressed and understood (truth) by an insider group.

sense of how relationship-building is progressing between his company, himself and his Japanese counterparts. Therefore, ethnographic understanding of ritual drinking is imperative (Table 6).

"Know how to sing," was the key learned by Pharmco management before going out drinking after dinner. Drinking in Karaoke bars is the ultimate socializing and relationship-building mechanism with and among Japanese. Power and social distance are almost completely broken down at the bars. The president as well as the most junior person present will sing, tell jokes, and generally relax. Although there is still not a round table, all the people together act as though they are at one. The environment has also changed substantially from that of the office. The bar is smaller than the office, and women are an important addition as they are to provide conversation and pour the drinks.[2] The tables are laid out so that there is little structure in the physical environment. A basic assumption is that this is the one place in the entire social milieu where uncertainty is acceptable. The assumption is that, with drink, it is totally acceptable to say what is on your mind to whomever you want. A further assumption is that whatever is said cannot be held against a person after leaving the bar.

Being there makes one an insider for the time spent together in the bar. "Insidership" is created only if the proper bar is chosen—one befitting the status of the group. Unlike choosing a restaurant, however, the foreigner must ask his Japanese associates for advice as to where to go, for they know that the foreigner lacks the knowledge to make a proper selection. A Pharmco executive experienced near-disaster the one time he selected a bar without consulting a Japanese businessman. He had found the hotel social relations director helpful with restaurants so [he] thought that person would be a good source of information for bars. He was not. As soon as he walked in the bar rec-

ommended by the director, he knew there was a problem: Except for one or two Japanese, only foreigners were present; the bar was almost empty; and the hostesses ranged in age from 40 to 50—far too old for the tastes of the Japanese guests. Fortunately, relationships between the Pharmco executive and his Japanese guests [were] strong enough for everyone to get a good laugh from the situation. He is still periodically reminded of the incident.

Business is usually not done at the bar, where drinking offers the Japanese an opportunity to express *honne* opinions about his relationships with colleagues, both foreign and Japanese. These opinions are tolerable as they are expressed when the person expressing them is acceptably drunk. Within the drinking context, everyone is in the same social circle. For this reason, one must constantly be alert for signals that might indicate something is on a colleague's mind. At one drinking session, a Pharmco manager felt that something was bothering his Japanese counterpart but, as the evening wore on, nothing was said. Just before it ended, the Japanese manager put his face down on the table and muttered that he had something important to say. The American leaned forward and asked what it was. All the Japanese said was "Your Johns-san is an asshole." Nothing more was said and the subject was never raised again. The American assumed that just stating the opinion was enough to relieve the tension the Japanese had. The opinion was not reported to Johns. The next business day discussions with the Japanese gentlemen were more relaxed than had been previously experienced.

PHARMCO BUSINESS IMPROVEMENTS

Three critical factors were deemed necessary for the program to be judged a success: (1) effective working relationships with Japanese executives; (2) shortened

TABLE 7 Critical Factors Outcome

Effective working relationships

1. Pharmco employees are more self-assured when meeting Japanese in Japan.

2. Their Japanese counterparts state they prefer working with Pharmco over other foreign companies.

Shortened project times

1. Prior to introducing the cultural material, projects between Pharmco and Diversity averaged 15 months to completion.

2. Projects run by executives applying cultural methodologies shortened project completion times to an average of 8 months, while all others remain at 15 months.

Improved financial returns

1. Financial returns based on contracts negotiated by personnel not exposed to the cultural material average gross income of 6% of sales.

2. Financial returns of contracts negotiated by personnel applying the anthropological techniques provide gross income equal to 18% of sales.

project times; and (3) improved financial returns. The project is successful based on these factors (Table 7) and is in the process of being applied to other countries.

Before learning the methodologies and skills outlined in this paper, Pharmco executives avoided travel to Japan and working with Japanese whenever possible. Fifty Pharmco executives have been through the training program. Before the program, they were asked to evaluate their comfort level of working with Japanese and their enjoyment of business trips to Japan. The rating scale was 1 to 10 with 1 expressing no comfort and no enjoyment to 10 expressing total comfort and enjoyment. The average score was 3 with a range of 1 to 5. After exposure to the concepts, tools, and material, the average score increased to 6, with a range of 5 to 9. The final measurement was based on 15 executives who used the concepts and tools in their next series of meetings. The average score of this group was 8, with a low score of 5 and a high score of 10. Before the program, most employees wanted to be accompanied to Japan by a person experienced in Japan. After the exposure, almost all are comfortable making these trips on their own. This willingness to work in and with Japan has improved the personal effectiveness of all these employees working on Japanese projects.

Late delivery of projects was costly to Pharmco and discouraged Diversity managers from working with their Pharmco counterparts. In one case the delays were estimated to cost Pharmco $90 million over a ten-year period. The delays were of a nature that a competitor entered the market with a similar product, thereby denying innovator status to Pharmco. The improved delivery times are helping both Diversity and Pharmco in gaining valuable marketing time over their key competitors.

SUMMARY

The ability to work with and within a foreign culture requires an organization to adopt and implement an interpretive strategy that permits its practitioners to set out to work proactively within the perceived meaning of the foreign environment. This strategy requires managers to become transformational in order to operate successfully in other social and institutional environments. Successful implementation of such a strategy demands the use of both business and anthropological tools and skills. By creating a base of these skills and providing a training environment in which employees individually could learn and implement such a strategy, Pharmco achieved dramatic improvements in its Japanese business relationships and business results. This success has led to adapting the training to other countries.

NOTES

1. In Japan, the concept of apology involves a great shame for not having behaved correctly or done something in the right way. To apologize is traumatic for a Japanese.

2. Apologies are necessary to my female colleagues for this chauvinistic viewpoint. It is how things are in Japan, however. I would like to point out that should a female colleague be part of the group visiting the bar, she

would be treated as a colleague by her peers and be well received by the employees in the bar.

REFERENCES

Brislin, Richard W., Kenneth Cushner, Craig Cherrie, and Mehalahi Yong. 1986. *Intercultural Interactions: A Practical Guide.* Beverly Hills, CA: Sage.

Campbell, Joseph. 1960. *The Masks of God: Primitive Mythology.* New York: Viking Press.

———. 1989. *The Hero with a Thousand Faces.* New York: Viking Press.

David, Kenneth. 1985. *Participant Observation in Pharmaceutical Field Selling.* Norwich, CT: Norwich Eaton Pharmaceutical Co., Inc.

Doi, Takeo. 1990a. *The Anatomy of Dependence.* Tokyo: Kodansha International.

———. 1990b. *The Anatomy of Self.* Tokyo: Kodansha International.

Hall, Edward T., and Mildred R. Hall. 1987. *Hidden Differences.* New York: Anchor Press.

Hamada, Tomoko. 1991. *American Enterprise in Japan.* Albany: SUNY Press.

Hayashi, Shuji. 1988. *Culture and Management in Japan.* Tokyo: University of Tokyo Press.

Hofstede, Geert. 1980. *Culture's Consequences: International Differences in Work-Related Values.* Beverly Hills, CA: Sage.

Ishida, Eiichiro. 1974. A Culture of Love and Hate. In *Japanese Culture and Behavior,* Takie Sugiyama Lebra and William P. Lebra, eds. Pp. 27–36. Honolulu: University Press of Hawaii.

Kluckhohn, F. R., and F. L. Strodbeck. 1961. *Variations in Value Orientations.* Westport, CT: Greenwood Press.

Lebra, Takie Sugiyama. 1976. *Japanese Patterns of Behavior.* Honolulu: University Press of Hawaii.

Matsumoto, Michihiro. 1988. *The Unspoken Way.* Tokyo: Kodansha International.

Nakane, Chie. 1970. *Japanese Society.* Tokyo: Charles E. Tuttle Co.

Pelzel, John C. 1974. Human Nature in the Japanese Myths. In *Japanese Culture and Behavior,* Takie Sugiyama Lebra and William P. Lebra, eds. Pp. 3–26. Honolulu: University Press of Hawaii.

Reeves-Ellington, Richard H. 1988. Relationships Between Multinationals and Peasants. Paper presented at the annual meeting of the American Anthropological Association, Chicago.

Reeves-Ellington, Richard H., and Paul Steidlmeier. 1991. *Total Quality, Institutionalism and the Retooling of American Business.* Binghamton, NY: SUNY-Binghamton, School of Management.

23

Family Planning Outreach and Credit Programs in Rural Bangladesh

Sidney Ruth Schuler and Syed M. Hashemi

In many parts of the world, high fertility rates threaten women's health and lead to a variety of negative consequences associated with exploding populations. Many applied anthropologists argue that stabilizing population growth is critical for increased quality of life in developing nations. Yet the paradoxical coexistence of high birthrates in tandem with starvation and poverty is all too common. Governments and nongovernmental agencies spend millions and millions of dollars each year trying to reduce birthrates. Certainly there has been much success, but there is a long way to go.

As we have seen repeatedly, anthropology teaches us of the interrelationships between the various segments of our social order. If we wish to reduce the birthrate, for example, there may be ways that are less intrusive than family planning and that have additional benefits for women and their communities.

Women's participation in the economic sphere is linked to their status in society. Low status, isolation, dependence, and lack of mobility to even visit with other women limit women's opportunities and ability to act in their own interests. Empowering women by enhancing their economic role in society can have many consequences, one of which is an increased use of contraceptives.

This intriguing selection examines the case of a Grameen Bank program that provides loans for poor women in rural Bangladesh.

As you read this selection, ask yourself the following questions:

- Who should make judgments about whether the fertility rate in Bangladesh is too high? And who has the right to implement programs that change the social order?

- How does purdah limit women's access to family planning services?

- What is Grameen Bank's strategy for reducing women's isolation?

- How are economic conditions linked to the use of contraceptives?

- Should family planning workers assist women in using contraceptive methods secretly?

- What do women mean when they say that through Grameen Bank they have "learned to talk"?

The following terms discussed in this selection are included in the Glossary at the back of the book:

dependent variable	*qualitative methods*
hypothesis	*random sample*
purdah	*TFR (total fertility rate)*

In rural Bangladesh, women's ability to seek out family planning services is limited by their isolation and their economic and social dependence on men. Large numbers of female outreach workers—about 28,000— are being employed by the government and non-

governmental programs to bring family planning services to women in their homes. Program evaluations and research studies have documented the effectiveness of this strategy, particularly in increasing use of the oral pill and other temporary contraceptive methods. Recent studies show substantial increases in contraceptive use and a decline in estimated fertility rates —from TFR[1] of about 7 in the late 1960s and early 1970s to about 5 in 1989—and attribute this change in large part to the expansion in access to family planning services in recent years, mainly through female

Reprinted with permission of Society for Applied Anthropology from *Human Organization* 54(4): 455–61, 1995.

community-based workers (Cleland et al. 1994; Larson and Mitra 1992; World Bank 1992).

While the intensive door-to-door delivery strategy has been effective in raising levels of contraceptive use from low to moderate levels (e.g., from 19% in 1983 to 40% in 1991), it is obvious that intensification of service delivery can only go so far, and that other strategies will be needed if levels of contraceptive use are to be increased to a level that would stabilize population growth. Improvements in the quality of services are needed, both for achievement of higher levels of contraceptive use, and from the perspective of women's rights to better health and reproductive autonomy. Another strategy would be interventions that increase women's ability to take an active role in getting access to services—for example, programs that strengthen women's economic roles and increase their mobility. This article examines the effects of the Grameen Bank program that provides small loans for women's self-employment activities in rural Bangladesh. Survey and ethnographic research findings are used to analyze the effects of the Grameen Bank, community-based family planning outreach, and women's relative levels of physical mobility on their practice of contraception. The effects of exposure to the Grameen Bank and home visits by family planning workers are compared for members and nonmembers living in Grameen Bank villages.

BACKGROUND

Among the poor in rural Bangladesh, women's lives are severely restricted by their social and economic dependence on men. Because of *purdah* (a system based on an ideology concerned with secluding and protecting women to uphold social standards of modesty and morality) women's contacts with the world outside of the family are extremely limited. Many cannot avail themselves of family planning, health and other services that may be available unless these services are brought to their homes. Bringing services to women in or near their homes is the principal strategy of the Bangladesh Government's family planning program and of many of the nongovernmental organizations providing family planning services in rural areas. As noted above, this strategy has been very effective in increasing contraceptive use.

Grameen Bank is a quasi-governmental organization involved in lending to the poor in nearly half of all villages in rural Bangladesh. Its two million female members (and about two hundred thousand male members) come from landless rural poor families, most of whom have very few assets of any kind. The program attempts to draw women out of isola-

tion by providing them with credit, to enable them to earn a cash income through various types of self-employment activities. In addition to supporting economic activities that require interactions in the public sphere, it increases women's mobility and access to information by requiring that they attend regular meetings. The rituals of membership help women to create a sense of identity outside of the family. Grameen Bank does not provide family planning services. We have argued, based on a previous analysis, that the program influences contraceptive use by strengthening women's economic roles and contributing to their empowerment, increasing their ability to overcome obstacles to use of contraception. The same analysis suggested that BRAC (Bangladesh Rural Advancement Committee), whose program focus is similar but somewhat broader, doe not have the same effect on contraceptive use because it is less effective in strengthening women's economic roles and in helping them to establish identities outside of the family (Schuler and Hashemi 1994).

A number of studies (e.g., Koenig et al. 1992) have assessed the effects of family planning outreach on use of contraception in Bangladesh. Two recent studies (Simmons et al. 1988, 1992) argue that the role of the female family planning worker in Bangladesh goes beyond the conventional concept of "supply" of family planning methods and services, so that they function as change agents in the communities where they work. In this article we focus on the effects of credit rather than family planning programs in transforming reproductive norms, and we attempt to highlight the interactive effects of the two types of interventions.

METHODOLOGY

Data Sources

The analysis is based on a survey conducted in late 1992 to measure the impact of participation in credit programs on contraceptive use. It included four separately selected samples. The first two were random samples of Grameen Bank and BRAC members.[2] . . . With a few exceptions, the women in these two samples have been members of the programs for a minimum of 18 months. The third was a comparison group consisting of nonmembers from Grameen Bank villages who would be eligible to join BLAC or Grameen Bank (i.e., poor and functionally landless). The fourth was a second comparison group consisting of women living in villages not served by either program, who would be eligible to join the programs. One adult woman was selected from each household. The interviewers were Bangladeshi women who had previous experience in conducting demographic surveys. They received more training during the process of pretesting the questionnaires. In addition to questions related to contraceptive use, the survey included questions related to women's status within the family and community, their physical mobility and their economic roles. A total of 1305 married women younger than 50 were interviewed.[3]

The data from concurrent ethnographic research in six villages describes the credit programs in operation, from the perspectives of the field research team as well as participants in the programs. The team consisted of six women and six men, all Bangladeshi, most of whom had master's degrees. The team received intensive training in qualitative research methods at the beginning of the project, and the principal investigators provided continuing informal training throughout the study. The male-female team in each village conducted in-depth interviews to document change processes, both in women's roles and status and in norms related to reproduction and use of contraception. This article is based primarily on the survey data, but data from the ethnographic study is taken into account in interpreting the survey results.

Hypotheses

The following analysis is intended to test several specific hypotheses. Underlying all of them is the more general hypothesis that women's isolation, dependence, and lack of mobility inhibit use of contraception, and that a variety of programmatic strategies can be used to lessen these effects. The specific hypotheses are:

1. Home visits by family planning fieldworkers are positively related to contraceptive use.

2. Membership in credit programs and residence in villages where such programs are present increases the likelihood that a woman will use contraception.

3. Women's relative physical mobility is positively related to use of contraception.

4. The higher level of physical mobility of credit program participants does not fully explain their greater propensity to use contraception.

Variables

Dependent Variable. The dependent variable indicates whether or not the respondent is currently using any method of contraception.

Exposure to Credit Programs. These variables indicate whether the respondent was a Grameen Bank member, a nonparticipant living in a Grameen Bank village, or a resident of a comparison village, where no credit program existed.

Control Variables. In order to distinguish between effects of credit program participation per se and effects of other variables that are believed to affect contraceptive use in Bangladesh, several control variables are included. These are respondent's age, whether she ever attended school, number of surviving children, existence of at least one surviving son, existence of at least one surviving daughter, and an indicator of the relative economic level of the respondent's household. The latter is a composite measure based on the number of items owned from the following list: bed, blanket/quilt, shawl/sweater/coat, radio/TV, cow/buffalo.

Indicators of Access to Family Planning Services. We include two indicators of access to family planning services. The first of these is whether the respondent was ever visited by a family planning worker and the second is whether she was visited in the three months prior to the survey. Because of the strong emphasis on community-based services in the Bangladesh family planning program, these are generally thought to be the best indicators of access to family planning services in rural Bangladesh.

Indicators of Women's Physical Mobility. For this analysis we consolidated the variables related to women's mobility to create a single score. In the survey interview the respondent was presented with a list of places (the market, a medical facility, the movies, outside the village) and asked if she had ever gone there. She was given one point for each place she had visited and an additional point if she had ever gone there alone. A dichotomous variable was then created, in which a respondent with a score of 3 or better was classified as "more mobile."

Frequency distributions and means, as applicable, for the dependent and independent variables are presented in Table 1.

STATISTICAL RESULTS

The first section of the analysis compares women living in villages where Grameen Bank is present with women living in villages without a credit program. As Table 1 indicates, there is a dramatic difference in levels of contraceptive use between Grameen Bank members and women living in comparison villages—a difference of 16 percentage points. . . . The presence of the Grameen Bank program in a village has a significant effect on use of contraception, both among members and nonmembers, which is not explained by the

TABLE 1 Characteristics of Study Samples

	GB	GB Non-members	Comparison
% using contraception	59.0	48.0	43.0
Mean age (in years)	31.0	26.0	29.0
Mean no. surviving children	3.5	2.6	3.3
Mean no. surviving sons	1.8	1.3	1.7
Mean no. surviving daughters	1.7	1.3	1.6
% attended school	29.0	18.0	18.0
Mean wealth score	2.5	1.7	1.6
% ever visited by FP worker	83.0	67.0	78.0
% visited in past 3 months	36.0	38.0	35.0
Mean mobility score	2.3	2.1	1.9
Mean duration of membership (in months)	50.0	—	—
N of cases	312	315	424

effects of outreach. Visits by family planning workers (both recent and "ever") also appear to have strong independent effects, as do age, relative wealth, and presence of a surviving son.

. . . [Further,] women who are "more mobile" are considerably more likely to use contraception. Sixty percent of the "more mobile" group were using a contraceptive method, compared with 46% of the "less mobile" group. The relatively higher level of mobility of women in Grameen Bank villages explains, at least in part, the higher level of contraceptive use.

COMBINED EFFECTS OF GRAMEEN BANK AND FAMILY PLANNING OUTREACH

Previous studies in Bangladesh have found contact with female family planning workers to be one of the most important determinants of contraceptive use. . . . In general the findings indicate that family planning outreach has a highly significant effect on contraceptive use and that the presence of Grameen Bank in a village has an added effect. However, another dimension is added when contraceptive use rates among women who have/have not been visited by family planning workers are examined separately for each of the three groups (Figure 1).

For the comparison group and for nonmembers in Grameen Bank villages, rates of contraceptive use among women who have been visited by a family planning worker are 21 and 30 points higher, respectively, than for women who have never been visited. However, for members of Grameen Bank, the rate of contraceptive use is consistently high (59%), regardless of whether the women have ever been visited by a family planning worker. This suggests that the poten-

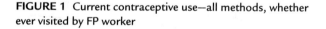

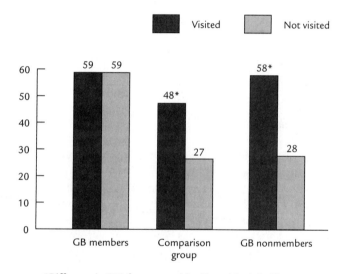

*Difference in CPR for women visited/not visited significant at $p<.001$ in chi square test.

FIGURE 1 Current contraceptive use—all methods, whether ever visited by FP worker

tial of Grameen Bank to influence contraceptive use is particularly important for women whose access to family planning services is relatively limited. For nonparticipating women in Grameen Bank villages who have been visited by a family planning fieldworker, the rate of contraceptive use is almost as high as among Grameen Bank members in the same communities—58%, compared with 48% for women in the comparison group. For the nonparticipants, the combined effect of the presence of Grameen Bank in a village and family planning outreach is even more evident when one looks at visits by family planning workers within the past three months (Figure 2). Among women who were not visited within the three

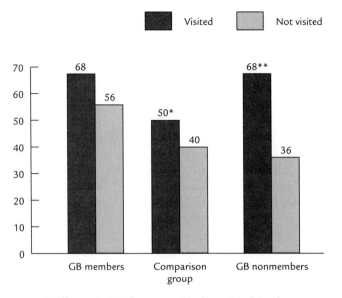

*Difference in CPR for women visited/not visited significant at p<.05 in chi square test.

**Difference in CPR for women visited/not visited significant at p<.001 in chi square test. (For GB members difference not significant at p<.05 level.)

FIGURE 2 Current contraceptive use—all methods, whether ever visited by FP worker past three months

months preceding the survey, the rates of contraceptive use are about the same for the comparison group, and about 20 points lower than among Grameen Bank members. The rates of contraceptive use among women who were visited by a family planning worker within the past three months are 9 point higher for Grameen Bank members, 11 points higher for the comparison group, and 32 points higher for Grameen Bank nonmembers (65%, 50%, and 68%, respectively).

. . . Family planning outreach is an important factor explaining the relatively high level of contraceptive use among nonparticipants in Grameen Bank villages, but . . . the even higher level of contraceptive use among participants is due to other factors.

DISCUSSION AND CONCLUSION

The strong effect of visits by community-based family planning fieldworkers on use of contraception supports the findings of previous research in Bangladesh. Because of their social and economic dependence on men, and their limited physical mobility, most women in rural Bangladesh cannot get access to family planning methods and services without assistance. As one of the respondents put it,

> I am not allowed to go out and work even though we are so poor that we are sometimes desperate. Neither

my husband nor his parents will let me go out to work . . . I had wanted to use family planning before my two daughters were born. I asked my husband several times to bring me a family planning method but he wouldn't listen . . . I am a woman—I could not get it for myself.

The ethnographic study data indicate that men often fail to provide this assistance because they are generally apathetic about fertility control, or because they fear that side effects will lead to economic losses—either by interfering with work or by incurring monetary costs for treatment. Since most women are prevented from working outside of the home, and perceived as economically nonproductive, their husbands and in-laws often feel that it is wrong for them to incur expenses (Schuler et al. 1995).

In this context the presence of a community-based fieldworker, whether employed by the government or a nongovernmental organization, can make a great difference. By providing information and services in the home, they preempt the need for most women to go to clinics or other sources for family planning methods. They provide free pills and suggest things that women can say to persuade their husbands to allow them to use contraception. In cases where persuasion seems unlikely to be effective, they often assist women in using contraceptive methods secretly.

The survey findings suggest that, in addition to "supply-side" strategies, it is possible to influence fertility through programs that decrease women's isolation and their economic dependence on men. Such programs can help women to overcome obstacles to contraceptive use such as lack of mobility, lack of cash, lack of information about contraceptive methods and services, and opposition or lack of cooperation from their husbands and other family members. Grameen Bank strengthens women's economic roles through credit, enabling them to contribute more substantially to their families' support. Even in cases where the woman hands her loan money over to her husband, there is usually some acknowledgment from the family that she is a source of income. Involvement in the program also gives women a socially legitimate purpose to participate in a group outside of the family. The opportunity for involvement in a nonfamily group can be important as a source of identity, new experiences, and ideas.

The ethnographic and the survey findings from this study generally support Grameen Bank's own contention that strengthening women's economic roles gives them more autonomy and more control over important decisions affecting themselves and their families, as well as contributing to their self-confidence and propensity to plan for the future. It promotes women's relative freedom to move about in

TABLE 2 Comparison of Method Mix in Grameen Bank Villages Versus Comparison Villages (N = 1051)

	Grameen Bank Villages	Comparison Villages
Modern Methods		
Pills	22%	15%
Condom	1%	—
Injectables	5%	1%
IUDs	1%	1%
Female Sterilization	18%	18%
Male Sterilization	2%	3%
Traditional Methods		
Rhythm Method	4%	4%
Withdrawal	1%	—
Abstinence	1%	—
Other	1%	1%
No Method	46%*	56%*

Totals not equal to 100% because of rounding.

public and to travel outside of the village. Where more women are employed outside of the home, and are required to walk along roads or use buses or other forms of transport, it is less difficult for them to travel within and outside of their villages to get services.

Participation in the Grameen Bank program also makes members more experienced in interacting with men outside of the family and with authority figures. Although the interactions that take place in weekly meetings with bank staff clearly cast the women in a subservient role, this nevertheless seems to give them a certain self-confidence. In all interactions with government officials and even representatives of nongovernmental organizations, the poor are in a subservient role, and at least in this case it is the woman rather than her husband who is doing the interacting. Several of the women in our study told our field investigators that through Grameen Bank they had "learned to talk," and now they were not afraid to talk to outsiders. This probably increases their ability to avail themselves of family planning and health services.

Through a combination of intimidation and confidence-building, Grameen helps women to stand up to their husbands. Normally, any savings or asset that a women might have could be legitimately (at least from her husband's point of view) appropriated by him. Having recognized that this would be a central problem in a loan program for women, Grameen Bank tells women what to say when their husbands try to take their loan money. Case studies suggest that women who have developed the self-confidence to try to protect their assets and earnings from their husbands are more likely to take initiative in other areas, such as practicing family planning.

The Grameen Bank program can produce high rates of contraceptive use among members, even if they are not exposed to family planning outreach. The very high rates of contraceptive use among nonmembers in Grameen Bank villages who are visited by a family planning fieldworker suggest that the presence of Grameen Bank's program in a village in combination with family planning outreach can increase use of contraception dramatically, even among women who do not join Grameen Bank. The probably explanation is that reproductive norms are changing in Grameen Bank villages, but that diffusion of innovations takes time. Nonmembers, whose level of dependence on men has not been reduced because they have not participated in the program, typically require the support of family planning workers to follow the reproductive norms that are emerging.

In considering the implications of these findings, it is important to avoid overestimating the magnitude of the changes occurring in gender relations. The vast majority of women—including those who participate in the Grameen Bank program—are able to make only small cash or kind contributions to the family's support, and many have little or no control over the income. Only a quarter of the Grameen Bank members in our survey said that their contribution represented half or more of the family's income, and only 7% of the nonmembers in Grameen Bank villages and 4% in comparison villages said this. Socially, and psychologically as well, the typical Grameen Bank member, like other women, is extremely dependent on her husband, and simply has to accept inequities, extreme limitations on her autonomy, and in some cases physical abuse. Watching the realities of poverty and gender-based subordination being played out in social life in the six ethnographic study villages, most of the members of our research team did not expect to find that the small changes occurring in women's lives as a result of Grameen Bank were having a measurable impact on contraceptive use.

Our ethnographic study provided some insight into the processes through which women are asserting themselves in making reproductive decisions, but it also revealed continuing obstacles to increased and more effective fertility control. The most significant of these seems to be fear—related to method side effects, health problems that may be perceived as side effects, and the widespread belief that contraceptive methods cause physical weakness and other problems. In some cases lingering ideas that contraceptive use may be sinful are reinforced when contraceptive users suffer from side effects or experience other types of misfortunes. In addition to physical suffering and even death, contraceptive users and their families fear inability to work, and the possibility that the problems resulting from contraceptive use will require costly medical treatments. Because most women do not have an independent income or control over money, they know that if something happens to them they will be dependent on others—in most cases their husbands—to arrange and pay for medical treatment. Generally the fieldworkers who come to their doors have limited training and are only minimally equipped to treat health problems. Women's restricted physical mobility and their economic dependence on men, as well as their general condition of poverty, limit their ability to seek treatment. In our view, a continuous and increased focus on providing economic opportunities for women and, simultaneously, on improving poor women's access to health services and improving the quality of contraceptive services is needed.

NOTES

1. TFR, or Total Fertility Rate, is the average number of children born to a woman during her lifetime.
2. Since the previous analysis suggested that BRAC does not affect the level of contraceptive use among its members it was excluded from the present analysis.
3. See Schuler and Hashemi 1994 for a more detailed description of the survey methodology.

REFERENCES

Cleland, John, James E. Phillips, Sajeda Amin, and G. M. Kasmal. 1994. The Determinants of Reproductive Change in Bangladesh: Success in a Challenging Environment. World Bank Regional and Sectoral Studies. Washington DC: The World Bank.

Koenig, Michael A., Ubaidur Rob, Mehrab Jali Khan, J. Chakraborty, and Vincent Fauveau. 1992. Contraceptive Use in Matlab, Bangladesh in 1990: Levels, Trends, and Explanations. *Studies in Family Planning* 23(6): 352–364.

Larson, Ann and S. N. Mitra. 1992. Family Planning in Bangladesh: An Unlikely Success Story. *International Family Planning Perspectives* 18(4):123–129.

Mauldin, W. Parker and John A. Ross. 1991. Family Planning Programs: Efforts and Results, 1982–89. *Studies in Family Planning* 22(6):350–367.

Mitra, S. N., Ann Larson, Gilliam Foo, and Shahidul Islam. 1992. *Bangladesh Contraceptive Prevalence Survey. July 1991: Key Findings.* Dhaka: Mitra and Associates.

Schuler, Sidney Ruth and Syed M. Hashemi. 1994. Credit Programs, Women's Empowerment and Contraceptive Use in Rural Bangladesh. *Studies in Family Planning* 25(2):65–76.

Schuler, Sidney Ruth, Syed M. Hashemi and Ann Hendrix. 1995. Bangladesh's Family Planning Success Story: A Gender Perspective. *International Family Planning Perspectives* 27:6.

Simmons, Ruth, Laila Baqee, Michael A. Koenig, and James E. Phillips. 1988. Beyond Supply: The Importance of Female Family Planning Workers in Rural Bangladesh. *Studies in Family Planning* 19(1):29–38.

Simmons, Ruth, Rezina Mita, and Michael A. Koenig. 1992. Employment in Family Planning and Women's Status in Bangladesh. *Studies in Family Planning* 23(2):97–109.

The World Bank. 1992. Population and the World Bank: Implications from Eight Case Studies. Operations Evaluations Department. Washington, DC: The World Bank.

24

Anthropology in the Technology Industry

Greg Guest

When people imagine anthropologists and anthropological work, they often envision the lone anthropologist living in a grass-roofed hut in the high mountains of New Guinea or in a canvas tent only a stone's throw away from an exciting archaeological dig. These images are not exactly wrong: Anthropologists are still doing such fieldwork in remote places, and such "exotic" work is still necessary for furthering our understanding of humankind. On the other hand, those images are quite incomplete, since many anthropologists work closer to home. Twenty-first century anthropology encompasses an exceptionally broad range of topics and research settings. Anthropologists are applying the theories and research methods honed in the Australian outback or the Kalahari Desert to modern settings, lending new and innovative insights and creating novel solutions.

This profile describes the work of anthropologists doing ethnographic analysis to help create solutions in the technology industry. The effectiveness of new technologies depends upon their acceptability to consumers; the design of "user-friendly" systems requires companies to understand the beliefs and behaviors of their consumers. Greg Guest, the author and anthropologist described in this profile, uses his anthropological training to become an "Experience Modeler" at Sapient Corporation, a consulting group that helps companies integrate into the new economy.

As you read this selection, ask yourself the following questions:

- What does the author mean by "contextual user research"?
- How would doing ethnographic field research differ from the use of surveys or focus groups? What are some of the advantages of each?
- When an anthropologist is employed by a company like Sapient, is she or he still doing anthropology?

The following terms discussed in this selection are included in the Glossary at the back of the book:

ethnography   *holistic*

focus groups   *participant observation*

What do anthropologists do in the technology industry? In brief, we use ethnography to better understand users and inform design. Our tradition *in situ* participant-observation and our holistic perspective can be used to gain a deeper understanding of the complex interaction between individuals, sociocultural factors, activities and design. Ethnography has an advantage over other forms of research—surveys and focus groups, to name two common examples—because it can reveal user needs in the context of the activity a given design is intended to support. This gives designers opportunities to make a closer match between products and user experience.

While the value of contextual user research may seem obvious to anthropologists, many designers and corporate decision-makers still push the supply side of technology and build systems that make sense to experts or marketers but not to the average end-user. This is why offices have phone systems or photocopiers that employees can't operate and homes are cluttered with electronic appliances that are difficult to use.

Computers and computer software have also become increasingly complicated, a fact attested to by

Reprinted with permission of the American Anthropological Association from *Anthropology News,* February 2001, p. 28.

the number of help lines necessary to support the industry. Rather than endeavoring to better understand users, companies have instead engaged in a race to simply add features. MSWord, for example, had 311 features in 1992. By 1997, the number of features had risen to 1033, most of which are not used by the typical user.

Anthropologists can make a difference in this techno-centric environment. I was recently working on a project in which a client—a large multinational—wanted our company to design a system that would better facilitate interaction between the client's project managers and external consultants. The client initially envisioned a standardized system that would support an idealized workflow model. Our research team went to the field, conducting interviews and observing participants in their offices. By working with users in the field, we were better able to describe their work process, because participants could show us the many artifacts they use to support their work processes such as Post-its and Gant charts.

Our research revealed that the workflow in this collaborative process is extremely dynamic and that users' needs are much more variable than originally anticipated in the corporate vision. The nature of the work in this collaborative space is constantly changing and unpredictable. In such a chaotic environment a system needs to be responsive to change and variation in order to be useful. Our team, therefore, made recommendations for a more flexible and customizable system, with features that could accommodate such dynamism and variability.

One of Sony's cordless phone models provides another example. Ethnographic research in homes showed that when people spend a lot of time on the phone, their arms become fatigued because they can't shift their arms without also moving the ear piece away from their ears. Sony developed a floating ear-piece to address this problem. This ear-piece, which came to market two years ago, is attached to the body of the phone by a floating hinge. The design allows users to move their arms while keeping the ear-piece on the ears. It has been a popular seller.

What anthropologists do in the technology industry is really not that different from what we do in more traditional engagements. My dissertation research, for example, dealt with shrimp fishermen in Ecuador. After spending a year in a small fishing village, two things became clear: (1) the current regulations were not effective in mitigating over-fishing and (2) the primary reason for the ineffectiveness was a poor understanding, on the government's part, of the local fishermen and their social conditions. Government regulations prohibit shrimp fishing for eight weeks of the year, and yet every fisherman finds a way of circumventing this restriction. This is not surprising, given that the imposed hiatus, if respected, would disrupt a series of social relationships in the community and would mean severe economic hardship for many families. One of my policy recommendations, therefore, was to regulate by geographic area, making certain ecologically important regions out of bounds for fishing, instead of restricting fishing activity based on time. This would defray negative economic impacts and would be more compatible with the local social structure.

Just as shrimp fishermen in Ecuador perceive fishing regulations—created in top-down fashion—to be incomprehensible, so too do many end-users of technological systems find themselves frustrated with inappropriate designs that result from a lack of, or poorly executed, user research. Whether it is fishery policy or technological design, an anthropological lens and methodology can make significant contributions to how the world is shaped. Using ethnography, anthropologists can help solve complex problems and make a difference.

25

Society and Sex Roles

Ernestine Friedl

Americans pride themselves on their concern for social justice. We believe, or at least say we believe, in equal rights and equal access to education, jobs, and other opportunities. As such, understanding the social and historical origins of inequality should be important to us for both intellectual and policy reasons. One of the many inequalities that remain in our society and in societies throughout the world is the asymmetrical relationship between men and women. Indeed, the dominant position of men is so pervasive that people often assume that this is the "natural" (read biological) relationship between the sexes. Anthropology, as we have seen, is a discipline that challenges us to question such fundamental assumptions.

In this selection, Ernestine Friedl examines contemporary hunter-gatherer societies and in so doing suggests that male dominance stems from economic control over resources. Differences in cultural perception about gender are closely related not only to economic patterns but also to the organization of families and the institution of marriage.

As you read this selection, ask yourself the following questions:

- Looking at the historical and anthropological records, how frequently do we find gender equality?
- What is the source of male power in hunter-gatherer societies?
- Why don't women hunt?
- Based on this reading, how will the changing position of women in the American labor force affect gender roles?
- What is the value of cross-cultural studies for understanding problems such as sexism in our own society?

The following terms discussed in this selection are included in the Glossary at the back of the book:

egalitarian society	nomadic band
gender	reciprocal gift
human universal	sex roles
hunter-gatherers	shaman

"Women must respond quickly to the demands of their husbands," says anthropologist Napoleon Chagnon describing the horticultural Yanomamo Indians of Venezuela. When a man returns from a hunting trip, "the woman, no matter what she is doing, hurries home and quietly but rapidly prepares a meal for her husband. Should the wife be slow in doing this, the husband is within his rights to beat her. Most reprimands . . . take the form of blows with the hand or with a piece of firewood. . . . Some of them chop their

From "Society and Sex Roles" by Ernestine Friedl from *Human Nature* magazine, April 1978. Copyright © 1978 by Human Nature, Inc. Reprinted by permission of Harcourt Brace & Company.

wives with the sharp edge of a machete or axe, or shoot them with a barbed arrow in some nonvital area, such as the buttocks or leg."

Among the Semai agriculturalists of central Malaya, when one person refuses the request of another, the offended party suffers *punan,* a mixture of emotional pain and frustration. "Enduring *punan* is commonest when a girl has refused the victim her sexual favors," reports Robert Dentan. "The jilted man's 'heart becomes sad.' He loses his energy and his appetite. Much of the time he sleeps, dreaming of this lost love. In this state he is in fact very likely to injure himself 'accidentally.'" The Semai are afraid of violence; a man would never strike a woman.

The social relationship between men and women has emerged as one of the principal disputes occupying the attention of scholars and the public in recent years. Although the discord is sharpest in the United States, the controversy has spread throughout the world. Numerous national and international conferences, including one in Mexico sponsored by the United Nations, have drawn together delegates from all walks of life to discuss such questions as the social and political rights of each sex, and even the basic nature of males and females.

Whatever their position, partisans often invoke examples from other cultures to support their ideas about the proper role of each sex. Because women are clearly subservient to men in many societies, like the Yanomamo, some experts conclude that the natural pattern is for men to dominate. But among the Semai no one has the right to command others, and in West Africa women are often chiefs. The place of women in these societies supports the argument of those who believe that sex roles are not fixed, that if there is a natural order, it allows for many different arrangements.

The argument will never be settled as long as the opposing sides toss examples from the world's cultures at each other like intellectual stones. But the effect of biological differences on male and female behavior can be clarified by looking at known examples of the earliest forms of human society and examining the relationship between the technology, social organization, environment, and sex roles. The problem is to determine the conditions in which different degrees of male dominance are found, to try to discover the social and cultural arrangements that give rise to equality or inequality between the sexes, and to attempt to apply this knowledge to our understanding of the changes taking place in modern industrial society.

As Western history and the anthropological record have told us, equality between the sexes is rare; in most known societies females are subordinate. Male dominance is so widespread that it is virtually a human universal; societies in which women are consistently dominant do not exist and have never existed.

Evidence of a society in which women control all strategic resources like food and water, and in which women's activities are the most prestigious has never been found. The Iroquois of North America and the Lovedu of Africa came closest. Among the Iroquois, women raised food, controlled its distribution, and helped to choose male political leaders. Lovedu women ruled as queens, exchanged valuable cattle, led ceremonies, and controlled their own sex lives. But among both the Iroquois and the Lovedu, men owned the land and held other positions of power and prestige. Women were equal to men; they did not have ultimate authority over them. Neither culture was a true matriarchy.

Patriarchies are prevalent, and they appear to be strongest in societies in which men control significant goods that are exchanged with people outside the family. Regardless of who produces food, the person who gives it to others creates the obligations and alliances that are at the center of all political relations. The greater the male monopoly on the distribution of scarce items, the stronger their control of women seems to be. This is most obvious in relatively simple hunter-gatherer societies.

Hunter-gatherers, or foragers, subsist on wild plants, small land animals, and small river or sea creatures gathered by hand; large land animals and sea mammals hunted with spears, bows and arrows, and blow guns; and fish caught with hooks and nets. The 300,000 hunter-gatherers alive in the world today include the Eskimos, the Australian aborigines, and the Pygmies of Central Africa.

Foraging has endured for two million years and was replaced by farming and animal husbandry only 10,000 years ago; it covers more than 99 percent of human history. Our foraging ancestry is not far behind us and provides a clue to our understanding of the human condition.

Hunter-gatherers are people whose ways of life are technologically simple and socially and politically egalitarian. They live in small groups of 50 to 200 and have neither kings, nor priests, nor social classes. These conditions permit anthropologists to observe the essential bases for inequalities between the sexes without the distortions induced by the complexities of contemporary industrial society.

The source of male power among hunter-gatherers lies in their control of a scarce, hard to acquire, but necessary nutrient—animal protein. When men in a hunter-gatherer society return to camp with game, they divide the meat in some customary way. Among the !Kung San of South Africa, certain parts of the animal are given to the owner of the arrow that killed the beast, to the first hunter to sight the game, to the one who threw the first spear, and to all men in the hunting party. After the meat has been divided, each hunter distributes his share to his blood relatives and his in-laws, who in turn share it with others. If an animal is large enough, every member of the band will receive some meat.

Vegetable foods, in contrast, are not distributed beyond the immediate household. Women give food to their children, to their husbands, to other members of the household, and rarely, to the occasional visitor. No one outside the family regularly eats any of the wild fruits and vegetables that are gathered by the women.

The meat distributed by the men is a public gift. Its source is widely known, and the donor expects a reciprocal gift when other men return from a successful hunt. He gains honor as a supplier of a scarce item and simultaneously obligates others to him.

These obligations constitute a form of power or control over others, both men and women. The opinions of hunters play an important part in decisions to move the village; good hunters attract the most desirable women; people in other groups join camps with good hunters; and hunters, because they already participate in an internal system of exchange, control exchange with other groups for flint, salt, and steel axes. The male monopoly on hunting unites men in a system of exchange and gives them power; gathering vegetable food does not give women equal power even among foragers who live in the tropics, where the food collected by women provides more than half the hunter-gatherer diet.

If dominance arises from a monopoly on big-game hunting, why has the male monopoly remained unchallenged? Some women are strong enough to participate in the hunt and their endurance is certainly equal to that of men. Dobe San women of the Kalahari Desert in Africa walk an average of 10 miles a day carrying from 15 to 33 pounds of food plus a baby.

Women do not hunt, I believe, because of four interrelated factors: variability in the supply of game; the different skills required for hunting and gathering; the incompatibility between carrying burdens and hunting; and the small size of seminomadic foraging populations.

Because the meat supply is unstable, foragers must make frequent expeditions to provide the band with gathered food. Environmental factors such as seasonal and annual variation in rainfall often affect the size of the wildlife population. Hunters cannot always find game, and when they do encounter animals, they are not always successful in killing their prey. In northern latitudes, where meat is the primary food, periods of starvation are known in every generation. The irregularity of the game supply leads hunter-gatherers in areas where plant foods are available to depend on these predictable foods a good part of the time. Someone must gather the fruits, nuts, and roots and carry them back to camp to feed unsuccessful hunters, children, the elderly, and anyone who might not have gone foraging that day.

Foraging falls to the women because hunting and gathering cannot be combined on the same expedition. Although gatherers sometimes notice signs of game as they work, the skills required to track game are not the same as those required to find edible roots or plants. Hunters scan the horizon and the land for traces of large game; gatherers keep their eyes to the ground, studying the distribution of plants and the texture of the soil for hidden roots and animal holes. Even if a woman who was collecting plants came across the track of an antelope, she could not follow it; it is impossible to carry a load and hunt at the same time. Running with a heavy load is difficult, and should the animal be sighted, the hunter would be off balance and could neither shoot an arrow nor throw a spear accurately.

Pregnancy and child care would also present difficulties for a hunter. An unborn child affects a woman's body balance, as does a child in her arms, on her back, or slung at her side. Until they are two years old, many hunter-gatherer children are carried at all times, and until they are four, they are carried some of the time.

An observer might wonder why young women do not hunt until they become pregnant, or why mature women and men do not hunt and gather on alternate days, with some women staying in camp to act as wet nurse for the young. Apart from the effects hunting might have on a mother's milk production, there are two reasons. First, young girls begin to bear children as soon as they are physically mature and strong enough to hunt, and second, hunter-gatherer bands are so small that there are unlikely to be enough lactating women to serve as wet nurses. No hunter-gatherer group could afford to maintain a specialized female hunting force.

Because game is not always available, because hunting and gathering are specialized skills, because women carrying heavy loads cannot hunt, and because women in hunter-gatherer societies are usually either pregnant or caring for young children, for most of the last two million years of human history men have hunted and women have gathered.

If male dominance depends on controlling the supply of meat, then the degree of male dominance in a society should vary with the amount of meat available and the amount supplied by the men. Some regions, like the East African grasslands and the North American woodlands, abounded with species of large mammals; other zones, like tropical forests and semi-deserts, are thinly populated with prey. Many elements affect the supply of game, but theoretically, the less meat provided exclusively by the men, the more egalitarian the society.

All known hunter-gatherer societies fit into four basic types: those in which men and women work together in communal hunts and as teams gathering edible plants, as did the Washo Indians of North America; those in which men and women each collect their own plant foods although the men supply some meat to the group, as do the Hadza of Tanzania; those in which male hunters and female gatherers work apart but return to camp each evening to share their acquisitions, as do the Tiwi of North Australia; and those in which the men provide all the food by hunting large game, as do the Eskimo. In each case the extent of male dominance increases directly with the proportion of meat supplied by individual men and small hunting parties.

Among the most egalitarian of hunter-gatherer societies are the Washo Indians, who inhabited the valleys of the Sierra Nevada in what is now southern California and Nevada. In the spring they moved north to Lake Tahoe for the large fish runs of sucker and native trout. Everyone—men, women, and children—participated in the fishing. Women spent the summer gathering edible berries and seeds while the men continued to fish. In the fall some men hunted deer but the most important source of animal protein was the jack rabbit, which was captured in communal hunts. Men and women together drove the rabbits into nets tied end to end. To provide food for the winter, husbands and wives worked as teams in the late fall to collect pine nuts.

Since everyone participated in most food-gathering activities, there were no individual distributors of food and relatively little difference in male and female rights. Men and women were not segregated from each other in daily activities; both were free to take lovers after marriage; both had the right to separate whenever they chose; menstruating women were not isolated from the rest of the group; and one of the two major Washo rituals celebrated hunting while the other celebrated gathering. Men were accorded more prestige if they had killed a deer, and men directed decisions about the seasonal movement of the group. But if no male leader stepped forward, women were permitted to lead. The distinctive feature of groups such as the Washo is the relative equality of the sexes.

The sexes are also relatively equal among the Hadza of Tanzania but this near-equality arises because men and women tend to work alone to feed themselves. They exchange little food. The Hadza lead a leisurely life in the seemingly barren environment of the East African Rift Gorge that is, in fact, rich in edible berries, roots, and small game. As a result of this abundance, from the time they are 10 years old, Hadza men and women gather much of their own food. Women take their young children with them into the bush, eating as they forage, and collect only enough food for a light family meal in the evening. The men eat berries and roots as they hunt for small game, and should they bring down a rabbit or a hyrax, they eat the meat on the spot. Meat is carried back to the camp and shared with the rest of the group only on those rare occasions when a poisoned arrow brings down a large animal—an impala, a zebra, an eland, or a giraffe.

Because Hadza men distribute little meat, their status is only slightly higher than that of the women. People flock to the camp of a good hunter and the camp might take on his name because of his popularity, but he is in no sense a leader of the group. A Hadza man and woman have an equal right to divorce and each can repudiate a marriage simply by living apart for a few weeks. Couples tend to live in the same camp as the wife's mother but they sometimes make long visits to the camp of the husband's mother. Although a man may take more than one wife, most Hadza males cannot afford to indulge in this luxury. In order to maintain a marriage, a man must support both his wife and his mother-in-law with some meat and trade goods, such as beads and cloth, and the Hadza economy gives few men the wealth to provide for more than one wife and mother-in-law. Washo equality is based on cooperation; Hadza equality is based on independence.

In contrast to both these groups, among the Tiwi of Melville and Bathurst Islands off the northern coast of Australia, male hunters dominate female gatherers. The Tiwi are representative of the most common form of foraging society, in which the men supply large quantities of meat, although less than half the food consumed by the group. Each morning Tiwi women, most with babies on their backs, scatter in different directions in search of vegetables, grubs, worms, and small game such as bandicoots, lizards, and opossums. To track the game, they use hunting dogs. On most days women return to camp with some meat and with baskets full of *korka*, the nut of the native palm, which is soaked and mashed to make a porridge-like dish. The Tiwi men do not hunt small game and do not hunt every day, but when they do they often return with kangaroo, large lizards, fish, and game birds.

The porridge is cooked separately by each household and rarely shared outside the family, but the meat is prepared by a volunteer cook, who can be male or female. After the cook takes one of the parts of the animal traditionally reserved for him or her, the animal's "boss," the one who caught it, distributes the rest to all near kin and then to all others residing with the band. Although the small game supplied by the women is distributed in the same way as the big game supplied by the men, Tiwi men are dominant because the game they kill provides most of the meat.

The power of Tiwi men is clearest in their betrothal practices. Among the Tiwi, a woman must always be married. To ensure this, female infants are betrothed at birth and widows are remarried at the gravesides of their late husbands. Men form alliances by exchanging daughters, sisters, and mothers in marriage and some collect as many as 25 wives. Tiwi men value the quantity and quality of food many wives can collect and the many children they can produce.

The dominance of the men is offset somewhat by the influence of adult women in selecting their next husbands. Many women are active strategists in the political careers of their male relatives, but to the exasperation of some sons attempting to promote their own futures, widowed mothers sometimes insist on selecting their own partners. Women also influence the marriages of their daughters and granddaughters, especially when the selected husband dies before the bestowed child moves to his camp.

Among the Eskimo, representative of the rarest type of forager society, inequality between the sexes is matched by inequality in supplying the group with food. Inland Eskimo men hunt caribou throughout the year to provision the entire society, and maritime Eskimo men depend on whaling, fishing, and some hunting to feed their extended families. The women process the carcasses, cut and sew skins to make clothing, cook, and care for the young; but they collect no food of their own and depend on the men to supply all the raw material for their work. Since men provide all the meat, they also control the trade in hides, whale oil, seal oil, and other items that move between the maritime and inland Eskimos.

Eskimo women are treated almost exclusively as objects to be used, abused, and traded by men. After puberty all Eskimo girls are fair game for any interested male. A man shows his intentions by grabbing the belt of a woman and if she protests, he cuts off her trousers and forces himself upon her. These encounters are considered unimportant by the rest of the group. Men offer their wives' sexual services to establish alliances with trading partners and members of hunting and whaling parties.

Despite the consistent pattern of some degree of male dominance among foragers, most of these societies are egalitarian compared with agricultural and industrial societies. No forager has any significant opportunity for political leadership. Foragers, as a rule, do not like to give or take orders, and assume leadership only with reluctance. Shamans (those who are thought to be possessed by spirits) may be either male or female. Public rituals conducted by women in order to celebrate the first menstruation of girls are common, and the symbolism in these rituals is similar to that in the ceremonies that follow a boy's first kill.

In any society, status goes to those who control the distribution of valued goods and services outside the family. Equality arises when both sexes work side by side in food production, as do the Washo, and the products are simply distributed among the workers. In such circumstances, no person or sex has greater access to valued items than do others. But when women

make no contribution to the food supply, as in the case of the Eskimo, they are completely subordinate.

When we attempt to apply these generalizations to contemporary industrial society, we can predict that as long as women spend their discretionary income from jobs on domestic needs, they will gain little social recognition and power. To be an effective source of power, money must be exchanged in ways that require returns and create obligations. In other words, it must be invested.

Jobs that do not give women control over valued resources will do little to advance their general status. Only as managers, executives, and professionals are women in a position to trade goods and services, to do others favors, and therefore to obligate others to them. Only as controllers of valued resources can women achieve prestige, power, and equality.

Within the household, women who bring in income from jobs are able to function on a more nearly equal basis with their husbands. Women who contribute services to their husbands and children without pay, as do some middle-class Western housewives, are especially vulnerable to dominance. Like Eskimo women, as long as their services are limited to domestic distribution they have little power relative to their husbands and none with respect to the outside world.

As for the limits imposed on women by their procreative functions in hunter-gatherer societies, childbearing and child care are organized around work as much as work is organized around reproduction. Some foraging groups space their children three to four years apart and have an average of only four to six children, far fewer than many women in other cultures. Hunter-gatherers nurse their infants for extended periods, sometimes for as long as four years. This custom suppresses ovulation and limits the size of their families. Sometimes, although rarely, they practice infanticide. By limiting reproduction, a woman who is gathering food has only one child to carry.

Different societies can and do adjust the frequency of birth and the care of children to accommodate whatever productive activities women customarily engage in. In horticultural societies, where women work long hours in gardens that may be far from home, infants get food to supplement their mothers' milk, older children take care of younger children, and pregnancies are widely spaced. Throughout the world, if a society requires a woman's labor, it finds ways to care for her children.

In the United States, as in some other industrial societies, the accelerated entry of women with preschool children into the labor force has resulted in the development of a variety of child-care arrangements. Individual women have called on friends, relatives, and neighbors. Public and private child-care centers are growing. We should realize that the declining birth rate, the increasing acceptance of childless or single-child families, and a de-emphasis on motherhood are adaptations to a sexual division of labor reminiscent of the system of production found in hunter-gatherer societies.

In many countries where women no longer devote most of their productive years to childbearing, they are beginning to demand a change in the social relationship of the sexes. As women gain access to positions that control the exchange of resources, male dominance may be archaic, and industrial societies may one day become as egalitarian as the Washo.

26

Our Babies, Ourselves

Meredith F. Small

Nature or nurture? Genes or environment? A perennial question in anthropology is the relative importance of innate human biology or particular cultural and early-childhood influences in people's social and psychological development. Cross-cultural variation in thought and behavior patterns is the hallmark of human diversity. Most anthropologists believe that there is individual variation within cultural variation. That is, members of a society share ideas of appropriate behavior, including the ways to raise children, and those shared ideas supercede individual variation. The influence of culture on personality development has been a theme in cultural anthropology since the days of Margaret Mead. These questions require us to study child-raising practices in a cross-cultural perspective.

This selection describes how parenting behaviors vary across societies. The way in which we interact with our own babies and children influences the adults they become. Sometimes we use the computer analogy of biology being the hardware (the brain) and culture as the software (the models with which we think and pattern our behavior) to think about nature and nurture. That analogy misses the fact that as babies learn they are physically shaping their neural pathways. With this in mind, the study of parenting and child development is even more important. In this regard, so-called traditional societies might have a lot

to teach us. People may be reticent to learn from others ("If it was good enough for us . . .") or to change behaviors, like extended breast-feeding.

As you read this selection, ask yourself the following questions:

- Why do Americans put babies in their own cribs, or feed them on schedules, or "let them cry it out"? What underlying cultural values might parents be trying to teach?

- How might high infant mortality risk affect parents' behaviors?

- How much stimulation for infants is appropriate? Why did the Dutch mother put her baby down for a nap right after the bath?

- Who is best to take care of a baby? How do people decide that?

- Why do anthropologists report that babies in traditional societies like the !Kung do not cry as much?

The following terms discussed in this selection are included in the Glossary at the back of the book:

adaptation	socialization
ethnopediatrics	weaning

During one of his many trips to Gusiiland in southwestern Kenya, anthropologist Robert LeVine tried an experiment: he showed a group of Gusii mothers a videotape of middle-class American women tending their babies. The Gusii mothers were appalled. Why does that mother ignore the cries of her unhappy baby during a simple diaper change? And how come that grandmother does nothing to soothe the screaming baby in her lap? These American women, the Gusii

concluded, are clearly incompetent mothers. In response, the same charge might be leveled at the Gusii by American mothers. What mother hands over her tiny infant to a six-year-old sister and expects the older child to provide adequate care? And why don't those Gusii women spend more time talking to their babies, so that they will grow up smart?

Both culture—the traditional way of doing things in a particular society—and individual experience guide parents in their tasks. When a father chooses to pick up his newborn and not let it cry, when a mother decides to bottle-feed on a schedule rather then breast-feed on demand, when a couple bring the newborn into their bed at night, they are prompted by what they believe to be the best methods of caregiving.

Reprinted with permission from *Natural History,* October 1997, pp. 42–51. American Museum of Natural History.

GUSII SURVIVAL SKILLS
By Robert A. LeVine

Farming peoples of subSaharan Africa have long faced the grim reality that many babies fail to survive, often succumbing to gastrointestinal diseases, malaria, or other infections. In the 1970s, when I lived among the Gusii in a small town in southwestern Kenya, infant mortality in that nation was on the decline but was still high—about eighty deaths per thousand live births during the first year, compared with about ten in the United States at that time and six to eight in Western Europe.

The Gusii grew corn, millet, and cash crops such as coffee and tea. Women handled the more routine tasks of cultivation, food processing, and trading, while men were supervisors or entrepreneurs. Many men worked at jobs outside the village, in urban centers or on plantations. The society was polygamous, with perhaps 10 percent of the men having two or more wives. A woman was expected to give birth every two years, from marriage to menopause, and the average married woman bore about ten live children—one of the highest fertility rates in the world.

Nursing mothers slept alone with a new infant for fifteen months to insure its health. For the first three to six months, the Gusii mothers were especially vigilant for signs of ill health or slow growth, and they were quick to nurture unusually small or sick infants by feeding and holding them more often. Mothers whose newborns were deemed particularly at risk—including twins and those born prematurely—entered a ritual seclusion for several weeks, staying with their infants in a hut with a constant fire.

Mothers kept infants from crying in the early months by holding them constantly and being quick to comfort them. After three to six months—if the baby was growing normally—mothers began to entrust the baby to the care of other children (usually six to twelve years old) in order to pursue tasks that helped support the family. Fathers did not take care of infants, for this was not a traditional male activity.

Because they were so worried about their children's survival, Gusii parents did not explicitly strive to foster cognitive, social, and emotional development. These needs were not neglected, however, because from birth Gusii babies entered an active and responsive interpersonal environment, first with their mothers and young caregivers, and later as part of a group of children.

For decades, anthropologists have been recording how children are raised in different societies. At first, the major goals were to describe parental roles and understand how child-rearing practices and rituals helped to generate adult personality. In the 1950s, for example, John and Beatrice Whiting, and their colleagues at Harvard, Yale, and Cornell Universities, launched a major comparative study of childhood, looking at six varied communities in different regions: Okinawa, the Philippines, northern India, Kenya, Mexico, and New England. They showed that communal expectations play a major role in setting parenting styles, which in turn play a part in shaping children to become accepted adults.

More recent work by anthropologists and child-development researchers has shown that parents readily accept their society's prevailing ideology on how babies should be treated, usually because it makes sense in their environmental or social circumstances. In the United States, for example, where individualism is valued, parents do not hold babies as much as in other cultures, and they place them in rooms of their own to sleep. Pediatricians and parents alike often say this fosters independence and self-reliance. Japanese parents, in contrast, believe that individuals should be well integrated into society, and so they "indulge" their babies. Japanese infants are held more often, not left to cry, and sleep with their parents. Efe parents in Congo believe even more in a communal life, and their infants are regularly nursed, held, and comforted by any number of group members, not just parents. Whether such practices help form the anticipated adult personality traits remains to be shown, however.

Recently, a group of anthropologists, child-development experts, and pediatricians have taken the cross-cultural approach in a new direction by investigating how differing parenting styles affect infant health and growth. Instead of emphasizing the development of adult personality, these researchers, who call themselves ethnopediatricians, focus on the child as an organism. Ethnopediatricians see the human infant as a product of evolution, geared to enter a particular environment of care. What an infant actually gets is a compromise, as parents are pulled by their offspring's needs and pushed by social and personal expectations.

Compared with offspring of many other mammals, primate infants are dependent and vulnerable. Baby monkeys and apes stay close to the mother's body, clinging to her stomach or riding on her back, and nursing at will. They are protected in this way for many months, until they develop enough motor and cognitive skills to move about. Human infants are at the extreme: virtually helpless as newborns, they need twelve months just to learn to walk and years of social learning before they can function on their own.

AN INFANT'S THREE Rs

By Sara Harkness and Charles M. Super

You are an American visitor spending a morning in a pleasant middle-class Dutch home to observe the normal routine of a mother and her six-month-old baby. The mother made sure you got there by 8:30 to witness the morning bath, an opportunity for playful interaction with the baby. The baby was then dressed in cozy warm clothes, her hair brushed and styled with a tiny curlicue atop her head. The mother gave her the midmorning bottle, then sang to her and played patty-cake for a few minutes before placing her in the playpen to entertain herself with a mobile while the mother attended to other things nearby. Now, about half an hour later, the baby is beginning to get fussy.

The mother watches her for a minute, then offers a toy and turns away. The baby again begins to fuss. "Seems bored and in need of attention," you think. But the mother looks at the baby sympathetically and in a soothing voice says, "Oh, are you tired?" Without further ado she picks up the baby, carries her upstairs, tucks her into her crib, and pulls down the shades. To your surprise, the baby fusses for only a few more moments, then is quiet. The mother returns looking serene. "She needs plenty of sleep in order to grow," she explains. "When she doesn't have her nap or go to bed on time, we can always tell the difference—she's not so happy and playful."

Different patterns in infant sleep can be found in Western societies that seem quite similar to those of the United States. We discovered the "three Rs" of Dutch child rearing—*rust* (rest), *regelmaat* (regularity) and *reinheid* (cleanliness)—while doing research on a sample of sixty families with infants or young children in a middle-class community near Leiden and Amsterdam, the sort of community typical of Dutch life styles in all but the big cities nowadays. At six months, the Dutch babies were sleeping more than a comparison group of American babies—a total of fifteen hours per day compared with thirteen hours for the Americans. While awake at home, the Dutch babies were more often left to play quietly in their playpens or infant seats. A daily ride in the baby carriage provided time for the baby to look around at the passing scene or to doze peacefully. If the mother needed to go out for a while without the baby, she could leave it alone in bed for a short period or time her outing with the baby's nap time and ask a neighbor to monitor with a "baby phone."

To understand how Dutch families manage to establish such a restful routine by the time their babies are six months old, we made a second research visit to the same community. We found that by two weeks of age, the Dutch babies were already sleeping more than same-age American babies. In fact, a dilemma for some Dutch parents was whether to wake the baby after eight hours, as instructed by the local health care providers, or let them sleep longer. The main method for establishing and maintaining this pattern was to create a calm, regular, and restful environment for the infant throughout the day.

Far from worrying about "adequate stimulation," these mothers were conscientious about avoiding overstimulation in the form of late family outings, disruptions in the regularity of eating and sleeping, or too many things to look at or listen to. Few parents were troubled by their babies' nighttime sleep routines. Babies's feeding schedules were structured following the guidelines of the local baby clinic (a national service). If a baby continued to wake up at night when feeding was no longer considered necessary, the mother (or father) would most commonly give it a pacifier and a little back rub to help it get back to sleep. Only in rare instances did parents find themselves forced to choose between letting the baby scream and allowing too much night waking.

Many aspects of Dutch society support the three Rs throughout infancy and childhood—for example, shopping is close to home, and families usually have neighbors and relatives nearby who are available to help out with child care. The small scale of neighborhoods and a network of bicycle paths provide local play sites and a safe way for children to get around easily on their own (no "soccer moms" are needed for daily transportation!). Work sites for both fathers and mothers are also generally close to home, and there are many flexible or part-time job arrangements.

National policies for health and other social benefits insure universal coverage regardless of one's employment status, and the principle of the "family wage" has prevailed in labor relations so that mothers of infants and young children rarely work more than part-time, if at all. In many ways, the three Rs of Dutch child rearing are just one aspect of a calm and unhurried life style for the whole family.

Dependence during infancy is the price we pay for being hominids, members of the group of upright-walking primates that includes humans and their extinct relatives. Four million years ago, when our ancestors became bipedal, the hominid pelvis underwent a necessary renovation. At first, this new pelvic architecture presented no problem during birth because the early hominids, known as australopithecines, still had rather small brains, one-third the present size. But starting about 1.5 million years ago, human brain size ballooned. Hominid babies now had to twist and bend to pass through the birth canal, and more important, birth had to be triggered before the skull grew too big.

DOCTOR'S ORDERS
By Edward Z. Tronick

In Boston, a pediatric resident is experiencing a vague sense of disquiet as she interviews a Puerto Rican mother who has brought her baby in for a checkup. When she is at work, the mother explains, the two older children, ages six and nine, take care of the two younger ones, a two-year-old and the three-month-old baby. Warning bells go off for the resident: young children cannot possibly be sensitive to the needs of babies and toddlers. And yet the baby is thriving; he is well over the ninetieth percentile in weight and height and is full of smiles.

The resident questions the mother in detail: How is the baby fed? Is the apartment safe for a two-year-old? The responses are all reassuring, but the resident nonetheless launches into a lecture on the importance of the mother to normal infant development. The mother falls silent, and the resident is now convinced that something is seriously wrong. And something is—the resident's model of child care.

The resident subscribes to what I call the "continuous care and contact" model of parenting, which demands a high level of contact, frequent feeding, and constant supervision, with almost all care provided by the mother. According to this model, a mother should also enhance cognitive development with play and verbal engagement. The pediatric resident is comfortable with this formula—she is not even conscious of it—because she was raised this way and treats her own child in the same manner. But at the Child Development Unit of Children's Hospital in Boston, which I direct, I want residents to abandon the idea that there is only one way to raise a child. Not to do so may interfere with patient care.

Many models of parenting are valid. Among Efe foragers of Congo's Ituri Forest, for example, a newborn is routinely cared for by several people. Babies are even nursed by many women. But few individuals ever play with the infant; as far as the Efe are concerned, the baby's job is to sleep.

In Peru, the Quechua swaddle their infants in a pouch of blankets that the mother, or a child caretaker, carries on her back. Inside the pouch, the infant cannot move, and its eyes are covered. Quechua babies are nursed in a perfunctory fashion, with three or four hours between feedings.

As I explain to novice pediatricians, such practices do not fit the continuous care and contact model; yet these babies grow up just fine. But my residents see these cultures as exotic, not relevant to the industrialized world. And so I follow up with examples closer to home: Dutch parents who leave an infant alone in order to go shopping, sometimes pinning the child's shirt to the bed to keep the baby on its back; or Japanese mothers who periodically wake a sleeping infant to teach the child who is in charge. The questions soon follow. "How could a mother leave her infant alone?" "Why would a parent ever want to wake up a sleeping baby?"

The data from cross-cultural studies indicate that child-care practices vary, and that these styles aim to make the child into a culturally appropriate adult. The Efe make future Efe. The resident makes future residents. A doctor who has a vague sense that something is wrong with how someone cares for a baby may first need to explore his or her own assumptions, the hidden "shoulds" that are based solely on tradition. Of course, pediatric residents must make sure children are cared for responsibly. I know I have helped residents broaden their views when their lectures on good mothering are replaced by such comments as "What a gorgeous baby! I can't imagine how you manage both work and three others at home!"

As a result, the human infant is born neurologically unfinished and unable to coordinate muscle movement. Natural selection has compensated for this by favoring a close adult–infant tie that lasts years and goes beyond meeting the needs of food and shelter. In a sense, the human baby is not isolated but is part of a physiologically and emotionally entwined dyad of infant and caregiver. The adult might be male or female, a birth or adoptive parent, as long as at least one person is attuned to the infant's needs.

The signs of this interrelationship are many. Through conditioning, a mother's breast milk often begins to flow at the sound of her own infant's cries, even before the nipple is stimulated. New mothers also easily recognize the cries (and smells) of their infants over those of other babies. For their part, newborns recognize their own mother's voice and prefer it over others. One experiment showed that a baby's heart rate quickly synchronizes with Mom's or Dad's, but not with that of a friendly stranger. Babies are also predisposed to be socially engaged with caregivers. From birth, infants move their bodies in synchrony with adult speech; they are hard-wired to absorb the cadence of speech and the general nature of language. Babies quickly recognize the arrangement of a human face—two eyes, a nose, and a mouth in the right place—over other more Picasso-like rearrangements. And mothers and infants will position themselves face-to-face when they lie down to sleep.

Babies and mothers seem to follow a typical pattern of play, a coordinated waltz that moves from attention to inattention and back again. This innate social connection was tested experimentally by Jeffrey

THE CRYING GAME
By Ronald G. Barr

All normal human infants cry, although they vary a great deal in how much. A mysterious and still unexplained phenomenon is that crying tends to increase in the first few weeks of life, peaks in the second or third month, and then decreases. Some babies in the United States cry so much during the peak period—often in excess of three hours a day—and seem so difficult to soothe that parents come to doubt their nurturing skills or to begin to fear that their offspring is suffering from a painful disease. Some mothers discontinue nursing and switch to bottle-feeding because they believe their breast milk is insufficiently nutritious and that their infants are always hungry. In extreme cases, the crying may provoke physical abuse, sometimes even precipitating the infant's death.

A look at another culture, the !Kung San hunter-gatherers of southern Africa, provides us with an opportunity to see whether caregiving strategies have any effect on infant crying. Both the !Kung San and Western infants escalate their crying during the early weeks of life, with a similar peak at two or three months. A comparison of Dutch, American, and !Kung San infants shows that the number of individual crying episodes are virtually identical. What differs is their length: !Kung San infants cry about half as long as Western babies. This implies that caregiving can influence only some aspects of crying, such as duration.

What is particularly striking about child-rearing among the !Kung San is that infants are in constant contact with a caregiver; they are carried or held most of the time, are usually in an upright position, and are breast-fed about four times an hour for one to two minutes at a time. Furthermore, the mother almost always responds to the smallest cry or fret within ten seconds.

I believe that crying was adaptive for our ancestors. As seen in the contemporary !Kung San, crying probably elicited a quick response, and thus consisted of frequent but relatively short episodes. This pattern helped keep an adult close by to provide adequate nutrition as well as protection from predators. I have also argued that crying helped an infant forge a strong attachment with the mother and—because new pregnancies are delayed by the prolongation of frequent nursing—secure more of her caregiving resources.

In the United States, where the thread of predation has receded and adequate nutrition is usually available even without breast-feeding, crying may be less adaptive. In any case, caregiving in the United States may be viewed as a cultural experiment in which the infant is relatively more separated—and separable—from the mother, both in terms of frequency of contact and actual distance.

The Western strategy is advantageous when the mother's employment outside of the home and away from the baby is necessary to sustain family resources. But the trade-off seems to be an increase in the length of crying bouts.

Cohn and Edward Tronick in a series of three-minute laboratory experiments at the University of Massachusetts, in which they asked mothers to act depressed and not respond to baby's cues. When faced with a suddenly unresponsive mother, a baby repeatedly reaches out and flaps around, trying to catch her eye. When this tactic does not work, the baby gives up, turning away and going limp. And when the mother begins to respond again, it takes thirty seconds for the baby to reengage.

Given that human infants arrive in a state of dependency, ethnopediatricians have sought to define the care required to meet their physical, cognitive, and emotional needs. They assume there must be ways to treat babies that have proved adaptive over time and are therefore likely to be most appropriate. Surveys of parenting in different societies reveal broad patterns. In almost all cultures, infants sleep with their parents in the same room and most often in the same bed. At all other times, infants are usually carried. Caregivers also usually respond quickly to infant cries; mothers most often by offering the breast. Since most hunter-gatherer groups also follow this overall style, this is probably the ancestral pattern. If there is an exception to these generalizations, it is the industrialized West.

Nuances of caretaking, however, do vary with particular social situations. !Kung San mothers of Botswana usually carry their infants on gathering expeditions, while the forest-living Ache of Paraguay, also hunters and gatherers, usually leave infants in camp while they gather. Gusii mothers working in garden plots leave their babies in the care of older children, while working mothers in the West may turn to unrelated adults. Such choices have physiological or behavioral consequences for the infant. As parents navigate between infant needs and the constraints of making a life, they may face a series of trade-offs that set the caregiver–infant dyad at odds. The areas of greatest controversy are breast-feeding, crying, and sleep—the major preoccupations of babies and their parents.

Strapped to their mothers' sides or backs in traditional fashion, human infants have quick access to the breast. Easy access makes sense because of the nature of human milk. Compared with that of other mam-

WHEN TO WEAN
By Katherine A. Dettwyler

Breast-feeding in humans is a biological process grounded in our mammalian ancestry. It is also an activity modified by social and cultural constraints, including a mother's everyday work schedule and a variety of beliefs about personal autonomy, the proper relationship between mother and child (or between mother and father), and infant health and nutrition. The same may be said of the termination of breast-feeding, or weaning.

In the United States, children are commonly bottle-fed from birth or weaned within a few months. But in some societies, children as old as four or five years may still be nursed. The American Academy of Pediatrics currently advises breast-feeding for a minimum of one year (this may be revised upward), and the World Health Organization recommends two years or more. Amid conflicting advice, many wonder how long breast-feeding should last to provide an infant with optimal nutrition and health.

Nonhuman primates and other mammals give us some clues as to what the "natural" age of weaning would be if humans were less bound by cultural norms. Compared with most other orders of placental mammals, primates (including humans) have longer life spans and spend more time at each life stage, such as gestation, infant dependency, and puberty. Within the primate order itself, the trend in longevity increases from smaller-bodied, smaller-brained, often solitary prosimians through the larger-bodied, larger-brained, and usually social apes and humans. Gestation, for instance, is eighteen weeks in lemurs, twenty-four weeks in macaques, thirty-three weeks in chimpanzees, and thirty-eight weeks in humans.

Studies of nonhuman primates offer a number of different means of estimating the natural time for human weaning. First, large-bodied primates wean their offspring some months after the young have quadrupled their birth weight. In modern humans, this weight milestone is passed at about two and a half to three years of age. Second, like many other mammals, primate offspring tend to be weaned when they have attained about one third of their adult human weight; humans reach this level between four and seven years of age. Third, in all species studied so far, primates also wean their offspring at the time the first permanent molars erupt; this occurs at five and a half to six years in modern humans. Fourth, in chimpanzees and gorillas, breast-feeding usually lasts about six times the duration of gestation. On this basis, a human breast-feeding would be projected to continue for four and a half years.

Taken together, these and other projections suggest that somewhat more than two and a half years is the natural minimum age of weaning for humans and seven years the maximum age, well into childhood. The high end of this range, six to seven years, closely matches both the completion of human brain growth and the maturation of the child's immune system.

In many non-Western cultures, children are routinely nursed for three to five years. Incidentally, this practice inhibits ovulation in the mother, providing a natural mechanism of family planning. Even in the United States, a significant number of children are breast-fed beyond three years of age. While not all women are able or willing to nurse each of their children for many years, those who do should be encouraged and supported. Health care professionals, family, friends, and nosy neighbors should be reassured that "extended" breast-feeding, for as long as seven years, appears physiologically normal and natural.

Substantial evidence is already available to suggest that curtailing the duration of breast-feeding far below two and a half years—when the human child has evolved to expect more—can be deleterious. Every study that includes the duration of breast-feeding as a variable shows that, on average, the longer a baby is nursed, the better its health and cognitive development. For example, breast-fed children have fewer allergies, fewer ear infections, and less diarrhea, and their risk for sudden infant death syndrome (a rare but devastating occurrence) is lower. Breast-fed children also have higher cognitive test scores and lower incidence of attention deficit hyperactivity disorder.

In many cases, specific biochemical constituents of breast milk have been identified that either protect directly against disease or help the child's body develop its own defense system. For example, in the case of many viral diseases, the baby brings the virus to the mother, and her gut-wall cells manufacture specific antibodies against the virus, which then travel to the mammary glands and go back to the baby. The docosahexanoic acid in breast milk may be responsible for improved cognitive and attention functions. And the infant's exposure to the hormones and cholesterol in the milk appears to condition the body, reducing the risk of heart disease and breast cancer in later years. These and other discoveries show that breast-feeding serves functions for which no simple substitute is available.

mals, primate milk is relatively low in fat and protein but high in carbohydrates. Such milk is biologically suitable if the infant can nurse on a frequent basis. Most Western babies are fed in a somewhat different

way. At least half are bottle-fed from birth, while others are weaned from breast to bottle after only a few months. And most—whether nursed or bottle-fed—are fed at scheduled times, waiting hours between

BEDTIME STORY

By James J. McKenna

For as far back as you care to go, mothers have followed the protective and convenient practice of sleeping with their infants. Even now, for the vast majority of people across the globe, "cosleeping" and nighttime breast-feeding remain inseparable practices. Only in the past 200 years, and mostly in Western industrialized societies, have parents considered it normal and biologically appropriate for a mother and infant to sleep apart.

In the sleep laboratory at the University of California's Irvine School of Medicine, my colleagues and I observed mother–infant pairs as they slept both apart and together over three consecutive nights. Using a polygraph, we recorded the mother's and infant's heart rates, brain waves (EEGs), breathing, body temperature, and episodes of nursing. Infrared video photography simultaneously monitored their behavior.

We found that bed-sharing infants face their mothers for most of the night and that both mother and infant are highly responsive to each other's movements, wake more frequently, and spend more time in lighter stages of sleep than they do while sleeping alone. Bed-sharing infants nurse almost twice as often, and three times as long per bout, than they do while sleeping alone. But they rarely cry. Mothers who routinely sleep with their infants get at least as much sleep as mothers who sleep without them.

In addition to providing more nighttime nourishment and greater protection, sleeping with the mother supplies the infant with a steady stream of sensations of the mother's presence, including touch, smell, movement, and warmth. These stimuli can perhaps even compensate for the human infant's extreme neurological immaturity at birth.

Cosleeping might also turn out to give some babies protection from sudden infant death syndrome (SIDS), a heartbreaking and enigmatic killer. Cosleeping infants nurse more often, sleep more lightly, and have practice responding to maternal arousals. Arousal deficiencies are suspected in some SIDS deaths, and long periods in deep sleep may exacerbate this problem. Perhaps the physiological changes induced by cosleeping, especially when combined with nighttime breast-feeding, can benefit some infants by helping them sleep more lightly. At the same time, cosleeping makes it easier for a mother to detect and respond to an infant in crisis. Rethinking another sleeping practice has already shown a dramatic effect: In the United States, SIDS rates fell at least 30 percent after 1992, when the American Academy of Pediatrics recommended placing sleeping babies on their backs, rather than face down.

The effect of cosleeping on SIDS remains to be proved, so it would be premature to recommend it as the best arrangement for all families. The possible hazards of cosleeping must also be assessed. Is the environment otherwise safe, with appropriate bedding materials? Do the parents smoke? Do they use drugs or alcohol? (These appear to be the main factors in those rare cases in which a mother inadvertently smothers her child.) Since cosleeping was the ancestral condition, the future for our infants may well entail a borrowing back from ancient ways.

feedings. Long intervals in nursing disrupt the manufacture of breast milk, making it still lower in fat and thus less satisfying the next time the nipple is offered. And so crying over food and even the struggles of weaning result from the infant's unfulfilled expectations.

Sleep is also a major issue for new parents. In the West, babies are encouraged to sleep all through the night as soon as possible. And when infants do not do so, they merit the label "sleep problem" from both parents and pediatricians. But infants seem predisposed to sleep rather lightly, waking many times during the night. And while sleeping close to an adult allows infants to nurse more often and may have other beneficial effects, Westerners usually expect babies to sleep alone. This practice has roots in ecclesiastical laws enacted to protect against the smothering of infants by "lying over"—often a thinly disguised cover for infanticide—which was a concern in Europe beginning in the Middle Ages. Solitary sleep is reinforced by the rather recent notion of parental privacy. Western parents are also often convinced that solitary sleep will mold strong character.

Infant care is shaped by traditions, fads, science, and folk wisdom. Cross-cultural and evolutionary studies provide a useful perspective for parents and pediatricians as they sift through the alternatives. Where these insights fail to guide us, however, important clues are provided by the floppy but interactive babies themselves. Grinning when we talk to them, crying in distress when left alone, sleeping best when close at heart, they teach us that growth is a cooperative venture.

27

New Women of the Ice Age

Heather Pringle

Anthropology is primarily a comparative study. We compare the human experience across cultures (as in the last selection) and across diverse periods of time. This selection asks a question about early European ancestors from the Paleolithic age, specifically a period of cold temperatures and glaciation. The central question regards gender roles and the interpretation of a certain type of artifact—the so-called Venus figurines. What can these sculptures tell us about the position of women in prehistoric societies?

Gender is not biology. It is a social construction, a cultural agreement about who men and women are and how they should behave. Cross-cultural comparison of gender shows that gender ideologies are correlated to other aspects of society, particularly the economy.

Archaeologists interpret the meaning and function of cultural artifacts in the context of ecology. They do this, in large part, by making ethnographic analogies with societies that have been studied by ethnographers. Archaeologists try to reconstruct the economy and the social system; finally, they interpret clues about the belief system. The problem is that such interpretations may be wrong. The archaeologists may be influenced by their own cultural biases, or they may be dealing with a sociocultural system that is extinct—and was never described by ethnographers. For example, the ethnographic record does not provide evidence of a truly matriarchal society (where political authority is controlled by women). On the other hand, there are certainly many cases of matrilineal societies (where kinship and descent are traced exclusively through the female line) with matrilocal postmarriage residence rules (the new couple lives with the bride's mother). While these societies afford women a great deal of influence and covert political power, they are not matriarchal. This does not mean, however, that matriarchal societies never existed in the past; rather, they may have become extinct.

The status of women in a society depends in large measure on their role in the economy. The reinterpretation of the Paleolithic past centers on new views of the role of women in the food-foraging economy. Historically, archaeological anthropologists first described a division of labor in which men hunted for meat and women gathered plants. This view has been rejected for three reasons: (1) it underemphasizes the importance of gathered foods in the diet; (2) in food-foraging societies women occasionally hunt small game and men gather; and (3) there is evidence to suggest that meat was obtained by scavenging from the kill-sites of carnivores rather than by hunting.

Discovering how gender systems worked in the past requires anthropologists to rethink their interpretations and to reanalyze previously excavated artifacts. This selection provides an excellent case study of that process.

As you read this selection, ask yourself the following questions:

- Was the interpretation of the Venus figurines wrong? If so, why did people believe it for such a long time?

- How might the anthropologist's own cultural notions about gender affect the interpretation of the prehistoric past?

- In what way might archaeological interpretations of Venus figurines have been different in the 1950s than today? Why?

- Would hunting with nets have been different in regard to gender and cooperation?

- How might anthropological analysis of the Venus figurines force us to reinterpret the meaning of art?

- How might the concept of "man the hunter" have shaped our cultural notions of male gender?

The following terms discussed in this selection are included in the Glossary at the back of the book:

hearth	radiocarbon dating
lithic	shaman

The Black Venus of Dolní Věstonice, a small, splintered figurine sensuously fashioned from clay, is an envoy from a forgotten world. It is all soft curves, with breasts like giant pillows beneath a masked face. At nearly 26,000 years old, it ranks among the oldest known portrayals of women, and to generations of researchers, it has served as a powerful—if enigmatic—clue to the sexual politics of the Ice Age.

Excavators unearthed the Black Venus near the Czech village of Dolní Věstonice in 1924, on a hillside among charred, fractured mammoth bones and stone tools. (Despite its nickname, the Black Venus is actually reddish—it owes its name to the ash that covered it when it was found.) Since the mid-nineteenth century, researchers had discovered more than a dozen similar statuettes in caves and open-air sites from France to Russia. All were cradled in layers of earth littered with stone and bone weaponry, ivory jewelry, and the remains of extinct Ice Age animals. All were depicted naked or nearly so. Collectively, they came to be known as Venus figurines, after another ancient bare-breasted statue, the Venus de Milo. Guided at least in part by prevailing sexual stereotypes, experts interpreted the meaning of the figurines freely. The Ice Age camps that spawned this art, they concluded, were once the domain of hardworking male hunters and secluded, pampered women who spent their days in idleness like the harem slaves so popular in nineteenth-century art.

Over the next six decades, Czech archeologists expanded the excavations at Dolní Věstonice, painstakingly combing the site square meter by square meter. By the 1990s they had unearthed thousands of bone, stone, and clay artifacts and had wrested 19 radiocarbon dates from wood charcoal that sprinkled camp floors. And they had shaded and refined their portrait of Ice Age life. Between 29,000 and 25,000 years ago, they concluded, wandering bands had passed the cold months of the year repeatedly at Dolní Věstonice. Armed with short-range spears, the men appeared to have been specialists in hunting tusk-wielding mammoths and other big game, hauling home great mountains of meat to feed their dependent mates and children. At night men feasted on mammoth steaks, fed their fires with mammoth bone, and fueled their sexual fantasies with tiny figurines of women carved from mammoth ivory and fired from clay. It was the ultimate man's world.

Or was it? Over the past few months, a small team of American archeologists has raised some serious

doubts. Amassing critical and previously overlooked evidence from Dolní Věstonice and the neighboring site of Pavlov, Olga Soffer, James Adovasio, and David Hyland now propose that human survival there had little to do with manly men hurling spears at big-game animals. Instead, observes Soffer, one of the world's leading authorities on Ice Age hunters and gatherers and an archeologist at the University of Illinois in Champaign-Urbana, it depended largely on women, plants, and a technique of hunting previously invisible in the archeological evidence—net hunting. "This is not the image we've always had of Upper Paleolithic macho guys out killing animals up close and personal," Soffer explains. "Net hunting is communal, and it involves the labor of children and women. And this has lots of implications."

Many of these implications make her conservative colleagues cringe because they raise serious questions about the focus of previous studies. European archeologists have long concentrated on analyzing broken stone tools and butchered big-game bones, the most plentiful and best preserved relics of the Upper Paleolithic era (which stretched from 40,000 to 12,000 years ago). From these analyses, researchers have developed theories about how these societies once hunted and gathered food. Most researchers ruled out the possibility of women hunters for biological reasons. Adult females, they reasoned, had to devote themselves to breast-feeding and tending infants. "Human babies have always been immature and dependent," says Soffer. "If women are the people who are always involved with biological reproduction and the rearing of the young, then that is going to constrain their behavior. They have to provision that child. For fathers, provisioning is optional."

To test theories about Upper Paleolithic life, researchers looked to ethnography, the scientific description of modern and historical cultural groups. While the lives of modern hunters do not exactly duplicate those of ancient hunters, they supply valuable clues to universal human behavior. "Modern ethnography cannot be used to clone the past," says Soffer. "But people have always had to solve problems. Nature and social relationships present problems to people. We use ethnography to look for theoretical insights into human behavior, test them with ethnography, and if they work, assume that they represent a universal feature of human behavior."

But when researchers began turning to ethnographic descriptions of hunting societies, they unknowingly relied on a very incomplete literature. Assuming that women in surviving hunting societies were homebodies who simply tended hearths and suckled children, most early male anthropologists

Heather Pringle/© 1998 *Discover* magazine.

spent their time with male informants. Their published ethnographies brim with descriptions of males making spears and harpoons and heaving these weapons at reindeer, walruses, and whales. Seldom do they mention the activities of women. Ethnography, it seemed, supported theories of ancient male big-game hunters. "When they talked about primitive man, it was always 'he,'" says Soffer. "The 'she' was missing."

Recent anthropological research has revealed just how much Soffer's colleagues overlooked. By observing women in the few remaining hunter-gatherer societies and by combing historical accounts of tribal groups more thoroughly, anthropologists have come to realize how critical the female half of the population has always been to survival. Women and children have set snares, laid spring traps, sighted game and participated in animal drives and surrounds—forms of hunting that endangered neither young mothers nor their offspring. They dug starchy roots and collected other plant carbohydrates essential to survival. They even hunted, on occasion, with the projectile points traditionally deemed men's weapons. "I found references to Inuit women carrying bows and arrows, especially the blunt arrows that were used for hunting birds," says Linda Owen, an archeologist at the University of Tübingen in Germany.

The revelations triggered a volley of new research. In North America, Soffer and her team have found tantalizing evidence of the hunting gear often favored by women in historical societies. In Europe, archeobotanists are analyzing Upper Paleolithic hearths for evidence of plant remains probably gathered by women and children, while lithics specialists are poring over stone tools to detect new clues to their uses. And the results are gradually reshaping our understanding of Ice Age society. The famous Venus figurines, say archeologists of the new school, were never intended as male pornography: instead they may have played a key part in Upper Paleolithic rituals that centered on women. And such findings, pointing toward a more important role for Paleolithic women than had previously been assumed, are giving many researchers pause.

Like many of her colleagues, Soffer clearly relishes the emerging picture of Upper Paleolithic life. "I think life back then was a hell of a lot more egalitarian than it was with your later peasant societies," she says. "Of course the Paleolithic women were pulling their own weight." After sifting through Ice Age research for nearly two decades, Soffer brings a new critical approach to the notion—flattering to so many of her male colleagues—of mighty male mammoth hunters. "Very few archeologists are hunters," she notes, so it never occurred to most of them to look into the mechanics of hunting dangerous tusked animals. They just accepted the ideas they'd inherited from past work.

But the details of hunting bothered Soffer. Before the fifth century B.C., no tribal hunters in Asia or Africa had ever dared make their living from slaying elephants; the great beasts were simply too menacing. With the advent of the Iron Age in Africa, the situation changed. New weapons allowed Africans to hunt elephants and trade their ivory with Greeks and Romans. A decade ago, keen to understand how prehistoric bands had slaughtered similar mammoths, Soffer began studying Upper Paleolithic sites on the Russian and Eastern European plains. To her surprise, the famous mammoth bone beds were strewn with cumbersome body parts, such as 220-pound skulls, that sensible hunters would generally abandon. Moreover, the bones exhibited widely differing degrees of weathering, as if they had sat on the ground for varying lengths of time. To Soffer, it looked suspiciously as if Upper Paleolithic hunters had simply camped next to places where the pachyderms had perished naturally—such as water holes or salt licks—and mined the bones for raw materials.

Soffer began analyzing data researchers had gathered describing the sex and age ratios of mammoths excavated from four Upper Paleolithic sites. She found many juveniles, a smaller number of adult females, and hardly any males. The distribution mirrored the death pattern other researchers had observed at African water holes, where the weakest animals perished closest to the water and the strongest farther off. "Imagine the worst time of year in Africa, which is the drought season," explains Soffer. "There is no water, and elephants need an enormous amount. The ones in the worst shape—your weakest, your infirm, your young—are going to be tethered to that water before they die. They are in such horrendous shape, they don't have any extra energy to go anywhere. The ones in better shape would wander off slight distances and then keel over farther away. You've got basket cases and you've got ones that can walk 20 feet."

To Soffer, the implications of this study were clear. Upper Paleolithic bands had pitched their camps next to critical resources such as ancient salt licks or water holes. There the men spent more time scavenging bones and ivory from mammoth carcasses than they did risking life and limb by attacking 6,600-pound pachyderms with short-range spears. "If one of these Upper Paleolithic guys killed a mammoth, and occasionally they did," concedes Soffer dryly, "they probably didn't stop talking about it for ten years."

But if Upper Paleolithic families weren't often tucking into mammoth steaks, what were they hunting and how? Soffer found the first unlikely clue in 1991, while sifting through hundreds of tiny clay fragments recovered from the Upper Paleolithic site of Pavlov, which lies just a short walk from Dolní Věstonice. Under a magnifying lens, Soffer noticed something strange on a few of the fragments: a series of parallel lines impressed on their surfaces. What could have left such a regular pattern? Puzzled, Soffer photographed the pieces, all of which had been unearthed from a zone sprinkled with wood charcoal that was radiocarbon-dated at between 27,000 and 25,000 years ago.

When she returned home, Soffer had the film developed. And one night on an impulse, she put on a slide show for a visiting colleague, Jim Adovasio. "We'd run out of cable films," she jokes. Staring at the images projected on Soffer's refrigerator, Adovasio, an archeologist at Mercyhurst College in Pennsylvania and an expert on ancient fiber technology, immediately recognized the impressions of plant fibers. On a few, he could actually discern a pattern of interlacing fibers—weaving.

Without a doubt, he said, he and Soffer were gazing at textiles or basketry. They were the oldest—by nearly 7,000 years—ever found. Just how these pieces of weaving got impressed in clay, he couldn't say. "It may be that a lot of these [materials] were lying around on clay floors," he notes. "When the houses burned, the walked-in images were subsequently left in the clay floors."

Soffer and Adovasio quickly made arrangements to fly back to the Czech Republic. At the Dolní Věstonice branch of the Institute of Archeology, Soffer sorted through nearly 8,400 fired clay pieces, weeding out the rejects. Adovasio made positive clay casts of 90. Back in Pennsylvania, he and his Mercyhurst colleague David Hyland peered at the casts under a zoom stereomicroscope, measuring warps and wefts. Forty-three revealed impressions of basketry and textiles. Some of the latter were as finely woven as a modern linen tablecloth. But as Hyland stared at four of the samples, he noted something potentially more fascinating: impressions of cordage bearing weaver's knots, a technique that joins two lengths of cord and that is commonly used for making nets of secure mesh. It looked like a tiny shred of a net bag, or perhaps a hunting net. Fascinated, Soffer expanded the study. She spent six weeks at the Moravian Museum in Brno, sifting through the remainder of the collections from Dolní Věstonice. Last fall, Adovasio spied the telltale impressions of Ice Age mesh on one of the new casts.

The mesh, measuring two inches across, is far too delicate for hunting deer or other large prey. But hunters at Dolní Věstonice could have set nets of this size to capture hefty Ice Age hares, each carrying some six pounds of meat, and other furbearers such as arctic fox and red fox. As it turns out, the bones of hares and foxes litter camp floors at Dolní Věstonice and Pavlov. Indeed, this small game accounts for 46 percent of the

individual animals recovered at Pavlov. Soffer, moreover, doesn't rule out the possibility of turning up bits of even larger nets. Accomplished weavers in North America once knotted mesh with which they captured 1,000-pound elk and 300-pound bighorn sheep. "In fact, when game officials have to move sheep out west, it's by nets," she adds. "You throw nets on them and they just lie down. It's a very safe way of hunting."

In many historical societies, she observes, women played a key part in net hunting since the technique did not call for brute strength nor did it place young mothers in physical peril. Among Australian aborigines, for example, women as well as men knotted the mesh, laboring for as much as two or three years on a fine net. Among Native American groups, they helped lay out their handiwork on poles across a valley floor. Then the entire camp joined forces as beaters. Fanning out across the valley, men, women, and children alike shouted and screamed, flushing out game and driving it in the direction of the net. "Everybody and their mother could participate," says Soffer. "Some people were beating, others were screaming or holding the net. And once you got the net on these animals, they were immobilized. You didn't need brute force. You could club them, hit them any old way."

People seldom returned home empty-handed. Researchers living among the net-hunting Mbuti in the forests of Congo report that they capture game every time they lay out their woven traps, scooping up 50 percent of the animals encountered. "Nets are a far more valued item in their panoply of food-producing things than bows and arrows are," says Adovasio. So lethal are these traps that the Mbuti generally rack up more meat than they can consume, trading the surplus with neighbors. Other net hunters traditionally smoked or dried their catch and stored it for leaner times. Or they polished if off immediately in large ceremonial feasts. The hunters of Dolní Věstonice and Pavlov, says Soffer, probably feasted during ancient rituals. Archeologists unearthed no evidence of food storage pits at either site. But there is much evidence of ceremony. At Dolní Věstonice, for example, many clay figurines appear to have been ritually destroyed in secluded parts of the site.

Soffer doubts that the inhabitants of Dolní Věstonice and Pavlov were the only net makers in Ice Age Europe. Camps stretching from Germany to Russia are littered with a notable abundance of small-game bones, from hares to birds like ptarmigan. And at least some of their inhabitants whittled bone tools that look much like the awls and net spacers favored by historical net makers. Such findings, agree Soffer and Adovasio, reveal just how shaky the most widely accepted reconstructions of Upper Paleolithic life are. "These terribly stilted interpretations," says Adovasio, "with men hunting big animals all the time and the poor females waiting at home for these guys to bring home the bacon—what crap."

In her home outside Munich, Linda Owen finds other faults with this traditional image. Owen, an American born and raised, specializes in the microscopic analysis of stone tools. In her years of work, she often noticed that many of the tools made by hunters who roamed Europe near the end of the Upper Paleolithic era, some 18,000 to 12,000 years ago, resembled pounding stones and other gear for harvesting and processing plants. Were women and children gathering and storing wild plant foods?

Most of her colleagues saw little value in pursuing the question. Indeed, some German archeologists contended that 90 percent of the human diet during the Upper Paleolithic era came from meat. But as Owen began reading nutritional studies, she saw that heavy meat consumption would spell death. To stoke the body's cellular engines, human beings require energy from protein, fat, or carbohydrates. Of these, protein is the least efficient. To burn it, the body must boost its metabolic rate by 10 percent, straining the liver's ability to absorb oxygen. Unlike carnivorous animals, whose digestive and metabolic systems are well adapted to a meat-only diet, humans who consume more than half their calories as lean meat will die from protein poisoning. In Upper Paleolithic times, hunters undoubtedly tried to round out their diets with fat from wild game. But in winter, spring, and early summer, the meat would have been very lean. So how did humans survive?

Owen began sifting for clues through anthropological and historical accounts from subarctic and arctic North America. These environments, she reasoned, are similar to that of Ice Age Europe and pose similar challenges to their inhabitants. Even in the far north, Inuit societies harvested berries for winter storage and gathered other plants for medicines and for fibers. To see if any of the flora that thrived in Upper Paleolithic Europe could be put to similar uses, Owen drew up a list of plants economically important to people living in cold-climate regions of North America and Europe and compared it with a list of species that botanists had identified from pollen trapped in Ice Age sediment cores from southern Germany. Nearly 70 plants were found on both lists. "I came up with just a fantastic list of plants that were available at that time. Among others, there were a number of reeds that are used by the Eskimo and subarctic people in North America for making baskets. There are a lot of plants with edible leaves and stems, and things that were used as drugs and dyes. So the plants were there."

The chief plant collectors in historical societies were undoubtedly women. "It was typically women's work," says Owen. "I did find several comments that the men on hunting expeditions would gather berries or plants for their own meals, but they did not participate in the plant-gathering expeditions. They might go along, but they would be hunting or fishing."

Were Upper Paleolithic women gathering plants? The archeological literature was mostly silent on the subject. Few archeobotanists, Owen found, had ever looked for plant seeds and shreds in Upper Paleolithic camps. Most were convinced such efforts would be futile in sites so ancient. At University College London, however, Owen reached a determined young archeobotanist, Sarah Mason, who had analyzed a small sample of charcoal-like remains from a 26,390-year-old hearth at Dolní Věstonice.

The sample held more than charcoal. Examining it with a scanning electron microscope, Mason and her colleagues found fragments of fleshy plant taproots with distinctive secretory cavities—trademarks of the daisy and aster family, which boasts several species with edible roots. In all likelihood, women at Dolní Věstonice had dug the roots and cooked them into starchy meals. And they had very likely simmered other plant foods too. Mason and her colleagues detected a strange pulverized substance in the charred sample. It looked as if the women had either ground plants into flour and then boiled the results to make gruel or pounded vegetable material into a mush for their babies. Either way, says Soffer, the results are telling. "They're stuffing carbohydrates."

Owen is pursuing the research further. "If you do look," she says, "you can find things." At her urging, colleagues at the University of Tübingen are now analyzing Paleolithic hearths for botanical remains as they unearth them. Already they have turned up more plants, including berries, all clearly preserved after thousands of years. In light of these findings, Owen suggests that it was women, not men, who brought home most of the calories to Upper Paleolithic families. Indeed, she estimates that if Ice Age females collected plants, bird eggs, shellfish, and edible insects, and if they hunted or trapped small game and participated in the hunting of large game—as northern women did in historical times—they most likely contributed 70 percent of the consumed calories.

Moreover, some women may have enjoyed even greater power, judging from the most contentious relics of Ice Age life: the famous Venus figurines. Excavators have recovered more than 100 of the small statuettes, which were crafted between 29,000 and 23,000 years ago from such enduring materials as bone, stone, antler, ivory, and fired clay. The figurines share a strange blend of abstraction and realism. They bear prominent breasts, for example, but lack nipples. Their bodies are often minutely detailed down to the swaying lines of their backbones and the tiny rolls of flesh—fat folds—beneath their shoulder blades, but they often lack eyes, mouths, and any facial expression. For years researchers viewed them as a male art form. Early anthropologists, after all, had observed only male hunters carving stone, ivory, and other hard materials. Females were thought to lack the necessary strength. Moreover, reasoned experts, only men would take such loving interest in a woman's body. Struck by the voluptuousness of the small stone, ivory, and clay bodies, some researchers suggested they were Ice Age erotica, intended to be touched and fondled by their male makers. The idea still lingers. In the 1980s, for example, the well-known American paleontologist Dale Guthrie wrote a scholarly article comparing the postures of the figurines with the provocative poses of *Playboy* centerfolds.

But most experts now dismiss such contentions. Owen's careful scouring of ethnographic sources, for example, revealed that women in arctic and subarctic societies did indeed work stone and ivory on occasion. And there is little reason to suggest the figurines figured as male erotica. The Black Venus, for example, seems to have belonged to a secret world of ceremony and ritual far removed from everyday sexual life.

The evidence, says Soffer, lies in the raw material from which the Black Venus is made. Clay objects sometimes break or explode when fired, a process called thermal-shock fracturing. Studies conducted by Pamela Vandiver of the Smithsonian Institution have demonstrated that the Black Venus and other human and animal figurines recovered from Dolní Věstonice —as well as nearly 2,000 fired ceramic pellets that litter the site—were made from a local clay that is resistant to thermal-shock fracturing. But many of the figurines, including the celebrated Black Venus, bear the distinctive jagged branching splinters created by thermal shock. Intriguingly, the fired clay pellets do not.

Curious, Vandiver decided to replicate the ancient firing process. Her analysis of the small Dolní Věstonice kilns revealed that they had been fired to temperatures around 1450 degrees Fahrenheit—similar to those of an ordinary hearth. So Vandiver set about making figurines of local soil and firing them in a similar earthen kiln, which a local archeological crew had built nearby. To produce thermal shock, she had to place objects larger than half an inch on the hottest part of the fire; moreover, the pieces had to be so wet they barely held their shape.

To Vandiver and Soffer, the experiment—which was repeated several times back at the Smithsonian Institution—suggests that thermal shock was no acci-dent. "Stuff can explode naturally in the kiln," says Soffer, "or you can make it explode. Which was going on at Dolní Věstonice? We toyed with both ideas. Either we're dealing with the most inept potters, people with two left hands, or they are doing it on purpose. And we reject the idea that they were totally inept, because other materials didn't explode. So what are the odds that this would happen only with a very particular category of objects?"

These exploding figurines could well have played a role in rituals, an idea supported by the location of the kilns. They are situated far away from the dwellings, as ritual buildings often are. Although the nature of the ceremonies is not clear, Soffer speculates that they might have served as divination rites for discerning what the future held. "Some stuff is going to explode. Some stuff is not going to explode. It's evocative, like picking petals off a daisy. She loves me, she loves me not."

Moreover, ritualists at Dolní Věstonice could have read significance into the fracturing patterns of the figurines. Many historical cultures, for example, attempted to read the future by a related method called scapulimancy. In North America, Cree ceremonialists often placed the shoulder blade, or scapula, of a desired animal in the center of a lodge. During the ceremonies, cracks began splintering the bone: a few of these fractures leaked droplets of fat. To Cree hunters, this was a sign that they would find game if they journeyed in the directions indicated by the cracks.

Venus figurines from other sites also seem to have been cloaked in ceremony. "They were not just something made to look pretty," says Margherita Mussi, an archeologist at the University of Rome-La Sapienza who studies Upper Paleolithic figurines. Mussi notes that several small statuettes from the Grimaldi Cave carvings of southern Italy, one of the largest troves of Ice Age figurines ever found in Western Europe, were carved from rare materials, which the artists obtained with great difficulty, sometimes through trade or distant travel. The statuettes were laboriously whittled and polished, then rubbed with ocher, a pigment that appears to have had ceremonial significance, suggesting that they could have been reserved for special events like rituals.

The nature of these rites is still unclear. But Mussi is convinced that women took part, and some archeologists believe they stood at the center. One of the clearest clues, says Mussi, lies in a recently rediscovered Grimaldi figurine known as Beauty and the Beast. This greenish yellow serpentine sculpture portrays two arched bodies facing away from each other and joined at the head, shoulders, and lower extremities. One body is that of a Venus figurine. The other is a strange creature that combines the triangular head of a reptile, the pinched waist of a wasp, tiny arms, and horns. "It is clearly not a creature of this world," says Mussi.

The pairing of woman and supernatural beast, adds Mussi, is highly significant. "I believe that these women were related to the capacity of communicating with a different world," she says. "I think they were believed to be the gateway to a different dimension." Possessing powers that far surpassed others in their communities, such women may have formed part of a spiritual elite, rather like the shamans of ancient Siberia. As intermediaries between the real and spirit worlds, Siberian shamans were said to be able to cure illnesses and intercede on behalf of others for hunting success. It is possible that Upper Paleolithic women performed similar services for their followers.

Although the full range of their activities is unlikely ever to be known for certain, there is good reason to believe that Ice Age women played a host of powerful roles—from plant collectors and weavers to hunters and spiritual leaders. And the research that suggests those roles is rapidly changing our mental images of the past. For Soffer and others, these are exciting times. "The data do speak for themselves," she says finally. "They answer the questions we have. But if we don't envision the questions, we're not going to see the data."

28

Doing Gender, Doing Surgery

Women Surgeons in a Man's Profession

Joan Cassell

American women are gaining increasing access to careers that historically have been the exclusive domain of men. Some people think that access to new opportunities instantly puts everyone on an equal footing and that once one has a new job, one simply performs it. A female police officer simply patrols, and a firefighter simply fights fires. But this view ignores the power of culture to establish expected behaviors based on gender. Gender is not the same as "sex" but rather an important part of culture. Gender is learned and negotiated in a social context.

Traditional societies often have sharply defined gender roles and clearly delimited spaces for men and women. In New Guinea, for example, groups of men live in separate men's houses that women are not allowed to enter. Similarly, industrialized societies maintain gender-specific spaces and occupations, such as firehouses and fishing boats. Since the late 1960s, feminist challenges to such exclusionary practices have brought about important changes in hiring practices. But the mere fact that women are allowed into a profession does not necessarily mean that they are welcomed or that the workplace is accommodating; discrimination can continue to be practiced in subtle (sometimes illegal) cultural forms.

Surgery is a traditionally male occupation dominated by martial metaphors and an ethos of classically masculine attributes: arrogance, aggressiveness, courage, and the ability to make split-second decisions. Although there has been a tenfold increase in the number of women surgeons since 1970, women still make up a tiny portion of this powerful medical specialty. In this selection, Joan Cassell examines differences between women and men and how gender roles play out in the surgical setting. The number of women surgeons has increased, but what is the cultural impact of this change?

Do women surgeons display traditionally female characteristics such as sensitivity, warmth, and compassion—and if so, how does the ethos of the operating room change when women become surgeons? What happens when women gain entrance to this traditionally male occupation—into the "men's house," as it were? Cassell shows how women surgeons themselves bring the ideology of differences between men and women to their analysis of such changes, arguing that they bring more empathy to their relationships with patients than the typical male surgeon. Yet anthropological research finds that reality is more complex, ambiguous, and interesting than the academic *difference theory* would have predicted. There are two cultural questions involved in considering the interaction of the dual identities of woman and surgeon. One question is how culture constructs (or defines) appropriate behavior for men and women; anthropological research shows that this varies between societies. Similarly, culture constructs the expected ways that a surgeon, as a subtype of medical doctor, acts, talks, and interacts. The second question involves the *social context* in which one set of behaviors is appropriate. In other words, when is this person a woman and when is she a surgeon? In a traditionally male space, women surgeons are continually forced to alternate between the behaviors and attitudes required by their profession and those required by their gender. This selection demonstrates the ways in which gender is as much a carefully rehearsed performance as it is an essential (biological) reality.

As you read this selection, ask yourself the following questions:

- Which professions in our society are still defined in terms of gender?

- What kinds of behaviors (including ways of talking) are expected from you, personally, because of your gender? What behaviors are discouraged or taboo?

- What is the difference between the view that gender is *essentialist* and the view that gender is *constructed*?

Human Organization, vol. 56, no. 1, 1997. Copyright © 1997 by the Society for Applied Anthropology. With permission from the publisher.

- What happens when a culture begins to challenge the roles and definitions of gender classification? How might society resolve such challenges?
- Will the entry of women into the traditionally male world of surgery have a positive impact on patient care, training, and leadership in the hospital? Why or why not?

The following terms discussed in this selection are included in the Glossary at the back of the book:

embodied   gender
essentialist   Gordian knot
ethos   social construction

....

When I began studying surgeons more than a decade ago, I was struck by the martial, masculine ambience of surgery. The surgical temperament or ethos (Bateson 1936; Cassell 1987a, 1991) involves characteristics that are traditionally ascribed to men: arrogance, aggressiveness, courage, and the ability to make split-second decisions in the face of life-threatening risks. Surgeons take the metaphor of the war on disease literally: from "the front lines" or "trenches," they carry out "blind maneuvers," attack "invading tumors," and conduct "search and destroy" missions. I found a certain distrust and exclusion of women. In the 1980s, surgery was a "men's club"—it still is, in many ways, although the number of women in surgery has increased almost tenfold from 1970 to 1993 and is still growing.[1] Similar distrust and exclusion of women is found in all the "adrenalized vocations": (Dorothy J. Douglas, personal communication) firefighting (Kaprow 1991), waging war (New York Times 1994), test piloting (Wolfe 1979). Such masculine thinking is familiar to anthropologists: the sacred flutes, trumpets, bull-roarers, will lose their potency if women learn their mysteries (Murphy and Murphy 1974:85–100; Gillison 1993:265–276), and in fact, Kaprow (1990) compares the all-male firehouse to an Amazonian men's house.

During thirty-three months of research in the 1980s, I met only seven senior female general surgeons.[2] When I finished my study of general surgeons (Cassell 1986, 1987a, 1987b, 1989, 1991), I resolved to study women in surgery. I wanted to learn whether the women were different from the men, and what went on when women gained entrance to the men's house.

GENDER DIFFERENCES

In the last fifteen years, the study of gender (or gender-related) differences has grown exponentially (see Haraway 1991). A central issue, under debate by scholars, scientists, and philosophers, is whether women and men are fundamentally different or essentially the same. The "difference theorists" (Gilligan 1982; Chodorow 1978; Ruddick 1989) contend that women are, or tend to be, more nurturant, caring, and cooperative as opposed to men, who are more independent, detached, and hierarchical. "An ethic built on caring is, I think, characteristically and essentially feminine," says Noddings (1984:8), adding a cautionary, "which is not to say, of course, that it cannot be shared by men." (Noddings attributes the ethic of caring to "our experiences as women, just as the traditional logical approach to ethical problems arises more obviously from masculine experience.") In a similar vein, Gilligan and Wiggans (1988:112) assert that "stereotypes of males as aggressive and females as nurturant, however distorting and limited, have some empirical basis."

Observations by women surgeons echo the arguments of the difference theorists. "The surgeon is seen as a John Wayne type," notes a woman surgeon, who criticizes this macho, martial approach; she suggests that "qualities that women in general bring quite unselfconsciously to patient care and resident and student teaching," such as sensitivity, warmth, and compassion, might improve the way surgery is taught, learned, and practiced (Kinder 1985:103). A number of her female colleagues agree. One contrasts the "female" with the "male" operating room, the atmosphere "of peace, tranquility, and contentment" when a woman surgeon is in charge, is opposed to the "tense, hostile, and even explosive" atmosphere generated by a "typical male surgeon" (Anon. 1986). Another woman, discussing her relationship with patients, says: "I spend more time [than male surgeons] in empathy, talking, explaining, teaching, and it's a much more equal power relationship"; she noted that she holds the patient's hand before that person is anesthetized, while "the boys scrub, then come in when the patient's asleep" (Klass 1988).

Kessler and McKenna (1978) point to a significant weakness of such binary comparisons: one cannot talk about differences without classifying the members of the two categories being compared. Thus, in order to compare "women" and "men," *one must already know what women and men are, and who belongs to each category.* They note that among biological, social, and behavioral scientists alike, classification precedes comparison, the basis for classification being the "incorrigible proposition" that humans are "naturally" divided into two genders.

In contrast to such dichotomies, some sociologists examine the effects of structural issues, such as opportunity, power, and relative numbers, upon the way men and women behave at work. Kanter (1977a, 1977b) challenges the view that "women are different," showing how apparent differences in attitudes or behavior can be explained by situation. She describes the effects of relative numbers on "tokens" (people whose type is represented in very small proportion in a particular role): their heightened visibility increases pressures to perform well; they feel isolated from informal social and professional networks; and they are encapsulated into gender-stereotyped roles. Kanter's interesting and insightful work, however, is placed firmly within the positivist sociological tradition; she tends to reify "structural factors" and organizes findings in terms of ranked, testable hypotheses. Such an approach flattens the give and take of human interaction, as though "variables" are interacting in a magisterial, relatively predictable pattern. The liveliness, interest, and suspense of human interaction is transformed into a "parsimonious" over-determined and essentially unreal construction. The more "scientific" such work attempts to be, the more distant it becomes from the "booming buzzing confusion" of human reality, human motivations, and in the end, human behavior. Other sociologists, such as Lorber (1994), who argue that gender and even sex differences are wholly social constructions, focus on the economic, social, political, and emotional advantages to men of the current systems of gender inequality.

GENDER DIFFERENCES AMONG SURGEONS

When I designed a pilot study of women surgeons in the early 1990s, I thought in terms of *difference.* Although I planned to explore the structural constraints discussed by Kanter, my primary focus was on contrasting women's perspectives, values, and behavior with those of men. My research inquired whether women surgeons differed from their male colleagues, if so, how, and whether such differences might affect patient care. I envisioned the possibility of two overlapping bell-shaped curves, with the female central tendency more in the direction of caring, cooperation, and compassion.

For my pilot study of women surgeons, carried out in a medium-sized city in the United States, I used the medical grapevine to list every senior woman surgeon and chief resident (excluding ophthalmology and ob-gyn, which were treated as separate populations[3]). I managed to study 18 of the 24 I located, spending five working days, from dawn to dark, with each. Subsequently, I conducted research in four additional geographic areas within eastern and midwestern North America (three in the U.S. and one in Canada). In these sites, I made a lessened effort to recruit all the women surgeons, and concentrated upon finding women who appeared to be significantly different: if I learned of a surgeon who was African American or Orthodox Jewish, or one in a specialty I had not yet observed, or in a particularly interesting personal or professional situation, I tried to study her. In addition, I spent time observing 3 (of the 7) women surgeons whom I had met and spent time with ten years ago when studying general surgeons (Cassell 1991). I spent two to five days with each woman, depending upon her schedule and my own. I then conducted a tape-recorded open-ended interview with each,[4] inquiring about her surgical education and training, having a mentor, being a mentor, ideas about differences between men and women surgeons, and relationships with superiors, colleagues, and subordinates.

My findings were more complex, ambiguous, and interesting than "difference theory" would have predicted. I observed women surgeons who acted nurturant and caring, as did some men; others appeared as detached and hierarchical as many of their male colleagues. When questioned, some women asserted that women surgeons were more compassionate and caring; others denied any difference between the behavior of female and male surgeons: admitting that some surgeons were more caring than others, these women rejected any relation of caring to gender. Although I observed the phenomena described by Kanter, I was unable to correlate the presence or absence of "gender differences" with the structural features she implicates. At the same time, I observed exchanges between women surgeons and patients, nurses, chiefs of surgery, colleagues, and residents, where *expressions of difference* were elicited and rewarded, while agonistic "masculine" displays were sanctioned.

GENDER AS INTERACTIONAL PROCESS

While struggling with the relation of my findings to the concepts of the difference theorists, I encountered a small body of recent theory and research that focuses on gender as a negotiated and constructed category (West and Zimmerman 1987; Coltrane 1989; Ginsburg and Tsing 1990; DeVault 1991; Unger 1989). Gender, in this view, is not a *Ding an sich*, a thing in itself; instead, it is *produced*. Discussing West and Zimmerman's formulation, DeVault explains:

> Doing gender, in this approach, is not just an individual performance, but an interactional process, a process of collective production and recognition of 'adequate' women and men through concerted activity (DeVault 1991:118).

Without negating the path-breaking research, insights, and theories of the difference theorists, or those of Kanter, this research alters the emphasis. Rather than examining differences *per se*, these scholars explore the *social construction* of such differences. Unlike Kanter's positivist search for law-like generalizations, which simplifies complexity into "variables," this processual approach to gender does not attempt to prune the richness and diversity of human interaction. As Ginsburg and Tsing (1991:2) explain their approach:

> By "gender" we mean the ways a society organizes people into male and female categories and the ways meanings are produced around these categories . . . gender is not seen as fixed or "natural" but rather as a category subject to change and specifically to *negotiation*. As ethnographers, we pay attention to the ways in which people learn, accept, negotiate and resist the categories of "difference" that define and constrain them in everyday life.

Focusing on process and interaction rather than searching for "deep structure" makes profound sense when conducting ethnographic research. Although the question of whether women and men are fundamentally similar or basically different has profound epistemic and political import, observed behavior provides inconsistent evidence for either contention. Gender is a slippery and on occasion contradictory category (Unger 1989:15). The more one reflects on its complexities, the more ambiguous it becomes. Unlike sex, which is a relatively fixed classification based on perceived morphological criteria—defining an individual as male, female, or hermaphrodite—gender is a socio-cultural construction, which is not necessarily binary (Kessler and McKenna 1978; Herdt 1994), or even tripartite (Jacobs and Cromwell 1992). Based on beliefs, behavior, and interaction, gender may be done, or enacted most successfully by someone of the opposite sex (Garfinkel 1967). The notion of "gender difference," even when softened as "gender-associated difference" has a certain circular quality: differences that members of various cultures believe exist and therefore focus on. Biological determinism (Wilson 1975, 1978; Moir 1991) cuts through such Gordian knots; in this view, a binary sexual division, based on physiological and anatomical differences, underlies gender assignment, making gender differences both natural and necessary; anatomy, in short, is destiny. A social scientist who refuses to be tempted by the simplicity, parsimony (and perhaps mythology) of such genetic exegeses, however, may wonder whether the term "gender difference" is not more a description of behavior than an explanation for it (Unger 1989:15). Even the *comparison* of gender differences may be epistemologically suspect. As Kessler and McKenna (1978) indicate, investigators begin with the "incorrigible proposition" that humans are divided into two and only two genders, then describe and classify the behavior of those whom they have placed in these dichotomous categories.

The notion of *doing* gender helped make sense of my otherwise ambiguous and confusing data. I observed the unspoken "rules" of the surgical gender game in action and noted what happened to those who violated these rules. Exempted from having to speculate about whether a particular woman surgeon was different from or similar to her male colleagues (which colleagues? when? in what ways?), absolved from generalizations on "deep structure" or conjectures about what someone was "really like," I was free to focus on observable phenomena. They were not only observable, they were important: I could investigate the elicitation, encouragement, and enforcement of gender-appropriate behavior among women in surgery. I found that patients, chiefs of surgery, colleagues, and subordinates all had notions of appropriate female conduct; all had techniques for invoking their categories of difference. Naturally, the women themselves possessed categories and behaviors that emerged in response to such definitions and constraints.

Otherwise puzzling incidents and remarks observed during research make sense when viewed through the lens of "doing gender." For example, a chief resident described how all her male colleagues confide in her about their romantic difficulties. "I don't know why they're telling me this," she protested. Here, we see the gender-appropriate characteristics of sympathy and empathy being elicited. Whether or not she was particularly interested, as the only woman in the training program, she was expected to be the repository of emotional confidences. A plastic surgeon complained that in the operating room (OR), she can only ask for one instrument at a time or the nurses label her as "demanding." "The guys ask for three or four at once and no one bats an eye," she complained. The nurses are encouraging, perhaps enforcing, the gender-appropriate trait of "thoughtfulness." Operating room (OR) nurses invariably inquire about surgeons' partners, spouses, children; they do such "sentimental work" (Strauss et al. 1985) with both male and female surgeons. But the female surgeon who does not remember and inquire about the *nurses'* partners, spouses, children is labeled "cold," "snobby," and "standoffish." This personal interest is not expected from the men, nor is its absence apparently resented.

The *enforcement* of gender-appropriate behavior is even more visible. A transplant surgeon described how, during an emergency when she was a chief resident, a hospital operator was obtuse and obstructive; the surgeon finally said, "Goddamit, someone's dying, get me Dr. so-and-so!" The operator reported her to the chief of surgery. Male surgeons do this all the time; there is no way a man would be sanctioned for (merely) swearing. Every woman studied agreed that women surgeons are not allowed to throw (what the male mentor of one woman called) "doctor fits." A male surgeon who has tantrums in the OR is characterized as "temperamental" or "high strung" (Cassell 1991:128–152). Nurses may joke and complain behind his back, but in the OR they pay scrupulous attention to his wants and needs, acting as though he were a volatile substance that might ignite if they make the wrong move. A woman surgeon who throws a "fit" is described as a "bitch"—the women I studied were unanimous about this. Rather than being more attentive, nurses become slow and sulky in the face of female tantrums; a slow operation is more dangerous to the patient, who is kept under anesthesia for a longer period of time.

Interested in female styles of leadership, I extended my observations from senior attending surgeons to chief residents, whose tasks include teaching and supervising the junior residents. I learned that, whether or not they wished to do so, women are not permitted to employ a common surgical teaching style, which I think of as "teaching by humiliation." This ranges from displays of rage, to ferocious teasing, including brutal nicknames, to commemorate less-than-optimum performance; although the "victim" may not relish such treatment, he (and it usually is he) is in no position to complain.

> After watching an intern close a breast biopsy very very slowly, as the surgeon stood above him, slowly shaking her head, as she instructed him, I later commented to her about the ugliness of the closing. She agreed, but said that making him feel bad wouldn't improve his performance; he'd just get sullen and conclude he couldn't work with her. "I know what I wanted to say, though," she told me: "What's the matter, first day with a new hand?" I suspect that's what novices were told in the prestigious, brutal program where she, herself, was trained.

Even firmness from female chief residents rankled. "You had a leadership choice," explained one woman: "You could be a pushover or a bitch." (The male equivalent of a "bitch" would be a "strong" chief resident.) Another described how the male residents gave her a "whip lady" award, with one remarking that doing rounds with her was like making stations of the cross. Her chief of surgery asked why she was so "castrating" to the residents under her.

Many of the women I observed had devised alternate, "feminine" ways of teaching juniors, relating to nurses, and running an operating room. One described how, when she was a chief resident leading rounds on hospitalized patients (when chief residents query juniors on correct procedures, medications, and treatment plans), she would send an intern to buy a bag of candies. Each correct response to her questions was rewarded by a candy. The same young surgeon had a sure-fire way to obtain a missing instrument in the OR: she would plaintively say, "I'll give ten cents to anyone who'll find me a bipolar Bovie [or whatever else she needed]; amid laughter, someone would run and get it."

When questioned about differences between a "female" and a "male" operating room, a neurosurgeon responded:[5]

> I do think that a woman surgeon's leadership qualities have to be Captain of the Team as opposed to King of the Hill. And so women surgeons, l think, recognize that they will not get the cooper . . . [she interrupts herself, and says]—they'll have more trouble than men will trying to exert their authority through force. And therefore have learned, one way or another, have learned in order to get the results they need they have to be the captain of a team and encourage each player to feel their part is important to the workings of the team.

Discussing her relationship with nurses, a high-ranking woman said:[6]

> I think that the nurses, especially in the operating room, and perhaps in the intensive care units, are probably nurses that are at a very high level of achievement, often. And, uh, frankly would rather be doctors than nurses, I suspect that's the underlying difficulty. And they are very resentful of women who make demands on them. (JC: Which means that you have to make demands in a different way?) I think so. I think quite differently. I think that it's important to be firm with the nurses, but not to be at all petty with them. And even being firm is often not a successful tactic. But certainly resorting to, 'oh, why did you do this to me again' sort of behavior is simply not a successful tactic. (JC: And you can't have what someone I knew called a "doctor fit"?) No, you really can't. And I learned that

probably the hard way. (JC: By having them.) (She laughs) By having them and having them totally unsuccessful!

Are these women fundamentally different from their male colleagues? It is impossible to determine. But it is clear that they cannot afford not to *act* differently. Moreover, someone who has been socialized all her life to produce gender-appropriate behavior, who finds that tantrums and shows of force invoke rebellion rather than compliance, already possesses a rich repertoire of "feminine" stratagems she can employ to ease her way.

Nurses act as "enforcers" of gender-appropriate behavior. The husband of a woman surgeon, also a surgeon, wrote:

> . . . women surgeons who happen to have "male surgeon"–type personalities are not accepted as quickly by the nursing staff (predominantly female). This is in sharp contrast to women surgeons who have a more traditional "female surgeon"–type personality. It is expected that male surgeons throw tantrums, whine, and complain. However, when this behavior comes from a woman and is directed at women nurses, tension escalates much more rapidly (personal communication).

Kanter (1977:204) notes that powerless women resent a boss's advantage, particularly if they think they could just as easily be the boss. True, so far as it goes, but why do powerless nurses resent women surgeons and not men? Because only when women become surgeons does the nurses' lack of mobility become apparent to them? Because, as "tokens," women are more vulnerable than the men? Then why do nurses resent those who do *not* produce gender-appropriate behavior more than those who do? Is gender-appropriate behavior rather like Nora's "squirrel dance" in Ibsen's *A Doll's House*: does it demonstrate that a woman, even a woman surgeon in a super-ordinate position, "knows her place"—which is *with* the other women, not above them? Same-sex policing is a particularly effective way of maintaining gender categories. Who has a better knowledge of the refinements of the "natural" behavior that defines and creates a gender category, and the "unnatural" behavior that challenges it, than those who have a lifetime's exposure to the same distinctions, values, and constraints?

Before examining doing masculine gender, let's think about Nora's squirrel dance in *A Doll's House*. Nora uses this "adorable" performance to beguile and manipulate her husband: enacting smallness, cuteness, and harmlessness emphasizes (or, more correctly, generates) a complementary expansiveness, assertiveness, and power in her husband, who then benevolently does what she wishes. It is a common reciprocal

form of gender interaction. The woman's diminishment of self amplifies the man's consciousness and enactment of grandeur. Is it possible that similar diminution is enacted by OR nurses? Is the surgeon "pumped up"—the way body builders pump up their muscles before competitions—by the nurses' self-constriction? Are the women (West and Zimmerman 1987:146) "doing deference" so that the men can "do dominance?" Although sterility has its demands, it is conceivable that interactions between nurses and surgeons, in the OR, are more impelled by the requisites of doing gender than the exigencies of sterility. For example, why do nurses scrub, dry their hands, don their own sterile gowns and gloves, give surgeons towels to dry their hands, and then gown and glove the surgeons (see Felker 1983:354–355)? It's a balletic ritual: each step is precisely choreographed as the subordinate nurses wait upon the super-ordinate surgeons. On occasion, I've seen hard-pressed women surgeons dress themselves, but I have never observed a male surgeon gown or glove himself. If the nurses' "sterile dance" is seen as a way of amplifying the surgeon's greatness, instrumentality, power—in short, his "masculinity"—it becomes clearer why nurses might resent "pumping up" other women. In return for nurses' enactments of gender subservience, women surgeons may also be required to do gender, portraying cooperation and a kind of egalitarianism as opposed to the dominance and hierarchy acted out by the men: Captain of the Team, not King of the Hill.

Men surgeons are particularly adept at producing agonistic gender displays (Cassell 1991). Surgeons whom I interviewed in the 1980s compared themselves to test pilots (Wolfe 1979; Cassell 1987a), and indeed, the legendary Chuck Yeager, who walked away from demolished planes to become the first man to fly faster than the speed of sound, might well exemplify the western warrior masculine gender ideal: taking risks, defying death, coming close to the edge, and carrying it off. "The right stuff" (Wolfe 1979) can be decoded as the quintessential masculine performative elements—no wonder there's no word for this ineffable assemblage, a name might destroy its quasi-magical power.

The surgeons I observed in the 1980s characterized colleagues who produced inadequate gender performances as "wimps" (Cassell 1986). A wimp is the symbolic inversion of the heroic masculine exemplar; he does *not* portray nerve, daring, self-confidence, flair, machismo. A "wimp," like a "bitch," exhibits behaviors associated with the opposing category. In surgery (as in the other "adrenalized vocations," I suspect) super-ordinate men, as opposed to subordinate women in the case of nurses, police the performances of other men.

Although gender is a binary classification defined through its "opposite," the relation of male gender to its opposing category is not isomorphic. The extreme "adrenalized" enactments of masculine gender have need of women, not only as wives, sexual conquests, and servitors—but perhaps most importantly *as a category to be excluded.* This renders displays of "the right stuff" somewhat fragile: the participation of women is perceived as radically destructive to the entire enterprise. This does not seem to be true of all-female gender displays (Kaprow 1990). If we think of the "adrenalized vocations" as a kind of essential or archetypal western male gender display, it seems logical that there should be similar archetypal female vocations, with associated gender enactments. And yet, so far as I can tell, there is only one: motherhood (Ruddick 1989). All others—sex goddess, seductress, beauty queen, et al.—seem to be invented by, or primarily reacted to by men. Psychoanalytically inclined commentators have suggested that the institution, idea, and reality of motherhood are so overwhelming to the male child that the entire complex of masculine gender elaborations have been developed to cope with its power and terror.

Anthropologists have noted the myths and fantasies of "male parthogenesis" associated with ritualized male development in societies where warlike males are needed and highly valued; Adams (1993) discerns a similar theme, of monosexual male procreation, in the rituals of a Southern all-male military college; and Kaprow (1991:102) observes that firefighters think of their heroic activities in terms of "giving life." Would the very presence of women in such all-male groups invalidate the "mythic scenario" (Herdt 1981:277) of men giving birth? Objections to the participation of women in the western "adrenalized vocations" are always vague; there are no words for the devastation that the presence of women would inevitably wreak; they would destroy "morale," "efficiency," "unit cohesion"—or as the senior cadet president of the all-male military college declared: "The very thing that women are seeking would no longer be there" (Adams 1993:3).

If such speculations have validity, what can they tell us about a phallic vocation where women have managed to gain entrance? Perhaps, they suggest that the very thing (the men believed) that the women were seeking in surgery *is* no longer there: that women have gained entry into the "men's house" because economic and political factors were already in the process of transforming the hypermasculine surgeon-warrior into an endangered and, even, extinct species.[7]

FINAL REFLECTIONS

I have described how my exploration into differences between women surgeons and their male colleagues challenged dichotomous categorizations. The more I attempted to grasp and apply notions of "gender difference," the more evanescent they became. Concepts of "doing" or "negotiating" gender were more effective in helping to illuminate my findings. But although I am convinced that gender is indeed "negotiated" and "done," there is more to gender than social structure, process, and interaction. Something else is going on, something deeper, less easily altered or eradicated. I now believe that gender exists not only "in the head," although it surely is a social and conceptual phenomenon, but also "in the body." In other words, gender is not only *performed,* it is *embodied* (Cassell 1996).

NOTES

1. The number of women surgeons grew from 485 in 1970 to 4754 in 1993 (Rogers 1995). The proportion of women in surgery increased more slowly, from less than 1% in 1970 to 5% in 1993.

2. By "senior," I mean above the rank of house officer. Of these, 3 had finished their surgical training within the past two years.

3. These specialties have separate training programs and (I believe) somewhat different temperaments. Every surgeon I discussed the issue with agreed that they were a separate population. (Interestingly, the ob-gyns I talked to were offended by this exclusion; they claimed they were "just like" the surgeons.)

4. With the exception of one woman, who refused to be interviewed.

5. This is from a tape-recorded interview, where a surgeon was asked to respond to the following quotation by an anonymous woman surgeon:

   "The atmosphere in an operating room in which there is a woman surgeon in charge is generally one of peace, tranquility, and contentment; when a typical male surgeon is in charge, the atmosphere tends to be tense, hostile, and even explosive at times."

6. This, too, comes from a tape-recorded interview, in response to a question about what she did, when she walked into an operating room, and found the instruments she had requested for the procedure were not there. Before the passage quoted, she responded: "I probably reacted in ineffective ways. I became angry, resentful, critical, and that usually reinforced the behavior of the nurses. And so, uh, I don't think that's an effective behavior for women surgeons. It's clearly what men do all the time, but the women should not do that with their nursing colleagues." The quote cited fol-

lowed, when I asked her if she would elaborate on that. ("JC" indicates my questions and remarks.)

7. A similar politically and economically induced "proletarianization" or "routinization of charisma" seems to be occurring in firefighting, at a time when women are beginning to gain entry (Kaprow n.d.).

REFERENCES CITED

Adams, Abigail E. 1993. Dyke to dyke: Ritual reproduction at a U.S. men's military college. *Anthropology Today* 9(5):3–6.

Anonymous. 1986. Why would a girl go into surgery? *Journal of the American Medical Women's Association* 41(2): 59–61.

Bateson, Gregory. 1951. *Naven: A Study of the Problems Suggested by a Composite Picture of the Culture of a New Guinea Tribe Drawn from Three Points of View.* Stanford, CA: Stanford University Press. (Originally published in 1936.)

Cassell, Joan. 1986. Dismembering the image of God: Surgeons, wimps, heroes and miracles. *Anthropology Today* 2(2):13–16.

———. 1987a. Of control, certitude and the "paranoia" of surgeons. *Culture, Medicine and Psychiatry* 11(2):229–249.

———. 1987b. The good surgeon. *International Journal of Moral and Social Studies* 2(2):155–171.

———. 1989. The fellowship of surgeons. *International Journal of Moral and Social Studies* 4(3):195–212.

———. 1991. *Expected Miracles: Surgeons at Work.* Philadelphia: Temple University Press.

———. 1996. The woman in the surgeon's body: Understanding difference. *American Anthropologist* 98(1):41–53.

Chodorow, Nancy. 1978. *The Reproduction of Mothering: Psychoanalysis and the Sociology of Gender.* Berkeley: University of California Press.

Coltrane, Scott. 1989. Household labor and the routine production of gender. *Social Problems* 36(5):473–490.

DeVault, Marjorie L. 1991. *Feeding the Family: The Social Organization of Caring as Gendered Work.* Chicago: University of Chicago Press.

Felker, Marcie Eliott. 1983. Ideology and order in the operating room. In *The Anthropology of Medicine: From Culture to Method.* Lola Romanucci-Ross, Daniel E. Moerman, Laurence R. Tancredi, M.D., and contributors. South Hadley, MA: J. F. Bergin, Publishers.

Fine, Michelle. 1992. *Disruptive Voices: The Possibilities of Feminist Research.* Ann Arbor, MI: University of Michigan Press.

Garfinkel, Harold. 1967. *Studies in Ethnomethodology.* Englewood Cliffs, NJ: Prentice-Hall.

Gilligan, Carol. 1982. *In a Different Voice: Psychological Theory and Women's Development.* Cambridge, MA: Harvard University Press.

Gilligan, Carol, and Grant Wiggans. 1988. The origins of morality in early childhood relationships. In *Mapping the Moral Domain: A Contribution of Women's Thinking to Psychological Theory and Education,* pp. 111–137, eds. Carol Gilligan, Janie Victoria Ward, Jill McLean Taylor, with Betty Bardige. Cambridge, MA: Harvard University Press.

Gillison, Gillian. 1993. *Between Culture and Fantasy: A New Guinea Highlands Mythology.* Chicago: University of Chicago Press.

Ginsburg, Faye, and Anna Lowenhaupt Tsing. 1990. In *Uncertain Terms: Negotiating Gender in American Culture,* pp. l–16, ed. F. Ginsburg and A. L. Tsing. Boston: Beacon Press.

Haraway, Donna J. 1991. 'Gender' for a Marxist dictonary: The sexual politics of a word. In *Simians, Cyborgs, and Women: The Reinvention of Nature,* pp. 127–148. New York: Routledge, Chapman and Hall, Inc.

Herdt, Gilbert H. 1981. *Guardians of the Flutes: Idioms of Masculinity.* New York: Columbia University Press.

———. 1994. *Third Sex, Third Gender: Beyond Sexual Dimorphism in Culture and History.* Cambridge, MA: Zone Books/ MIT Press.

Horney, Karen. 1932. The dread of women. *International Journal of Psycho-Analysis* 13:348–360.

Jacobs, Sue-Ellen, and Jason Cromwell. 1992. Visions and revisions of reality: Reflections on sex, sexuality, gender, and gender variance. *Journal of Homosexuality* 23(4): 43–69.

Kanter, Rosabeth Moss. 1977a. *Men and Women of the Corporation.* New York: Basic Books.

———. 1977b. Some effects of proportions on group life: Skewed sex ratios and responses to token women. *American Journal of Sociology* 82:985–990.

Kaprow, Miriam Lee. 1990. *Men's Studies, Male Firefighters.* Paper presented at the V Congreso de Antropologia, Granada (Spain).

———. 1991. Magical work: Firefighters in New York. *Human Organization* 50(1):97–103.

———. n.d. *Genteel Proletarianization: Regulating Leisure Domesticating the Citizenry.* Unpublished manuscript.

Kessler, Suzanne J., and Wendy McKenna. 1978. *Gender: An Ethnomethodological Approach.* New York: John Wiley & Sons.

Kinder, Barbara K. 1985. Women and men as surgeons: Are the problems really different? *Current Surgery* 42: 101–103.

Klass, Perri. 1988. Are women better doctors? *New York Times Magazine* (April 10).

Lorber, Judith. 1994. *Paradoxes of Gender.* New Haven and London: Yale University Press.

Moir, Anne. 1991. *Brain Sex: The Real Difference Between Men and Women.* New York: Carol Publishing Group.

Murphy, Yolanda, and Robert F. Murphy. 1974. *Women of the Forest.* New York: Columbia University Press.

New York Times. 1994. Generals oppose combat by women (June 17).

Noddings, Nell. 1984. *Caring: A Feminine Approach to Ethics and Moral Education.* Berkeley: University of California Press.

Rogers, Carolyn M., ed. 1995. *Socio-Economic Fact Book for Surgery 1995.* Chicago: American College of Surgeons.

Ruddick, Sarah. 1989. *Maternal Thinking: Toward a Politics of Peace.* Boston: Beacon Press.

Strauss, Anselm, Shizuko Fagerhaugh, Barbara Suczek, and Carolyn Weiner. 1985. *Social Organization of Medical Work.* Chicago: University of Chicago Press.

Unger, Rhoda K. 1989. *Representations: Social Constructions of Gender.* Amityville, NY: Baywood Publishing Company, Inc.

West, Candace, and Don H. Zimmerman. 1987. Doing gender. *Gender and Society* 1(2):125–151.

Wilson, Edward O. 1975. Human decency is animal. *New York Times Magazine* (October 12).

———. 1978. *On Human Nature.* Cambridge, MA: Harvard University Press.

Wolfe, Tom. 1979. *The Right Stuff.* New York: Random House.

29

When Brothers Share a Wife

Melvyn C. Goldstein

Marriage is a social institution that formalizes certain aspects of the relationship between males and females. It is an institution that evokes in us deep-seated emotions about questions of right and wrong, good and evil, and traditional versus modern. Within families, arguments may occur about what is appropriate premarital behavior, what is a proper marriage ceremony, and how long a marriage should last. Although these arguments may be traumatic for parents and their offspring, from a cross-cultural perspective, they generally involve minor deviations from the cultural norms. In contrast, anthropology textbooks describe an amazing variety of marriage systems that fulfill both biological and social functions. This selection will show just how different things could be.

Social institutions are geared to operate within and adapt to the larger social and ecological environment. This was the case in the earlier selections on gender roles and family planning; the organization of the family must also be adapted to the ecology. For example, the nuclear family is more adapted to a highly mobile society than is an extended family unit that includes grandparents and others. As society increasingly focuses on technical education, career specialization, and therefore geographic mobility for employment purposes, a system has evolved that emphasizes the nuclear family over the extended family. In a similar way, fraternal polyandry in Tibet, as described in this selection, can meet the social, demographic, and ecological needs of its region.

As you read this selection, ask yourself the following questions:

- What is meant by the term *fraternal polyandry?*
- Is this the only form of marriage allowed in Tibet?
- How do husbands and wives feel about the sexual aspects of sharing a spouse?
- Why would Tibetans choose fraternal polyandry?
- How is the function of fraternal polyandry like that of nineteenth-century primogeniture in England?

The following terms discussed in this selection are included in the Glossary at the back of the book:

arable land	nuclear family
corvée	population pressure
fraternal polyandry	primogeniture
monogamy	

Eager to reach home, Dorje drives his yaks hard over the 17,000-foot mountain pass, stopping only once to rest. He and his two older brothers, Pema and Sonam, are jointly marrying a woman from the next village in a few weeks, and he has to help with the preparations.

Dorje, Pema, and Sonam are Tibetans living in Limi, a 200-square-mile area in the northwest corner of Nepal, across the border from Tibet. The form of marriage they are about to enter—fraternal polyandry in anthropological parlance—is one of the world's rarest forms of marriage but is not uncommon in Tibetan society, where it has been practiced from time immemorial. For many Tibetan social strata, it traditionally represented the ideal form of marriage and family.

The mechanics of fraternal polyandry are simple. Two, three, four, or more brothers jointly take a wife, who leaves her home to come and live with them. Traditionally, marriage was arranged by parents, with children, particularly females, having little or no say. This is changing somewhat nowadays, but it is still unusual for children to marry without their parents' consent. Marriage ceremonies vary by income and region and range from all the brothers sitting together as grooms to only the eldest one formally doing so. The age of the brothers plays an important role in determining this: very young brothers almost never participate in actual marriage ceremonies, although they typically join the marriage when they reach their midteens.

With permission from *Natural History*, vol. 96, no. 3. Copyright © 1987 the American Museum of Natural History.

The eldest brother is normally dominant in terms of authority, that is, in managing the household, but all the brothers share the work and participate as sexual partners. Tibetan males and females do not find the sexual aspect of sharing a spouse the least bit unusual, repulsive, or scandalous, and the norm is for the wife to treat all the brothers the same.

Offspring are treated similarly. There is no attempt to link children biologically to particular brothers, and a brother shows no favoritism toward his child even if he knows he is the real father because, for example, his older brothers were away at the time the wife became pregnant. The children, in turn, consider all of the brothers as their fathers and treat them equally, even if they also know who is their real father. In some regions children use the term "father" for the eldest brother and "father's brother" for the others, while in other areas they call all the brothers by one term, modifying this by the use of "elder" and "younger."

Unlike our own society, where monogamy is the only form of marriage permitted, Tibetan society allows a variety of marriage types, including monogamy, fraternal polyandry, and polygyny. Fraternal polyandry and monogamy are the most common forms of marriage, while polygyny typically occurs in cases where the first wife is barren. The widespread practice of fraternal polyandry, therefore, is not the outcome of a law requiring brothers to marry jointly. There is choice, and in fact, divorce traditionally was relatively simple in Tibetan society. If a brother in a polyandrous marriage became dissatisfied and wanted to separate, he simply left the main house and set up his own household. In such cases, all the children stayed in the main household with the remaining brother(s), even if the departing brother was known to be the real father of one or more of the children.

The Tibetans' own explanation for choosing fraternal polyandry is materialistic. For example, when I asked Dorje why he decided to marry with his two brothers rather than take his own wife, he thought for a moment, then said it prevented the division of his family's farm (and animals) and thus facilitated all of them achieving a higher standard of living. And when I later asked Dorje's bride whether it wasn't difficult for her to cope with three brothers as husbands, she laughed and echoed that rationale of avoiding fragmentation of the family land, adding that she expected to be better off economically, since she would have three husbands working for her and her children.

Exotic as it may seem to Westerners, Tibetan fraternal polyandry is thus in many ways analogous to the way primogeniture functioned in nineteenth-century England. Primogeniture dictated that the eldest son inherited the family estate, while younger sons had to leave home and seek their own employment—

for example, in the military or the clergy. Primogeniture maintained family estates intact over generations by permitting only one heir per generation. Fraternal polyandry also accomplishes this but does so by keeping all the brothers together with just one wife so that there is only one set of heirs per generation.

While Tibetans believe that in this way fraternal polyandry reduces the risk of family fission, monogamous marriages among brothers need not necessarily precipitate the division of the family estate: brothers could continue to live together, and the family land could continue to be worked jointly. When I asked Tibetans about this, however, they invariably responded that such joint families are unstable because each wife is primarily oriented to her own children and interested in their success and well-being over that of the children of other wives. For example, if the youngest brother's wife had three sons while the eldest brother's wife had only one daughter, the wife of the youngest brother might begin to demand more resources for her children since, as males, they represent the future of the family. Thus, the children from different wives in the same generation are competing sets of heirs, and this makes such families inherently unstable. Tibetans perceive that conflict will spread from the wives to their husbands and consider this likely to cause family fission. Consequently, it is almost never done.

Although Tibetans see an economic advantage to fraternal polyandry, they do not value the sharing of a wife as an end in itself. On the contrary, they articulate a number of problems inherent in the practice. For example, because authority is customarily exercised by the eldest brother, his younger male siblings have to subordinate themselves with little hope of changing their status within the family. When these younger brothers are aggressive and individualistic, tensions and difficulties often occur despite there being only one set of heirs.

In addition, tension and conflict may arise in polyandrous families because of sexual favoritism. The bride normally sleeps with the eldest brother, and the two have the responsibility to see to it that the other males have opportunities for sexual access. Since the Tibetan subsistence economy requires males to travel a lot, the temporary absence of one or more brothers facilitates this, but there are also other rotation practices. The cultural ideal unambiguously calls for the wife to show equal affection and sexuality to each of the brothers (and vice versa), but deviations from this ideal occur, especially when there is a sizable difference in age between partners in the marriage.

Dorje's family represents just such a potential situation. He is fifteen years old and his two older brothers are twenty-five and twenty-two years old. The new

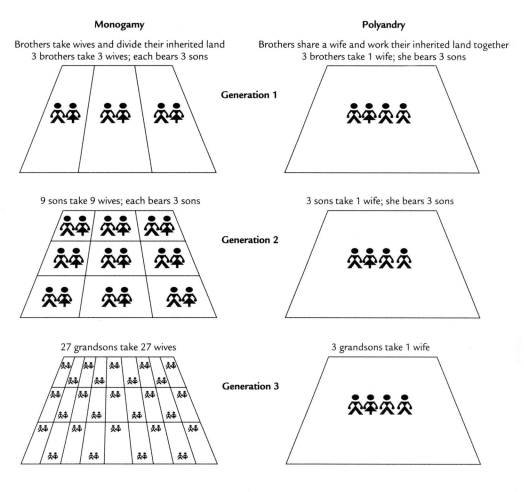

Monogamy

Brothers take wives and divide their inherited land
3 brothers take 3 wives; each bears 3 sons

Polyandry

Brothers share a wife and work their inherited land together
3 brothers take 1 wife; she bears 3 sons

Generation 1

9 sons take 9 wives; each bears 3 sons

3 sons take 1 wife; she bears 3 sons

Generation 2

27 grandsons take 27 wives

3 grandsons take 1 wife

Generation 3

bride is twenty-three years old, eight years Dorje's senior. Sometimes such a bride finds the youngest husband immature and adolescent and does not treat him with equal affection; alternatively, she may find his youth attractive and lavish special attention on him. Apart from this consideration, when a younger male like Dorje grows up, he may consider his wife "ancient" and prefer the company of a woman his own age or younger. Consequently, although men and women do not find the idea of sharing a bride or a bridegroom repulsive, individual likes and dislikes can cause familial discord.

Two reasons have commonly been offered for the perpetuation of fraternal polyandry in Tibet: that Tibetans practice female infanticide and therefore have to marry polyandrously, owing to a shortage of females; and that Tibet, lying at extremely high altitudes, is so barren and bleak that Tibetans would starve without resort to this mechanism. A Jesuit who lived in Tibet in the eighteenth century articulated this second view: "One reason for this most odious custom is the sterility of the soil, and the small amount of land that can be cultivated owing to the lack of water. The crops may suffice if the brothers all live together, but if

they form separate families they would be reduced to beggary."

Both explanations are wrong, however. Not only has there never been institutionalized female infanticide in Tibet, but Tibetan society gives females considerable rights, including inheriting the family estate in the absence of brothers. In such cases, the woman takes a bridegroom who comes to live in her family and adopts her family's name and identity. Moreover, there is no demographic evidence of a shortage of females. In Limi, for example, there were (in 1974) sixty females and fifty-three males in the fifteen- to thirty-five-year age category, and many adult females were unmarried.

The second reason is also incorrect. The climate in Tibet is extremely harsh, and ecological factors do play a major role perpetuating polyandry, but polyandry is not a means of preventing starvation. It is characteristic, not of the poorest segments of the society, but rather of the peasant landowning families.

In the old society, the landless poor could not realistically aspire to prosperity, but they did not fear starvation. There was a persistent labor shortage throughout Tibet, and very poor families with little or no land and few animals could subsist through agricultural labor, tenant farming, craft occupations such as carpentry, or by working as servants. Although the per person family income could increase somewhat if brothers married polyandrously and pooled their wages, in the absence of inheritable land, the advantage of fraternal polyandry was not generally sufficient to prevent them from setting up their own households. A more skilled or energetic younger brother could do as well or better alone, since he would completely control his income and would not have to share it with his siblings. Consequently, while there was and is some polyandry among the poor, it is much less frequent and more prone to result in divorce and family fission.

An alternative reason for the persistence of fraternal polyandry is that it reduces population growth (and thereby reduces the pressure on resources) by relegating some females to lifetime spinsterhood. Fraternal polyandrous marriages in Limi (in 1974) averaged 2.35 men per woman, and not surprisingly, 31 percent of the females of child-bearing age (twenty to forty-nine) were unmarried. These spinsters either continued to live at home, set up their own households, or worked as servants for other families. They could also become Buddhist nuns. Being unmarried is not synonymous with exclusion from the reproductive pool. Discreet extramarital relationships are tolerated, and actually half of the adult unmarried women in Limi had one or more children. They raised these children as single mothers, working for wages or weaving cloth and blankets for sale. As a group, however, the unmarried women had far fewer offspring than the married women, averaging only 0.7 children per woman, compared with 3.3 for married women, whether polyandrous, monogamous, or polygynous. While polyandry helps regulate population, this function of polyandry is not consciously perceived by Tibetans and is not the reason they consistently choose it.

If neither a shortage of females nor the fear of starvation perpetuates fraternal polyandry, what motivates brothers, particularly younger brothers, to opt for this system of marriage? From the perspective of the younger brother in a landholding family, the main incentive is the attainment or maintenance of the good life. With polyandry, he can expect a more secure and higher standard of living, with access not only to his family's land and animals, but also to its inherited collection of clothes, jewelry, rugs, saddles, and horses. In addition, he will experience less work pressure and much greater security because all responsibility does not fall on one "father." For Tibetan brothers, the question is whether to trade off the greater personal freedom inherent in monogamy for the real or potential economic security, affluence, and social prestige associated with life in a larger, labor-rich polyandrous family.

A brother thinking of separating from his polyandrous marriage and taking his own wife would face various disadvantages. Although in the majority of Tibetan regions all brothers theoretically have rights to their family's estate, in reality Tibetans are reluctant to divide their land into small fragments. Generally, a younger brother who insists on leaving the family will receive only a small plot of land, if that. Because of its power and wealth, the rest of the family usually can block any attempt of the younger brother to increase his share of land through litigation. Moreover, a younger brother may not even get a house and cannot expect to receive much above the minimum in terms of movable possessions, such as furniture, pots, and pans. Thus, a brother contemplating going it on his own must plan on achieving economic security and the good life not through inheritance but through his own work.

The obvious solution for younger brothers—creating new fields from virgin land—is generally not a feasible option. Most Tibetan populations live at high altitudes (above 12,000 feet), where arable land is extremely scarce. For example, in Dorje's village, agriculture ranges only from about 12,900 feet, the lowest point in the area, to 13,300 feet. Above that altitude, early frost and snow destroy the staple barley crop. Furthermore, because of the low rainfall caused by the Himalayan rain shadow, many areas in Tibet and northern Nepal that are within appropriate altitude range for agriculture have no reliable sources of irrigation. In the end, although there is plenty of unused land in such areas, most of it is either too high or too arid.

Even where unused land capable of being farmed exists, clearing the land and building the substantial terraces necessary for irrigation constitute a great undertaking. Each plot has to be completely dug out to a depth of two to two and a half feet so that the large rocks and boulders can be removed. At best, a man might be able to bring a few new fields under cultivation in the first years after separating from his brothers, but he could not expect to acquire substantial amounts of arable land this way.

In addition, because of the limited farmland, the Tibetan subsistence economy characteristically includes a strong emphasis on animal husbandry. Tibetan farmers regularly maintain cattle, yaks, goats, and sheep, grazing them in the areas too high for agriculture. These herds produce wool, milk, cheese, butter, meat, and skins. To obtain these resources, however, shepherds must accompany the animals on a daily basis. When first setting up a monogamous household, a younger brother like Dorje would find it difficult to both farm and manage animals.

In traditional Tibetan society, there was an even more critical factor that operated to perpetuate fraternal polyandry—a form of hereditary servitude somewhat analogous to serfdom in Europe. Peasants were tied to large estates held by aristocrats, monasteries, and the Lhasa government. They were allowed the use of some farmland to produce their own subsistence but were required to provide taxes in kind and corvée (free labor) to their lords. The corvée was a substantial hardship, since a peasant household was in many cases required to furnish the lord with one laborer daily for most of the year and more on specific occasions such as the harvest. This enforced labor, along with the lack of new land and the ecological pressure to pursue both agriculture and animal husbandry, made polyandrous families particularly beneficial. The polyandrous family allowed an internal division of adult labor, maximizing economic advantage. For example, while the wife worked the family fields, one brother could perform the lord's corvée, another could look after the animals, and a third could engage in trade.

Although social scientists often discount other people's explanations of why they do things, in the case of Tibetan fraternal polyandry, such explanations are very close to the truth. The custom, however, is very sensitive to changes in its political and economic milieu and, not surprisingly, is in decline in most Tibetan areas. Made less important by the elimination of the traditional serf-based economy, it is disparaged by the dominant non-Tibetan leaders of India, China, and Nepal. New opportunities for economic and social mobility in these countries, such as the tourist trade and government employment, are also eroding the rationale for polyandry, and so it may vanish within the next generation.

30

African Polygyny

Family Values and Contemporary Changes

Philip L. Kilbride

Marriage is a cultural universal, although particular forms of marriage and family structure vary throughout the world. In the United States, polygamy, or plural marriage, is illegal. People have very strong feelings about what marriage is supposed to be like. The ideal of romantic love and lifelong monogamous marriage between people who are intimate companions—even best friends—is a dominant theme in American culture. Yet in all societies, including our own, there are significant differences between the sociocultural ideals and social realities. Divorce is so common in American society that many anthropologists and sociologists say that we actually practice serial monogamy; that is, we have more than one spouse but not at the same time. The nature of marriage is also being debated in our society in regard to gay and lesbian couples and adoption of children by gay couples.

In this selection, Philip Kilbride argues that marriage has much more to do with children and community than it does with sex. Divorce, he says, has negative effects on children's psychological and economic well-being. Deadbeat dads who fail to pay court-ordered child support are a major cause of the impoverishment of single-parent households and are a national disgrace. Teenage pregnancy is yet another problem to contend with.

From the child's point of view, is it better to have blended families linked through plural marriages? In contemporary Africa, this subject raises lively discussion—in part because it pits traditional culture against Christian morality and in part because marriage structure is a critical factor for understanding gender relations. Kilbride has examined polygyny in Africa and among Mormons and has also studied a phenomenon called "man sharing" in the African American community. It is a controversial topic that has led him to some TV talk shows. But for an anthropologist to stir up controversy—that's nothing new.

As you read this selection, ask yourself the following questions:

- Why do Americans think that polygamy is immoral?

- Is the author correct in saying that American men might be mildly for polygyny but American women are strongly against it? Why would this be so?

- Even in societies that allow polygyny, most people live in monogamous marriages. The author says that this is because polygyny is too expensive. What social functions does marriage serve that involve economic resources?

- Would the problem of deadbeat dads go away if polygyny were an option?

- Why do Africans see the American marriage system, with its high frequency of divorce, as inferior to traditional polygyny? Is this really from the child's perspective?

The following terms discussed in this selection are included in the Glossary at the back of the book:

extended family   polygyny
polyandry   serial monogamy
polygamy

RETHINKING POLYGAMY

In the Western world today, the term *marriage* is defined as a social institution that legally joins one man and one woman at the same time; that is, it is synonymous with monogamy. Nevertheless, anthropologists define marriage more broadly as to include cultural variation, such as number of mates, at the same time recognizing the universal function of marriage as a public contract that makes socially legitimate any offspring resulting from the marital union or unions. Anthropologists tell us that monogamy is the norm around the world (Fisher 1992). This assertion is correct in the pragmatic sense because even in cultures that permit polygyny, or marriage between one man and more than one woman at a time, the majority of individuals, in actuality, are married monogamously. Nevertheless, in the majority of the world's cultures, polygyny exists along with monogamy as a viable and, in many cases, ideal form of marriage. Ford and Beach (1951), for example, found that in 84 percent of the 185 cultures they studied, men were permitted to have more than one wife at a time. One common misconception in the West about polygyny is that its function is primarily one of sexual gratification. That this is not the case can be derived from the sociology of polygynous family life, which reveals that in all cultures in which polygyny is practiced, there are a number of commonalities. Ideally, for example, work is divided evenly among wives; the fair practice visiting rule requires the husband to visit each wife equally; wives usually have separate houses and sleeping quarters; and the first wife is given the most respected status of senior wife.

One of the best-known cases of polygyny comes from the Islamic religion. An important ordinance in Islam provides limits on the institution of polygyny: "And if you fear that you cannot act equitably toward orphans, then marry such women as seem good to you, 2, 3, or 4, or if you fear you will not do justice (between them) then marry only one or what your right hand possesses" (the Koran 4:3). Polygyny, in this case, cannot be understood apart from community obligations toward widows and children. The actual practice allows considerable variation, although as set forth as a religious ideology in the Koran, its basis is understood best in a humanitarian, communitarian context.

Polyandry, found in less than 1 percent of the world's cultures, always exists in combination with polygyny. Among the Irigwe of Nigeria (Sangree 1969), there are two basic types of marriage. The first type, the "primary marriage," is arranged by parents prior to the couple's adolescence. "Second marriage" is arranged later by the couple itself. When a woman leaves her primary husband and goes to a secondary husband or later on to still another secondary husband, she leaves behind everything except the clothes and jewelry she is wearing. She may be fetched back by her former husband, or she may decide to stay and take up residence with her new husband, who then provides her with a house and everything she needs for housekeeping. The traditional Irigwe marriage system has no divorce. A woman's prior marriages are not terminated by her switching residence to another spouse. At any point in time, she may return to any of her spouses and resume residence with him. Paternity is settled by consensus, and a husband competes with his wife's other husbands for the paternity of the child she bears.

Advocates for Euro-American polygamy have met with stiff resistance. For example, the great nineteenth-century explorer Captain Richard Francis Burton shocked and angered the Victorians by writing openly about sexual matters. He also angered his wife with his private opinions concerning polygamy. Nevertheless, he believed that polygamy would help keep families stable, lessen the need for prostitutes, and help the single wife with her many household chores. Although Victorians may not have understood Burton's opinion, it is probably fair to say that most Irigwe men and women would have agreed with him.

AFRICAN POLYGYNY AS A CULTURAL VALUE

In her research on family structure among the Yoruba of Nigeria, Sudarkasa (1982) describes the typical situation. Whether or not a husband is polygynous, he has his own room separate from that of his wife or wives who, in turn, have their own rooms and their own household belongings. Although separated physically at times, the polygynous family should be thought of as one family, not as separate families sharing a common husband. Sudarkasa points out that the latter view would rule out the very significant role that the senior wife plays in the polygynous family. The senior wife must be a confidant and a cowife to the other wives, and she sometimes serves as an intermediary between her cowives and their common husband. Wives of the same husband frequently cooperate in economic activities. Distinction is made between children of the same father and children of the same mother by the same father. Sudarkasa emphasizes that for certain purposes, a mother and her children constitute a "*subunit* within the family, but they do not constitute a separate *unit* within the family" (p. 142).

After her many years of studying African social organization, it is her opinion that widespread in Africa is the preference for a system of cowives rather than one where women bear children outside of marriage or where women may choose to live as childless spinsters. In Africa, spinsterhood would be perceived as very much outside the normal range of human behavior.

The anthropological literature frequently reports that African cultures in fact value polygyny; however, some evidence suggests that this may be primarily a male's point of view. At a minimum, this requires us to consider a possible gender bias in this generalization. There is evidence that women, in fact, do traditionally value polygyny. There is also evidence that suggests that men value it even more. There is also strong evidence that modernizing or Westernizing women most likely value it not at all. We will consider some evidence in this direction, since the gender question has occurred over and over again when polygyny is considered in any particular cultural context. Sudarkasa writes that before being bombarded with Western propaganda against polygyny, African women valued the companionship of cowives. In fact, in one study of Nigerian women conducted within the last 15 years, a majority of the women interviewed stated that they would be "pleased" to have a second wife in the home (Ware 1979). The negative bias of some Western-educated African women toward polygyny cannot, Sudarkasa emphasizes, be taken as indicative of the traditional attitude toward it.

On many occasions, female students from Bryn Mawr College have been taken to Uganda and Kenya, where they lived with families in both urban and rural locations. When the subject of polygyny has been introduced into our "theoretical" discussions, these highly educated students who, by their academic training, are sympathetic toward and knowledgeable about cultural variation, uniformly expressed unfavorable comments concerning the practice or even the concept of polygyny in our initial discussions. A conversation that took place in a Nairobi pub one evening is a good illustration of the cultural gap between Western-educated male and female values and East African male values concerning polygyny.

Two female students had been living in the home of one of the married Kenyan men present in the pub with us. They had quickly become attached to his wife and children and sympathized with her when her husband was not present at dinnertime because, like many urban Kenyan men, he stopped regularly at a pub after work before going home. Nevertheless, they could see that he was a good father and provider for his family. Although not meeting their Western ideal of the "husbandly role," they liked him very much and

could understand why he might be thought of favorably by his family, friends, and colleagues. They were therefore somewhat shocked and dismayed when he mentioned to the group that he was thinking about taking a second wife. With such a charming, intelligent, and attractive wife at home, the students especially could not understand why he should be contemplating this. He explained that he was getting a lot of pressure from his mother to do so because she was all alone in the rural area and needed someone to help her farm. His mother also stated that there were many single women in her village who needed husbands, and she wanted grandchildren who would live near or with her rather than far away in the city. This man's wife opposed the idea because she was afraid that there would then not be enough money to pay for her own children's school fees. Besides, the second wife might want to come to the city to live also. He said that he told his wife that he would make sure that she stayed on the farm. One African man who pragmatically supported monogamy stated that there was no way to guarantee that the second wife wouldn't want to come to the city. He stated that he might consider polygyny himself if he could insure that one would stay in the rural area, but he didn't think that was probable.

For the sake of argument (and because one might accept the practice of polygyny under the right circumstances), the professor asked whether a "feminist" perspective shouldn't look favorably on this man being compassionate to the needs of an older woman, his mother, should he decide to marry a second wife. To make more salient to the students the cultural influence on their negative attitudes toward polygyny, another dimension to our cross-cultural discussion of marriage was added. The group was asked their opinion of two men marrying each other and adopting children. While the two students, in conformity with their liberal ideology and anthropological training, felt that this would be perfectly reasonable, the reaction of the African males present was one of stunned silence followed by asking the professor to repeat what their ears could not have heard correctly. When he did so, these men, who had just been divided on the question of polygyny, laughed heartily and stated that this would be impossible because it was not natural. Their disbelief and laughter at what *to them* was such a culturally dissonant idea were still evident on the way home.

POLYGAMY AND GENDER

While there appears to be a female bias against the institution of polygamy among Western-educated women, including those in Africa, there is considerable evidence that traditional African women do value polygyny, at least under certain circumstances. At this time, it may be informative for us to consider some of the evidence for this contention. Those Africans who have written in praise of polygyny have invariably been men, but some African women have noted that polygyny is to be preferred over stigmatized concubinage. In general, little is known about the issue of "women's views of polygyny in the broad context of their perceptions of marriage and women's issues as a whole" (Ware 1979). A survey of over 6,000 Yoruba females, ranging in age from 15 to 59, from the city of Ibadan, Nigeria, found that about one wife in two lives in a polygynous marriage; the proportion for women over 40 rises to about two out of three. About 60 percent of the women in the survey reported that they would be "pleased" if their husbands took another wife. They would then have some companionship and someone with whom they could share housework, husband care, and child care. Only 23 percent expressed anger at the idea of sharing with another wife. More traditionally oriented women without education (67 percent) were more favorable toward polygyny than women with some formal education (54 percent).

Ware (1979) suggests that sharing economic and domestic responsibilities among women might well appeal to modern feminists. She goes on to point out that the sharing of a husband might be viewed as a detriment or an advantage, depending on the extent to which husbands as such are considered to be assets or liabilities. Some Ibadan wives see little value in having a husband except as a "recognized progenitor for their children" (1979:190). When these women, who live in a society where 99 percent of women marry by the age of 40, were asked whether there was a need for a husband apart from his role in begetting children, 47 percent answered that women do not need husbands. They felt that there were many disadvantages in marriage, and since women were equal to men, they often did better on their own. Those women who did consider other roles played by husbands (in addition to progenitor) mentioned companionship most frequently.

Around the time of the Ware study, a survey was undertaken in western Kenya by a Catholic nun and a Kenyan nurse. Lwanga (1976) reports the following concerning their discussions of polygyny with 27 Samia women living in a remote rural area of western Kenya. Many women felt that polygyny can be a happy and beneficial experience if the cowives cooperate with each other. They caution, however, that this is not likely to happen unless the husband allows the senior wife the chance to look for a second wife. Then she may choose a relative or the daughter of another family of which she approves. If he should require a

third wife, these two wives would then be informed so that they could help to look for someone with whom they would wish to share their lives and work. Women felt that the most common reason a wife would advise her husband to take another wife was that he was a rich man with lots of cattle and land, too much for one wife to handle alone. Twenty-five out of the 27 women considered polygyny to be better than monogamy. Other studies have also suggested that traditional (usually rural, uneducated) women view polygyny more positively than their educated counterparts.

Susan Whyte (1980) provides information from Marachi, Kenya, on the practice known as *okhwenda eshiebo*, in which a wife could bring her sister's or brother's daughter or occasionally her mother's brother's daughter to be her cowife. She points out that this often happened at the instigation of the husband, but the Mariachi view of it is that "it is the woman who brings herself a cowife" (p. 137). Whyte states that polygyny has become more problematic in today's deteriorating economic climate. Many men still want the respect they can gain by having many wives and children, but women emphasize the difficulties of polygyny due to a shortage of land and labor and an increasing need for money for school fees, clothing, labor, and food. Whyte points out that while polygyny, in her opinion, has never been popular with women, it is even less so at present because the resources of individual men are becoming less adequate; thus, there is an increase in competition for the already scarce resources of the polygynous husband.

Studying another Kenyan society, Monique Mulder (1992) found that married women have strong views concerning polygyny that are generally positive. Seventy-six percent of the women in her survey viewed polygyny favorably. In general, cowife relations are not full of tension, nor do polygynously married women suffer reproductive costs. Neither women nor their parents expressed antipathy toward polygyny (Mulder 1989:179).

Whatever the value orientation is toward polygyny, the reality is that throughout Africa, most men turn out to be monogamous. A recent study among the Zulu of southern Africa by Moller and Welch (1990) helps explain this male point of view regarding polygyny. Among the Zulus, polygynists account for about 10 percent of rural married men. There continues to be a shift from overt polygyny to covert polygyny or monogamy owing to several factors. Among these are (1) a shortage of agriculturally productive land and other economic changes; (2) social pressures to accept the values of politically and socially dominant whites; and (3) the inflexible teachings and policy of Christian mission churches. From their research surveys, Moller and Welch (1990) found that a majority of monogamist and polygynist men reported both economic advantages and disadvantages to the practice of polygyny, although most men professed to favor monogamy. In the views of the majority who favored monogamy, the main disadvantage of polygyny, as they saw it, was an economic one. They found, for example, that the notion of the large polygynous family as a social security investment is now being replaced by the problems associated with educating children during an extended period of their life cycle. It must be pointed out, however, that these are view of men who are faced with the prospect of polygyny in a modern economy for which many of the advantages of the past are not available to them. One of the frequently mentioned circumstances resulting in polygyny is the practice of labor migration, in which many Africans travel away from their home areas in search of cash income. For these men, polygyny provides a solution to the problem of being required to spend lengthy periods away from their home families. Thus, one wife may visit the husband in town while the other one cares for the rural homestead. Polygynist wives may also share labor and keep each other company in the rural area when the husband is away (Moller and Welch 1990:208).

One serendipitous finding from this study was that polygynist men reported higher-quality work lives than did monogamous men. The former had higher job satisfaction, more voluntary retirement, better health, and higher degrees of social adjustment, including a better adjustment to aging and retirement. Very significantly, Moller and Welch discovered that in a mood index analysis, polygynous men overall felt less lonely and neglected than other men in the survey. It may be that part of this positive mood adjustment can be seen by reference to spiritual values in Zulu society as men age. The older cohorts of returned migrants are more likely to be traditionally oriented and therefore more likely to choose polygynous lifestyles, since it may be seen as pleasing to the ancestors. More research needs to be done in this area, however, before one can conclude that the practice of polygyny per se has a directly positive effect on the morale of these men.

There is not much evidence available to consider whether polygyny does cut down on male infidelity, but one recent study conducted in Nigeria by Orubuloye, Caldwell, and Caldwell (1990) suggests that it might. In this extensive survey done in the Akiki district of Nigeria, the researchers found that for monogamous males in the rural area, 56 percent of their most recent sexual experiences were outside their marriages; this figure rose to 67 percent in the urban area. Contributing to this practice is sexual abstinence dur-

ing pregnancy and for two years postpartum, but also the belief common in polygynous societies that men need more than one woman. Sexual variety may be achieved by acquiring another wife. Polygynous men are more likely to turn to one of their other wives for gratification while another one is sexually abstaining. Only 38 percent of polygynous men in the rural area had their most recent sexual experience outside of marriage, and in the urban area 44 percent of polygynous men's most recent sexual partners were women other than their wives. These data suggest that, at least in this society, monogamous men are much more likely to have extramarital partners than are polygynous men. However, we see the opposite pattern for female respondents. Thirty-four percent of rural polygynous wives and 47 percent of urban polygynous wives reported that their most recent sexual encounter was an extramarital one. Only 14 percent of monogamous rural women and 36 percent of their urban counterparts reported that their most recent sexual partner was someone other than their spouse (Orubuloye, J. Caldwell, and P. Caldwell 1990:12). Thus, it appears that polygyny allows greater sexual equality, at least in terms of extramarital sexual relations, than does monogamy. Future research on marital relationships within monogamous and polygynous households should attempt a closer examination of de facto male and female balance of power and responsibilities within these two marital forms.

DELOCALIZED POLYGYNY

The fate of polygyny in Africa is very much caught up in the processes of moral and economic change. The churches vary considerably in terms of overt condemnation of polygyny, with the mainstream churches being predominantly opposed and many independent churches being favorable toward polygyny. Community sanctions traditionally at work in regulating polygyny have changed as well, and elders and other traditional moral leaders have lost the authority they had in the past when practices like polygyny were closely monitored. One finds, for example, that today in Kenya, many men who traditionally would not have been considered acceptable as polygynists in terms of their economic resources are practicing polygyny because community sanctions no longer operate with the same degree of salience as in the past. As traditions change and the modern economy and moral order impose themselves more and more into the everyday lives of people, polygyny increasingly takes on a negative ambiance. Much of the current female opposition to polygyny may in fact be related to the irresponsible practice of this custom by many men in modernizing circumstances throughout the African continent. A few examples drawn from the Kenya media will provide readers with a sense of the tone surrounding what can be thought of as a public discourse concerning doubts over the suitability of polygyny in contemporary times.

Kilbride and Kilbride (1990), in discussing the modernization of tradition in East Africa, present excerpts from newspapers and magazines published in Nairobi, Kenya. The gist of the polygyny debate as seen in mass media discourse will be presented here. Many Western-educated, urban Kenyan women no longer find polygyny acceptable. One prominent female Kenyan politician, in her address at a seminar on "Women and the Church," urged that the churches ban polygyny, which she described as "more dangerous than malaria" (*Daily Nation*, May 18, 1985). She was, however, compassionate with the plight of single women who, because of an imbalance in the sex ratio, found themselves chasing after other women's husbands or settling for second or third wives. As the following argument from a male Kenyan politician will illustrate, modern educated men tend to be more favorable to polygyny. In his view, foreign influences are responsible for present social ills. To counteract this moral decline, he suggests returning to their traditions, including polygyny, which he believes would "help reduce the number of unmarried women roaming the streets as prostitutes" (*Daily Nation*, July 9, 1985).

Unlike the Roman Catholic Church, which is officially opposed to the practice of polygyny, some Protestant churches are becoming more tolerant of it. A bishop of the Anglican Church in Kenya stated that while monogamy may be ideal "for the expression of love between a husband and wife," the church should consider that in certain cultures polygyny is socially acceptable and that the belief that polygyny is contrary to Christianity was no longer tenable (*The Weekly Review*, August 1, 1987). The Catholic Archbishop of Nairobi, who himself was raised in a polygynous home, expressed the Catholic Church's opposition to it when he spoke to a gathering of young people about the sacrament of marriage. He admonished them to do "the will of God" rather than blindly following their customs. As he put it, "God wanted one Adam and one Eve, not one Adam and three Eves nor five Adams and one Eve" (*Daily Nation*, February 11, 1985). Sometimes differences of opinion regarding polygyny erupt within splinter groups of a particular religion. The Friends Church in Kakamega, Kenya, for example, faced a leadership crisis between its "old and monogamist founders" and its "young and polygamist followers" who formed a splinter group over the parent church's opposition to polygyny (*Sunday Nation*, January 6, 1985).

GROWING UP IN A POLYGYNOUS HOME

In general, our interviews revealed that East Africans have both positive and negative memories about growing up in polygynous homes. Although jealousy and conflict were present, especially between cowives concerning economic injustices, this was less likely to be the case when the polygynous home was a wealthy one. Importantly, in keeping with traditional values, whether talking about the past or the present, more positive impressions about life in a polygynous home as parents or as children were given if the family was rich. Two cases from Kenyan research will illustrate this variation.

The first case deals with the recollections of a Ugandan woman, here called Marjorie, who is 40 years old; she is a high school graduate whose father is a wealthy agricultural officer. He has four wives and 25 children. Her own mother was the senior wife. Before taking a second wife, her father provided her mother with her own home and land near to where two of her other children were attending boarding school. When Marjorie was in sixth grade, she went to live with her father and his second wife and her children so that she could attend school nearby their residence. Interestingly, she states that although her stepmother gave her a lot of chores to do, she didn't mind. She liked her stepmother, whom she described as being good. On school holidays, she went back to her own mother, who was even stricter with her because it was her mother's job to teach Marjorie all her female duties. Marjorie states that although their family was large, everyone always had enough to eat and plenty of land to farm. The children treated each other well. "Myself and the stepsisters, we don't say, 'Who is your mother?' We are all like sisters and brothers" (Kilbride and Kilbride 1990:207). As behooves a good polygynous husband, her father showed no favoritism—at least as could be perceived by Marjorie. She stated that she never knew who her father loved best. The cowives also followed the traditional custom of giving respect and deference to the senior wife. Marjorie also reported that she liked her father very much.

Our next account is a less favorable recollection of growing up in a polygynous home by a man in his mid-20s, here called Robert. His father, like Marjorie's, also has four wives. Unfortunately, this man's economic situation is much less favorable. He has 31 children, thus far, with his youngest being less than one year old. Also, Robert's mother is not in as favorable a position economically or in terms of respect in that she is his father's second wife. In Robert's early childhood, his father had only two wives, both of whom Robert called "mother." It was not until he was seven years old that he began to question his status. When he was eight years old, he recollects going to school for awhile with the sons of the first wife. It was not a pleasant memory in that his stepbrothers beat him, made him carry their books to and from school, and forced him to get money from his mother to give to them for their own lunches. He finally refused to go to that school, which was 10 kilometers away, so he was transferred to a school near his home. After fourth grade, he states that he was forced to go to another primary school near the home of the fourth wife. While living at her house, which is 15 miles from the home of his mother and the other two wives, who all share the same compound, Robert complains that he was forced to do many household chores, including cooking, cleaning, and tending livestock, at times going without food from breakfast until dinner. He also disliked the fact that when he had friends over to visit, his stepmother would say that he wasn't living in the home of his mother. "It made me feel that I was born somewhere else but was now under the control of another person" (Kilbride and Kilbride 1990:208).

As an adult, Robert understands that there are some advantages to polygyny, such as sharing the workload, protection from outsiders, helping to care for other family members when they or their children are sick, and preventing childlessness and thus gaining immortality through one's children. Nevertheless, the disadvantages he has experienced personally, which he sees as being mainly the result of a lack of sufficient economic resources on the part of his father, who married more wives and had more children than he could support, makes him unfavorable to polygyny and what he perceives to be its many problems of jealousy and conflict over insufficient resources for food, clothing, and education. He reports that during times of food shortage, each mother looked after only her own children rather than sharing with the others, while his father tended to "disappear" until the worst was over. In Robert's case, we can see the workings of modernized polygyny in that his father did not fit the traditional ideal of being wealthy enough to be a polygynist, at least on the scale that he practiced it. There are indications that two wives would have been better for all concerned.

MONOGAMY RECONSIDERED

A very different definite pattern is visible in Kenya today: professional women rejecting marriage altogether because many of them feel that men on the whole are unsympathetic to their attempts to have careers, to seek education beyond the B.A., and to practice independent lifestyles frequently associated with modern, professional occupations. At the same time, many women feel that men involve themselves too frequently with other women (mistresses) while they expect their wives to remain at home caring for the children. There is also the problem of wife beating, which women have traditionally agreed is the "right" of the husband if they do not perform their duties or act properly. Although many professional women are opting against marriage, they have not given up on their desire to have children. For this reason, such women frequently find themselves in a position of seeking out a man, married or single, to give them a child or to become a father to that child or to one that they already have.

Perlez (1991) reports the views of a Miss Makuku, who is a postgraduate student in French at Nairobi University and a former schoolteacher. She sees herself ten years from now as a single parent with a male companion, but not a husband. She points out that this is a choice made not only by herself but by many of her over-30 female friends with occupations ranging from television producers to professors. For example, many educated women are delaying marriage; more than half of the 16 female law graduates of Nairobi University in 1980 are still single. Miss Makuku admonishes that traditionally, African men looked after their women, but today the average man contributes to the rent if one is lucky while using the rest for mistresses and beer. According to Perlez, anecdotal evidence from Kenya abounds concerning professional women who have been previously married but have left their husbands because they cannot tolerate the restrictions imposed by these men. Eventually, these women seek a relationship of some kind with a man. Miss Makuku points out that it is difficult to raise a child without the financial help of a man. By the age of 35, however, most of her economically self-sufficient, single, female friends have decided to have children even though they are not married. Some choose to have a child by a younger man because he is less likely to "boss them around" than would an older man. A second choice would be to have a child by a married man, paradoxically choosing to do one of the very things that has turned them against marriage to begin with.

We see here that exclusive monogamy, in Kenya as in the United States, does not appear to be working very well. There seems to be a tendency for polygyny to be reinvented as more and more single women have relationships with married men. Perhaps these men will involve themselves in the role of father to their outside children. Here we have a situation, similar to that described for man sharing in the African American community, developing in the East African setting where, ironically, polygamy was, until recently, the ideal. Very much present in Kenya at this time is a consciousness of the importance of having fathers for children. For example, the July 18, 1993, issue of the *Sunday Nation,* a prominent Kenyan newspaper, published a cartoon that accompanied a story entitled "Choice: The New Trend." The cartoon shows a woman dressed in fashionable clothing and a young boy, presumably her son, leaning against their car with a man standing beside them looking at them. The woman says, "I have everything I want, a good job, a good house, and a good child. Why should I need a man?" The child, however, is shown to be thinking: "But a daddy, we don't have." The story itself reported that in nearly all their interviews, women stated that they would find it acceptable having children without marriage if they were financially secure. One woman who is a company executive replied that she had reached the age where she was ready for a child, but not a husband, since she wanted to advance in her career and found that men were usually intolerant of ambitious women. Many of the single women interviewed were involved with men who were already married. While encouraging his mistress to have his child, he may promise that he is going to divorce his wife, which ten years later she finally realizes will never happen. At this point, the woman may feel that it is too late for her, given her increasing age, to meet anyone else. The article does not offer any analysis of this situation in terms of whether or not, on balance, quasi-polygyny is more or less desirable than divorce, especially when children are involved.

The interview material with Kenyan men in Kilbride and Kilbride (1990) presents a similar picture of frustration and difficulties associated with the current situation. One man in his late 40s, for example, responded to the AIDS crisis by curtailing his outside girlfriends so that he had a long-standing relationship with a single woman from an ethnic group other than his own. He required secrecy from this woman so that his wife and family would not be offended. The child that resulted from this relationship, who is now a young girl, is presently being raised entirely by her mother, since my informant no longer gives her any support. In spite of this, he seemed to feel that everything would be fine for his daughter. Another informant who spoke openly about polygyny is a wealthy Kenyan who is Roman Catholic and states that although he does not himself favor polygyny, he is not opposed to others practicing it. He believes that it is, in fact, a fairly common practice. He himself has been "offered" a wife when he has gone into rural areas, although he has not involved himself because of his wife's opposition to polygyny. He nevertheless confesses that at present he has numerous girlfriends and would like to know whether his wife would prefer him to be polygynous with a small number of wives or monogamous with the large number of mistresses that he now has. Moreover, each of his mistresses is unaware of the other women in his life and are themselves in search of a permanent relationship. Some of his girlfriends do not even know that he is married.

PLURAL MARRIAGE AS A REINVENTED OPTION

Is it worth considering plural marriage as a morally viable option for American men and women, particularly in light of our national family crisis and increased calls for cultural pluralism? A myriad of legal considerations, including property ownership, inheritance, child disciplinary obligations, and health insurance, to name but a few, will require special study and legal adjustment. In the United States, the monogamous companionate marriage, though viewed as an ideal, is not in the majority. In fact, given our high divorce rate, it can be argued that the United States now has a high rate of informal, unrecognized polygyny, at least as we would infer from Remi Clignet's comment that "Africans argue that remarriage subsequent to a divorce is merely another form of polygyny, one less desirable because it imposes on Westerners succession and discontinuity in married life" (1970:3). Blended families are known to be particularly stressful for children, given the ambiguous status of this rapidly emerging family structure. Once marriage is consistently considered from the perspective of children, perhaps more people will come to see that seemingly radical forms of now improper plurality are actually "smart" opportunities for children to have multiple parents and often access to a better life through foster parents or blended parents who are *added* to their biological family.

REFERENCES

Clignet, R. 1970. *Many Wives, Many Powers: Authority and Power in Polygynous Families.* Evanston, IL: Northwestern University Press.

Fisher, H. E. 1992. *Anatomy of Love: The Natural History of Monogamy, Adultery, and Divorce.* New York: W. W. Norton and Company.

Ford, C., and F. Beach. 1951. *Patterns of Sexual Behavior.* New York: Harper & Row.

Kilbride, P. L., and J. E. Kilbride. 1990. *Changing Family Life in East Africa: Women and Children at Risk.* University Park: Pennsylvania State University Press.

Lwanga, G. 1976. Report on the Health Education of Clan Health Workers. Nangina Hospital, Nangina, Kenya.

Moller, V., and G. J. Welch. 1990. Polygamy, Economic Security, and Well-being of Retired Zulu Migrant Workers. *Journal of Cross-Cultural Gerontology* 5:205–216.

Mulder, M. 1989. Polygyny and the Extent of Women's Contributions to Subsistence: A Reply to White. *American Anthropologist* 91:178–180.

———. 1992. Women's Strategies in Polygynous Marriage. *Human Nature* 3(1):45–70.

Orubuloye, I. O., J. Caldwell, and P. Caldwell. 1990. Experimental Research on Sexual Networking in the Ekti District of Nigeria. Health Transition Working Paper No. 3.

Perlez, J. 1991. Elite Kenyan Women Avoid a Rite: Marriage. *The New York Times,* March 3, p. 14.

Sangree, W. 1969. Going Home to Mother: Traditional Marriage Among the Irigwe of Benue-Plateau State, Nigeria. *Journal of the American Anthropological Association* 71(6): 946–1056.

Sudarkasa, N. 1982. African and Afro-American Family Structure. In *Anthropology for the Eighties,* J. Cole, ed. Pp. 132–161. New York: Free Press.

Ware, H. 1979. Polygyny, Women's Views in a Transitional Society, Nigeria 1975. *Journal of Marriage and the Family* 41(1):185–195.

Whyte, S. 1980. Wives and Co-wives in Marachi, Kenya. *Folk* 21–22; 134–136.

31

Law, Custom, and Crimes Against Women

The Problem of Dowry Death in India

John van Willigen and V. C. Channa

Anthropologists find many societies with unusual customs, beliefs, and behaviors. Usually they discover, after careful study and reflection, that these perform some useful function within the society, as in the case of polyandry discussed in the previous selection. But is this always the case? Must we assume that simply because a custom exists it is healthy for the members of society? We think not, and the Christians who were fed to lions and the Aztec slaves who were sacrificed to a bloodthirsty god would most likely agree.

Times change; hunters and gatherers plant crops, tribal people rush headlong into peasantry, and small-scale farmers become urban wage earners. Traditions that helped maintain a healthy society in one context may become dysfunctional in another. For better or worse, traditions and beliefs run deep and are almost impossible to unlearn. It is the nature of culture to resist change.

As you will read, the practice of dousing a bride with kerosene and creating a human torch certainly indicates that the payment of dowry is a traditional practice gone awry. That said, what can be done? Laws, even those that carry serious penalties, are light ammunition against the armor of strongly held cultural beliefs. Governments will solve such problems only through public policy based on in-depth cultural understanding.

As you read this selection, ask yourself the following questions:

- What do you think the authors mean when they suggest that dowry death presents a problem for ethnologists because of ethnological theory's functional cast?

- Why does the institution of dowry make college education problematic for some young women?

- What are the present-day approaches to solving the dowry death problem?

- How can women's access to production roles and property, delocalization of social control, and economic transformation affect the problem of dowry death?

- Dowry-related violence in India is related to the economic value of women. What might be said about the relationship between the economic position and the social status of women in America?

The following terms discussed in this selection are included in the Glossary at the back of the book:

caste	*ethnology*
cultural materialism	*peasants*
demography	*sex roles*
dowry	

A 25-year-old woman was allegedly burnt to death by her husband and mother-in-law at their East Delhi home yesterday. The housewife, Mrs. Sunita, stated before her death

Reproduced by permission of the Society for Applied Anthropology from *Human Organization,* vol. 50, no. 4, 1991, pp. 369–377.

at the Jaya Prakash Narayana Hospital that members of her husband's family had been harassing her for bringing inadequate dowry.

The woman told the Shahdara subdivisional magistrate that during a quarrel over dowry at their Pratap Park house yesterday, her husband gripped her from behind while the mother-in-law poured kerosene over her clothes.

Her clothes were then set ablaze. The police have registered a case against the victim's husband, Suraj Prakash, and his mother.

—*Times of India*, February 19, 1988

This routinely reported news story describes what in India is termed a "bride-burning" or "dowry death." Such incidents are frequently reported in the newspapers of Delhi and other Indian cities. In addition, there are cases in which the evidence may be ambiguous, so that deaths of women by fire may be recorded as kitchen accidents, suicides, or murders. Dowry violence takes a characteristic form. Following marriage and the requisite giving of dowry, the family of the groom makes additional demands for the payment of more cash or the provision of more goods. These demands are expressed in unremitting harassment of the bride, who is living in the household of her husband's parents, culminating in the murder of the woman by members of her husband's family or by her suicide. The woman is typically burned to death with kerosene, a fuel used in pressurized cook stoves, hence the use of the term "bride-burning" in public discourse.

Dowry death statistics appear frequently in the press and parliamentary debates. Parliamentary sources report the following figures for married women 16 to 30 years of age in Delhi: 452 deaths by burning for 1985; 478 for 1986 and 300 for the first six months of 1987 (Bhatia 1988). There were 1,319 cases reported nationally in 1986 (*Times of India*, January 10, 1988). Police records do not match hospital records for third degree burn cases among younger married women; far more violence occurs than the crime reports indicate (Kumari 1988).

There is other violence against women related both directly and indirectly to the institution of dowry. For example, there are unmarried women who commit suicide so as to relieve their families of the burden of providing a dowry. A recent case that received national attention in the Indian press involved the triple suicide of three sisters in the industrial city of Kanpur. A photograph was widely published showing the three young women hanging from ceiling fans by their scarves. Their father, who earned about 4,000 Rs. [rupees] per month, was not able to negotiate marriage for his oldest daughter. The grooms were requesting approximately 100,000 Rs. Also linked to the dowry problem is selective female abortion made possible by amniocentesis. This issue was brought to national attention with a startling statistic reported out of a seminar held in Delhi in 1985. Of 3,000 abortions carried out after sex determination through amniocentesis, only one involved a male fetus. As a result of these developments, the government of the state of Maharashtra banned sex determination tests except those carried out in government hospitals.

The phenomenon of dowry death presents a difficult problem for the ethnologist. Ethnological theory, with its residual functionalist cast, still does not deal effectively with the social costs of institutions of what might be arguably referred to as custom gone bad, resulting in a culturally constituted violence syndrome.

This essay examines dowry and its violent aspects, and some of the public solutions developed to deal with it in India. Our work consists of a meta-analysis of some available literature. We critique the legal mechanisms established to regulate the cultural institution of dowry and the resultant social evils engendered by the institution, and argue that policies directed against these social evils need to be constructed in terms of an underlying cause rather than of the problem itself. We consider cause, an aspect of the problem infrequently discussed in public debate. As Saini asserts, "legal academicians have shown absolutely no interest in the causal roots of dowry as practiced in contemporary India" (1983:143).

THE INSTITUTION

Since ancient times, the marriage of Hindus has required the transfer of property from the family of the bride to the family of the groom. Dowry or *daan dehej* is thought by some to be sanctioned by such religious texts as the *Manusmriti*. Seen in this way, dowry is a religious obligation of the father of a woman and a matter of *dharma* (religious duty) whereby authority over a woman is transferred from her father to her husband. This transfer takes different forms in different communities in modern India (Tambiah 1973). In public discussion, the term "dowry" covers a wide range of traditional payments and expenses, some presented to the groom's family and others to be retained by the bride. Customs have changed through time. The financial burdens of gifts and the dowry payments per se are exacerbated by the many expenses associated with the marriage celebration itself, but dowry payment is especially problematic because of its open-ended nature. As Tambiah notes, "marriage payments in India usually comprise an elaborate series of payments back and forth between the marrying families" and "this series extends over a long period of time and persists after marriage" (1973:92). Contemporary cases such as the death of Mrs. Sunita, often revolve around such continued demands.

A daughter's marriage takes a long time to prepare and involves the development of an adaptive strategy on the part of her family. An important part of the strategy is the preparation for making dowry payments; family consumption may be curtailed so as to allow accumulation of money for dowry. Seeing to marriage arrangements may be an important aspect of retirement planning. The dowries that the family receives on behalf of their sons may be "rolled over" to deal with the daughter's requirements. Families attempt to cultivate in both their sons and daughters attributes that will make them more attractive in marriage negotiations. Many things besides dowry are considered in negotiations: "non-economic" factors have demonstrable effect on the expectations for dowry and the family's strategy concerning the dowry process.

Education is a variable to be considered in the negotiation process. Education of young women is somewhat problematic because suitable husbands for such women must also be college educated. The parents of such young men demand more dowry for their sons. A consideration in sending a young woman to college will therefore be her parents' capacity to dower her adequately so as to obtain an appropriate groom. In any case, education is secondary to a man's earning power and the reputation of a woman's family. Education is, however, important in the early stages of negotiation because of the need to coordinate the level of the education of the men and women. Education qualifications are also less ambiguously defined than other dimensions of family reputation. Physical attractiveness is a consideration, but it is thought somewhat unseemly to emphasize this aspect of the decision.

Advertisements in newspapers are used for establishing marriage proposals (Aluwalia 1969, Niehoff 1959, Weibe and Ramu 1971), but contacts are more typically established through kin and other networks. Some marriages may be best termed "self-arranged," and are usually called "love marriages." In these cases, young men and women may develop a relationship independent of their families and then ask that negotiations be carried out on their behalf by family representatives.

Analysis of matrimonial advertisements shows some of the attributes considered to be important. Listed in such advertisements are education, age, income and occupation, physical attributes, gotra (a kind of unilineal descent group) membership, family background, place of residence, personality features, consideration of dowry, time and type of marriage, and language.

Consideration of dowry and other expenditures are brought out early in the negotiations and can serve as a stumbling block. Dowry negotiations can go on for some time. The last stage is the actual "seeing of the groom" and the "seeing of the bride," both rather fleeting encounters whose position at the end of the process indicates their relative lack of importance.

Marriage is a process by which two families mutually evaluate each other. The outcome of the negotiations is an expression of the relative worth of the two persons, a man and a woman, and, by extension, the worth of their respective families. This estimation of worth is expressed in marriage expenditures, of which dowry is but a part. There are three possible types of expenditures: cash gifts, gifts of household goods, and expenditures on the wedding celebration itself. The cash gift component of the dowry goes to the groom's father and comes to be part of his common household fund. The household goods are for use by the groom's household, although they may be used to establish a separate household for the newlyweds. When separate accommodations are not set up, the groom's family may insist that the goods do not duplicate things they already have.

Dates for marriages are set through consideration of horoscopes; horoscopy is done by professional astrologers (pandits). This practice leads to a concentration of marriage dates and consequent high demand for marriage goods and services at certain times of the year. During marriage seasons, the cost of jewelry, furniture, clothes, musicians' services and other marriage related expenditures goes up, presumably because of the concentration of the demand caused by the astrologers.

The expenditures required of the woman's family for the wedding in general and the dowry in particular are frequently massive. Paul reports, for a middle-class Delhi neighborhood, that most dowries were over 50,000 Rs. (1986). Srinivas comments that dowries over 200,000 Rs. are not uncommon (1984).[1]

ETHNOLOGICAL THEORIES ABOUT DOWRY

Dowry had traditionally been discussed by ethnologists in the context of the functionalist paradigm, and much theorizing about dowry appears to be concerned with explaining the "contribution" that the institution makes to social adaptation. The early theoretician Westermarck interpreted dowry as a social marker of the legitimacy of spouse and offspring, and as a mechanism for defining women's social roles and property rights in the new household (Westermarck 1921:428). Murdock suggests that dowry may confirm the contract of marriage (1949). Dowry is interpreted by Friedl as a means to adjust a woman to her affinal home as it rearranges social relationships including the social separation of the man from his parents (1967). Dowry payments are public expressions of the new relationship between the two families, and of the social status of the bride and groom.

Dowry is seen in the social science literature as a kind of antemortem or anticipated inheritance by which a widow is assured of support, and provision for her offspring (Friedl 1967; Goody 1973, 1976). It transfers money to where the women will be and where they will reproduce; as a result, resources are also placed where the children will benefit, given the practice of patrilineal inheritance of immovable, economically valuable property like farm land.

In India, dowry is also seen as an expression of the symbolic order of society. According to Dumont, dowry expresses the hierarchal relations of marriage in India and lower status of the bride (Dumont 1957). The amount of dowry given is an expression of prestige. The capacity to buy prestige through dowry increases the potential for social mobility (Goody 1973). Dowry is a kind of delayed consumption used to demonstrate or improve social rank (Epstein 1960).

There is a significant discontinuity between discussions of dowry in the ethnological theory and in public discourse. Certainly the dowry problem does appear in the writing of contemporary ethnologists, but it is simply lamented and left largely uninterpreted and unexplained.

THE EXTANT SOLUTIONS TO THE PROBLEM

The Dowry Prohibition Act of 1961, as amended in 1984 and 1986, is the primary legal means for regulating the dowry process and controlling its excesses. The laws against dowry are tough. Dowry demand offenses are "cognizable" (require no warrant) and nonbailable, and the burden of proof is on the accused. There are, in fact, convictions under the law.

The act defines dowry as "any property of valuable security given or agreed to be given either directly or indirectly—(a) by one party to a marriage to the other party to a marriage; or (b) by parents of either party to a marriage or by any other person, to either party to the marriage or to any other person" (Government of India 1986:1). The act makes it illegal to give or take dowry, "If any person after the commencement of this act, gives or takes or abets the giving or taking of dowry, he shall be punishable with imprisonment for a term which shall be not less than five years; and with fine which shall not be less than fifteen thousand rupees or the amount of the value of such dowry which ever is more" (Government of India 1986:1). While this section unambiguously prohibits dowry, the third section allows wedding presents to be freely given. Thus the law does not apply to "presents which are given at the time of marriage to the bride (without demand having been made in that behalf)" (Government of India 1986:1). Identical provi-

sions apply to the groom. Furthermore, all such presents must be listed on a document before the consummation of the marriage. The list is to contain a brief description and estimation of the value of the gifts, name of presenting person, and the relationship that person has with the bride and groom. This regulation also provides "that where such presents are made by or on the behalf of the bride or any other person related to the bride, such presents are of a customary nature and the value thereof is not excessive having regard to the financial status of the person by whom, or on whose behalf, such presents are given" (Government of India 1986:2). Amendments made in 1984 make it illegal for a person to demand dowry with the same penalty as under the earlier "giving and taking" provision. It was also declared illegal to advertise for dowry, such an offense being defined as not bailable, with the burden of proof on the accused person.

This legislation was coupled with some changes in the Indian Penal Code that legally established the concept of "dowry death." That is, "where the death of a woman is caused by any burns or bodily injury or occurs otherwise than under normal circumstances within seven years of her marriage and it is shown that soon before her death she was subjected to cruelty or harassment by her husband or any relative of her husband for, or in connection with, any demand for dowry, such death shall be called 'dowry death,' and such husband or relative shall be deemed to have caused her death" (Government of India 1987:4). The Indian Evidence Act of 1871 was changed so as to allow for the presumption of guilt under the circumstances outlined above. Changes in the code allowed for special investigation and reporting procedures of deaths by apparent suicide of women within seven years of marriage if requested by a relative. There were also newly defined special provisions for autopsies.

To this point, however, these legal mechanisms have proved ineffective. According to Sivaramayya, the "act has signally failed in its operation" (1984:66). Menon refers to the "near total failure" of the law (1988:12). A similar viewpoint is expressed by Srinivas, who wrote, "The Dowry Prohibition Act of 1961 has been unanimously declared to be an utterly ineffective law" (1984:29).

In addition to the legal attack on dowry abuses, numerous public groups engage in public education campaigns. In urban settings, the most noteworthy of these groups are specialized research units such as the Special Cell for Women of the Tata Institute of Social Sciences (Bombay), and the Center for Social Research (New Delhi). Also involved in the effort are private voluntary organizations such as the Crimes Against Women Cell, Karmika, and Sukh Shanti.

These groups issue public education advertising on various feminist issues. The anti-dowry advertisement of the Federation of Indian Chambers of Commerce and Industry Ladies Organization exemplifies the thrust of these campaigns. In the following advertisement, which was frequently run in the winter of 1988 in newspapers such as the *Times of India*, a photograph of a doll dressed in traditional Indian bridal attire was shown in flames.

> Every time a young bride dies because of dowry demands, we are all responsible for her death. Because we allow it to happen. Each year in Delhi hospitals alone, over 300 brides die of third degree burns. And many more deaths go unreported. Most of the guilty get away. And we just shrug helplessly and say, "what can we do?" We can do a lot.
>
> Help create social condemnation of dowry. Refuse to take or give dowry. Protest when you meet people who condone the practice. Reach out and help the girl being harassed for it. Act now.
>
> Let's fight it together.
>
> As parents, bring up educated, self-reliant daughters. Make sure they marry only after 18. Oppose dowry; refuse to even discuss it. If your daughter is harassed after marriage stand by her.
>
> As young men and women, refuse marriage proposals where dowry is being considered. As friends and neighbors, ostracize families who give or take dowry. Reach out to help victims of dowry harassment.
>
> As legislators and jurists, frame stronger laws. Ensure speedy hearings, impose severe punishments. As associations, give help and advice. Take up the challenge of changing laws and attitudes of society. Let us all resolve to fight the evil. If we fight together we can win.
>
> SAY NO TO DOWRY.

Also engaged in anti-dowry work are peasant political action groups such as Bharatiya Kisan Union (BKU). BKU consists of farmers from western Uttar Pradesh whose political program is focused more generally on agricultural issues. The group sponsored a massive 25-day demonstration at Meerut, Uttar Pradesh, in 1988. The leadership used the demonstration to announce a social reform program, most of it dealing with marriage issues. According to news service reports, "The code of social reforms includes fixing the maximum number of persons in a marriage party at 11, no feasts relating to marriage, and no dowry except 10 grams of gold and 30 grams of silver" (*Times of India*, February 11, 1988). Buses plying rural roads in western Uttar Pradesh are reported to have been painted with the slogan "The bride is the dowry." Private campaigns against dowry occur in the countryside as well as among the urban elites,

although it is likely that the underlying motivations are quite different.

POLICY ANALYSIS

Our argument is based on the assumption that social problems are best dealt with by policies directed at the correction of causative factors, rather than at the amelioration of symptoms. While current legal remedies directly confront dowry violence, the linkage between cause and the problematic behavior is not made. Here we develop an argument consisting of three components: women's access to production roles and property; delocalization of social control; and economic transformation of society. The pattern of distribution of aspects of the institution of dowry and its attendant problems is important to this analysis. Although dowry practices and the related crimes against women are distributed throughout Indian society, the distribution is patterned in terms of geography, caste rank, socioeconomic rank, urban/rural residence, and employment status of the women. In some places and among some people there is demonstrably more violence, more intensity of dowry practices, and more commitment to dowry itself. Much of the distributional data are problematic in one way or another. The most frequent problem is that the studies are not based on national samples. Furthermore, the interpretation of results is often colored by reformist agendas. There is a tendency to deemphasize differences in frequency from one segment of the population to another so as to build support of dowry death as a general social reform issue. Nevertheless, while the data available for these distributions are of inconsistent quality, they are interpretable in terms of our problem.

Women's Access to Production Roles and Property

Dowry violence is most frequent in north India. Some say that it is an especially severe problem in the Hindi Belt (i.e., Uttar Pradesh, Haryana, Punjab, Delhi, Bihar) (Government of India 1974:75). It is a lesser, albeit increasing problem in the south. There is also a north/south difference in the marriage institution itself. To simplify somewhat, in the north hypergamy is sought after in marriage alliances, in which case brides seek grooms from higher rank descent groups within their caste group (Srinivas 1984). In the south, marriages are more typically isogamous.

The literature comparing north and south India indicates important contrasts at both the ecological and the institutional levels. Based on conceptions developed by Boserup (1970) in a cross-cultural comparative framework on the relationship between the farming system and occupational role of women, Miller (1981) composed a model for explaining the significant north-south differences in the juvenile sex ratio [the ratio of males to females ten years of age and below]. The farming systems of the north are based on "dry-field plow cultivation," whereas in the south the farming systems are dominated by "swidden and wet-rice cultivation" (Miller 1981:28). These two systems make different labor demands. In the wet rice or swidden systems of the south, women are very important sources of labor. In the north, women's involvement in agricultural production is limited. According to Miller, women in the north are excluded from property holding and receive instead a "dowry of movables." In the south, where women are included in the production activities, they may receive "rights to land" (Miller 1981:28). In the north, women are high-cost items of social overhead, while in the south, women contribute labor and are more highly valued. In the north there is a "high cost of raising several daughters" while in the south there is "little liability in raising several daughters." There is thus "discrimination against daughters" and an "intense preference for sons" in the north, and "appreciation for daughters" and "moderate preference for sons" in the south. Miller thus explains the unbalanced-toward-males juvenile sex ratios of the north and the balanced sex ratios of the south (Miller 1981:27–28). The lower economic value of women in the north is expressed in differential treatment of children by sex. Females get less food, less care, and less attention, and therefore they have a higher death rate. In general the Boserup and Miller economic argument is consistent with Engels's thesis about the relationship between the subordination of women and property (Engels 1884, Hirschon 1984:1).

Miller extended her analysis of juvenile sex ratios to include marriage costs (including dowry), female labor participation, and property owning, and found that property owning was associated with high marriage costs and low female labor force participation, both of which were associated with high juvenile sex ratios. That is, the death rate of females is higher when marriage costs are high and women are kept from remunerative employment. Both of these patterns are associated with the "propertied" segment of the population (Miller 1981:156–159). Her data are derived from the secondary analysis of ethnographic accounts. The literature concerning the distribution of dowry practices and dowry death is consistent with these results.

Miller's analysis shows a general pattern of treatment of females in India. Their access to support in various forms is related to their contribution to production (Miller 1981). This analysis does not explain the problem of dowry violence, but it does demonstrate a fundamental pattern within which dowry violence can be interpreted.

The distribution of dowry varies by caste. In her study of dowry violence victims in Delhi, Kumari found that members of the lower ranking castes report less "dowry harassment" than do those in higher ranking castes (Kumari 1988:31). These results are consistent with Miller's argument since the pattern of exclusion of women from economic production roles varies by caste. Women of lower castes are less subject to restrictions concerning employment outside the realm of reproduction within the household. These women are often poor and uneducated, and are subject to other types of restrictions.

In the framework of caste, dowry practices of higher caste groups are emulated by lower caste groups. This process is known as "Sanskritization" and it may relate to the widely held view that dowry harassment is increasing in lower ranking castes. Sanskritization is the process by which lower ranked caste groups attempt to raise their rank through the emulation of higher rank castes. The emulation involves discarding certain behaviors (such as eating meat or paying bride price) and adopting alternatives (Srinivas 1969). Attitudinal research shows that people of the lower socio-economic strata have a greater commitment to dowry than do those of higher strata (Hooja 1969, Khanna and Verghese 1978, Paul 1986). Although the lower and middle classes are committed to dowry, the associated violence, including higher death rates, is more typically a middle class problem (Kumari 1988).

Employment status of women has an effect on dowry. In her survey of dowry problems in a south Delhi neighborhood, Paul (1986) found that the amount of dowry was less for employed middle class women than it was for the unemployed. This pattern is also suggested by Verghese (1980) and van der Veen (1972:40), but disputed by others (Murickan 1975). This link is also manifested among tribal people undergoing urbanization. Tribal people, ranked more toward the low end of the social hierarchy, typically make use of bride price (i.e., a payment to the bride's family) rather than dowry (Karve 1953). As these groups become more integrated into national life, they will shift to dowry practices to emulate high castes while their women participate less in gainful employment (Luthra 1983). Croll finds a similar relationship in her analysis of post-revolutionary China. She says, "it is the increased value attributed to women's labor which is largely responsible for the decline in the dowry" (1984:58).

Both Kumari (1988) and Srinivas (1984) developed arguments based on non-economic factors. Kumari in effect indicated that if dowry could be explained in economic terms, marriage would be simply a calculation of the value of a woman: if the value were high, bride price would be paid, and if the value were low, dowry transactions would occur. This formulation was presented as a refutation of Madan's dowry-as-compensation argument (Kumari 1988). We agree that reducing this practice to purely economic terms is an absurdity. The argument is not purely economic, but it is certainly consistent with a cultural materialist perspective (Harris 1979) in which symbolic values are shaped by an underlying material relationship that is the basis for the construction of cultural reality.

Delocalization of Social Control

Dowry violence is more frequent in cities (Saini 1983). Delhi has the reputation of having a high frequency of problems of dowry (Srinivas 1984:7). The urban-rural distribution pattern may be a manifestation of the effects of the delocalization of dowry. Dowry, when operative in the relationships among local caste groups in related villages, was to an extent self-regulating through caste *panchayats* (councils) and by the joint families themselves. These groups easily reach into peoples' lives. By contrast, the national level laws have inadequate reach and cannot achieve regulation. While in some areas caste groups continue to function to limit abuses, these groups are less effective in urban settings. Population movements and competition with state level social control mechanisms limit the effectiveness of self-regulation. A government commission study of women's status argues "that because of changed circumstances in which a son generally has a separate establishment and has a job somewhere away from home, the parents cannot expect much help from him, and so they consider his marriage as the major occasion on which their investment in his education can be recovered" (Government of India 1974:74). These views are consistent with the research results reported by Paul, who demonstrates that dowry amounts are higher among people who have migrated to Delhi and those who live in nuclear families, because the families in general and the women in particular are less subject to social constraints (Paul 1986). New brides do not seem to have adequate support networks in urban settings.

Economic Transformation of Society

The custom of dowry has been thrown into disarray by inflationary pressures. The consumer price index for urban non-manual workers has increased from its reference year of 1960 value of 100 to 532 for 1984–85 (Government of India 1987). The media of dowry exchange have changed dramatically because of the increasing availability of consumer goods. It has become increasingly difficult to prepare for giving dowry for a daughter or a sister. Sharma argues that, in part, dowry problems are caused by rapid change in the nature of consumer goods which made it no longer possible to accumulate gift goods over a long period as the latest styles in material goods could not be presented (1984: 70–71).

The current regime of individual dowry seeking and giving is constituted as a kind of rational behavior. That is, it is achieved through choice, is consistent with certain values, and serves to increase someone's utility. There are a number of things sought by the groom's family in these transactions. Wealth and family prestige are especially important. The family prestige "bought" with marriage expenditures, which is relevant to both the bride and groom's side in the transaction, is no doubt very much worth maximizing in the Indian context. From the perspective of the bride's family, dowry payments involve trading present consumption for future earning power for their daughter through acquiring a groom with better qualities and connections. In a two-tier, gender segregated, high unemployment, inflationary economy such as that of India, one can grasp the advantage of investing in husbands with high future earning potential. It is also possible to argue that in societies with symbolic mechanisms of stratification, it is expected that persons will attempt to make public displays of consumption in order to improve their overall performance and so to take advantage of the ambiguities of the status hierarchy system. The demand for both symbolic goods and future earnings is highly elastic. Family connections, education, and wealth seem especially important in India, and they all serve as hedges against inflation and poverty. With women having limited access to jobs and earning lower pay, it is rational to invest in a share of the groom's prospects. If you ask people why they give dowry when their daughters are being married they say, "because we love them." On the other hand, grooms' families will find the decision to forgo dowry very difficult.

SUMMARY

The distributional data indicate that the relationship between the way females are treated in marriage and their participation in economic production is consistent with Miller's development of the Boserup hypothesis. It is assumed that the pattern of maltreatment of females has been subject to various controls operating at the levels of family, caste, and community. Urbanization reduces the effectiveness of these mechanisms, thus increasing the intensity of the problem. This trend is exacerbated by the economic transformations within contemporary Indian society. It is our viewpoint that policies developed to reduce dowry-related violence will fail if they do not increase the economic value of women.

The criminalization of dowry may have been a politically useful symbol, but it has not curtailed the practice. As dowry is attacked, the state has not adequately dealt with the ante-mortem inheritance aspect of the custom. If dowry continues to provide a share of the family wealth to daughters before the death of the parents, then legally curtailing the practice is likely to damage the economic interests of women in the name of protecting them. One might argue that the primary legal remedy for the dowry problem actually makes it worse because it limits the transfer of assets to women. Perhaps this is why research on attitudes toward dowry indicates a continued positive commitment to the institution (Mathew 1987). India is a society in which most people (most particularly the elite) have given and received dowry; most people are even today giving and taking dowries. Declaring dowry a crime creates a condition in which the mass of society are technically criminals. The moral-legal basis of society suffers, and communal, parochial, and other fissiparous forces are encouraged.

To be effective, anti-dowry legislation must make sure that the social utility provided by dowry practices be displaced to practices that are less problematic, and that the apparent causes of the practice be attacked. To do so would mean that attempts to eradicate the social evils produced by the dowry institution need to be based on an examination of women's property rights so as to increase their economic access. Traditional Hindu customs associated with inheritance give sons the right from birth to claim the so-called ancestral properties. This principle is part of the Mitakshara tradition of Hindu law, which prevails throughout India except in Bengal, Kerala, Assam, and northern parts of Orissa. These properties are obtained from father, paternal grandfather, or paternal great-grandfather. According to Sivaramayya (1984:71), "The Hindu Succession Act (the law which controls inheritance) did not abrogate this right by birth which exists in favor of a son, paternal grandson and paternal great grandson. The availability of the right in favor of these male descendants only is a discrimination against daughters." The right is derived from ancient texts. According to Tambiah (1973:95), the Dharmasastras provide that it is "essentially males who inherit the patrimony while women are entitled to maintenance, marriage

expenses and gifts." While the Hindu Succession Act abrogates much traditional law, it specifically accepts the principle of male birth right to the property of the joint family. That is, "When a male Hindu dies after the commencement of the Act, having at the time of death an interest in a Mitakshara coparcenary property, his interest in the property shall devolve by survivorship upon the surviving members of the coparcenary and not in accordance with this Act" (Government of India 1985:3). The Hindu Succession Act in its most recent form provides for the intestate or testamentary inheritance of a female of a share of the family property. Yet the prior right of males at birth is not abrogated. Hindu males own a share of the family rights at birth; females can inherit it. Testamentary succession overrides the principle of intestate succession, and therefore the interests of females can be usurped simply by writing a will. The other procedures for a female to renounce an interest in family property are very simple. Moreover, according to Sivaramayya (1984:58), "no specific formality is required for the relinquishment of the interest beyond the expression of a clear intention to that effect." Instruments of relinquishment can be and are forged.

The antemortem inheritance function of dowry has been eroded or perhaps supplanted by transfer of goods to the groom's family for their consumption and the expression of the so-called prestige of the family. Indeed social science commentary on dowry in India suggests that this aspect of dowry is relatively unimportant in any case because only a small portion of the total marriage expenditure is under the bride's control. There is evidence that even the clothing and ornaments and other personal property of the bride are being usurped (Verghese 1980). Implementation of a gender-neutral inheritance law as advocated by the Government of India Committee on the Status of Women may serve to increase the economic value of women in general, while it serves as an alternative to the ante-mortem inheritance aspect of dowry. Since dowry constitutes a kind of ante-mortem inheritance, it is logical to change the inheritance laws in conjunction with the restrictions on dowry behavior. Sisters as well as brothers need to have a share in the family wealth from birth, and that right should be associated with legal procedures that increase the difficulty of alienation of property rights. There is no question that such a procedure would serve to erode the stability of the patrilineal family by diluting its economic base.

The Government of India has passed legislation such as the Hindu Succession Act (1956) and the Hindu Adoption and Maintenance Act (1956), both of which inter-alia provide for a woman's right of inheritance from her father. For example, under the Adoption and Maintenance Act, a woman has a claim of rights of maintenance from her husband's father in case she is widowed. Moreover, she has the right to claim inheritance from her deceased husband's estate. In spite of these changes, inheritance provisions are quite different for males and females. The Chief Justice of the Supreme Court of India, Honorable Mr. Justice Y. V. Chandrachud, wrote that in spite of changes, "some inequalities like the right of birth in favor of a son, paternal grandson and paternal great grandson still persist" (1984:vii). Provision of females with equal rights to inherit ancestral property from birth, or from a bequest, or at the death may reduce dowry problems. Furthermore, property that is allowed to remain in the name of the deceased for any length of time, as is frequently the case in India, should revert to the state. As it stands, property may remain in the name of a deceased ancestor, while his descendants divide it informally among themselves.

The establishment of a gender-neutral inheritance law represents a significant shift in public policy. We argue that there is a link between pro-male property laws and violence toward women. While we assert this position, we also need to recognize that the property laws give coherence and stability to an essential Indian institution, the joint family. The Mitakshara principle of male inheritance rights is both a reflection and a cause of family solidarity. Modifying this principle in an attempt to reduce violence toward women could have a deleterious effect on family coherence. In addition, the fundamental nature of these institutions makes it inconceivable that there would be substantial resistance to these changes. Yet if one considers this issue in historic terms, it is apparent that during the 20th century, legal change is in the direction of gender neutrality, a process that started with the Hindu Law of Inheritance (Amendment) Act (1929) and the Hindu Succession Act (1956), and continues through judicial decisions to the present (Diwan 1988:384). As Diwan notes in reference to the changes brought by the Hindu Succession Act of 1956, "the Mitakshara bias towards preference of males over females and of agnates over cognates has been considerably whittled down" (1988:358). Such change is not easy. The changes brought with the Hindu Succession Act in 1956 were achieved only after overcoming "stiff resistance from the traditionalists" (Government of India 1974:135). The same report states, "The hold of tradition, however, was so strong that even while introducing sweeping changes, the legislators compromised and retained in some respects the inferior position of women" (Government of India 1974:135). It must be remembered that the texts that are the foundations of contemporary law include legislation (such as the

Hindu Succession Act itself), case law, and religious texts, so that the constitutional question is also a question for religious interpretation, despite the constitutional commitment to secularim.

We are advocating further steps toward gender neutrality of the inheritance laws so that women and men will receive an equal share under intestate succession, and have an equal chance to be testamentary heirs. The law should thus be gender-neutral while still permitting a range of decisions allowing property to stay in a male line if the holder of the property so chooses. The required social adjustment could be largely achieved through the decisions of a family, backed by the power of the state. Families could express their preferences, but the state would not serve to protect the economic interests of males. The process could involve the concept of birthright as well as succession at death. We do not choose to engage those arguments, but do point out that the rapid aging of the Indian population may suggest that a full abrogation of the Mitakshara principle of birthright would be the best social policy because doing so would give older people somewhat greater control over their property in an economy virtually devoid of public investment in social services for older people (Bose and Gangrade 1988, Sharma and Dak 1987).

There are precedents for such policy at the state level. In Andhra Pradesh, the Hindu Succession Act was amended to provide for a female's birthright interest in the Mitakshara property. In Kerala, the Mitakshara property concept was legally abrogated altogether. Other gender asymmetries in the laws of India need to be attacked. The overall goal of policy should be to increase the economic value of women.

Ethnological theory directs our attention to social recognition of marriage and property transfer as functionally important features of the institution. The state can provide a means of socially recognizing marriage through registration and licensure. The law expresses no explicit preference for traditional marriage ritual, and it is possible to have a civil marriage under the provisions of the Special Marriage Act (1954) through registration with a magistrate. Nevertheless, this system co-exists parallel with the traditional system of marriage, which is beyond the reach of state control. Other marriages may be registered under this act if the persons involved so choose, and if a ceremony has been carried out. These special marriages are an alternative to an unregistered marriage.

We conclude that a useful mechanism for state control of dowry problems is the establishment of universal marriage registration, which does not exist at the present time. Marriage registration is also called for by the first Round Table on Social Audit of Implementation of Dowry Legislation (Bhatia 1988), which may serve to provide some monitoring of dowry abuses and perhaps to manifest the state's interest in an effective marriage institution. It would be naive to assume that such a policy would be widely honored, but as it is, low-income persons do not get married because they do not have the resources for marriage under the traditional non-state controlled regime. There are numerous reform groups that organize mass marriage ceremonies of village people so as to help them escape the burden of marriage expenditures. The point is that compliance is a large problem even under current circumstances.

In conclusion, we feel that the causes of the dowry problems are a product of the low economic value of women, loss of effective social control of abuse through delocalization, and pressures caused by economic transformation. The traditional family, caste group, and community controls which have been reduced in effectiveness should be replaced by state functions. The foundation of state control is universal marriage registration and licensure. The impact of the economic value of women on the problem is indicated by the transition from bride price to dowry among tribal people. It is also associated with a reduction in the extent of gainful employment and lower dowry amounts demonstrated for employed women. A broad program to increase the economic value of women would be the most useful means of dealing with the problem of dowry. Further restrictions on dowry without providing for a radically different property right for females is probably not in the interests of Indian women, since dowry represents ante-mortem inheritance. This underlying paradox may explain the commitment to dowry revealed in attitudinal research with Indian women, even though it is also an important feminist issue. The alternatives include the abolishment of the legal basis for the joint family as a corporate unit as has been done in Kerala, or the legal redefinition of the joint family as economically duolineal, as has occurred in Andhra Pradesh.

NOTE

1. For purposes of comparison, a mid-career Indian academic might be paid 60,000 Rs. per year.

REFERENCES

Aluwalia, H. 1969. Matrimonial Advertisements in Panjab. *Indian Journal of Social Work* 30:55–65.

Bhatia, S. C. 1988. Social Audit of Dowry Legislation. Delhi: Legal Literacy Project.

Bose, A. B., and K. D. Gangrade. 1988. *The Aging in India, Problems and Potentialities*. New Delhi: Abhinav.

Boserup, Ester. 1970. *Women's Role in Economic Development*. New York: St. Martin's Press.

Chandrachud, Y. V. 1984. Foreword. In *Inequalities and the Law*. B. Sivaramayya, ed. Pp. iv–vi. Lucknow: Eastern Book Company.

Croll, Elisabeth. 1984. The Exchange of Women and Property: Marriage in Post-revolutionary China. In *Women and Property—Women as Property*. Renee Hirschon, ed. Pp. 44–61. London/New York: Croom Helm/St. Martin's Press.

Diwan, Paras. 1988. *Modern Hindu Law, Codified and Uncodified*. Allahabad: Allahabad Law Agency.

Dumont, Louis. 1957. *Hierarchy and Marriage Alliance in South Indian Kinship*. London: Royal Anthropological Institute.

Engels, Fredrich. 1884. *The Origin of Family, Private Property and the State*. New York: International.

Epstein, T. Scarlett. 1960. Peasant Marriage in South India. *Man in India* 40:192–232.

Friedl, Ernestine. 1967. *Vasilika, A Village in Modern Greece*. New York: Holt, Rinehart and Winston.

Goody, Jack. 1973. Bridewealth and Dowry in Africa and Eurasia. In *Bridewealth and Dowry*. Jack Goody and S. J. Tambiah, eds. Pp. 1–58. Cambridge: Cambridge University Press.

———. 1976. *Production and Reproduction, A Comparative Study of the Domestic Domain*. Cambridge: Cambridge University Press.

Government of India. 1974. *Towards Equality: Report of the Committee on the Status of Women*. New Delhi: Government of India, Ministry of Education and Social Welfare.

———. 1985. The Hindu Succession Act. New Delhi: Government of India.

———. 1986. The Dowry Prohibition Act, 1961 (Act No. 28 of 1961) and Connected Legislation (as on 15th January, 1986). New Delhi: Government of India.

———. 1987. *India 1986, A Reference Manual*. Delhi: Ministry of Information and Broadcasting.

Harris, Marvin. 1979. *Cultural Materialism: The Struggle for a Science of Culture*. New York: Random House.

Hirschon, Renee. 1984. Introduction: Property, Power and Gender Relations. In *Women and Property—Women as Property*. Renee Hirschon, ed. Pp. 1–22. London/New York: Croom Helm/St. Martin's Press.

Hooja, S. L. 1969. *Dowry System in India*. New Delhi: Asia Press.

Karve, Irawati. 1953. *Kinship Organization in India*. Bombay: Asia Publishing.

Khanna, G. and M. Verghese. 1978. *Indian Women Today*. New Delhi: Vikas Publishing House.

Kumari, Ranjana. 1988. Practice and Problems of Dowry: A Study of Dowry Victims in Delhi. In *Social Audit of Dowry Legislation*. S. C. Bhatia, ed. Pp. 27–37. Delhi: Legal Literacy Project.

Luthra, A. 1983. Dowry Among the Urban Poor, Perception and Practice. *Social Action* 33:207.

Mathew, Anna. 1987. Attitudes Toward Dowry. *Indian Journal of Social Work* 48:95–102.

Menon, N. R. Madhava. 1988. The Dowry Prohibition Act: Does the Law Provide the Solution or Itself Constitute the Problem? In *Social Audit of Dowry Legislation*. S. C. Bhatia, ed. Pp. 11–26. Delhi: Legal Literacy Project.

Miller, Barbara D. 1981. *The Endangered Sex, Neglect of Female Children in Rural North India*. Ithaca, NY: Cornell University Press.

Murdock, George P. 1949. *Social Structure*. New York: Macmillan.

Murickan, J. 1975. Women in Kerala: Changing Socioeconomic Status and Self Image. In *Women in Contemporary India*. A. de Souza, ed. Pp. 73–95. Delhi: Manohar.

Niehoff, Arthur H. 1959. A Study of Matrimonial Advertisements in North India. *Eastern Anthropologist* 12:37–50.

Paul, Madan C. 1986. *Dowry and the Position of Women in India. A Study of Delhi Metropolis*. New Delhi: Inter India Publishers.

Saini, Debi. 1983. Dowry Prohibition Law, Social Change and Challenges in India. *Indian Journal of Social Work* 44(2):143–147.

Sharma, M. L. and T. Dak. 1987. *Aging in India, Challenge for the Society*. Delhi: Ajanta Publications.

Sharma, Ursula. 1984. Dowry in North India: Its Consequences for Women. In *Women and Property—Women as Property*. Renee Hirschon, ed. Pp. 62–74. London/New York: Croom Helm/St. Martin's Press.

Sivaramayya, B. 1984. *Inequalities and the Law*. Lucknow: Eastern Book Company.

Srinivas, M. N. 1969. *Social Change in Modern India*. Berkeley, CA: University of California Press.

——. 1984. *Some Reflections on Dowry*. Delhi: Oxford University Press.

Tambiah, S. J. 1973. Dowry and Bridewealth and the Property Rights of Women in South Asia. In *Bridewealth and Dowry*. Jack Goody and S. J. Tambiah, eds. Pp. 59–169. Cambridge: Cambridge University Press.

van der Veen, Klaus W. 1972. *I Give Thee My Daughter—A Study of Marriage and Hierarchy Among the Anavil Brahmins of South Gujarat*. Assen: Van Gorcum.

Verghese, Jamila. 1980. *Her Gold and Her Body*. New Delhi: Vikas Publishing House.

Weibe, P. O. and G. N. Ramu. 1971. A Content Analysis of Matrimonial Advertisements. *Man in India* 51:119–120.

Westermarck, Edward. 1921. *The History of Human Marriage*. London: MacMillan and Co.

32

PROFILE OF AN ANTHROPOLOGIST

Crossing the Minefield
Politics of Refugee Research and Service

Jeffery L. MacDonald

A fundamental idea of anthropology is that other cultures must be understood in their own terms, and that people should struggle against their tendency towards ethnocentrism and cultural bias. Anthropologists believe that such intolerant ethnocentrism, in combination with competition for economic resources, is at the root of much political conflict and warfare. This selection shows that as members of society, anthropologists are also tempted by ethnocentrism. Anthropologists themselves can bring stereotypes and political ideologies to their fieldwork, often because they see themselves as speaking up for the rights of disenfranchised peoples.

This selection is a profile of an anthropologist at work, doing both research and service with a group of people who are war refugees now living in the United States. In the world today around 20 million refugees are displaced because of war.

While working with refugee Iu-Mien peoples (from Laos) in Portland, Oregon, Jeffery MacDonald was faced with several obstacles because of his own cultural perspectives. MacDonald, like many anthropologists, was greatly suspicious of missionary work in Southeast Asia. This was because Christian missionaries often actively attempt to erase native cultural and religious traditions. In addition, MacDonald held a negative view of the U.S. involvement in the Vietnam War. The problem was that the Iu-Mien refugees were predominantly Christian converts and overwhelmingly conservative and critical of the United States for pulling out of Vietnam. In order to work in this society effectively, he had to hold his tongue and understand the political tensions within the refugee community. As the author says, this seemed like crossing a minefield.

As we have seen in many of the selections in this book, cultures are always changing, and people usually have good practical reasons for making specific choices; the challenge is to see the situation from their own point of view. MacDonald found that Iu-Mien people were motivated to abandon their traditions, even to the point of burning their Taoist ritual books, in part because the disastrous war that had led them to becoming refugees was seen as bad luck and the traditional spirit world had not helped them. In addition, refugees are faced with overwhelming challenges when they try to adapt to a new language and culture. By turning away from some parts of their tradition, refugees may choose strategies to help them adapt, not necessarily because their host society demands that they do so.

It is commonplace in discussions of fieldwork and ethnographic method for the first people with whom one makes contact in a community to be marginal. Associating with marginal people can sometimes be a barrier to working with the wider community. In MacDonald's case, his "outspoken" political views and his association with Taoist Iu-Mien made the majority of the community, who were Christians, view him with suspicion. Applied anthropologists are not simply observers; very often they have access to resources, information, and power structures. They are sometimes manipulated by the local community. It is difficult to judge people's motivations when one first arrives in the "field," yet it is essential to learn the political culture of the community in order to avoid stepping on diplomatic landmines.

As you read this selection, ask yourself the following questions:

- How can identifying your own preconceptions and stereotypes become an important part of your ethnographic data?

- How can one reconcile one's emotional need for friendship and reciprocity in fieldwork with the need to be wary of people's motives?

Reprinted with permission from *Practicing Anthropology*, 1996.

- What strategies can anthropologists use to avoid becoming embroiled with one political faction?
- How can anthropological awareness of culturally variable rules of communication be useful in other fields?

For the past seven years I have worked in dual roles as an ethnographic researcher and an applied anthropologist/social worker in the Southeast Asian refugee community in Portland, Oregon. I began doing research within a single ethnic community of Iu-Mien (Yao) refugees from Laos. Like many refugee researchers, I soon became an applied anthropologist, first providing services for the Iu-Mien. Later, I took a position in a refugee resettlement social service agency where I began to work with other Southeast Asian ethnic communities, providing direct client services and training, doing needs assessment research, and managing and designing culturally specific programs for Southeast Asians.

My research and applied roles necessarily involve me with a variety of political issues both internal and external to the community. I have often likened this to "crossing a minefield," because in order to be successful one has not only to balance these often opposed, dual roles, but also to understand how one's own political biases, alliances with community leaders, and sensitivity to interethnic political relationships affect each role. One misstep, one personal slight or oversight in dealing with community leaders, or one misunderstanding about political relationships can affect not only your research but your job survival as well.

In the process of learning to negotiate the minefields of internal community, interethnic, and agency politics, my own political roles, views, activities, and awareness were transformed. I became far more politicized in the way I view interpersonal and professional relationships, diplomatic and negotiating skills, and the long-term consequences of my actions and words. In the following pages I explore three levels of personal political transformation I experienced in working with Southeast Asian refugees in the United States and discuss how each affected my work.

TRANSFORMATIONS IN POLITICAL VIEWS

Due to the profoundly political nature of the refugee experience, the researcher must be aware of how the political views and opinions which he or she brings to the field affect and in turn will be challenged by the research and by the refugees themselves. I brought two political biases to the field: a negative view of Christian missionary activity among Southeast Asians and a critical view of American policy and actions in the Vietnam War. Both biases were quickly confronted. I realized that if I wanted to be successful in conducting my research I had to change my attitude, be more open minded, and silence my often outspoken opinions with regard to both issues.

Since my research interests centered on traditional religion, I was especially concerned about how missionary activities were altering Iu-Mien culture. Ironically, my chief sponsor for community entrée and research was a Christian convert who held a vision of a new, Christian Iu-Mien society not only in the U.S. but around the world. I soon became involved with other Christian converts and with Euro-American missionaries as well. They viewed me and my activities suspiciously since I spent most of my research time attending traditional Taoist rituals and relatively little time at Christian activities. I realized that my views needed to be suppressed in order to carry out my research and maintain my personal relationships. I also realized that I needed to broaden and refocus my research interests from simply traditional religion to how religious change interrelated with community politics.

I recorded many reports of Iu-Mien families who had burned their traditional Taoist ritual books and genealogical texts when they converted to Christianity. As a scholar, I found book burning to be abhorrent, and the Iu-Mien variety is all the more shocking when one realizes that these traditional texts were handmade books, many decades old, that families had perilously carried on their backs as they fled through the jungles of Laos and Thailand. (The mother in one family had even sneaked back into Laos to retrieve books left behind.) It was easy to blame the missionaries for encouraging book burning and the destruction of other ritual objects.

Once I realized that casting Iu-Mien converts as victims of the stereotypical culture-destroying missionary was too simplistic, I had to ask *why* people converted to Christianity and subsequently burnt their books. I found an answer in the convergence of the fundamentalist Christian teaching that the Iu-Mien spirit world is essentially evil and the refugees' experience of death, bad luck, disease, and the like which they attributed to vengeful ancestors and angry spirits. Expensive Taoist ceremonies had not solved their spirit problems. Christianity offered them a new, simpler way to control the spirits, and burning their books helped them sever all ties to the spirit world.

The conversion of many Iu-Mien to Christianity had led to a split in the ritual ties that helped bind the community—a split that was mirrored in the political organization, with Christian and Taoist leaders each having their own base of support. Christianity also seemed to confer adaptive advantages in the U.S. context; Christian Iu-Mien received church support in becoming economically self-sufficient and in learning English.

Such insights about the relationship between conversion, politics, and adaptation helped me in my research, analysis, and applied roles with the Iu-Mien. It also gave me more empathy and understanding when working in applied settings with other groups, such as Soviet refugees who had joined Pentecostal denominations.

My views on the Vietnam War were similarly challenged and transformed. Like many who grew up during the 1960s and 1970s, I viewed the war as immoral and illegal and believed the U.S. should have withdrawn far sooner than it did. I saw the suffering the war had brought to Americans. Southeast Asian refugees saw the suffering endured by themselves and their compatriots, and they felt that the U.S. had abandoned them after promising to fight with them to victory.

The conservative, generally Republican, anticommunist politics of Southeast Asian refugees made it difficult for me not to voice my opinions on many occasions. Nevertheless, by keeping my mouth shut, I learned the valuable political skills of diplomacy, tact, and consensus building. Such demeanor was often viewed by my Iu-Mien friends as an expression of humility, a highly valued trait in their society, which in turn advanced my status as a scholar and increased community trust in me.

The tempering of my political views also served me well when I later began to work in the social service agency with former refugees from Southeast Asia. Keeping an open mind when hearing their stories helped build trust between us as well as deepening my understanding. The agency's executive director, a Cambodian, was closely involved with the Cambodian peace process on the side of Prince Sihanouk. Had I not learned to practice some discretion in the expression of my political views, my ability to advance in the agency might well have been blocked.

Transformations in my religious and political views led me to consider how transnational political forces of war and religious conversion had helped create, sustain, and transform refugee identity. My research trajectory and interests were completely altered by my own experience and transformation with regard to these issues. Such transformations also made it possible for me to work closely and supportively with Southeast Asians from all backgrounds in my subsequent role as an applied anthropologist.

TRANSFORMATIONS IN POLITICAL STRATEGIES

The second level of transformation involved political strategies and accommodations adopted in order to negotiate complex political relationships within the Iu-Mien community and to understand how that community fits into the power relationships of the larger Southeast Asian refugee community.

My alliance with a man who was simultaneously a local Portland ethnic leader, a national U.S. ethnic leader, and a Christian leader had both positive and negative consequences. His deep understanding of internal Iu-Mien politics helped me see how the political structure of the Iu-Mien in the United States was a mixture of U.S. political practices and of political institutions and leadership structures from Laos. I also learned how political divisions and factions had grown up in the community between Christians and traditional Taoists. This individual's sponsorship separated me from other rival community leaders, but such a separation was probably inevitable since I could not have functioned in their society without a sponsor.

My relationship with my Iu-Mien sponsor led me to reexamine my own understanding of friendship and professional relationships. His alliance with me as a scholar/researcher fit into his political agenda and enhanced his status. I was often shown off in public meetings as his ally and advisor. In addition, he quickly put me to work writing grants at a time when I really knew little about Iu-Mien culture or how my activities fit into my sponsor's political agenda.

While I recognized the need for reciprocity—in friendship and professional relationships—my rapidly evolving, somewhat competing roles as a researcher and an applied anthropologist caused me some ethical concerns. These concerns expanded when I was appointed to the board of directors of the Iu-Mien Association of Oregon. How can one voice opinions on what a community should be doing while maintaining impartiality as a researcher? While this is a question that has bedeviled many anthropologists, it was not an issue for my Iu-Mien colleagues.

Besides learning to look for hidden political agendas and reciprocal responsibilities in my interpersonal relationships with the Iu-Mien, I gained other valuable political skills and knowledge by working closely with this Iu-Mien leader. He helped me understand the complexities of interethnic politics among Southeast Asian refugees, including how groups viewed themselves relative to others and how these self-perceptions were based upon former relations in Southeast Asia. He also introduced me to many key community leaders among the Lao, the Hmong, the Cambodians, and the Vietnamese, and he helped me understand which leaders were allies and which were enemies and how these relationships could change dramatically in different contexts.

My contacts with these community leaders helped me secure a position at a community-based refugee resettlement agency operated largely by Southeast Asian management. Many of the community leaders were then my coworkers or supervisors, and others were on the agency's board of directors. Knowledge gained from research helped me avoid stepping on interethnic land mines in the agency. At the same time, my work as an applied anthropologist in the agency expanded my understanding of interethnic politics and introduced me to a wider range of community members and leaders.

The agency, which provides employment services, vocational training, and other social services to refugees, was formed in 1984 as a merger of two mutual assistance associations. In this merger, certain ethnic leaders advanced their positions, while others lost their jobs or their agency leadership roles. Anger still lingers, as I discovered recently when a Southeast Asian leader whom I had previously counted as a supporter suddenly became an enemy. His attacks on me were a means to get back at senior management staff from another ethnic community.

As I have become more knowledgeable of interethnic politics and community needs, my roles in the agency have evolved and expanded. From preemployment instructor I became community researcher and program coordinator of a project for Lao, Iu-Mien, and Hmong teen mothers. I had little knowledge of or personal ability to counsel Southeast Asian teen moms, and I often lay awake at night wondering how a white male could end up in such a position! Based on this experience, however, I began developing new services such as parent education, child care training, intervention with gang-involved youth, and recreational activities for youth and their parents. My current job description includes program development, grant writing, needs assessment research, staff supervision, and provision of cross-cultural training.

Over the years, I have also learned how interethnic politics affect the delivery of social services. For example, ethnic groups not represented in the management structure tend to receive fewer special services—a pattern to which I too have contributed. Although I try to ensure that services are delivered equitably to all groups based on need, I have tended to employ direct service staff from the Lao, Iu-Mien, and Hmong communities because of my previous research. As a result, other communities may be underserved. In addition, certain social service needs, such as alleviation of domestic violence, may remain unmet because agency management will either not acknowledge such problems or not address them for fear of upsetting power relationships within the community. As an applied anthropologist/social worker, one needs to know what subjects are taboo and what social service proposals will be dead on arrival.

Knowledge of ethnic power structures is also important in doing interethnic community research. Without such knowledge, it is easy to overlook significant issues or to make the fatal error of not including key community leaders in your research. This detracts from your reputation as knowledgeable and, more importantly, insults community leaders by devaluing their importance and reputation in the community. For many Southeast Asians, a mistake of this kind can create barriers for research as well as for developing and delivering social services.

Another important transformation in my political skills was learning different communication styles. Speaking strategically, being diplomatic and tactful, and building consensus are all part of an indirect or "spiraling" communication style common within many Southeast Asian communities. Being able to practice this style of communication has proven very valuable in my work. Without the necessary cultural background knowledge and skills, many new social workers in our agency do not understand the hidden meanings and agendas being communicated. One learns to look for the implicit, rather than the literal meaning of what is being said.

TRANSFORMATIONS IN POLITICAL ACTIVISM

As my reputation has grown in the Southeast Asian community as an expert sympathetic to community needs, and as my job responsibilities have expanded at my agency, I have had to take on the roles of advocate for individuals and of community political activist. As part of my job, I advocate for and assist clients who are not receiving services from other agencies or from the government. I also advocate for individuals as part of my reciprocal responsibilities to community leaders and friends. In addition, I can hardly refuse any requests from my chief sponsor that I take on explicitly political roles as a community advocate.

Serving as an advocate or political activist can generate new research material. For example, a close personal friend and traditional religious leader in the Iu-Mien community called on me to assist his family when wedding plans for his nephew were disrupted by a city official's decision to ban large wedding parties in apartments. I was able to mobilize many Southeast Asian and mainstream leaders to force the city to back down on the basis of racial and religious discrimination. Taking this action allowed me in turn to learn much about wedding ceremonies. The chief priest had to write out a schedule of events, which had never been done before, and explain each step of the ceremony for city officials.

In 1992 I was contracted to conduct a study on the causes of juvenile delinquency in the Southeast Asian community and to make program and service recommendations to solve the problem. This was an explicitly political task from the beginning. Early on it involved me in infighting between Asian American county officials, who had had the money earmarked for Southeast Asian youth, and state officials, who felt that the funds should be used for African American youth. The Southeast Asian community was eager to see the study go forward because it would provide them a forum for expressing their needs and concerns to government.

Part of the reason I was given the task was my expertise and good relationships in the community. I could be expected not to weigh the findings in favor of one ethnic group over another. In addition, Southeast Asian community leaders felt I would be discreet in what I revealed about the community as a whole. Knowledge of the complex internal and external political implications of my research findings allowed me to write a report which was accurate but which also discreetly skirted sensitive issues.

Since completion of the study in January 1993, its recommendations have been adopted by the county as a blueprint for developing new services for Southeast Asian families and youth. While this is personally gratifying, it has thrust me further into the role of political activist, as I have been asked to testify at meetings and to lend my support in other ways. Despite the faith which many of my Southeast Asian friends and colleagues place in me, I am very uncomfortable in this role. I feel it is neither politically nor culturally correct for me to represent the Southeast Asian community in an activist role at a government hearing or other community forum. Ideally, my role should be advisory, and my knowledge and writings should be used to empower Southeast Asians themselves to advocate for their communities.

The latter has actually occurred in the last two years. A group of Southeast Asian leaders used the study's recommendations to develop a proposal for an Asian Family Center. In May of 1994, they took their proposal to the county board of commissioners and successfully lobbied the board for funding. Following budget approval, they asked me and my agency to develop the center and implement the new programs. Operating since November 1994, the Asian Family Center is maintaining close community ties through an advisory board composed of members of each of Portland's Asian ethnic groups. While the advisory board is still in its infancy, its members have taken on the key advocacy functions which will be critical to community empowerment and to continued funding for the center.

CONCLUSION

Other anthropologists who work in applied fields while simultaneously carrying out ethnographic research experience similar personal transformations. Many of us slowly move from pure research into applied roles as professional development opportunities arise and as we deepen our awareness of the needs of our research communities. In the process, we learn that research and applied roles may actually be more complementary than conflicting, as advocacy and activism lead to new research insights. Certainly this is true for many of us who work in such multiple roles in refugee communities.

Transformations of this type will become increasingly important issues for all anthropologists as interactions between ethnic, cultural, and linguistic groups expand worldwide. Anthropologists will need to take on enlarged and often multiple roles as political activists, researchers, and designers of social service, health care, and cultural preservation programs. If our vast accumulation of cultural, linguistic, and social knowledge and analysis is to become more than just an internal discourse within our profession, or archival material in a museum or library, we as anthropologists must transform our own political consciousness and activities beyond academia. We must take responsibility for assuring that our knowledge is of use to the communities that we have studied.

33

The Kpelle Moot

James L. Gibbs Jr.

Some scholars argue that law, like marriage, is a major institution found in all societies, although in widely divergent forms. Others argue that law exists only where some individual or group possesses the authority to impose punishments. Debates about what is and what isn't law aside, conflict exists in all societies. Further, all societies have culturally defined mechanisms by which people attempt to settle their differences.

Conflict-management procedures must be geared to meet the needs of particular social systems. In the urban centers of Western society, people live in faceless anonymity. Relations between people can be characterized as single interest. For example, generally a person's landlord is neither kin nor neighbor. The landlord-tenant relationship is not complicated by any other social bonds. A person who has a car accident is unlikely to have run into a friend or a relative. Our legal system, with its narrow focus on the grievance itself, fits our social system of one-dimensional relationships.

In small-scale social systems, people are often involved with one another on multiple levels. A landlord may also be a neighbor and a relative. In such settings, people are born, grow up, grow old, and die in the same community. Because their social relationships are long-term and highly valued, people in such communities need to resolve disputes in a way that maintains good relations.

Today in the United States, government agencies and grassroots organizations are establishing programs—Neighborhood Justice Centers or Dispute Resolution Centers—based on models of consensus and conciliation. According to the *Citizen's Dispute Resolution Handbook*, the potential of local-level conflict resolution was originally recognized in the work of an anthropologist who had described these processes in Africa.

As you read this selection, ask yourself the following questions:

- How are formal courtroom hearings different from moots?
- In what kinds of cases is the formal court effective and in what kinds is it ineffective?
- How is a mediator different from a judge?
- What is the function of the blessing at the beginning of the moot?
- In contrast to the official court, how does the procedure used during the moot facilitate harmony and reconciliation?
- Why does the author consider the moot therapeutic?

The following terms discussed in this selection are included in the Glossary at the back of the book:

clan	multiplex relationships
culture area	palaver
extended family	patrilineal
mediator	single-interest relationship
moot	social control

Africa as a major culture area has been characterized by many writers as being marked by a high development of law and legal procedures.[1] In the past few years research on African law has produced a series of highly competent monographs such as those on law among the Tiv, the Barotse, and the Nuer.[2] These and related shorter studies have focused primarily on formal processes for the settlement of disputes, such as those which take place in a courtroom, or those which are, in some other way, set apart from simpler measures of social control. However, many African societies have informal, quasi-legal, dispute-settlement procedures, supplemental to formal ones, which have not been as well studied, or—in most cases—adequately analysed.

Reprinted from James L. Gibbs, "The Kpelle Moot," *Africa*, vol. 33, no. 1, 1963.

In this paper I present a description and analysis of one such institution for the informal settlement of disputes, as it is found among the Kpelle of Liberia; it is the moot, the *bɛrɛi mu meni saa* or "house palaver." Hearings in the Kpelle moot contrast with those in a court in that they differ in tone and effectiveness. The genius of the moot lies in the fact that it is based on a covert application of the principles of psychoanalytic theory which underlie psychotherapy.

The Kpelle are a Mande-speaking, patrilineal group of some 175,000 rice cultivators who live in Central Liberia and the adjoining regions of Guinea. This paper is based on data gathered in a field study which I carried out in 1957 and 1958 among the Liberian Kpelle of Panta Chiefdom in north-east Central Province.

Strong corporate patrilineages are absent among the Kpelle. The most important kinship group is the virilocal polygynous family which sometimes becomes an extended family, almost always of the patrilineal variety. Several of these families form the core of a residential group, known as a village quarter, more technically, a clan-barrio.[3] This is headed by a quarter elder who is related to most of the household heads by real or putative patrilineal ties.

Kpelle political organization is centralized although there is no single king or paramount chief, but a series of chiefs of the same level of authority, each of whom is superordinate over district chiefs and town chiefs. Some political functions are also vested in the tribal fraternity, the Poro, which still functions vigorously. The form of political organization found in the area can thus best be termed the polycephalous associational state.

The structure of the Kpelle court system parallels that of the political organization. In Liberia the highest court of a tribal authority and the highest tribal court chartered by the Government is that of a paramount chief. A district chief's court is also an official court. Disputes may be settled in these official courts or in unofficial courts, such as those of town chiefs or quarter elders. In addition to this, grievances are settled informally in moots, and sometimes by associational groupings such as church councils or cooperative work groups.

In my field research I studied both the formal and informal methods of dispute settlement. The method used was to collect case material in as complete a form as possible. Accordingly, immediately after a hearing, my interpreter and I would prepare verbatim transcripts of each case that we heard. These transcripts were supplemented with accounts—obtained from respondents—of past cases or cases which I did not hear litigated. Transcripts from each type of hearing were analysed phrase by phrase in terms of a frame of reference derived from jurisprudence and ethno-law. The results of the analysis indicate two things: first, that courtroom hearings and moots are quite different in their procedures and tone, and secondly, why they show this contrast.

Kpelle courtroom hearings are basically coercive and arbitrary in tone. In another paper[4] I have shown that this is partly the result of the intrusion of the authoritarian values of the Poro into the courtroom. As a result, the court is limited in the manner in which it can handle some types of disputes. The court is particularly effective in settling cases such as assault, possession of illegal charms, or theft where the litigants are not linked in a relationship which must continue after the trial. However, most of the cases brought before a Kpelle court are cases involving disputed rights over women, including matrimonial matters which are usually cast in the form of suits for divorce. The court is particularly inept at settling these numerous matrimonial disputes because its harsh tone tends to drive spouses farther apart rather than to reconcile them. The moot, in contrast, is more effective in handling such cases. The following analysis indicates the reasons for this.[5]

The Kpelle *bɛrɛi mu meni saa*, or "house palaver," is an informal airing of a dispute which takes place before an assembled group which includes kinsmen of the litigants and neighbors from the quarter where the case is being heard. It is a completely ad hoc group, varying greatly in composition from case to case. The matter to be settled is usually a domestic problem: alleged mistreatment or neglect by a spouse, an attempt to collect money paid to a kinsman for a job which was not completed, or a quarrel among brothers over the inheritance of their father's wives.

In the procedural description which follows I shall use illustrative data from the Case of the Ousted Wife:

Wama Nya, the complainant, had one wife, Yua. His older brother died and he inherited the widow, Yokpo, who moved into his house. The two women were classificatory sisters. After Yokpo moved in, there was strife in the household. The husband accused her of staying out late at night, of harvesting rice without his knowledge, and of denying him food. He also accused Yokpo of having lovers and admitted having had a physical struggle with her, after which he took a basin of water and "washed his hands of her."

Yokpo countered by denying the allegations about having lovers, saying that she was accused falsely, although she had in the past confessed the name of one lover. She further complained that Wama Nya had assaulted her and, in the act, had committed the indignity of removing her headtie, and had expelled her from the house after the ritual hand-washing. Finally, she alleged that she had been thus cast out of the house at the instigation of the other wife who, she asserted, had great influence over their husband.

Kɔlɔ Waa, the Town Chief and quarter elder, and the brother of Yokpo, was the mediator of the moot, which decided that the husband was mainly at fault, although Yua and Yokpo's children were also in the wrong. Those at fault had to apologize to Yokpo and bring gifts of apology as well as local rum[6] for the disputants and participants in the moot.

The moot is most often held on a Sunday—a day of rest for Christians and non-Christians alike—at the home of the complainant, the person who calls the moot. The mediator will have been selected by the complainant. He is a kinsman who also holds an office such as town chief or quarter elder, and therefore has some skill in dispute settlement. It is said that he is chosen to preside by virtue of his kin tie, rather than because of his office.

The proceedings begin with the pronouncing of blessings by one of the oldest men of the group. In the Case of the Ousted Wife, Gbenai Zua, the elder who pronounced the blessings, took a rice-stirrer in his hand and, striding back and forth, said:

This man has called us to fix the matter between him and his wife. May γala (the supreme, creator deity) change his heart and let his household be in good condition. May γala bless the family and make them fruitful. May He bless them so they can have food this year. May He bless the children and the rest of the family so they may always be healthy. May He bless them to have good luck. When Wama Nya takes a gun and goes in the bush, may he kill big animals. May γala bless us to enjoy the meat. May He bless us to enjoy life and always have luck. May γala bless all those who come to discuss this matter.

The man who pronounces the blessings always carries a stick or a whisk (*kpung*) which he waves for effect as he paces up and down chanting his injunctions. Participation of spectators is demanded, for the blessings are chanted by the elder (*kpung namu* or "*kpung* owner") as a series of imperatives, some of which he repeats. Each phrase is responded to by the spectators who answer in unison with a formal response, either *e ka ti* (so be it), or a low, drawn-out *eeee*. The *kpung namu* delivers his blessings faster and faster, building up a rhythmic interaction pattern with the other participants. The effect is to unite those attending in common action before the hearing begins. The blessing focuses attention on the concern with maintaining harmony and the well-being of the group as a whole.

Everyone attending the moot wears their next-to-best clothes or, if it is not Sunday, everyday clothes. Elders, litigants, and spectators sit in mixed fashion, pressed closely upon each other, often overflowing onto a veranda. This is in contrast to the vertical spatial separation between litigants and adjudicators in the courtroom. The mediator, even though he is a chief, does not wear his robes. He and the oldest men will be given chairs as they would on any other occasion.

The complainant speaks first and may be interrupted by the mediator or anyone else present. After he has been thoroughly quizzed, the accused will answer and will also be questioned by those present. The two parties will question each other directly and question others in the room also. Both the testimony and the questioning are lively and uninhibited. Where there are witnesses to some of the actions described by the parties, they may also speak and be questioned. Although the proceedings are spirited, they remain orderly. The mediator may fine anyone who speaks out of turn by requiring them to bring some rum for the group to drink.

The mediator and others present will point out the various faults committed by both the parties. After everyone has been heard, the mediator expresses the consensus of the group. For example, in the Case of the Ousted Wife, he said to Yua: "The words you used towards your sister were not good, so come and beg her pardon."

The person held to be mainly at fault will then formally apologize to the other person. This apology takes the form of the giving of token gifts to the wronged person by the guilty party. These may be an item of clothing, a few coins, clean hulled rice, or a combination of all three. It is also customary for the winning party in accepting the gifts of apology to give, in return, a smaller token such as a twenty-five cent piece[7] to show his "white heart" or good will. The losing party is also lightly "fined"; he must present rum or beer to the mediator and the others who heard the case. This is consumed by all in attendance. The old man then pronounces blessings again and offers thanks for the restoration of harmony within the group, and asks that all continue to act with good grace and unity.

An initial analysis of the procedural steps of the moot isolates the descriptive attributes of the moot and shows that they contrast with those of the courtroom hearing. While the airing of grievances is incomplete in courtroom hearings, it is more complete in the moot. This fuller airing of the issues results, in many marital cases, in a more harmonious solution. Several specific features of the house palaver facilitate this wider airing of grievances. First, the hearing takes place soon after a breach has occurred, before the grievances have hardened. There is no delay until the complainant has time to go to the paramount chief's or district chief's headquarters to institute suit. Secondly, the hearing takes place in the familiar surroundings of a home. The robes, writs, messengers, and other symbols of power which subtly intimidate and inhibit the parties in the courtroom, by reminding them of the physical force which underlies the procedures, are absent. Thirdly, in the courtroom the conduct of the hearing is firmly in the hands of the judge but in the moot the investigatory initiative rests much more with the parties themselves. Jurisprudence suggests that, in such a case, more of the grievances lodged between the parties are likely to be aired and adjusted. Finally, the range of relevance applied to matters which are brought out is extremely broad. Hardly anything mentioned is held to be irrelevant. This too leads to a more thorough ventilation of the issues.

There is a second surface difference between court and moot. In a courtroom hearing, the solution is, by and large, one which is imposed by the adjudicator. In the moot the solution is more consensual. It is, therefore, more likely to be accepted by both parties and hence more durable. Several features of the moot contribute to the consensual solution: first, there is no unilateral ascription of blame, but an attribution of fault to both parties. Secondly, the mediator, unlike the chief in the courtroom, is not backed by political authority and the physical force which underlies it. He cannot jail parties, nor can he levy a heavy fine. Thirdly, the sanctions which are imposed are not so burdensome as to cause hardship to the losing party or to give him or her grounds for a new grudge against the other party. The gifts for the winning party and the potables for the spectators are not as expensive as the fines and the court costs in a paramount chief's court. Lastly, the ritualized apology of the moot symbolizes very concretely the consensual nature of the solution.[8] The public offering and acceptance of the tokens of apology indicate that each party has no further grievances and that the settlement is satisfactory and mutually acceptable. The parties and spectators drink together to symbolize the restored solidarity of the group and the rehabilitation of the offending party.

This type of analysis describes the courtroom hearing and the moot, using a frame of reference derived from jurisprudence and ethno-law which is explicitly comparative and evaluative. Only by using this type of comparative approach can the researcher select features of the hearings which are not only unique to each of them, but theoretically significant in that their contribution to the social-control functions of the proceedings can be hypothesized. At the same time, it enables the researcher to pin-point in procedures the cause for what he feels intuitively: that the two hearings contrast in tone, even though they are similar in some ways.

However, one can approach the transcripts of the trouble cases with a second analytical framework and emerge with a deeper understanding of the implications of the contrasting descriptive attributes of the court and the house palaver. Remember that the coercive tone of the courtroom hearing limits the court's effectiveness in dealing with matrimonial disputes, especially in effecting reconciliations. The moot, on the other hand, is particularly effective in bringing about reconciliations between spouses. This is because the moot is not only conciliatory, but *therapeutic*. Moot procedures are therapeutic in that, like psychotherapy, they re-educate the parties through a type of social learning brought about in a specially structured interpersonal setting.

Talcott Parsons[9] has written that therapy involves four elements: support, permissiveness, denial of reciprocity, and manipulation of rewards. Writers such as Frank,[10] Klapman,[11] and Opler[12] have pointed out that the same elements characterize not only individual psychotherapy, but group psychotherapy as well. All four elements are writ large in the Kpelle moot.

The patient in therapy will not continue treatment very long if he does not feel support from the therapist or from the group. In the moot the parties are encouraged in the expression of their complaints and feelings because they sense group support. The very presence of one's kinsmen and neighbors demonstrates their concern. It indicates to the parties that they have a real problem and that the others are willing to help them to help themselves in solving it. In a parallel vein, Frank, speaking of group psychotherapy, notes that: "Even anger may be supportive if it implies to a patient that others take him seriously enough to get angry at him, especially if the object of the anger feels it to be directed toward his neurotic behavior rather than himself as a person."[13] In the moot the feeling of support also grows out of the pronouncement of the blessings which stress the unity of the group and its harmonious goal, and it is also undoubtedly increased by the absence of the publicity and expressive symbols of political power which are found in the courtroom.

Permissiveness is the second element in therapy. It indicates to the patient that everyday restrictions on making anti-social statements or acting out anti-social impulses are lessened. Thus, in the Case of the Ousted Wife, Yua felt free enough to turn to her ousted co-wife (who had been married leviratically) and say:

> You don't respect me. You don't rely on me any more. When your husband was living, and I was with my husband, we slept on the farm. Did I ever refuse to send you what you asked me for when you sent a message? Didn't I always send you some of the meat my husband killed? Did I refuse to send you anything you wanted? When your husband died and we became co-

wives, did I disrespect you? Why do you always make me ashamed? The things you have done to me make me sad.

Permissiveness in the therapeutic setting (and in the moot) results in catharsis, in a high degree of stimulation of feelings in the participants and an equally high tendency to verbalize these feelings.[14] Frank notes that: "Neurotic responses must be expressed in the therapeutic situation if they are to be changed by it."[15] In the same way, if the solution to a dispute reached in a house palaver is to be stable, it is important that there should be nothing left to embitter and undermine the decision. In a familiar setting, with familiar people, the parties to the moot feel at ease and free to say *all* that is on their minds. Yokpo, judged to be the wronged party in the Case of the Ousted Wife, in accepting an apology, gave expression to this when she said:

> I agree to everything that my people said, and I accept the things they have given me—I don't have *anything else* about them on my mind. *(My italics.)*

As we shall note below, this thorough airing of complaints also facilitates the gaining of insight into and the unlearning of idiosyncratic behaviour which is socially disruptive. Permissiveness is rooted in the lack of publicity and the lack of symbols of power. But it stems, too, from the immediacy of the hearing, the locus of investigatory initiative with the parties, and the wide range of relevance.

Permissiveness in therapy is impossible without the denial of reciprocity. This refers to the fact that the therapist will not respond in kind when the patient acts in a hostile manner or with inappropriate affection. It is a type of privileged indulgence which comes with being a patient. In the moot, the parties are treated in the same way and are allowed to hurl recriminations that, in the courtroom, might bring a few hours in jail as punishment for the equivalent of contempt of court. Even though inappropriate views are not responded to in kind, neither are they simply ignored. There is denial of *congruent* response, not denial of *any* response whatsoever. In the *bɛrɛi mu meni saa*, as in group psychotherapy, "private ideation and conceptualization are brought out into the open and all their facets or many of their facets exposed. The individual gets a 'reading' from different bearings on the compass, so to speak,[16] and perceptual patterns . . . are joggled out of their fixed positions. . . ."[17]

Thus, Yua's outburst against Yokpo quoted above was not responded to with matching hostility, but its inappropriateness was clearly pointed out to her by the group. Some of them called her aside in a huddle and said to her:

You are not right. If you don't like the woman, or she doesn't like you, don't be the first to say anything. Let her start and then say what you have to say. By speaking, if she heeds some of your words, the wives will scatter, and the blame will be on you. Then your husband will cry for your name that you have scattered his property.

In effect, Yua was being told that, in view of the previous testimony, her jealousy of her co-wife was not justified. In reality testing, she discovered that her view of the situation was not shared by the others and, hence was inappropriate. Noting how the others responded, she could see why her treatment of her co-wife had caused so much dissension. Her interpretation of her new co-wife's actions and resulting premises were not shared by the co-wife, nor by the others hearing a description of what had happened. Like psychotherapy, the moot is gently corrective of behavior rooted in such misunderstandings.

Similarly, Wama Nya, the husband, learned that others did not view as reasonable his accusing his wife of having a lover and urging her to go off and drink with the suspected paramour when he passed their house and wished them all a good evening. Reality testing for him taught him that the group did not view this type of mildly paranoid sarcasm as conducive to stable marital relationships.

The reaction of the moot to Yua's outburst indicates that permissiveness in this case was certainly not complete, but only relative, being much greater than in the courtroom. But without this moderated immunity the airing of grievances would be limited, and the chance for social relearning lessened. Permissiveness in the moot is incomplete because, even there, prudence is not thrown to the winds. Note that Yua was not told not to express her feelings at all, but to express them only after the co-wife had spoken so that, if the moot failed, she would not be in an untenable position. In court there would be objection to her blunt speaking out. In the moot the objection was, in effect, to her speaking *out of turn*. In other cases the moot sometimes fails, foundering on this very point, because the parties are *too* prudent, all waiting for the others to make the first move in admitting fault.

The manipulation of rewards is the last dimension of therapy treated by Parsons. In this final phase of therapy[18] the patient is coaxed to conformity by the granting of rewards. In the moot one of the most important rewards is the group approval which goes to the wronged person who accepts an apology and to the person who is magnanimous enough to make one.

In the Case of the Ousted Wife, Kɔlɔ Waa, the mediator, and the others attending decided that the husband and the co-wife, Yua, had wronged Yokpo. Kɔlɔ Waa said to the husband:

From now on, we don't want to hear of your fighting. You should live in peace with these women. If your wife accepts the things which the people have brought you should pay four chickens and ten bottles of rum as your contribution.

The husband's brother and sister also brought gifts of apology, although the moot did not explicitly hold them at fault.

By giving these prestations, the wrong-doer is restored to good grace and is once again acting like an "upright Kpelle" (although, if he wishes, he may refuse to accept the decision of the moot). He is eased into this position by being grouped with others to whom blame is also allocated, for, typically, he is not singled out and isolated in being labelled deviant. Thus, in the Case of the Ousted Wife, the children of Yokpo were held to be at fault in "being mean" to their step-father, so that blame was not only shared by one "side," but ascribed to the other also.

Moreover, the prestations which the losing party is asked to hand over are not expensive. They are significant enough to touch the pocketbook a little; for the Kpelle say that if an apology does not cost something other than words, the wrong-doer is more likely to repeat the offending action. At the same time, as we noted above, the tokens are not so costly as to give the loser additional reason for anger directed at the other party which can undermine the decision.

All in all, the rewards for conformity to group expectations and for following out a new behaviour pattern are kept within the deviant's sight. These rewards are positive, in contrast to the negative sanctions of the courtroom. Besides the institutionalized apology, praise and acts of concern and affection replace fines and jail sentences. The mediator, speaking to Yokpo as the wronged party, said:

> You have found the best of the dispute. Your husband has wronged you. All the people have wronged you. You are the only one who can take care of them because you are the oldest. Accept the things they have given to you.

The moot in its procedural features and procedural sequences is, then, strongly analogous to psychotherapy. It is analogous to therapy in the structuring of the role of the mediator also. Parsons has indicated that, to do his job well, the therapist must be a member of two social systems: one containing himself and his patient; and the other, society at large.[19] He must not be seduced into thinking that he belongs only to the therapeutic dyad, but must gradually pull the deviant back into a relationship with the wider group. It is significant, then, that the mediator of a moot is a kinsman who is also a chief of some sort. He thus represents both the group involved in the dispute and the wider community. His task is to utilize his position as kinsman as a lever to manipulate the parties into living up to the normative requirements of the wider society, which, as chief, he upholds. His major orientation must be to the wider collectivity, not to the particular goals of his kinsmen.

When successful, the moot stops the process of alienation which drives two spouses so far apart that they are immune to ordinary social-control measures such as a smile, a frown, or a pointed aside.[20] A moot is not always successful, however. Both parties must have a genuine willingness to cooperate and a real concern about their discord. Each party must be willing to list his grievances, to admit his guilt, and make an open apology. The moot, like psychotherapy, is impotent without well-motivated clients.

The therapeutic elements found in the Kpelle moot are undoubtedly found in informal procedures for settling disputes in other African societies also; some of these are reported in literature and others are not. One such procedure which seems strikingly parallel to the Kpelle *bɛrɛi mu meni saa* has been described by J. H. M. Beattie.[21] This is the court of neighbors or *rukurato rw'enzarwa* found in the Banyoro kingdom of Uganda. The group also meets as an ad hoc assembly of neighbors to hear disputes involving kinsmen or neighbors.[22]

The intention of the Nyoro moot is to "reintegrate the delinquent into the community and, if possible, to achieve reconciliation without causing bitterness and resentment; in the words of an informant, the institution exists 'to finish off people's quarrels and to abolish bad feeling.'"[23] This therapeutic goal is manifested in the manner in which the dispute is resolved. After a decision is reached the penalty imposed is always the same. The party held to be in the wrong is asked to bring beer (four pots, modified downwards according to the circumstances) and meat, which is shared with the other party and all those attending the *rukurato*. The losing party is also expected to "humble himself, not only to the man he has injured but to the whole assembly."[24]

Beattie correctly points out that, because the council of neighbors has no power to enforce its decision, the shared feast is *not* to be viewed primarily as a penalty, for the wrong-doer acts as a host and also shares in the food and drink. "And it is a praiseworthy thing; from a dishonourable status he is promoted to an honourable one . . ."[25] and reintegrated into the community.[26]

Although Beattie does not use a psychoanalytic frame of reference in approaching his material, it is clear that the communal feast involves the manipulation of rewards as the last step in a social-control measure which breaks the progressive alienation of the deviance cycle. The description of procedures in the *rukurato* indicates that it is highly informal in nature, convening in a room in a house with everyone "sitting around." However, Beattie does not provide enough detail to enable one to determine whether or not the beginning and intermediate steps in the Nyoro moot show the permissiveness, support, and denial of reciprocity which characterize the Kpelle moot. Given the structure and outcome of most Nyoro councils, one would surmise that a close examination of their proceedings[27] would reveal the implicit operation of therapeutic principles.

The fact that the Kpelle court is basically coercive and the moot therapeutic does not imply that one is dysfunctional while the other is eufunctional. Like Beattie, I conclude that the court and informal dispute-settlement procedures have separate but complementary functions. In marital disputes the moot is oriented to a couple as a dyadic social system and serves to reconcile them wherever possible. This is eufunctional from the point of view of the couple, to whom divorce would be dysfunctional. Kpelle courts customarily treat matrimonial matters by granting a divorce. While this may be dysfunctional from the point of view of the couple, because it ends their marriage, it may be eufunctional from the point of view of society. Some marriages, if forced to continue, would result in adultery or physical violence at best, and improper socialization of children at worst. It is clear that the Kpelle moot is to the Kpelle court as the domestic and family relations courts (or commercial and labour arbitration boards) are to ordinary courts in our own society. The essential point is that both formal and informal dispute-settlement procedures serve significant functions in Kpelle society and neither can be fully understood if studied alone.[28]

NOTES

1. The field work on which this paper is based was carried out in Liberia in 1957 and 1958 and was supported by a grant from the Ford Foundation, which is, of course, not responsible for any of the views presented here. The data were analyzed while the writer was the holder of a predoctoral National Science Foundation Fellowship. The writer wishes to acknowledge, with gratitude, the support of both foundations. This paper was read at the Annual Meeting of the American Anthropological Association in Philadelphia, Pennsylvania, in November 1961.

    The dissertation, in which this material first appeared, was directed by Philip H. Gulliver, to whom I am indebted for much stimulating and provocative discussion of many of the ideas here. Helpful comments and suggestions have also been made by Robert T. Holt and Robert S. Merrill.

Portions of the material included here were presented in a seminar on African Law conducted in the Department of Anthropology at the University of Minnesota by E. Adamson Hoebel and the writer. Members of the seminar were generous in their criticisms and comments.

2. Paul J. Bohannan, *Justice and Judgment among the Tiv*, Oxford University Press, London, 1957; Max Gluckman, *The Judicial Process among the Barotse of Northern Rhodesia*, Manchester University Press, 1954; P. P. Howell, *A Handbook of Nuer Law*, Oxford University Press, London, 1954.

3. Cf. George P. Murdock, *Social Structure*, Macmillan, New York, 1949, p. 74.

4. James L. Gibbs, Jr., "Poro Values and Courtroom Procedures in a Kpelle Chiefdom," *Southwestern Journal of Anthropology* (in press) [1963, 18:341–350]. A detailed analysis of Kpelle courtroom procedures and of procedures in the moot together with transcripts appears in: James L. Gibbs, Jr., *Some Judicial Implications of Marital Instability among the Kpelle* (unpublished Ph.D. Dissertation, Harvard University, Cambridge, Mass., 1960).

5. What follows is based on a detailed case study of moots in Panta Chiefdom and their contrast with courtroom hearings before the paramount chief of that chiefdom. Moots, being private, are less susceptible to the surveillance of the anthropologist than courtroom hearings, thus I have fewer transcripts of moots than of court cases. The analysis presented here is valid for Panta Chiefdom and also valid, I feel, for most of the Liberian Kpelle area, particularly the north-east where people are, by and large, traditional.

6. This simple distilled rum, bottled in Monrovia and retailing for twenty-five cents a bottle in 1958, is known in the Liberian Hinterland as "cane juice" and should not be confused with imported varieties.

7. American currency is the official currency of Liberia and is used throughout the country.

8. Cf. J. F. Holleman, "An Anthropological Approach to Bantu Law (with special reference to Shona law)" in the *Journal of the Rhodes-Livingstone Institute*, vol. x, 1950, pp. 27–41. Holleman feels that the use of tokens for effecting apologies—or marriages—shows the proclivity for reducing events of importance to something tangible.

9. Talcott Parsons, *The Social System*, The Free Press, Glencoe, Ill., 1951, pp. 314–19.

10. Jerome D. Frank, "Group Methods in Psychotherapy," in *Mental Health and Mental Disorder: A Sociological Approach*, edited by Arnold Rose, W. W. Norton Co., New York, pp. 524–35.

11. J. W. Klapman, *Group Psychotherapy: Theory and Practice*, Grune & Stratton, New York, 1959.

12. Marvin K. Opler, "Values in Group Psychotherapy," *International Journal of Social Psychiatry*, vol. iv, 1959, pp. 296–98.

13. Frank, op. cit., p. 531.

14. Ibid.

15. Ibid.

16. Klapman, op. cit., p. 39.

17. Ibid., p. 15.

18. For expository purposes the four elements of therapy are described as if they always occur serially. They may, and do, occur simultaneously also. Thus, all four of the factors may be implicit in a single short behavioural sequence. Parsons (op. cit.) holds that these four elements are common not only to psychotherapy but to all measures of social control.

19. Parsons, op. cit., p. 314. Cf. loc. cit., chap. 10.

20. Cf. Parsons, op. cit., chap. 7. Parsons notes that in any social-control action the aim is to avoid the process of alienation, that "vicious-cycle" phenomenon whereby each step taken to curb the non-conforming activity of the deviant has the effect of driving him further into his pattern of deviance. Rather, the need is to "reach" the deviant and bring him back to the point where he is susceptible to the usual everyday informal sanctions.

21. J. H. M. Beattie, "Informal Judicial Activity in Bunyoro," *Journal of African Administration,* vol. ix, 1957, pp. 188–95.

22. Disputes include matters such as a son seducing his father's wives, a grown son disobeying his father, or a husband or wife failing in his or her duties to a spouse. Disputes between unrelated persons involve matters like quarrelling, abuse, assault, false accusations, petty theft, adultery, and failure to settle debts. (Ibid., p. 190.)

23. Ibid., p. 194.

24. Beattie, op. cit., p. 194.

25. Ibid., p. 193.

26. Ibid., p. 195. Moreover, Beattie also recognizes the functional significance of the Nyoro moots, for he notes that: "It would be a serious error to represent them simply as clumsy, 'amateur' expedients for punishing wrong-doers or settling civil disputes at an informal, sub-official level." (Ibid.)

27. The type of examination of case materials that is required demands that field workers should not simply record cases that meet the "trouble case" criterion (cf. K. N. Llewellyn and E. A. Hoebel, *The Cheyenne Way,* Norman, Okla., University of Oklahoma Press, 1941; and E. A. Hoebel, *The Law of Primitive Man,* Cambridge, Mass., Harvard University Press, 1954), but that cases should be recorded in some transcript-like form.

28. The present study has attempted to add to our understanding of informal dispute-settlement procedures in one African society by using an eclectic but organized collection of concepts from jurisprudence, ethno-law, and psychology. It is based on the detailed and systematic analysis of a few selected cases, rather than a mass of quantitative data. In further research a greater variety of cases handled by Kpelle moots should be subjected to the same analysis to test its merit more fully.

34

Contemporary Warfare
in the New Guinea Highlands

Aaron Podolefsky

Within political units—whether tribes or nations—there are well-established mechanisms for handling conflict nonviolently. Anthropologists have described a wide range of conflict resolution mechanisms within societies. Between politically autonomous groups, however, few mechanisms exist. Consequently, uncontained conflict may expand into armed aggression—warfare. In both primitive and modern forms, warfare always causes death, destruction, and human suffering. It is certainly one of the major problems confronting humankind.

New Guinea highlanders can tell you why they go to war—to avenge ghosts or to exact revenge for the killing of one of their own. As we have seen in previous selections, people do not seem to comprehend the complex interrelationship among the various parts of their own social system. Throughout the world, anthropologists find that people do not fathom the causes of their own social behavior. If they did, finding solutions would certainly be a far simpler matter.

The leaders of Papua New Guinea see intertribal fighting as a major social problem with severe economic consequences. Although fighting itself may be age-old, the reemergence of warfare in this area in the 1970s appears to have a new set of causes. In this selection, Aaron Podolefsky shows how the introduction of Western goods may have inadvertently resulted in

changes in economic arrangements, marriage patterns, and, ultimately, warfare.

As you read this selection, ask yourself the following questions:

- What is the theoretical orientation (research strategy) of this paper?
- When did tribal fighting reemerge as a national problem in New Guinea?
- How did intertribal marriage constrain the expansion of minor conflict into warfare?
- How has the rate of intertribal marriage changed? Why did it change?
- How are the introduction of Western goods, trade, marriage, and warfare interrelated?

The following terms discussed in this selection are included in the Glossary at the back of the book:

affinal kin	hypothesis
aggression	lineage
agnates	multiplex relationships
blood relatives	pacification
cross-cutting ties	tribe
cultural materialism	

From *Ethnology*, 1984. Reprinted by permission of *Ethnology*.

After decades of pacification and relative peace, intergroup warfare reemerged in the Papua New Guinea highlands during the late 1960s and early 1970s, only a few years before national independence in 1975. Death and destruction, martial law, and delay

in highlands development schemes have been the outcome.

Most explanations of the resurgence either posit new causes (such as psychological insecurity surrounding political independence from Australian rule or disappointment at the slow speed of development) or attribute the increased fighting to relaxation of government controls which suppressed fighting since the pacification process began. None of the explanations thus far advanced has looked at changes in the structure or infrastructure of highlands societies themselves which could account for behavioral changes in the management of conflict.

This paper employs a cultural materialist strategy in which the efficacy of explanatory models are ranked: infrastructure, structure, and superstructure.[1] From a macrosociological perspective, infrastructural changes unintentionally induced during the colonial era resulted in changes in the structural relations between groups. These changes reduced existing (albeit weak) indigenous mechanisms constraining conflict. Traditionally, groups maintained differential access to resources such as stone used for axes and salt. Axe heads and salt were produced in local areas and traded for valuables available elsewhere. I argue that the introduction and distribution of items such as salt and steel axes reduced the necessity for trade, thereby altering the need for intertribal marriage as well as reducing extratribal contacts of a type which facilitated marriage between persons of different tribes. The reduction of intertribal marriage, over time, resulted in a decay of the web of affinal and nonagnatic kin ties which had provided linkages between otherwise autonomous tribal political units. Thus, the resurgence of tribal fighting is, in part, a result of the reduction of constraints which might otherwise have facilitated the containment of conflict rather than its expansion into warfare. This view sees warfare as one possible end result of a process of conflict management.

An advantage of this strategy is that it suggests a testable hypothesis which runs counter to conventional wisdom and informed opinion that the rate of intertribal marriage would increase after pacification. Some researchers believed that once tribal fighting ended men would be able to wander farther afield and develop relationships with single teenage girls over a wide area. Pacification, then, might reasonably be expected to result in an increase in intertribal marriage. An increase or lack of change in the rate of intergroup marriage since contact would invalidate the explanation. The hypothesis will be tested on data collected in the Gumine District, Simbu (formerly Chimbu) Province, Papua New Guinea.

BACKGROUND

Warfare in traditional highlands societies has been regarded as chronic, incessant, or endemic, and is said to have been accepted as a part of social living in most areas. Indeed, the pattern of warfare was one of the most continuous and violent on record.

However, hostilities were neither random nor did highlanders live in a perpetual state of conflict with all surrounding groups. Some neighboring groups maintained relations of permanent hostility and had little to do with one another. In contrast, most neighboring tribes intermarried and attended one another's ceremonies.

Pacification was an early goal of the colonial administration. By the end of the 1930s fighting was rare in the vicinity of Simbu province government stations. By 1940 Australian authority was accepted and attacks on strangers and tribal fighting had nearly ended, although the entire highlands was not pacified until the 1960s. This period also witnessed the introduction of Western goods such as salt and the steel axe.

Change came quickly to New Guinea. Sterling writes in 1943: "Headhunters and cannibals a generation ago, most of the natives of British New Guinea have now become so accustomed to the ways of the whites that they have been trained as workers and even to assist in administering the white man's law."

From the end of World War II through the 1970s, educational and business opportunities expanded, local government and village courts were introduced, and national self-government was attained in 1975. Highlanders came to expect that development would lead to material gains.[2]

Tribal warfare began to reemerge as a significant national problem in about 1970, five years before independence. By 1973 the government had become concerned that the situation might deteriorate to a point that they could no longer effectively administer parts of the highlands. In 1972, according to government report, 28 incidents involving 50 or more persons were reported in the Western Highlands District. A decade later, Bill Wormsley (1982) reports 60 fights per year in the Enga Province (the figures are of course not directly comparable). Although the level of fighting declined in Enga during 1980 due to the declaration of a state of emergency, it increased again in 1981 and 1982. Martial law has also been declared in the Simbu Province. Deaths lead to payback killing and to demands for compensation payments. Inflated demands for "excess" compensation further compound the problem.

Of the five major theories of warfare outlined by Koch in 1974 (biological evolution, psychological theories, cultural evolution, ecological adaptation, and social-structure analysis), scholars have used only psychological theories and social-structural analysis to explain the recent emergence of tribal warfare.

Some researchers favor explanations which combine the traditional cultural heritage of violence with issues in development. Others seem to argue that the problem lies in the Enga's perception that the government, especially the courts, has become weaker and that this had led to the breakdown in law and order. Rob Gordon notes, however, that the police force in Enga has increased from 72 in 1970 to 300 in 1981, and that the average sentence for riotous behavior has grown from 3 months in 1970 to 9.6 months in 1978–9 with no apparent deterrent effect. Kiaps (field officers), Gordon suggests, have in fact lost power for several reasons. Most interesting from the perspective of the present analysis involves the kiaps' loss of control over access to goods. He (1983:209) states that "The importance that the Enga attach to trade-goods should not be underestimated." An old Engan is quoted as saying "The first Kiaps gave beads, salt, steel axes— everyone wanted it so they all followed the Kiap and stopped fighting. We stopped fighting because we did not want to lose the source of these things." I would add that once they "followed the kiaps" for these goods, previous important trade relations no longer needed to be kept up. In a 1980 study, Gordon also acknowledges problems created by intergroup suspicion, generational conflict exacerbated by education, and decline in men's houses and clan meetings. Similarly, Paula Brown (1982a) believes that pacification was a temporary effect in which fighting was suppressed. The Simbu do not see the government as holding power.

Explanations also combine development problems with psychologically oriented theories. Contemporary violence is sometimes thought to be a protest rising out of psychological strain created by the drastic social change of an imposed economic and political system. In a 1973 paper Bill Standish describes the period leading up to independence as one of stress, tension, and insecurity. He argues that the fighting is an expression of primordial attachments in the face of political insecurity surrounding national independence from Australian colonial rule. Paula Brown (1982a, 1982b) suggests that during the colonial period expectations for the future included security, wealth, and the improvement of life. "Disappointment that these goals have not been realized is expressed in disorder." She suggests that what is needed is a political movement rather than the imposition of Western institutions and suppression of fighting.

The present paper cannot and does not formally refute any of these explanations. Indeed, some make a great deal of sense and fill in part of a very complex picture. However, it is difficult to evaluate the validity of these explanations since very little data are presented. For example, Standish (1973) presents no evidence to assess whether, in fact, the level of stress has changed over time (precontact, postcontact, or independence era), or whether stress is associated with fighting or even with differential levels of awareness about independence, the latter likely expressing itself

geographically around centers of population and development.

ETHNOGRAPHIC BACKGROUND— THE MUL COMMUNITY

Mul lies approximately 3 miles east of the Gumine District Headquarters and 32 miles south of Kundiawa, the capital of the Simbu province. The Gumine patrol post was established in 1954. During the early 1960s a dirt road was constructed linking Gumine to the capital and within a few years the road was extended through Mul. Lying at an elevation of about 5,500 feet, Mul is the central portion of a larger tribal territory which extends steeply from the southern edge of the Marigl Gorge to elevations of 8 to 9,000 feet.

The area is densely populated. Land is either cultivated or fallow in grass or scrub regrowth. Individually owned trees are scattered and there are a yearly increasing number of coffee trees. With 295 persons per square mile on cultivatable land, this density is high compared with other highland groups (see Brown and Podolefsky 1976).

The people of Mul are Simbus. Social relations and cultural patterns follow in most important respects those extensively documented by Paula Brown in numerous publications. I will describe here only those dimensions of organization most directly relevant to the resurgence of tribal fighting.

Mul residents trace kinship through males, and their social groupings are patrilineal. Hierarchical segments link themselves as father/son, while parallel segments are seen as brothers. Individuals, however, are less concerned with this overall construct and tend to interact in terms of group composition and alignments. The likelihood of an individual conflict escalating into warfare is directly related to the structural distance between conflicting parties.

The largest political group to unite in warfare is the tribe, a group of several thousand individuals. Tribes are segmented into clans whose members see themselves as a unified group. Generally, individually owned plots of land tend to cluster and people can point out rough boundaries between adjacent clans. Plots of land belonging to members of a particular subclan tend to cluster within the clan area. The subclan section (or one-blood group) is the first to mobilize for warfare. The potential for expansion of such conflicts depends to a large degree on whether the relative position of the groups in the segmentary system lends itself to opposing alignments at the higher levels of segmentation and upon the past relations between the groups.

Unlike subclan sections in most highlands societies there is no restriction upon fighting between sections of the subclan. Within the subclan section, however, there are moral restrictions on internal fighting. If comembers become extremely angry they may attack with fists, clubs, or staffs, but not with axes, arrows, or spears. These restrictions are related to the notion that members of the subclan have "one-blood," and that this common blood should not be shed.

Segmentary principles operate in situations of cooperation as well as conflict. Members of a subclan section may enclose garden plots within a single fence and cooperate in the construction of men's houses. Brown (1970:99–103) similarly notes that in the central Simbu transactions between clans and tribes are competitive while those within the clan are reciprocal. Generally speaking, in terms of proximity of land holdings and residence, cooperation in gardening and house construction and the willingness to unite in common defense and ceremonial exchange, the solidarity of a social group is inversely related to the position in the segmentary hierarchy.

Cross-cutting these segmentary principles are a variety of interpersonal ties (e.g., affinal and other non-agnatic relations, exchange ties and personal friendships) which affect behavior in conflict situations. It is these ephemeral or transitory linkages which provide the avenues through which structurally autonomous tribal groups interact.

MARRIAGE AND WARFARE

Marriage and warfare are linked in the minds of New Guinea highlanders. Early writers report indigenous notions that highlanders marry their enemies. The Siane say, "They are our affinal relatives; with them we fight" (Salisbury 1962:25). Enga informants report, "We marry those whom we fight" (Meggitt 1958:278). In an extensive study of Enga warfare, Meggitt (1977: 42) supports these assertions by reporting quite strong correlations between rates of intergroup marriage and killing.

While there is little doubt that there is a strong association between marriage and warfare, it is not clear at all that they are causally related in any direct fashion, i.e., warfare causing marriage or marriage causing warfare. It is highly unlikely that warfare causes marriage. Researchers have noted the difficulty in arranging marriages between hostile groups. It is similarly unlikely that marriage causes warfare (although exceptions can certainly be pointed out). While disputes may arise between bride and groom or their families, the relations are generally highly valued and long term. The association between mar-

riage and warfare can be reduced to two separate relationships. First, highlanders most frequently marry their neighbors. Second, highlanders most frequently go to war with their neighbors. This is because in the highlands, where travel is restricted and relations are multiplex, neighbors are the parties most likely to be involved in a dispute. Thus propinquity is causally related to both marriage and warfare; the positive correlation between marriage and warfare is spurious. Indeed, the essence of the argument made here is that if other variables could be "controlled" the association between warfare and marriage would in fact be negative.

The notion that there is no direct (as opposed to inverse) causal relationship between warfare and marriage is critical. Warfare results from precipitating disputes in the absence of sufficiently powerful third party mechanisms and other constraints which control the dispute. One dimension of constraint stems from marriage links.

In her paper "Enemies and Affines," Paula Brown (1964) carefully describes the relevant social relations among the central Simbu. During wedding ceremonies speeches proclaim that the groups of the bride and groom (consisting of subclansmen, some clansmen, kin, and affines) should remain on friendly terms and exchange visits and food. The marriage creates individual ties and obligations outside the clan which, while not institutionalized, are not wholly voluntary. At various stages in the life cycle payments are obligatory. Given the widely documented emphasis on transaction in highlands social relations, it is important to note that whenever a formal food presentation occurs between clans, the donors and recipients are related to one another through marriage. Extratribal relatives play an important role in conflict situations.

> The prevailing hostility between neighboring tribes gives extratribal relatives a special complex role. Men try not to injure their close kin and affines in any conflict between their agnatic group and the group of their relatives, but they may not attempt to prevent or stop hostilities. In any dealings between neighboring tribes, men with connections in both take a leading part; their political sphere of action encompasses both. When intermediaries and peacemakers are required these men are active (Brown 1964:348).

Thus, in Central Simbu, affines played some role in attempting to prevent warfare and were important in restoring peace. No amount of oral history data will tell us how many wars did not occur due to efforts made through these channels. Nor can such data tell us how many wars were shorter or less intense than they would have been had there been fewer cross-cutting ties. The importance of cross-cutting ties is recognized among the densely populated Enga.

TABLE 1   Marriage Ties by Time Period

	Before Contact		After Contact	
	N	%	N	%
Between tribes	85	75%	30	40%
Within tribes	29	25%	44	60%
Total	114	100%	74	100%

chi squared = 21.86 1 df

p < 0.001 (one tail)

phi = .341

Even while or after two men or groups fight over an issue, others may intervene to urge negotiation and compromise. . . . Whether, however, noncombatants initiate some kind of conciliation or simply stand by and watch the fighting spread depends on a complex set of conditions . . . relevant factors . . . include, for instance, the importance traditionally ascribed to the object in contention (is it a pig or a sweet potato garden?), the number of antagonists, the kinship, affinal, or exchange connections among some or all of them, and between them and interested noncombatants (Meggitt 1977:12).

Moreover, the frequency of intergroup marriage is related to the expansion or containment of a dispute. That is, the more intermarriage the greater the chance that disputes will be handled without violence or that the violence can be contained.

Especially within the tribe, the supporters of each party include men with affines on the other side, most of whom are on good terms with their in-laws and have no wish to offend them. In such cases some men stay out of the fight while others, while participating, avoid meeting their affines in combat. This may serve to confine interclan conflict. Between tribes, similar serious disputes can more easily lead to fighting because fewer men have close ties which restrain them from supporting their fellow tribesmen (Brown 1964:352).

In sum, while there is an apparent correlation between marriage and warfare, marriage, in fact, establishes a social relationship which acts primarily as a constraint upon the expansion of a dispute. Second, as Meggitt suggests, it is not merely the marriage ties between the two groups, but also between them and their allies, i.e., the web of affinal relations. Third, the frequency of marriage, or density of the web, is related to efficacy of conflict management processes.

CHANGING PATTERN OF INTERTRIBAL MARRIAGE

A null hypothesis that the proportion of intertribal marriages has gone up or remained the same can be

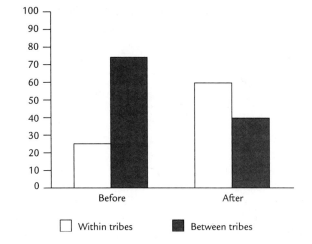

FIGURE 1   Percentage of Marriage Ties

rejected ($p < 0.001$) on the basis of the data shown in Table 1. Thus, we tend to believe, based upon these data, that there has in fact been an overall decline in intertribal marriage.

The data reveal a statistically significant change in the marriage pattern in the anticipated direction. Figure 1 describes the proportion of marriage ties within and between tribes, before and after Western influence. Comparing the intertribal (between) and intratribal (within) marriage rates in the precontact sample (labeled before), we see that intertribal marriage was nearly three times as frequent as intratribal marriage. Of the 114 marriage ties recorded in the precontact sample, 85 (75 percent) were between members of different tribes while only 29 (25 percent) were within the tribe. This allowed for a dense network of affinal ties between autonomous political groups. In the recent postcontact period (labeled after), in contrast, the number of intertribal marriages drops below the number of intratribal marriages. Of the 74 marriage ties in the postcontact sample, only 30 (40 percent) were between persons of different tribes while 44 (60 percent) were within the tribe. The intertribal marriage rate in the recent period is nearly half that of the precontact period.

The argument presented in this paper is that the dramatic reduction of intertribal marriage rates had significant implications for the structure of relations between politically autonomous tribal groups.

A Secondary Analysis

Sometimes it is possible to replicate one's findings by performing a secondary analysis on data collected by other researchers.

In 1964, Paula Brown published data on the marriage of some men in the Naregu tribe who live in the

TABLE 2 Marriages of Some Men in the Naregu Tribe

	Pre-1930 (Before)		Post-1930 (After)	
	N	%	N	%
Between tribes	154	60%	130	47%
Within tribes	102	40%	144	53%
Total	256	100%	274	100%

chi squared = 8.597 1 df

p < 0.005 (one tail)

phi = .1272

central Simbu near the capital of Kundiawa. Data for two clans are divided into previous generations (prior to 1930) and present generation. Brown's categories for marriage ties may be collapsed to match those used above.

What should we expect, a priori? Since Brown did not arrange the data to address this particular question, we expect some differences. Her temporal dichotomy is previous and present generation rather than before and after contact. Europeans did not reach this area until the mid-1930s and Brown's data are dichotomized at 1930. This means that precontact marriages are included in the present generation sample. Neither do Brown's data allow for a decade of transition. Based upon these differences in the data sets, we would expect the difference between the previous and present samples to be less extreme than the difference between the before and after sample in the Mul data (i.e., we expect a lower measure of association).

The data in Table 2 reveal a statistically significant change in the marriage pattern, although the association is lower (as we expected it would be) than in Mul. The between-tribe marriage rate (in the sample) dropped from 60 to 47 percent. This change was sufficient to draw Brown's attention. While the analysis fits our predictions, we cannot be certain that the change in marriage pattern observed by Paula Brown in central Simbu represents the same process occurring in Mul nearly twenty years later. Nevertheless, the analysis is intriguing. I think Brown was observing the initial stages of a process of change initiated by a reduction in the necessity for trade.[3]

TRADE AND MARRIAGE

Given the conventional wisdom that pacification would lead to greater intertribal contact and, therefore, an increase in the rate of intertribal marriage, it remains to be explained why the proportion of inter-

tribal marriages decreased. In other words, what forces or situations affected the marriage pattern?

Interviews with young men of marriageable age and some of the oldest men in the community elicited two different perspectives. (Unfortunately, it was not possible for me, being a male, to maintain serious conversation with women on this topic.) Young men typically explained that they do not find wives from other areas because they are "tired"; they just do not have any desire to travel the long distances to visit women of other areas when there are women close at hand. This emic explanation is not particularly satisfactory from an anthropological perspective.

While the older men could not explain why the distribution of marriages in their younger days differed from that of more recent years, they were able to describe the ways young men and women met prospective spouses from other tribes prior to the coming of Europeans scarcely twenty years earlier. The old men reported that when they were young trade was very important. Salt, stone axes, bird of paradise feathers, shells of different kinds, pandanus oil, carpul fur, and the like were traded between tribes during trading expeditions. Figure 2 maps the trade network as described by the older residents of Mul.

When they were young, the old men reported, they would dress in their finest decorations and travel to the places described in Figure 2. The women at these places, they said, would see them arrayed in all their finery and want to marry them. Of course, the situation may not have been quite this straightforward.

These reports drew my attention to the link between intertribal marriage and trade for scarce necessary and luxury resources. What would be the effect of the introduction of European goods upon trade? And, could this affect marriage patterns?

According to the old men, pigs from Mul were traded south to the lower elevation, less densely populated areas in return for bird of paradise feathers and carpul fur (see Figure 2). Some of the fur and feathers were traded for cowrie shells with people from Sina. Cowries, in turn, were traded to the Gomgales for kina shells. Carpul fur and pandanus oil were traded to the east for salt. Finally, some of the fur and feathers obtained from the south and the salt obtained from the east were traded to the northeast for stone axes and small shells, which had in turn been brought in from even further off.

Enter the ubiquitous steel axe; exit the stone axe. No one in Mul today would use a stone axe. Indeed, it was difficult to find someone who recalled how to attach stone to handle. The effect was that the primary reason for trade between the peoples of Mul and Era (i.e., the need for stone axes) was eliminated and the Muls' need for fur, feathers, and salt was reduced

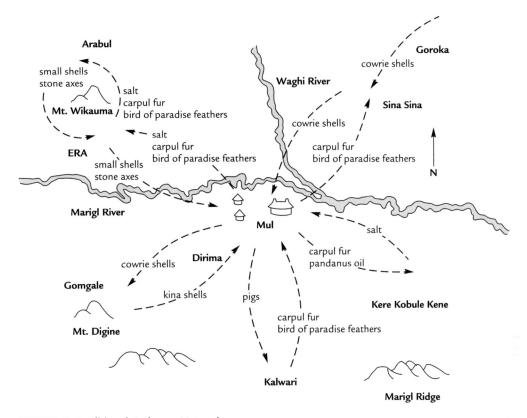

FIGURE 2 Traditional Exchange Network

(what may have begun to increase was a need for cash). Similarly, salt increasingly became more readily available. Nowadays it can be purchased at the store on the government station or in small trade stores which stock, for example, three bags of salt, two packs of cigarettes, a bit of rice, and two or three tins of mackerel. The availability of salt locally eliminates the need to trade for it and further reduces the need for fur. Thus, two of the five trade routes shown on Figure 2 become totally unnecessary and the usefulness of trade items from a third is reduced.

The elimination of the need to trade for necessary scarce resources allowed some trade relations to atrophy. I use the term *atrophy* since the process was probably one of gradual disuse of trade networks rather than a catastrophic change. The remaining trade relations were reliant upon the need for luxury items such as shells and feathers. Scholars who have done long-term research in New Guinea have described the highlanders' declining interest in these decorative items.

With the introduction of Western goods and the reduction of trade, both the need and the opportunity for intermarriage declined. Intertribal marriage was functional in that it facilitated intergroup economic transactions. While there are a range of rights and obligations as well as affective ties which make marriage into neighboring groups preferable, more distant marriages have recognized importance. This same point was made by Roy Rappaport in his study of the Tsembaga Maring:

> While unions between men and women of a single local group are generally preferred, the Tsembaga recognize certain advantages in marriage to members of other local groups . . . unions with groups north of the Sambai River and south of the Bismarks strengthen trading relationships. Bird-of-paradise plumes and shell ornaments are still obtained from these groups and until the 1950s stone axes from the Jimi Valley were traded for salt manufactured in the Simbai Valley (1969:121).

An early paper on the Siani linked trade and marriage directly by focusing on the exchange of nonutilitarian valuables which occurred at marriage and at the rites of passage for children of the marriage (Salisbury 1956). Valuables were traded in from the coast about 70 miles to the northeast. Trading took the form of ceremonial gift exchange between affines. At the same time, Salisbury reports a statistically significant trend for Siane men to obtain wives from the south and west while their sisters marry into groups from the north and east (the direction from which valuables come).

Even more interesting for the present purpose is Salisbury's report on the effect of the introduction of

European wealth goods. The European settlements nearest the Siane were in Goroka and Asaroka, 30 miles to the east and north. Groups nearest these (who were already closer than the Siane to coastal wealth) quickly became wealthy in shells, cloth, and other European goods. Salisbury reports that, as a result of this increased wealth, the movement of women in that direction became more pronounced. He also notes that "Neither the wealth difference nor the movement of women is recognized in Siane ideology."

Thus, Salisbury clearly links marriage patterns to the need to obtain wealth not locally available, although no mention is made of utilitarian goods. While the initial response to "wealthy neighbors" is to increase "wife giving," it is easy to see that once wealth is more evenly (and locally) distributed this reason for marrying out will no longer be of major consequence.

Particularly in the many areas of the highlands where marriages were arranged by families with minimal, if any, consultation with the bride or groom, consideration of trade relations was likely to play a role in the selection of a spouse. Families had an interest in the establishment or maintenance of trade relations.

At the same time that the function of intertribal marriage for maintaining the economic system in terms of access to necessary resources was eliminated, the decline in trade itself reduced the opportunity to make marriage arrangements between non-adjacent groups. Generally speaking, opportunity for marriage is not random but may be structured by factors such as class, caste, religious affiliation, sorority membership, or political borders. Changes in this structure of opportunity may lead to observable changes in marriage patterns. In other words, a change in the visiting (or trading) pattern between autonomous political groups could affect the structure of opportunity. The importance of opportunity remains whether the individuals are free to choose their own mates or whether such choices are made for them.

In central Simbu elders choose a person's spouse for them and, although they can refuse, the bride and groom usually accept even though they may never have met. Brown (1969) reports that some groups do not intermarry because of the lack of opportunity to make arrangements.

Administrative policy and mission influence may have speeded the process. In some areas, such as South Fore or Manga, Australian patrol officers insisted (or at least strongly urged) that brides consent and that women have a right to choose a spouse. Nowadays in central Simbu more marriages are being initiated by the couples themselves. Choice in a mate is likely to further increase the importance of the structure of opportunity.

In sum, the argument here is that the replacement, by Western goods, of resources secured through trade reduced the economic need (function) for intergroup marriage and the opportunity to arrange such marriages. The effects of these changes were not felt immediately because of the extant relations between groups. Over time fewer and fewer intertribal marriages were arranged to replace those of the passing generation. The net effect was a gradual decay of the web of affinal and non-agnatic ties which cut across tribal boundaries.

CONCLUSION

Gordon (1980) has insightfully pointed out that there is very little sense in talking about or planning development if people live in fear of renewed tribal fighting. Moreover, he notes that this is a testing time for anthropologists "who find that their explanatory models are somewhat inadequate." Indeed, few of the explanations begin from a particular theoretical position nor even a unified conceptual model; there is little discussion of the mechanisms by which suggested "causes" result in the behavior being explained; and, little evidence is presented to test the explanations.

In this paper, I have employed a particular theoretic strategy, namely, cultural materialism, in which the efficacy of explanatory models are ranked: infrastructure, structure, and superstructure.

Prior to contact with the outside world, stone axe heads and salt were produced in local areas where these resources were available. Redistribution was accomplished through trade. One of the functions of intertribal marriage was the facilitation of trade between autonomous political groups. With the early introduction of Western goods, particularly steel axes and salt, local production was discontinued and marriage was no longer necessary to maintain these trade relations. As trade was discontinued, so declined the opportunity to make marriage arrangements between non-adjacent groups. Of course, existing marriage ties facilitated continued contact between groups, but probably less frequently, and there was no pragmatic reason for young people to marry others from distant areas. Particularly in the case of women, where such a marriage necessitated a move far from her natal family, there were distinct disadvantages. Thus, as older people died and fewer marriages were arranged between groups, the web of affinal and non-agnatic kin ties decayed. Intertribal marriages provided a linkage through which groups could communicate, and a mechanism and reason for containing conflict. With the decline in intergroup marriage over time, the likelihood of a dispute expanding into full-scale warfare increased.

This explanation began with infrastructural conditions (production) and showed how they were causally related to structural changes (trade relations) which in turn caused further structural changes (the web of kin ties), finally leading to changes in conflict behaviors. I have tried to explain each of the stages in this temporal process, i.e., the relationship between trade and marriage and the relationship between marriage and warfare.

Scientific hypotheses and models can be tested by examining predictions which can be deduced from them. The model which I have outlined predicts the unlikely occurrence that, with pacification and the ability to wander further afield without the threat of life and limb, intertribal marriage actually declined rather than rose as was thought would be the case. The hypothesis was tested on genealogical data collected in this research site as well as on data published earlier from a different area of the Simbu province. This is but a single case study and there is no statistical reason to extend the findings to other areas of the highlands. However, the inability to falsify the hypothesis in this case lends support to the general efficacy of the explanation.

NOTES

1. Financial support from the National Science Foundation (Grant No. BNS76-218 37) is gratefully acknowledged.

2. For a more extensive discussion of this period with special reference to the resurgence of fighting, see Brown 1982a and 1982b.

3. Paula Brown reports (pers. comm.) that recently many Simbu women are marrying outside the Simbu to men they had met in the district or on visits. She notes that there are, now, advantages for older men having a daughter married to a prestigious outsider. Naregu men who migrate probably also marry outsiders.

    Such marriages further the process described here since, although they are extra-tribal, they do not link neighboring potential enemy groups.

REFERENCES

Brown, P. 1964. Enemies and Affines. *Ethnology* 3:335–356.

——. 1969. Marriage in Chimbu. In R. M. Glasse and M. Meggitt (eds.), *Pigs, Pearlshells and Women*, pp. 77–95. Englewood Cliffs, NJ: Prentice-Hall.

——. 1970. Chimbu Transactions. *Man* 5:99–117.

——. 1982a. Conflict in the New Guinea Highlands. *Journal of Conflict Resolution* 26:525–546.

——. 1982b. Chimbu Disorder: Tribal Fighting in Newly Independent Papua New Guinea. *Pacific Viewpoint* 22:1–21.

Brown, P. and A. M. Podolefsky. 1976. Population Density, Agricultural Intensity, Land Tenure, and Group Size in the New Guinea Highlands. *Ethnology* 15:211–238.

Gordon, R. 1980. Rituals of Governance and the Breakdown of Law and Order in Papua New Guinea. Paper presented at the annual meeting of the American Anthropological Association. Washington, D.C.

——. 1983. The Decline of the Kiapdom and the Resurgence of "Tribal Fighting" in Enga. *Oceania* 53:205–223.

Howlett, D., et al. 1976. *Chimbu: Issues in Development*. Development Studies Centre Monograph No. 4 Canberra.

Koch, K. 1974. *The Anthropology of Warfare*. Addison-Wesley Module in Anthropology No. 52.

Meggitt, M. 1958. The Enga of the New Guinea Highlands. *Oceania* 28:253–330.

——. 1977. *Blood Is Their Argument: Warfare Among the Mae Enga Tribesmen of the New Guinea Highlands*. Palo Alto, CA: Mayfield.

Rappaport, R. 1969. Marriage Among the Maring. In R. M. Glasse and M. Meggitt (eds.), *Pigs, Pearlshells and Women*, pp. 117–137. Englewood Cliffs, NJ: Prentice-Hall.

Salisbury, R. F. 1956. Asymmetrical Marriage Systems. *American Anthropologist* 58:639–655.

——. 1962. *From Stone to Steel*. London: Cambridge University Press.

Standish, B. 1973. The Highlands. *New Guinea* 8:4–30.

Wormsley, W. 1982. Tribal Fighting, Law and Order, and Socioeconomic Development in Enga, Papua New Guinea. Paper presented at the meeting of the American Anthropological Association. Washington, D.C.

35

The Power of Islam

Lincoln Keiser

We begin this section on religion, ritual, and curing with a selection describing the way Islam, one of the world's great religions, is interpreted in a geographic region of particular contemporary interest—the borderlands between Afghanistan and Pakistan. The setting is Thull, a Kohistani tribal community of 6,000 people in the Hindu-Kush mountains of Pakistan on the northeastern border of Afghanistan.

This selection, and the book from which it is drawn, focus on what is called *death enmity* (blood vengeance or death vengeance) and how it defines relationships within the Thull community. In Thull, a man's most prized possession may be his expensive, Russian-made AK-47. And death may result from the most innocent affront to a man's honor or his integrity. Staring at another man's wife, daughter, or marriageable-age sister demands the offender's death.

Those who know orthodox Islam may be surprised that anyone could possibly believe that death vengeance constitutes religious piety. Islam neither advocates violence nor condones murder. Yet, the men of Thull, following their particular version of Islamic ideology, argue that taking vengeance is a religious act.

Although competing ethnic (tribal) groups have long been a key element in traditional Kohistani society, the obsession with death vengeance developed as a central tenet of Thull social organization only in the last few decades, the same period that witnessed economic and political modernization. As global powers like the Soviet Union, and now the United States, have become involved in warfare in Afghanistan, there have been new, more complex, and more deadly social stressors.

As we know all too well since the devastation of September 11, 2001, the doctrine of death vengeance associated with some versions of Islam has become a national and international concern. Awareness of other core principles—such as the obligation to give refuge to anyone (even a mortal enemy) asking for it—help us comprehend the impact of culture on complex and inscrutable current events.

As you read this selection, ask yourself the following questions:

- How difficult was it for Keiser to gain permission to live in Thull and gain acceptance in the community? Explain why this was the case, and how it was overcome.

- What is the first, most fundamental component of Islamic faith, and what is the minimal obligation for believers? What are the "five pillars" of Islam?

- What things are forbidden to Islamic women and why? How does the honor of women affect the status of a man in the community?

- How are honor and integrity related to revenge and death enmity? How do these ideas fit with the Kohistani tribal code of conduct?

The following terms discussed in this selection are included in the Glossary at the back of the book:

infidel	*mosque*
Islam	*Muslim*
Koran	

Visitors to Thull see mosques everywhere they look. I counted eighteen but was never certain I had found them all. They range from simple wooden platforms scattered along the road and next to the river, to ornately decorated buildings situated at the center of settlement clusters. In the plains beneath the Malakand Pass villagers construct concrete mosques, but in Kohistan men build mosques primarily of wood and stone. The roof of the community's central mosque, located in the core settlement (called "Thull Proper," using a borrowed English word), rests on

Reprinted with permission from *Friend by Day, Enemy by Night: Organized Vengeance in a Kohistani Community.* Wadsworth (original Holt, Rinehart & Winston) © 1991, pp. 29–43.

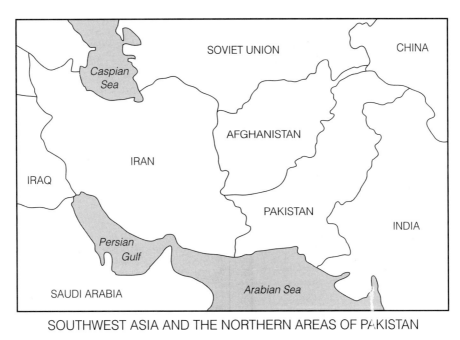

SOUTHWEST ASIA AND THE NORTHERN AREAS OF PAKISTAN

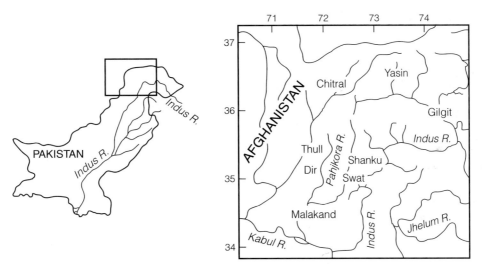

gigantic wood columns covered with carved geometric figures of fantastic design.

From the central mosque one can easily find the low one-story house, whose considerable size distinguishes it from its neighbors. In this building resides one of the most influential religious leaders in Thull, a learned Muslim scholar who teaches Islamic faith in the local primary school. He wields considerable power in community affairs because of his reputation for religious learning and piety. The building's large, flat roof, called *torwalo shan* ("Torwal's roof") after its original builder, provides a site for town meetings and is a constant reminder of the political vigor of Islam. Indeed Islam lies over, under, in front of, behind, around, and beyond society and culture in Thull; nothing escapes its sway.

I first saw *torwalo shan* during my initial visit to Thull, when I attended a town council (*jirga*), an unfor-

gettable experience, to say the least. Dilaram Sher and Gul Shah, two important town leaders, called the meeting to decide whether I could reside in the community. Both men stand out because of their openness to contacts with the outside world. Dilaram Sher's lucrative timber business requires that he develop and maintain relations with government bureaucrats. Frequent business trips outside Thull gave him a taste for cosmopolitan ideas and imported consumer goods. He once appeared at my door, sporting an AK-47 assault rifle, a fishing rod, a camera, a bandolier of bullets, and a thermos jug with the smile logo and English motto "Have a Happy Day" printed on its front. Gul Shah's reputation comes from his learning, intelligence, reputation for religious piety, and his wealth. He continually searches for ways to tear down barriers and in the process open Thull to the wider pan-Islamic community. Both men are "progressives" in their own way, dedicated to changing Thull; both sponsored me because of their connections to my government sponsors outside the community.

Over four hundred men attended, most squatting on their haunches (with their heels flat to the ground) in rows lined on three sides of the roof. Gul Shah and Dilaram Sher led my research assistant, Shahid Mahmood, and me to a row of chairs facing the crowd. No one smiled, at least no one I could see, many scowled, and some even spat on the ground in my general direction. I was unnerved to say the least, feeling like a lost sheep in a wolf pack. From that inauspicious beginning, events rapidly proceeded downhill. Dilaram Sher's short opening speech preceded Gul Shah's more lengthy oration. Later I learned that Dilaram Sher had introduced my request, whereas Gul Shah had argued its merits. As my friend Anwar explained, "Dilaram Sher shot his rifle from Gul Shah's shoulder." The meeting then opened to general debate. Only grey-bearded men of haughty demeanor spoke. Although I understood no Kohistani at the time, their harsh, bellicose voices and cruel-looking eyes conveyed a world of meaning. I was not surprised, therefore, when Gul Shah turned and said to my assistant in Urdu, "They oppose us. The elders say we should never allow foreigners to live in Thull. *Kafir* (roughly, "infidel") foreigners cannot be trusted. He should not stay."

Shahid, my research assistant, slowly rose to face the crowd and, with his head bowed and his hands outstretched, began to recite the *Kalima*, the Muslim witness to faith. The angry muttering hushed as the beautiful tones of his almost musical chant transformed the moment. When the last words of the sacred text died away, *"Allah Akbar! Allah Akbar! Allah Akbar!"* ("God is great! God is great! God is great!") quietly resonated through the gathering. The tones of voice, expressions of emotion, and body postures appropriate to political debate suddenly became unsuitable, indeed unacceptable. The *Kalima* demanded a new propriety.

A moment of silence passed, and then Shahid began speaking to the gathering in Urdu; Gul Shah translated his words into Kohistani for the benefit of the old men who could not understand. Political oratory constitutes high art in South Asia and Shahid mastered the craft long ago during his days as a student politician. He took the style of extemporaneous speech developed by Muslim fundamentalist preachers as the model for his creation, clothing our request in religion. After introducing each of us, he briefly explained that I wished to study the history and customs of the community. Then he began to construct his major theme, that our living in the village would strengthen Islam. Initially he talked about personal safety. We feared nothing, he said, for our fate, as everyone's fate, lies in the hands of God. Fate deter-

mines life and death, but our honor depends on how we revere God, and respecting God protects our honor. So whether we live or die means nothing. No government, no weapons, no human authority can provide true sanctuary, for one finds that only within God. But we also feared nothing because the people of Thull had a superb reputation for Muslim piety and hospitality. We wished to live in Thull precisely because of the piety of its people, since it made them excellent teachers of religion. Moreover, our learning about Islam would strengthen it. Although others had asked us to live with them, we could learn more about religion in Thull. Finally, the people of Thull would collect God's reward if our living in their community actually strengthened Islam.

Shahid's words ended. After a moment of silence first one, then another, then another, and finally every man attending the meeting waved their hands in unison. Gul Shah leaned toward us and, with a dazed look on his face, said the council had decided we could live in Thull. The clerk for the District Commissioner accompanying us shook his head in disbelief. The men of Thull, he told us, almost never agree to any proposal from outside the community.

The effect of Shahid's speech dramatically introduced me to the power of Islam in Kohistani social relations. Contrary to Shahid's words, most people throughout the Northwest Frontier believe Kohistanis are savages. They judge them as rude barbarians who only recently converted to Islam and practice its tenets poorly at best. The people of Thull know how neighboring ethnic groups judge them. Yet the roots of Kohistani sense of self lie in Muslim identity, and Thull men obsess over demonstrating their Muslim piety. Shahid's speech forced them into a corner with its subtle but clear subtext—namely, everyone knows Muslims have a duty to convert Kafirs to Islam. I wished to live in Thull to learn about Islam. Teaching me Islam would provide an excellent opportunity to convert me. Therefore refusing my request meant refusing to take seriously the responsibility to convert Kafirs and would reconfirm that the people of Thull practice their religion only half-heartedly at best, as their neighbors claimed. Almost the entire male population adamantly opposed my staying in town for more than a short time (and the shorter the better). Yet they could publicly admit to a superficial commitment to Islam only at great personal cost. Shahid had struck at the community's poor reputation for religious piety and subtly played both on their need for others to see them, and their need to see themselves, as good, pious Muslims. Thus I became the first Kafir ever to live in Thull for more than ten days. Unfortunately, in spite of Shahid's best efforts, most people continued to dislike and distrust me. Many never stopped thinking I secretly intended to steal their forest, and some always called me *kafrot*—which stands in relation to Kafir as "spic" stands to Hispanic, and "nigger" stands to Negro. From the beginning I knew I would never make it to honorary-member-of-the-tribe status.

Who cares, though, if anthropologists get ulcers doing research in Thull? And whether religious fanaticism reigns supreme in Kohistan depends on one's perspective. However, looking at my experiences in entering the community makes it easier to understand the impact of Islam on social relations. More to the point, they help us understand its power in shaping death enmity. Although formulated as cultural rules for behavior, Thull's version of Islamic ideology does not determine what its people do in any mechanical fashion. Instead Islam possesses the power to distort action—to bend, twist, unshape, and reshape it. In many instances Islam culturally defines meaningful options. Sometimes it weights these differently so that people pay prices and obtain rewards for choosing to act in particular ways. It also corners people, severely limiting their choices so that their behavior appears almost predetermined. No matter what the actions of people are in Thull, Islam always affects their consequences. Finally, Islam creates and releases powerful emotions, which propel people toward certain behaviors despite personal costs by virtue of the part these play in constructing self.

. . .

THE AXIOMATIC FEATURES OF ISLAM

Islam possesses a simple beauty and exquisite complexity at the same time. I can only describe a small part of Islam here, for volumes fail to treat its subtleties and intricacies in their entirety. I can, however, outline some of the more significant characteristics for the people of Thull, especially those related to *dushmani* [enmity]. I once asked a Kohistani friend to tell me the most important aspects of Islam. He answered, "the *Kalima*, prayer, fast, and faith." These four features make up the heart of Islam in Thull, although others are also meaningful to Kohistanis. And basic to their belief is a conception of God.

God in Thull does not resemble some distant father who rarely sees his children except during Christmas and Easter, or on Sunday morning. No. God in Thull "sticks right in your face." Constantly repeating "Allah" in formal greetings, casual conversations, and even in most arguments makes God's presence a part of everyday reality. His relevancy is overwhelmingly clear to everyone. Additionally Allah does not wear the clothes of a loving parent but appears as an imperious ruler, who demands that his subjects unconditionally submit to his will. Fundamentally

Islam means submission (as well as peace, with the implication that one achieves peace by submitting to God's will).

Submitting to God's will is the first fundamental component of Islamic faith, bearing witness to its central truths the second. One generally bears witness by reciting the lines of the *Kalima*.

> I witness that Allah is the only God.
> I witness that Allah is the only God.
> I witness that Mohammed is his prophet.
> I witness that Mohammed is his prophet.

Reciting the *Kalima* automatically makes one a Muslim, according to the people of Thull. Consequently, when I attempted to elicit Kohistani vocabulary from the village children, they often tried to trick me into converting to Islam by telling me the Arabic words of the *Kalima* instead. Pious Kohistanis keep the *Kalima* close to their lips, for they must continually witness their faith by reciting its words. The constant repetition helps create and recreate Muslim identity, and situates Islam at the center of self.

The *Kalima* forms a pivotal part of Muslim prayer, and praying constitutes the most notable act of submission to God the people of Thull perform. Religious leaders constantly exhort Kohistanis to pray. Mullana Fakir, leader of the largest mosque in Thull, even preaches that men should admonish their wives to pray. "If they don't," he advises, "then beat them. If they still don't, then divorce them."

THE RITUAL OF PRAYER

While reading the following account of Muslim prayer, one might question the need for such detailed ethnographic description. But prayer brings into play dominant symbols and arouses powerful emotions that continually fashion and refashion an organization of self circling Muslim identity. This process is revealed in the complexity of Muslim prayer. Moreover, experiencing firsthand the complexity of detail will help the reader understand the critical importance of prayer to Kohistanis, although in themselves the details may appear inconsequential.

The language of Muslim prayer is Arabic. Hence Kohistanis intone their prayers in a ritual language that many understand either incompletely, or not at all. Consequently praying is a time-consuming and demanding task, as the complexity of the following description (which repeats the Kohistani pronunciation of Arabic words) makes evident. Yet Kohistanis believe that saying one's prayers correctly and at the specified times is the minimal obligation of good Muslims. Few fail to fulfill this obligation.

Prayer in Thull is of two kinds, *du'a* and *namaz*. Kohistanis say *du'a* prayers in a variety of contexts. For example, after eating they give thanks to God in a kind of prayer called *du'ai shukraraj*. When someone dies, people pray that his/her soul may rest in peace, intoning a *du'ai maghfarat*, and those initiating any kind of major project (constructing a house, for instance) say a *du'ai barkat*. Purifying the worshipper by raising the hands to touch facial orifices marks *du'a* prayers.

The pious always say *du'a* prayers on all appropriate occasions, but when most Kohistanis talk about saying their prayers, they mean *namaz*. *Namaz* forms a ritual cycle that punctuates each day at five specified times. While all *namaz* rituals vary on a common theme, each has its own peculiarities and each its own name:

Fajar—the morning prayer said just before dawn
Zohar—the noon prayer
Asar—the afternoon prayer said about 5:30 P.M.
Maghrib—the evening prayer said just after sunset
Isha—the night prayer said about 9:30 P.M.

The call to prayer, called *azan*, always initiates *namaz*. Usually, a religious leader—a *mullana*, *mulvi*, or *mullah*—chants *azan* from the mosque, which signals all those in the nearby vicinity to gather for prayer. Sometimes the leader of the mosque asks a guest to give *azan*, especially if he possesses skill at chanting. In the hands of a skilled chanter, *azan* has a beauty and power to evoke emotions difficult to describe adequately. *Azan* translates as follows:

God is great!
God is great!
I witness that no one is worthy of worship except God.
I witness that no one is worthy of worship except God.
I witness that Mohammed is the prophet of God.
I witness that Mohammed is the prophet of God.
Come to prayer.
Come to prayer.
Come to success.
Come to success.
God is great.
God is great.
No one is worthy of worship except God.

The call to *Fajar*, the morning prayer, varies slightly in that the chanter inserts the twice repeated phrase "Prayer is better than sleep," immediately following the second "Come to success." At 5:30 in the morning this always made me think the Prophet (peace be upon him) possessed a definite sense of humor.

As the men gather (Islam forbids women to enter mosques; they must pray alone), each faces the holy city of Mecca in Saudi Arabia to perform a sequence of prescribed rituals by himself. When the majority finish, the worshippers, called *muktadids*, form rows headed by an *imam* ("leader"), again all facing toward Mecca. A ritual specialist appointed by the *imam*,

called a *moazan*, begins by intoning the *aqamat*. This comprises a special version of *azan*, distinguished by the twice-repeated phrase "Stand still for prayer," inserted after "Come to success." The *imam* then chants "God is great," and the main part of the ritual begins.

Complex units of ritual action, called *rakats*, make up *namaz*. . . . Like *namaz* itself, *rakats* vary—in small but significant details of ritual action and in function. Distinctive dimensions of contrast differentiate four kinds of *rakats*: *faras*, *sunnat*, *nafal*, and *vitar*. Worshippers render the ritual actions of *faras rakats* collectively under the leadership of the *imam*, who chants its phrases while performing the other three *rakats* individually, their phrases repeated silently. Kohistanis must perform both *sunnat* and *vitar rakats* (failing to do so constitutes a serious sin). They distinguish between them by their contrastive purposes. Worshippers render *sunnat rakats* for the holy prophet, *vitar rakats* for themselves. Conversely, people can choose not to perform *nafal rakats*, though doing so demonstrates piety and helps the worshipper gain paradise.

Both number, sequence, and kind of *rakats* change with various kinds of *namaz* prayer. *Fajar* [morning prayer] has two *sunnat rakats*, for example, whereas *zohar* [noon prayer] has six. *Maghrib* [evening prayer] has three *faras rakats* whereas *isha* [night prayer] has four. And only *isha* has *vitar rakats*, three in all. Sequences of body movements in conjunction with spoken phrases constitute the *rakats* themselves. Raising the hands to the ears, crossing the arms over the stomach, bowing while placing the hands on the knees, prostrating the body with the head touching the ground, and raising the index finger while moving it from one ear to the other comprise some of the movements. Lines from the Koran and the *Kalima*, affirmations of God's greatness, and formulaic blessings and praises to God make up the core of the spoken phrases. The phrases and movements intertwine in involved and complex progressions.

A careful look at the verbal and kinetic components of *namaz* points out that prayer in Thull does not so much communicatively link Man with God. On the contrary, it asserts fundamental truths of Islam. Pointing the index finger asserts God's oneness. Crossing the arms over the stomach, bowing while placing the hands on the knees, and touching the head to the ground submit the worshipper to God, the imperious ruler. Similarly, such verbal phrases as "God is great!," "Praises are for my God who is great!," "All good traits are for God!," and "All praises are for my God who is best!" profess the greatness of God in relation to the humbleness of humans.

In sum, *namaz* prayer in Thull involves long and complex rituals. It demands that participants devote considerable time and concentration to worship. By doing so, *namaz* dedicates and rededicates worshippers to Islam, and in the process recreates Muslim identities located at the center of self.

THE RITUAL OF FAST

Keeping the fast during *Ramazan* (called *Ramadan* in the western part of the Muslim world), the month-long period set aside for that purpose, distinguishes pious Muslims from those who casually follow Islam's precepts. Repeated exhortations to fast and to pray make up two of the triumvirate themes dominating religious preaching in Thull. No one in the community publicly admits to breaking the fast. Accordingly, accusing anyone in Thull of failing to fast constitutes a serious charge that can lead to fighting, bloodshed, and even murder.

Fasting has simple, unambiguous rules; during Ramazan nothing should pass one's lips during the time between the calls to morning and evening prayers. Particularly Muslims should not eat, drink, smoke, or take snuff. Nor should Muslims reorganize their daily activities to escape feeling the uncomfortable effects of the fast. One should not sleep excessive amounts of time during the day but, to the contrary, should fully experience fasting so that one contemplates and, most importantly, wholly embraces Islamic faith. Keeping the fast, therefore, continually reinvigorates the power of Muslim identity to dominate self.

The Islamic faith (*iman*) that must be wholly embraced includes belief in angels; in God's omnipotence and His oneness; in a day of judgment; and in the sending by God of a series of prophets to spread the divine message on earth, Mohammad being the last of the series. Muslims believe God will send no one to follow Mohammad because he brought mankind the perfect truth. *Iman* has an additional meaning to Kohistanis as well. They also understand it as a particular kind of gift from God consisting primarily of *ghrairat* (honor in the sense of personal integrity). God gives *ghrairat* to all male Muslims at birth. No Kohistani can gain it by his actions, but anyone can lose *ghrairat* by failing to protect it. With few exceptions, protecting *ghrairat* requires taking revenge. Kohistanis believe Muslims must protect God's gift by taking vengeance at appropriate times, or they forsake their obligations to him. Kohistani notions of *iman* thus inject vengeance into Muslim identity and help create sociocultural context that incubate death enmity.

The pace of life in Thull dramatically changes during *Ramazan*. A kind of tense stillness hovers in the air. Both speech and the way men move their bodies, become slow, studied, controlled, and a faint threat of violence continually lurks just beneath the surface. Hunger and thirst create volatile tempers, and embracing *iman* means embracing one's obligations for vengeance. *Ramazan* is the season for revenge, as everyone in Thull knows.

FUNDAMENTALIST ISLAM IN THULL

Religious beliefs in Thull form an especially streamlined version of Sunni Islam. The *Kalima*, prayer, fast, giving alms to the poor and making the pilgrimage to Mecca compose what Muslims everywhere call "the five pillars of Islam." Kohistanis recognize that one should contribute alms and give considerable respect to those who make the pilgrimage. They show much less concern for these last two obligations, however, because the *Kalima*, prayer, and fast constitute more fundamental "pillars."

Yet Sunni fundamentalism in Kohistan differs from the brand of Shi'a Islam so politically significant in Iran and Lebanon. Religious figures in Thull do not boast the kind of institutionalized political authority possessed by fundamentalist Shi'a leaders. . . .

Still, the men occupying positions ranked by degrees of religious competency have no secular authority. In other words, the titles they hold do not confer special rights to make secular political decisions binding on members of the community. People think of them primarily as scholars, men whose special learning gives them the right to speak with authority only on matters pertaining to religion. Mullana Fakir, for instance, never gave his opinions in council debates, nor would anyone have listened to him if he had. Nevertheless he spoke unhesitatingly to the throng that gathered around two accident victims at a wedding. A man had attempted to ignite a dynamite stick during the celebration, but the fuse had burned too fast, exploding the dynamite prematurely. The explosion blew off the man's hand and blinded a young bystander. When the crowd heard Mullana Fakir's voice coming over the loud-speaker in the mosque, conversation immediately hushed. He spoke authoritatively and directly to the point. "Exploding dynamite at weddings is un-Islamic, like singing and dancing, and should cease!" People listened with respect.

Islam in Thull also differs from more orthodox fundamentalism found in other parts of the Muslim world by a special set of accretions. These elements of Islamic ideology focus on death enmity, molding it in specific ways. Kohistanis have competed with their politically powerful Pathan neighbors for centuries. Accordingly the peculiar nature of Pathan Islam made a deep and lasting impact on Kohistani culture. Pathans differentiate themselves from surrounding people by strictly adhering to a tribal code of conduct called *pakhtunwali*. At its core lie four obligations: to commit vengeance, to provide hospitality, to give refuge to anyone asking for it (even a mortal enemy), and to treat with generosity a fallen advisory who sues for peace. *Pakhtunwali* and Islam interconnect in Pathan culture in an ambiguous way. Most Pathans claim their common ancestor converted to Islam at an early date, allegedly becoming one of the first of Mohammad's converts. Consequently most Pathans see themselves as archetypal Muslims, believing their way of life to be fundamentally and profoundly Islamic. At the same time, Pathans set themselves above other Muslims by strictly adhering to their distinctive code of conduct. Some Pathans will occasionally admit that *pakhtunwali* superficially makes them poor Muslims, because orthodox Islamic teaching does not recognize it. Nonetheless they declare everything Pathan to be Islamic, almost by definition. I heard an educated Pathan, a graduate student in a major American university, argue for the Islamic quality of Pathan culture. He said in the same breath, "No. Of course *pakhtunwali* is not Islamic. But yes, it is Islamic."

Kohistanis borrowed the essential features of *kakhtunwali* over the last three hundred years of contact with the Yusufzai, the dominant Pathan group in Dir. Taking revenge, providing hospitality, giving refuge, and being generous to a fallen enemy became accepted rules of behavior in Thull. Even so, no Kohistani ever claimed to follow *pakhtunwali*, for one must be Pathan to do that. Nevertheless Kohistanis accepted the rules of *pakhtunwali* as integral to Islam because they bought Pathans' claims to be archetypal Muslims. Friends unhesitatingly told me that because the Koran (the holy book of God) and the Hadith (the holy prophet's sayings) prominently displayed them, following these rules demonstrated Muslim piety. Revenge, consequently, became a defining characteristic of the Muslim identity located at the center of self.

THE BROTHERHOOD OF PREACHERS

To better understand how Islam in Thull empowers revenge we must also discuss the most recent change in Kohistani religion, the birth of the *Tablighi Jamma'at* or *Jamma'at al-Tabligh*. In the last few years this organization surged through Pakistan, as well as Pakistani communities in the United States and Europe, like a hurricane tidal wave. *Tablighi Jamma'at* ("community of evangelists," or "preachers") even operates in Muslim areas of the Soviet Union according to members in Thull. Unquestionably the organization has become one of the most potent forces in Kohistan.

The Community of Preachers dedicates itself to uniting Muslims of all sects and persuasions so that Islam can counteract the power of secular Western states. The organization argues that all Muslims must unite to struggle effectively against the powers of Satan. Accordingly it emphasizes those aspects of Islam unifying Muslims (the five pillars of Islam and correct moral behavior), while minimizing the sectarian, ethnic, regional, and national differences dividing them.

Tablighi Jamma'at began sometime in the 1950s in the village of Raivind near Lahore in the Punjab. Mullana Mohammed Zikria, a wealthy textile mill owner and noted religious scholar, founded the organization. His book *Tablighi Nisab*, "Syllabus for Preaching," remains today the group's charter of purpose, and copies exist in most rural villages in Pakistan. Muslim scholars translated the book into several South Asian languages; a Pushto version resides in the library of the main mosque in Thull. Raivind remains today the center for the group's activities, it's headquarters located in a large mosque and *madrasa* (religious school) in that village. The community of scholars in residence there forms a kind of semiofficial leadership for the organization. Once each year members from all over the world gather in Raivind, while similar, but smaller, gatherings periodically occur in the various administrative districts in Pakistan. Chitral hosted a gathering numbering more than 1000 members in 1984.

No clear-cut rules dictate *Tablighi* membership, for any man can join. Participating in the group's preaching automatically makes one a member, and those who take part regularly become known as *tablighis*, or "preachers." Members of the group begin their activities by visiting the people living in a chosen locality, usually near members' homes. At other times *tablighis* travel to different neighborhoods in the same community. Sometimes deputations journey outside their home villages, and on rare occasions even outside their native country. Men in Thull visited cities in India, and one man from London visited Thull as a member of a *Tablighi* deputation. When traveling in distant areas the group sleeps at a local mosque, visiting the homes of the people who frequent it.

Those wishing to participate in the activities of the group in Thull gather at a chosen mosque about one hour before noon or afternoon prayer. After the members assemble they must choose a leader (*amir*), who in turn appoints a spokesman (*mutakalam*). The group then leaves the mosque to begin their duties, headed by the leader. *Tablighi* deputations walk in single file, with heads bowed, and with a look of sanctity on their faces. The members carry bedding on their heads when they plan to spend the night at the mosque. There they propound Islamic morality to one another and anyone else who happens to be present.

Members of the deputation recite the *Kalima*, the affirmation of faith, repeatedly to themselves, as they walk with their heads bowed. No one speaks aloud except the spokesman. He talks only when the group encounters a man on the path or at the door of his house. He says, "We are from the mosque. Because of God's blessings we are Muslims. Our deeds should be as our words. Please join us in our virtuous work." Most men cannot refuse the invitation. About fifteen minutes before the call to prayer, the deputation, swollen in size by those who joined along the way, turns toward the mosque. After it arrives, the spokesman asks everyone present to remain after prayer for preaching to be led by the *amir*, although other members of the group participate if they wish. Preaching focuses on prayer, fast, and moral behavior. "Moral behavior" signifies the morality of Muslims as contrasted to the evil decadence of Kafirs, for *Tablighi* preaching continually propounds the holiness of Islam relative to the sinfulness of Kafirs. Participation in the group's activities creates new contexts for constructing Muslim identity and reinforces a self defined primarily in its terms. Emphasizing moral behavior also reinforces the passion for revenge, as discussed below.

WOMEN, HONOR, AND REVENGE

Moral behavior leads us to the third major theme in sermons (whether sermons of recognized religious scholars, or preachings of the *Tablighi Jamma'at*), and the last feature of Islam to be considered here. Along with saying prayers and keeping the fast, preachers in Thull repeatedly admonish men to control their women. Women's behavior becomes a matter of male Muslim identity because the way women act directly impacts on *ghrairat*, men's gift of personal integrity from God. Women must never walk outside their husband's (or father's) house without proper escort, preachers proclaim. Women must never speak to an unrelated man. No man's direct gaze should fall on another's wife or daughter. Women (men too, but especially women) must not sing or dance, particularly at weddings. Finally, women should always comport themselves with modesty to protect their shame (*sharam*)—hiding, controlling, minimizing, and denying their sexuality completely if possible. Men who allow their women freedom become *baghrairatman* ("men without personal integrity"). So do those who refuse to retaliate violently against anyone purposely threatening their women's shame.

The number of women whose shame puts a man's integrity at risk varies with the situation, but can be extensive. This factor alone intensifies death enmity in the community. Wives, daughters, and sisters always possess the power to endanger men's integrity. Additionally, men's vulnerability can extend to other women under a variety of circumstances. The men who owned the house where I lived always guarded my research assistant's wife with their rifles whenever she left our compound. Yet they knew she needed little protection, as only a minimal threat to her physical safety existed. But because she lived in their house, any attack on her shame by men outside the household, even a simple stare, threatened their integrity as well. By guarding her, they guarded themselves.

Men's vulnerability to attacks on women's shame can even stretch further than the household. Once I asked Anwar to arrange a visit to a Kohistani house in the neighboring Swat Valley for a group of American teachers traveling through Pakistan under the auspices of the Fullbright program. After we finished our obligatory tea and left the house, a woman in the group asked one of the Kohistani men present to have his picture taken with her. Unfortunately, Kohistanis interpret such actions as explicit sexual invitations; the man responded by attempting to embrace her. Visibly shaken, she asked me to tell Anwar, but I refused, knowing the potential for deadly violence in the situation. "Terrific!" I thought, as I imagined the field day newspapers and magazines would have with the story if anyone were killed.

I did tell Anwar what happened three days later, after we returned to Thull. He immediately demanded to know the name of the culprit. He arranged the visit, making him responsible for the women in the group, and putting his personal integrity at risk. "Why didn't you tell me this immediately? I should have given the man an instant gift of bullets! Tell me who he is now, so I can kill him! He has made my *ghrairat* (personal integrity) bad." Fortunately, I did not know the man's name.

Our study of Islam in Thull concentrated on the relation between religious ideology and death enmity. We learned how men create and recreate vengeance as part of a Muslim identity crucial in constructing self, and how vengeance becomes a passion, endowed with the power to move men to violence. Yet the religious ideology I have described is unorthodox in many ways. Understanding how it became such an important part of Kohistani culture will help to explain what generated blood feuding in Thull. Accordingly, I take a historical perspective in the next chapter, tracing the sociocultural transformations leading to changes in religious ideology. At the same time, changes in Thull's economic system also worked to implement death enmity, reinforcing the effects of changes in the system of Islamic beliefs.

Students who find themselves particularly interested in how cultural codes of conduct, which now affect world peace, developed in this region of the world should have a look at the book from which this chapter is drawn.—EDS.

36

Hallucinogenic Plants
and Their Use in Traditional Societies

Wade Davis

In Western society, drugs are used for either medicinal purposes or pleasure. Our culture sometimes defines those who use drugs for nonmedicinal purposes as deviant, and we have begun to view the use of drugs as a pathological condition unique in the annals of human history. The illegal use of drugs is considered a major social problem. In Selection 4, an ethnography of "Crack Street," we saw the human dimension of that problem.

The use of drugs is widespread in traditional cultures around the world. However, in traditional societies hallucinogenic plants are used for religious purposes and in ritual settings. Throughout history, people have sought ways to see beyond the normal reality of everyday life. They have endured the risk of poison in experimenting with ways to prepare mind-altering substances. These substances may be smoked, chewed, eaten, sniffed, drunk, rubbed onto the skin or into cuts, or even taken as intoxicating enemas. They have taken these risks, not for pleasure or kicks, but for curing illnesses through magic, divining truth, peering into the future, and making contact with the spirit world. This is serious and important for the people involved.

Another difference highlighted by the comparative study of drug use is the important effect of culture and context on the drug experience. Used in different settings, under different sets of expectations, the same drug may cause very different reactions, from nausea on the one hand to a religious experience on the other. Today we may find it odd that Native Americans

(Amerindians) smoked tobacco to cause giddiness (one of the universal symptoms of ecstasy) and to open the pathways through which shamans disassociated themselves from the normal state of awareness.

In light of America's drug problem, getting a broader historical and comparative vision of the role of drugs in society makes sense.

As you read this selection, ask yourself the following questions:

- Were hallucinogenic plants discovered by chance?
- What is the relationship between medicinal drugs, psychotropic drugs, and poisons?
- What factors influence what an individual sees under the influence of hallucinogens?
- How do ritual and the role of the shamanistic leader create a different context for the use of hallucinogenic drugs in traditional and modern societies?
- Do drug users in our society have their own secular rituals?

The following terms discussed in this selection are included in the Glossary at the back of the book:

Amerindian	*psychoactive drugs*
decoction	*rite of passage*
hallucinogen	*ritual*
indigenous	*sorcery*

The passionate desire which leads man to flee from the monotony of everyday life has made him instinctively discover strange substances. He has done so, even where nature has been most niggardly in producing them and

where the products seem very far from possessing the properties which would enable him to satisfy this desire.

Thus early in this century did Lewis Lewin, perhaps the preeminent pioneer in the study of psychoactive drugs, describe the primal search that led to man's discovery of hallucinogens. Strictly speaking, a hallucinogen is any chemical substance that distorts the senses and produces hallucinations—perceptions or experi-

From *Cultural Survival* 9(4):2–5, 1985. Reprinted by permission of *Cultural Survival*.

ences that depart dramatically from ordinary reality. Today we know these substances variously as psychotomimetics (psychosis mimickers), psychotaraxics (mind disturbers) and psychedelics (mind manifesters); dry terms which quite inadequately describe the remarkable effects they have on the human mind. These effects are varied but they frequently include a dreamlike state marked by dramatic alterations "in the sphere of experience, in the perception of reality, changes even of space and time and in consciousness of self. They invariably induce a series of visual hallucinations, often in kaleidoscopic movement, and usually in indescribably brilliant and rich colours, frequently accompanied by auditory and other hallucinations"—tactile, olfactory, and temporal. Indeed the effects are so unearthly, so unreal that most hallucinogenic plants early acquired a sacred place in indigenous cultures. In rare cases, they were worshipped as gods incarnate.

The pharmacological activity of the hallucinogens is due to a relatively small number of types of chemical compounds. While modern chemistry has been able in most cases successfully to duplicate these substances, or even manipulate their chemical structures to create novel synthetic forms, virtually all hallucinogens have their origins in plants. (One immediate exception that comes to mind is the New World toad, *Bufo marinus*, but the evidence that this animal was used for its psychoactive properties is far from complete.)

Within the plant kingdom the hallucinogens occur only among the evolutionarily advanced flowering plants and in one division—the fungi—of the more primitive spore bearers. Most hallucinogens are alkaloids, a family of perhaps 5,000 complex organic molecules that also account for the biological activity of most toxic and medicinal plants. These active compounds may be found in the various concentrations in different parts of the plant—roots, leaves, seeds, bark and/or flowers—and they may be absorbed by the human body in a number of ways, as is evident in the wide variety of folk preparations. Hallucinogens may be smoked or snuffed, swallowed fresh or dried, drunk in decoctions and infusions, absorbed directly through the skin, placed in wounds or administered as enemas.

To date about 120 hallucinogenic plants have been identified worldwide. On first glance, given that estimates of the total number of plant species range as high as 800,000, this appears to be a relatively small number. However, it grows in significance when compared to the total number of species used as food. Perhaps 3,000 species of plants have been regularly consumed by some people at some period of history, but today only 150 remain important enough to enter world commerce. Of these a mere 12–15, mostly domesticated cereals, keep us alive.

In exploring his ambient vegetation for hallucinogenic plants, man has shown extraordinary ingenuity, and in experimenting with them all the signs of pharmacological genius. He has also quite evidently taken great personal risks. Peyote (*Lophophora williamsii*), for example, has as many as 30 active constituents, mostly alkaloids, and is exceedingly bitter, not unlike most deadly poisonous plants. Yet the Huichol, Tarahumara and numerous other peoples of Mexico and the American Southwest discovered that sundried and eaten whole the cactus produces spectacular psychoactive effects.

With similar tenacity, the Mazatec of Oaxaca discovered amongst a mushroom flora that contained many deadly species as many as 10 that were hallucinogenic. These they believed had ridden to earth upon thunderbolts, and were reverently gathered at the time of the new moon. Elsewhere in Oaxaca, the seeds of the morning glory (*Rivea corymbosa*) were crushed and prepared as a decoction known at one time as ololiuqui—the sacred preparation of the Aztec, and one that we now realize contained alkaloids closely related to LSD, a potent synthetic hallucinogen. In Peru, the bitter mescaline-rich cactus *Trichocereus pachanoi* became the basis of the San Pedro curative cults of the northern Andes. Here the preferred form of administration is the decoction, a tea served up at the long nocturnal ceremonies during which time the patients' problems were diagnosed. At dawn they would be sent on the long pilgrimages high into the mountains to bathe in the healing waters of a number of sacred lakes.

Lowland South America has provided several exceedingly important and chemically fascinating hallucinogenic preparations, notably the intoxicating yopo (*Anadenanthera peregrina*) and ebene (*Virola calophylla, V. calophylloidea, V. theiodora*) snuffs of the upper Orinoco of Venezuela and adjacent Brazil and the ayahuasca-caapi-yagé complex (*Banisteriopsis caapi*) found commonly among the rainforest peoples of the Northwest Amazon. Yopo is prepared from the seeds of a tall forest tree which are roasted gently and then ground into a fine powder, which is then mixed with some alkaline substance, often the ashes of certain leaves. Ebene is prepared from the blood red resin of certain trees in the nutmeg family. Preparations vary but frequently the bark is stripped from the tree and slowly heated to allow the resin to collect in a small earthenware pot where it is boiled down into a thick paste, which in turn is sun dried and powdered along with the leaves of other plants. Ayahuasca comes from the rasped bark of a forest liana which is carefully heated in water, again with a number of admixture plants, until a thick decoction is obtained. All three products are violently hallucinogenic and it is of some significance that they all contain a number of subsidiary plants that, in ways not yet fully understood, intensify or lengthen the psychoactive effects of the principal ingredients. This is an important feature of many folk preparations and it is due in part to the fact that different chemical compounds in relatively small concentrations may effectively potentiate each other, producing powerful synergistic effects—a biochemical version of the whole being greater than the sum of its parts. The awareness of these properties is evidence of the impressive chemical and botanical knowledge of the traditional peoples.

In the Old World may be found some of the most novel means of administering hallucinogens. In southern Africa, the Bushmen of Dobe, Botswana, absorb the active constituents of the plant kwashi (*Pancratium trianthum*) by incising the scalp and rubbing the juice of an onion-like bulb into the open wound. The fly agaric (*Amanita muscaria*), a psychoactive mushroom used in Siberia, may be toasted on a fire or made into a decoction with reindeer milk and wild blueberries. In this rare instance the active principals pass through the body unaltered, and the psychoactive urine of the intoxicated individual may be consumed by the others. Certain European hallucinogens—notably the solanaceous belladonna (*Atropa belladonna*), henbane (*Hyoscyamus niger*), mandrake (*Mandragora officinarum*) and datura (*Datura metel*)—are topically active; that is the active principals are absorbed through the skin. We now know, for example, that much of the behavior associated with the medieval witches is as readily attributable to these drugs as to any spiritual communion with the diabolic. The witches commonly rubbed their bodies with hallucinogenic ointments. A particularly efficient means of self-administering the drug for women is through the moist tissue of the vagina; the witches broomstick or staff was considered the most effective applicator. Our own popular image of the haggard woman on a broomstick comes from the medieval belief that the witches rode their staffs each midnight to the sabbat, the orgiastic assembly of demons and sorcerers. In fact, it now appears that their journey was not through space but across the hallucinatory landscape of their minds.

There is in the worldwide distribution of the hallucinogenic plants a pronounced and significant discrepancy that has only inadequately been accounted for but which serves to illustrate a critical feature of their role in traditional societies. Of the 120 or more such plants found to date, over 100 are native to the Americas; the Old World has contributed a mere 15–20 species. How might this be explained? To be sure it is in part an artifact of the emphasis of academic research. A good many of these plants have entered the literature due to the efforts of Professor R. E. Schultes and his colleagues at the Harvard Botanical Museum and elsewhere, and their interest has predominantly been in the New World. Yet were the hallucinogenic plants a dominant feature of traditional cultures in Africa and Eurasia, surely they would have shown up in the extensive ethnographic literature and in the journals of traders and missionaries. With few notable exceptions, they don't. Nor is this discrepancy due to floristic peculiarities. The rainforests of West Africa and Southeast Asia, in particular, are exceedingly rich and diverse. Moreover, the peoples of these regions have most successfully explored them for pharmacologically active compounds for use both as medicines and poisons. In fact, as much as any other material trait the manipulation of toxic plants remains a consistent theme throughout sub-Saharan African cultures. The Amerindians, for their part, were certainly no strangers to plant toxins which they commonly exploited as fish, arrow and dart poisons. Yet it is a singular fact that while the peoples of Africa consistently used these toxic preparations on each other, the Amerindian almost never did. And while the Amerindian successfully explored his forest for hallucinogens, the African did not. This suggests the critical fact that the use of any pharmacologically active plant —remembering that the difference between hallucinogen, medicine and poison is often a matter of dosage —is firmly rooted in culture. If the peoples of Africa did not explore their environment for psychoactive drugs, surely it is because they felt no need to. In many Amerindian societies the use of plant hallucinogens lies at the very heart of traditional life.

To begin to understand the role that these powerful plants play in these societies, however, it is essential to place the drugs themselves in proper context. For one, the pharmacologically active components do not produce uniform effects. On the contrary, any psychoactive drug has within it a completely ambivalent potential for good or evil, order or chaos. Pharmacologically it induces a certain condition, but that condition is mere raw material to be worked by particular cultural or psychological forces and expectations. This is what our own medical experts call the "set and setting" of any drug experience. *Set* in these terms is the individual's expectation of what the drug will do to him; *setting* is the environment—both physical and social—in which the drug is taken. This may be illustrated by an example from our own country. In the northwest rainforests of Oregon are a native species of hallucinogenic mushrooms. Those who go out into the forest deliberately intending to ingest these mushrooms generally experience a pleasant intoxication. Those who inadvertently consume them while foraging for edible mushrooms invariably end up in the poison unit of the nearest hospital. The mushroom itself has not changed.

Similarly the hallucinogenic plants consumed by the Amerindian induce a powerful but neutral stimulation of the imagination; they create a template, as it were, upon which cultural beliefs and forces may be amplified a thousand times. What the individual sees in the visions is dependent not on the drug but on other factors—the mood and setting of the group, the physical and mental states of the participants, his own expectations based on a rich repository of tribal lore and, above all in Indian societies, the authority, knowledge and experience of the leader of the ceremony. The role of this figure—be it man or woman, shaman, curandero, paye, maestro or brujo—is pivotal. It is he who places the protective cloak of ritual about the participants. It is he who tackles the bombardment of visual and auditory stimuli and gives them order. It is he who must interpret a complex body of belief, reading the power in leaves and the meaning in stones, who must skillfully balance the forces of the universe and guide the play of the winds. The ceremonial use of hallucinogenic plants by the Amerindian is (most often) a collective journey into the unconscious. It is not necessarily, and in fact rarely is, a pleasant or an easy journey. It is wondrous and it may be terrifying. But above all it is purposeful.

The Amerindian enters the realm of the hallucinogenic visions not out of boredom, or to relieve an individual's restless anxiety, but rather to fulfill some collective need of the group. In the Amazon, for example, hallucinogens are taken to divine the future, track the paths of enemies, ensure the fidelity of women, diagnose and treat diseases. The Huichol in Mexico eat their peyote at the completion of long arduous pilgrimages in order that they may experience in life the journey of the soul of the dead to the underworld. The Amahuaca Indians of Peru drink yage that the nature of the forest animals and plants may be revealed to their apprentices. In eastern North America during puberty rites, the Algonquin confined adolescents to a longhouse for two weeks and fed them a beverage based in part on datura. During the extended intoxication and subsequent amnesia—a pharmacological feature of this drug—the young boys forgot what it was to be a child so that they might learn what it meant to be a man. But whatever the ostensible purpose of the hallucinogenic journey, the Amerindian imbibes his plants in a highly structured manner that places a ritualistic framework of order around their use. Moreover the experience is explicitly sought for positive ends. It is not a means of escaping from an uncertain existence; rather it is perceived as a means of contribution to the welfare of all one's people.

37

AIDS as Human Suffering

Paul Farmer and Arthur Kleinman

Our environment is constantly changing, and the necessity of adapting to environmental change is a fundamental challenge for every species. Often, when people think of the "environment," they envision trees, mountains, water, and animals. Few people think of invisible life forms, like bacteria and viruses, as part of our environment—but they are. Disease organisms themselves are constantly changing, and the kinds of diseases that afflict a social group are largely determined by their ecology and culture.

In the last two decades, humans have been faced by the challenge of a new virus (HIV) causing a lethal disease—acquired immune deficiency syndrome (AIDS)—that has spread throughout the world. In the United States we tend to think of AIDS as a disease that affects "risk groups" like gay men and intravenous drug users. But on a global basis, an estimated three-quarters of AIDS sufferers contracted the HIV virus through heterosexual intercourse. In the United States, much of the public discussion about AIDS reflects moral judgments about people's lifestyles and places the blame for the disease on the sufferers. For people with AIDS, such cultural attitudes and stigmatization significantly compound their suffering.

In this selection, we see that social reactions to AIDS vary among cultures. The cross-cultural comparison of Robert and Anita, both dying from AIDS but in very different settings, has much to tell us about the cultures themselves. In this selection, two prominent medical anthropologists make the case that on a human plane the way that we think about AIDS and its victims compounds the suffering and tragedy of this epidemic.

In the history of this epidemic, anthropologists have played a role in describing and understanding the behavioral practices related to the transmission of the HIV virus. The biomedical challenge of AIDS is great, but the challenge of coping with the human dimensions of AIDS is enormous, requiring both compassion and cross-cultural understanding.

As you read this selection, ask yourself the following questions:

- How might culture be a factor in the distribution of a disease (that is, in determining who gets the disease and who doesn't)?

- What are the main ways in which the deaths of Robert and Anita were different? How do those differences reflect cultural values?

- What are some practical suggestions for reducing the human suffering caused by AIDS?

- How is the cost of AIDS different in the United States and Third World countries?

The following terms discussed in this selection are included in the Glossary at the back of the book:

AIDS	lexicon
AZT	medical anthropology
cultural values	SIDA
HIV	stigma

That the dominant discourse on AIDS at the close of the twentieth century is in the rational-technical language of disease control was certainly to be expected and even necessary. We anticipate hearing a great deal about the molecular biology of the virus, the clinical epidemiology of the disease's course, and the pharmacological engineering of effective treatments. Other of contemporary society's key idioms for describing life's troubles also express our reaction to AIDS: the political-economic talk of public-policy experts, the social-welfare jargon of the politicians and bureaucrats, and the latest psychological terminology of mental-health professionals. Beneath the action-oriented verbs and reassuringly new nouns of these experts' distancing terminology, the more earthy, emotional rumblings of the frightened, the accusatory, the

"AIDS as Human Suffering" reprinted by permission of *Daedalus*, Journal of the American Academy of Arts and Sciences, from the issue, "Living with AIDS," spring 1989, vol. 118, no. 2.

hate-filled, and the confused members of the public are reminders that our response to AIDS emerges from deep and dividing forces in our experience and our culture.

AIDS AND HUMAN MEANINGS

Listen to the words of persons with AIDS and others affected by our society's reaction to the new syndrome:

- "I'm 42 years old. I have AIDS. I have no job. I do get $300 a month from social security and the state. I will soon receive $64 a month in food stamps. I am severely depressed. I cannot live on $300 a month. After $120 a month for rent and $120 a month for therapy, I am left with $60 for food and vitamins and other doctors and maybe acupuncture treatments and my share of utilities and oil and wood for heat. I'm sure I've forgotten several expenses like a movie once in a while and a newspaper and a book."[1]
- "I don't know what my life expectancy is going to be, but I certainly know the quality has improved. I know that not accepting the shame or the guilt or the stigma that people would throw on me has certainly extended my life expectancy. I know that being very up-front with my friends, and my family and coworkers, reduced a tremendous amount of stress, and I would encourage people to be very open with friends, and if they can't handle it, then that's their problem and they're going to have to cope with it."
- "Here we are at an international AIDS conference. Yesterday a woman came up to me and said, 'May I have two minutes of your time?' She said, 'I'm asking doctors how they feel about treating AIDS patients.' And I said, 'Well, actually I'm not a doctor. I'm an AIDS patient,' and as she was shaking hands, her hand whipped away, she took two steps backward, and the look of horror on her face was absolutely diabolical."
- "My wife and I have lived here [in the United States] for fifteen years, and we speak English well, and I do O.K. driving. But the hardest time I've had in all my life, harder than Haiti, was when people would refuse to get in my cab when they discovered I was from Haiti [and therefore in their minds, a potential carrier of HIV]. It got so we would pretend to be from somewhere else, which is the worst thing you can do, I think."

All illnesses are metaphors. They absorb and radiate the personalities and social conditions of those who experience symptoms and treatments. Only a few illnesses, however, carry such cultural salience that they become icons of the times. Like tuberculosis in *fin de siècle* Europe, like cancer in the first half of the American century, and like leprosy from Leviticus to the present, AIDS speaks of the menace and losses of the times. It marks the sick person, encasing the afflicted in an exoskeleton of peculiarly powerful meanings: the terror of a lingering and untimely death, the panic of contagion, the guilt of "self-earned" illness.

AIDS has offered a new idiom for old gripes. We have used it to blame others: gay men, drug addicts, inner-city ethnics, Haitians, Africans. And we in the United States have, in turn, been accused of spreading and even creating the virus that causes AIDS. The steady progression of persons with AIDS toward the grave, so often via the poor house, has assaulted the comforting idea that risk can be managed. The world turns out to be less controllable and more dangerous, life more fragile than our insurance and welfare models pretend. We have relegated the threat of having to endure irremediable pain and early death—indeed, the very image of suffering as the paramount reality of daily existence—to past periods in history and to other, poorer societies. Optimism has its place in the scale of American virtues; stoicism and resignation in the face of unremitting hardship—unnecessary character traits in a land of plenty—do not. Suffering had almost vanished from public and private images of our society.

Throughout history and across cultures, life-threatening disorders have provoked questions of control (What do we do?) and bafflement (Why me?). When bubonic plague depopulated fourteenth-century Europe by perhaps as many as half to three-fourths of the population, the black death was construed as a religious problem and a challenge to the moral authority as much or even more than as a public-health problem. In the late twentieth century, it is not surprising that great advances in scientific knowledge and technological intervention have created our chief responses to questions of control and bafflement. Yet bafflement is not driven away by the advance of scientific knowledge, for it points to another aspect of the experience of persons with AIDS that has not received the attention it warrants. It points to a concern that in other periods and in other cultures is at the very center of the societal reaction to dread disease, a concern that resonates with that which is most at stake in the human experience of AIDS even if it receives little attention in academic journals—namely, suffering.

A mortal disease forces questions of dread, of death, and of ultimate meaning to arise. Suffering is a culturally and personally distinctive form of affliction of the human spirit. If pain is distress of the body, suffering is distress of the person and of his or her family and friends. The affliction and death of persons with AIDS create master symbols of suffering; the ethical and emotional responses to AIDS are collective representations of how societies deal with suffering. The stories of sickness of people with AIDS are texts of suffering that we can scan for evidence of how cultures and communities and individuals elaborate the unique textures of personal experience out of the impersonal cellular invasion of viral RNA. Furthermore, these illness narratives point toward issues in the AIDS epidemic every bit as salient as control of the spread of infection and treatment of its biological effects.

Viewed from the perspective of suffering, AIDS must rank with smallpox, plague, and leprosy in its capacity to menace and hurt, to burden and spoil human experience, and to elicit questions about the nature of life and its significance. Suffering extends from those afflicted with AIDS to their families and intimates, to the practitioners and institutions who care for them, and to their neighborhoods and the rest of society, who feel threatened by perceived sources of the epidemic and who are thus affected profoundly yet differently by its consequences. If we minimize the significance of AIDS as human tragedy, we dehumanize people with AIDS as well as those engaged in the public-health and clinical response to the epidemic. Ultimately, we dehumanize us all.

ROBERT AND THE DIAGNOSTIC DILEMMA

It was in a large teaching hospital in Boston that we first met Robert, a forty-four-year-old man with AIDS.[2] Robert was not from Boston, but from Chicago, where he had already weathered several of the infections known to strike people with compromised immune function. His most recent battle had been with an organism similar to that which causes tuberculosis but is usually harmless to those with intact immune systems. The infection and the many drugs used to treat it had left him debilitated and depressed, and he had come east to visit his sister and regain his strength. On his way home, he was prevented from boarding his plane "for medical reasons." Beset with fever, cough, and severe shortness of breath, Robert went that night to the teaching hospital's emergency ward. Aware of his condition and its prognosis, Robert hoped that the staff there would help him to "get into shape" for the flight back to Chicago.

The physicians in the emergency ward saw their task as straightforward: to identify the cause of Robert's symptoms and, if possible, to treat it. In contemporary medical practice, identifying the cause of respiratory distress in a patient with AIDS entails following what is often called an algorithm. An algorithm, in the culture of biomedicine, is a series of

sequential choices, often represented diagrammatically, which helps physicians to make diagnoses and select treatments. In Robert's case, step one, a chest X-ray, suggested the opportunistic lung parasite *Pneumocystis* as a cause for his respiratory distress; step two, examination of his sputum, confirmed it. He was then transferred to a ward in order to begin treatment of his lung infection. Robert was given the drug of choice, but did not improve. His fever, in fact, rose and he seemed more ill than ever.

After a few days of decline, Robert was found to have trismus: his jaw was locked shut. Because he had previously had oral candidiasis ("thrush"), his trismus and neck pain were thought to suggest the spread of the fungal infection back down the throat and pharynx and into the esophagus—a far more serious process than thrush, which is usually controlled by antifungal agents. Because Robert was unable to open his mouth, the algorithm for documenting esophagitis could not be followed. And so a "GI consult"—Robert had already had several—was called. It was hoped that the gastroenterologists, specialists at passing tubes into both ends of the gastrointestinal tract, would be better able to evaluate the nature of Robert's trismus. Robert had jumped ahead to the point in the algorithm that called for "invasive studies." The trouble is that on the night of his admission he had already declined a similar procedure.

Robert's jaw remained shut. Although he was already emaciated from two years of battle, he refused a feeding tube. Patient refusal is never part of an algorithm, and so the team turned to a new kind of logic: Is Robert mentally competent to make such a decision? Is he suffering from AIDS dementia? He was, in the words of one of those treating him, "not with the program." Another member of the team suggested that Robert had "reached the end of the algorithm" but the others disagreed. More diagnostic studies were suggested: in addition to esophagoscopy with biopsy and culture, a CT scan of the neck and head, repeated blood cultures, even a neurological consult. When these studies were mentioned to the patient, his silent stare seemed to fill with anger and despair. Doctors glanced uncomfortably at each other over their pale blue masks. Their suspicions were soon confirmed. In a shaky but decipherable hand, Robert wrote a note: "I just want to be kept clean."

Robert got a good deal more than he asked for, including the feeding tube, the endoscopy, and the CT scan of the neck. He died within hours of the last of these procedures. His physicians felt that they could not have withheld care without having some idea of what was going on.

In the discourse of contemporary biomedicine, Robert's doctors had been confronted with "a diagnostic dilemma." They had not cast the scenario described above as a moral dilemma but had discussed it in rounds as "a compliance problem." This way of talking about the case brings into relief a number of issues in the contemporary United States—not just in the culture of biomedicine but in the larger culture as well. In anthropology, one of the preferred means of examining culturally salient issues is through ethnology: in this case, we shall compare Robert's death in Boston to death from AIDS in a radically different place.

ANITA AND A DECENT DEATH

The setting is now a small Haitian village. Consisting of fewer than a thousand persons, Do Kay is composed substantially of peasant farmers who were displaced some thirty years ago by Haiti's largest dam. By all the standard measures, Kay is now very poor; its older inhabitants often blame their poverty on the massive buttress dam a few miles away and note bitterly that it has brought them neither electricity nor water.

When the first author of this paper began working in Kay, in May of 1983, the word *SIDA*, meaning AIDS, was just beginning to make its way into the rural Haitian lexicon. Interest in the illness was almost universal less than three years later. It was about then that Anita's intractable cough was attributed to tuberculosis.

Questions about her illness often evoked long responses. She resisted our attempts to focus discussions. "Let me tell you the story from the beginning," she once said; "otherwise you will understand nothing at all."

As a little girl, Anita recalls, she was frightened by the arguments her parents would have in the dry seasons. When her mother began coughing, the family sold their livestock in order to buy "a consultation" with a distinguished doctor in the capital. Tuberculosis, he told them, and the family felt there was little they could do other than take irregular trips to Port-au-Prince and make equally irregular attempts to placate the gods who might protect the woman. Anita dropped out of school to help take care of her mother, who died shortly after the girl's thirteenth birthday.

It was very nearly the *coup de grâce* for her father, who became depressed and abusive. Anita, the oldest of five children, bore the brunt of his spleen. "One day, I'd just had it with his yelling. I took what money I could find, about $2, and left for the city. I didn't know where to go." Anita had the good fortune to find a family in need of a maid. The two women in the household had jobs in a U.S.-owned assembly plant; the husband of one ran a snack concession out of the house. Anita received a meal a day, a bit of dry floor to sleep on, and $10 per month for what sounded like incessant labor. She was not unhappy with the arrangement, which lasted until both women were fired for participating in "political meetings."

Anita wandered about for two days until she happened upon a kinswoman selling gum and candies near a downtown theater. She was, Anita related, "a sort of aunt." Anita could come and stay with her, the aunt said, as long as she could help pay the rent. And so Anita moved into Cité Simone, the sprawling slum on the northern fringes of the capital.

It was through the offices of her aunt that she met Vincent, one of the few men in the neighborhood with anything resembling a job: "He unloaded the whites' luggage at the airport." Vincent made a living from tourists' tips. In 1982, the year before Haiti became associated, in the North American press, with AIDS, the city of Port-au-Prince counted tourism as its chief industry. In the setting of an unemployment rate of greater than 60 percent, Vincent could command considerable respect. He turned his attention to Anita. "What could I do, really? He had a good job. My aunt thought I should go with him." Anita was not yet fifteen when she entered her first and only sexual union. Her lover set her up in a shack in the same neighborhood. Anita cooked and washed and waited for him.

When Vincent fell ill, Anita again became a nurse. It began insidiously, she recalls: night sweats, loss of appetite, swollen lymph nodes. Then came months of unpredictable and debilitating diarrhea. "We tried everything—doctors, charlatans, herbal remedies, injections, prayers." After a year of decline, she took Vincent to his hometown in the south of Haiti. There it was revealed that Vincent's illness was the result of malign magic: "It was one of the men at the airport who did this to him. The man wanted Vincent's job. He sent an AIDS death to him."

The voodoo priest who heard their story and deciphered the signs was straightforward. He told Anita and Vincent's family that the sick man's chances were slim, even with the appropriate interventions. There were, however, steps to be taken. He outlined them, and the family followed them, but still Vincent succumbed. "When he died, I felt spent. I couldn't get out of bed. I thought that his family would try to help me to get better, but they didn't. I knew I needed to go home."

She made it as far as Croix-des-Bouquets, a large market town at least two hours from Kay. There she collapsed, feverish and coughing, and was taken in by a woman who lived near the market. She stayed for a month, unable to walk, until her father came to take her back home. Five years had elapsed since she'd last seen him. Anita's father was by then a friendly but broken-down man with a leaking roof over his one-room, dirt-floor hut. It was no place for a sick woman, the villagers said, and Anita's godmother, honoring twenty-year-old vows, made room in her over-crowded but dry house.

Anita was diagnosed as having tuberculosis, and she responded to antituberculosis therapy. But six months after the initiation of treatment, she declined rapidly. Convinced that she was indeed taking her medications, we were concerned about AIDS, especially on hearing of the death of her lover. Anita's father was poised to sell his last bit of land in order to "buy more nourishing food for the child." It was imperative that the underlying cause of Anita's poor response to treatment be found. A laboratory test confirmed our suspicions.

Anita's father and godmother alone were apprised of the test results. When asked what she knew about AIDS, the godmother responded, "AIDS is an infectious disease that has no cure. You can get it from the blood of an infected person." For this reason, she said, she had nothing to fear in caring for Anita. Further, she was adamant that Anita not be told of her diagnosis—"That will only make her suffer more"—and skeptical about the value of the AIDS clinic in Port-au-Prince. "Why should we take her there?" asked Anita's godmother wearily. "She will not recover from this disease. She will have to endure the heat and humiliation of the clinic. She will not find a cool place to lie down. What she might find is a pill or an injection to make her feel more comfortable for a short time. I can do better than that."

And that is what Anita's godmother proceeded to do. She attempted to sit Anita up every day and encouraged her to drink a broth promised to "make her better." The godmother kept her as clean as possible, consecrating the family's two sheets to her god-daughter. She gave Anita her pillow and stuffed a sack with rags for herself. The only thing she requested from us at the clinic was "a beautiful soft wool blanket that will not irritate the child's skin."

In one of several thoughtful interviews accorded us, Anita's godmother insisted that "for some people, a decent death is as important as a decent life. . . . The child has had a hard life; her life has always been difficult. It's important that she be washed of bitterness and regret before she dies." Anita was herself very philosophic in her last months. She seemed to know of her diagnosis. Although she never mentioned the word *SIDA*, she did speak of the resignation appropriate to "diseases from which you cannot escape." She stated, too, that she was "dying from the sickness that took Vincent," although she denied that she had been the victim of witchcraft—"I simply caught it from him."

Anita did not ask to be taken to a hospital, nor did her slow decline occasion any request for further diagnostic tests. What she most wanted was a radio—"for the news and the music"—and a lambswool blanket. She especially enjoyed the opportunity to "recount my life," and we were able to listen to her narrative until hours before her death.

AIDS IN CULTURAL CONTEXT

The way in which a person, a family, or a community responds to AIDS may reveal a great deal about core cultural values. Robert's story underlines our reliance on technological answers to moral and medical questions. "Americans love machines more than life itself," asserts author Philip Slater in a compelling analysis of middle-class North American culture. "Any challenge to the technological-over-social priority threatens to expose the fact that Americans have lost their manhood and their capacity to control their environment."[3] One of the less noticed but perhaps one of the farthest-reaching consequences of the AIDS epidemic has been the weakening of North America's traditional confidence in the ability of its experts to solve every kind of problem. In the words of one person with the disorder, "The terror of AIDS lies in the collapse of our faith in technology."[4]

This core cultural value is nowhere more evident than in contemporary tertiary medicine, which remains the locus of care for the vast majority of AIDS patients. Despite the uniformity of treatment outcome, despite the lack of proven efficacy of many diagnostic and therapeutic procedures, despite their high costs, it has been difficult for practitioners to limit their recourse to these interventions. "When you're at Disney World," remarked one of Robert's physicians ironically, "you take all the rides."

Robert's illness raises issues that turn about questions of autonomy and accountability. The concept of autonomous individuals who are solely responsible for their fate, including their illness, is a powerful cultural premise in North American society. On the positive side, this concept supports concern for individual rights and respect for individual differences and achievement. A more ominous aspect of this core cultural orientation is that it often justifies blaming the victims. Illness is said to be the outcome of the free choice of high-risk behavior.

This has been especially true in the AIDS epidemic, which has reified an invidious distinction between "innocent victims"—infants and hemophiliacs—and, by implication, "the guilty"—persons with AIDS who are homosexuals or intravenous drug users. Robert's lonely and medicalized death is what so many North Americans fear: "He was terrified. He knew what AIDS meant. He knew what happens. Your friends desert you, your lover kicks you out into the street. You get fired, you get evicted from your apartment. You're a leper. You die alone."[5] The conflation of correlation and responsibility has the effect of making sufferers feel guilt and shame. The validity of their experience is contested. Suffering, once delegitimated, is complicated and even distorted; our response to the sufferer, blocked.

In contrast, in Haiti and in many African and Asian societies, where individual rights are often underemphasized and also frequently unprotected, and where the idea of personal accountability is less powerful than is the idea of the primacy of social relationships, blaming the victim is also a less frequent response to AIDS. Noticeably absent is the revulsion with which AIDS patients have been faced in the United States, in both clinical settings and in their communities. This striking difference cannot be ascribed to Haitian ignorance of modes of transmission. On the contrary, the Haitians we have interviewed have ideas of etiology and epidemiology that reflect the incursion of the "North American ideology" of AIDS—that the disease is caused by a virus and is somehow related to homosexuality and contaminated blood. These are subsumed, however, in properly Haitian beliefs about illness causation. Long before the advent of AIDS to Do Kay, we might have asked the following question: some fatal diseases are known to be caused by "microbes" but may also be "sent" by someone; is *SIDA* such a disease?

Differences in the responses of caregivers to Robert and Anita—such as whether to inform them of their diagnosis or undertake terminal care as a family or a community responsibility—also reflect the egocentered orientation in North American cities and the more sociocentric orientation in the Haitian village. An ironic twist is that it is in the impersonal therapeutic setting of North American healthcare institutions that concern for the patient's personhood is articulated. It is, however, a cool bioethical attention to abstract individual rights rather than a validation of humane responses to concrete existential needs. Perhaps this cultural logic—of medicine as technology, of individual autonomy as the most inviolable of rights, and so of individuals as responsible for most of the ills that befall them—helps us to understand how Robert's lonely death, so rich in all the technology applied to his last hours, could be so poor in all those supportive human virtues that resonate from the poverty-stricken village where Anita died among friends.

A core clinical task would seem to be helping patients to die a decent death. For all the millions of words spilled on the denial of death in our society and the various psychotechniques advertised to aid us to overcome this societal silence, AIDS testifies vividly that our secular public culture is simply unable to come to terms with mortality.

A final question might be asked in examining the stories of Robert and Anita: just how representative are they of the millions already exposed to HIV? As a middle-class, white gay male, Robert is thought by many to be a "typical victim of AIDS." But he is becoming increasingly less typical in the United States, where the epidemic is claiming more and more blacks and Hispanics, and Robert would not be sociologically representative of the typical AIDS patient in much of the rest of the world. In many Third World settings, sex differences in the epidemiology of HIV infection are unremarkable: in Haiti, for example, there is almost parity between the sexes. Most importantly, most people with AIDS are not middle-class and insured. All this points to the fact that the virus that causes AIDS might exact its greatest toll in the Third World.

AIDS IN GLOBAL CONTEXT

Although the pandemic appears to be most serious in North America and Europe, per capita rates reveal that fully seventeen of the twenty countries most affected by AIDS are in Africa or the Caribbean. Further, although there is heartening evidence that the epidemic is being more effectively addressed in the North American gay community, there is no indication that the spread of HIV has been curbed in the communities in which women like Anita struggle. Although early reports of high HIV seroprevalence were clearly based on faulty research, even recent and revised estimates remain grim: "In urban areas in some sub-Saharan countries, up to 25% of young adults are *already* HIV carriers, with rates among those reporting to clinics for sexually transmitted diseases passing 30%, and among female prostitutes up to 90%."[6] In other words, the countries most affected are precisely those that can least afford it.

These figures also remind us that AIDS has felled many like Anita—the poor, women of color, victims of many sorts of oppression and misfortune. Although heterosexual contact seems to be the means of spreading in many instances, not all who contract the disease are "promiscuous," a label that has often offended people in Africa, Haiti, and elsewhere. *Promiscuous* fails utterly to capture the dilemmas of millions like Anita. In an essay entitled "The Myth of African Promiscuity," one Kenyan scholar refers to the "'new poor': the massive pool of young women living in the most deprived conditions in shanty towns and slums across Africa, who are available for the promise of a meal, new clothes, or a few pounds."[7]

Equally problematic, and of course related, is the term *prostitute*. It is often used indiscriminately to refer to a broad spectrum of sexual activity. In North America, the label has been misused in investigations of HIV seroprevalence: "the category *prostitute* is taken as an undifferentiated 'risk group' rather than as an occupational category whose members should, for epidemiological purposes, be divided into IV drug users and nonusers—with significantly different rates of HIV infection—as other groups are."[8] A more historical view reminds us that prostitutes have often been victims of scapegoating and that there has long been more energy for investigation of the alleged moral shortcomings of sex workers than for the economic underpinnings of their work.

The implications of this sort of comparative exercise, which remains a cornerstone of social anthropology, are manifold. The differences speak directly to those who would apply imported models of prevention to rural Haiti or Africa or any other Third World setting. A substantial public-health literature, reflecting the fundamentally interventionist perspective of that discipline, is inarguably necessary in the midst of an epidemic without cure or promising treatment. The same must be true for the burgeoning biomedical literature on AIDS. But with what consequences have these disciplines ignored the issue of AIDS as suffering? Whether reduced to parasite-host interactions or to questions of shifting incidence and prevalence among risk groups, AIDS has meant suffering on a large scale, and this suffering is not captured in these expert discourses on the epidemic.

The meaning of suffering in this context is distinctive not only on account of different beliefs about illness and treatment responses but because of the brute reality of grinding poverty, high child and maternal mortality, routinized demoralization and oppression, and suffering as a central part of existence. The response to AIDS in such settings must deal with this wider context of human misery and its social sources. Surely it is unethical—in the broadest sense, if not in the narrow technical biomedical limits to the term—for international health experts to turn their backs on the suffering of people with AIDS in the Third World and to concentrate solely on the prevention of new cases.

DEALING WITH AIDS AS SUFFERING

To what practical suggestions does a view of AIDS as human suffering lead?

Suffering Compounded by Inappropriate Use of Resources

The majority of all medical-care costs for AIDS patients is generated by acute inpatient care. In many ways, however, infection with HIV is more like a chronic disease. Based on cases of transfusion-associated HIV transmission in the United States, the mean time between exposure to the virus and the development of AIDS is over eight years. This period may well be lengthened by drugs already available. And as the medical profession becomes more skilled at managing the AIDS condition, the average time of survival of patients with the full-blown syndrome will also be extended. For many with AIDS, outpatient treatment will be both more cost-effective and more humane. For the terminally ill, home or hospice care may be preferred to acute-care settings, especially for people who "just want to be kept clean." Helping patients to die a decent death was once an accepted aspect of the work of health professionals. It must be recognized and appropriately supported as a core clinical task in the care of persons with AIDS.

Not a small component of humane care for people with AIDS is soliciting their stories of sickness, listening to their narratives of the illness, so as to help them give meaning to their suffering. Restoring this seemingly forgotten healing skill will require a transformation in the work and training of practitioners and a reorganization of time and objectives in health-care delivery systems.

The practitioner should initiate informed negotiation with alternative lay perspectives on care and provide what amounts to brief medical psychotherapy for the threats and losses that make chronic illness so difficult to bear. But such a transformation in the provision of care will require a significant shift in the allocation of resources, including a commitment to funding psychosocial services as well as appropriate providers—visiting nurses, home health aides, physical and occupational therapists, general practitioners, and other members of teams specializing in long-term, outpatient care.

Suffering Magnified by Discrimination

In a recent study of the U.S. response to AIDS, the spread of HIV was compared to that of polio, another virus that struck young people, triggered public panic, and received regular attention in the popular media. "Although these parallels are strong," notes the author, "one difference is crucial: there was little early sympathy for victims of AIDS because those initially at risk—homosexual men, Haitian immigrants, and drug addicts—were not in the main-stream of society. In contrast, sympathy for polio patients was extensive."[9] "This lack of sympathy is part of a spectrum that extends to hostility and even violence, and that has led to discrimination in housing, employment, insurance, and the granting of visas."[10] The victims of such discrimination have been not only people with AIDS or other manifestations of HIV infection but those thought to be in "risk groups."

In some cases, these prejudices are only slightly muted in clinical settings. In our own experience in U.S. hospitals, there is markedly more sympathy for those referred to as "the innocent victims"—patients with transfusion-associated AIDS and HIV-infected babies. At other times, irrational infection-control precautions do little more than heighten patients' feelings of rejection. Blame and recrimination are reactions to the diseases in rural Haiti as well—but there the finger is not often pointed at those with the disease.

Although the President's Commission on AIDS called for major coordinated efforts to address discrimination, what has been done has been desultory, unsystematic, and limited in reach. While legislation is crucial, so too is the development of public-education programs that address discrimination and suffering.

Suffering Augmented by Fear

Underlying at least some of the discrimination, spite, and other inappropriate responses to AIDS is fear. We refer not to the behavior-modifying fear of "the worried well" but to the more visceral fear that has played so prominent a role in the epidemic. It is fear that prompts someone to refuse to get into a taxi driven by a Haitian man; it is fear that leads a reporter to wrench her hand from that of a person with AIDS; it is fear that underpins some calls for widespread HIV-antibody testing, and fear that has led some health professionals to react to patients in degrading fashion. The fact that so much of this fear is "irrational" has thus far had little bearing on its persistence.

Dissemination of even a few key facts—by people with AIDS, leaders of local communities, elected officials and other policy-makers, teachers, and health professionals—should help to assuage fear. HIV is transmitted through parenteral, mucous-membrane, or open-wound contact with contaminated blood or body fluids and not through casual contact. Although the risk of transmission of HIV to health-care professionals is not zero, it is extremely low, even after percutaneous exposure (studies show that, of more than 1,300 exposed health-care workers, only four seroconverted[11]).

Suffering Amplified by Social Death

In several memoirs published in North America, persons with AIDS have complained of the immediate social death their diagnosis has engendered. "For some of my friends and family, I was dead as soon as they heard I had AIDS," a community activist informed us. "That was over two years ago." Even asymptomatic but seropositive individuals, whose life expectancy is often better than that of persons with most cancers and many common cardiovascular disorders, have experienced this reaction. Many North Americans with AIDS have made it clear that they do not wish to be referred to as victims: "As a person with AIDS," writes Navarre, "I can attest to the sense of diminishment at seeing and hearing myself referred to as an AIDS victim, an AIDS sufferer, an AIDS case—as anything but what I am, a person with AIDS. I am a person with a condition. I am not that condition."[12]

It is nonetheless necessary to plan humane care for persons with a chronic and deadly disease—"without needlessly assaulting my denial," as a young man recently put it. The very notion of hospice care will need rethinking if its intended clients are a group of young and previously vigorous persons. Similarly, our cross-cultural research has shown us that preferred means of coping with a fatal disease are shaped by biography and culture. There are no set "stages" that someone with AIDS will go through, and there can be no standard professional response.

Suffering Generated by Inequities

AIDS is caused, we know, by a retrovirus. But we need not look to Haiti to see that inequities have sculpted the AIDS epidemic. The disease, it has been aptly noted, "moves along the fault lines of our society."[13] Of all infants born with AIDS in the United States, approximately 80 percent are black or Hispanic.[14] Most of these are the children of IV drug users, and attempts to stem the virus may force us to confront substance abuse in the context of our own society. For as Robert Gallo and Luc Montagnier assert, "efforts to control AIDS must be aimed in part at eradicating the conditions that give rise to drug addiction."[15]

There are inequities in the way we care for AIDS patients. In the hospital where Robert died, AZT—the sole agent with proven efficacy in treating HIV infection—is not on formulary. Patients needing the drug who are not in a research protocol have to send someone to the drugstore to buy it—if they happen to have the $10,000 per year AZT can cost or an insurance policy that covers these costs. Such factors may prove important in explaining the striking ethnic differences in average time of survival following diagnosis of AIDS. In one report it was noted that, "while the average lifespan of a white person after diagnosis is two years, the average minority person survives only 19 weeks."[16]

From rural Haiti, it is not the local disparities but rather the international inequities that are glaring. In poor countries, drugs like AZT are simply not available. As noted above, the AIDS pandemic is most severe in the countries that can least afford a disaster of these dimensions. A view of AIDS as human suffering forces us to lift our eyes from local settings to the true dimensions of this worldwide tragedy.

Compassionate involvement with persons who have AIDS may require listening carefully to their stories, whether narratives of suffering or simply attempts to recount their lives. Otherwise, as Anita pointed out, we may understand nothing at all.

NOTES

We thank Carla Fujimoto, Haun Saussy, and Barbara de Zalduondo for their thoughtful comments on this essay.

1. The first three of the four quotations cited here are the voices of persons with AIDS who attended the Third International Conference on AIDS, held in Washington, D.C. in June 1987. Their comments are published passim in 4 (1) (Winter/Spring 1988) of *New England Journal of Public Policy*. All subsequent unreferenced quotations are from tape-recorded interviews accorded the first author.

2. All informants' names are pseudonyms, as are "Do Kay" and "Ba Kay." Other geographical designations are as cited.

3. Philip Slater, *The Pursuit of Loneliness: American Culture at the Breaking Point* (Boston: Beacon Press, 1970), 49, 51.

4. Emmanuel Dreuilhe, *Mortal Embrace: Living with AIDS* (New York: Hill and Wang, 1988), 20.

5. George Whitmore, *Someone Was Here: Profiles in the AIDS Epidemic* (New York: New American Library, 1988), 26.

6. RenEe Sabatier, *Blaming Others: Prejudice, Race, and Worldwide AIDS* (Philadelphia: New Society Publishers, 1988), 15.

7. Professor Aina, ibid., 80.

8. Jan Zita Grover, "AIDS: Keywords," in *AIDS: Cultural Analysis/Cultural Activism* (Cambridge: MIT Press, 1988), 25–26.

9. Sandra Panem, *The AIDS Bureaucracy* (Cambridge: Harvard University Press, 1988), 15.

10. See Sabatier for an overview of AIDS-related discrimination. As regards Haiti and Haitians, see Paul Farmer, "AIDS and Accusation: Haiti, Haitians, and the Geography of Blame," in *Cultural Aspects of AIDS: Anthropology and the Global Pandemic* (New York: Praeger, in press). The degree of antipathy is suggested by a recent *New York Times*–CBS News poll of 1,606 persons: "Only 36 percent of those interviewed said they had a lot or some sympathy for 'people who get AIDS from homosexual activity,' and 26 percent said they had a lot or some sympathy for 'people who get AIDS from sharing needles while using illegal drugs'" (*New York Times*, 14 October 1988, A12).

11. Infectious Diseases Society of America, 276.

12. Max Navarre, "Fighting the Victim Label," in *AIDS: Cultural Analysis/Cultural Activism* (Cambridge: MIT Press, 1988), 143.

13. Mary Catherine Bateson and Richard Goldsby, *Thinking AIDS: The Social Response to the Biological Threat* (Reading, Mass.: Addison-Wesley, 1988), 2.

14. Samuel Friedman, Jo Sotheran, Abu Abdul-Quadar, Beny Primm, Don Des Jarlais, Paula Kleinman, Conrad Mauge, Douglas Goldsmith, Wafaa El-Sadr, and Robert Maslansky, "The AIDS Epidemic Among Blacks and Hispanics," *The Milbank Quarterly* 65, suppl. 2 (1987): 455-99.

15. Robert Gallo and Luc Montagnier, "AIDS in 1988," *Scientific American* 259 (4) (October 1988):48.

16. Sabatier, 19.

38

Circumcision, Pluralism, and Dilemmas of Cultural Relativism

Corinne A. Kratz

One of the things about studying anthropology is that we encounter cultural ideas and practices that are very alien to our own. Encountering the "other" can be a challenge in two ways. On an intellectual level, it can be a challenge to understand vastly different cultures and customs—why do people do/believe that? How does it fit within the wider context of their lives? The second of these challenges can be on a personal level, because the beliefs and practices of others might offend our own notions of morality and propriety. Studying and living in other cultures sometimes brings up our own ugly ethnocentrism.

At the same time, it is fair to ask, Are there limits to cultural relativism? Looking cross-culturally, anthropologists can identify some universal (or at least extremely common) elements in cultural codes about proper personal conduct. All societies follow the ethnocentric line of thought that *their own traditions* are correct and right, but at the same time there are gigantic areas of controversy. In a complex society, the laws that are recognized and enforced often reflect the interests of the dominant social group.

The topic of this selection, female circumcision, really bothers some students; they can hardly believe that such cultural practices exist in the twenty-first century. In Africa, female circumcision has been a controversial topic for nearly a century, and there have been repeated international efforts to "eradicate" the custom, as if it were a disease. But this is not simply a medical issue, and to oversimplify the complex issue misses the point.

It is important to recognize that the single term *FGM* (*female genital modification* or *mutilation*) refers to a wide variety of surgeries with different levels of invasiveness. It is also important to remember that the symbolic and ritual meanings of this practice also vary among cultures. Finally, as students of anthropology, we need to recognize that there are at least two different views of what is at stake here, and, as in many other arenas of public controversy, there is real value to a sympathetic understanding of both sides.

This selection has two parts. The first provides a description of female circumcision in Africa—reporting the "facts" almost as it might be reported in a reference book. The second part discusses the author's strategies for *teaching* about the female circumcision controversy in the college classroom context. This controversy is both local and global—it involves traditional cultures, immigrants, and international nongovernmental organizations (NGOs). Understanding the different dimensions of the argument is an important educational goal; hopefully, it will also challenge you to come to your own well-informed opinion.

As you read this selection, ask yourself the following questions:

- For the women in the societies that practice it, FGM is related to beliefs about aesthetics of the body. Can you think of traditions in your own culture that transform or modify the body for purposes of beauty or identity? (Try relating this to Miner's description of body ritual among the Nacirema in Selection 1.)

- What are the potential health complications of female circumcision? What are the possible social complications of not being circumcised?

- What are the human rights issues involved? Is this a question where local societies should debate it themselves, or is international intervention necessary?

- Why does this tradition persist even when it is made against the law? Why would loving parents have this done to their daughters?

- Is the analogy to male circumcision in the West appropriate?

The following terms discussed in this selection are included in the Glossary at the back of the book:

clitorectomy	infibulation
FGM	neocolonial
human rights	sunna circumcision

Differences of social and cultural practice have been a source of both puzzlement and edification around the world and throughout human history, interpreted and treated in vastly different ways in different circumstances.[1] They have been perennial resources through which people form their own identities, defining themselves through contrasts with other cultures. Distinctions in dress, cuisine, language, music, and ritual are particularly common as such markers of identity and difference. When ethnic or religious groups and minorities are reviled, differences in cultural practice have been used to help justify derogatory attitudes and discrimination. In other settings, cultural difference and diversity have been celebrated through various forms of multiculturalism.

With such remarkable diversity in the world, however, situations inevitably arise where incompatible social and cultural values, practices, and aesthetics produce conflict or controversy. How should they be dealt with? Cultural relativism would suggest that each set of practices and understandings is valid within its own circumstances and way of life. Yet plural societies combine and blend different beliefs and practices within the same social settings. Further, certain practices seem to challenge the nonjudgmental tolerance that cultural relativism implies (Shweder 2002) and raise serious questions about how to define human rights and who should define them. To many Americans, for instance, religious practices of discipline and self-mortification might seem extreme when they include self-flagellation, or political martyrdom might be taken as a sign of fanaticism. To people in other parts of the world, on the other hand, certain American economic practices might seem exploitative and certain modes of American dress might be seen as indecent or immoral.

Anthropologists seek to understand cultural production, i.e., how cultural meanings and social worlds continually take shape and change through daily interaction, communication, and exchange, through interpretations of personal and community histories and negotiations of political economic differences. They seek to understand the range of experience, meanings, and values produced by the world's diverse societies and cultures, examining how people perceive and make sense of lives and circumstances as different as those of African pastoralists caught in a long civil war, Chinese women working in a silk factory, men in an urban homeless shelter in the United States, contemporary Australians maintaining complex ritual traditions and fighting for land and mining claims, or radical political activists in Europe (Hutchinson 1996; Rofel 1999; Desjarlais 1997; Dussart 2000; Holmes 2000). In doing so, anthropologists may move beyond simple relativism to develop knowledge and judgments based on pluralism. Philosopher and social theorist Isaiah Berlin describes the distinction between relativism and pluralism (1991:10–11):

> "I prefer coffee, you prefer champagne. We have different tastes. There is no more to be said." That is relativism. . . . [Pluralism is] the conception that there are many different ends that men [sic] may seek and still be fully rational, fully men [sic], capable of understanding each other and sympathising and deriving light from each other, as we derive it from reading Plato or the novels of medieval Japan—worlds, outlooks, very remote from our own.
>
> Members of one culture can, by the force of imaginative insight, understand . . . the values, the ideals, the forms of life of another culture or society, even those remote in time or space. They may find these values unacceptable, but if they open their minds sufficiently they can grasp how one might be a full human being, with whom one could communicate, and at the same time live in the light of values widely different from one's own, but which nevertheless one can see to be values, ends of life, by the realisation of which men [sic] could be fulfilled.

Anthropological research may not be able to resolve conflicts and controversies that emerge from social and cultural difference, but the knowledge produced can provide the foundation of understanding needed for engagement and debate grounded in pluralism. It can help to identify the basic value contradictions and issues at stake as well as the different positions and interests in play. It is also important to pay attention to such controversies and debates themselves as cultural phenomena, analyzing their rhetorics, weighing competing arguments, and placing them within their own social and historical contexts. These analytical skills are important in understanding debates concerning issues of social justice, abortion rights, defining human rights, or controversial practices such as *sati* in India, and they are critical to effective political action related to any of these issues.

This essay considers a widespread cultural practice that has many different forms and meanings throughout the world and a long history of sparking debate and controversy at different times and places: forms of genital modification commonly called circumcision. Vehement debates have swirled around male and female circumcision alike, but the essay focuses particularly on practices of female genital

---

Original publication to this volume.

modification because they currently receive the greatest attention and are at the center of recent contention. After outlining the varied practices of female genital modification and some of the meanings associated with them, the essay will turn to controversies and debates about these cultural practices.

THE VARIED PRACTICES AND MEANINGS OF FEMALE GENITAL MODIFICATION

Female circumcision is a term commonly used to refer to surgical operations performed in over thirty African, Middle Eastern, and Southeast Asian countries, by immigrants from those communities living elsewhere, and for roughly a century (about 1850 to 1950) by physicians in Europe and the United States. As this geographic and historical span suggests, the operations are embedded in a wide range of cultural and historical contexts and can be quite different in definition, meaning, and effect. All involve surgical modification of female genitals in some way, though this ranges from relatively minor marking for symbolic purposes to the most radical operation, infibulation.[2]

The general term *female circumcision* includes at least three clinically distinct kinds of surgery. Clitoridectomy removes all or part of the clitoris and the hood, or prepuce, covering it.[3] The second type, excision, includes clitoridectomy but also removes some or all of the labia minora; all or part of the labia majora might also be cut. The most extreme form of circumcision, infibulation, goes beyond excision.[4] After removing the labia, the sides of the vulva are joined so that scar tissue forms over the vaginal opening, leaving a small gap for urination and menstruation. Infibulated women often require surgical opening to allow first intercourse and birthing; in many cases women are reinfibulated after each childbirth. In addition to these three well-recognized types of female circumcision, a fourth is sometimes included. The mildest form, this involves a symbolic pricking or slight nicking of the clitoris or prepuce. Excision and infibulation are the most widely practiced types of female genital modification. In Africa, infibulation is common primarily in the Horn of Africa (Somalia, Sudan, Djibouti, Ethiopia).

Whether and how circumcision practices affect women's sexuality is much debated. It is important to distinguish sexual desire, sexual activity, and sexual pleasure when considering this question. Sexual desire and sexual activity may not diminish with female genital operations. Evidence about sexual feeling and pleasure is variable, difficult to define or measure, and hard to come by.[5] Euro-American opponents of the practices assert that circumcised women feel no sexual pleasure, but a number of African women disagree with these assertions. Studies suggest that the effect varies widely with type of operation, with prior sexual experience, and other circumstances as well. Some African activists also suggest that the stress on sexual pleasure in anticircumcision campaigns reflects a recent, primarily Western concept of sexuality.[6]

The operations have also been said to carry a number of health risks. While the range of possible health problems is well known, there has been little epidemiological research to determine how widespread each problem might be in different areas. Immediate risks include infection, shock, excessive bleeding, and urinary retention, risks that are related to hygienic conditions and care during and after the operations. Longer term health problems are most common with infibulation but can be associated with excision as well. Most of these problems are related to heavy scarring and to covering over of vaginal and urinary openings after infibulation: keloid scars, vulvar cysts, retention of urine or menses, painful menstruation, difficulty urinating, and chronic pelvic infections. Clinical studies on the relation between these health problems and genital modification are contradictory, however, and a recent study in Gambia found that many negative consequences commonly cited for the operations were not significantly more common in women who had been cut (Morison et al. 2001).[7]

In many places where female circumcision is practiced, the physical operation is but one moment in an elaborate ceremony that contains many other events. For Okiek people in Kenya, for instance, initiation into adulthood includes circumcision for boys and excision for girls, but the full initiation process continues for several months and includes much more as well: moral teaching, family and community engagement, the negotiation of new social relationships, and important cultural meanings and values. While the operations are a central initiation trial and create a permanent physical mark of adulthood, initiation cannot be reduced to circumcision or excision alone. In many other societies, initiation does not involve circumcision at all.

In every case the purposes and meanings of female genital modification are related to specific cultural understandings of identity, personhood, morality, adulthood, gender, bodily aesthetics, and other important issues. In the Sudan, for instance, it is seen as enhancing a woman's purity, cleanliness, and beauty. For the Kikuyu people of Kenya, circumcision was the foundation of moral self-mastery for women and men alike, performed as part of initiation into adulthood. The age of those circumcised varies widely according to these cultural understandings. In much of Mali and the Sudan, for instance, girls are circumcised at six to eight years, while various communities in Kenya and Sierra Leone perform the operation in the early teens. Yoruba people in Nigeria often circumcise their children at just a few days old, much like male circumcision in the United States and Europe. Circumcision and excision are not connected with initiation for the Yoruba people, but they do relate the operations to moral concepts associated with shame and fertility. Circumcision is not regularly performed after puberty in Africa, where the operation is usually seen as related to a person's social and moral development.[8] The history of female circumcision in Europe and the United States contrasts with most of the world with regard to circumcision age. For roughly a century beginning in the 1850s, clitoridectomy was prescribed for adult women in Europe and the United States as medical treatment for insomnia, sterility, and masturbation (which was defined as an ailment at that time).

Many societies practice male but not female circumcision, but the reverse is rare. Where both are practiced, they can only be understood fully when considered together, in relation to one another. In many societies, cultural meanings and patterns link the two and equate them. A single word refers to both operations in many African languages, and this correspondence is often central to the way their practitioners understand them. The English translation, "female circumcision," maintains this parallel between male and female genital operations, though anticircumcision activists have criticized the term for being misleading (as discussed below).

DEBATES AND CONTROVERSIES ABOUT CIRCUMCISION

Both male and female genital operations have engendered long histories of debate and opposition; these have often involved cross-cultural disagreements about the meaning and worth of the practices. The value of Jewish male circumcision, for instance, was debated in Rome during the first century A.D., and male circumcision has become a topic of heated opposition in the United States again today. The most widespread and vociferous opposition currently centers on female genital modification, but these practices have been the subject of international political controversies and abolition campaigns since at least the 1910s.[9] Contemporary campaigns continue the tradition and rhetoric of colonial and missionary opposition and also build on decades of Africa-based activism. Health consequences have consistently been part of the debate,

particularly in relation to infibulation, but the issues have also been defined at times in terms of colonialism, neocolonialism, feminism, sexuality, and human rights.

Controversies can be confusing. Heated arguments based on strong convictions are rarely presented in ways that make clear the different assumptions, perspectives, and interests fueling contention. When controversies cross cultural and national boundaries, they can be very complicated indeed. To begin to understand circumcision debates, it is important to first identify the grounds of controversy: Who is involved, what is it about, and what is at issue. Circumcision controversies concern a wide variety of actors and cross a number of social and legal arenas, from family and household relations to international tribunals. This renders it impossible to characterize the debates in simple terms. It is inaccurate and misleading to describe them merely as contests of women versus men or Africans versus outsiders.

To understand today's debates, it is helpful to think about them in relation to several contexts. Most central are the sociocultural contexts of the varied practices at issue and the history and contexts of the current controversies themselves. An effective way to highlight the issues and perspectives involved is to consider these contexts comparatively, to relate different situations and practices, or to explore similarities and differences between several controversies (e.g., debates about male and female genital operations, debates that occur at different historical periods, or debates that might concern different practices but are presented in similar ways (such as *sati* in India[10]). Examining cultural practices in context also means identifying the different actors, perspectives, and meanings involved (see below). It is important to recognize that trying to understand unfamiliar practices does not necessarily mean supporting them. However, to oppose or help alter practices that some might consider problematic, it is essential to work *with* the people involved, as equal peers. Such understanding is critical to effective engagement.

One of the best-documented historical examples of circumcision controversy took place in central Kenya during the colonial era. Colonial missionaries and administrators there made judgments about which local customs violated Christian behavior and sought to discourage them. Campaigns to abolish female circumcision in central Kenya were among these efforts. When the Church of Scotland Mission and segments of the Church Missionary Society tried to prohibit the practice in the 1910s and 1920s, Kikuyu female circumcision became connected with the anticolonial movement and defense of cultural tradition (Murray 1974, 1976). Jomo Kenyatta, later president of

Kenya, was a prominent opponent of colonial attempts to alter Kikuyu custom. These local protests against abolishing female circumcision provided an impetus for starting independent schools and churches in central Kenya.

Arenas encompassed in this debate, then, included British politics (with pressure from feminist parliamentarians and anticolonial activists), rivalries between Christian denominations with missions in Kenya, the colonial administration in Kenya, and local Kenyan communities. In addition to anticolonial movements and defense of cultural tradition, the debate also became connected with relations of authority between men and women and between women of different generations, and even the introduction of maternity clinics.[11] Since 1979, the Kenyan government has conducted several anticircumcision campaigns that were tinged with Christian and colonial overtones, banning female circumcision in 1982, but with little effect. In 1996, a national organization proposed an alternative initiation ceremony as a substitute. Like Kenya, each country has its own such history of circumcision debates and policies.

To place contemporary controversies in context, we should also consider their own history and the different arenas where debates occur. The debates have been related to feminist movements in various times and places, to colonial administration and missionary campaigns, to Islamic religious movements, and a number of other issues. Arenas of debate shift as different parties become involved. Several decades after the Kenyan controversy, in the late 1950s, international efforts to have the World Health Organization (WHO) address female circumcision were not effective. Later, in the 1970s, a number of publicizing efforts and publications converged to galvanize international attention. These included articles in African publications in the mid-1970s, a press conference held in Switzerland before the WHO assembly in 1977, and publications by Fran Hosken (1979) and Mary Daly (1990) in the United States. The Inter-African Committee on Traditional Practices affecting the Health of Women and Children was formed in Geneva in 1977. A 1979 WHO seminar in Khartoum helped to begin regular discussion of female genital operations by international bodies and at regular conferences. The resurgence of anticircumcision activity in the 1970s was also buoyed by the United Nations Decade of Women (1975–1985).

Since the early 1990s, international debates about female genital modification have again become increasingly heated and highly politicized. Greater media coverage in the 1990s and publicity over legal cases concerning African immigrants in France and the United States brought the debates to a wider public than previously.[12] In the United States, involvement by such well-known figures as novelist Alice Walker also helped to publicize and polarize the debate. A number of African scholars and activists based in the United States (such as Seble Dawit, Salem Mekuria, and Micere Mugo) have been highly critical of the way Walker and others have represented female circumcision in Africa.[13] They argue that Walker and others are engaged in neocolonial depictions that demonize African practitioners, distort the social meanings and contexts involved, portray African women only as victims, ignore decades of activism in Africa, and isolate female circumcision from other issues of women's health, economic status, and education.

Both practices of female genital modification and the arenas of debate have shifted over the years as other circumstances changed and different constituencies became involved. Public health education about the potential risks of the operations has increased in most countries where they are practiced. Similarly, an increasing number of female genital modifications are being performed either by specialists who have received some hygienic training or in health clinics and hospitals. As noted above, alternative rituals have also been proposed in some countries, though it is not clear whether they will be widely adopted. Shifts in practice also include adoption of genital modification by noncircumcising communities (Leonard 1999) and modification of long-standing rituals toward what I call "circumcision by pronouncement" or "performative circumcision," i.e., substituting a verbal formula for actual cutting (Abusharaf 1999:7; Hernlund 1999). There are intense debates among African activists about whether a medicalized, minor form of female genital modification should be promoted as an interim substitute for more severe operations (Obiora 1997; Shell-Duncan 2001). African immigrant communities in Europe and the United States often continue traditional practices in new ways in their new homes. Their preservation of the practices has brought all these debates to the fore in those countries as immigrant communities and their children have grown in recent decades. Sweden, Switzerland, the United Kingdom, and several other European countries passed laws restricting the operations in the 1980s and early 1990s. The United States followed suit in 1997.

CONTEXTS FOR UNDERSTANDING THE DEBATES AND ISSUES

These examples illustrate how many different parties and perspectives can become involved in these controversies. In tracing the shape of today's debates, it is useful to distinguish the following three interacting arenas. The social, cultural, and historical contexts of debates about female and male genital operations can be examined for each:

1. *Home countries* are countries in Africa, the Middle East, and Southeast Asia where circumcising practices have traditional standing. There may be a variety of traditions and practices that include genital modification within each home country and a number of different positions within each community, if the practices are debated.

2. The *United States* and *Europe* are the second arena to consider. These countries also have a history of genital operations for both boys and girls. The histories are related to changing understandings of health, class, ethnicity, gender, and sexuality. In the U.K., for instance, male circumcision had become a middle-class fashion by the 1920s (Lonsdale 1992:388). In Nazi Germany, it was taken as a mark of Jewish identity. In the United States today, white men are more likely to be circumcised than African Americans or Hispanics; higher education levels are also related to higher circumcision rates (Laumann et al. 1997: 1053–1054). Clitoridectomy was a recognized medical treatment for women in these countries for decades, as noted above. Concern about female genital operations within these countries is now related particularly to immigrants from home countries.

3. The third arena is that of *international campaigns*. Though obviously related to the other two, it is useful to consider how international campaigns differ from debates within the other arenas, how international bodies and action groups establish their legitimacy to intervene in other countries, and how the international arena redefines issues central to particular communities and nations.[14]

In addition to identifying the complex social geographies and range of actors involved, it is equally important to pay attention to the ways that language and rhetoric shape the presentation of issues and convey particular values and judgments. For instance, the growing intensity of the debates became encapsulated in the very terms used for female genital operations between the 1970s and 1990s, illustrating the political divisions and rhetorics involved. *Female circumcision* was the most common term for decades, the English phrase ordinarily used in the debates about British colonial attempts to outlaw female genital operations in Kenya in the 1920s–30s. In the 1970s, anticircumcision activists increasingly criticized the term *female circumcision*, claiming that it condoned a brutal custom by creating what they considered false similarities between male and female circumcision.[15] A more par-

tisan alternative was coined and eventually popularized: *female genital mutilation*.[16] The new term did not attempt impartial description, but condemned the practices through a label that defined them all as intentional mistreatment and disfigurement. Promotion of the new "mutilation" term was part of an escalating anticircumcision campaign that used more sensationalism and gory images.[17] As this term became more common, it was shortened to an acronym, "FGM." Others reject this term as misrepresenting the intentions of African families, criminalizing parents and relatives, and judging them through Euroamerican cultural values.

The increasingly heated and polarized nature of the debate thus became embedded in its very terms. Attempting to find an appropriate phrase, *New York Times* reporter Celia Duggers used the term *genital cutting* in her late 1996 articles, a term she adopted from demographic and health surveys.[18] A number of other alternative terms also came into use in the mid-1990s, seeking more neutral ground: genital surgery, genital operations, genital modification, and body modification. This last term acknowledges broad similarities among such practices as male and female genital surgeries, genital/body piercing, and other cosmetic surgery. Female circumcision, genital cutting, and FGM remain the most common terms in English, though the acronym FGM has now also been redefined as "female genital *modification*" in efforts to use less polarizing, descriptive language.

Whatever terms are used, the topic at the center of controversy is a generalized category defined and shaped by that very debate. The category is created by extracting and combining fragments from many different cultural practices found in dozens of countries, a variety of practice described above. The fragments all concern genital modification but may share little else. Taken out of their social and cultural contexts, they combine to form a new, abstract category (e.g., "female circumcision"). Scientific, medical language is an important tool in this process. The clinical emphasis makes the general category seem like an objective and universal way to talk about women's bodies, but it also narrows the range of information defined as relevant to the debate. For instance, the physically different operations described above are combined and treated as the same thing, though they vary considerably in extent and effects. The rest of the ceremonies in which the physical operations may be embedded are often ignored.

The terms used in circumcision controversies convey different impressions of the people involved as well. A number of African women and others have objected to the word *mutilation*, for instance, because it misrepresents parents and families. It suggests that they intend harm to their children, likening to child abuse what they themselves might see as a cultural triumph, "carried out for the noblest of reasons, the best of intentions, and in good faith" (Iweriebor 1996). Accounts often demonize women who perform the operations as well. In recent French legal cases, for instance, they were portrayed as avaricious and predatory and received the harshest rulings.

A prominent example concerns the way African or "Third World" women in general are represented as a single, unified group, as seen across a range of sources: news media, informational publicity material produced by action groups, scholarly writing, or novels.[19] This stereotyped concept of "African women" is usually formed by homogenizing divergent circumstances; it assumes women to be a pre-existent, coherent group with shared interests and desires. This requires removing the concept of "woman" from any specific cultural context and isolating it from related notions that help form understandings of gender. How are differences based on nationality, class, ethnicity, religion, education, or age accommodated in this generalized figure and how might these variations affect the debates? The "average" Third World woman that emerges is set in contrast to elite women, though the contrast is often implicit. Elite women are presented as self-conscious, active, choice-making agents. They are not exclusively Western, but also include women born in the Third World who have joined the campaign against female genital modification. Yet African activists consistently protest that their work is rarely recognized when controversies are described. The rhetoric and structure of these controversies might be examined further by looking at how different kinds of men are portrayed, or by considering parallel cases in contemporary campaigns against male genital operations, abortion, or welfare.[20]

These different portrayals of Third World women and other actors in circumcision controversies are often bound up with notions of "progress" and other values as they have been defined in Euroamerican contexts. But conflicting values are the very crux of controversy. Diverse social and political positions inform the perspectives of those involved, but they are also grounded in different cultural frameworks, competing definitions of the practices at issue, and what seem to be irreconcilable values. In seeking to understand circumcision debates, it can be helpful to identify the various positions on each issue, along with the priorities and cultural values associated with each. Issues at stake would include the following:

Human Rights Circumcision debates presented in human rights terms often emphasize the integrity and inviolability of the human body, sometimes using analogies with torture and child abuse. As noted above, this falsely attributes evil intent to parents and relatives. "Human rights" as a concept is itself under considerable debate. Should social and economic rights be included? Whose values will be enshrined as universal when there are fundamental disagreements (An-Na'im 1992; An-Na'im and Deng 1990)? How might the language of human rights accommodate the diverse people, practices, and circumstances involved?

Self-Determination The human rights approach does not fit easily with another common way that circumcision debates are framed, in terms of self-determination.[21] However, self-determination can be defined in relation to individuals, families, or communities, each with rather different implications. Upholding family autonomy, community values, or religious freedom would seem to support continuing traditional practices understood as central to personal and community identity. Does this include male and female initiation ceremonies? How does individual self-determination apply in the intricate contexts of family and community relations? How do questions of self-determination apply to children of different ages?

Health Issues and Sexuality These were discussed earlier in this essay. Both have been central to debates about female genital modification. Questions of sexuality have also figured in opponents' efforts to explain the operations. They commonly assert that male desire to control female sexuality is the origin and reason for all such practices. This universal conspiracy theory, however, does not correspond to what is known about circumcising practices. There is no evidence or discussion of when or how this might have happened in so many places, how this explanation would account for the variety of circumcising practices, why women also staunchly defend them, or how the theory relates to explanations offered by practitioners.[22]

Yet even when the issues and stances in circumcision controversies are delineated, the fact remains that the debates involve fundamentally different perceptions and lived understandings of aesthetics, morality, society, and personhood that come together with questions of authority, class, power, gender, and history.[23] There are no simple, single answers to the issues they raise. They pinpoint a nexus whose very opaqueness of understanding illustrates recalcitrant problems and issues of cultural translation. In this respect, recent circumcision controversies draw attention to the limits and dilemmas of cultural relativism and moral judgments. How are such judgments, choices, and even laws to be made in plural societies (which ultimately means all societies)? Can incommensurable values be accommodated? As Sir Isaiah Berlin noted, "A certain humility in these matters is very necessary" (1991:18).

CULTURAL AND MORAL VALUES: DILEMMAS OF RELATIVISM

Many people would agree that cultural difference and diversity should be recognized, respected, and accommodated. Cultural relativism has fairly wide currency in the United States as a general way to approach cultural difference, though it coexists with popular notions of cultural evolution and civilizational hierarchy. The relativist view that each society's practices and values are valid and understandable in the particular context of their lives may be easiest to hold, however, when applied to distant people or to practices that seem strange but harmless. What happens when people with incompatible practices and values live closely together, when culturally justified practices seem to be physically harmful, or when an overarching national legal system must deal with radically different values? Does cultural relativism imply moral relativism as well?

The controversies over genital operations present such dilemmas and flashpoints. Usually associated with ceremonial performances, the songs, dances, costumes, and other beliefs that give meaning to the ceremonies are readily accepted as part of "tradition," as markers of particular forms of ethnic or religious identity. Scarification or tattooing might also be recognized and appreciated as part of a different aesthetic or religion, so what is different about genital operations? Why are they seen as an exception that raises this moral dilemma? What other practices pose similar dilemmas?

In the last decade, legal cases dealing with African immigrants in the United States and Europe have raised these issues in particularly clear and urgent ways. Examining these cases—particularly court procedure and sections of testimony—provides a way to again consider the different actors and interests involved, this time in situations even closer to home (Kratz 2002). Among the many questions that these cases raise are the following:

- Legislation is written in general terms, intended as applicable to the broadest range of cases. However, laws are interpreted through individual cases and precedents. Should a case about, for instance, Somali immigrants (who practice infibulation for young girls) serve as precedent for families from Sierra Leone (where initiated individuals are older, the operation is less severe, and family relations are quite different)?

- Whose legal rights should be protected and when? Parents' rights to raise their children in accordance with their beliefs and traditions? What if parents disagree? The rights of the girls affected? What if they *choose* to undergo the operation? What if they are minors legally?
- When female genital operations are outlawed, who is legally responsible and liable for prosecution? At different times and places, the accused have included fathers, mothers, initiates, and surgeons. What constructions of actors, intentions, and meanings are involved in each of these scenarios?
- When court proceedings involve immigrants, how are issues of adequate translation and adequate legal representation handled? These were important problems in the way French cases in the 1990s were handled.
- Are judges, juries, lawyers, and those concerned with civil liberties informed about the communities and cultural values involved? For instance, a lawyer in one case argued that the girls affected would have psychological problems when they realized they were not like other women, but the "other women" assumed in this statement were not women of the immigrant community. In fact, most women in their own ethnic community had had the operation, making the argument one that would more appropriately support the operation (cf. Matias 1996:4).
- How do gendered differences in immigrant experiences influence knowledge about relevant laws and services and the ways people participate in legal proceedings?

These questions raise some of the difficult practical implications of general issues of cultural translation and the moral dilemmas involved. They provide another way to ground the circumcision debates in specific questions and situations. Such groundings provide useful ways to understand and engage with controversies that are puzzling and sometimes troubling in their passions and complexities.

NOTES

1. This paper includes portions of Kratz (1999a) and (1999b) that have been combined, revised, and updated for inclusion here.
2. Wide variation in female genital modification can be found on the African continent alone, where it is practiced across a band of the continent that includes parts of Mauritania, Senegal, Gambia, Guinea-Bissau, Sierra Leone, Liberia, Mali, Burkina Faso, Côte d'Ivoire, Ghana, Togo, Benin, Niger, Nigeria, Chad, Cameroon,

Central African Republic, Democratic Republic of the Congo (formerly Zaire), Sudan, Egypt, Eritrea, Ethiopia, Djibouti, Somalia, Kenya, Tanzania, and Uganda. The percentage of women circumcised in each country varies considerably (e.g., 5–10% in Uganda, 25–30% in Ghana, 80% in the Sudan), as does the kind of operation practiced, its cultural and personal significance, and its history. Female circumcision is not practiced at all in some communities within this broad area, but it is commonplace in others. Regional, ethnic, and religious variation in practice is considerable. Christians, Muslims, and followers of traditional religions all might practice forms of female circumcision. Communities have adopted, abandoned, and modified the practices in various ways over the centuries, in keeping with the complex histories of political and religious influence and interaction among societies on the African continent.

3. This is sometimes called *sunna circumcision*, though *sunna circumcision* might also refer to preputial cutting alone. The name *sunna* relates the practice to Islamic traditions, though most Muslim scholars and theologians deny Koranic justification for female circumcision.

4. Infibulation is also called *pharaonic circumcision*, a name originating in beliefs that the practice was part of ancient Egyptian life.

5. See Apena (1996:8); Kratz (1994:345–346); Lyons (1981:507, 510); Obiora (1997:298). Matias (1996:3) and Ogbu (1997:414–415) cite examples where they are seen as enhancing sexuality. Again, the type of operation is critical. Infibulation is more often discussed as reducing desire (Boddy 1989:54), though Obiora (1997:310) cites another study in the Sudan to opposite effect. As for sexual pleasure, according to Gruenbaum (also writing about the Sudan), some infibulated women do have orgasms, perhaps because "many midwives, fearing hemorrhage, leave much of the clitoral (erectile) tissue intact beneath the infibulation when they perform the surgeries" (1996:462). She notes, though, that other infibulated women report finding sex unsatisfying. See also Parker (1995:514); Obiora (1997:308–310); Koso-Thomas (1987:37–42). Several of these sources note that reports of sexual pleasure are related to sexual experience before circumcision as well as other factors.

6. Even in Europe and the United States, the pleasure-oriented definition of sexuality became prominent in recent decades. In this view, recent international debates about female genital operations have taken a form that resonates particularly with recent Western concerns and anxieties (Parker 1995). The paradoxical nature of questions of sexuality can be brought into relief through comparison. Historically, classical theologians and philosophers made parallel claims about men; they promoted male circumcision because it reduces male sexual passion (Boyarin 1992:486–487; Lyons 1981:503–504). Though circumcised men today might not agree, similar assumptions still inform medical research. A study publicized on National Public Radio in 1997 found that circumcised men are more "sexually adventurous," but explained this as compensation for loss of sexual feeling (Laumann et al. 1997). "Adventurousness" was defined through behavioral range and frequencies, suggesting that sexual interest, desire, and activity were actually greater with circumcision. Considering such gender reversals can raise critical questions about all these claims and show that understandings of sexuality are neither universal nor unchanging.

7. Obiora (1997:292) cites studies that show no obstetric or gynecological complication when infibulation is performed at an early age. Parker (1995:514–516) notes that findings in some studies of health risks from other forms of genital operations are not clear, though it is generally accepted that some complications can occur.

8. See Shell-Duncan and Hernlund (2000) for a collection of case studies on female genital modification in various parts of Africa.

9. Far earlier, in the 1820s, circumcising practices were also at the center of debates in the Sudan (Abusharaf 1999).

10. In the Hindu practice of *sati*, a widow immolates herself on her husband's funeral pyre. *Sati* became the subject of considerable debate in India during British colonial rule, leading to abolition in 1829. The *sati* controversy, like debates about female genital operations, involves a wide range of perspectives and has been framed at various times in terms of women's status, issues of tradition, authority, religious rights, personal autonomy, and humanitarianism. Outlawing *sati* did not make it disappear entirely. "Through the 1970s and 1980s . . . [the same time when circumcision controversies were heating up], either incidents of *sati* increased or greater scrutiny was brought to bear on the issue, primarily by women's organizations" (Courtright 1994:47). In September 1987, the case of Roop Kanwar, a young Hindu woman who burned in Rajasthan, galvanized national debate. Nandy (1988) and Mani (1990b) have noted continuities of language and argument between contemporary Indian positions and earlier colonial debates, parallels similar to those in circumcision controversies. Both debates involve "instabilities of perspective, of meaning, of judgment," and provide avenues for considering the "social history of moral imagination" (Geertz 1983:42). See also Mani (1990a), Nandy (1975), and Teltscher (1995:37–72).

11. Different aspects of this debate are described in Murray (1974; 1976), Pederson (1991), and Lonsdale (1992:388–397). Descriptions of Kikuyu initiation and contemporary women's attitudes can be found in Davison et al. (1989). Thomas discusses debates in nearby Meru, Kenya, and their connections with many other domains of life (1996; 1997).

12. For instance, several 1990s immigration cases and asylum claims in the United States have been based on arguments about the persecution of women through genital operations. Lydia Oluloro, a Nigerian woman, fought deportation on the grounds that she was protecting her daughters from the procedure. Her case was profiled in newspapers and on television in a segment

of *Sixty Minutes* in 1994. A woman from Togo, Fauziya Kassindja, was also granted asylum in 1996, and a woman calling herself "Adelaide Abankwah" received asylum in the United States in 1999. Highly publicized cases in France in the 1990s prosecuted immigrant parents and ritual surgeons who continued the practice in their new country (Verdier 1992; Winter 1994). Kratz (2002) analyzes several asylum cases heard in the United States.

13. See for example Dawit (1997).

14. Actors and institutions involved in each arena might include the following. (1) *In each home country:* National governments and politicians' local NGOs and national action groups; international action groups; churches; religious and ethnic communities whose circumcising practice may differ and whose histories of education and involvement with government also differ. Within each circumcising community, differences of age, gender, education, religion, and wealth also influence positions. For instance, a Christian mother, her non-Christian husband, his educated brother, and their school-child daughter might disagree about whether the girl should participate with her friends in initiation ceremonies during a school holiday. Peters (1997:484–486) discusses the different positions within the Togolese family and community in the asylum case of Fauziya Kassindja as an actual example. See Gruenbaum (1996:463–470) and the film *Bintou in Paris* for other examples. (2) *In the United States and Europe:* Female genital modification was historically recognized as a viable medical procedure in these countries, "cosmetic" labial surgery on women is currently performed, and male circumcision is also widely practiced. Current female genital operations within their borders are usually debated in relation to immigrant families and communities from various "home countries." Some families and communities have lived outside their home countries for quite a while, with some children born and raised in the United States and Europe. Actors involved in these debates include immigrants themselves (again with differences of gender, religion, ethnicity, education, length of residence, etc.); their community organizations and spokespersons; national, state, and municipal governments, judiciaries, and agencies dealing with immigrants (e.g., Immigration and Naturalization Service, Health and Human Services, child welfare services, etc.); national action groups and organizations concerned with women and children; and international action groups. (3) *In international campaigns:* These actors may also be engaged with those in "home countries" and in the United States or Europe, but they reach beyond national boundaries as well. They include international action groups based in various countries; the United Nations, World Health Organization, and related international agencies and NGOs; journalists; religious officials; national governments and politicians who seek conditionality clauses for foreign policy and provision of aid.

15. In many contexts, however, ritual meanings and patterns unite the two for practitioners, who often use a single word for both operations in local languages.

16. Fran Hosken may have coined the term, though I could not verify this. She certainly played a key role in popularizing it through the Women's International Network (WIN) newsletter she wrote. By the time she wrote the Hosken Report in 1979, *female genital mutilation* had become her standard term. Before 1975, she vacillated between that term and *female circumcision.* Mary Daly also used "genital mutilations" in her 1978 book. In the British parliamentary debates about Kenya, the word *mutilation* was used at times to distinguish between two different types of genital operations (infibulation was not at issue in this controversy), but it did not become the primary term of reference (Pederson 1991:666). The Church of Scotland Mission, however, did begin to use the term *sexual mutilation* (Pederson 1991:671).

17. There are striking parallels between these shifts in rhetoric and tactics and the rhetoric of radical anti-abortion organizations such as Operation Rescue.

18. Duggers eschewed the automatic condemnation of "mutilation," the medical implications of "surgery," and what she considered the "mildness" of "female circumcision" (Moses 1997:4).

19. A number of scholarly papers discuss the problems with these generalized images and show how they are constructed; Mohanty (1988) and Stephens (1989) are a good starting place. Alice Walker's books, *Possessing the Secret of Joy* and *Warrior Marks,* are commonly used as novelistic examples. Walker's representations of African women have also been discussed by a number of scholars; Obiora (1997:323–328) and Mugo (1997) are examples focused on their relation to controversies about female genital modification.

20. Information about campaigns against male genital operations is available from NOCIRC (National Organization of Circumcision Information Resource Centers) or NOHARMM (National Organization to Halt the Abuse and Routine Mutilation of Males). Both can be found through Web searches.

21. Examples of different body modifications illustrate the different kinds and contexts of "choice" involved in self-determination. Operations for breast reduction or enhancement, multiple ear piercings, and body piercings (including genital piercings) are modifications often presented by their American or European practitioners as ways to take control of one's body. These self-definitions are very much like local definitions of female genital operations in initiation, also seen as a sign of self-control, maturity, and both social and personal change. In both cases, the practices are linked to understandings of the body, aesthetics, sexuality, and gender relations, but the understandings are rather different, as are their social and institutional settings.

22. See Gruenbaum (1996:460–463) for further discussion of so-called false consciousness and the costs and benefits of female genital operations for various segments of Sudanese communities.

23. I have talked with many people in the United States who seek a "logical" explanation or rationale for traditions of female genital modification. When I summarize

what Okiek in Kenya might say in response—e.g., that initiation is necessary for children to become adults—Americans have a hard time understanding and accepting these as "reasons." What for Okiek are logically satisfying, deeply felt, and natural understandings do not have for Americans the same intuitive sense and resonance. It is equally hard to answer Okiek questions about Americans, whom they sometimes encounter as tourists: Why do the women paint their mouths to look like they drink blood? Why do they walk about without clothing (e.g., in bathing suits)? Don't they feel shame? Why aren't girls initiated—how can they live their entire lives as children?

REFERENCES

Abusharaf, Rogaia Mustafa. 1999. Beyond "The External Messiah Syndrome": What Are Sudanese People Doing to End Ritualized Genital Surgeries? Paper presented at the Annual Meetings of the American Anthropological Association, Chicago. Session on Female Genital Cutting: Local Dynamics of a Global Debate.

An-Na`im, Abdullahi, ed. 1992. *Human Rights in Cross-Cultural Perspectives: A Quest for Consensus.* Philadelphia: University of Pennsylvania Press.

An-Na`im, Abdullahi, and Francis Deng, eds. 1990. *Human Rights in Africa : Cross-Cultural Perspectives.* Washington, DC: The Brookings Institution.

Apena, Adeline. 1996. Female Circumcision in Africa and the Problem of Cross-Cultural Perspectives. *Africa Update* 3(2):7–8 (see below for Web version).

Berlin, Isaiah. 1991. *The Crooked Timber of Humanity.* New York: Alfred A. Knopf.

Boddy, Janice. 1989. *Wombs and Alien Spirits.* Madison: University of Wisconsin Press.

Boyarin, Daniel. 1992. "This We Know to Be Carnal Israel": Circumcision and the Erotic Life of God and Israel. *Critical Inquiry* 18(3):474–505.

Courtright, Paul. 1994. The Iconographies of Sati. In *Sati, the Blessing and the Curse.* Ed. John S. Hawley. New York: Oxford University Press.

Daly, Mary. 1990. African Genital Mutilation: The Unspeakable Atrocities. In *Gyn/ecology.* Boston: Beacon Press (originally 1978).

Davison, Jean, with the women of Mutira. 1989. *Voices from Mutira: Lives of Rural Gikuyu Women.* Boulder: Lynn Rienner.

Dawit, Seble. 1997. Letter from a Female Circumcision Activist. *Colloquium: The On-line Magazine of the Case Western Reserve Law Review.* November 1997:lawwww.cwru.edu/cwrulaw/publications/colloquium/dawitfea.html.

Desjarlais, Robert. 1997. *Shelter Blues: Sanity and Selfhood Among the Homeless.* Philadelphia: University of Pennsylvania Press.

Dussart, Françoise. 2000. *The Politics of Ritual in an Aboriginal Settlement: Kinship, Gender and the Currency of Knowledge.* Washington, DC: Smithsonian Institution Press.

Geertz, Clifford. 1983. Found in Translation: On the Social History of Moral Imagination. In *Local Knowledge.* New York: Basic Books.

Gruenbaum, Ellen. 1996. The Cultural Debate over Female Circumcision: The Sudanese Are Arguing This One Out for Themselves. *Medical Anthropology Quarterly* 10(4): 455–475.

Hernlund, Ylva. 1999. Ritual Negotiations and Cultural Compromise: An Alternative Initiation in the Gambia. Paper presented at the Annual Meetings of the American Anthropological Association, session on Female Genital Cutting: Local Dynamics of a Global Debate.

Holmes, Douglas R. 2000. *Integral Europe: Fast-Capitalism, Multiculturalism, Neofascism.* Princeton, NJ: Princeton University Press.

Hosken, Fran. 1979. *The Hosken Report.* Lexington, MA: Women's International Network News.

Hutchinson, Sharon. 1996. *Nuer Dilemmas.* Berkeley: University of California Press.

Iweriebor, Ifeyinwa. 1996. Brief Reflections on Clitoridectomy. *Africa Update* 3(2):2 (see below for Web version).

Koso-Thomas, Olayinka. 1987. *The Circumcision of Women: A Strategy for Eradication.* London: Zed Books.

Kratz, Corinne. 1994. *Affecting Performance: Meaning, Movement, and Experience in Okiek Women's Initiation.* Washington, DC: Smithsonian Institution Press.

———. 1999a. Contexts, Controversies, Dilemmas: Teaching Circumcision." In *Great Ideas for Teaching About Africa.* Eds. Misty Bastian and Jane Parpart. Boulder: Lynne Rienner, pp. 103–118.

———. 1999b. Female Circumcision in Africa. In *Africana: Encyclopedia of the African and African American Experience.* Eds. Kwame Anthony Appiah and Henry Louis Gates, Jr. New York: Perseus Publishing. Co-published with CD-ROM version by Microsoft.

———. 2002. Circumcision Debates and Asylum Cases: Intersecting Arenas, Contested Values, and Tangled Webs. In *Engaging Cultural Differences: The Multicultural Challenge in Liberal Democracies.* Eds. Richard A. Shweder, Hazel R. Markus, and Martha Minow. New York: Russell Sage Foundation.

Laumann, E. O., C. M. Masi, and E. W. Zuckerman. 1997. Circumcision in the United States: Prevalence, Prophylactic Effects, and Sexual Practice. *Journal of the American Medical Association* 277(13):1052–1057.

Leonard, Lori. 1999. "We Did It for Pleasure Only": Hearing Alternative Tales of Female Circumcision. Paper presented at the Annual Meetings of the American Anthropological Association, session on Female Genital Cutting: Local Dynamics of a Global Debate.

Lonsdale, John. 1992. Wealth, Poverty, and Civic Virtue in Kikuyu Political Thought. In B. Berman and J. Lonsdale, *Unhappy Valley: Conflict in Kenya and Africa.* London: James Currey.

Lyons, Harriet. 1981. Anthropologists, Moralities, and Relativities: The Problem of Genital Mutilations. *Canadian Review of Sociology and Anthropology* 18(4):499–518.

Mani, Lata. 1990a. Contentious Traditions: The Debate on *Sati* in Colonial India. In *The Nature and Context of Minority Discourse*. Eds. A. JanMohamed and D. Lloyd. Oxford: Oxford University Press.

———. 1990b. Multiple Mediations: Feminist Scholarship in the Age of Multinational Reception. *Feminist Review* 35:24–40.

Matias, Aisha Samad. 1996. Female Circumcision in Africa. *Africa Update* 3(2):3–6.

Mohanty, Chandra. 1988. Under Western Eyes: Feminist Scholarship and Colonial Discourses. *Feminist Review* 30:61–88.

Morison, Linda, Caroline Scherf, Gloria Ekpo, et. al. 2001. The Long-term Reproductive Health Consequences of Female Genital Cutting in Rural Gambia: A Community-Based Survey. *Tropical Medicine and International Health* 6(8):643–653.

Moses, Meredith. 1997. Watching the Watchdog: Female Circumcision in *The New York Times.* Student paper, Emory University.

Mugo, Micere. 1997. Elitist Anti-Circumcision Discourse as Mutilating and Anti-Feminist. *Case Western Reserve Law Review* 47(2):461–80.

Murray, Jocelyn. 1974. The Kikuyu Female Circumcision Controversy, with Special Reference to the Church Missionary Society's "Sphere of Influence." Ph.D. dissertation, University of California, Los Angeles.

———. 1976. The Church Missionary Society and the "Female Circumcision" Issue in Kenya, 1929–1932. *Journal of Religion in Africa* 8(2):92–104.

Nandy, Ashis. 1975. Sati: A Nineteenth Century Tale of Women, Violence, and Protest. In *Rammohun Roy and the Process of Modernization in India*. Ed. V. C. Joshi. Delhi: Vikas Publishing House.

———. 1988. The Human Factor. *The Illustrated Weekly of India*, 17 January, pp. 20–23.

Obiora, L. Amede. 1997. Bridges and Barricades: Rethinking Polemics and Intransigence in the Campaign Against Female Circumcision. *Case Western Reserve Law Review* 47(2):275–378.

Ogbu, M. A. 1997. Comment on Obiora's "Bridges and Barricades." *Case Western Reserve Law Review* 47(2):411–422.

Parker, Melissa. 1995. Rethinking Female Circumcision. *Africa* 65(4):506–524.

Pederson, Susan. 1991. National Bodies, Unspeakable Acts: The Sexual Politics of Colonial Policymaking. *Journal of Modern History* 63:647–680.

Peters, Pauline. 1997. Another Bridge to Cross: Between "Outside" and "Inside." *Case Western Reserve Law Review* 47(2):481–490.

Rofel, Lisa. 1999. *Other Modernities: Gendered Yearnings in China After Socialism.* Berkeley: University of California Press.

Shell-Duncan, Bettina. 2001. The Medicalization of Female "Circumcision": Harm Reduction or Promotion of a Dangerous Practice? *Social Science and Medicine* 52: 1013–1028.

Shell-Duncan, Bettina, and Ylva Hernlund, eds. 2000. *Female "Circumcision" in Africa: Culture, Controversy and Change.* Boulder, CO: Lynne Rienner.

Shweder, Richard. 2002. What About Female Genital Mutilation? And Why Understanding Culture Matters in the First Place. In *Engaging Cultural Differences: The Multicultural Challenge in Liberal Democracies*. Eds. Richard A. Shweder, Hazel R. Markus, and Martha Minow. New York: Russell Sage Foundation.

Stephens, Julie. 1989. Feminist Fictions: A Critique of the Category "Non-Western Woman" in Feminist Writings on India. In *Subaltern Studies VI.* Ed. R. Guha. New York: Oxford University Press.

Teltscher, Kate. 1995. *India Inscribed: European and British Writing on India, 1600–1800.* Oxford: Oxford University Press.

Thomas, Lynn. 1996. "Ngaitana (I will circumcise myself)": The Gender and Generational Politics of the 1956 Ban on Clitoridectomy in Meru, Kenya. *Gender and History* 8(3):338–363.

———. 1997. Imperial Concerns and "Women's Affairs": State Efforts to Regulate Clitoridectomy and Eradicate Abortion in Meru, Kenya, c. 1920–1950. *Journal of African History*.

Verdier, Raymond. 1992. The *Exiseuse* in Criminal Court: the Trial of Soko Aramata Keita. *Passages* 3:1–3 (originally in *Droit et Cultures: Revue semestrielle d'anthropologie et d'histoire*, 1991).

Winter, Bronwyn. 1994. Women, the Law, and Cultural Relativism in France: The Case of Excision. *Signs* 19(4):939–974.

39

Advertising and Global Culture

Noreene Janus

Cultures have always undergone change, whether slow and evolutionary or rapid and revolutionary. Sometimes these changes make people's lives better and sometimes they make them worse. Some social change is spontaneous and unplanned; at other times change is the result of conscious efforts. Planned change can produce socially disastrous results or significant social benefits.

In this selection, Noreene Janus describes changes that are occurring on a global scale. The change agents —those creating the change—are transnational corporations and transnational advertising agencies. Through their efforts, Western goods and Western values are being introduced throughout the Third World, causing significant cultural transformations.

This selection raises the question of conflicting inalienable rights among the members of our global village. Some people believe that transnational advertisers have the inalienable right to sell their products in a free market without worrying about the burden of long-term social consequences. Most Third World people feel they have the right to access the world's consumer goods. But in doing so, are they aware of the long-term consequences that buying into the Western consumer model may have on the continuation of their cultural heritage? Some people think that Third World leaders should be warned of these consequences and have the opportunity to reject the consumer model by restricting advertising. The big question is whether Third World peoples are the beneficiaries or the victims of this global process of change.

As you read this selection, ask yourself the following questions:

- Are these global cultural changes spontaneous or planned? Who is responsible?
- What is the underlying value, the core, of transnational culture?
- What do you think is meant by "consumer democracy"?
- Do transnational advertisers seem to have their own culture, or set of values, about the legitimacy of their work?
- Do you think transnational advertisers have an inalienable right to advertise, or should restrictions be imposed on them?

The following terms discussed in this selection are included in the Glossary at the back of the book:

economy *transnational culture*

social stratification *values*

N o one can travel to Africa, Asia, or Latin America and not be struck by the Western elements of urban life. The symbols of transnational culture—automobiles, advertising, supermarkets, shopping centers, hotels, fast food chains, credit cards, and Hollywood movies—give the feeling of being at home. Behind these tangible symbols are a corresponding set of values and attitudes about time, consumption, work relations, etc. Some believe global culture has resulted from gradual spontaneous processes that depended solely on technological innovations—increased international trade, global mass communications, jet travel. Recent studies show that the processes are anything but spontaneous; that they are the result of tremendous investments of time, energy and money by transnational corporations.

This "transnational culture" is a direct outcome of the internationalization of production and accumulation promoted through standardized development models and cultural forms.

From *Cultural Survival* 7(2): 28–31, 1983. Reprinted with permission of *Cultural Survival*.

The common theme of transnational culture is consumption. Advertising expresses this ideology of consumption in its most synthetic and visual form.

Advertisers rely on few themes: happiness, youth, success, status, luxury, fashion, and beauty. In advertising, social contradictions and class differences are masked and workplace conflicts are not shown. Advertising campaigns suggest that solutions to human problems are to be found in individual consumption, presented as an ideal outlet for mass energies . . . a socially acceptable form of action and participation which can be used to defuse potential political unrest. "Consumer democracy" is held out to the poor around the world as a substitute for political democracy. After all, as the advertising executive who transformed the U.S. Pepsi ad campaign "Join the Pepsi Generation" for use in Brazil as "Join the Pepsi Revolution" explains, most people have no other means to express their need for social change other than by changing brands and increasing their consumption.

Transnational advertising is one of the major reasons both for the spread of transnational culture and the breakdown of traditional cultures. Depicting the racy foreign lifestyles of a blond jetsetter in French or English, it associates Western products with modernity. That which is modern is good; that which is traditional is implicitly bad, impeding the march of progress. Transnational culture strives to eliminate local cultural variations. Barnett and Muller (1974:178) discuss the social impact of this process:

> What are the long range social effects of advertising on people who earn less than $200 a year? (Peasants, domestic workers, and laborers) learn of the outside world through the images and slogans of advertising. One message that comes through clearly is that happiness, achievement, and being white have something to do with one another. In mestizo countries (sic) such as Mexico and Venezuela where most of the population still bear strong traces of their Indian origin, billboards depicting the good life for sale invariably feature blond, blue-eyed American-looking men and women. One effect of such "white is beautiful" advertising is to reinforce feelings of inferiority which are the essence of a politically immobilizing colonial mentality. . . . The subtle message of the global advertiser in poor countries is "Neither you nor what you create are worth very much; *we will sell you a civilization*" (emphasis added).

But global culture is the incidental outcome of transnational marketing logic more than it is the result of a conscious strategy to subvert local cultures. It is marketing logic, for example, that created the "global advertising campaign," one single advertising message used in all countries where the product is made or distributed. This global campaign is both more efficient and less expensive for a firm. Thus, before the

intensification of violence in rural Guatemala, for example, farmers gathered around the only television set in their village to watch an advertisement for Revlon perfume showing a blonde woman strolling down Fifth Avenue in New York—the same advertisement shown in the U.S. and other countries.

Transnational firms and global advertising agencies are clearly aware of the role of advertising in the creation of a new consumer culture in Third World countries. A top Israeli advertising executive says,

> Television antennas are gradually taking the place of the tom-tom drums across the vast stretches of Africa. Catchy jingles are replacing tribal calls in the Andes of Latin America. Spic-and-span supermarkets stand on the grounds where colorful wares of an Oriental Bazaar were once spread throughout Asia. Across vast continents hundreds of millions of people are awakening to the beat of modern times. Is the international advertiser fully aware of the magnitude of this slow but gigantic process? Is he alert to the development of these potential markets? Does he know how to use and apply the powerful tools of modern advertising to break into these vast areas of emerging consumers despite the barriers of illiteracy, tribal customs, religious prejudices and primitive beliefs? How great is the potential, and how promising are the prospects of the pioneer industrialist, marketer or advertiser who will venture into this vast Terra Incognita? [Tal, 1974].

Increasingly advertising campaigns are aimed at the vast numbers of poor in Third World countries. As one U.S. advertising executive observes about the Mexican consumer market, even poor families, when living together and pooling their incomes, can add up to a household income of more than $10,000 per year. He explains how they can become an important marketing target:

> The girls will need extra for cosmetics and clothes, but Jaime needs date money and, of course, something is going into the bank to send Carlito to the university. Once all day-to-day expenses have been covered there will come the big decisions that change lifestyles from month to month.
>
> First will probably be a TV set. Nobody can visit Latin America and not be shocked at the number of antennas on top of shacks. And once the TV set goes to work the Fernandez family is like a kid in a candy store. They are the audience that add up to five and one-half hours of viewing a day. They are pounded by some 450 commercials a week. They see all the beautiful people and all the beautiful things. And what they see, they want [Criswell, 27 October 1975].

Since an important characteristic of transnational culture is the speed and breadth with which it is transmitted, communications and information systems play an important role, permitting a message to be distributed globally through television series, news, magazines, comics, and films. The use of television to spread transnational culture is especially effective with illiterates. Grey Advertising International undertook a worldwide study of television to determine its usefulness as an advertising channel and reported that:

> Television is undisputedly the key communications development of our era. It has demonstrated its power to make the world a global village; to educate and inform; to shape the values, attitudes, and lifestyles of generations growing up with it. In countries where it operates as an unfettered commercial medium it has proven for many products the most potent of all consumer marketing weapons as well as a major influence in establishing corporate images and affecting public opinion on behalf of business [Grey Advertising International, 1977].

What do we know about the impact of transnational culture on Third World cultures? Personal observations are plentiful. Anyone who has heard children singing along with television commercials and introducing these themes into their daily games begins to see the impact. There are more extensive analyses as well. Pierre Thizier Seya studied the impact of transnational advertising on cultures in the Ivory Coast. He notes that transnational firms such as Colgate and Nestle have helped to replace traditional products—often cheaper and more effective—with industrialized toothpastes and infant formulas.

> By consuming Coca-Cola, Nestle products, Marlboro, Maggi, Colgate or Revlon, Ivorians are not only fulfilling unnecessary needs but also progressively relinquishing their authentic world outlook in favor of the transnational way of life [Seya, 1982:17].

Advertising of skin-lightening products persuades the African women to be ashamed of their own color and try to be white.

> In trying to be as white as possible, that is to say, in becoming ashamed of their traditional being, the Ivorians are at the same time relinquishing one of the most powerful weapons at their disposal for safeguarding their dignity as human beings: their racial identity. And advertising is not neutral in such a state of affairs [Seya, 1982:18].

He also mentions that advertising is helping to change the Ivorian attitude toward aging, making women fear looking older and undermining the traditional respect for elders.

The consumption of soft drinks and hard liquor points to another social change. Traditionally drinks are consumed only in social settings, as evidenced by the large pot where they are stored. Yet, the advertising of Coca-Cola and Heineken portrays drinking as an individual act rather than a collective one.

A study carried out in Venezuela explores the relationship between television content and children's attitudes. Santoro (1975) analyzed a week of television programming and interviewed 900 sixth-grade children. The children were asked to invent a story by drawing the characters in a television screen and then to describe what they had drawn. The imaginary scenes were primarily stories about violence, crime, physical force, and competition, and the large majority of them depicted destructive actions motivated by greed. The "good" characters were primarily from the U.S., white, rich, of varied professions and English surnames. The "bad" characters were mostly from other countries including China and Germany, of black color, poor, workers or office personnel, and with English or Spanish surnames. Santoro concluded that these stereotypes held by children were largely the same ones to be found in typical Venezuelan television and advertising contents.

In another study carried out in Mexico by the National Consumer's Institute in 1981, more than 900 sixth-grade children were quizzed on the contents of their textbooks and the contents of commercial television. They knew more about television personalities than about national heroes and recognized more trademarks for snacks, soft drinks, chewing gum and so on than national symbols such as the flag, a map of the country, the major party's symbol, etc. They knew much more about soap operas and action series than they did about episodes of Mexican history. The researchers concluded that advertising and the television medium are far more effective teachers than the public school system. If children are learning about consumption, soap operas and transnational symbols, their parents must be also.

In another research project, seven-year-old Mexican children from different economic backgrounds were interviewed to determine the role of the mass media—primarily television—as sources of information, the relationship established between children and television, and the degree to which the children have internalized transnational consumption patterns (Janus, 1982).

Children were shown pictures of the same man in three different settings—family, nature, and luxury possessions and asked to choose which of these three was the happiest. The question was meant to show the degree to which the children accept the fundamental assumption of advertising: consumption brings happiness. While slightly more than half of the children chose the family scene, poorer children were significantly more likely to associate the luxury possessions with happiness than the rich children.

In the same study, children were shown a series of industrial products along with the traditional products they had replaced: Tang and fresh orange juice, Wonder bread and traditional rolls, Nescafe and coffee beans. The question was designed to determine the degree to which these children actually thought of the industrialized product as the principal form of the food. Again, poor children more often answered that Nescafe *is* coffee, and Tang *is* orange juice.

Perhaps the most interesting result of the study concerns the ability of children to analyze consumption in terms of class. They were shown different categories of consumer products such as cigarettes and television sets, and asked which a rich person could buy and which a poor person could buy. Virtually every child showed an acute awareness of the different access to these products by class. They knew very well that a rich person could buy any or all of the products whereas the poor could buy only the cigarettes, the Coca-Cola, the snackfoods, and the lipstick.

These results, while very tentative, suggest that the impact of transnational culture is greater among the poor—the very people who cannot afford to buy the lifestyle it represents. The poor are more likely to associate consumption with happiness and feel that industrialized products are better than the locally made ones. But at the same time they are painfully aware that only the rich have access to the lifestyle portrayed.

This leads us to the most important questions. What political impact does the spread of transnational culture have on the poor for whom luxury lifestyles are not possible? How do they deal with the daily contradictions that this awareness implies? How much will they accept and how much will they reject? How can they maintain their own identities in the face of transnational culture?

REFERENCES

Barnett, R. and R. Muller, 1974. *Global Reach*. New York: Simon and Schuster.

Criswell, R. 1975. "Keeping up with the Fernandez." *Advertising Age*. October 27.

Grey Advertising International. 1977. "Survey of International Television." *Grey Matter*.

Instituto Nacional del Consumidor (INCO). 1981. *La Television y Los Niños: Conocimiento de la "Realidad Televisiva" vs. Conocimiento de la "Realidad Nacional."* Mexico City: INCO.

Janus, N. 1982. "Spiderman Drinks Tang: Television and Transnational Culture in Mexican Children." Mexico: Instituto Latinoamericano de Estudios Transnacionales (ILET).

Santoro, E. 1975. *La Television Venezolana y La Formacion de Estereotipos en el Niño*. Caracas: Universidad Central de Venezuela.

Seya, P. T. 1982. "Advertising as an Ideological Apparatus of Transnational Capitalism in the Ivory Coast." Mimeographed copy.

40

How Sushi Went Global

Theodore C. Bestor

Cultures are always changing. If we take the broad anthropological view of cultural change in human prehistory and history, it is clear that the world is getting "smaller and smaller." In addition to the remarkable technological advances in electronic media and jet travel, the world is "smaller" because there is less cultural diversity in the world, as evidenced, in part, by the rapid decline in the number of remaining human languages. Particularly in the past decade, societies all around the world have become more closely linked within a single world capitalist system. This type of cultural and economic change has both good and bad aspects, although many people would argue that, in general, the good aspects are enjoyed by the relatively rich and the negative aspects tend to burden the relatively poor. Local societies experience and interpret global changes in different ways: People are influenced not only by their own traditions and customs but also by the attractive, exotic, and luxurious aspects of "modern" cultural traditions.

This selection provides a good illustration of two different processes of culture change that are often discussed under the term *globalization*. One process links tuna fishermen in Maine with the fresh sushi market in Tokyo (while being influenced by new businesses of tuna-fattening lots off the coast of Spain and Morocco). The second change involves the spread of sushi into societies such as the United States where the raw sliced fish rolls have become a popular, cosmopolitan, and elite food item. When we first started teaching anthropology, students were revolted when they heard of the Japanese cuisine consisting of raw fish, seaweed, and rice. Cultures are always changing.

Globalization is a pattern of economic and cultural change involving the mutual influence of previously separate and distinct societies. This is not a new phenomenon, because the entire period of colonialization was one of unequal transnational economic and cultural exchange. In the postcolonial world, the processes of globalization are made possible by the advent of world capitalism. Multinational corporations are now world powers operating in a world market. On the local level, the flow of investment, profit, and consumer goods across borders can provide

access to cash for the producers of some luxury goods. In the long run, however, the evidence indicates that peripheral peoples become less well-off because of globalization, while wealth becomes more and more concentrated in the hands of a small elite.

In this selection we see that fishermen (following an ancient hunting-gathering tradition) do not eat what they catch but rather sell their fish on a world market. Japanese merchants travel halfway around the world to buy the fresh seafood, and the huge tuna is flown to Tokyo to be sold the next day. Indeed, it has become a small world, a global village.

As you read this selection, ask yourself the following questions:

- Why has sushi become popular in the United States? What is the attraction?

- What might be the ecological impact of the processes of globalization? For example, what will happen if the Atlantic tuna fishery is poorly regulated and becomes overfished?

- Is world cultural diversity diminishing through the process of global homogenization? Why?

- How is the value of Atlantic bluefin tuna sold on a little dock in Maine controlled by a Japanese fish market in Tokyo and influenced by a mishap that occurred off the southern coast of Spain?

- Do you eat sushi? Do the Atlantic fishermen eat sushi? Why are aesthetics part of the sushi experience?

The following terms discussed in this selection are included in the Glossary at the back of the book:

CITES (Convention on International Trade and Endangered Species)

globalization

luxury

regional economy

sushi

A 40-minute drive from Bath, Maine, down a winding two-lane highway, the last mile on a dirt road, a ramshackle wooden fish pier stands beside an empty parking lot. At 6:00 p.m. nothing much is happening. Three bluefin tuna sit in a huge tub of ice on the loading dock.

Between 6:45 and 7:00, the parking lot fills up with cars and trucks with license plates from New Jersey, New York, Massachusetts, New Hampshire, and Maine. Twenty Tuna buyers clamber out, half of them Japanese. The three bluefin, ranging from 270 to 610 pounds, are winched out of the tub, and buyers crowd around them, extracting tiny core samples to examine their color, fingering the flesh to assess the fat content, sizing up the curve of the body.

After about 20 minutes of eyeing the goods, many of the buyers return to their trucks to call Japan by cellphone and get the morning prices from Tokyo's Tsukiji market—the fishing industry's answer to Wall Street—where the daily tuna auctions have just concluded. The buyers look over the tuna one last time and give written bids to the dock manager, who passes the top bid for each fish to the crew that landed it.

The auction bids are secret. Each bid is examined anxiously by a cluster of young men, some with a father or uncle looking on to give advice, others with a young woman and a couple of toddlers trying to see Daddy's fish. Fragments of concerned conversation float above the parking lot: "That's all?" "Couldn't we do better if we shipped it ourselves?" "Yeah, but my pickup needs a new transmission now!" After a few minutes, deals are closed and the fish are quickly loaded onto the backs of trucks in crates of crushed ice, known in the trade as "tuna coffins." As rapidly as they arrived, the flotilla of buyers sails out of the parking lot—three bound for New York's John F. Kennedy Airport, where their tuna will be airfreighted to Tokyo for sale the day after next.

Bluefin tuna may seem at first an unlikely case study in globalization. But as the world rearranges itself—around silicon chips, Starbucks coffee, or sashimi-grade tuna—new channels for global flows of capital and commodities link far-flung individuals and communities in unexpected new relationships. The tuna trade is a prime example of the globalization of a regional industry, with intense international competition and thorny environmental regulations; centuries-old practices combined with high technology; realignments of labor and capital in response to international regulation; shifting markets; and the diffusion of culinary culture as tastes for sushi, and bluefin tuna, spread worldwide.

GROWING APPETITES

Tuna doesn't require much promotion among Japanese consumers. It is consistently Japan's most popular seafood, and demand is high throughout the year. When the Federation of Japan Tuna Fisheries Cooperative (known as Nikkatsuren) runs ad campaigns for tuna, they tend to be low-key and whimsical, rather like the "Got Milk?" advertising in the United States. Recently the federation launched "Tuna Day" (Maguro no hi), providing retailers with posters and recipe cards for recipes more complicated than "slice and serve chilled." Tuna Day's mascot is Goro-kun, a colorful cartoon tuna swimming the Australian crawl.

Despite the playful contemporary tone of the mascot, the date selected for Tuna Day carries much heavier freight. October 10, it turns out, commemorates the date that tuna first appeared in Japanese literature, in the eighth-century collection of imperial court poetry known as the *Man'yoshu*—one of the towering classics of Japanese literature. The neat twist is that October 10 today is a national holiday, Sports Day. Goro-kun, the sporty tuna, scores a promotional hat trick, suggesting intimate connections among national culture, healthy food for active lives, and the family holiday meal.

Outside of Japan, tuna, especially raw tuna, hasn't always had it so good. Sushi isn't an easy concept to sell to the uninitiated. And besides, North Americans tend to think of cultural influence as flowing from West to East: James Dean, baseball, Coca-Cola, McDonald's, and Disneyland have all gone over big in Tokyo. Yet Japanese cultural motifs and material—from Kurosawa's *The Seven Samurai* to Yoda's Zen and Darth Vader's armor, from Issey Miyake's fashions to Nintendo, PlayStation, and Pokémon—have increasingly saturated North American and indeed the entire world's consumption and popular culture. Against all odds, so too has sushi.

In 1929, the *Ladies' Home Journal* introduced Japanese cooking to North American women, but discreetly skirted the subject of raw fish: "There have been purposely omitted . . . any recipes using the delicate and raw tuna fish which is sliced wafer thin and served iced with attractive garnishes. [These] . . . might not sound so entirely delicious as they are in reality." Little mention of any Japanese food appeared in U.S. media until well after World War II. By the 1960s, articles on sushi began to show up in lifestyle magazines like *Holiday* and *Sunset*. But the recipes they suggested were canapés like cooked shrimp on caraway rye bread, rather than raw fish on rice.

Reprinted with permission from *Foreign Policy*, November/December 2000, pp. 54–63.

STATELESS FISH

As the bluefin business grows ever more lucrative, the risk of overfishing has become ever more real. The question of who profits form the world's demand for sushi makes for battles among fishers, regulators, and conservationists.

Bluefin tuna have been clocked at 50 miles per hour, and tagged fish have crossed the Atlantic in about two months. Since bluefin swim across multiple national jurisdictions, international regulations must impose political order on stateless fish.

Charged with writing those regulations is the International Commission for the Conservation of Atlantic Tunas (ICCAT), which assigns quotas for bluefin tuna and related species in the North Atlantic and the Mediterranean and directs catch reporting, trade monitoring, and populations assessments. Based in Madrid since its founding in 1969, ICCAT now has 28 members, including Atlantic and Mediterranean fishing countries and three global fishing powers: South Korea, China, and Japan.

In recent years, conservation groups have criticized ICCAT for not regulating more aggressively to prevent or reverse an apparent bluefin population decline in the Western Atlantic. Some activists have campaigned to have bluefin tuna protected under the Convention on International Trade in Endangered Species, or CITES. At least in part to keep that from happening, Japan and ICCAT have implemented new systems to track and regulate trade; "undocumented fish" from nations that fail to comply with ICCAT regulations are now banned from Japanese markets.

Regulations, though, are complicated by how far and fast these fish can travel: No one can say for certain whether there is one bluefin population in the Atlantic or several. ICCAT, the U.S. National Academy of Sciences, the National Audubon Society, and industry groups disagree over how many bluefin migrate across the Atlantic, and whether or not they are all part of the same breeding stock. What's the big deal? If there are two (or more) stocks, as ICCAT maintains, then conservation efforts can vary from one side of the Atlantic to the other.

When ICCAT registered a dramatic decline in bluefin catches off North America, it imposed stringent quotas on North America's mainly small-scale fishing outfits. On the European side of the Atlantic, however, industrial-strength fishing efforts continued. American fishers, not surprisingly, point to evidence of cross-Atlantic migration and genetic studies of intermingling to argue that Europeans need to conserve bluefin more strenuously as well. ICCAT's regulations, they argue, protect bluefin at America's expense only, and ultimately, fishers from other countries pocket Japanese yen.

—T.C.B.

A decade later, however, sushi was growing in popularity throughout North America, turning into a sign of class and educational standing. In 1972, the *New York Times* covered the opening of a sushi bar in the elite sanctum of New York's Harvard Club. *Esquire* explained the fare in an article titled "Wake up Little Sushi!" Restaurant reviewers guided readers to Manhattan's sushi scene, including innovators like Shalom Sushi, a kosher sushi bar in SoHo.

Japan's emergence on the global economic scene in the 1970s as the business destination du jour, coupled with a rejection of hearty, red-meat American fare in favor of healthy cuisine like rice, fish, and vegetables, and the appeal of the high-concept aesthetics of Japanese design all prepared the world for a sushi fad. And so, from an exotic, almost unpalatable ethnic specialty, then to haute cuisine of the most rarefied sort, sushi has become not just cool, but popular. The painted window of a Cambridge, Massachusetts, coffee shop advertises "espresso, cappuccino, carrot juice, lasagna, and sushi." Mashed potatoes with wasabi (horseradish), sushi-ginger relish, and seared sashimi-grade tuna steaks show Japan's growing cultural influence on upscale nouvelle cuisine throughout North America, Europe, and Latin America. Sushi has even become the stuff of fashion, from "sushi" lip gloss, col-ored the deep red of raw tuna, to "wasabi" nail polish, a soft avocado green.

ANGLING FOR NEW CONSUMERS

Japan remains the world's primary market for fresh tuna for sushi and sashimi; demand in other countries is a product of Japanese influence and the creation of new markets by domestic producers looking to expand their reach. Perhaps not surprisingly, sushi's global popularity as an emblem of a sophisticated, cosmopolitan consumer class more or less coincided with a profound transformation in the international role of the Japanese fishing industry. From the 1970s onward, the expansion of 200-mile fishing limits around the world excluded foreign fleets from the prime fishing grounds of many coastal nations. And international environmental campaigns forced many countries, Japan among them, to scale back their distant water fleets. With their fishing operations curtailed and their yen for sushi still growing, Japanese had to turn to foreign suppliers.

Jumbo jets brought New England's bluefin tuna into easy reach of Tokyo, just as Japan's consumer economy—a byproduct of the now disparaged "bubble" years—went into hyperdrive. The sushi business boomed. During the 1980s, total Japanese imports of fresh bluefin tuna worldwide increased from 957 metric tons (531 from the United States) in 1984 to 5,235 metric tons (854 from the United States) in 1993. The average wholesale price peaked in 1990 at 4,00 yen (U.S. $34) per kilogram, bones and all, which trimmed out to approximately U.S.$33 wholesale per edible pound.

Not surprisingly, Japanese demand for prime bluefin tuna—which yields a firm red meat, lightly marbled with veins of fat, highly prized (and priced) in Japanese cuisine—created a gold-rush mentality on fishing grounds across the globe wherever bluefin tuna could be found. But in the early 1990s, as the U.S. bluefin industry was taking off, the Japanese economy went into a stall, then a slump, then a dive. U.S. producers suffered as their high-end export market collapsed. Fortunately for them, the North American sushi craze took up the slack. U.S. businesses may have written off Japan, but Americans' taste for sushi stuck. An industry founded exclusively on Japanese demand survived because of Americans' newly trained palates and a booming U.S. economy.

A TRANSATLANTIC TUSSLE

Atlantic bluefin tuna ("ABT" in the trade) are a highly migratory species that ranges from the equator to Newfoundland, from Turkey to the Gulf of Mexico. Bluefin can be huge fish; the record is 1,496 pounds. In more normal ranges, 600-pound tuna, 10 feet in length, are not extraordinary, and 250- to 300-pound bluefin, six feet long, are commercial mainstays.

Before bluefin became a commercial species in New England, before Japanese buyers discovered the stock, before the 747, bluefin were primarily sports fish, caught with fighting tackle by trophy hunters out of harbors like Montauk, Hyannis, and Kennebunkport. Commercial fishers, if they caught bluefin at all, sold them for cat food when they could and trucked them to town dumps when they couldn't. Japanese buyers changed all of that. Since the 1970s, commercial Atlantic bluefin tuna fisheries have been almost exclusively focused on Japanese markets like Tsukiji.

In New England waters, most bluefin are taken one fish at a time, by rod and reel, by hand line, or by harpoon—techniques of a small-scale fisher, not of a factory fleet. On the European side of the Atlantic, the industry operates under entirely different conditions. Rather than rod and reel or harpooning, the typical gear is industrial—the purse seiner (a fishing vessel closing a large net around a school of fish) or the long line (which catches fish on baited hooks strung along lines played out for many miles behind a swift vessel). The techniques may differ from boat to boat and from country to country, but these fishers are all angling for a share of the same Tsukiji yen—and in many cases, some biologists argue, a share of the same tuna stock. Fishing communities often think of themselves as close-knit and proudly parochial; but the sudden globalization of this industry has brought fishers into contact—and often into conflict—with customers, governments, regulators, and environmentalists around the world [see box on page 369].

Two miles off the beach in Barbate, Spain, a huge maze of nets snakes several miles out into Spanish waters near the Strait of Gibraltar. A high-speed, Japanese-made workboat heads out to the nets. On board are five Spanish hands, a Japanese supervisor, 2,500 kilograms of frozen herring and mackerel imported from Norway and Holland, and two American researchers. The boat is making one of its twice-daily trips to Spanish nets, which contain captured Mediterranean tuna being raised under Japanese supervision for harvest and export to Tsukiji.

Behind the guard boats that stand watch over the nets 24 hours a day, the headlands of Morocco are a hazy purple in the distance. Just off Barbate's white cliffs to the northwest, the light at the Cape of Trafalgar blinks on and off. For 20 minutes, the men toss herring and mackerel over the gunwales of the workboat while tuna the size (and speed) of Harley-Davidsons dash under the boat, barely visible until, with a flash of silver and blue, they wheel around to snatch a drifting morsel.

The nets, lines, and buoys are part of an *almadraba*, a huge fish trap used in Spain as well as Sicily, Tunisia, and Morocco. The *almadraba* consists of miles of nets anchored to the channel floor suspended from thousands of buoys, all laid out to cut across the migration routes of bluefin tuna leaving the strait. This *almadraba* remains in place for about six weeks in June and July to intercept tuna leaving the Mediterranean after their spawning season is over. Those tuna that lose themselves in the maze end up in a hug pen, roughly the size of a football field. By the end of the tuna run through the strait, about 200 bluefin are in the pen.

Two hundred fish may not sound like a lot, but if the fish survive the next six months, if the fish hit their target weights, if the fish hit the market at the target price, these 200 bluefin may be worth $1.6 million dollars. In November and December, after the bluefin season in New England and Canada is well over, the tuna are harvested and shipped by air to Tokyo in time for the end-of-the-year holiday spike in seafood consumption.

The pens, huge feed lots for tuna, are relatively new, but *almadraba* are not. A couple of miles down the

TOKYO'S PANTRY

Tsukiji, Tokyo's massive wholesale seafood market, is the center of the global trade in tuna. Here, 60,000 traders come each day to buy and sell seafood for Tokyo's 27 million mouths, moving more than 2.4 million kilograms of it in less than 12 hours. Boosters encourage the homey view that Tsukiji is *Tokyo no daidokoro*—Tokyo's pantry—but it is a pantry where almost $6 billion worth of fish change hands each year. New York City's Fulton Fish Market, the largest market in North America, handles only about $1 billion worth, and only about 13 percent of the tonnage of Tsukiji's catch.

Tuna are sold at a "moving auction." The auctioneer, flanked by assistants who record prices and fill out invoice slips at lightning speed, strides across the floor just above rows and rows of fish, moving quickly from one footstool to the next without missing a beat, or a bid. In little more than half an hour, teams of auctioneers from five auction houses sell several hundred (some days several thousand) tuna. Successful buyers whip out their cellphones, calling chefs to tell them what they've got. Meanwhile, faxes with critical information on prices and other market conditions alert fishers in distant ports to the results of Tsukiji's morning auctions. In return, Tsukiji is fed a constant supply of information on tuna conditions off Montauk, Cape Cod, Cartagena, Barbate, and scores of other fishing grounds around the world.

Tsukiji is the command post for a global seafood trade. In value, foreign seafood far exceeds domestic Japanese products on the auction block. (Tsukiji traders joke that Japan's leading fishing port is Tokyo's Narita International Airport.) On Tsukiji's slippery auction floor, tuna from Massachusetts may sell at auction for over $30,000 apiece, near octopus from Senegal, eel from Guangzhou, crab from Sakhalin, salmon from British Columbia and Hokkaido, snapper from Kyushu, and abalone from California.

Given the sheer volume of global trade, Tsukiji effectively sets the world's tuna prices. Last time I checked, the record price was over $200,000 for a particularly spectacular fish from Turkey—a sale noteworthy enough to make the front pages of Tokyo's daily papers. But spectacular prices are just the tip of Tsukiji's influence. The auction system and the commodity chains that flow in and out of the market integrate fishers, firms, and restaurants worldwide in a complex network of local and translocal economies.

As an undisputed hub of the fishing world, Tsukiji creates and deploys enormous amounts of Japanese cultural capital around the world. Its control of information, its enormous role in orchestrating and responding to Japanese culinary tastes, and its almost hegemonic definitions of supply and demand allow it the unassailable privilege of imposing its own standards of quality—standards that producers worldwide must heed.

—T.C.B.

coast from Barbate is the evocatively named settlement of Zahara de los Atunes (Zahara of the Tunas) where Cervantes lived briefly in the late 16th century. The centerpiece of the village is a huge stone compound that housed the men and nets of Zahara's *almadraba* in Cervantes's day, when the port was only a seasonally occupied tuna outpost (occupied by scoundrels, according to Cervantes). Along the Costa de la Luz, the three or four *almadraba* that remain still operate under the control of local fishing bosses who hold the customary fishing rights, the nets, the workers, the boats, and the locally embedded cultural capital to make the *almadraba* work—albeit for distant markets and in collaboration with small-scale Japanese fishing firms.

Inside the Strait of Gibraltar, off the coast of Cartagena, another series of tuna farms operates under entirely different auspices, utilizing neither local skills nor traditional technology. The Cartagena farms rely on French purse seiners to tow captured tuna to their pens, where joint ventures between Japanese trading firms and large-scale Spanish fishing companies have set up farms using the latest in Japanese fishing technology. The waters and the workers are Spanish, but almost everything else is part of a global flow of techniques and capital: financing from major Japanese trading companies; Japanese vessels to tend the nets; aquacultural techniques developed in Australia; vitamin supplements from European pharmaceutical giants packed into frozen herring from Holland to be heaved over the gunwales for the tuna; plus computer models of feeding schedules, weight gains, and target market prices developed by Japanese technicians and fishery scientists.

These "Spanish" farms compete with operations throughout the Mediterranean that rely on similar high-tech, high-capital approaches to the fish business. In the Adriatic Sea, for example, Croatia is emerging as a formidable tuna producer. In Croatia's case, the technology and the capital were transplanted by émigré Croatians who returned to the country from Australia after Croatia achieved independence from Yugoslavia in 1991. Australia, for its part, has developed a major aquacultural industry for southern bluefin tuna, a species closely related to the Atlantic bluefin of the North Atlantic and Mediterranean and almost equally desired in Japanese markets.

CULTURE SPLASH

Just because sushi is available, in some form or another, in exclusive Fifth Avenue restaurants, in baseball stadiums in Los Angeles, at airport snack carts in Amsterdam, at an apartment in Madrid (delivered by motorcycle), or in Buenos Aires, Tel Aviv, or Moscow, doesn't mean that sushi has lost its status as Japanese cultural property. Globalization doesn't necessarily homogenize cultural differences nor erase the salience of cultural labels. Quite the contrary, it grows the franchise. In the global economy of consumption, the brand equity of sushi as Japanese cultural property adds to the cachet of both the country and the cuisine. A Texan Chinese-American restauranteur told me, for example, that he had converted his chain of restaurants from Chinese to Japanese cuisine because the prestige factor of the latter meant he could charge a premium; his clients couldn't distinguish between Chinese and Japanese employees (and often failed to notice that some of the chefs behind his sushi bars were Latinos).

The brand equity is sustained by complicated flows of labor and ethnic biases. Outside of Japan, having Japanese hands (or a reasonable facsimile) is sufficient warrant for sushi competence. Guidebooks for the current generation of Japanese global *wandervogel* sometimes advise young Japanese looking for a job in a distant city to work as a sushi chef; U.S. consular offices in Japan grant more than 1,000 visas a year to sushi chefs, tuna buyers, and other workers in the global sushi business. A trade school in Tokyo, operating under the name Sushi Daigaku (Sushi University) offers short courses in sushi preparation so "students" can impress prospective employers with an imposing certificate. Even without papers, however, sushi remains firmly linked in the minds of Japanese and foreigners alike with Japanese cultural identity. Throughout the world, sushi restaurants operated by Koreans, Chinese, or Vietnamese maintain Japanese identities. In sushi bars from Boston to Valencia, a customer's simple greeting in Japanese can throw chefs into a panic (or drive them to the far end of the counter).

On the docks, too, Japanese cultural control of sushi remains unquestioned. Japanese buyers and "tuna techs" sent from Tsukiji to work seasonally on the docks of New England laboriously instruct foreign fishers on the proper techniques for catching, handling, and packing tuna for export. A bluefin tuna must approximate the appropriate *kata*, or "ideal form," of color, texture, fat content, body shape, and so forth, all prescribed by Japanese specifications. Processing requires proper attention as well. Special paper is sent from Japan for wrapping the fish before burying them in crushed ice. Despite high shipping costs and the fact that 50 percent of the gross weight of a tuna is unusable, tuna is sent to Japan whole, not sliced into salable portions. Spoilage is one reason for this, but form is another. Everyone in the trade agrees that Japanese workers are much more skilled in cutting and trimming tuna than Americans, and no one would want to risk sending botched cuts to Japan.

Not to impugn the quality of the fish sold in the United States, but on the New England docks, the first determination of tuna buyers is whether they are looking at a "domestic" fish or an "export" fish. On that judgment hangs several dollars a pound for the fisher, and the supply of sashimi-grade tuna for fishmongers, sushi bars, and seafood restaurants up and down the Eastern seaboard. Some of the best tuna from New England may make it to New York or Los Angeles, but by way of Tokyo—validated as top quality (and top price) by the decision to ship it to Japan by air for sale at Tsukiji, where it may be purchased by one of the handful of Tsukiji sushi exporters who supply premier expatriate sushi chefs in the world's leading cities.

PLAYING THE MARKET

The tuna auction at Yankee Co-op in Seabrook, New Hampshire, is about to begin on the second-to-last day of the 1999 season. The weather is stormy, few boats are out. Only three bluefin, none of them terribly good, are up for sale today, and the half-dozen buyers at the auction, three Americans and three Japanese, gloomily discuss the impending end of a lousy season.

In July, the bluefin market collapsed just as the U.S. fishing season was starting. In a stunning miscalculation, Japanese purse seiners operating out of Kesennuma in northern Japan managed to land their entire year's quota from that fishery in only three days. The oversupply sent tuna prices at Tsukiji through the floor, and they never really recovered.

Today, the news from Spain is not good. The day before, faxes and e-mails from Tokyo brought word that a Spanish fish farm had suffered a disaster. Odd tidal conditions near Cartagena led to a sudden and unexpected depletion of oxygen in the inlet where one of the great tuna nets was anchored. Overnight, 800 fish suffocated. Divers hauled out the tuna. The fish were quickly processed, several months before their expected prime, and shipped off to Tokyo. For the Japanese corporation and its Spanish partners, a harvest potentially worth $6.5 million would yield only a tiny fraction of that. The buyers at the morning's auctions in New Hampshire know they will suffer as well. Whatever fish turn up today and tomorrow, they will arrive at Tsukiji in the wake of an enormous glut of hastily exported Spanish tuna.

Fishing is rooted in local communities and local economies—even for fishers dipping their lines (or nets) in the same body of water, a couple hundred miles can be worlds away. Now, a Massachusetts fisher's livelihood can be transformed in a matter of hours by a spike in market prices halfway around the globe or by a disaster at a fish farm across the Atlantic. Giant fishing conglomerates in one part of the world sell their catch alongside family outfits from another. Environmental organizations on one continent rail against distant industry regulations implemented an ocean away. Such instances of convergence are common in a globalizing world. What is surprising, and perhaps more profound, in the case of today's tuna fishers, is the complex interplay between industry and culture, as an esoteric cuisine from an insular part of the world has become a global fad in the span of a generation, driving, and driven by, a new kind of fishing business.

Many New England fishers, whose traditional livelihood now depends on unfamiliar tastes and distant markets, turn to a kind of armchair anthropology to explain Japan's ability to transform tuna from trash into treasure around the world. For some, the quick answer is simply national symbolism. The deep red of tuna served as sashimi or sushi contrasts with the stark white rice, evoking the red and white of the Japanese national flag. Others know that red and white is an auspicious color combination in Japanese ritual life (lobster tails are popular at Japanese weddings for just

this reason). Still others think the cultural prize is a fighting spirit, pure machismo, both their own and the tuna's. Taken by rod and reel, a tuna may battle the fisher for four or five hours. Some tuna literally fight to the death. For some fishers, the meaning of tuna—the equation of tuna with Japanese identity—is simple: Tuna is nothing less than the samurai fish!

Of course, such mystification of a distant market's motivations for desiring a local commodity is not unique. For decades, anthropologists have written of "cargo cults" and "commodity fetishism" from New Guinea to Bolivia. But the ability of fishers today to visualize Japanese culture and the place of tuna within its demanding culinary tradition is constantly shaped and reshaped by the flow of cultural images that now travel around the globe in all directions simultaneously, bumping into each other in airports, fishing ports, bistros, bodegas, and markets everywhere. In the newly rewired circuitry of global cultural and economic affairs, Japan is the core, and the Atlantic seaboard, the Adriatic, and the Australian coast are all distant peripheries. Topsy-turvy as Gilbert and Sullivan never imagined it.

Japan is plugged into the popular North American imagination as the sometimes inscrutable superpower, precise and delicate in its culinary tastes, feudal in its cultural symbolism, and insatiable in its appetites. Were Japan not a prominent player in so much of the daily life of North Americans, the fishers outside of Bath or in Seabrook would have less to think about in constructing their Japan. As it is, they struggle with unfamiliar exchange rates for cultural capital that compounds in a foreign currency.

And they get ready for next season.

41

The Price of Progress

John H. Bodley

Anthropologists are not against progress: We do not want everyone to return to the "good old days" of our Paleolithic ancestors. On the other hand, the discoveries of cultural anthropologists have made us painfully aware of the human costs of unplanned social and economic change. Anthropologists do not want our society to plunge blindly into the future, unaware and unconcerned about how our present decisions will affect other people or future generations. Cultures are always changing, and the direction of that change is toward a single world system. As seen in the previous selection on advertising, cultures change because a society's economy is pulled into the world economy. "Progress" is a label placed on cultural and economic change, but whether something represents "progress" or not depends on one's perspective.

In this selection, John Bodley reviews some of the unexpected consequences of economic development in terms of health, ecological change, quality of life, and relative deprivation. We have seen this same theme in several previous selections—the invention of agriculture, for example. The benefits of economic development are not equally distributed within a developing society. In this selection, we see the relative costs and benefits of economic progress for some of the most marginalized people of the world—the tribal peoples who have been the traditional focus of cultural anthropology research. We believe that the problems detailed here should make our society think about the way cultural change can make people's lives worse; these are issues of social justice.

Anthropologists have been active in seeking solutions to many serious problems. At the same time, most anthropologists believe that tribal peoples have a right to lead their traditional lifestyles and not to be forced into change. In this regard, an organization called Cultural Survival has been active in the international political arena in protecting the land and rights of native peoples.

As you read this selection, ask yourself the following questions:

- What is meant by quality of life? Why might it increase or decrease for a population?
- What are the three ways in which economic development can change the distribution of disease?
- Why do people's diets change? Do people choose diets and behaviors that are harmful to them?
- What is meant by relative deprivation? Can you think of other examples of this process?
- Are tribal peoples more vulnerable to the negative impact of social and economic change than larger industrial societies?

The following terms discussed in this selection are included in the Glossary at the back of the book:

dental anthropology	*relative deprivation*
ecosystem	*self-sufficient*
ethnocentrism	*swidden cultivation*
nomadic band	*tribe*
population pressure	*urbanization*

In aiming at progress . . . you must let no one suffer by too drastic a measure, nor pay too high a price in upheaval and devastation, for your innovation.

—Maunier, 1949:725

From *Victims of Progress*, Fourth Edition by John Bodley, by permission of Mayfield Publishing Company. Copyright © 1999 by Mayfield Publishing Company.

Until recently, government planners have always considered economic development and progress beneficial goals that all societies should want to strive toward. The social advantages of progress—as defined in terms of increased incomes, higher standards of living, greater security, and better health—are thought to be positive, *universal* goods, to be obtained at any price. Although one may argue that tribal peoples must sacrifice their traditional cultures to obtain these benefits, government planners generally feel that this is a small price to pay for such obvious advantages.

In earlier chapters, evidence was presented to demonstrate that autonomous tribal peoples have not *chosen* progress to enjoy its advantages, but that governments have *pushed* progress upon them to obtain tribal resources, not primarily to share with the tribal peoples the benefits of progress. It has also been shown that the price of forcing progress on unwilling recipients has involved the deaths of millions of tribal people, as well as their loss of land, political sovereignty, and the right to follow their own life style. This chapter does not attempt to further summarize that aspect of the cost of progress, but instead analyzes the specific effects of the participation of tribal peoples in the world-market economy. In direct opposition to the usual interpretation, it is argued here that the benefits of progress are often both illusory and detrimental to tribal peoples when they have not been allowed to control their own resources and define their relationship to the market economy.

PROGRESS AND THE QUALITY OF LIFE

One of the primary difficulties in assessing the benefits of progress and economic development for any culture is that of establishing a meaningful measure of both benefit and detriment. It is widely recognized that *standard of living*, which is the most frequently used measure of progress, is an intrinsically ethnocentric concept relying heavily upon indicators that lack universal cultural relevance. Such factors as GNP, per capita income, capital formation, employment rates, literacy, formal education, consumption of manufactured goods, number of doctors and hospital beds per thousand persons, and the amount of money spent on government welfare and health programs may be irrelevant measures of actual *quality* of life for autonomous or even semiautonomous tribal cultures. In its 1954 report, the Trust Territory government indicated that since the Micronesian population was still largely satisfying its own needs within a cashless subsistence economy, "Money income is not a significant measure of living standards, production, or well-being in this area" (TTR, 1953:44). Unfortunately, within a short time the government began to rely on an enumeration of certain imported goods as indicators of a higher standard of living in the islands, even though many tradition-oriented islanders felt that these new goods symbolized a lowering of the quality of life.

A more useful measure of the benefits of progress might be based on a formula for evaluating cultures devised by Goldschmidt (1952:135). According to

these less ethnocentric criteria, the important question to ask is: Does progress or economic development increase or decrease a given culture's ability to satisfy the physical and psychological needs of its population, or its stability? This question is a far more direct measure of quality of life than are the standard economic correlates of development, and it is universally relevant. Specific indication of this *standard* of living could be found for any society in the nutritional status and general physical and mental health of its population, the incidence of crime and delinquency, the demographic structure, family stability, and the society's relationship to its natural resource base. A society with high rates of malnutrition and crime, and one degrading its natural environment to the extent of threatening its continued existence, might be described as at a lower standard of living than is another society where these problems did not exist.

Careful examination of the data, which compare, on these specific points, the former condition of self-sufficient tribal peoples with their condition following their incorporation into the world-market economy, leads to the conclusion that their standard of living is *lowered*, not raised, by economic progress—and often to a dramatic degree. This is perhaps the most outstanding and inescapable fact to emerge from the years of research that anthropologists have devoted to the study of culture change and modernization. Despite the best intentions of those who have promoted change and improvement, all too often the results have been poverty, longer working hours, and much greater physical exertion, poor health, social disorder, discontent, discrimination, overpopulation, and environmental deterioration—combined with the destruction of the traditional culture.

DISEASES OF DEVELOPMENT

> Perhaps it would be useful for public health specialists to start talking about a new category of diseases. . . . Such diseases could be called the "diseases of development" and would consist of those pathological conditions which are based on the usually unanticipated consequences of the implementation of development schemes (Hughes & Hunter, 1972:93).

Economic development increases the disease rate of affected peoples in at least three ways. First, to the extent that development is successful, it makes developed populations suddenly become vulnerable to all of the diseases suffered almost exclusively by "advanced" peoples. Among these are diabetes, obesity, hypertension, and a variety of circulatory problems. Second, development disturbs traditional environmental balances and may dramatically increase certain bacterial and parasite diseases. Finally, when development goals prove unattainable, an assortment of poverty diseases may appear in association with the crowded conditions of urban slums and the general breakdown in traditional socioeconomic systems.

Outstanding examples of the first situation can be seen in the Pacific, where some of the most successfully developed native peoples are found. In Micronesia, where development has progressed more rapidly than perhaps anywhere else, between 1958 and 1972 the population doubled, but the number of patients treated for heart disease in the local hospitals nearly tripled, mental disorder increased eightfold, and by 1972 hypertension and nutritional deficiencies began to make significant appearances for the first time (TTR, 1959, 1973, statistical tables).

Although some critics argue that the Micronesian figures simply represent better health monitoring due to economic progress, rigorously controlled data from Polynesia show a similar trend. The progressive acquisition of modern degenerative diseases was documented by an eight-member team of New Zealand medical specialists, anthropologists, and nutritionists, whose research was funded by the Medical Research Council of New Zealand and the World Health Organization. These researchers investigated the health status of a genetically related population at various points along a continuum of increasing cash income, modernizing diet, and urbanization. The extremes on this acculturation continuum were represented by the relatively traditional Pukapukans of the Cook Islands and the essentially Europeanized New Zealand Maori, while the busily developing Rarotongans, also of the Cook Islands, occupied the intermediate position. In 1971, after eight years of work, the team's preliminary findings were summarized by Dr. Ian Prior, cardiologist and leader of the research, as follows:

> We are beginning to observe that the more an islander takes on the ways of the West, the more prone he is to succumb to our degenerative diseases. In fact, it does not seem too much to say our evidence now shows that the farther the Pacific natives move from the quiet, carefree life of their ancestors, the closer they come to gout, diabetes, atherosclerosis, obesity, and hypertension (Prior, 1971:2).

In Pukapuka, where progress was limited by the island's small size and its isolated location some 480 kilometers from the nearest port, the annual per capita income was only about thirty-six dollars and the economy remained essentially at a subsistence level. Resources were limited and the area was visited by trading ships only three or four times a year; thus, there was little opportunity for intensive economic development. Predictably, the population of Pukapuka was characterized by relatively low levels of imported sugar and salt intake, and a presumably related low level of heart disease, high blood pressure, and diabetes. In Rarotonga, where economic success was introducing town life, imported food, and motorcycles, sugar and salt intakes nearly tripled, high blood pressure increased approximately ninefold, diabetes two- to threefold, and heart disease doubled for men and more than quadrupled for women, while the number of grossly obese women increased more than tenfold. Among the New Zealand Maori, sugar intake was nearly eight times that of the Pukapukans, gout in men was nearly double its rate on Pukapuka, and diabetes in men was more than fivefold higher, while heart disease in women had increased more than sixfold. The Maori were, in fact, dying of "European" diseases at a greater rate than was the average New Zealand European.

Government development policies designed to bring about changes in local hydrology, vegetation, and settlement patterns and to increase population mobility, and even programs aimed at reducing certain diseases, have frequently led to dramatic increases in disease rates because of the unforeseen effects of disturbing the preexisting order. Hughes and Hunter (1972) published an excellent survey of cases in which development led directly to increased disease rates in Africa. They concluded that hasty development intervention in relatively balanced local cultures and environments resulted in "a drastic deterioration in the social and economic conditions of life."

Traditional populations in general have presumably learned to live with the endemic pathogens of their environments, and in some cases they have evolved genetic adaptations to specific diseases, such as the sickle-cell trait, which provided an immunity to malaria. Unfortunately, however, outside intervention has entirely changed this picture. In the late 1960s, sleeping sickness suddenly increased in many areas of Africa and even spread to areas where it did not formerly occur, due to the building of new roads and migratory labor, both of which caused increased population movement. Large-scale relocation schemes, such as the Zande Scheme, had disastrous results when natives were moved from their traditional disease-free refuges into infected areas. Dams and irrigation developments inadvertently created ideal conditions for the rapid proliferation of snails carrying schistosomiasis (a liver fluke disease), and major epidemics suddenly occurred in areas where this disease had never before been a problem. DDT spraying programs have been temporarily successful in controlling malaria, but there is often a rebound effect that increases the problem when spraying is discontinued, and the malarial mosquitoes are continually evolving resistant strains.

Urbanization is one of the prime measures of development, but it is a mixed blessing for most former tribal peoples. Urban health standards are abysmally poor and generally worse than in rural areas for the detribalized individuals who have crowded into the towns and cities throughout Africa, Asia, and Latin America seeking wage employment out of new economic necessity. Infectious diseases related to crowding and poor sanitation are rampant in urban centers, while greatly increased stress and poor nutrition aggravate a variety of other health problems. Malnutrition and other diet-related conditions are, in fact, one of the characteristic hazards of progress faced by tribal peoples and are discussed in the following sections.

The Hazards of Dietary Change

The traditional diets of tribal peoples are admirably adapted to their nutritional needs and available food resources. Even though these diets may seem bizarre, absurd, and unpalatable to outsiders, they are unlikely to be improved by drastic modifications. Given the delicate balances and complexities involved in any subsistence system, change always involves risks, but for tribal people the effects of dietary change have been catastrophic.

Under normal conditions, food habits are remarkably resistant to change, and indeed people are unlikely to abandon their traditional diets voluntarily in favor of dependence on difficult-to-obtain exotic imports. In some cases it is true that imported foods may be identified with powerful outsiders and are therefore sought as symbols of greater prestige. This may lead to such absurdities as Amazonian Indians choosing to consume imported canned tunafish when abundant high-quality fish is available in their own rivers. Another example of this situation occurs in tribes where mothers prefer to feed their infants expensive and nutritionally inadequate canned milk from unsanitary, but *high status,* baby bottles. The high status of these items is often promoted by clever traders and clever advertising campaigns.

Aside from these apparently voluntary changes, it appears that more often dietary changes are forced upon unwilling tribal peoples by circumstances beyond their control. In some areas, new food crops have been introduced by government decree, or as a consequence of forced relocation or other policies designed to end hunting, pastoralism, or shifting cultivation. Food habits have also been modified by massive disruption of the natural environment by outsiders—as when sheepherders transformed the Australian Aborigine's foraging territory or when European invaders destroyed the bison herds that were the primary element in the Plains Indians' subsistence patterns. Perhaps the most frequent cause of diet change occurs when formerly self-sufficient peoples find that wage labor, cash cropping, and other economic development activities that feed tribal resources into the world-market economy must inevitably divert time and energy away from the production of subsistence foods. Many developing peoples suddenly discover that, like it or not, they are unable to secure traditional foods and must spend their newly acquired cash on costly, and often nutritionally inferior, manufactured foods.

Overall, the available data seem to indicate that the dietary changes that are linked to involvement in the world-market economy have tended to *lower* rather than raise the nutritional levels of the affected tribal peoples. Specifically, the vitamin, mineral, and protein components of their diets are often drastically reduced and replaced by enormous increases in starch and carbohydrates, often in the form of white flour and refined sugar.

Any deterioration in the quality of a given population's diet is almost certain to be reflected in an increase in deficiency diseases and a general decline in health status. Indeed, as tribal peoples have shifted to a diet based on imported manufactured or processed foods, there has been a dramatic rise in malnutrition, a massive increase in dental problems, and a variety of other nutrition-related disorders. Nutritional physiology is so complex that even well-meaning dietary changes have had tragic consequences. In many areas of Southeast Asia, government-sponsored protein supplementation programs supplying milk to protein-deficient populations caused unexpected health problems and increased mortality. Officials failed to anticipate that in cultures where adults do not normally drink milk, the enzymes needed to digest it are no longer produced and milk *intolerance* results (Davis & Bolin, 1972). In Brazil, a similar milk distribution program caused an epidemic of permanent blindness by aggravating a preexisting vitamin A deficiency (Bunce, 1972).

Teeth and Progress

There is nothing new in the observation that savages, or peoples living under primitive conditions, have, in general excellent teeth. . . . Nor is it news that most civilized populations possess wretched teeth which begin to decay almost before they have erupted completely, and that dental caries is likely to be accompanied by periodontal disease with further reaching complications (Hooton, 1945:xviii).

Anthropologists have long recognized that undisturbed tribal peoples are often in excellent physical condition. And it has often been noted specifically that dental caries and the other dental abnormalities that plague industrialized societies are absent or rare among tribal peoples who have retained their traditional diets. The fact that tribal food habits may contribute to the development of sound teeth, whereas modernized diets may do just the opposite, was illustrated as long ago as 1894 in an article in the *Journal of the Royal Anthropological Institute* that described the results of a comparison between the teeth of ten Sioux Indians and a comparable group of Londoners (Smith, 1894:109–116). The Indians were examined when they came to London as members of Buffalo Bill's Wild West Show and were found to be completely free of caries and in possession of all their teeth, even though half of the group were over thirty-nine years of age. Londoners' teeth were conspicuous for both their caries and their steady reduction in number with advancing age. The difference was attributed primarily to the wear and polishing caused by the traditional Indian diet of coarse food and the fact that they chewed their food longer, encouraged by the absence of tableware.

One of the most remarkable studies of the dental conditions of tribal peoples and the impact of dietary change was conducted in the 1930s by Weston Price (1945), an American dentist who was interested in determining what caused normal, healthy teeth. Between 1931 and 1936, Price systematically explored tribal areas throughout the world to locate and examine the most isolated peoples who were still living on traditional foods. His fieldwork covered Alaska, the Canadian Yukon, Hudson Bay, Vancouver Island, Florida, the Andes, the Amazon, Samoa, Tahiti, New Zealand, Australia, New Caledonia, Fiji, the Torres Strait, East Africa, and the Nile. The study demonstrated both the superior quality of aboriginal dentition and the devastation that occurs as modern diets are adopted. In nearly every area where traditional foods were still being eaten, Price found perfect teeth with normal dental arches and virtually no decay, whereas caries and abnormalities increased steadily as new diets were adopted. In many cases the change was sudden and striking. Among Eskimo groups subsisting entirely on traditional food he found caries totally absent, whereas in groups eating a considerable quantity of store-bought food approximately 20 percent of their teeth were decayed. The figure rose to more than 30 percent with Eskimo groups subsisting almost exclusively on purchased or government-supplied food, and reached an incredible 48 percent among the Vancouver Island Indians. Unfortunately for many of these people, modern dental treatment

did not accompany the new food, and their suffering was appalling. The loss of teeth was, of course, bad enough in itself, and it certainly undermined the population's resistance to many new diseases, including tuberculosis. But new foods were also accompanied by crowded, misplaced teeth, gum diseases, distortion of the face, and pinching of the nasal cavity. Abnormalities in the dental arch appeared in the new generation following the change in diet, while caries appeared almost immediately even in adults.

Price reported that in many areas the affected peoples were conscious of their own physical deterioration. At a mission school in Africa, the principal asked him to explain to the native schoolchildren why they were not physically as strong as children who had had no contact with schools. On an island in the Torres Strait the natives knew exactly what was causing their problems and resisted—almost to the point of bloodshed—government efforts to establish a store that would make imported food available. The government prevailed, however, and Price was able to establish a relationship between the length of time the government store had been established and the increasing incidences of caries among a population that showed an almost 100 percent immunity to them before the store had been opened.

In New Zealand, the Maori, who in their aboriginal state are often considered to have been among the healthiest, most perfectly developed of peoples, were found to have "advanced" the furthest. According to Price:

> Their modernization was demonstrated not only by the high incidence of dental caries but also by the fact 90 percent of the adults and 100 percent of the children had abnormalities of the dental arches (Price, 1945:206).

Malnutrition

Malnutrition, particularly in the form of protein deficiency, has become a critical problem for tribal peoples who must adopt new economic patterns. Population pressures, cash cropping, and government programs all have tended to encourage the replacement of traditional crops and other food sources that were rich in protein with substitutes high in calories but low in protein. In Africa, for example, protein-rich staples such as millet and sorghum are being replaced systematically by high-yielding manioc and plantains, which have insignificant amounts of protein. The problem is increased for cash croppers and wage laborers whose earnings are too low and unpredictable to allow purchase of adequate amounts of protein. In some rural areas, agricultural laborers have been forced systematically to deprive nonproductive members (principally children) of their households of their minimal nutritional requirements to satisfy the need of the productive members. This process has been documented in northeastern Brazil following the introduction of large-scale sisal plantations (Gross & Underwood, 1971). In urban centers the difficulties of obtaining nutritionally adequate diets are even more serious for tribal immigrants, because costs are higher and poor quality foods are more tempting.

One of the most tragic, and largely overlooked, aspects of chronic malnutrition is that it can lead to abnormally undersized brain development and apparently irreversible brain damage; it has been associated with various forms of mental impairment or retardation. Malnutrition has been linked clinically with mental retardation in both Africa and Latin America (see, for example, Mönckeberg, 1968), and this appears to be a worldwide phenomenon with serious implications (Montagu, 1972).

Optimistic supporters of progress will surely say that all of these new health problems are being overstressed and that the introduction of hospitals, clinics, and the other modern health institutions will overcome or at least compensate for all of these difficulties. However, it appears that uncontrolled population growth and economic impoverishment probably will keep most of these benefits out of reach for many tribal peoples, and the intervention of modern medicine has at least partly contributed to the problem in the first place.

The generalization that civilization frequently has a broad negative impact on tribal health has found broad empirical support (see especially Kroeger & Barbira-Freedman [1982] on Amazonia; Reinhard [1976] on the Arctic; and Wirsing [1985] globally), but these conclusions have not gone unchallenged. Some critics argue that tribal health was often poor before modernization, and they point specifically to tribals' low life expectancy and high infant mortality rates. Demographic statistics on tribal populations are often problematic because precise data are scarce, but they do show a less favorable profile than that enjoyed by many industrial societies. However, it should be remembered that our present life expectancy is a recent phenomenon that has been very costly in terms of medical research and technological advances. Furthermore, the benefits of our health system are not enjoyed equally by all members of our society. High infant mortality could be viewed as a relatively inexpensive and egalitarian tribal public health program that offered the reasonable expectation of a healthy and productive life for those surviving to age fifteen.

Some critics also suggest that certain tribal populations, such as the New Guinea highlanders, were "stunted" by nutritional deficiencies created by tribal culture and are "improved" by "acculturation" and cash cropping (Dennett & Connell, 1988). Although this argument does suggest that the health question requires careful evaluation, it does not invalidate the empirical generalizations already established. Nutritional deficiencies undoubtedly occurred in densely populated zones in the central New Guinea highlands. However, the specific case cited above may not be widely representative of other tribal groups even in New Guinea, and it does not address the facts of outside intrusion or the inequities inherent in the contemporary development process.

ECOCIDE

"How is it," asked a herdsman . . . "how is it that these hills can no longer give pasture to my cattle? In my father's day they were green and cattle thrived there; today there is no grass and my cattle starve." As one looked one saw that what had once been a green hill had become a raw red rock (Jones, 1934).

Progress not only brings new threats to the health of tribal peoples, but it also imposes new strains on the ecosystems upon which they must depend for their ultimate survival. The introduction of new technology, increased consumption, lowered mortality, and the eradication of all traditional controls have combined to replace what for most tribal peoples was a relatively stable balance between population and natural resources, with a new system that is imbalanced. Economic development is forcing *ecocide* on peoples who were once careful stewards of their resources. There is already a trend toward widespread environmental deterioration in tribal areas, involving resource depletion, erosion, plant and animal extinction, and a disturbing series of other previously unforeseen changes.

After the initial depopulation suffered by most tribal peoples during their engulfment by frontiers of national expansion, most tribal populations began to experience rapid growth. Authorities generally attribute this growth to the introduction of modern medicine and new health measures and the termination of intertribal warfare, which lowered mortality rates, as well as to new technology, which increased food production. Certainly all of these factors played a part, but merely lowering mortality rates would not have produced the rapid population growth that most tribal areas have experienced if traditional birth-spacing mechanisms had not been eliminated at the same time. Regardless of which factors were most important, it is clear that all of the natural and cultural checks on population growth have suddenly been pushed aside by culture change, while tribal lands have been steadily reduced and consumption levels have risen. In many tribal areas, environmental deterioration due to over-use of resources has set in, and in other areas such deterioration is imminent as resources continue to dwindle relative to the expanding population and increased use. Of course, population expansion by tribal peoples may have positive political consequences, because where tribals can retain or regain their status as local majorities they may be in a more favorable position to defend their resources against intruders.

Swidden systems and pastoralism, both highly successful economic systems under traditional conditions, have proven particularly vulnerable to increased population pressures and outside efforts to raise productivity beyond its natural limits. Research in Amazonia demonstrates that population pressures and related resource depletion can be created indirectly by official policies that restrict swidden peoples to smaller territories. Resource depletion itself can then become a powerful means of forcing tribal people into participating in the world-market economy—thus leading to further resource depletion. For example, Bodley and Benson (1979) showed how the Shipibo Indians in Peru were forced to further deplete their forest resources by cash cropping in the forest area to replace the resources that had been destroyed earlier by the intensive cash cropping necessitated by the narrow confines of their reserve. In this case, a certain species of palm trees that had provided critical housing materials were destroyed by forest clearing and had to be replaced by costly purchased materials. Research by Gross (1979) and others showed similar processes at work among four tribal groups in central Brazil and demonstrated that the degree of market involvement increases directly with increases in resource depletion.

The settling of nomadic herders and the removal of prior controls on herd size have often led to serious overgrazing and erosion problems where these had not previously occurred. There are indications that the desertification problem in the Sahel region of Africa was aggravated by programs designed to settle nomads. The first sign of imbalance in a swidden system appears when the planting cycles are shortened to the point that garden plots are reused before sufficient forest regrowth can occur. If reclearing and planting continue in the same area, the natural pattern of forest succession may be disturbed irreversibly and the soil can be impaired permanently. An extensive tract of tropical rainforest in the lower Amazon of Brazil was reduced to a semiarid desert in just fifty years through such a process (Ackermann, 1964). The soils in the Azande area are also now seriously threatened with laterization and other problems as a result of the government-promoted cotton development scheme (McNeil, 1972).

The dangers of overdevelopment and the vulnerability of local resource systems have long been recognized by both anthropologists and tribal peoples themselves, but the pressures for change have been overwhelming. In 1948 the Maya villagers of Chan Kom complained to Redfield (1962) about the shortening of their swidden cycles, which they correctly attributed to increasing population pressures. Redfield told them, however, that they had no choice but to go "forward with technology" (Redfield, 1962:178). In Assam, swidden cycles were shortened from an average of twelve years to only two or three within just twenty years, and anthropologists warned that the limits of swiddening would soon be reached (Burling, 1963:311–312). In the Pacific, anthropologists warned of population pressures on limited resources as early as the 1930s (Keesing, 1941:64–65). These warnings seemed fully justified, considering the fact that the crowded Tikopians were prompted by population pressures on their tiny island to suggest that infanticide be legalized. The warnings have been dramatically reinforced since then by the doubling of Micronesia's population in just the fourteen years between 1958 and 1972, from 70,600 to 114,645, while consumption levels have soared. By 1985 Micronesia's population had reached 162,321.

The environmental hazards of economic development and rapid population growth have become generally recognized only since worldwide concerns over environmental issues began in the early 1970s. Unfortunately, there is as yet little indication that the leaders of the now developing nations are sufficiently concerned with environmental limitations. On the contrary governments are forcing tribal peoples into a self-reinforcing spiral of population growth and intensified resource exploitation, which may be stopped only by environmental disaster or the total impoverishment of the tribals.

The reality of ecocide certainly focuses attention on the fundamental contrasts between tribal and industrial systems in their use of natural resources. In many respects the entire "victims of progress" issue hinges on natural resources, who controls them, and how they are managed. Tribal peoples are victimized because they control resources that outsiders demand. The resources exist because tribals managed them conservatively. However, as with the issue of the health consequences of detribalization, some anthropologists minimize the adaptive achievements of tribal groups and seem unwilling to concede that ecocide might be a consequence of cultural change. Critics attack an exaggerated "noble savage" image of tribals living in perfect harmony with nature and having no visible impact on their surroundings. They then show that tribals do in fact modify the environment, and they conclude that there is no significant difference between how tribals and industrial societies treat their environments. For example, Charles Wagley declared that Brazilian Indians such as the Tapirape

> are not "natural men." They have human vices just as we do. . . . They do not live "in tune" with nature any more than I do; in fact, they can often be as destructive of their environment, within their limitations, as some civilized men. The Tapirape are not innocent or child-like in any way (Wagley, 1977:302).

Anthropologist Terry Rambo demonstrated that the Semang of the Malaysian rain forests have measurable impact on their environment. In his monograph *Primitive Polluters,* Rambo (1985) reported that the Semang live in smoke-filled houses. They sneeze and spread germs, breathe, and thus emit carbon dioxide. They clear small gardens, contributing "particulate matter" to the air and disturbing the local climate because cleared areas proved measurably warmer and drier than the shady forest. Rambo concluded that his research "demonstrated the essential functional similarity of the environmental interactions of primitive and civilized societies" (1985:78) in contrast to a "noble savage" view (Bodley, 1983) which, according to Rambo (1985:2), mistakenly "claims that traditional peoples almost always live in essential harmony with their environment."

This is surely a false issue. To stress, as I do, that tribals tend to manage their resources for sustained yield within relatively self-sufficient subsistence economies is not to make them either innocent children or natural men. Nor is it to deny that tribals "disrupt" their environment and may never be in absolute "balance" with nature.

The ecocide issue is perhaps most dramatically illustrated by two sets of satellite photos taken over the Brazilian rain forests of Rôndonia (Allard & McIntyre, 1988:780–781). Photos taken in 1973, when Rôndonia was still a tribal domain, show virtually unbroken rain forest. The 1987 satellite photos, taken after just fifteen years of highway construction and "development" by outsiders, show more than 20 percent of the forest destroyed. The surviving Indians were being concentrated by FUNAI (Brazil's national Indian foundation) into what would soon become mere islands of forest in a ravaged landscape. It is irrelevant to quibble about whether tribals are noble, childlike, or innocent, or about the precise meaning of balance with nature, carrying capacity, or adaptation, to recognize that for the past 200 years rapid environmental deterioration on an unprecedented global scale

has followed the wresting of control of vast areas of the world from tribal groups by resource-hungry industrial societies.

DEPRIVATION AND DISCRIMINATION

> Contact with European culture has given them a knowledge of great wealth, opportunity and privilege, but only very limited avenues by which to acquire these things (Crocombe, 1968).

Unwittingly, tribal peoples have had the burden of perpetual relative deprivation thrust upon them by acceptance—either by themselves or by the governments administering them—of the standards of socioeconomic progress set for them by industrial civilizations. By comparison with the material wealth of industrial societies, tribal societies become, by definition, impoverished. They are then forced to transform their cultures and work to achieve what many economists now acknowledge to be unattainable goals. Even though in many cases the modest GNP goals set by development planners for the developing nations during the "development decade" of the 1960s were often met, the results were hardly noticeable for most of the tribal people involved. Population growth, environmental limitations, inequitable distribution of wealth, and the continued rapid growth of the industrialized nations have all meant that both the absolute and the relative gap between the rich and poor in the world is steadily widening. The prospect that tribal peoples will actually be able to attain the levels of resource consumption to which they are being encouraged to aspire is remote indeed except for those few groups who have retained effective control over strategic mineral resources.

Tribal peoples feel deprivation not only when the economic goals they have been encouraged to seek fail to materialize, but also when they discover that they are powerless, second-class citizens who are discriminated against and exploited by the dominant society. At the same time, they are denied the satisfactions of their traditional cultures, because these have been sacrificed in the process of modernization. Under the impact of major economic change family life is disrupted, traditional social controls are often lost, and many indicators of social anomie such as alcoholism, crime, delinquency, suicide, emotional disorders, and despair may increase. The inevitable frustration resulting from this continual deprivation finds expression in the cargo cults, revitalization movements, and a variety of other political and religious movements that have been widespread among tribal peoples following their disruption by industrial civilization.

REFERENCES

Ackermann, F. L. 1964. *Geologia e Fisiografia da Região Bragantina, Estado do Pará.* Manaus, Brazil: Conselho Nacional de Pesquisas, Instituto Nacional de Pesquisas da Amazônia.

Allard, William Albert, and Loren McIntyre. 1988. Rôndonia's settlers invade Brazil's imperiled rain forest. *National Geographic* 174(6):772–799.

Bodley, John H. 1983. The World Bank tribal policy: Criticisms and recommendations. *Congressional Record,* serial no. 98-37, pp. 515–521. (Reprinted in Bodley, 1988.)

Bodley, John H., and Foley C. Benson. 1979. Cultural ecology of Amazonian palms. *Reports of Investigations,* no. 56. Pullman: Laboratory of Anthropology, Washington State University.

Bunce, George E. 1972. Aggravation of vitamin A deficiency following distribution of non-fortified skim milk: An example of nutrient interaction. In *The Careless Technology: Ecology and International Development,* ed. M. T. Farvar and John P. Milton, pp. 53–60. Garden City, N.Y.: Natural History Press.

Burling, Robbins. 1963. *Rengsanggri: Family and Kinship in a Garo Village.* Philadelphia: University of Pennsylvania Press.

Crocombe, Ron. 1968. Bougainville!: Copper, R. R. A. and secessionism. *New Guinea* 3(3):39–49.

Davis, A. E., and T. D. Bolin. 1972. Lactose intolerance in Southeast Asia. In *The Careless Technology: Ecology and International Development,* ed. M. T. Farvar and John P. Milton, pp. 61–68. Garden City, N.Y.: Natural History Press.

Dennett, Glenn, and John Connell. 1988. Acculturation and health in the highlands of Papua New Guinea. *Current Anthropology* 29(2):273–299.

Goldschmidt, Walter R. 1952. The interrelations between cultural factors and acquisition of new technical skills. In *The Progress of Underdeveloped Areas,* ed. Bert F. Hoselitz, pp. 135–151. Chicago: University of Chicago Press.

Gross, Daniel R., and Barbara A. Underwood. 1971. Technological change and caloric costs: Sisal agriculture. *American Anthropologist* 73(3):725–740.

Gross, Daniel R., et al. 1979. Ecology and acculturation among native peoples of Central Brazil. *Science* 206(4422):1043–1050.

Hooton, Earnest A. 1945. Introduction. In *Nutrition and Physical Degeneration: A Comparison of Primitive and Modern Diets and Their Effects* by Weston A. Price. Redlands, Calif.: The author.

Hughes, Charles C., and John M. Hunter. 1972. The role of technological development in promoting disease in Africa. In *The Careless Technology: Ecology and International Development,* ed. M. T. Farvar and John P. Milton, pp. 69–101. Garden City, N.Y.: Natural History Press.

Jones, J. D. Rheinallt. 1934. Economic condition of the urban native. In *Western Civilization and the Natives of South Africa,* ed. I. Schapera, pp. 159–192. London: George Routledge and Sons.

Keesing, Felix M. 1941. *The South Seas in the Modern World.* Institute of Pacific Relations International Research Series. New York: John Day.

Kroeger, Axel, and Françoise Barbira-Freedman. 1982. *Culture Change and Health: The Case of South American Rainforest Indians.* Frankfurt am Main: Verlag Peter Lang. (Reprinted in Bodley, 1988:221–236).

Maunier, René. 1949. *The Sociology of Colonies.* Vol. 2. London: Routledge and Kegan Paul.

McNeil, Mary. 1972. Lateritic soils in distinct tropical environments: Southern Sudan and Brazil. In *The Careless Technology: Ecology and International Development,* ed. M. T. Farvar and John P. Milton, pp. 591–608. Garden City, N.Y.: Natural History Press.

Mönckeberg, F. 1968. Mental retardation from malnutrition. *Journal of the American Medical Association* 206:30–31.

Montagu, Ashley. 1972. Sociogenic brain damage. *American Anthropologist* 74(5):1045–1061.

Price, Weston Andrew. 1945. *Nutrition and Physical Degeneration: A Comparison of Primitive and Modern Diets and Their Effects.* Redlands, Calif.: The author.

Prior, Ian A. M. 1971. The price of civilization. *Nutrition Today* 6(4):2–11.

Rambo, A. Terry. 1985. *Primitive Polluters: Semang Impact on the Malaysian Tropical Rain Forest Ecosystem.* Anthropological Papers no. 76, Museum of Anthropology, University of Michigan.

Redfield, Robert. 1962. *A Village That Chose Progress: Chan Kom Revisited.* Chicago: University of Chicago Press, Phoenix Books.

Reinhard, K. R. 1976. Resource exploitation and the health of western arctic man. In *Circumpolar Health: Proceedings of the Third International Symposium, Yellowknife, Northwest Territories,* ed. Roy J. Shephard and S. Itoh, pp. 617–627. Toronto: University of Toronto Press. (Reprinted in Bodley, 1988.)

Smith, Wilberforce. 1894. The teeth of ten Sioux Indians. *Journal of the Royal Anthropological Institute* 24:109–116.

TTR: TTR, United States, Department of the Interior, Office of the Territories. 1953. Report on the Administration of the trust territories of the Pacific Islands for the period of July 1, 1951 to June 30, 1952.

United States, Department of State. 1955. *Seventh Annual Report to the United Nations on the Administration of the Trust Territory of the Pacific Islands* (July 1, 1953, to June 30, 1954).

——. 1959. *Eleventh Annual Report to the United Nations on the Administration of the Trust Territory of the Pacific Islands* (July 1, 1957, to June 30, 1958).

——. 1973. *Twenty-Fifth Annual Report to the United Nations on the Administration of the Trust Territory of the Pacific Islands* (July 1, 1971, to June 30, 1972).

Wagley, C. 1977. *Welcome of Tears: The Tapirape Indians of Central Brazil.* New York: Oxford University Press.

Wirsing, R. 1985. The health of traditional societies and the effects of acculturation. *Current Anthropology* 26: 303–322.

IN THE SUPERIOR COURT OF DARROW COUNTY

STATE OF NITA

THE PEOPLE OF THE STATE OF NITA)
)
vs.)
) Case No. YR-0 CR 324
JOHN BURNS,)
) JURY VERDICT
Defendant.)

We, the Jury, return the following verdict, and each of us concurs in this verdict:

[Choose the appropriate verdict for each charge]

I. ARMED ROBBERY

We, the Jury, find the defendant, John Burns, NOT GUILTY of Armed Robbery.

_____

Foreperson

We, the Jury, find the defendant, John Burns, GUILTY of Armed Robbery.

_____

Foreperson

If, and only if, you find the defendant guilty of Armed Robbery, then you must consider the additional charge of Murder in the First Degree.

II. MURDER IN THE FIRST DEGREE

We, the Jury, find the Defendant, John Burns, NOT GUILTY of Murder in the First Degree.

_____

Foreperson

We, the Jury, find the Defendant, John Burns, GUILTY of Murder in the First Degree.

_____

Foreperson